C000165609

Financial Management
An Irish Text

Tom Power, Stephen Walsh
and Paul O Meara

GILL & MACMILLAN

Gill & Macmillan Ltd
Hume Avenue
Park West
Dublin 12
with associated companies throughout the world
www.gillmacmillan.ie

© 2001 Tom Power, Stephen Walsh and Paul O Meara
0 7171 3192
Index compiled by
Matthew Seal
Print origination in Ireland by
Carrigboy Typesetting Services, County Cork.

Dedications

To my mother and in memory of my father
T.P.

To Jack and Paddy — accountants from different spheres
P.O'M.

To my family and my late father Joe
S.W.

Contents

PART 2: Valuations

Chapter 4. The Time Value of Money   81

Chapter 5. Introduction to Bond Valuations   102

PART 7: Special Topics in Finance and Investment

Contents Explained

Brief Contents

For short courses we have provided a possible course lay-out that should encompass all of the basic principles in financial management.

Preface

From our combined years of lecturing (too many to tell you about) to a wide variety of students with different backgrounds doing different courses we have discovered that students find this subject probably the most difficult that they will encompass during their years at college. We have also discovered that students want to know not just about corporate finance but about the related area of the investment market as well. The financial investment products along with institutional changes brought about by the single currency have changed the face of the Irish investment market. We have incorporated these changes into this book along with the new developments in corporate finance.

This book on finance covers the areas of management, valuations, and investment. Corporate financial management is of course an essential ingredient in any textbook of this nature because most students studying finance will end up working in corporations in one capacity or another. In recent years, a greater emphasis on valuations, particularly on shareholder value, is evident from both the academic literature and in corporate reporting. Many students, in addition to corporate financial management will benefit from an introduction to the Irish investment market. This area is becoming increasingly more important and an understanding of the various investment products and markets are both necessary and useful.

In essence this book includes the following:

- The standard time-honoured basic principles of financial management with an emphasis on shareholder value.
- The Irish investment market.
- Risk management and derivatives.

Target audience

This book is mainly designed for undergraduate students of commerce, accounting and finance, business studies, business management, economics, banking, valuations/property, as well as for M.B.A. and M.Sc. students where finance is a subject. It is expected that students will have completed some introductory course in financial accounting and basic mathematics. However, the book does review some basic accounting concepts in Chapter 2.

In addition, practitioners will find this book very useful because it encompasses concepts and material they work at on a daily basis. Finally, students who take professional examinations will find this book essential reading material. These courses will include:

- Institute of Chartered Accountants in Ireland
- Society of Chartered Surveyors

- Chartered Institute of Bankers
- Chartered Institute of Public Accountants
- Chartered Institute of Management Accountancy
- Chartered Association of Certified Accountants
- Certificate Diploma in Accounting and Finance.

Pedagogical guide

The structure of this book is such that individual lecturers can customise to suit their own individual styles without lack of continuity. It can, for example, be customised to suit **short courses** in finance. At the beginning we provide a possible lay-out for a short course. Of course, the book is also suitable for more advanced and detailed courses. We have included a comprehensive reference and additional reading material for students who want to advance their knowledge of the areas in greater depth.

The lay-out of this book is designed principally to enhance student learning. These include:

- Each chapter begins with a set of learning objectives to be achieved by the student.
- Each chapter ends with a comprehensive executive summary.
- Many chapters incorporate newspaper vignettes, which bring real world examples into the text. These are taken mostly from *The Irish Times*, so they mainly involve Irish case studies.
- About 400 end of chapter questions. These include general review and concept questions and computational and mathematical questions and problems, which we know from our experience students like to get their teeth into.
- Each chapter contains worked answers and solutions to illustrate various themes.
- References and further additional material is provided for students who want to explore certain topics in more detail.
- A glossary of finance and investment terms is provided at the end of the book.

For the lecturer

A website which includes:

- Solutions to all end of chapter questions and problems. This forms an effective solutions manual.
- Power point presentation material (in colour) covering all of the main issues presented in the text. These include graphs, tables etc.

Acknowledgments

We would like to acknowledge the contribution and help we received from the following people and institutions:

Ailbhe O'Reilly and Deirdre Greenan of Gill & Macmillan. Their workload in overseeing this text was invaluable and we are very grateful for their patience and perseverance.

The staff at the DIT, in particular Anne Russell and Tracy Pickerill, who provided valuable information and comments, and to our colleagues who have passed through Room 4 at AIT.

Thanks to our many legions of students down through the years who provided us with a source of inspiration.

Gerry Pickerill who worked on many of the diagrams in the book.

A special word of thanks must go to the academics throughout the country that reviewed earlier drafts of this book. Indeed their comments and insights were truly invaluable.

We got a wealth of information from different sources and sectors to whom we are truly grateful: Mr. Felix O'Regan of the Irish Bankers' Federation, NTMA, AIB Capital Markets, Irish Association of Pension Funds and the Software Vineyard.

Finally, we would like to thank Dr Eleanor O'Higgins, Dr John Teeling, Roger Acton, Carol Power, Dominic Coyle, Rory Kelliher, *The Irish Times* and the *Sunday Business Post* for permission to reproduce articles in the book.

Part 1

Overview of Financial Management

1
An Overview of Finance

CHAPTER OBJECTIVES

Having studied this chapter the student will be able to:

1. appreciate the objectives of financial management
2. understand the role of the financial manager
3. distinguish between the different forms of business organisations
4. understand the concept of shareholder value.

INTRODUCTION

When we decided to write this textbook we were motivated by two basic ideas:

1. to produce a textbook that would cover the fundamental principles of finance in a rigorous but at the same time succinct format that would incorporate Irish themes.
2. to relate the fundamentals of the Irish investment market as recognition that finance also involves the study of the investment market. Many textbooks we feel miss this important connection. For example, if one works in the money and capital markets dealing with stocks, bonds, mutual funds, pension funds etc., a sound understanding of financial management is necessary because investments of this nature will necessitate an understanding of the financial performance of the firm. Investment advice from stockbrokers to their clients presupposes an understanding of financial management. In addition, financial managers will need an understanding of how the investment market views companies and how security prices are set. Another example is the economics of interest rate determination. This does not simply come within the sphere of the investment market. It is crucially important to the corporate financial manager, as we shall discuss in Chapter 13 on cash management.

Students of finance will specialise in one of these areas in higher courses of finance, but this text will provide students with foundations that will enable them to understand the fundamentals of finance and investment. For this reason we believe that this text is unique. For non-finance specialists this text will provide all the necessary information to interpret and understand the financial literature. It is important for many students of finance to seek out a quantitative approach to problem-solving; for others an intuitive approach is more advisable. We feel that students should adopt both approaches and we hope this text accomplishes this objective.

1.1 What is finance?

Finance is about managing money. You can readily appreciate this if you think of the basic issues to be considered in setting up a business. Your first consideration will be (after you have put your business plan together) to determine how much cash you will need to finance the business. This is the budgeting process, which involves assessing the firm's long-term investment projects. It is at this stage that we begin the discussion on the most fundamental principle in finance — **net present value (NPV)**. Investment projects are undertaken when their market value is greater than their cost. This will involve an assessment of the future timing and risk of future cash flow generated by these investments. We develop these themes in detail throughout this book.

You will then need to consider where this cash will come from, i.e. will you have sufficient savings of your own to fund the operation or will you need to bring in outside investment in the form of a partnership or loans from financial institutions? This is the **capital structure decision**, which is crucial for the financial manager to get right if he/she is to maximise the return on investment to the owners.

Managing the day-to-day working capital (stock, cash, debtors and creditors) will absorb considerable time, but decisions made here will have a huge bearing on the company's profitability and liquidity. These issues are discussed in the chapters on **working capital**.

There is however one overriding consideration included in all of these decisions (budgeting, capital structure and working capital), and that is that these investments must be managed in a way that maximises the owner's wealth. We discuss this briefly next.

1.2 Maximising shareholder value

Emanating from the United States in the 1990s and increasingly taking a foothold in Europe is the concept of value creation. Shareholders are the owners of corporations. They elect directors who in turn appoint managers to run the company. It seems reasonable that shareholders will want managers to manage the company in such a way that will maximise shareholders' wealth. The wealth of shareholders is the number of shares they hold multiplied by the market price of the share. For example, Mr Richard Hewat of Heiton Holdings plc has a beneficial ownership of 495,731 ordinary shares.[1] The quoted share price as at 1 June 2000 was €3.23, giving a shareholder value of €1,601,211. Therefore shareholder value maximisation means maximising the price of the company's shares. It is not surprising therefore that a system of compensation packages which remunerate managers and employees based on value creation has developed. We will return to this concept and look at how we can best calculate value added in later chapters.

Nevertheless the idea that maximising shareholder value should be the sole consideration in business seems insidious. Surely there are other and perhaps more important goals of business, such as the maximisation of employee welfare, and the reduction in pollution. Proponents of value creation will insist that maximising share price benefits everybody in society and society itself.[2]

Share ownership is increasing because of the proliferation of growth in pension funds, life insurance companies and unit-linked funds. This is why, particularly in the US, pension funds and mutual fund managers are seeking out companies that are adopting shareholder value added financial systems. With the advent of the internet and e-commerce more and more individuals are trading in stocks and shares online, sometimes for very short periods like a day (day trading). Around the world share ownership is increasing because of government commitment to the privatisation of public utilities. Therefore, because more and more people are now becoming shareholders, maximising share price can increase the wealth of many more people.

1.3 What maximises share price?

The value of a share, indeed the value of any financial asset, depends on the ability of a company to generate cash flows both now and in the future. In finance, 'cash is king'. Cash is what is used by companies to invest in **value-creating** projects and to pay dividends.

Shareholder value is maximised by generating cash flow and not necessarily maximising profits. The remuneration package of company executives will depend on how successful they are at maximising shareholder value. For example, the stated remuneration policy as expressed in the directors' report of Heiton Holdings[3] recognises that 'employment and remuneration conditions for senior executives should properly reward and motivate them to perform in the best interests of shareholders'. On the other hand the stated policy in the directors' report of the Barlo Group[4] is 'not to pay performance related annual bonuses to executive directors'. However this policy was under review and the report goes on to say: 'Executives will participate in an annual bonus scheme under which payments will be made based on performance criteria.' **Profit maximisation should not necessarily be a goal of financial management**. For example, developing a new product may involve a lot of time, money, risk and effort. It will reduce short-term profitability. However, if the future cash flows of the project are more than enough to offset the initial capital outlay, then shareholder wealth will increase. Concentrating on short-term profitability may destroy shareholder value.

The **timing** of cash flows is also important in enhancing shareholder value. Cash received sooner is more valuable because it can be reinvested in the company to generate more cash or paid to shareholders as dividends.[5]

Finally, investors will pay more for shares that are less risky. Therefore reducing the **riskiness of the expected cash flows** can enhance share price (shareholder wealth).

To summarise, maximising shareholder wealth means maximising share price. The price (or value) of a share depends on:

1. the ability of the company (i.e. share) to generate cash flow
2. the timing of these cash flows
3. the riskiness of these cash flows.

Therefore to maximise share price (i.e. to maximise shareholder value) requires:

1. generating as much cash flow as possible
2. getting these cash flows into the company as quickly as possible and
3. doing all this while minimising risk.

1.4 What doesn't maximise share price?

Shareholders appoint directors who in turn appoint managers. Managers act as agents for owners. Managers are assumed to make decisions that enhance shareholder value. Sometimes, however, managers make decisions that suit themselves at the expense of shareholders. **Agency theory** deals with the conflict of interest between managers and their shareholders, and between shareholders and creditors.[6] Agents work on behalf of others. The people agents represent are called principals. For example senior management and the board of directors of the Smurfit Group act as agents for their shareholders or principals. The directors and management have a legal and ethical responsibility to enhance their shareholders' interests, i.e. shareholder value. **An agency cost** is any benefit a manager receives from a company that is not part of the manager's remuneration package and which does not enhance shareholder value. For example agency costs may include golf in the afternoon, fancy offices and the use of luxurious company cars where smaller less expensive ones would do, the use of company helicopters and perhaps jets (see Box 1.1).

Another example of an agency cost is managers deciding not to embark on projects that are risky, even though such projects may be potentially lucrative if they pay off. Managers will have a lot more to lose (they may lose their jobs) than individual shareholders who may have only a small proportion of their capital tied up in the company. Agency costs also include the expenditure incurred by shareholders designed to investigate and control managerial actions, such as audit costs on internal control. In addition, agency costs involve the appointment of outside specialists to the board of directors in order to limit and control the actions of managers. Controlling agency costs is difficult, particularly for large companies where individual shareholders will not have the power to control managers who are not acting in the best interests of their shareholders. There are a number of ways that agency costs can be reduced:

1. One way to reduce agency costs is the threat of takeovers. A **takeover** is likely to replace inefficient and wasteful managers.[7] If managers are only interested in **lining their own pockets** at the expense of shareholders, the threat of a takeover is likely to ensure that such managers will be replaced after the takeover.
2. **Stock options** may be a means of synchronising the interests of managers to that of shareholders. Stock options are increasingly becoming a part of employee and management remuneration packages.[8] Managers are more likely to act in the interest of shareholder wealth maximisation if they are themselves significant shareholders.[9] For example in the annual report of the directors of the Kerry Group,[10] a reference to share options states: 'A total of 1,010,000 shares have been granted under option to the executive directors.'
3. Finally, **pension fund managers** who control large blocks of shares in companies can take action to deal with the agency problem:

   (a) action against managers of companies (in the form of advice, or the imposition of outside directors on the board of management) if their actions are in conflict with shareholders' interests. This is the best course of action for fund managers to take.
   (b) They could exit the market by selling their shares in the company. However, because they hold such large portfolios of shares, selling those shares would depress the market price.

Box 1.1 Mercs, perks and clubs define the modern Irish manager

The typical Irish business leader over 45 years of age drives a Mercedes, likes to play golf . . . Those under 45 are likely to drive a BMW . . . and are less company loyal than their older counterparts. These are the results of a survey carried out by KPMG Consultants. . . . Companies were chosen from the business and finance top 1,000 companies.

Ella Shanahan, *The Irish Times*, 26 May 2000

Figure 1.1 illustrates the major factors affecting share prices. These are broadly divided into **internal** and **external** factors, and the impact of the business/economic environment.

Figure 1.1 Major factors affecting share value

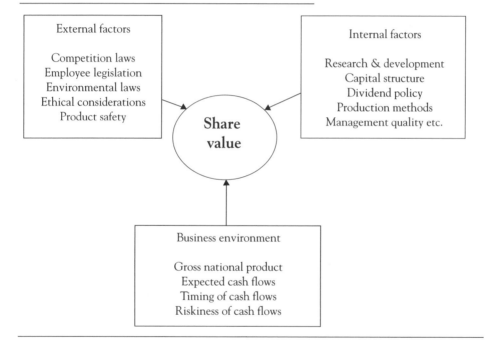

1.5 Ethics in business

Ethical issues challenge the function of business and financial management. These include the civil rights of employees and consumers, environmental pollution concerns, workplace health and safety issues, ethical responsibilities of management towards shareholders, fair employment opportunities, product safety, ethical advertising standards, bribery and corruption and insider dealing.

There is a fundamental shift throughout the world to have big business incorporate ethical issues in their investment policies. A move in Britain to have pension fund trustees look beyond a simple narrow financial focus will have repercussions in Ireland (see Box 1.2).

Box 1.2 Ethics takes centre stage in pension market

The business and financial world has recently become the target for campaigners, sometimes violent, who do not like what it does with its power and money.

Last year witnessed increased opposition to big business at a number of points throughout the world, including the well-organised demonstrations at the World Trade Organisation in Seattle as well as more violent bomb threats against investors in certain companies.

While these activists hit the headlines, a much more fundamental and peaceful shift is underway behind the scenes particularly in Britain. We in Ireland would do well to take notice of emerging developments.

From 3 July this year British pension fund trustees will have to move beyond their traditional, narrow financial focus and inform their members about the ethics that lie behind their investment policies.

The significance of this development should not be underestimated. Already the largest fund management groups are organising to monitor companies they invest in on issues ranging from energy use to labour conditions in their factories. It has been predicted that sterling £100 billion of pension fund money will soon be invested according to some kind of ethical criteria.

Most major consulting actuary firms have already set up teams to look at socially responsible investment (SRI).

Also, all the major institutions are now trying to decide how to provide these services to their customers.

The impetus for this dramatic development came originally from local authorities and others concerned about where their members' savings were going. For years, such pension trustees were read about whether they were legally allowed to discriminate between the company investments on anything other than financial grounds. The traditional view was that trustees' fiduciary duties prevented them from worrying about what the companies were doing, or how they were doing it.

The only issue to guide investment decisions was supposedly the duty to maximise financial returns for members.

During the 1990s this dictum was diluted. While trustees still had to look after members' money as best they could, as long as financial returns were not threatened they could discriminate on social and environmental grounds.

This approach mirrored the traditional ethical investment stance avoiding activities such as arms, tobacco and alcohol manufacturing, and gambling.

But the new pensions regulation moves the argument on well beyond that exclusionary approach to what has become known as 'engagement'.

Following an amendment to the 1995 British Pensions Act, trustees must declare, in their annual statement of investment principles: 'The extent (if at all) to which social, environmental or ethical considerations are taken into account in the selection, the extent and realisation of investments; and their policy (if any) directing the exercise of rights (including voting rights) attaching to investments.'

Ministers have made it clear that this is not intended to drive investments away from unpopular sectors. Instead it is based on two notions: the right of pension scheme members to know where their money is being invested; and the view that responsible businesses will be more profitable in the long term. This latter view is reflected in the ethical statement

$\longrightarrow$

which has been drawn up by Hermes, the investment manager in charge of BT's sterling £29 billion fund which is the largest in Britain and the first leading company to respond to the new regulation.

BT's fund managers will be required to consider that 'the company run in the long-term interests of its shareholders will need to manage effectively relationships with employees, suppliers and customers, to behave ethically and to have regard for the environment and society as a whole'.

This injunction is similar to the approach to be taken by the third largest British fund, the University Superannuation Scheme.

The US finally caved in last December after a long campaign by its lecturer members, and agreed to 'engage' companies about their non-financial policies and performance.

Other funds would follow suit over the next few months, but it will be some time after 3 July this year before the full impact on the business world is felt.

It is expected that trustees are taking the view that they need to respond positively to this development. They will need to because they will be targeted by dissatisfied members if they stick to the position that ethics have no place in fund management. And in the nervous world of pensions, there is also likely to be concern in some trustees' minds about their legal liability if members can be shown in a few years' time that funds which do take ethics seriously have performed better.

As a result, chief executives and finance directors are going to find themselves facing questions about their carbon dioxide emissions and human rights policies — not from campaigners whose job it is to go on about these things, but from pension fund managers.

For years companies have complained that market pressure for short-term results prevented them from taking environmental and social issues more seriously. Chief executives have frequently promised that they would be able to improve their green performance if only analysts and fund managers understood the issues and the importance of addressing subjects such as global warming or Third World labour conditions.

This argument will no longer apply. There might be some concerns regarding costs in that adding new dimensions to investment managers' research responsibilities will clearly add to costs at a time when the industry is seeking to pare expenses in pursuit of better returns for funds.

However it is possible to track indices which take account of ethical issues. And since the end of last year, investors have been able to follow the Dow Jones Sustainability Index, comprising international companies leading the field in pursuit of sustainable development. Also, while remembering that the new regulation is supposed to be about engagement, fund managers should continue to raise social and environmental issues in routine company meetings along with more mainstream issues such as investment, cost-cutting and dividend policy.

The new pensions regulation in Britain will make trustees take social and environmental issues seriously. This is clearly a welcome development in a world that is becoming increasingly conscious of the environment.

While there are a number of smaller-scale funds operating within Ireland that could be described as socially and environmentally responsible, the fact is we have not yet become alive to the demands and the opportunities such a departure will present. A new challenge has now been posed to fund managers and indeed government in Ireland to keep abreast of these exciting initiatives.

Roger Acton (head of ACCA Ireland) *Sunday Business Post*, 7 May 2000

There have been many examples of unethical business behaviour. Many of these have involved the collusion of the world of politics and business. In the late 1990s the Irish Government set up several inquiries to investigate unethical practices. These included how some of Ireland's financial institutions were involved in successful attempts to allow some investors to avoid paying deposit interest retention tax (the so called DIRT Inquiry presided over by the Dáil's Public Accounts Committee). (See Box 1.3.)

At the time of writing, there is an ongoing tribunal of inquiry into payments made to politicians in the planning process. Elected county councillors have the power to zone designated lands for commercial and residential development.

While these have all been high profile cases, companies and management must be made to understand that **ethical business behaviour can have long-term profitability gains.** It will avoid the possibility of hefty legal expenses, gain more business from customers who support ethical business policies, and it will attract high-calibre employees.

Box 1.3 Learning to recognise the law and ethics divide

Always tell the truth. That way you don't have to remember anything, declared Mark Twain.

The often contradictory memories of events recounted to the different tribunals and inquiries in Ireland suggest some witnesses have failed to take Mark Twain's advice.

An interesting example is the inquiry by the Dáil Committee of Public Accounts into DIRT. Did or did not AIB Bank have a tacit agreement with the Revenue to ignore a tax liability of up to €127.1 million? As the cat and mouse game between politicians, bankers, Revenue and barristers is played out, it is obvious the issue is being treated primarily as one of legal compliance, rather than of value systems and integrity.

Even if AIB had an amnesty from the Revenue, does that excuse its behaviour and attitude? The crux is that AIB, indeed all the banks with bogus foreign accounts, aided and abetted tax evaders. With or without Revenue agreement, their behaviour could be deemed unethical. This is the core issue, even if there is room for argument about personal responsibility of those involved.

The explanations—indeed justifications—of the behaviour of the banks and their bogus account holders typify the rationalisations often heard when unethical choices have been made: for example, 'everybody else does it' or 'if we don't do it, someone else will'. Defence of unethical behaviour on the basis of its frequent occurrence or that you will lose out to a competitor is not acceptable ethical reasoning.

'It doesn't really hurt anyone' is another justification. Tax evasion, social welfare fraud and false compensation claims fall into this category. This is because the victims of these transgressions are usually faceless, for example Dublin Corporation or insurance companies.

'The system is unfair'—tax evasion in the 1980s has been justified by way of the 'crucifying' tax rates prevailing at the time. Moreover, those who facilitated bogus foreign accounts to evade taxes have actually defended this practice on the basis that there would have been a flight of capital out of the State had they not acted as they did.

'We'll wait until the lawyers tell us it's wrong'—the philosophy of those appearing before the different inquiries with their teams of legal advisers. This attempts to equate law with ethics, not always a perfect match. There are many situations where behaviour is perfectly

$\longrightarrow$

legal but totally unethical, for example, when banks forgive large debts or influential debtors under political pressure but relentlessly pursue smaller less powerful debtors, the moral reasoning used is at a low level.

In fact, an element considered to influence ethical judgment and action is the maturity in moral reasoning attained by the individual. Lawrence Kohlberg, an American psychologist, has devised a theoretical framework that describes development in moral reasoning.

Kohlberg's theory consists of six stages of moral reasoning. The stages are sequential and invariable in their order.

At the first two stages, the person accepts good/bad or right/wrong as being externally imposed by some authority figure. In childhood, it is the parents, in adulthood, it may be the boss. At the first stage, the person 'has a punishment and obedience orientation' and does what is expected by the authority figure to avoid punishment. In business life, this childish orientation is paralleled by the mentality that nothing is wrong if you can get away with it and avoid punishment.

At the second stage, 'instrumental purpose and exchange', the individual has stepped outside him/herself to an awareness that others too have needs. In fact, the person realises that s/he can trade in the satisfaction of these needs. For instance, an employee can be encouraged to sell high margin but unsuitable products to a vulnerable class of customers. The seller might make a high rate of commission. At this development stage, the incentive of the remuneration is the main consideration of employee and employer.

At the third and fourth stages, the individual takes up group expectations as standards of moral behaviour. Conformity to the norms of one's family, or social, professional or ethnic/national groups is given as the reason for choosing one behaviour over another.

At stage three, 'good' behaviour is used to gain approval from those to whom one has an emotional or social dependency relationship. This involves the mutual maintenance of trust, loyalty, respect and gratitude to consolidate such relationships. At stage three reasoning, an employee may mis-sell products under the direction of a manager in order to retain good working relationships with the superior, and with peers engaged in the same practice for the same reasons. Of course, these practices might be disapproved of by those outside the workplace, creating a conflict of moral judgment.

In stage four, the basis of approved behaviour moves to obligations to society and the common good. The rationale for moral behaviour is to keep the institution going, to avoid a break-down in the system 'if everyone did it'. Those who have reached this stage might refuse to mis-sell products because it could harm consumers and thereby, society.

The fifth and sixth stages involve 'principled thinking', when people see beyond law for the sake of law and order, or social norms. Instead, principles guide moral behaviour. At stage five, the emphasis is still on rules and laws, but these should protect people's rights. So, an employee refusing to mis-sell products at this point would justify the refusal on the grounds that it violates the rights of customers to know the full truth.

Stage six thinking appeals to universal ethical principles. These tend to be abstract, dealing with justice, equality of human rights, respect for the dignity of human beings and the concept that human beings are ends in themselves, not instruments. At this stage, the person will have the insight to grasp complexity, the existence of conflicting principles, and the difficulty of resolving them.

$\longrightarrow$

For example companies setting up in countries where child labour and corruption are rampant have a conflict between providing indirect support for regimes which violate human rights and freedoms, and providing a livelihood, food and shelter for the citizens of those regimes.

According to Kohlberg's research, fewer than 20% of the population achieved principled thinking: most stop at stage five.

Kohlberg considers the higher stages morally preferable to lower ones. Of course, a high moral reasoning level does not guarantee moral conduct, since other factors, such as personality and organisational culture, influence behaviour. But research studies have found a moderate relationship between lower moral reasoning stages and behaviour, ranging from delinquency and fraud, to cheating at exams.

Moral reasoning stages are measurable through psychometric tests, although they are rarely used as an assessment instrument in Ireland. Had they been used, who knows? The Irish taxpayer might have been deprived of the hours of riveting entertainment showing at all the tribunals and inquiries.

Dr Eleanor O'Higgins (UCD), *The Irish Times*, 1 November 1999

1.6 Forms of business organisation

There are three main legal forms of business organisation: sole proprietorship, partnerships and limited liability companies.

Sole trader

Sole proprietorship is the most prevalent form of business organisation in Ireland and around the world. This is a business formed and owned by one individual. The general features of sole proprietorship are:

- It is independent, easily and inexpensively formed.
- It avoids corporation tax and profits are taxed at the rate of personal income tax.
- There are no requirements under the Companies Act for disclosure to the public of its accounts.
- It has the limitations that it doesn't have access to large sums of capital and has unlimited liability.
- The life of a sole proprietorship is legally limited to the life of the founder.

Partnership

A partnership exists whenever two to twenty persons carry on a business with the view of making a profit. It has the following characteristics:

- Partnerships can be formal when formed under a written deed of partnership, or informal oral agreements.
- It can easily be formed and is relatively inexpensive.
- The liability of the partners is unlimited.

- It can be in two forms: (a) **general partnership** where each partner contributes an agreed amount, and (b) **limited partnership** where some of the partners are liable for all the debts of the firm and other partner(s) are liable only for their financial contribution to the firm.
- General partnerships can be dissolved after a fixed term or after the completion of a specific venture for which the partnership was set up in the first place, the bankruptcy or death of a partner, legally on the grounds of insanity, misconduct of a partner, or viability of the business. Limited partnerships cannot be dissolved on the death, bankruptcy or lunacy of a limited partner.
- Profits are taxed at the appropriate income tax rate.

Limited liability company or the corporation

A limited liability company is a legal entity separate from its owners. The formation of a limited liability company takes the following form:[11]

- The articles of association: The rules governing the organisation are set out by the owners in a contract known as the articles of association. These govern the internal workings of the company. They set out the relative rights and duties of the management of the company and its shareholders. The main elements of the articles of association include:
  - (a) the authorised share capital of the company and its division into shares
  - (b) the voting rights of these shares
  - (c) powers of directors
  - (d) meeting of the shareholders and procedures at such meetings.
- Memorandum of association: The document governing the relationship between the company and others is set out in the memorandum of association. The main contents of the memorandum are:
  - (a) the name of the company. If the company is a public company, the words **public limited company (plc)** should be included in the name. If it is a private company the word **Limited** or **Ltd** should be included.[12]
  - (b) the main areas of activity in which the group intends to operate
  - (c) the authorised or nominal share of capital
  - (d) a statement that the liability of the members is limited.

These documents, together with a list of the directors, are sent to the registrar of companies, and if everything is in order, he/she will issue a certificate of incorporation.

The fact that the corporation is a separate legal entity (from its owners) means that it can have unlimited life and will continue after the life of its owners. Transferability of ownership is easier than in a partnership or a sole proprietorship because the ownership of a limited liability company can be divided into a number of shares which are more easily transferred. Easier transferability of shares improves liquidity, which means that it is easier to convert shares (assets) into cash.[13] The liability of a limited liability company is, as the name suggests, limited. The risk borne by the investors of a corporation is limited, which means that investors cannot lose more than the amount they invested when buying the shares. The ability of a corporation to attract capital is greater than that of a partnership or a sole trader. Consequently, growth opportunities for corporations are better.

1.7 Current trends in financial management

Currently the focus in financial management is on shareholder wealth creation. Increasingly managerial and employee remuneration packages are linked to shareholder value added. In addition, two other trends have become important, globalisation and information technology.

Globalisation and information technology

The currency crisis in south-east Asia in 1997 sparked off a global financial crisis and led to a slowdown in global economic growth. Because of economic globalisation and financial integration, virtually all businesses are affected by events in the world economy. Some multinational companies generate more in sales and output than the total GNP of some countries. Multinational companies can shift their production to different parts of the world where costs are lowest. If domestic production costs are high, survival will depend on the ability to shift production to countries where they can compete.

The forces driving outward investment range from declining global transportation and communication costs to market deregulation. The United Nations counted 572 regulatory changes affecting foreign investment worldwide, over the 1991–1996 period, which were directed at greater investment liberalisation.

Table 1.1 World average annual FDI outflows

Time	$ Billions
1970–1979	27.7
1980–1984	49.5
1985–1989	136.4
1990–1996	256.7

Source: *101 Trends every investor should know about the global economy*, J. Quinlan, K. Stevens

Advances in communication technology, computers, the World Wide Web and the Internet are changing the face of financial decision-making. 'This **new economy** has three distinguishing characteristics: it is global; it favours intangible things—ideas, information and relationships; and it is intensely interlinked. These three attributes produce a new type of marketplace and society, one that is rooted in ubiquitous electronic networks.'[14] This new economy is about communications and financial managers are able to analyse information more readily and speedily than before.

SUMMARY

- Finance is about managing money. The most fundamental principle in finance is net present value—is the market value of an investment greater than its cost?
- Finance also involves the study of the investment market.
- Shareholders will want management to manage the company so that shareholder wealth is maximised.

- Cash is king—the value of any financial asset depends on the ability of the asset to generate cash flows both now and in the future.
- Profit maximisation should not necessarily be a goal of financial management.
- Cash received sooner is more valuable.
- Reducing the riskiness of cash flows increases share value.
- Agency theory deals with the conflict of interest between managers and shareholders.
- Ethical issues challenge the function of business and financial management.
- There are three legal forms of business organisation: partnership, limited liability companies and sole proprietorship.
- Advances in technology, the Internet and the World Wide Web are changing the face of financial and investment decision-making.

QUESTIONS

1. What is finance about?
2. Explain the link between the study of finance and the study of investment markets.
3. What do you understand by the term 'shareholder value'?
4. Should profit maximisation be an objective of financial management? Explain your answer.
5. In finance 'Cash is king.' Discuss.
6. Illustrate and outline the factors influencing share value.
7. Define agency theory.
8. Define (a) sole trader, (b) partnership and (c) corporation.
9. 'Surely if the firm maximises profits it will simultaneously maximise share price.' Would you agree?
10. Describe the legal and ethical challenges that face the financial manager.
11. For class discussion: Should managers be interested only in the maximisation of shareholder wealth or should they be also interested in the welfare of society at large?

NOTES

1. Heiton Holdings plc, Report and Financial Statement 1999.
2. See 'The Goals of the Corporation', in *Financial Management—Theory and Practice*, 9th edn, Bringham, Gapenski and Ehrhardt, chapter 1.
3. Heiton Holdings plc, Report and Financial Statement 1999.
4. 'A year of Progress', Barlo Group Annual Report 1998.
5. The 'time value of money' is discussed in Chapter 4.
6. See 'Theory of the Firm, Managerial Behaviour, Agency Costs and Ownership Structure', M.C. Jensen and W.J. Meckling in the *Journal of Financial Economics*, October 1976.
7. Takeovers and mergers are discussed in Chapter 19.
8. Stock options are discussed in Chapter 17.
9. Economic value added (EVA) is a way of measuring true company profitability. By maximising EVA, managers maximise shareholder value. We discuss EVA in detail in subsequent chapters.
10. Kerry Group Annual Report & Accounts 1998.

11. These are set out in the Companies Act 1963, Table A.
12. We will discuss in more detail the difference between a public and a private company in Chapter 11.
13. Liquidity is discussed in detail in Chapters 3, 13 and 15.
14. *New Rules for the New Economy*, Kevin Kelly.

2
Financial Statements and Cash Flow

CHAPTER OBJECTIVES

At the end of this chapter the student will be able to:

1. understand the relevant features of financial statements
2. appreciate the distinction between cash flow and profitability
3. understand the concepts of operating cash flow and free cash flow
4. understand that operating performance is measured by reference to free cash flow.

INTRODUCTION

This chapter examines financial statements and cash flow. Chapter 1 emphasised that shareholder value maximisation depends on the generation of cash flow. The starting point in forecasting future cash flows begins in the financial statements. This chapter does not deal with the preparation of financial statements. It emphasises that financial statements provide information for management in their decision-making.

2.1 The balance sheet

A balance sheet is a list of a company's assets, liabilities and equity at any one point in time. It is a snapshot of the company. The reader might like to draw up his/her own balance sheet by making a list of his/her assets and liabilities. **Assets** are what you own (e.g. cash, property, books etc.) or what is owed to you (people who owe you money). **Liabilities** are what you owe to other people (loans to the bank or building society, to your class mate). The difference between the value of your assets and your liabilities is your equity or net worth.

This is expressed in the balance sheet equation:

$$\textbf{Assets} = \textbf{Liabilities} + \textbf{Equity} \qquad (2.1)$$

Balance sheets are divided into five sections:

1. Fixed assets
2. Current assets
3. Current liabilities
4. Long-term debt
5. Equity.

Figure 2.1 shows how the balance sheet is constructed. On the left-hand side is a list of the assets and on the right-hand side is a list of the company's liabilities and equity.

Figure 2.1 The balance sheet

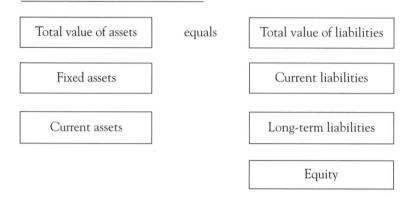

The balance sheet of a hypothetical company Genesis Ltd is provided in Table 2.1. The current year (2001) and the previous year's (2000) data is provided.

Fixed assets

Fixed assets are assets that are expected to provide a benefit to the firm for more than one year. They are held for long-term use in the business. For example, plant and machinery is described as a tangible fixed asset. Similarly, intangible fixed assets such as trademarks and patents have a life that can span over many years. Genesis Ltd has fixed assets of €2,640,000 at book value.

Current assets

On the other hand, current assets have a life of less than one year. It is expected that current assets will be converted into cash within one year. For example, stock would normally be sold within a year. The exception of course is stock that has remained unsold during the year. In this case, the closing stock would be carried forward to the following year. Cash and debtors (or accounts receivables) are also current assets. Genesis has €1,747,000 in current assets. This is made up of €890,000 in stock, which is what the company has produced but has not sold to its customers. It has €850,000 in debtors. This is what customers owe to Genesis.[1] It has cash of €7,000.[2]

Table 2.1 Balance sheet as at 31 December 2001   (€000)

	2001	2000
Fixed assets		
Plant and machinery (net)	2,640	1,923
Current assets		
Stock	890	830
Debtors	850	630
Short-term investments		130
Cash	7	70
	1,747	1,660
Amounts falling due within one year (current liabilities)		
Creditors	120	60
Bank overdraft	220	120
	340	180
Net current assets	1,407	1,480
Total assets *less* current liabilities	4,047	3,403
Amounts falling due after more than one year		
Long-term debt	1,700	1,160
Capital and reserves		
Preference shares	80	80
Ordinary shares	220	220
Retained earnings	2,047	1,943
	4,047	3,403

Current liabilities

Current liabilities have a life of less than one year. In other words, it is expected that they will be paid within 12 months. Creditors are companies and individuals to whom the firm owes money. Genesis owes suppliers €120,000 for materials it purchased on credit.[3] It has a bank overdraft of €220,000.[4] This is a short-term loan which is repayable to the bank within a year.

Net working capital

Net working capital (NWC) is current assets *minus* current liabilities:

$$\text{Net working capital} = \text{Current assets} - \text{Current liabilities} \qquad (2.2)$$

NWC is positive when current assets are greater than current liabilities. This would be the normal case for healthy companies. For Genesis, this is €1,747,000 – €340,000 = €1,407,000. This is sometimes shown as **net current assets**.

Long-term liabilities

Any debt that is not due within the year is a long-term liability. Firms borrow in the long term from a number of different sources and for different reasons.[5] Genesis has €1,700,000 in long-term debt. The figure on the balance sheet refers only to the **principal** or the actual amount borrowed. The interest paid on the debt appears in the profit and loss account, which we discuss in the next section.

Shareholders' equity (or net worth)

The difference between the value of the firm's assets and the firm's liabilities is the company's equity. In a sense, this figure makes the balance sheet balance. This is depicted in equation 2.1 and is referred to as the balance sheet equation. Genesis has a net worth of €2,347,000.

The equity section shows preference shares, ordinary shares and retained earnings. A fixed rate of dividends is paid on preference shares and they have priority on dividend payments over ordinary shareholders. The ordinary share capital is the original investment made by the shareholders. This is the **book value** of their investment. The **market value** of their investment will depend on the market price of the shares. We discuss this in more detail in Chapter 8.

The figure for retained earnings is the sum of all the earnings that have been available to ordinary shareholders since the inception of the business *less* all dividends paid to ordinary shareholders since its inception. This amounts to €2,047,000 for Genesis. **This does not constitute cash**. Earnings retained by the company over the years will have been invested in various projects by the company or may have been used to pay off some outstanding debts.

2.2 The profit and loss account or income statement

The profit and loss account is a summary of the performance of the firm over a certain period—a year or a quarter of a year. The profit and loss account equation is:

$$\text{Income (profit)} = \text{Revenue} - \text{Expenses} \qquad (2.3)$$

Revenues are the gross income (sales) of the company. Expenses represent the costs incurred in generating this revenue. The profit and loss account of Genesis is given in Table 2.2.

Table 2.2 Genesis Ltd

Profit and loss account for the year ended 31 December 2001   (€000)

	2001	2000
Turnover	6,000	5,700
Cost of sales	3,260	3,104
Gross profit	2,740	2,596
Selling and distribution	1,086	1,034
Administration	923	879
Depreciation	162	155
Profit before interest and tax (PBIT)	569	528
Interest paid	180	120
Profit before taxation (PBT)	389	408
Taxation (30%)	117	125
Profit after tax (PAT)	272	283
Preference dividends	8	8
Profit available for ordinary shareholders	264	275
Ordinary dividends	160	170
Retained earnings	104	105

Turnover

This is the revenue or sales generated by Genesis which came to €6,000,000.

Cost of goods sold

This represents the direct costs of the goods sold, e.g. direct labour, materials and direct overheads. These costs come to 54.3% of sales income. Deducting the cost of sales from sales we get gross profit which equals €2,740,000.

Selling, distribution and administration

These include salaries paid to sales people, marketing expenses, insurance and other office expenses. This figure is deducted from gross profit. The total for Genesis is €2,009,000.

Depreciation

Assets generate sales. Depreciation is that part of a fixed asset consumed when generating the sales. It is an expense and like all expenses will be entered as expenses in the profit and loss account.

Operating profit

Having deducted the cost of goods sold, selling, distribution, administration and depreciation expenses from gross profit we are left with profit before interest and tax (PBIT) or **operating profit**. This is an extremely significant figure, as we shall see later on in the chapter. Genesis's operating income is €569,000.

Profit before tax

The interest paid on the company's borrowings is deducted from the operating profit to arrive at the profit before taxes (PBT). For Genesis this is €389,000.

Profit after tax (PAT)

Having deducted all operating expenses and financing costs, we are left with net profit (income) or profit after tax. The PAT for Genesis is €272,000.

Preference dividends

Once the net profit has been determined, the preference shareholders receive their dividends. What is left is profit available for the ordinary shareholders. Preference dividends to Genesis's preference shareholders came to €8,000.

Ordinary dividends

Dividend policy is discussed in Chapter 12 but, in a nutshell, a company can pay out all of the remaining profit (after paying preference shareholders their dividends) or reinvest the profits in the company or lay out some of the earnings and reinvest the remainder.[6] Retained earnings are that proportion of the profit after tax that is retained (reinvested) in the firm. The rest is paid out as dividends to the ordinary shareholders. Of the €264,000 profit after tax and preference dividends for Genesis, €160,000 (60%) is given to shareholders as dividends, while the remainder €104,000 (40%) is retained in the company. For convenience we have rounded off these figures.

2.3 Statement of cash flows

Although companies can make large profits during the year, the amount of cash the company reports in its balance sheet may be the same at the end of the year as it was at the beginning of the year—it may be even less. The net profit made during the year is not always kept as cash. It can be used in a variety of ways. For example, it could be used to purchase fixed assets, to finance an increase in debtors or stock, or to pay dividends to its shareholders. The statement of cash flows shows how cash flows into and out of a business over a period. The statement of cash flows is constructed by distinguishing between cash flow and income in the profit and loss account, and by comparing the changes in the balance sheet between the beginning and the end of the accounting period. Have a look at Genesis's cash flow for the year 2001 in Table 2.3.

Table 2.3 Statement of cash flows for 2001—Genesis Ltd

Operating profit	€569
Depreciation	€162
Increase in stocks	€(60)
Increase in debtors	€(220)
Increase in creditors	€60
Operating cash flow before interest and tax	€511
Less Servicing of finance	
Interest paid	€(180)
Less	
Taxation paid	€(117)
Net cash flow before investing and financing	€214
Less Dividend payments	€(168)
Capital expenditure	
Purchase of fixed assets[7]	€(879)
Net cash flow before financing	€(833)
Financing activities	
Sale of short-term investments	€130
Increase in long-term debt	€540
Decrease in cash during the year	€(163)
Summary of change in cash[8]	
Change in cash	€(163)
Cash at the beginning	€(50)
Cash at the end	€(213)

Depreciation

Net profit is arrived at after depreciation is calculated and deducted as an expense. Depreciation is included with all the other expenses, administration, distribution etc. There is one important distinction between depreciation and these other expenses— **depreciation does not involve a movement of cash**. The financial manager does not sign a cheque for depreciation. Therefore, since depreciation does not involve the movement of cash (it is a non-cash expense), it must be added back to net profit when calculating the company's cash flow.

Changes in current assets and current liabilities

Any changes in the company's balance sheet during the year will indicate changes in the company's cash flow.

An increase in current assets (except cash) will decrease cash. A decrease in current assets increases cash balances. Buying additional stock, for instance, will mean that the company will have to use some of its cash balance to pay for the additional inventory. On the other hand, if stock decreases from one year to the next, the company must be selling more stock than it is buying and so cash will be increasing. In addition, an increase in accounts payable (creditors) will mean the company is getting more time to pay its bills, which saves cash. A decrease in creditors will mean a reduction in cash. These changes along with depreciation are referred to as changes in operating activities.

Servicing of finance

Interest on debt involves a cash outlay, as does taxation paid on company profits.

Changes in fixed assets

Buying fixed assets will reduce cash and the sale of fixed assets will increase cash. These are investing activities.

Changes in share capital and borrowings

Selling additional shares or bonds will increase cash. On the other hand, the company could use some of its cash to buy back shares,[9] pay dividends to its shareholders or pay off some of its outstanding debt.

2.4 Importance of the statement of cash flows

The cash flow statement is probably the most important financial statement because of the information that it provides. **The financial manager will need to know if the company is generating sufficient cash flow to finance additional fixed assets to generate further growth and repay debt.** Genesis's net profit (profit after tax) is €272,000. Adding the non-cash charge for depreciation (€162,000) to the net profit gives the **net cash flow** of €434,000. However, it has used €220,000 to finance increases in working capital[10] to give a net cash flow from operations of €214,000. **This figure (net cash flow from operations) is a hugely important figure in finance. Companies can report net profits but simultaneously have negative operational cash flow.** As we will see in Chapter 6, profits can be manipulated in a variety of ways but it is not possible to manipulate operational cash flow. **So in this respect the cash flow from operational activities can be much more reliable in assessing the financial 'well-being' of a company.**

Genesis purchased fixed assets (gross) €879,000 in 2001. The company raised an additional €540,000 in borrowings and €130,000 by selling short-term investments. It paid out €168,000 in dividends to preferred and ordinary shareholders. Considering all these activities we find that Genesis's cash outflows were greater than its cash inflows by €163,000. The good news from the cash flow statement is that it has a positive cash flow from operating activities. However, it purchased additional fixed assets while borrowing heavily and paying out cash to shareholders. This situation could have long-term repercussions for Genesis.

2.5 Operating performance

In the opening chapter, we said that one of the primary goals of financial management is shareholder wealth maximisation. Shareholders are the owners of companies and they appoint directors to direct the operations. Directors in turn appoint managers to run the company by investing shareholders' money in a way that maximises shareholder value. Managers will in turn be compensated by reference to how successful they have been in meeting this objective. However it would only be fair to assess managers' performance by looking at the operating income they have generated with the assets they have under their control. In other words, **operating profit (profit before interest and tax) is the appropriate yardstick.** Companies will have different capital structures (debt in relation to equity) and consequently different interest payments. The capital structure decision is a decision taken outside the realm of operational management. Consequently, an inappropriate capital structure could wipe out an otherwise impressive operating profit. Similarly companies can have different tax structures. Therefore it would be unfair to compare two companies with different tax structures by looking at their profit after tax. Profit after tax is an unsound way of evaluating the performance of a company's employees and operating managers.

2.6 Net operating profit after tax (NOPAT)

The best measure of a company's operating performance is net operating profit after tax.[11] It would be unfair to measure the performance of managers and employees alike by looking at net profit because this figure is calculated after interest is paid on debt. The amount of debt a company takes on is a decision taken by the directors of the company. In other words, a good operating performance by managers and employees could be destroyed by interest payments. **NOPAT is the after-tax profit earned if the company had no debt.**

Net operating profit after tax is defined as:

$$NOPAT = PBIT(1-T) \qquad (2.4)$$

where PBIT is profit before interest and tax, and T is the corporation tax rate the company pays on its profits, in this case 30%.

For Genesis the NOPAT = €569,000(1 − 0.3) = €398,300.

2.7 Calculating free cash flow[12]

The concept of **free cash flow** is a crucially important concept in finance, a concept we will return to in Chapter 6 on company valuations.

We have already noted that net cash flow is net profit *plus* any non-cash flow items like depreciation. However some of this cash flow must be used to replace fixed assets and working capital (operating capital) in order to continue and expand operations. Therefore **free cash flow** refers to what is left (free) to distribute to shareholders and lenders. Therefore increasing shareholder value means increasing free cash flow.

The first step in calculating free cash flow is to define and distinguish between operating and non-operating assets. Operating assets are assets used to operate the business. Operating assets are divided into operating working capital (cash, debtors, stock) and operating fixed assets (plant and machinery). Non-operating assets will include marketable securities, investments in land for future use and subsidiaries etc. The current assets included in operating working capital are those that *do not pay interest*. Companies will tend to hold a certain amount of cash for operating purposes as well as minimum amounts of stock and debtors. Investments in, say, marketable securities are excluded because these are decisions made by the directors of the company and are not part of core operations.

The current liabilities included in operating working capital are those that *do not charge interest*. These include creditors and accruals. Bank overdrafts and short-term loans are excluded in calculating net operating working capital because they are treated as investment capital.

Therefore

Total operating capital = Net operating working capital + Net fixed assets   (2.5)

and

Net operating working capital = (Stock + debtors + cash) – (Creditors + accruals)   (2.6)

For Genesis we have

Net operating working capital =(€890,000 + €850,000 + €7,000) – (€120,000) = €1,627,000

and

Net fixed assets = €2,640,000, which gives

Total operating capital (2001) = €1,627,000 + 2,640,000 = €4,267,000

For the year 2000 the total operating capital is

Net operating working capital = (€830,000 + €630,000 + €70,000) – (€60,000) = €1,470,000

Net fixed assets = €1,923,000. This gives

Total operating capital (2000) = €1,470,000 + €1,923,000 = €3,393,000[13]

The increase in total net operating capital from the year 2000 to 2001 is €874,000. A summary of the change in total net operating working capital is given in Table 2.4.

Table 2.4 Summary of changes in total net operating capital

(Genesis Ltd)

	2001	2000
	€	€
Plant & machinery	2,640	1,923
Stock	890	830
Debtors	850	630
Cash	7	70
Creditors	(120)	(60)
	4,267	3,393
	Change of €874,000	

2.8 Operating cash flow

Operating cash flow is NOPAT *plus* non-cash adjustments such as depreciation.

$$\text{Operating cash flow} = \text{NOPAT} + \text{Depreciation} \qquad (2.7)$$

For Genesis this is

$$\text{NOPAT} + \text{Depreciation}$$
$$= €398,300 + €162,000 = €560,300$$

Remember that free cash flow is operating cash flow *less* any gross investment in operating capital, i.e. in net operating working capital and in net fixed assets.

$$\text{Free cash flow} = \text{Operating cash flow} - \text{Gross investment in operating capital} \quad (2.8)$$

where

$$\textbf{Gross investment in operating capital} =$$
$$\textbf{Net investment in operating capital} + \textbf{Depreciation} \qquad (2.9)$$

For Genesis

Gross investment in operating capital = Net investment in operating capital + Depreciation
$$€1,036,000 = €874,000 + €162,000$$

Therefore free cash flow is

$$\text{Free cash flow} = \text{Operating cash flow} - \text{Gross investment in operating capital}$$
$$€(475,700) = €560,300 - 1,036,000$$

There are two alternative definitions of free cash flow, both providing the same result:

1. **Free cash flow (FCF) = NOPAT – Net investment in operating capital**   **(2.10)**

Equation 2.10 gives the same result as equation 2.8:

Free cash flow (FCF) = NOPAT – Net investment in operating capital
(€475,700) = €398,300 – €874,000

2. **Free cash flow** = $\left(\begin{array}{c} \textbf{Operating} \\ \textbf{cash flow} \end{array} \right) - \left(\begin{array}{c} \textbf{Expenditure} \\ \textbf{on fixed assets} \end{array} \right) + \left(\begin{array}{c} \textbf{Increase in} \\ \textbf{operating} \\ \textbf{working capital} \end{array} \right)$ (2.11)

Equation 2.11 gives the same result as equations 2.10 and 2.11:

Free cash flow = $\left(\begin{array}{c} \text{Operating} \\ \text{cash flow} \end{array} \right) - \left(\begin{array}{c} \text{Expenditure} \\ \text{on fixed assets} \end{array} \right) + \left(\begin{array}{c} \text{Increase in} \\ \text{operating} \\ \text{working capital} \end{array} \right)$

(€475,700) = €560,300 – (€879,000 + €157,000)

Equation 2.11 can be shown in tabular format as

Free cash flow =	
Operating cash flow	€560,300
Less Expenditure on fixed assets	€(879,000)
Plus Increase in operating working capital	€(157,000)
= Free cash flow	€(475,700)

The investments it made during the year in operating capital have wiped out the positive NOPAT. Free cash flow is what is left over for investors. Not only was there nothing left over but also additional investor capital was provided in the form of debt capital. There are two points to remember here:

1. If the NOPAT is negative, it probably spells something fundamentally wrong with operations.
2. **A negative free cash flow is not always a bad sign**. In fact, it might prove to be very positive. If the additional investments in operating capital are used for positive NPV projects, it will add value to the firm in the form of higher free cash flows in the future. In fact, many so called growth companies have positive NOPAT but negative free cash flows. This is because they are at the growth stage of their business cycle and will incur significant expenditures to launch their product.

SUMMARY

- Balance sheets are lists of companies' assets and liabilities
- The profit and loss account is a statement of the financial performance over a period.
- The statement of cash flow is a summary of the number of euros that came into the business and the number of euros that went out of the business.

- Cash flow is important because investors know that it is cash flow (not profits as reported on the profit and loss account) that will pay creditors, dividends and fund additional investment projects.
- Net operating capital is the amount of capital that the company needs to continue operations.
- Net operating profit after tax (NOPAT) is the profit after tax that a company would have if it had no debt. It excludes the impact of financing activities and is therefore a better measure of the operating performance of the operating managers and employees.
- Free cash flow is the amount of cash that is available for distribution to shareholders and investors. Maximising free cash flow maximises shareholder value.

QUESTIONS

1. Explain each of the following terms:
    (a) the five sections of the balance sheet
    (b) the income statement
    (c) the cash flow statement
    (d) net worth
    (e) net operating working capital
    (f) total operating working capital
    (g) net cash flow
    (h) NOPAT.
2.♦ Explain the significance of the difference between NOPAT and PAT.
3. Explain operating cash flow and net cash flow.
4. The figures shown on the profit and loss account may not represent the cash position of the company at the end of the year. Why? Discuss.
5. If a company's free cash flow is negative, is this a bad sign? What about operating cash flow?
6. How would you explain a negative change in net working capital during the year?
7.♦ Lexus Ltd has €30,000 in fixed assets, €10,000 in current assets, €3,000 in current liabilities, €15,000 in debentures. Calculate the net worth and net working capital.
8. Sales for Quirkie & Co. for the year just ended came to €1,000,000. Costs incurred amounted to €600,000. Depreciation on fixed assets was €10,000 and interest charges came to €5,000. Calculate the net profit assuming taxation of 15%. If it pays out 10% in dividends, what is the addition to retained earnings?
9.♦ Sales for the year amounted to €1,000,000. The cost of goods sold was €600,000. Depreciation was €12,000 and interest charges came to €5,000. Tax was at the rate of 15%. Calculate the operating cash flow.
10. The following information is provided from the profit and loss account and balance sheet of Dominican Limited for the year 2000.

Sales	€100,000
Cost of sales	€60,000
Administration expenses	€5,000
Depreciation	€7,000
Interest paid	€12,000
Taxation	€6,000
Dividends	€6,500
Ordinary shares issued during the year	€2,000
Redeemed long-term debt	€6,000

Calculate: (a) The operating cash flow for the year 2000.
(b) The cash flow to shareholders.
(c) Cash flow to creditors.

11.   The total assets of Alpha Ltd is €4,000,000. It has to pay creditors €3,600,000 during the year. Calculate the value of shareholders' funds.

12.♦ The following information is available from the accounts of Alexis Ltd:

Sales	€1,000,000
Cost of sales	€600,000
Depreciation	€10,000
Interest charges	€3,000
Dividends paid	€4,000
Change in fixed assets (net) during the year	€30,000
Change in current assets	€6,000
Change in current liabilities	€2,500
Taxation (15%)	

Calculate: (i) the net profit; (ii) operating cash flow; (iii) free cash flow

13.♦ A company's profit after tax for the year was €1m and its profit before interest and tax was €3m. The company's corporate tax rate is 15%. How much did it pay in interest charges?

14.   The profit before interest and tax of O'Keeffe Ltd is €600,000. The company's tax rate is 20% and it has no debt. Depreciation of fixed assets was €100,000. Calculate the company's net cash flow and its operating cash flow.

15.   The financial statements of Beta Ltd are as follows:

Profit and loss account for year ended 31 December

	2001	2000
Turnover	€1,500	€1,000
Cost of sales	€1,200	€800
Gross profit	€300	€200
Depreciation	€35	€25
Profit before interest and taxes	€265	€175
Interest	€27	€17
Profit before taxes	€238	€158
Taxes (20%)	€48	€32
Profit after tax	€190	€126
Ordinary dividends	€139	€88

Balance sheet as at 31 December	2001	2000
Fixed assets (net)	€400	€260
Current assets		
Stock	€225	€250
Debtors	€200	€125
Cash	€16	€11
Total current assets	€441	€386
Current liabilities		
Creditors	€148	€95
Short-term debt	€85	€53
Accrued expenses	€90	€65
Total current liabilities	€323	€213
Net working capital	€118	€173
Net total assets	€518	€433
Long-term debt	€185	€185
Ordinary share capital	€60	€60
Retained earnings	€273	€188
	€518	€433

Calculate
(a) NOPAT for 2001.
(b) Net operating working capital for 2000 and 2001.
(c) Total operating capital for 2000 and 2001.
(d) Free cash flow for 2001.

NOTES

1. The management of debtors or accounts receivable is explored in Chapter 14.
2. The appropriate or optimum amount of cash a company should hold is discussed in Chapter 13 on cash management.
3. The management of inventory and accounts payable (creditors) is discussed in Chapter 14.
4. Sources of short-term finance are discussed in Chapter 15.
5. The amount of money borrowed by firms is a crucial decision in financial management and is discussed in detail in Chapter 8.
6. There is another option and that is to repurchase some of the shares. Share purchase is discussed in Chapter 12.
7. There was a net increase in fixed assets of €2,640 − £1,923 = €717. This is the net increase *after* the deduction for this year's depreciation. Therefore, the depreciation expense should be added back in to show the total increase in *gross* fixed assets.
8. Remember that an **overdraft** is seen as **negative** cash. So therefore the opening cash is €70 − €120 (overdraft) = €50. Cash at the end of the year is €7 − €220 (overdraft) = €213.
9. Share buy-backs are discussed in Chapter 12.
10. Cash used for increases in stock €(60,000) + cash used to finance increases in debtors €(220,000) *less* an increase in cash from an increase in creditors €60,000 = €220,000.

11. Remember PAT is profit **after** tax and after interest is paid on company debt. NOPAT is profit after tax but **before** interest is paid on debt.
12. There are different methods used in calculating **free cash flow**. The general method used here is that used by Brigham, Gapenski and Ehrhardt (op. cit.).
13. We do not include the figure for short-term investments because these are investments made, which do not impact on operations. This is an asset which is not under the control of the operating managers.

3
Financial Statement Analysis

CHAPTER OBJECTIVES

Having completed this chapter the student will be able:

1. to interpret from financial statements:
   (a) the ability of companies to meet their short-term financial obligations—liquidity ratios
   (b) how efficiently the company is using their assets—asset management ratios
   (c) the extent to which the firm uses debt finance to fund their operations—gearing ratios
   (d) the overall effect of liquidity, asset management and gearing on company profitability—profitability ratios

2. and be able to:
   (a) show how the most important ratio in business, the return on equity (ROE) is affected by asset turnover, the profit margin and gearing—the Du Pont formula
   (b) show how liquidity, asset management, gearing and profitability affect market valuation—company valuation ratios.
   (c) assess the trends in financial ratios over periods of time—trend analysis
   (d) introduce the concepts of market value added (MVA) and economic value added (EVA)
   (e) understand the difficulties in making international accounting comparisons
   (f) highlight the weaknesses of ratio analysis.

INTRODUCTION

Financial statements provide a wealth of information about the financial health and state of affairs of companies. As we have seen in Chapter 1, the principal purpose of management is to maximise company value. Financial analysis will help in this regard by comparing and evaluating trends over time. Financial performance is often measured by using financial ratios. Ratio analysis is concerned with quantifying the relationship between key variables in a company's financial statements. The information provided by ratio analysis is used by different groups of people including management, employees, creditors, banks and the suppliers of goods and services. Information unlocked from company financial statements using financial analysis will show the ability the company has:

1. in meeting its day-to-day financial obligations (liquidity).
2. in calculating the rate of return it is getting from its capital invested (profitability).
3. in establishing the efficiency with which it is using its assets and the extent to which it has used borrowed funds to finance its operations (gearing).

In this chapter financial ratios will be calculated using hypothetical data.

3.1 Solvency—liquidity ratios

Solvency refers to the ability of a firm to pay its liabilities as they fall due. In other words, a firm must have sufficient liquid assets to meet its financial obligations. A liquid asset is one that can be quickly converted into cash.

A firm is liquid if
(a) the company's total assets exceed its total liabilities—a positive **net worth**. This is long-term solvency.
(b) the firm is able to pay all its short-term debts as they fall due. If its short-term assets exceed its short-term liabilities—short-term solvency.

3.1.1 The current ratio

Short-term (current) liabilities refer to **less than one year**. Therefore, in balance sheets the heading **amounts falling due within one year** refers to short-term debt, whereas **amounts falling due after more than one year** refers to long-term debt. Short-term liabilities consist of accounts payable, bank overdrafts, short-term loans, current maturities of long-term debt, accrued taxes (taxes due), and other accrued expenses such as wages.

Current assets are those that can be quickly converted into cash. Current assets normally include stocks, accounts receivable (debtors), marketable securities and cash.

The ratio of current assets to current (short-term) liabilities is referred to as the current ratio. The current ratio is calculated by dividing current assets by current liabilities:

$$\text{Current ratio} = \frac{\text{Current assets}}{\text{Current liabilities}} \tag{3.1}$$

At this stage it is important to point out that ratios on their own do not mean anything because a ratio is simply one number divided by another. We need to look behind the figures and analyse what items make up the assets and liabilities that constitute the ratio. We need to look at the trends in the company's ratios over a number of years to see if they are improving or not. Finally, we need to compare our company's ratios with ratios of similar companies in the same industry—this is known as **benchmarking**.

The data given in Tables 3.1, 3.2 and 3.3 is taken from a hypothetical company Genesis Ltd, which published its accounts as at 31 December 2001.

Table 3.1 Genesis Ltd

Balance sheet as at 31 December 2001	€000s	
	2001	2000
Fixed assets		
Plant and machinery (net)	2,640	1,923
Current assets		
Stock	890	830
Debtors	850	630
Short-term investments		130
Cash	7	70
	1,747	1,660
Amounts falling due within one year (current liabilities)		
Creditors	120	.60
Bank overdraft	220	120
	340	180
Net current assets	1,407	1,480
Total assets *less* current liabilities	4,047	3,403
Amounts falling due after more than one year		
Long-term debt	1,700	1,160
Capital and reserves		
Preference shares	80	80
Ordinary shares	220	220
Retained earnings	2,047	1,943
	4,047	3,403

We can see from the balance sheet for the year 2001 that Genesis has €1,747 in current assets and €340 in current liabilities. The current ratio is got by dividing current assets by current liabilities:

2001	2000	Industry average
Current ratio $\dfrac{€1,747}{€340} = 5.14$ times	$\dfrac{€1,660}{€180} = 9.2$ times	6 times

This means it has €5.14 in short-term assets for every €1 in current liabilities, which is lower than the average. Is this good or bad? To answer this question we need to consider the following:

(a)   What type of company we are looking at? For example, the current liabilities of food stores are usually greater than their current assets. They don't hold a great deal of stock (perishable goods), don't usually provide credit but they get the usual credit terms from their suppliers. Because cash flows into the shop on a daily basis, they can feel confident of meeting their short-term debts. On the other hand, manufacturers will usually have lots of cash tied up in raw materials, work-in-progress and finished goods, and will provide whatever the usual credit terms are to their customers (debtors). At the same time, the demand for cash will come from employees (wages), the banks (in the form of interest payments) and their suppliers (creditors).   Therefore, manufacturers will need to have more in current assets than current liabilities. How much more depends on the length of the **conversion cycle** or the **working capital cycle.**   The conversion cycle estimates the length of time it takes to convert raw materials back into cash. The longer this time period, the greater the need for a higher current ratio. For example a heavy engineering company's conversion cycle could be nine to twelve months and it will therefore need a high current ratio, whereas a bakery products company will need a lower current ratio.

(b)   A high current ratio does not necessarily mean that a company is liquid and a low current ratio does not necessarily mean that it is illiquid. An example should illustrate this point.

Example 3.1 Current ratios and liquidity

Firm A and firm B have the same current ratio but they have quite different liquidity profiles:

Current assets:	Firm A (€)	Firm B (€)
Stocks	20,000	10,000
Debtors	5,000	15,000
Cash	5,000	5,000
	30,000	30,000
Current liabilities	15,000	15,000
Current ratio	2:1	2:1

Firm B will have an inflow of cash from debtors of €15,000, while firm A, over the same period, will have an inflow of cash from debtors of just €5,000. The current ratio, on its own, doesn't show this.

(a)   Look at the ratio over a period. Is it improving or disimproving? Later on in this chapter we consider how this is done in the section on trend analysis.

(b)   Who is asking the question? For example, if **suppliers** were thinking of extending credit to a company, they would like to see a high current ratio. If current liabilities are rising faster than current assets, the current ratio will fall and this could spell trouble for suppliers. From the point of view of a **shareholder**, a high current ratio may not be good. Recently, for example, Fyffes plc had a lot of money tied up in non-productive assets such as excess cash. With interest rates so low, shareholders were not happy with the rate of return they were getting. They demanded that the company use the cash to invest in a suitable acquisition so those shareholders would see a higher rate of return. The situation was resolved when the company reduced its cash holding by making an acquisition.

(c)   Industry average ratios: If a firm's ratios are far removed from the industry average then this should act as a clear warning signal for management. Corrective and radical action may be needed. **However, reaching industry average ratios should not necessarily be the ultimate objective of management.** Some companies will exceed the industry average while other good companies may be below the industry average. A falling current ratio, for example, could mean that the company is very proficient in just-in-time stock control or it could mean that its stock control is very poor and so the company may be unable to meet orders and therefore sales. Genesis is below the industry average, which would indicate a relatively weak liquidity position. But at a ratio of 5.13:1, Genesis could liquidate their current assets at only 19.5% of their book value to pay off their current creditors in full ($1 \div 5.13 = 19.5\%$). It is often said that a current ratio of 2:1 should be the target. There is no scientific basis for this assertion except to say that it does seem to be a ratio which companies work towards, and in this sense it gains some validity.

3.1.2 Quick ratio or acid test ratio

The **quick or acid test ratio** is calculated by deducting inventories (stocks) from current assets and dividing the remainder by current liabilities. Stocks are usually the least liquid of a company's current assets because if the demand for a company's product falls off, then stocks won't be sold and are therefore not liquid.

$$\text{Quick ratio} \quad = \quad \frac{\text{Current assets } less \text{ stock}}{\text{Current liabilities}} \qquad (3.2)$$

	2001	2000	Industry average
Quick ratio	$\dfrac{(€1,747 - €890)}{€340} = 2.52$ times	$\dfrac{(€1,660 - €830)}{€180} = 4.6$ times	3 times

This means that, excluding stocks, for every €2.52 the company has in short-term assets it owes €1 to its creditors. In practice, companies will aim for a ratio of 1:1 (i.e. liquid assets are sufficient to cover short-term liabilities) but again, like the current ratio, a quick ratio of less than 1:1 does not necessarily spell disaster. For example, if a firm has liquid assets of £2,500 and current liabilities of £5,000 (a quick ratio of 0.5:1), the company would appear to have liquidity problems. Like the current ratio, the composition of liquid assets and current liabilities is important. Liquid assets could consist of €2,000 in cash and €500 in debtors, while the current liabilities could comprise €2,000 in creditors due in three months, and tax due of €3,000 to be paid in nine months' time. The firm will be able to meet its short-term obligations and will probably be able to generate enough cash flow in the remaining six months to cover its tax liability.

Genesis has a quick ratio less than the average for other firms in the same industry. However, if Genesis can collect accounts receivable (debtors) on time, it will be able to pay off current liabilities without having to liquidate its stock. The question to ask ourselves here is **what would happen if all the company's creditors asked for immediate payment**. Faced with this situation, the company would look to those assets that could easily be turned into cash within a short space of time (a day or a week). It may not be possible to sell off stocks in this space of time (if at all), particularly if it is a manufacturing company. However, some businesses such as retailers may be able to realise all of their assets including stocks.

3.1.3 Creditors payments period

Like the current ratio, we must look behind the quick ratio and ask how likely is it that company creditors will look for **immediate payment**. We can calculate on average how long it is taking the company to pay its creditors. How many days is the company allowed from the people it owes money to, before it has to pay them? To find this out we calculate a new ratio called the **creditors payments period**.

$$\text{Creditors payment period} = \frac{\text{Trade creditors}}{\text{Cost of sales}} \times \text{Number of days in the accounting period} \quad (3.3)$$

If the accounting period is one year, then we will use 365 as the number of days in the period.

	2001	2000	Industry average
Creditors payment period	$\frac{€120}{€3,260} \times 365 = 13 \text{ days}$	$\frac{€60}{€3,104} \times 365 = 7 \text{ days}$	20 days

This means that based on cost of sales the company is taking 13 days on average to pay its creditors. Genesis is not taking as long a period to pay its creditors as other companies are in the industry. This may mean that there is a demand for a shorter payment period from Genesis's customers. This puts pressure on company liquidity.[1]

3.1.4 Working capital to sales ratio

Working capital is defined as current assets *less* current liabilities. This working capital to sales ratio gives an indication of the capital necessary to fund the operation on a day-to-day basis. **It tells us how much the company needs in working capital to fund every €100 in sales.** It is calculated as

$$\text{Working capital ratio} = \frac{\text{Current assets } \textit{less} \text{ current liabilities}}{\text{Turnover (sales)}} \quad (3.4)$$

So, if the working capital ratio is given as €20 for every €100 in sales, a €100,000 order means that it will require €20,000 in working capital to fund the order. The sales figure will provide an indication of the cash flow for the company. If sales are increasing and the working capital ratio is static, the company is in danger of going into liquidation (the company doesn't have enough cash to meet the increased level of activity undertaken). This situation is known as **overtrading**.[2]

A declining working capital ratio would indicate a danger of overtrading. The working capital ratio for Genesis is

	2001	2000	Industry Average
Working capital ratio	$\dfrac{€1,407}{€6,000} = 0.23{:}1$	$\dfrac{€1,480}{€5,700} = 0.26{:}1$	$0.21{:}1$

Genesis's working capital ratio is slightly higher than the average for the industry, and is getting worse, which means:

1. it needs more working capital for every €100 in sales than the industry average.
2. it may need to reduce its working capital requirements. By cutting the amount of cash tied up in stocks and debtors and increasing the number of days before it pays its creditors (creditors payments period), it is possible to use the same amount of cash to fund an increasing amount of sales.

3.1.5 Other liquidity ratios

We briefly discuss two additional liquidity ratios. A creditor who needs payment very soon might be interested in the **cash ratio**:

$$\text{Cash ratio} \;=\; \frac{\textbf{Cash}}{\textbf{Current liabilities}} \qquad\qquad (3.5)$$

Short-term creditors of Genesis will be worried about its very poor cash ratio:

$$2001$$

$$\text{Cash ratio} \qquad \frac{€7}{€340} = 2\%$$

In addition, consider how long the company would have to survive, if for some reason (perhaps because of a lost export market) cash inflows began to dry up. To calculate the time involved we can use the ratio[3]

$$\text{Interval measure} \;=\; \frac{\textbf{Current assets}}{\textbf{Average daily operating costs}} \qquad\qquad (3.6)$$

Total operating costs for Genesis (excluding interest charges and depreciation—we don't include depreciation because it is a non-cash item, and interest payments are excluded because we are only concerned with operating costs) is €5,269. Average daily operating costs is €5,269/365 = €14.4. Therefore

$$2001$$

$$\text{Interval measure} \quad \frac{€1,747}{€14.4} = 121 \text{ days}$$

Genesis could hang on for about 4.5 months.

3.1.5 Long-term solvency

The long-term solvency of a company can be gauged by answering the following question:
    Do the company's total assets exceed its total liabilities?
    The difference between total assets and total liabilities is called **net worth**. If the reader added up all his/her assets (everything she/he owns or is owed) and deducted all his/her liabilities (all his/her debts), the result would be his/her individual net worth. Another name for this is the company's **net book value** or **shareholders' funds**. Positive net worth occurs when total assets are greater than total liabilities. Companies and individuals can suffer from the same problem. If the value of your mortgage is greater than the value of your house (if total liabilities are greater than total assets), there is negative net worth or negative equity. The net worth of Genesis for 2001 is €2,267. However, some practices need attention when using net worth as a measure of liquidity. These include the methods used in the revaluation of fixed assets and the provision for liabilities and charges. Appendix 3A provides a discussion of some of these practices.

3.2 Debt management ratios—gearing/leverage ratios

These ratios attempt to answer the following question:
    To what extent is the company in debt?
    Gearing or leverage is the proportion of debt the company has in its capital structure. Gearing can be calculated in different ways. This is because there are different definitions of what debt is. Debt can be defined as:

1. long-term loans only
2. long-term and short term loans
3. net debt (all loans *less* cash and short-term deposits)
4. total debt (short and long-term bank loans *plus* current liabilities and long-term liabilities).

The first three definitions are concerned with **formal, interest-bearing** debt. These are loans from financial institutions and individuals and are referred to as **financial gearing/leverage**. The final definition includes all money owed by the company, both to financial institutions and to all other creditors including trade creditors, the government (tax due) and money owed to shareholders in the form of dividend payments due. This is referred to as the total debt ratio. Interested parties will have their own favoured way of calculating gearing. Financial institutions will obviously be more interested in the first three definitions of debt, while management and business analysts will be more concerned with the total debt ratio. The debt ratios are calculated as follows:

1. **Long-term loans ratio** $=$ $\dfrac{\text{Long-term loans}}{\text{Capital employed}} \times 100$ $\qquad$ (3.7)

This shows the proportion of long-term capital that has been borrowed.
Capital employed = Total assets *less* Current liabilities.

	2001	2000
$\dfrac{\text{Long-term loans}}{\text{Capital employed}} \times 100$	$\dfrac{\text{€1,700}}{\text{€4,047}} \times 100 = 42\%$	$\dfrac{\text{€1,160}}{\text{€3,403}} \times 100 = 34\%$

2. **Long-term loans to equity ratio** $=$ $\dfrac{\text{Long-term loans}}{\text{Equity}}$ $\qquad$ (3.8)

	2001	2000
$\dfrac{\text{Long-term loans}}{\text{Equity}}$	$\dfrac{\text{€1,700}}{\text{€2,267}} = 75\%$	$\dfrac{\text{€1,160}}{\text{€2,163}} = 54\%$

This is the proportion of long-term loans to equity. In 2001, long-term loans were 75% of the firm's equity. This ratio is also referred to as the debt to equity ratio.

3. **Net debt** $=$ $\dfrac{\text{Formal debt } less \text{ cash and short-term deposits}}{\text{Capital employed}} \times 100$ $\quad$ (3.9)

	2001	2000
Net debt	$\dfrac{(\text{€1,700} + \text{€220}) - (\text{€7})}{\text{€4,047}} = 47\%$	$\dfrac{(\text{€1,160} + \text{€120}) - (\text{€70})}{\text{€3,403}} = 36\%$

Some companies may have cash balances and overdrafts. Consequently, by paying off their overdrafts with cash they could significantly reduce their gearing. This is the definition of gearing used mainly by financial analysts.

4. **Total debt ratio** $=$ $\dfrac{\text{Total debt}}{\text{Capital employed}} \times 100$ $\qquad$ (3.10)

	2001	2000
Total debt	$\dfrac{(\text{€1,700} + \text{€340})}{\text{€4,047}} = 50\%$	$\dfrac{(\text{€1,160} + \text{€180})}{\text{€3,403}} = 39\%$

This ratio shows the extent of companies' total indebtedness. (Note that all gearing figures need to be adjusted for **goodwill**. Appendix 3B, using the Kerry Group as an example, shows how the adjustment is made.)

For Genesis, the ratio of total debt to total capital employed is 50%. This may act as a warning signal to the management of Genesis because

1. borrowing more money may be difficult unless they can raise more equity
2. company creditors may be worried about Genesis's ability to pay.

Finally, financial leverage has an important implication for shareholder wealth maximisation. If a company earns more on investments that have been financed with borrowed funds than it pays in interest, then the return on equity (shareholder return) is enhanced or geared. The implications of capital structure are explored in Chapter 8. Appendix 3D at the end of this chapter gives an example illustrating the **gearing effect**.

3.2.1 Interest cover ratio

In addition to finding the extent to which the company is in debt, of more importance is the ability the company has in financing its debt. In other words, we need an answer to the following question:

Does the company have the ability to pay interest on its debt?

The interest cover ratio is calculated by dividing **profit before interest and taxes** by **interest payable**.[4]

$$\text{Interest cover ratio} = \frac{\text{PBIT (Operating profit)}}{\text{Interest payable}} \qquad (3.11)$$

Table 3.2 Genesis Ltd

Profit and loss account for the year ended 31 December 2001 (€000)

	2001	2000
Turnover	6,000	5,700
Cost of sales	3,260	3,104
Gross profit	2,740	2,596
Selling and distribution	1,086	1,034
Administration	923	879
Depreciation	162	155
Profit before interest and tax (PBIT)	**569**	**528**
Interest	180	120
Profit before taxation (PBT)	389	408
Taxation (30%)	117	123
Profit after tax (PAT)	272	285
Preference dividends	8	8
Profit available for ordinary shareholders	264	277
Ordinary dividends	160	170
Retained earnings	104	107

The interest cover data for Genesis Ltd:

	2001	2000	Industry average
Interest cover	$\dfrac{€569}{€180} = 3.2$ times	$\dfrac{€528}{€120} = 4.4$ times	5 times

It measures the number of times the firm's operating income covers its interest payments. Put another way, it measures the extent the firm's operating income can decline before it is unable to meet its annual interest costs. The ratio has deteriorated and is below the industry average and should act as a warning signal to the management of Genesis.[5]

The riskier the company, the higher this ratio should be. High levels of financial risk (high borrowings) and low interest cover can be a signal of future solvency problems for a company.

3.2.2 Fixed-charge coverage ratio

Many companies lease assets. These are fixed charges which, when added to interest charges, provide a more comprehensive view of a firm's long-term solvency.

$$\text{Fixed-charge coverage ratio} = \frac{(\text{PBIT} + \text{Lease payments})}{(\text{Interest charges} + \text{Lease payments})} \quad (3.12)$$

A note to the accounts of Genesis shows that lease payments amount to £30 million. Therefore the fixed-charge coverage ratio for Genesis is

	2001	2000	Industry average
Fixed-charge coverage	$\dfrac{€569 + €30}{€180 + €30} = 2.85$ times	$\dfrac{€528 + €30}{€120 + €30} = 3.72$ times	5 times

The ratio got worse, and like the last two ratios is below the industry average and simply reinforces the view that the company may encounter difficulties if it tries to increase its debt.

3.2.3 Cash interest cover ratio

Because **interest is paid out of cash,** it is necessary to find out the ability of the company to pay interest from operational cash flow. How many times does operational cash flow cover interest payments? We introduced cash flow statements in Chapter 2. The cash flow statement of Genesis is given in Table 3.3.

Table 3.3 Genesis Ltd statement of cash flows for 2001

Operating profit	€569
Depreciation	€162
Increase in stocks	€(60)
Increase in debtors	€(220)
Increase in creditors	€60
Operating cash flow before interest and tax	€511
Less Servicing of finance	
Interest paid	€(180)
Less	
Taxation paid	€(117)
Net cash flow before investing and financing	€214
Less Dividend Payments	€(168)
Capital expenditure	
Purchase of fixed assets	€(879)[6]
Net cash flow before financing	€(833)
Financing activities	
Sale of short-term investments	€130
Increase in long-term debt	€540
Decrease in cash during the year	€(163)
Summary of change in cash[7]	
Change in cash	€(163)
Cash at the beginning	€(50)
Cash at the end	€(213)

The number of times interest payments are covered by operational cash flow is

$$\text{Cash interest cover} \ = \ \frac{\text{Operational cash flow}}{\text{Interest payments}} \qquad (3.13)$$

For Genesis the cash interest cover is

	2001	Industry average
Cash interest cover	$\dfrac{€511}{€180} = 2.8 \text{ times}$	4.2 times

The operational cash flow is only just covering the interest bill 2.8 times. This is lower than the industry average, and it could result in liquidity problems.

When calculating interest cover we should remember that the interest reported in the profit and loss account is usually **net** interest after deducting interest receivable. Should this be included when calculating interest cover? Appendix 3C, using Unidare plc as an example, illustrates how interest receivable is treated.

3.3 Asset management ratios or efficiency ratios

These ratios measure the **efficiency** with which the company is utilising its assets. It is important that companies have the right amount of investment tied up in assets. Assets generate sales that in turn generate profits. It follows therefore that if a company does not have enough investment in assets it will lose sales, reduce cash inflow and adversely affect liquidity and profitability. On the other hand, if it has too much money tied up in assets, then its capital costs will be too high which will adversely affect cash inflow, liquidity and profitability. Therefore it is important to have the correct amount of investment in assets. It should not be too high or too low.

3.3.1 Stock turnover ratio

The stock turnover ratio is defined as sales divided by stock (inventories)

$$\text{Stock turnover ratio} = \frac{\text{Sales}}{\text{Stock}} \qquad (3.14)$$

	2001	2000	Industry average
Stock turnover ratio	$\dfrac{€6,000}{€890} = 6.7$ times	$\dfrac{€5,700}{€830} = 6.9$ times	7.5 times

This means that each item of stock is sold out or restocked (turned over) 6.7 times a year. Genesis's stock turn is below the industry average, which suggests too much stock. This suggests that too much investment (cash) is tied up in stocks, which are not being sold and therefore are not being converted back into cash. If this continues and stocks continue to increase then the company will find itself short of cash to pay creditors and to service its debts. So too much investment tied up in stock is unproductive and yields a low or zero rate of return.[8]

Because the sales figure is given at market prices (units sold × sales or market price) and the stock figure is usually given at cost price, the stock turnover figure is therefore overstated. It would be preferable to use the **cost of sales** as the numerator.

$$\text{Stock turnover} = \frac{\text{Cost of sales}}{\text{Stock}} \qquad (3.15)$$

	2001	2000	Industry average
Stock turnover	$\dfrac{€3,260}{€890} = 3.6$ times	$\dfrac{€3,104}{€830} = 3.7$ times	5 times

An alternative calculation shows how many days' sales the stock held represents.

$$\text{Stock turnover ratio} = \frac{\text{Stock}}{\text{Cost of sales}} \times 365 \qquad (3.16)$$

	2001	2000	Industry average
Stock turnover (days' sales)	$\dfrac{\text{€}890}{\text{€}3,260} \times 365 = 99$ days	$\dfrac{\text{€}830}{\text{€}3,104} \times 365 = 98$ days	70 days

Sometimes average stock (opening stock + closing stock + 2) is used. This might be preferred because sales occur over the entire year whereas stock is for one point at the end of the year. Preferably, if stock figures are given for each month of the year, then we could calculate the stock turn by summing the twelve months' stock and dividing by twelve. If this isn't possible, take the sum of the opening and closing stock and divide by 2.

$$\text{Stock turnover ratio} = \frac{\text{Average stock}}{\text{Cost of goods sold}} \times 365$$

The lower the stock relative to sales, the less capital is tied up. Stocks should be held to a minimum provided there is enough stock to meet customer requirements. A low turnover multiple or a high number of days' stock held (as it is for Genesis) might be an indication of:

- a fall-off in demand for the firm's product
- overproduction
- slow moving stock
- inefficiency in stock control.

3.3.2 Debtors collection period or average collection period

This ratio is an estimate of the number of days, on average, it takes for the people that owe you money (debtors) to pay. It is calculated by taking accounts receivable (debtors) and dividing by the average daily sales to find the number of days' sales that are tied up in debtors.

$$\text{Debtors collection period (DCP)} = \frac{\text{Debtors}}{\text{Average credit sales per day}} = \frac{\text{Debtors}}{\text{Annual credit sales}} \times 365 \qquad (3.17)$$

	2001	2000	Industry average
Debtors collection period	$\dfrac{\text{€}850}{\text{€}6,000} \times 365 = 52$ days	$\dfrac{\text{€}630}{\text{€}5,700} \times 365 = 40$ days	40 days

In 2001, Genesis waited on average 52 days before it received payment from its debtors. This is a deterioration from the previous year and is well above the industry average. Too much cash is tied up in debtors and is not being converted back into cash quickly enough. This situation is contributing to Genesis's poor liquidity position, as illustrated in the quick ratio and the interest cover ratios.[9]

It is useful to evaluate the debtors collection period with the credit terms being offered by the company. If the debtors collection period is greater than the credit terms given, then customers are not paying their bills on time.

The management of Genesis should watch this ratio because if the DCP is greater than the credit terms given then

- the customer may be in financial trouble if s/he is not paying his/her bills on time
- Genesis is not getting the cash in from its customers and this will put pressure on its liquidity position.

Genesis may have to resort to borrowing which adds to its capital costs.

3.3.3 Fixed asset turnover ratio

This ratio measures how efficiently the company is using its fixed assets. It is calculated by dividing sales by net fixed assets.

$$\text{Fixed asset turnover} = \frac{\text{Sales}}{\text{Net fixed assets}} = \text{Times} \qquad (3.18)$$

	2001	2000	Industry average
Fixed asset turnover	$\frac{€6,000}{€2,640} = 2.27$ times	$\frac{€5,700}{€1,923} = 3$ times	3 times

This measures the amount of sales a company generates with the amount of money it has tied up in fixed assets. In the case of Genesis, for every €100 in fixed assets the company generates €227 in sales. The worrying aspect is that it has deteriorated from the previous year. The company's assets are generating less income, which results in weaker cash flows and more liquidity worries.

Financial statements are drawn up on the **historical cost** basis of accounting. This means that the assets shown on balance sheets reflect the historical costs of the assets. Inflation causes fixed assets purchased in the past to be understated in current terms. Therefore, if we are comparing the fixed asset turnover of an old firm, which would have purchased its fixed assets at a low price in the past, with a new firm, which would have acquired its fixed assets recently, it is probable that the old firm would have a higher fixed asset turnover ratio. Making comparisons is therefore difficult. Nothing can be done about this until the accountancy profession comes up with a way of dealing with inflation and makes accounting statements deal with current values.

3.3.4 Total asset turnover

This ratio measures the efficiency with which it is utilising all of its assets.

$$\text{Total asset turnover} = \frac{\text{Sales}}{\text{Total assets}} = \text{Times} \qquad (3.19)$$

	2000	2001	Industry average
Total asset turnover	$\dfrac{€6,000}{€4,387}$ = 1.4 times	$\dfrac{€5,700}{€3,583}$ = 1.6 times	2 times

Is Genesis generating sufficient sales to justify capital invested in assets? It is below the industry average and efforts should be made to increase sales or reduce the investments tied up in assets.

3.4 Profitability ratios

Most of the ratios we have looked at so far have been calculated by using data from the balance sheet. Profitability ratios use data taken from the profit and loss account **and** the balance sheet. In calculating rates of return, profit figures (from the profit and loss account) are compared to various investment figures taken from the balance sheet. An outline profit and loss account and balance sheet shown in Table 3.4 provides different definitions of what profit means. Comparing these definitions of **profit** to the different definitions we find for **investment** in the balance sheet, we can calculate the rate of return the company is making on its investments. This is what profitability is. It calculates the percentage rate of return the company makes on different measures of investments. For example, if shareholders want to know the rate of return they are getting on their investment, the appropriate profit figure to use is **profit for ordinary shareholders**. This is divided into the appropriate investment figure from the balance sheet, which is shareholders' funds. A business analyst might be more interested in the rate of return on all capital employed, in which case the appropriate profit figure is **profit before interest and tax** and the appropriate balance sheet figure is **capital employed**. These ratios will be calculated in sections 3.4.5 and 3.4.7.

Profitability ratios, like the other ratios, are of little use on their own. We must look at trends and industry averages. In addition, for profitability ratios, a comparison with other rates of return in the investment markets would be very useful, e.g. gilts, bonds, cash, currencies and equities.

Table 3.4 Different definitions of profit and investment—calculating return

Profit and loss account	Balance sheet
Gross profit	Fixed assets
Profit before interest and tax (PBIT)	Current assets
Profit before tax (PBT)	Amounts falling due within one year
Profit after tax (PAT)	= Current liabilities
Profit for ordinary shareholders (PFO)	Capital employed (net total assets)
	Amounts falling due after more than one year
	Long-term loans
	Total assets *less* total liabilities
	= Net worth
	= Shareholders' funds

3.4.1 *Gross profit margin*

The gross profit margin measures the profit remaining after the costs of goods sold have been deducted from sales. The ratio is

$$\text{Gross profit margin} = \frac{\text{Gross profit}}{\text{Sales}} \times 100 \qquad (3.20)$$

	2001	2000	Industry average
Gross profit margin	$\frac{€2,740}{€6,000} = 46\%$	$\frac{€2,596}{€5,700} = 46\%$	50%

This ratio indicates that Genesis's cost of goods and services sold came to 46% of sales income. This left 54% of total sales income for other uses.

3.4.2 *Operating profit margin*

The operating profit margin is a measure of the costs of goods sold *plus* all other operating expenses. Operating profit is profit before interest and tax. It is calculated as follows:

$$\text{Operating profit margin} = \frac{\text{Profit before interest and tax}}{\text{Sales}} \times 100 \qquad (3.21)$$

For Genesis the operating profit margin is

	2001	2000	Industry average
Operating profit margin =	$\frac{€569}{€6,000} = 9.5\%$	$\frac{€528}{€5,700} = 9.3\%$	10%

Therefore, for Genesis, 9.5% of sales revenue remains after all operating expenses have been deducted. This ratio is useful when comparing companies with different tax and gearing structures. This is because the profit figure is taken before interest and tax.

3.4.3 *Operating profit margin after taxes*

Like many things in life, taxes have to be paid. Because of this certainty, a better measure of company profitability is the operating profit margin after taxes. In the previous chapter we defined net operating profit after taxes (NOPAT) as PBIT$(1 - T) = €569 (1 - 0.3) = €398$. The operating profit margin after the tax ratio is calculated is

$$\text{Operating profit margin after taxes} = \frac{\text{NOPAT}}{\text{Sales}} \times 100 \qquad (3.22)$$

The ratios for Genesis are

	2001	2000	Industry average
Operating profit margin after taxes	$\dfrac{€398}{€6,000} = 6.6\%$	$\dfrac{€370}{€5,700} = 6.5\%$	6.7%

Therefore, after all operating costs and taxes have been subtracted, Genesis is left with about 6.6 cents for every €1 of sales. **The operating profit margin after taxes is the true measure of the profitability of the company's operations.**

3.4.4 Net profit margin on sales

This measures the profit per one euro of sales. It measures the return the company generates for every €1 in sales. It is calculated as follows:

$$\textbf{Net profit margin} = \frac{\textbf{Profit for ordinary shareholders}}{\textbf{Sales}} \times 100 \qquad (3.23)$$

	2001	2000	Industry average
Net profit margin	$\dfrac{€264}{€6,000} = 4.4\%$	$\dfrac{€277}{€5,700} = 4.8\%$	4.8%

So from an accounting point of view, Genesis generates 4.8 cents profit on every €1 in sales.

The company's net margin on sales is lower than the average ratio for its competitors. This may indicate:

(a) the cost ratios of Genesis are too high or sales prices are too low.
(b) too much debt capital (remember that the profit figure used in this ratio is profit **after** interest has been paid on debt). Therefore if two companies have identical operating results in terms of sales, operating costs and operating profit, they will have different profit **after** tax figures if one firm has a greater amount of debt capital. And as we have seen earlier, the company with the low net margin may end up with a higher return on equity because of its greater use of debt (see Appendix 3D).

3.4.5 Return on capital employed (ROCE)

Capital employed, as we have seen earlier in our discussion on liquidity, is all long-term capital used by the company, both debt and equity. The profit figure we use is profit before interest and tax (PBIT). We use profit before interest and tax for a number of reasons.

(a) Since the denominator includes debt, the numerator must be the profit figure before interest is paid on that debt.
(b) It is necessary to use PBIT[10] when comparing companies with different capital structures. This is because interest is paid on profits **before** tax, while dividends are paid on profits **after** tax.

(c) Tax regulations can change from year to year. Therefore, if we want to compare a company's performance from one year to another, we must be consistent and use profit before any tax deductions.

$$\text{Return on capital employed (ROCE)} = \frac{\text{PBIT}}{\text{Capital employed}} \qquad (3.24)$$

	2001	2000	Industry average
ROCE	$\dfrac{€569}{€4,047} = 14\%$	$\dfrac{€528}{€3,403} = 15.5\%$	18%

What do these figures mean? Genesis is currently making a return of 14% on its capital employed.[11] This means that for every €100 in capital employed it is making a profit (a return) of €14. Is this good or bad? To answer this question we would need to know:

(a) What are the industry comparisons?
(b) What have been the trends in the company's own ROCE over the years?
(c) How does it compare with other market returns, e.g. gilts etc?

3.4.6 Return on total assets

This measures the return on total assets after interest and taxes have been paid, and after any dividends due to preferred stockholders have been paid.

$$\text{Return on total assets (ROTA)} = \frac{\text{Profit for ordinary shareholders}}{\text{Total assets}} \times 100 \qquad (3.25)$$

For Genesis the ROTA is

	2001	2000	Industry average
ROCE	$\dfrac{€264}{€4,387} = 6\%$	$\dfrac{€277}{€3,583} = 7.7\%$	8%

Genesis's ROTA is below the industry average because of its lower operating profit ratio and because it has a high level of debt in its capital structure. The high gearing will result in high interest charges and subsequently lower profit after tax.

3.4.7 Return on equity (ROE)

This ratio measures the return that ordinary shareholders get on their investment.

Taking the income available for ordinary shareholders and dividing it by equity gives the ROE.

$$\text{Return on equity (ROE)} = \frac{\text{Profit for ordinary shareholders}}{\text{Equity}} \qquad (3.26)$$

	2001	2000	Industry average
ROE	$\dfrac{€264}{€2,267} = 11.6\%$	$\dfrac{€277}{€2,163} = 12.8\%$	12.8%

Ordinary shareholders get an 11.6% return on every €100 invested. With equities providing investors with high returns on their investments, this will be a cause for concern for Genesis stockholders. This may be reflected in the market price for Genesis shares. **Interestingly the ROE is greater than the ROTA because of the use of deb**t. As explained in Appendix 3D, the use of debt can increase the return on equity because of its tax advantages, and because of the higher return required to compensate for the additional risk. This **gearing effect** will become more apparent after studying the following section on the Du Pont formula.

3.5 Ratio pyramids—the Du Pont system

This system of ratio pyramids brings all the ratios we have already calculated together and it shows how they are interrelated. It was first developed by the Du Pont organisation in America and hence its name. Ratio pyramids have the following characteristics:

1. They provide a reference for management to plan their overall profitability.
2. The ratios are interdependent and so the effects of a change in one ratio can be traced against changes in other ratios.
3. It shows how the return on equity is affected by asset turnover, the profit margin and gearing.

The Du Pont equation is given as

$$\textbf{Return on assets} = \textbf{Net margin} \times \textbf{Total asset turnover} \qquad (3.27)$$

$$\frac{\text{Net profit}}{\text{Total assets}} = \frac{\text{Net profit}}{\text{Sales}} \times \frac{\text{Sales}}{\text{Total assets}}$$

This equation is illustrated in the modified Du Pont chart in Figure 3.1. You can read the chart as follows:

1. The various costs are added together to give total costs.
2. Total costs are then subtracted from sales to give net profit.
3. Net profit is then divided by sales to give the net margin. Note that from a management point of view if the net margin is low it may be because the individual costs may be too high (by industry comparisons). The management can set in motion measures that will tackle this high cost structure, and so increase the profit margin.
4. On the other side of the chart, we calculate total assets (fixed assets + current assets).
5. Total assets are then divided into sales to give the number of times Genesis **turns over** its assets each year. In Genesis's case this is 1.36 times. For every €100 in total assets the company generates €136 in sales.

6. Finally, multiply the net profit margin by the total asset turnover to get the return on assets. This is the Du Pont equation.

Figure 3.1 Modified Du-Pont for Genesis

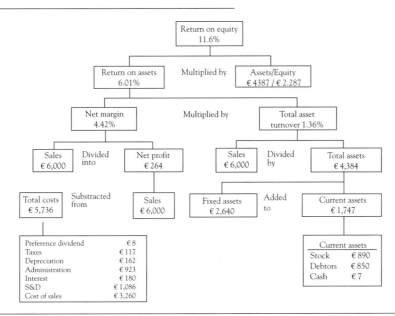

Genesis made €4.42 in net profit on every €100 in sales, a net margin of 4.42%. It turned over its assets 1.36 times in the year. Therefore, it generated a return of 6.01% on its total assets. So, in 2001 the Du Pont equation gives the following answer:

$$\text{Return on assets} = \text{Net margin} \times \text{Total asset turnover}$$

$$\frac{\text{Net profit}}{\text{Total assets}} = \frac{\text{Net profit}}{\text{Sales}} \times \frac{\text{Sales}}{\text{Total assets}}$$

$$6.01\% \quad = \quad 4.42\% \quad \times \quad 1.36$$

Supermarkets and general convenience shops would have a high total asset turnover because of the frequency with which it sells food and drink. However, they would have low net profit margins. On the other hand, heavy engineering firms would have low asset turnover but high profit margins.

In addition, the chart in Figure 3.1 shows how the return on equity (ROE) is affected by asset efficiency, net profit margin and gearing. Remember that if the company finances all of its assets with equity capital only, then the return on assets (ROA) would equal the return on equity (ROE). This is because total assets would equal total equity:

$$\text{ROA} = \frac{\text{Net profit}}{\text{Total assets}} = \frac{\text{Net profit}}{\text{Total equity}} = \text{ROE} \qquad (3.28)$$

However, if the company finances part of its total assets with debt, then the return on equity must be greater than the return on assets. In fact, the ROA is the product of the net profit margin, total asset turnover, and the **equity multiplier**. The equity multiplier is the ratio of total assets to common equity:

$$\text{Equity multiplier} = \frac{\text{Total assets}}{\text{Common equity}} \tag{3.29}$$

For Genesis, the equity multiplier is

$$\text{Equity multiplier} = \frac{€4,387}{€2,267} = 1.94$$

The company finances every €194 of total assets with €100 of equity. Therefore the modified Du Pont equation which gives the ROE is

$$\text{ROE} = \text{Net margin} \times \text{Total asset turnover} \times \text{Equity multiplier}$$

$$\frac{\textbf{Net profit}}{\textbf{Equity}} = \frac{\textbf{Net profit}}{\textbf{Sales}} \times \frac{\textbf{Sales}}{\textbf{Total assets}} \times \frac{\textbf{Total assets}}{\textbf{Equity}} \tag{3.30}$$

For Genesis, this works out as

$$11.6\% = \frac{€264}{€6,000} \times \frac{€6,000}{€4,387} \times \frac{€4,387}{€2,247}$$

$$11.6\% = 4.42\% \times 1.36 \times 1.94 \text{ (allowing for rounding)}$$

Obviously, if the firm were financed totally with equity, the equity multiplier would be equal to 1. Why? Remember from Chapter 2 the accounting equation

$$\text{Assets} = \text{Equity capital} + \text{Debt capital}$$

If all assets are financed by equity, with **no** debt, then the equity multiplier must be equal to 1:

$$\text{Equity multiplier} = \frac{\text{Total assets}}{\text{Common equity}} = 1$$

Therefore, if the equity multiplier is 1, the ROE must be the product of the net margin and the asset turnover ratio:

$$\text{Modified Du-Pont equation}$$
$$\text{ROE} = \text{Net margin} \times \text{Total asset turnover} \times \text{Equity multiplier}$$

$$\frac{\text{Net profit}}{\text{Equity}} = \frac{\text{Net profit}}{\text{Sales}} \times \frac{\text{Sales}}{\text{Total assets}} \times \frac{\text{Total assets}}{\text{Equity}}$$

$$6.01\% = \frac{€264}{€6,000} \times \frac{€6,000}{€4,387} \times \frac{1}{1}$$

$$6.01\% = 4.42\% \times 136$$

However, the equity multiplier for Genesis is 1.94 and this has the effect of increasing the ROE from 6.01% to 11.6%. **Shareholder value (ROE)** has been **geared up** by the use of debt capital.

The return on equity could also be derived by dividing the return on total assets by the equity fraction. The equity fraction is the proportion of equity in the capital structure. For Genesis, the equity fraction is €2,267/€4,387 = 52%. Therefore

$$\text{ROE} = \frac{\text{ROTA}}{\text{Equity fraction}} = \frac{6.01\%}{0.52} = 11.6\%$$

Looked at this way, **the Du Pont formula can be used by management to see how they can improve performance and hence shareholder value.** This means assessing the two ratios that make up the overall return on total assets and the company's use of debt.

3.6 Market valuation—maximising shareholder value

These ratios compare the book value of a company to its market value. The book value is the same as net worth. Taking all the company's assets and deducting all its liabilities, we are left with the company's net worth. The ratios we have already calculated— liquidity, asset efficiency, debt management and profitability—will determine what the book value is. If these ratios are good then this will be reflected in the book value. The book value will in turn be reflected in the market value of the company's shares. Financial management's primary goal is to maximise shareholders' wealth.

This is achieved by maximising the difference between the market value of shareholders' investment and the amount of capital supplied by shareholders. This difference is referred to as **market value added**.

Market value added	**=**	**Market value**	*minus*	**Equity capital supplied**	
(MVA)		**of equity**		**by shareholders**	**(3.31)**

The market value of equity is **the number of shares multiplied by the market price per share**. Equity capital supplied by shareholders is **total common equity *plus* reserves.**[12]

Example 3.2 Market value added—Unidare plc[13]

MVA calculation
Price per share	€2.35
Number of shares	19.8m
Market value	€46.53m
Equity + reserves	€34.55m

Unidare's MVA is therefore €46.53m *minus* €34.55m which equals €11.98m or 1.35 times shareholders' funds. Maximising this figure will enhance shareholder value.

A different form of the MVA ratio is the market to book ratio. In a sense, this ratio incorporates all the ratios we have already calculated and is a final overall assessment of company performance. It is calculated by taking the market capitalisation and dividing it by the shareholders' funds.

$$\text{Market to book ratio} = \frac{\text{Market capitalisation}}{\text{Shareholders' funds}} \qquad (3.32)$$

Genesis's market price is given at €5 per share. It has 520,000 shares in issue. This means that Genesis is valued at a slight premium to shareholders' investment. Each €100 share investment in Genesis is valued in the market at €146.

Obviously, companies will want to achieve a minimum ratio of 1:1 and preferably higher.

Table 3.5 Genesis Ltd market: book ratio

Market price	Number of shares	Market capitalisation	Shareholders' funds	Market: book ratio
€5	520,000	€2,600,000	€2,267,000	$\frac{€2,600,000}{€2,267,000} = 1.146:1$

3.7 Economic value added

Closely related to market value added is economic value added (EVA). It is a measure of how the firm has added to shareholder value. The profit and loss account shows what is left for ordinary shareholders after tax has been paid to the government and interest has been paid to the providers of debt capital. This is an **accounting** definition of what profit means. This definition only accounts for the cost of debt capital. However, if we were to deduct the cost of all capital **including the cost of equity capital,** we would be left with a true economic profit. As we will see in Chapter 8, equity capital has a cost because equity shareholders will require a rate of return to satisfy them for the risk they take in investing in the company. For shareholders there is an **opportunity cost** involved in their decision to buy equity. Shareholders give up the opportunity to invest funds elsewhere, of equal risk, where they could earn a rate of return. The cost of equity capital is the rate of return required to satisfy the providers of equity capital. What's left after tax and interest on debt has been paid is retained earnings. This belongs to equity shareholders. If all or part of this is distributed to the shareholders in the form of a dividend (shareholders' return), income tax will have to be paid by those who receive the dividend. Therefore, from the company's position this reduces the cost of equity capital. Therefore it is the after-tax cost of capital which is important.

EVA = PBIT (1–T) – (Total capital supplied by shareholders) (After-tax cost of capital)   (3.33)

Suppose that the after-tax cost of capital for Genesis is 12% (calculation of after-tax cost of capital will be given in Chapter 8). The operating profit to be used in EVA calculations is NOPAT, which is equal to PBIT $(1 - T)$ discussed in Chapter 2. Therefore for Genesis, EVA is

$$\text{EVA} = €569\,(1 - 0.3) - (€2{,}267)(0.12) = €398 - €272 = €126$$

This suggests that Genesis has added €126,000 to shareholder wealth during 2001.

Emanating from the United States, EVA is the new mantra in shareholder wealth maximisation. EVA differs from other corporate performance yardsticks (e.g. earnings per share) by charging profit for the cost of all capital employed, including equity capital. According to its proponents, by concentrating on EVA management can carry out its functions in a way consistent with maximising shareholder value. While a full discussion is beyond the scope of this book, we will return to its main theme in other chapters throughout the book.

3.8 Trend analysis

Ratios are useful, not on their own, but if they are seen over periods. Trends will provide clues as to whether the situation will improve or get worse. Trend analysis plots a ratio over time. Figure 3.3 illustrates the trend in the ROCE of Genesis from 1990 to 1998.

Fig. 3.2 Return on capital employed 1990–1998

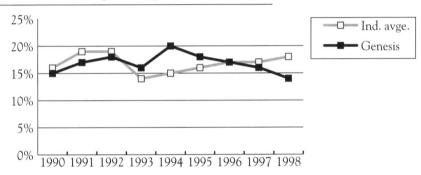

Financial analysts plot trends in ratios over time. To the financial analyst, the resulting graph is a very useful tool in spotting strengths and weaknesses.

3.9 Horizontal analysis

This involves comparing one year's figures with another and calculating the percentage change.[14] Tables 3.6 and 3.7 provide a horizontal analysis for Genesis, followed by an analysis of the results.

Table 3.6 Genesis horizontal analysis—profit and loss account

	2000	2001	% change
Turnover	5,700	6,000	5.2
Cost of sales	3,104	3,259	4.8
Gross profit	2,596	2,740	5.5
Administration	879	923	5.0
Selling and distribution	1,034	1,086	5.0
Depreciation	155	162	4.5
Interest	120	180	50.0

→

PBIT	528	569	7.7
Taxation	125	117	(6.41)
PAT	285	272	(4.5)
Profit for ordinary shareholders (PFO)	275	264	(4.0)
Ordinary dividends	170	160	(5.8)
Retained earnings	105	104	(0.009)

Table 3.7 Genesis Ltd horizontal analysis—balance sheet

	2000	2001	% Change
Fixed assets	1,923	2,640	37
Current assets	1,660	1,747	5.2
Cash	70	7	(91)
Debtors	630	850	34
Stock	830	890	7.2
Short-term investments	130	0	(100)
Current liabilities			
Creditors	60	120	100
Bank overdraft	120	220	83
Working capital (net current assets)	1,480	1,407	(4.9)
Total assets *less* current liabilities			
(capital employed)	3,403	4,047	18.9
Long-term debt	1,160	1,700	46
Shareholders' funds	2,163	2,267	4.8

Horizontal statement analysis

1. Sales increased by 5.2% during the year while cost of sales increased by 4.8%. This has led directly to a 5.5% increase in the gross profit.
2. However, because the long-term debt (46%) and the bank overdraft (83%) have increased, interest payments increases (50%) have wiped out the gain in gross profit.
3. Consequently, PAT and retained earnings have fallen.
4. As a result, shareholders have suffered a fall in dividend income.
5. While sales have increased (5%), working capital has decreased (4.9%). The working capital ratio is deteriorating and the consequence could be overtrading. Of particular concern to the management of Genesis will be the increase in stocks of 7.2%, while sales have increased by only 5%.

3.10 Common size statements (vertical analysis)

Items in the profit and loss account are expressed as percentages of sales. This tells us what percentage of sales income is profit and costs. Similarly, each item in the balance sheet is expressed as a percentage of capital employed or, alternatively, total assets. Tables 3.8 and 3.9 provide common size statements for Genesis followed by a common size statement analysis.

Table 3.8 Genesis Ltd common size statement—profit and loss account for the year end 31 December 2001

	2001	2000	2001 Industry average
Turnover	100%	100%	100%
Cost of sales	54.4%	54.4%	55%
Gross profit	45.6%	45.5%	45%
Operating expenses:			
Selling and distribution	18.1%	18.1%	16%
Administration	15.3%	15.4%	15.2%
Depreciation	2.7%	2.7%	2.6%
Profit before interest and tax (PBIT)	9.48%	9.26%	11.2%
Interest	3%	2.1%	1.2%
Profit before taxation (PBT)	6.48%	7.15%	10%
Taxation (30%)	1.95%	2.1%	2.0%
Profit after tax (PAT)	4.53%	5%	8.0%
Preference dividends	.0013%	.0014%	.1%
Profit available for ordinary shareholders	4.4%	4.8%	7.9%
Ordinary dividends	2.6%	3.0%	4.1%
Retained earnings	1.75%	1.9%	3.8%

Table 3.9 Genesis Ltd common size statement—balance sheet as at 31 December 2001

	2001	2000	1998 industry average
Fixed assets			
Plant and machinery (net)	65.20%	56.50%	60.0%
Current assets			
Cash	.0002%	.0205%	3.2%
Debtors	21.00 %	18.50%	17.0%
Stock	22.00 %	24.40%	19.1%
Short-term investments	–	.038%	1.0%
	43.00 %	42.95%	40.2%

Table 3.9 cont.	2001	2000	1998 industry average
Amounts falling due within one year (current liabilities)			
Creditors	3.0%	1.76%	3.5%
Bank overdraft	5.4%	3.50%	3.4%
	8.4%	5.26%	6.9%
Net current assets	34.7%	43.49%	33.3%
Total assets *less* current liabilities	100%	100%	100%
Amounts falling due after more than one year			
Long-term debt	42.00%	34.00%	33.00%
Preference shares	1.9 %	2.35%	.2 %
Capital and reserves			
Ordinary shares	5.4 %	6.4 %	7.8 %
Retained earnings	50.5 %	57.00%	59.2 %
	100%	100%	100%

Common size statement analysis

1. PBIT is below the average because selling/distribution costs are above the average.
2. Interest costs are higher than the average because of the company's greater reliance on borrowed funds, both short-term (bank overdraft) and long-term (debentures).
3. Taxation is currently lower because of lower PBIT.
4. Consequently, PAT and profit for ordinary shareholders are lower than the industry average.
4. The debtors figure is higher and this will have cash flow consequences. This is one of the contributory factors giving it a significantly lower end of year cash figure.
5. Stock accounts for 22% of total capital employed, above the industry average of 19%. The management of Genesis should now question why this is happening, and develop a policy of resolving the problem.

Using a method called **sensitivity testing**, we can measure how sensitive the overall return on investment is to changes in the individual cost ratios. We defer a discussion of this to Appendix 3E at the end of the chapter.

3.11 International accounting practices—accounting in different countries

Accounting is not a standardised exercise internationally. Consequently, because different accounting standards apply in different countries, it is very difficult for investors to make cross-border comparisons. The main reasons for this are:

- In Ireland, for example, net book value of assets is cost *less* accumulated depreciation. In other countries, an effort is made to try to make the asset values reflect current market values.
- Differences occur in the treatment of goodwill, leases, research and development costs and pension plans.
- Historical and political factors: Commonwealth countries have a legacy of UK accounting practices. French accounting practices have been influenced by the German occupation. Japanese accounting is a hybrid of UK and US practices. In addition, there will be increasing demands for a common European accounting practice because of the single currency.
- Ownership: In Germany and Japan the banks are the key source of both debt and equity capital. In the UK and US, the public capital markets are most important in raising capital. Therefore, there is a greater demand for more information from accounts in the US and the UK than there is in Germany and Japan who use very conservative reporting practices.

3.12 Limitations of ratio analysis

- Creative accounting can have the effect of manipulating profits:
  - (a) A change in the method used could have a serious impact on reported profits.
  - (b) Reducing **paper** charges (charges that don't require an invoice) made to the profit and loss account. Examples of **paper** charges are depreciation and provisions.
  - (c) Long-term contracts. Some companies have contracts which span several accounting periods. Construction companies are examples. When should the revenue from such contracts be recognised in the profit and loss account? This is usually done on a percentage completion basis. Different ways of calculating the percentage of contract completion will give different turnover figures.
  - (d) Raising short-term loans to reduce balances to creditors.
- Many large companies operate different divisions in different industries, and therefore industry comparisons are made difficult.
- The effect of inflation may be ignored. For example a volume increase in sales of, say, 5% could constitute a decline in real terms if inflation is running at a rate greater than 5%.
- Seasonal factors may distort figures. Company end of year figures may not reflect the position throughout the year.
- Generalising ratios. A high current ratio may be good or it may be bad. It may indicate a strong liquidity position but it may also indicate that the company is holding too much cash, which is unproductive.
- Financial ratios do not tell us to what extent a company's revenue is
  - (a) tied to one key product. This is important because while a single product company might be more focused in its operations, a lack of diversification increases the company's risk.
  - (b) tied to a single key customer. What happens company performance if the customer goes elsewhere?
  - (c) dependent on a single supplier. Any problems with this supplier will lead to shortages of essential raw materials.

(d) dependent on the legal and regulatory environment—the legal framework surrounding the regulation of, for example, the telecommunications industry, the tobacco industry and the banking sector.

SUMMARY

Information from financial statements is used by different groups of people. Shareholders use financial statements to see if their original investment in the company has increased in value. The providers of debt finance will want to know if the company can service their debts, as will suppliers of raw materials and services. The users of financial statements will require a proper financial assessment, which will include ratio analysis, trend analysis, common size statements, Du Pont and sensitivity analysis.

This chapter discussed the techniques used to answer these questions. The principal areas discussed were:

- Liquidity ratios—current and acid test ratios, and creditors collection period.
- Profitability ratios—gross and net margin, return on capital employed, return on total assets and return on equity.
- Debt management ratios or how efficiently the company is utilising its assets—stock turnover, debtors collection period, fixed asset turnover and total asset turnover.
- Debt management ratios—gearing ratios and the ability of the company to finance its debt.
- Trend analysis to plot the performance of a company over time.
- The concept of market value added and economic value added.
- How all the ratios combine to give the most important ratio in business—market: book ratio.
- The Du Pont system—showing how the pyramid of ratios interrelates to give the shareholder value—the return on equity.
- Sensitivity testing.
- The limitations of ratio analysis.

QUESTIONS

1. Explain the following:
   (a) Liquidity ratios
   (b) Debt management ratios
   (c) Asset management ratios
   (d) Profitability ratios
   (e) Trend analysis
   (f) Comparative ratios
   (g) Du Pont formula.
2.♦ The stock turnover ratios are more important for a manufacturing company than they are for a service company. Explain.
3. You are employed as a business analyst in a manufacturing company. The company's managing director brings you into his office and states: 'The current asset to current

liabilities ratio has increased. Total assets are generating less sales than the previous year. I also notice that sales have not increased, as has the fixed asset turnover ratio and quick ratio. What's going on?'

4.♦ Explain the impact inflation has on ratio analysis.

5. Ratios on their own don't mean anything—they are simply one number divided by another. Therefore, it is important to use some **benchmark** when analysing ratios. Explain and outline any significant problems there might be in this approach.

6. At the end of the month, a company pays off some of its creditors. What happens the current ratio if initially it is (a) >1 and (b) <1.

7. Explain the relationship between the ROE and the ROA.

8.♦ The profit and loss account of Dunmore Ltd is reproduced below. Construct a common size income statement.

Dunmore Ltd profit and loss account for year ended 31 December 2000

Sales	€400
Cost of sales	€260
Depreciation	€40
Profit before interest and tax	€100
Interest	€20
Profit before tax	€80
Tax 15%	€12
Profit after tax	€62
Dividends	€20
Retained earnings	€42

9.♦ The balance sheet and profit and loss account of Doyle Ltd for the year ended 31 December 2000 is as follows:

Balance sheet	€(000)	Profit and Loss account	
Fixed assets			
Plant & machinery (net)	€180	Sales	€126
Current assets		Cost of sales	€80
Stock	€9	Depreciation	€18
Debtors	€9	PBIT	€28
Cash	€6	Interest	€15
	€24	PBT	€13
Current liabilities		Tax (20%)	€3
Creditors	€6	PAT	€10
Short-term loans	€40		
	€46		
Net working capital	(€22)		
Net total assets	€158		
Financed by			
Debentures	€70		
Ordinary shares	€30		
Retained earnings	€58		
	€158		

(a) Calculate the following ratios:
- (i) Liquidity (current and acid test)
- (ii) Stock turnover
- (iii) Debtor turnover
- (iv) Days sales outstanding
- (v) Cash ratio
- (vi) Times interest earned
- (vii) Total debt ratio.

(b) Using the Du Pont identity, calculate the ROE and break it down into its different parts.

10. The balance sheet and income statement of Alpha Ltd is provided below and you are asked to calculate the various ratios that follow.

Profit and loss account	2001	2000
Turnover (net)	€100	€70
Cost of sales	€75	€48
Selling and admin. expenses	€8	€15
Depreciation	€1	€1
Profit before interest and tax	€16	€6
Interest	€2	€3
Profit before tax	€14	€3
Tax	€3	€0.6
Profit after tax	€11	€2.4
Balance sheet		
Fixed assets (net)	€20	€17
Current assets		
Stock	€10	€12
Debtors	€9	€5
Cash	€2	€3
Total current assets	€21	€20
Current liabilities		
Creditors	€3	€2
Short-term debt	€3	€2
Accruals	€4	€4
Total current liabilities	€10	€8
Working capital	€11	€12
Total net assets	€31	€29
Long-term debt	€9	€15
Ordinary shares	€1	€1
Retained earnings	€21	€13
	€31	€29

(a) Gross profit margin
(b) Operating profit margin
(c) Net profit margin
(d) Total asset turnover
(e) Fixed asset turnover
(f) Debtors turnover
(g) Stock turnover
(h) Current ratio
(i) Creditors payment period
(j) Debt ratio and equity multiplier
(k) TIE ratio
(l) ROE
(m) ROA.

11. Using the information from the balance sheet and income statement of Alpha Ltd, prepare a common size income statement and balance sheet.

12. From the information contained in the balance sheet and income statement of Alpha Ltd, construct a Du Pont analysis.

13.♦ Market to book ratios don't always tell the full story. Explain.

14. (a) Is it always good news when the current ratio increases?
    (b) If a firm has a low asset turnover ratio what does this mean and how can it be rectified?

15. The balance sheet and profit and loss account of Harry Murphy's DIY is as follows:

Balance sheet as at 31 December 2000 (€000)

Fixed assets (net)	€280
Current assets	
Stock	€300
Debtors	€120
Cash	€90
Total current assets	€510
Current liabilities	
Creditors	€100
Short-term loans	€90
Accruals	€40
Total current liabilities	€230
Working capital	€280
Total net assets	€560
Long-term debt	€50
Ordinary share capital	€230
Retained earnings	€280
	€560

Profit and loss account for the year ended
31 December 2000 (€000)

Net turnover	€1,600
Cost of goods sold	€1,280
Sales, general & distribution expenses	€140
Depreciation	€20
Profit before interest and tax	€160
Interest	€9
Profit before tax	€151
Tax	€23
Profit after tax	€128

The average financial ratios for the industry are as follows:

Fixed asset turnover	7x	Sales to stock	11x
Total asset turnover	3x	Debtors collection period	25 days
Net margin	4%	Times interest earned	6x
ROTA	10%	Current ratio	2.5 x
ROE	13%	Gearing (debt: TA)	35%

As a financial analyst you are asked to prepare a report on the performance of Murphy's DIY which should include:
   (a) a ratio analysis
   (b) a Du Pont equation
   (c) a comparison of Murphy's DIY with the industry average.

16. South East Manufacturing Ltd has total assets of €2m and an operating profit (PBIT/TA) of 25% on total assets. What would be the difference in the ROE if the company financed its operations with gearing of 40% or 100% equity? (Assume interest on debt of 5% and a corporation tax rate of 15%.)

17.♦ The net profit margin of Compu-Vision Ltd is 3% and the company's ROE is 16% and ROA = 11%. Calculate the equity multiplier.

18. Companies in the same industry will use standardised ratios that are meaningful and useful for that industry only. For example, hotels might use an income: cost per room ratio. Give examples of how different industries might use different ratios to standardise financial information.

19. Net income for the year is €100,000. The interest charges amount to €20,000 and depreciation charged is €5,000. Calculate the cash coverage ratio assuming a tax rate of 15%.

20. Express Cargo Ltd has a gearing ratio of 40%. The amount due in less than one year is €1,000 and it has a current ratio of 1.5. Its net profit margin is 6% on sales of €5,000. The company's ROE is 18%. How much does the company have invested in fixed assets?

21. Case Study—Unidare plc

The consolidated profit and loss account, and consolidated balance sheet for Unidare plc is shown below. Analyse.

Consolidated profit and loss account

	1993 (£000)	1994 (£000)	1995 (£000)	1996 (£000)	1997 (£000)
Turnover	104,697	169,939	151,552	131,028	125,286
Cost of sales	(82,222)	(133,804)	(100,519)	(100,519)	(95,857)
Gross profit	22,475	36,135	35,852	30,509	29,429
Distribution	(10,888)	(18,270)	(17,794)	(15,149)	(13,291)
Administration	(7,038)	(10,861)	(9,285)	(9,240)	(9,275)
Other trading income	634	147	169	3	140
Trading profit	5,184	7,151	8,942	6,123	7,003
Investment income	32	122	372	777	615
Interest payable	(724)	(1,156)	(1,286)	(1,030)	(743)
Exceptional charges		(7,579)	107	(1,430)	
PBT	4,492	(1,462)	8,135	4,440	6,875
Tax	(973)	(72)	(1,542)	(1,486)	(1,876)
Profit (loss) after tax	3,159	(1,543)	6,593	2,954	5,005
Minority interests	(290)	(108)	(301)	(182)	(215)
Net income (loss)	3,229	(1,642)	6,292	2,772	4,790

Consolidated balance sheets

	1993 (£000)	1994 (£000)	1995 (£000)	1996 (£000)	1997 (£000)
Fixed assets					
Tangible	25,580	18,502	10,919	9,519	11,254
Financial	9	9	9	9	–
	25,589	18,511	10,928	9,528	11,254
Current assets					
Stocks	28,928	26,447	20,168	18,477	21,840
Debtors	27,051	29,147	19,588	15,059	18,300
Prepayments/accruals	1,154	2,253	1,216	1,033	1,001
Tax recoverable			234	240	
Other debtors	756	344	511	1,024	930
Cash	4,137	4,828	18,387	16,243	10,024
Assets held for resale	—	2,053	1,271	1,271	1,271
	61,990	65,072	61,375	53,347	53,366

→

Creditors due within one year

Short-term debt	3,219	4,483	4,589	3,752	3,090
Trade creditors	17,170	21,021	15,222	11,370	15,101
Accruals	4,157	4,995	3,700	3,524	3,989
Revenue tax	1,769	1,428	1,782	1,115	796
Tax & social security	623	775	502	282	575
Taxation	1,764	1,098	541	730	786
Dividends	1,942	1,935	2,533	2,585	2,732
Other creditors	451	=	=	=	=
	31,167	35,734	28,869	23,358	27,069
Net current assets	30,823	29,338	32,506	29,989	26,297
Total assets *less* current liabilities	56,412	47,849	43,434	39,517	37,551

Amount due after more than one year

Long-term debt	11,987	13,951	10,676	8,017	4,069
Long-term gov. grants	1,202	1,107	831	394	363
Other long-term liabilities	2,915	–	–	–	–
	16,104	15,058	11,507	8,411	4,432
Provisions	2,595	4,561	653	469	980
Net assets	37,713	28,230	31,274	30,637	32,139
Capital and reserves	3,4630	3,5126	3,5232	3,5232	3,5232
Revaluation reserve	7,115	6,446	1,906	840	838
Goodwill reserve	(27,747)	(31,240)	(30,808)	(30,407)	(31,887)
P & L a/c	21,406	15,942	23,776	23,862	26,772
Other reserves	258	258	241	241	241
Shareholders' funds	35,662	26,532	30,354	29,768	31,196
Minority interests	2,051	1,698	920	869	943
Net assets	37,713	28,230	31,274	30,637	32,139

APPENDIX 3A

Practices we need to look out for when using net worth as a measure of company liquidity

• Revaluation of assets

If assets are revalued, the increase in value is added to the asset figure in the balance sheet. For the balance sheet to balance (recall the balance sheet equation where assets equal capital *plus* liabilities) an equal amount should be added to the capital section of the balance sheet, since any increase in value belongs to the shareholders.

Example Revaluation of assets and net worth

A company has tangible fixed assets of €1m and share capital of €1m. In 1995 the company bought property for €100,000 which it paid for out of its share capital. In 1998 it decided to revalue its property portfolio and since property prices have been rising it is now valued at €400,000. The company decides to incorporate this into its balance sheet:

Balance sheet before revaluation		Balance sheet after revaluation
Fixed assets	€1m	€1.4m
Share capital	€1m	€1m
Revaluation reserve		€0.4m

Asset revaluation is not an exact science and not all companies revalue their assets. One should ask therefore if the company's positive net worth is due to asset revaluation. The possibility arises that some companies may revalue their assets simply to show a positive net worth. One should ask who carried out the valuation and what method of valuation was used.

- Provisions for liabilities and charges

In their accounts, companies make provisions for possible future liabilities. Provisions that relate to a reduction of an asset are deducted from that asset. For example, bad debt provisions are deducted from debtors in the balance sheet. Other provisions relate to potential losses and are shown on the balance as **provision for liabilities and charges**. It is with these that potential difficulties can arise because some companies will use this technique to **window dress** their accounts. For example, companies will not like disclosing bumper year profits because markets prefer steady non-volatile growth in earnings. If the market expects profits of £50 million and the company reports profits of £60 million, then the market will expect profits of £70 million the following year. Therefore, reporting higher than expected profits can generate unrealistic expectations about the company. To prevent this from happening the company can camouflage its profits by increasing its provision for liabilities and charges. This will have the effect of lowering its reported net worth.

APPENDIX 3B

Adjusting gearing figures for goodwill

All gearing figures need to be adjusted for goodwill. Goodwill is the difference between the purchase price of an asset and its book value. If, for example, the book value of a company's assets is €100m and if the company is sold for €150m, goodwill is equal to €50m. Writing off goodwill reduces the gearing ratio as it reduces the capital and reserves. When looking at trends in a company's performance or inter-company comparisons, it is preferable to add back the figure for goodwill. The following example is taken from Kerry Group plc (1997).

Capital and reserves	€445,421
Goodwill reserve	€(357,357)
	€88,064

Kerry's long-term debt is given in note 14 to their accounts at €261,782. Total assets *less* current liabilities are given at €374,376. This is adjusted for the goodwill written off through reserves. Therefore the two gearing percentages are:*

Adjusted
*€261,782 ÷ 731,733 = 36%

Unadjusted
€261,782 ÷ 374,376 = 70%

*€731,733 = €374,376 + Goodwill reserve €357,357

APPENDIX 3C

Interest Cover and Interest Receivable

When calculating interest cover we should remember that the interest reported in the profit and loss account is usually **net** interest after deducting interest receivable. Should this be included when calculating interest cover? If interest receivable is a normal part of a company's profits then we should include it in calculating interest cover. If, on the other hand, interest received is not a normal part of business income then we should not include it in interest cover calculations.

Example Unidare plc

Note 7 to Unidare's annual report 1997 shows net interest expense as follows:

Net interest expense:
      Interest payable:
      Borrowings wholly repayable within five years:

– bank overdraft and loan	(€734)
– finance lease	(€9)
Interest receivable	€615
	(€128)

Profit before interest and tax for Unidare was €7,003 (000)

Interest cover (Unidare)

Including interest receivable
€7,618/€734 = 10.3 times

Excluding interest receivable
€7,003/€734 = 9.5 times

APPENDIX 3D

Why is Gearing/Leverage important?

Financial leverage has an important implication:
* If a company earns more on investments that have been financed with borrowed funds than it pays in interest, then the return on equity is enhanced or **geared**.

Example Gearing and return on equity

A company which has assets of €1m is financed totally with equity. It has no borrowed funds. The financial results of its first year of trading are:

Operating profit	€200,000
Taxation	€40,000
Profit after tax	€160,000

Therefore the return on equity (ROE) = PAT ÷ Equity = €160,000/€1m = 16%. For every €100 in equity the company makes €16 in profits after tax.

The company then decides to expand its business and invest a further €1m. This time it borrows the €1m from the bank at an interest rate of 7%. This additional investment of €1million generates the same amount of operating profit €200,000. A summary of its new financial position is as follows:

Operating profit	€400,000
Less interest	€70,000
Profit before tax (PBT)	€330,000
Taxation (20%)	€66,000
Profit after tax (PAT)	€264,000

Therefore the new return on equity = €264,000 ÷ €1m = 26.4%.

Therefore by using debt the company has **geared up** the return to equity shareholders. There are two reasons for this.

1. The interest paid on debt is tax deductible. In the above example the company pays €70,000 to the bank in interest charges. The corporation (company) tax rate is 20% on company profits. This tax is paid on £330,000, not £400,000. Therefore the company shareholders have an extra bonus of €14,000 (€70,000 × 20%).
2. Buying shares in a company is riskier than lending the company money. People and institutions that lend money to companies have a prior call on the company's assets. This means that they must be paid the interest on their loans before shareholders receive any return in the form of dividends. Banks, financial institutions and debenture holders must be paid the interest they are due. If this is not forthcoming, they have a right to enforce payment by forcing liquidation. On the other hand, shareholders will only be paid a dividend if the company directors decide that it is in the best interests of the firm. Therefore, because shareholders carry a greater risk, they require a higher rate of return to compensate for this higher risk.

In the above example, shareholders enhanced their return when the company increased the level of debt in the capital structure. The more gearing, the higher the return on equity. So why not have 100% gearing? The answer to this question depends on the overall level of risk attached to the firm. A firm has two types of risk associated with it:

- Business risk which relates to the type of business environment in which the company operates. The operations of a business will inherently face a certain amount of risk. This will relate to the type of business environment the business is in, e.g. the level of competition in the industry, industrial relations history etc., and on the level of operating leverage. Operating leverage refers to the proportion of total costs that are fixed. If a high proportion of a company's total costs are fixed, it will mean the company has high business risk. Capital intensive firms usually have high levels of fixed costs. This type of risk is business risk. Obviously some industries will face less business risk than others. Market share and profit margins will be tight in companies with high business risk. Any downturn in the company's fortunes (a fall-off in sales) could have serious implications for the company's profitability and survival. As we will see in Chapter 8, by using debt the company isolates business risk on to one type of investor—the ordinary shareholders.
- Financial risk refers to the level of debt the company has in its capital structure—its gearing. A company with a high level of debt has a high financial risk. The risk arises because interest on debt must be paid, whereas dividends do not have to be paid to equity shareholders.

A **general rule** is that companies with high business risk should carry low financial risk. Companies in very competitive environments should not carry high levels of debt. A company operating in a very competitive environment (high business risk) and therefore tight profit margins, runs the risk of going out of business if there is a slow-down in the economy or if there is a fall-off in the demand for its product or service because this will cut already tight profit margins. If a company has high operating leverage, a small change in sales will result in a large change in the return shareholders get on their investment. Interest on debt must be paid regardless of the amount of profits. A further example will help illustrate how financial leverage affects risk and return. Table 3D analyses two companies that are identical except for the way they are financed. Firm U (ungeared) has no debt, whereas firm G (geared) is financed half with equity and half with debt at 7% interest. Both companies have assets of €1,000 and sales of €1,000. Their **expected** operating profit (PBIT) is €400. Both firms **expect** to earn €400 in profits before tax on their assets. However, things could turn out to be not what was expected. There could be a bad year for sales. Operating profit could be lower, and in the second column of the table, we see operating profit declining from £400 to £50 under bad conditions. Under normal, (expected/good) conditions, firm G will provide a return to its equity shareholders of 51.1% versus only 28% for firm U. However, financial gearing can cut both ways. If sales are lower and costs higher than expected, the return on assets will be lower than expected. The geared firm's return on equity falls faster than that for the ungeared firm. Under the bad conditions, the debt free firm still shows a profit, but the geared firm shows a very low profit and return on equity. The geared firm needs cash to service its debt while the ungeared firm does not. Firm G must pay €35 in interest regardless of the levels of sales and profitability. If the economy is in recession, the firm is unlikely to be able to generate additional sales income to meet the interest payments. If the company doesn't have sufficient cash resources to meet the interest payment on its debt, it will either go into liquidation or it can try to raise additional equity capital. The latter option could prove to be very difficult when the firm is running at a loss. Selling shares does not prove attractive to potential shareholders when all the company wants to do is use the money raised to pay interest to banks and lower its debt:equity ratio. (A more detailed discussion of this will be given in Chapter 8.)

Table 3D Financial gearing and return on equity

Firm U (ungeared)		
Total assets	€1,000	
Financed by:		
Debt	€0	
Equity	€1,000	
	Good conditions	Poor conditions
Sales	€1,000	€500
Operating costs	€600	€450
Operating profit (profit before interest and tax)	€400	€50
Interest	–	–
Profit before tax (PBT)	€400	€50
Tax (30%)	€120	€15
Profit after tax	€280	€35
Return on Equity (ROE)	28%	3.5%

Geared firm (G)		
Total assets	€1,000	
Financed by:		
Debt (7%)	€500	
Equity	€500	
	Good conditions	Poor conditions
Sales	€1,000	€500
Operating costs	€600	€450
Operating profit	€400	€50
Interest	€35	€35
Profit before tax	€365	€15
Taxation (30%)	€109.5	€4.5
Profit after tax	€255.5	€10.5
Return on equity	51.1%	2.1%

To summarise:
- Firms with high debt ratios have higher than expected returns when the economy is normal, but they can suffer losses when the economy goes into recession.
- Firms with low debt ratios are less risky but they forgo the opportunity of **gearing up** their return on equity.

APPENDIX 3E

Sensitivity Testing

Sensitivity testing can help us understand how Genesis can improve its overall performance. By assuming possible improvements in the company's cost ratios and/or improvements in sale price, we can trace the impact of these changes in the company's overall return on total assets and shareholders' investments.

Explanation

1 Ratio	2 Old value %	3 Change by %	4 New PBIT/ sales	5 New ROI %	6 % change ROI	7 New PBIT €	8 Interest €	9 PBT €	10 Tax %	11 New PAT €
Cost of sales/ Sales	54.4	(2)	10.56	14.37	11.3	663.6	180	453.6	30	317.5
S + D/ Sales	18.1	(2)	9.84	13.4	3.9	590.4	180	410.4	30	287.28
Admin./ Sales	15.3	(5)	10.2	14	8.5	612	180	432	30	303
Sales/ Total assets	1.36	5	14	20	110	882	180	702	30	491

12 Pref. div. €	13 New PFO €	14 New PFO/ sales %	15 Asset turn times	16 New ROTA %	17 % change on ROTA	18 New equity	19 New multiplier	20 New ROE	21 Old EOE	22 % change
8	309.5	5.2	1.36	7	17	2066.8	2.12	14.9	11.6	28
8	279.9	4.7	1.36	6.3	5.3	2055	2.13	13.4	10.5	28
8	295	5	1.36	6.7	11.4	2061	2.12	14.3	10.5	35
8	483	7.6	1.43	11	83	2716	1.6	17.8	10.5	69

To help explain the sensitivity test, take the cost of sales ratio.

Cost of sales ratio
- The old value is 54.4%, given in the vertical analysis above.

- Reducing this by 2% increases the PBIT by 2%, and we get a new PBIT/sales of 10.56% (54.4% × .02 = 1.09 + 9.48% =10.56%).
- The new ROI is the product of the new PBIT/sales ratio and the old asset turnover ratio (10.56 × 1.36 = 14.37). This constitutes an 11.3% increase from the old ROI, which was 12.9%.
- The new PBIT is €633.6 (€6,000 × 10.56% = €633).
- Interest is deducted of €180 and this gives a profit before tax of €453.6.
- Tax of 30% is deducted, giving a profit after tax of €317.5.
- Preference dividends (€8) are deducted leaving €309.5 for ordinary shareholders.
- The new PFO/sales ratio is €309.5/€6,000 = 5.2%.
- Multiplying the new PFO/sales ratio by the original asset turnover ratio of 1.36, gives the new return on total assets of 7% (1.36 × 5.2%). This constitutes an increase in the old ROTA of 17%.
- Profit for ordinary shareholders has increased €264 to €309.5. The dividend pay-out ratio is 60% and 40% is added to retained earnings. Therefore €309.5 × 0.4 = €123.8 is added to retained earnings. This gives a new equity figure of €123.8 + €1,943 = €2,066.8.
- Total assets of €4,387 when divided by the new equity figure of €2,066.8 gives the new equity multiplier of 2.12
- Therefore, the new return on equity is 14.8% (2.12 × 7%), which constitutes an increase in the old ROE of 27%.

Sales/total assets
(Assumptions: an increase of 5% in selling price and no change in volume)

- The original asset turnover ratio is 1.36 times.
- Before any changes are made, €9.48 in every €100 sales income is operating profit. The other €90.52 goes to pay the operating costs. Given an increase of 5% in selling price, **and no other changes**, the operating costs as a percentage of sales falls to 86% (90.5 divided by 1.05). Therefore, the new PBIT/sales ratio is the residual 14% (100% *minus* 86%).
- Therefore the new sales to total asset ratio is 1.43 (6,000 × 1.05)/€4,387.
- The new ROI is now 20% (1.43 × 14%). This is an increase of 55% on the original ROI of 12.9%.
- The new PBIT figure is €882 (€6000 × 1.05 = €6,300 × 0.14).
- Deducting interest, tax and preference dividends gives a profit for ordinary shareholders of €483 and a new PFO/sales of 7.6% (483/6,300).
- The new ROTA is 11% (7.6% × new asset turn ratio of 1.43), which is a huge 82% increase in the ROTA (i.e. the original ROTA was 6.01%). **This shows the importance of price in the overall calculations**.
- Adding the increase in retained earnings (€483 × 0.4 = €193.2) gives the new equity figure of (€193.2 + €1,943 = €2,136.2) and a new equity multiplier of €4,387 ÷ €2,136.2 = 2.05.
- Consequently, the new ROE is 11% × 2.05 = 22.5%, or a 94% increase (from the original 11.6%).

Sensitivity testing can be performed for cost reductions (and/or price increases) or cost increases (and/or price reductions). In reality, it may be difficult, or impossible, in some situations to cut costs or increase prices. Even if costs can be reduced, it might have productivity side effects particularly in the area of labour relations and motivation. Nevertheless, sensitivity testing provides us with a useful tool in financial analysis.

NOTES

1. Sometimes cost of sales means different things to different companies, so turnover is often used instead of cost of sales in creditor payments period calculations.
2. A more detailed analysis of working capital and overtrading is given in Chapter 13.
3. The term interval measure is used by Ross, Westerfield & Jordan in 'Working with Financial Statements', op. cit.
4. The profit before interest and tax figure may include **exceptional items**. These are once off items, so when we calculate interest cover it is important to exclude exceptional items in the calculation:

Interest cover = PBIT and exceptional items/interest payments

5. Because interest is paid before tax is deducted, the numerator is PBIT because the full amount of operating income is available for interest payments.
6. There was a net increase in fixed assets of €2,460 *minus* £1,923 = €537. This is the net increase **after** the deduction for this year's depreciation. Therefore, the depreciation expense should be added back in to show the total increase in **gross** fixed assets.
7. Remember that an **overdraft** is seen as **negative** cash. So therefore the opening cash is €70 *minus* €120 (overdraft) = €50. Cash at the end of the year is €7 *minus* €220 (overdraft) = €213.
8. A more detailed discussion on this topic is provided in Chapter 14 on inventory and credit management.
9. The reader might find it useful to refer to Chapter 13 on Working Capital.
10. PBIT is earned throughout the year, while capital employed is an end of year calculation. Therefore, it would be better, where possible, to use average capital employed (opening capital + closing capital) ÷ 2).
11. Attention should be paid to the following factors in calculating capital employed:
    - Minority interests. Where one company has control over another company, the company must prepare consolidated accounts to show the financial position of both companies. Minority interests occur when companies have subsidiaries that are not wholly owned. Therefore, part of the profits in the consolidated profit and loss account do not belong to the shareholders. However, minority interests are included in calculating capital employed, because the profits earned from the company's subsidiaries are included in the PBIT figure.
    - Provisions for liabilities and charges. These have already been charged to the profit and loss account but have not been spent and should therefore be included in capital employed.
    - Reserves are included but attention should be paid to the company's accounting policies for revaluation.

- Goodwill: If goodwill is written off against reserves this will seriously distort the ROCE ratio. It will also increase the gearing because it has effectively reduced capital and reserves. When looking at trends in the company's return on capital employed over a period of time and for industry comparison purposes, it makes sense to add back the goodwill write-off.
- Profit (loss) on sale of assets. These profits are shown after operating profit but before tax and are therefore included in the ROCE calculation.
- Profit on sale of subsidiaries. These are **once off** and should **not** be included in ROCE calculations.
- Discontinued operations. If the assets and liabilities of the discontinued operations are still shown on the balance sheet, then they are included as part of capital employed, and any profit made from discontinued operations will be included in the PBIT.
- Share of associates' and joint venture profits and losses. These company investments are part of the capital employed and therefore the profits arising from these investments are included in the numerator.

12. In calculating MVA and market to book ratios, the following issues will need to be considered:

    (a) Goodwill: goodwill arising on acquisition should be amortised over its life. Assets are reduced by the amount of goodwill and reserves by the same amount. Using this method, profits are not affected and balance sheet totals are reduced. Rates of return on assets and equity will therefore increase because of this artificial reduction in assets. This will have the effect of enhancing the market to book ratio.

    (b) Revaluation of fixed assets. What effect will a company's revaluation policy have on valuation ratios? The increase in asset values will be matched by an increase in reserves. The revaluation does not affect the profit and loss account, as it is not a realised profit. The consequence of this is that the return on assets and the return on equity will get worse. This will not boost market to book ratios.

    (c) Pension funds. Surpluses or deficits in pension funds will impact on the company's value.

13. The share price and the number of shares were extracted from *The Irish Stock Manual 2000*. For simplicity, the share price is taken as the average between the high and low prices on offer for 1998. Shareholder funds is that reported in their balance sheet in 1998.

14. It is usual to extend this analysis to several years.

Part 2

Valuations

4
The Time Value of Money

CHAPTER OBJECTIVES

At the end of this chapter the student should be able to:

1. understand the concept of the time value of money
2. distinguish between simple and compound interest calculations and when to use each
3. understand the concept of discounting
4. understand the difference between the nominal and effective rates of interest
5. calculate the effective rate of interest from the nominal rate and vice versa
6. understand the difference between fixed and variable rates of interest
7. understand the concept of annuities
8. distinguish between present value and future value of an annuity
9. calculate the value of each of the four variables in both the present value and future value of an annuity formula, i.e. present/future value, interest rate, number of payments, periodic payments.

INTRODUCTION

If you were offered the following options

* €10,000 now or
* €10,000 in ten years' time

which would you choose?

It is almost certainly the case that your answer would be €10,000 now.

Why would everyone choose the first option? There are a number of possible reasons:

* risk of default, i.e. perhaps in ten years' time the person/institution offering the €10,000 will have disappeared and you won't get the money;
* inflation over the next ten years eats into the value of €10,000 and it is far less valuable then than now.

Let's exclude these two possibilities, i.e. the €10,000 is guaranteed with no default risk and inflation is guaranteed to be zero for the next ten years.

The third and most important reason why you would choose the €10,000 now is because money has a **time value**, i.e. money now is more desirable and valuable than the same amount at some date in the future. A simple rationale for this is that if you have the money now you could place it in a demand deposit account paying, say, 5% p.a. and have instant access to it. In technical terms you are receiving a **return** and have a **liquid** asset. If you left it there for ten years it would be worth a lot more than €10,000 (€16,288.94 — see below). Alternatively you could remove the interest each year, consume it and still leave the €10,000 intact.

Likewise if you are offered an investment which pays €10,000 in ten years' time, you won't pay €10,000 for it now. You will pay a sum less than that. Why? Because you want to make a return on your investment and you want to be rewarded for forgoing access to your money (i.e. liquidity).

4.1 Simple interest

Interest is the amount paid on a periodic basis on a savings account (or charged on a loan). It is usually calculated as a percentage of the amount (principal) in the account at the beginning of the period. Savers may choose to take the interest from the account at the end of each period. In this case the principal will remain intact at its original value. The interest earned over n periods of time by the saver, in this case, is referred to as simple interest and can be calculated from 4.1 below:

$$I = PV.r.n \qquad (4.1)$$

where   I = interest earned
  PV = present value (original principal)
   r = interest rate per period
   n = number of interest periods.

The value of any one of the four variables can be calculated from the other three.

If interest is taken from the account at the end of each period and held in a non-interest bearing form, e.g. a shoebox under the bed, the amount the saver will have after n periods is the original principal *plus* the simple interest.

$$FV = PV + I \qquad (4.2)$$

where FV = future value.

This can be written as FV = PV + PV.r.n

or

$$FV = PV (1 + r.n) \qquad (4.3)$$

where   PV = present value
  FV = future value
   r = interest rate per period
   n = number of interest periods/fraction of interest period.

Example 4.1 *Future value using simple interest*

Suppose €1,000 was deposited into an account paying 8% p.a. and left for 5 years. If the interest is withdrawn each year and held in a non-interest bearing form, then the total amount that the saver has at the end of 5 years is, from 4.3 above.

$$FV = 1,000(1 + (0.08) \times 5) = 1,400$$

While this is a somewhat artificial situation it is useful as a comparison with the equivalent compound interest calculation (see example 4.6 below).

If the principal is left in the account for less than a full interest period, then the interest is normally calculated as a fraction of the interest for the full period, e.g. if interest is paid annually and the saver withdraws the money after six months, the interest would be half of the stated annual rate.

Any one of the parameters in 4.3 can be calculated if the other three are known, through simple algebraic manipulation. The following examples assume that money is deposited for less than a full year.

Example 4.2 *Solving for future value*

A lady places €5,000 in a deposit account which pays 8% p.a. Interest is paid on a pro rata basis if left in the account for less than one year. If she closes the account 3 months later, how much money will she get?

Here   PV = 5,000
          r = 0.08
          n = $^1/4$

Using 4.3 $FV = 5,000 (1 + (0.08) . (^1/4)) = 5,100$

Example 4.3 *Solving for present value*

Suppose the same lady as above wished to have €5,600 after 3 months. How much would she have to put on deposit now?

Here   FV = 5,600
          r = 0.08
          n = $^1/4$

Using 4.3 $5,600 = PV (1 + (0.08) . (^1/4))$

$$PV = \frac{5,600}{(1 + (0.08) . (^1/4))} = 5,490.20$$

Example 4.4 Solving for the time factor

A lady places €5,000 in a deposit account which pays 8% p.a. Interest is paid on a pro rata basis on money on deposit for less than a year. How long will it take before she can withdraw €5,250?

Here   PV = 5,000
         FV = 5,250
          r = 0.08

Using 4.3 $5,250 = 5,000 (1 + (0.08).n) = 5,100$

$$n = \frac{\dfrac{5,250}{5,000} - 1}{0.08} = 0.625$$

The answer above is expressed as a fraction of a year. To convert it into days or months simply multiply it by 365 or 12, e.g. $0.625 \times 365 = 228$ days.

Example 4.5 Solving for the interest rate

A lady wishes to have €5,300 in six months' time. If she places €5,000 in a deposit account now, what annual rate of interest must she earn to reach her target? Assume that interest is paid on a pro rata basis if left in the account for less than one year.

Here   PV = 5,000
         FV = 5,300
          n = $^1/_2$

Using 4.3 $5,300 = 5,000 (1 + r. (^1/_2))$

$$r = \frac{\dfrac{5,300}{5,000} - 1}{^1/_2} = 0.12 = 12\%$$

4.2 Compound interest

The saver may choose to leave the interest in an account, in which case it is added to the principal at the end of each interest period. Interest is then earned on both the original principal and the interest earned to date. The fund is said to earn interest on a compound basis i.e. compound interest.

The value of the savings fund after n periods can be calculated from (4.4) below

$$FV = PV (1 + r)^n \qquad\qquad (4.4)$$

where   PV = present value (original principal)
   FV = future value
   r = interest rate per period
   n = number of interest periods.

Example 4.6 Compound interest

How much is in an account after five years if €1,000 is deposited and the fund earns interest at the rate of 8% p.a?

Using 4.4 above $FV = 1,000 (1.08)^5 = 1,469.32$

Note that the future value here is substantially greater than the value in example 4.1, which used simple interest. This illustrates the value of compounding. Section 4.4 below shows that the more frequent the interest compounding, the greater is the final value of the investment.

   Any one of the parameters in 4.4 can be calculated if the other three are known, through simple algebraic manipulation. Example 4.6 above showed how to calculate FV. The calculation of PV is left until section 4.3. The calculation of n and r are shown in examples 4.7 and 4.8 below. The value of n can be found using logarithms.

Example 4.7 Finding the time factor

A man deposits €5,000 into an account paying 8% p.a. compound. How long will it take for the value to grow to €8,000?
Here   PV = 5,000
   FV = 8,000
   r = 0.08.

The value of n can be found using logarithms.

From 4.4 $8,000 = 5,000 (1.08)^n$

Through algebraic manipulation this can be reduced to

$$n \times \log 1.08 = \log \frac{8,000}{5,000} = \log 1.6$$

$$n = \frac{\log 1.6}{\log 1.08} = 6.11$$

Thus it takes a little over 6 years to reach the target of €8,000.

Example 4.8 Finding the interest rate

A man deposits €5,000 into an account. He wishes to have €8,000 ten years later. What annual rate of interest must the account pay?

Here   PV = 5,000
          FV = 8,000
           n = 10.

From 4.4   8,000   = 5,000 (1 + r)^{10}
     This reduces to
                            (1 + r)^{10} = 1.6
                                1 + r = (1.6)$^{1/10}$ = 1.0481
                                    r = 0.0481   = 4.81%

In order to avoid repetitive calculations, the compound interest tables shown in the Appendix can be used. The columns give the rate of interest per period, while the rows give the number of periods. The entries in the body of the table show the value of a €1 investment for the specified period of time at the specified rate of interest per period. Thus to find the value of a €1 investment for 5 years at 6% p.a., simply read the relevant entry from the table, i.e. 1.3382 (the future value is €1.3382). The future value of any other investment amount is got by multiplying it by 1.3382, e.g. the value of a €6,000 investment at 6% p.a. for 5 years is found thus:

$$€6,000 \times 1.3382 = €8,029.2$$

4.3 Discounting and present value

Discounting is basically the opposite of compounding.

Discounting arises because **money has a time value**. As pointed out at the start of this chapter, money is worth more now than in the future if only because it can be invested and can earn a return.

Let's look at a simple example, first without discounting and then using a discounting approach.

Suppose an investment costs €500 now and pays €250 at the end of each of the next three years. Is this a good investment? Assume there is no default risk and there is no inflation in the economy over the three years. It looks like a good investment. The investor receives €750 over three years for a €500 outlay now. This looks like a 50% return over three years.

The above is misleading. It **may** be a good investment—this depends on the rate of interest in the economy.

Suppose the investor borrowed to buy the investment and suppose the bank charged an annual interest rate of 10%.

The investor's bank account might look like this:

Time	Borrow	Interest	Repay	Balance
0	500			− 500
1		50	250	− 300
2		30	250	− 80
3		8	250	162

This is a good investment. The investor ends up with €162 at the end of the third year.
Now repeat this exercise where the rate of interest charged by the bank is 30% p.a.

Time	Borrow	Interest	Repay	Balance
0	500			– 500
1		150	250	– 400
2		120	250	– 270
3		81	250	– 101

Now the investor makes a loss. The message here is that the value of the investment depends crucially on the rate of interest.

The figures of €162 profit and €101 loss might be termed the net terminal value of this investment.

Now look at this investment from a different perspective. Suppose the bank charges 10% p.a. on borrowed funds. How much could the investor borrow from the bank using this investment as security.

The €250 receivable in one year's time could support a borrowing of

$$\frac{€250}{1.1} \quad = \quad €227.27$$

In other words, if the investor borrowed €227.27 from the bank today, he could discharge this debt in one year's time with a payment of €250.

Likewise the receipts of €250 at the end of the second and third years could support borrowings of

$$\frac{250}{(1.1)^2} \quad \text{and} \quad \frac{250}{(1.1)^3} \quad = €206.61 \text{ and } €187.83 \text{ respectively.}$$

The three future receipts could together support a borrowing of €621.71 in total. Since the investment only costs €500 to buy, the investor can take a profit of €121.71 now.

The three numbers represent the discounted values or present values of future receipts. The sum of €621.71 is the total discounted or present value of the future stream of income and the net present value (see Chapter 7) of the investment is €121.71.

The student should now re-do the above calculation where the rate of interest is 30% on borrowed funds. This will show that the present value of the future receipts is €454.03 and the net present value of the investment is – €45.97.

Again it is clear that as the rate of interest increases, the present value of a future receipt decreases and vice versa.

The discounted or present value of a future sum can be calculated by inverting 4.4 above, i.e.

$$PV = \frac{FV}{(1 + r)^n} \tag{4.5}$$

Example 4.9 Finding the discounted value of a future receipt

An investment bond (bonds are dealt with in detail in Chapter 5) is due to pay €8,000 in five years' time. How much is it worth today if the rate of interest on such investments is 12% p.a?
   Using 4.5 above

$$PV = \frac{8000}{(1.12)^5} = 4,539.41$$

Discounting is the fundamental basis of discounted cash flow analysis as discussed in Chapter 7 and the mathematics of bond market investment as discussed in Chapter 5.

   Each of the other parameters in 4.5 can be calculated from the other three. This is not shown here as the approach is similar to that used in the compounding formula.

   Just as in the case of compounding, a set of mathematical tables may be used to avoid repetitive calculations in discounting. These discount tables as shown in the appendix can be used. The columns give the rate of interest per period, while the rows give the number of periods. The entries in the body of the table show the value today of a €1 receipt at a specified time in the future for a specified rate of interest per period. Thus to find today's value of €1 in 5 years' time where the rate of interest in the market is 6% p.a., simply read the relevant entry from the table, i.e. 0.7473 and the present value is €0.7473, i.e. just under 75 pence. The present value of any other future amount is got by multiplying it by 0.7473, e.g. the value of a €6,000 receipt in 5 years where the appropriate rate of interest is 6% p.a. is found by

$$€6,000 \times 0.7473 = €4,483.80$$

4.4 Nominal and effective rate of interest

Banks normally quote a rate of interest on an annual basis but may charge interest to the account more often than once a year. Likewise interest may be added to a savings account more often than once a year. The stated/advertised rate is referred to as the nominal rate. The actual rate that the borrower pays or the actual rate that the saver earns will be greater than the nominal rate if compounding takes place more often than once a year. The actual rate is referred to as the effective rate of interest or annual percentage rate (APR). It can be calculated from 4.6 below:

$$\textbf{Effective rate of interest} = \left(1 + \frac{j_m}{m}\right)^m - 1 \qquad\qquad \textbf{4.6}$$

where j_m = nominal rate of interest compounded m times per year.

Example 4.10 Effective rate of interest

(a) What is the effective rate of interest if the nominal rate of interest is 9% p.a. and interest is compounded quarterly?

Using formula 4.6

$$\text{Effective rate of interest} = \left(1 + \frac{0.09}{4}\right)^4 - 1 = 0.093 = 9.3\%$$

(b) What is the effective rate of interest p.a. if the nominal rate is 15% p.a. and interest is compounded monthly?

$$\text{Effective rate of interest} = \left(1 + \frac{0.15}{12}\right)^{12} - 1 = 0.1608 = 16.08\%$$

(c) At what nominal rate of interest compounded monthly must €1,000 be invested in order to double itself in eight years?

Here PV = 1,000
       FV = 2,000
        n = 96 months
        r = unknown, where r = monthly rate

Solve for r from formula 4.4 above.

$$2,000 = 1,000 \, (1 + r)^{96}$$
$$2 = (1 + r)^{96}$$
$$2^{1/96} = 1 + r$$
$$1.007246412 = 1 + r$$
$$0.007246412 = r$$

This gives r = 0.007246412

The nominal rate is therefore $12 \times 0.007246412 = 0.086956 = 8.7\%$

4.5 Fixed versus variable rates of interest

Banks may offer savers or borrowers an option to receive or pay a fixed rather than a variable rate of interest. In times of rising interest rates borrowers are protected by fixed rates, but do not get the benefit if rates fall. The opposite applies to savers.

Whether choosing a fixed rate over a variable rate is an efficient decision or not is really only answerable after the event. With a fixed rate borrowers are opting for certainty over uncertainty.

Example 4.11 Fixed and variable rates of interest

What fixed rate of interest p.a. payable for five years provides an equivalent compound investment return to a variable rate structure paying interest as follows?

Year	Rate of interest
1	10
2	12
3	14
4	9
5	15

The fixed rate is that which would produce the same future value after 5 years as the variable rate structure.

Variable rate
Let the initial investment be €1,000

$$FV = 1,000 \ (1.1) \ (1.12) \ (1.14) \ (1.09) \ (1.15) = 1,760.52$$
Fixed rate
$$1,760.52 = 1,000 \ (1 + r)^5$$
where r = fixed rate of interest p.a.
Solving the above equation gives r = 11.98%

$$Check \ 1,000 \ (1.1198)^5 = €1,760.77$$

Example 4.12 Fixed versus variable rate

What fixed nominal rate of interest p.a. compounded monthly would be equivalent to a variable rate structure over three years if the variable rate was

(a) 10% p.a. compounded quarterly in the first year?
(b) 12% p.a. compounded monthly in the second year?
(c) 14% p.a. compounded half-yearly in the third year?

Variable rate
Let initial investment = €1,000

$$FV = 1,000 \ (1.025)^4 \ (1.01)^{12} \ (1.07)^2 = 1,424.03$$

Fixed rate
$$1,424.03 = 1,000 \ (1+r)^{36} \text{ where r = monthly rate of interest}$$

Solving the equation gives r = 0.0098676
Nominal rate = $12 \times 0.0098676 = 0.1184 = 11.84\%$

4.6 Continuous streams of payments

Continuous regular streams of payments are a feature of many financial arrangements, either formally or informally.

- A young lady wishes to save for a deposit on a new apartment and decides that she can afford to save €300 per month. She may be interested in knowing how long it will take to reach a certain target figure or she may wish to know how much she will have saved after a certain period of time.
- Her brother wants to buy a new car. He does so by borrowing from a finance company. He will be interested in knowing what his regular repayment will be or how long it will take to pay off the loan.

The two examples illustrate the two principal driving forces of a continuous stream of payments, either a future value (FV) to be reached or a present value (PV), here a loan, to be paid off. The present value of a stream of payments also arises in relation to investment appraisal (see Chapter 7).

Future value of annuity

Using the example of the young lady saving for the deposit on the apartment, she lodges €300 into an account at the end of each month. The account pays a monthly interest rate of 0.5%. How much has she got in the account after three years, i.e. 36 deposits?

Each of the payments will earn compound interest at the same interest rate, but for a different length of time. The first payment will earn interest for 35 months, the second for 34 months and so on. The second last payment will earn one month's interest and the last deposit will earn no interest, if the account is valued at the end of the third year. The total value is therefore the sum of the 36 deposits *plus* the compound interest on each one. This can be calculated as follows:

$$FV @ time 36 = 300\,(1.005)^{35} + 300\,(1.005)^{34} + \dots + \dots 300(1.005)^{1} + 300$$

Calculating the value of this stream would involve 36 calculations. However, since all terms form a geometric progression, it can be easily shown that the sum is given by 4.7 below.

$$FV = P_t \left[\frac{(1 + r)^n - 1}{r} \right] \qquad (4.7)$$

where FV = future value
       P_t = periodic payment
       r = interest rate per compounding period
       n = number of payments.

Note that the fund is valued just as the last payment is being made and so the last payment earns no interest.

This stream of payments in this example forms an ordinary simple annuity. The conditions for an **ordinary simple annuity** in the future value case are:

- the rate of interest is paid at the same frequency as the payments are being made (here monthly)
- the interest is added to the account at the same time as the payments are being made (here at the end of the month)
- the fund is valued just at the point when the last payment is being made (here at the end of the 36th month).

Any one of the four variables can be calculated given the other three. Calculation of the number of payments required, i.e. n, requires the use of logarithms, while the calculation of the rate of interest requires a trial and error approach. The technique of linear interpolation can be used to find the value of r (see example 4.14 below).

In the example above, if payments had been made at the start of each month and the fund is valued at the end of the 36th month, then each payment earns an additional one month's interest. The value from the formula above would be multiplied by (1.005) or (1 + r) in the general case. This is referred to as a simple annuity due.

Example 4.13 Future value of an ordinary simple annuity

Solving for the future value

A young lady is saving for the deposit on the apartment. She lodges €300 into an account at the end of each month. The account pays a monthly interest rate of 0.5%. How much has she got in the account after three years?

Using 4.7 above

$$FV = 300 \left[\frac{(1.005)^{36} - 1}{0.005} \right] = 11,800.83$$

Annuity tables — future value

4.7 involves the calculation of the following:

$$\frac{(1 + r)^n - 1}{r}$$

This is a repetitive calculation, differing only in the value of the two parameters, n and r. In order to avoid such repetitive calculations, a set of annuity tables is provided in the Appendix. There are two sets, one for future value and the other for present value. The entries in the body of the future value annuity table give the future value, after n periods, of a regular stream of €1 deposits for n periods into an account paying r% per period, e.g. €1 invested each year for 12 years into an account paying 8% p.a. has a value at the end of the 12th year of €18.98, according to the tables.

This annuity factor, 18.98, can then be used to find the value of any other equal deposit for the same period at the same rate of interest, e.g. if the deposit had been €50, then the future value at the end of the 12th year is €50 × 18.98 = €949.

Each row represents a different time period and each column represents a different rate of interest.

Solving for the periodic payment

If one wished to set a target of €10,000, and wanted to know the size of the monthly deposit required, it can be solved from the expression. (The interest rate and the term are as above.)

$$10,000 = P_t \left[\frac{(1.005)^{36} - 1}{0.005} \right]$$

The value is solved by simple algebraic manipulation and is €254.22.

Solving for the number of payments

If one wished to know how long it would take to reach a target of €10,000 with payments of €300 per month, it can be solved from the expression

$$10,000 = 300 \left[\frac{(1.005)^n - 1}{0.005} \right]$$

The value is solved using logarithms.

$$(1.005)^n = \frac{10,000 \times 0.005}{300} + 1 = 1.166667$$

$$n \times \log(1.005) = \log 1.166667$$

$$n = \frac{\log 1.166667}{\log(1.005)} = 30.9$$

This can be interpreted as 30 full deposits and one final deposit at the end of the 31st month less than €300. It will not be equal to 0.9 of €300 since the relationship between Pt and n in 4.7 is not linear. In some instances there may be no need for a final smaller payment since the interest alone will carry the fund value over the target in the last month. This is covered in the end of chapter questions.

Since the monthly rate of interest is small in the above example, a different example is used to illustrate the calculation of the rate of interest.

Example 4.14 *Solving for the rate of interest*

A company has to repay a loan of €600,000 in eight years' time. It sets up a fund and deposits €50,000 at the end of each year for the eight years. Calculate, using the technique of linear interpolation, the annual rate of interest which the company must earn on the fund in order to pay off the loan in the time required. Answer to one place of decimals.

Using 4.7

$$600,000 = 50,000 \left[\frac{(1 + r)^8 - 1}{r} \right]$$

Since r appears in the formula above and below the line, there is no simple algebraic manipulation which can isolate it on one side of the equation. It must be solved by trial and error.

A number of trial values of r are inserted into the equation above. This is continued until two rates produce values either side of the target of €600,000.

Since the answer will be approximated between these two rates, the nearer they are, the more accurate the answer will be. All examples in this chapter (and in Chapters 5 and 20) approximate the answer to one place of decimals using the technique of linear interpolation between two interest rates which are one percentage point apart.

Using r = 10% produces FV = €571,794.41. This leaves the fund short of the target, therefore the rate of interest must be higher than 10%.

Using r = 11% produces FV = €592,971.71. This still leaves the fund short of the target, therefore the rate of interest must be higher than 11%.

Using r = 12% produces FV = €614,984.66. This is above the target and so the required rate is below 12%.

The rate is therefore between 11% and 12%. The answer can be approximated using linear interpolation.

The technique of linear interpolation assumes that the future value rises in a linear fashion as the rate of interest is increased. While the true relationship is non-linear, the assumption of linearity is a reasonable approximation for small changes in the rate of interest.

A one percentage point rise in r from 11% causes the future value to rise by €22,012.95 (614,984.66 − 592,971.71). What fraction of a 1 per cent increase in r from 11% would cause the future value to rise by €7,028.29 (600,000.00 − 592,971.71)? This is calculated as follows:

$$\frac{x}{1} = \frac{7,028.29}{22,012.95} = 0.3$$

The answer is therefore approximated as 11.3%. This can be checked by using 11.3% as the value of r in 4.7 and calculating FV. This produces FV = 599,486.51 which is €13.49 short of the target. To complete the answer, r should be increased to 11.4% and FV recalculated. This produces FV = 601,674.96, which is significantly above the target. The answer is therefore r = 11.3% correct to one place of decimals.

(Linear interpolation is discussed in more detail in Chapter 5.)

Present value of annuity

Using the example of the young man wishing to buy a new car, he reckons that he can repay €350 per month off a loan. The bank charges interest at the rate of 0.7% per month. He wishes to pay the loan off over a period of three years. How much can he afford to borrow?

Each of the monthly payments could themselves pay off a small loan. For example the payment of €350 in one month's time could pay off a loan taken out today. The bank would lend an amount of money so that when interest is added to it for one month, the debt to the bank would be €350 and the loan would be cleared with the single payment. The amount the bank would lend is simply the present value or discounted value of €350 payable in one month's time. This can be solved using 4.5 above.

$$PV = \frac{FV}{(1 + r)^n}$$

$$PV = \frac{350}{(1.007)^1} = 347.57$$

The bank would therefore lend the man €347.57 today which would be repaid in one month's time at €350.

Likewise the bank would lend a second amount which would be repaid in two months' time with a payment of €350. The amount of this loan can be calculated as

$$PV = \frac{350}{(1.007)^2} = 345.15$$

The 36 repayments can therefore be seen as repaying a succession of different loans, each one smaller as the payment period is further out into the future. The total that could be borrowed is therefore

$$PV = \frac{350}{(1.007)^1} + \frac{350}{(1.007)^2} \; ... + ... \; \frac{350}{(1.007)^{35}} + \frac{350}{(1.007)^{36}}$$

This involves 37 calculations. However since the terms form a geometric progression, it can easily be shown that the sum is given by 4.8 below

$$PV = P_t \left[\frac{1 - (1 + r)^{-n}}{r} \right] \qquad (4.8)$$

where PV = present value
  P_t = periodic payment
  r = interest rate per discounting period
  n = number of payments.

Note that the loan is valued at the start of the month but the first payment is made at the end of the month.

This stream of payments in this example forms an **ordinary simple annuity**. The conditions for an ordinary simple annuity in the present value case are:

- the rate of interest is paid at the same frequency as the payments are being made (here monthly)
- the interest is added to the account at the same time as the payments are being made (here at the end of the month)

- payments start at the end of the first interest period or one period after the loan is taken out (here at the end of the 1st month).

Any one of the four variables can be calculated given the other three. Calculation of the number of payments required, i.e. n, requires the use of logarithms, while the calculation of the rate of interest requires a trial and error approach. The technique of linear interpolation can be used to find the value of r (see example 4.16 above).

   In the example above, if the repayments had started at the beginning of the first month, one month's interest is saved and so a larger loan could be taken out. The value from the formula above would be multiplied by (1.005) or (1 + r) in the general case. This is referred to as a simple annuity due. This would be unusual in a lending situation but could arise in an investment appraisal situation (see Chapter 7).

Example 4.15 Present value of an ordinary simple annuity

Solving for the present value

A young man wishing to buy a new car reckons that he can repay €350 per month off a loan. The bank charges interest at the rate of 0.7% per month. He wishes to pay off the loan over a period of three years. How much can he afford to borrow?

Using 4.8, the PV can be solved as

$$PV = 350 \left[\frac{1 - (1.007)^{-36}}{0.007} \right]$$

This produces an answer of €11,103.63.

Annuity tables — present value

Formula 4.8 involves the calculation of the following

$$\frac{1 - (1 + r)^{-n}}{r}$$

This is a repetitive calculation, differing only in the value of the two parameters, n and r. Similar to the case of the future value, there is a set of annuity tables to obviate the need for such calculations in the present value case. The entries in the body of the present value annuity table give the present value of a regular stream of €1 payments for n periods where the discount rate is r% per period, e.g. a €1 repayment each year for 12 years against a loan which is charging interest at 8% p.a. can support a loan size of €7.54 today, according to the tables. This annuity factor, 7.54, can then be used to find the value of any other equal payment stream for the same period at the same rate of interest, e.g. if the repayment had been €50, then the present value is €50 × 7.54 = €377.

   Each row represents a different time period and each column represents a different rate of interest.

Solving for the periodic payment

Suppose the man wished to borrow €12,000 and wanted to know what the monthly repayments would be. The interest rate and term of the loan are as above.

Using 4.8

$$12,000 = Pt \left[\frac{1 - (1.007)^{-36}}{0.007} \right]$$

This produces an answer of = €378.25

Solving for the number of payments

Suppose the man can only afford to repay €300 per month and wants to borrow €12,000. How long would it take to clear the loan. The interest rate is as before.

Using 4.8

$$12,000 = 300 \left[\frac{1 - (1.007)^{-n}}{0.007} \right]$$

The solution requires the use of logarithms. The procedure is similar to that in the future case and is not reproduced here. The answer works out at n = 47.09. This can be interpreted as 47 monthly payments of €300 and a final smaller payment one month later. The final smaller payment will not be 0.09 of €300, since the relationship between Pt and n is not linear. Alternatively the loan could be cleared on the 47th month by increasing the €300 payment. The increased size of the 47th payment or the size of the 48th payment can be calculated by using the outstanding balance formula. This is discussed in Chapter 21.

Calculation of the rate of interest from 4.8 requires the use of linear interpolation. This is shown in the example below.

Example 4.16 *Solving for the rate of interest*

A company is repaying a loan of €800,000 with annual repayments of €120,000 over a period of twelve years, with the first repayment made one year after the loan is taken out. Calculate, using the technique of linear interpolation, the annual rate of interest which is being charged on the loan. Answer to one place of decimals.

Using 4.8

$$800,000 = 120,000 \left[\frac{1 - (1 + r)^{-12}}{r} \right]$$

As before, trial values of r are inserted into the equation above.

Using r = 10% produces PV = €817,643.02. This means that at a rate of interest of 10%, 12 annual payments of €120,000 would pay off a loan of €817,643.02. Since the loan is only €800,000, the rate of interest must be above 10%.

Using r = 11% produces PV = €779,082.74. This is below the loan size and so the required rate is below 11%.

The rate is therefore between 10% and 11%. The answer can be approximated using linear interpolation.

The technique of linear interpolation assumes that the present value falls in a linear fashion as the rate of interest is increased. While the true relationship is non-linear, the assumption of linearity is a reasonable approximation for small changes in the rate of interest.

A one percentage point rise in r from 10% causes the present value to fall by €38,560.28 (817,643.02 -- 779,082.74). What fraction of a one per cent increase in r from 10% would cause the present value to fall by €17,643.02 (817,643.02 – 800,000.00)? This is calculated as follows:

$$\frac{x}{1} = \frac{17,643.02}{38,560.28} = 0.46$$

The answer is therefore approximated as 10.5%. This can be checked by using 11.5% as the value of r in 4.8 and calculating PV. This produces PV = 797,995.72 which is €2,004.28 short of the given loan size. To complete the answer r should be reduced to 10.4% and PV recalculated. This produces PV = 801,865.31 which is just €1,865.31above the loan size. The answer is therefore r = 11.4% correct to one place of decimals.

SUMMARY

- Money has a time value, i.e. money received now is worth more than the same amount received at a time in the future.
- Money invested for a period of time grows in value at a compound rate.
- The process of discounting is used to find the present day equivalent (present value) of a future sum.
- The higher the discount factor, the lower the present value of a future receipt is.
- The annual effective rate of interest is higher than the nominal/stated rate if compounding takes place more often than once a year.
- Fixed rates of interest protect borrowers against the possibility of increased interest charges, but prevent them from benefiting if interest rates fall.
- Many financial arrangements involve a continuous stream of regular payments. This may be in the context of repaying a loan or receiving a pension or other payment.
- Loan repayments can often be treated as an ordinary simple annuity, where the loan size will equal the present value of the repayment stream discounted at the appropriate rate of interest.
- Regular savings contributions can often be treated as an ordinary simple annuity, where the value of the fund at a point in the future can be found as the future value of the stream of contributions.

QUESTIONS

1. What is the effective rate of interest p.a. if the nominal rate of interest is 12% and interest is compounded quarterly?

2.♦ If a savings account stands at €10,000 today, and no deposits have been made into it for the past seven years, how much was in it seven years ago if interest was earned at
(a) 12% p.a. compounded monthly for the seven years?
(b) 12 % p.a. compounded monthly for the past four years and 10% p.a. compounded half-yearly for the previous three years?

3. At what nominal rate of interest p.a. compounded quarterly must €1,000 be invested in order to double itself in four years?

4. (a) A loan of €45,000 is to be repaid with equal monthly payments (except the last) of €400 starting one month after the loan is taken out. The interest rate is 6% p.a. compounded monthly. Find the number of €400 payments.
(b) If the bank required that the above loan be repaid ten years after it is taken out, what is the size of the equal monthly payment, starting one month after the loan is taken out, required to clear the loan?

5. If a savings account stands at €8,000 today, and no deposits have been made into it for the past five years, how much was in it five years ago if interest was earned at
(a) 9% p.a. compounded monthly for the five years?
(b) 9% p.a. compounded monthly for the past three years and 12% p.a. compounded quarterly for the previous two years?

6.♦ A loan of €8,000 with interest at 1.1% per month is to be repaid over seven years with equal monthly payments starting one month after the loan is taken out. Calculate the amount of interest which will be paid over the life of the loan.

7.♦ A family wishes to have €15,000 in three years' time in order to undertake some refurbishment on their home. They place €5,000 into a fund today paying interest at 12% p.a. compounded monthly. They intend to deposit a fixed amount into the fund at the end of each month starting at the end of the current month. The fund pays interest on a simple interest basis on money on deposit for part of a month.
(a) What size must this monthly deposit be in order to have €15,000 in three years' time?
(b) Suppose the family only made the initial deposit of €5,000 and the first 30 of the intended 36 monthly deposits. How long would it take the fund to grow to €15,000?
(c) Going back to (a) above, suppose after two years the family realised that they would need €18,000 rather than €15,000 at the end of the third year and decided to increase the size of the monthly deposits in the third year to a new equal value. What would this new monthly deposit have to be?

8. Two proud grandparents decide to set up a fund to provide assistance towards a third level education for their new granddaughter. They deposit a single amount of money, on the day the child is born, into a fund paying interest at 12% p.a. compounded quarterly. The fund will allow the granddaughter to withdraw €1,000 on a quarterly basis for a total of 16 quarters, starting on her 17th birthday. What single deposit is required to establish the fund on the day of the child's birth?

9.♦ A farmer is buying a parcel of land from a neighbour. The seller wants either €200,000 immediately or €100,000 now and €30,000 at the end of each year for 5 years. Which option should the buyer choose if the rate of interest is
(a) 14.4% p.a. compounded monthly and is expected to remain so for 5 years?

(b) 14.4 % p.a. compounded monthly for the first two years, expected to rise to 15.6% p.a. compounded monthly for the third year, and to fall to 13.2% p.a. compounded quarterly for the last two years?

10. Joe is made redundant on his 50th birthday and receives a lump sum payment of €40,000. He finds another job and decides to invest the €40,000 into a fund paying interest at 1.2% per month. He retires from the new job on his 60th birthday and receives a lump sum payment of €10,000. He deposits this immediately into the same fund. He decides to make 180 equal monthly withdrawals from the fund, starting one month after his 60th birthday, so as to exhaust the fund with the last withdrawal.

(a) Find the size of the monthly withdrawals.

(b) Suppose Joe was forced to withdraw €15,000 from the fund on his 55th birthday to cover an unforeseen expense, but otherwise the conditions are similar to part (a) above. Calculate the size of the monthly withdrawals.

11. (a) A family wishes to have €25,000 in three years' time to build an extension to their home. They intend to deposit a fixed amount at the end of each month, starting at the end of the current month, into a fund paying interest at 13.2% p.a. compounded monthly. Interest is paid on a simple interest basis on money on deposit for a fraction of a month. Find the size of the monthly deposit.

(b) Suppose the family in part (a) above won €10,000 in a lottery at the end of the first year and placed this amount into the fund immediately.

(i) How long would it now take to reach the target of €25,000 if they continued with the existing monthly deposits?

(ii) If they decide to stick with the three year plan, and to reduce their monthly deposits in the second and third year to a new equal value, what size would these deposits be in order to reach the target of €25,000 at the end of the third year?

12. Jean is buying a business from the current owner. The owner wants €260,000 now or €100,000 now and a further €40,000 at the end of each year for the next four years and €60,000 five years from now. Which payment option should Jean choose if the rate of interest is

(a) 14% p.a. compounded quarterly and expected to remain so?

(b) 14% p.a. compounded quarterly at present, but expected to fall to 12% p.a. compounded monthly after two years and to 9% p.a. compounded monthly one year later?

13. (a) A family wishes to have €30,000 in four years' time to build an extension to their home. They intend to deposit a fixed amount at the end of each month, starting at the end of the current month, into a fund paying interest at 10.8% p.a. compounded monthly. Interest is paid on a simple interest basis on money on deposit for a fraction of a month. Find the size of the monthly deposit.

(b) Suppose the family in part (a) above won €12,000 in a lottery at the end of the second year and placed this amount into the fund immediately.

(i) How long would it now take to reach the target of €30,000 if they continued with the existing monthly deposits?

(ii) If they decide to stick with the four year plan, and to reduce their monthly deposits in the third and fourth year to a new equal value, what size would these deposits be in order to reach the target of €30,000 at the end of the fourth year?

14. A tenant renting an office from a landlord for five years beginning today is offered the following rental options:
    (a) €30,000 p.a. payable annually in advance (i.e. at the beginning of each year) or
    (b) €28,000 p.a. payable annually in advance *plus* 10% of annual turnover payable in arrears (i.e. at the end of each year). Turnover is forecast as follows:

Year	Turnover (€000)
1	20
2	25
3	30
4	35
5	40

Which option should the tenant choose if the current rate of interest is
(a) 12% p.a. compounded monthly and expected to remain so?
(b) 12% p.a. compounded monthly, but is expected to increase to 14% compounded quarterly after two years?

15.♦ A loan of €700,000 is repaid with annual payments of €100,000 over a period of 10 years, the first payment one year after the loan is taken out. Using the technique of linear interpolation, calculate the rate of interest (to one place of decimals) which is being charged on the loan.

16.♦ A company has a loan of €14,000 at a variable rate of interest. The loan is to be repaid within four years. It agrees to pay back €4,000 at the end of the first year, €5,000 at the end of the second year and €6,000 at the end of the third year. What single payment at the end of the fourth year will clear the loan if the rate of interest changes as follows:

Year	Rate of interest
1	15% p.a. compounded monthly?
2	12% p.a. compounded monthly?
3	9% p.a. compounded monthly?
4	12% p.a. compounded quarterly?

17. Explain the concept of the 'time value of money'.
18. Define the following:

   • Nominal rate of interest
   • Effective rate of interest
   • Ordinary simple annuity.

19. Distinguish between a fixed and variable rate of interest. What are the advantages and disadvantages of each?
20. Explain the purpose of discounting.

5
Introduction to Bond Valuations

CHAPTER OBJECTIVES

At the end of this chapter the student should understand:

1. the defining features of a fixed interest bond
   - face/nominal value
   - redemption value
   - coupon
   - redemption date
2. the defining features of a discount bond
3. the defining features of a perpetual bond
4. the defining features of a stepped-interest bond
5. and be able to calculate the yield measures
   - gross redemption yield
   - net redemption yield
   - gross flat/income/running yield
   - net flat/income/running yield
6. the relationship between bond prices and yield.

INTRODUCTION

This chapter provides an introduction to the mathematics of bonds and investment in the bond market. Chapter 16 deals with the structure and operation of the Irish bond market while Chapter 20 deals with more advanced aspects of bonds.

There are four underlying investment assets in a developed economy:

- equity
- bonds
- property/real estate
- cash and related investments.

Bonds represent, after equity, the largest asset category in institutional portfolios. Bonds can be viewed both from the issuer's and the investor's point of view. For the issuer they represent a funding mechanism, e.g. a company raising capital to undertake a research and development project or a government raising funds to meet a budget deficit. For the investor they represent a relatively low-risk investment opportunity in the case of government-issued bonds to a very risky investment in the case of *junk* bonds. The issuer will obviously attempt to issue the bond at the lowest possible cost to itself while the investor will be looking to generate the maximum return possible.

The bond market in Ireland is predominantly based on bonds issued by the Irish Government. There is a small market in corporate bonds. This chapter, therefore, focuses primarily on government-issued bonds.

5.1 Definition of a bond

A bond is basically a paper asset through which the issuer agrees to pay the purchaser some amount(s) of money at some agreed date(s) in the future, in exchange for a sum of money now.

There is an enormous range of bond types available to the investor. This chapter deals with the simplest types. The basic bond is one with a fixed coupon and a fixed redemption date. Section 5.4 describes some variations on the basic type.

5.2 Defining features of a bond

The key defining features of a bond are:

- Nominal or face value
  This is a notional amount which is used to calculate the periodic interest payment. It is normally a round figure such as €100 or €1,000 and represents the basic amount against which the % coupon is paid. It is usually the same as the redemption value.
- Redemption value
  This is the amount which will be repaid on the redemption date. It is typically €100 or €1,000.
- Coupon
  This is the periodic (e.g. annual or semi-annual) interest payment. It is expressed as a percentage of the face value. In the case of a fixed interest bond it does not change over the life of the bond. Note that the coupon rate and the market rate of interest are unrelated after issue. In the case of a floating rate bond, the coupon rate is adjusted periodically to reflect current market rates of interest. The rate is expressed as a margin over some reference rate, e.g. 3 month exchequer bill rate, or Euribor. As the reference rate changes, the coupon rate on the bond changes, normally at the end of each period, e.g. quarterly. This chapter is primarily concerned with fixed interest bonds.
- Redemption date
  This is the date on which the redemption value of the bond is to be paid.

5.3 Fixed coupon and fixed redemption date bond

The most typical bond is one which pays both a regular coupon and a final redemption value. Thus a bond with a nominal and redemption value of €1,000 and an annual coupon of 12% with 10 years to run to maturity will pay €120 p.a. for ten years and €1,000 at the end of the tenth year.

Figure 5.1 Typical fixed coupon and redemption date bond

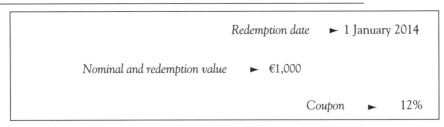

The above bond is issued on, say, 1 January 2004 and is redeemable by the issuer on 1 January 2014 at a redemption value of €1,000. It pays an annual coupon of €120 (12% of €1,000) on 1 January (unless otherwise indicated) each year up to and including 2014.

5.4 Alternatives to the fixed coupon and redemption bond

Pure discount bond/zero coupon bond

- The basic feature of a discount bond is that the value at redemption date is greater than the price at issue. The difference is known as the discount. There may be a coupon paid periodically in addition to the discount. If a coupon is paid, it will typically be below the going market rate for similar bonds. The investor is compensated by the capital bonus at redemption. In a pure discount bond the coupon is zero. In other words, the only return to the purchaser is in the form of a capital bonus or gain at the redemption date. A pure discount bond is often referred to as a zero coupon bond or simply a **zero**.
- A pure discount bond (zero coupon bond) may be used where the issuer could be faced with cash flow problems in the early years of the debt if annual interest payments have to be made. The solution is to issue a bond in which the interest **accrues** and is effectively paid as a single sum together with the capital sum on redemption.
- Zero coupon bonds are particularly useful in financing a project which will not generate a cash inflow for some time e.g. a property development with a construction period of, say, 2 years. The cash inflow will not arise until the development is sold or starts to generate a rent roll.

Figure 5.2 Typical zero coupon bond

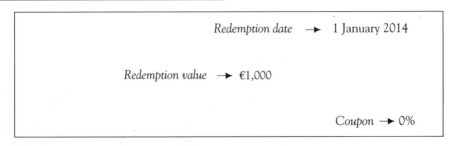

The above bond is issued on 1 January 2004 and is redeemable by the issuer on 1 January 2014 at a redemption value of €1,000. Since it does not pay any annual coupon it is sold by the issuer to the investor at a discount to its redemption value for a price of, say, €600. The investor receives a capital gain on redemption of €400 or two-thirds of the price paid.

Example 5.1 Zero coupon bond

A company wishes to raise €30 million to fund a new project. It wishes to do so through the issue of a 5 year zero coupon bond. The redemption yield (see section 5.6) on a 5 year government bond is 7% p.a. The market will require, say, a 2% p.a. margin over the government bond to reflect the additional risk. What is the sum repayable by the company at the end of 5 years?

Solution
The implicit annual interest rate is 7% + 2% = 9%. The amount repayable is the amount borrowed *plus* rolled-up interest

$$= €30 \text{ million } (1.09)^5 = €46.16 \text{ million}$$

Note that the interest is calculated on a compound rather than a simple basis.

Another way to look at this is that the company issues a zero coupon bond with a redemption value of €46.16 million at a price of €30 million, i.e. at a discount of 35%.

Irredeemable bond

An irredeemable bond is one where there is no redemption date and so no redemption value is paid. They are also called perpetual bonds. The coupon is calculated as a percentage of the nominal or face value.

This type of bond is not issued very frequently. In practice, it is usually redeemed for a nominal sum after a certain point.

Chapter 20, section 20.7 discusses the derivation of the true annual cost of finance for an irredeemable bond.

Figure 5.3 Typical perpetual bond

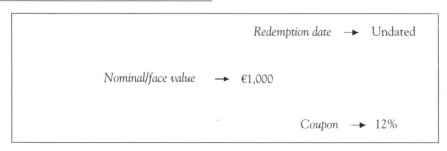

The above bond is issued on 1 January 2004 and pays an annual coupon of €120 (12% of €1,000) on 1 January (unless otherwise indicated) each year in perpetuity.

Callable bond/dual redemption-dated bond

Bonds may be issued with a range of redemption dates within which the issuer is free to call the bond in, i.e. to pay the investors the redemption value. No further coupon payments are made.

The decision to redeem the bond will depend on the relationship between the coupon rate on the bond and the market rate of interest at any time during the callable period. If the market rate is lower than the coupon rate, then it makes economic sense to redeem the bond early and to re-issue at the lower market rate.

Example 5.2 Callable bond

A 12% coupon bond with €100 face value and redemption value is issued on 1 January 2004. The final redemption date is 1 January 2014, but the issuer has an option to call the bond at any time after 31 December 2009. If the issuer raises €20 million at issue, then the annual interest charge is €2.4 million. If, after 6 years, the market rate of interest on similar investments (i.e. 4 year bonds since the bond now has only 4 years to go to the final maturity date) is 14%, the issuer will leave the bond in the market. If, however, the market rate of interest has fallen to 10% on 4 year bonds and the issuer believes that the market could hold an issue of €20 million, he would be expected to redeem the bond immediately and reissue a new 4 year bond (total value €20 million) at a coupon of 10% thus reducing the annual interest charge to €2 million. The proceeds from the new issue would be used to redeem the existing bond.

Chapter 20, section 20.4, discusses the pricing of callable bonds in more detail.

Stepped-interest bond

This is a bond where the coupon rises over the life of the bond in a predetermined manner.

Like the discount bond, it holds the rate of interest payable by the issuer down in the early years. Here, however, the purchaser is compensated by higher rates of interest in the later years, e.g. the coupon is set at 3% for the first 3 years rising by 2% each year for the remainder of the life of the bond.

A stepped-interest bond may be used with the coupon set at zero up to the point at which the project which is being funded starts to produce a positive cash flow, say, three years after issue, and then stepped up to a level consistent with the expected cash flow from the project.

Chapter 20, section 20.7, discusses the derivation of the true annual cost of finance for a stepped-interest bond.

Stripped zero coupon bonds

These are bonds which are issued such that the amount due for redemption is spread over a number of years. They are effectively a series of differently dated bonds. They may be used to fund, say, a property development where the development is sold off in parts over a number of years. The amount and maturity of each strip would be set to coincide with the expected value and date of each sale.

5.5 Comparison of coupon bond and pure discount bond

Two important distinctions arise between these two main types of bond, viz. reinvestment risk and relative volatility. While these are problems for the investor rather than the issuer they may be reflected in the yield required at the time of issue.

Reinvestment risk refers to the rate of interest at which coupon income from a bond can be reinvested in the financial markets. While the bond may have been issued at a coupon rate of 10%, the rate of interest may have fallen before the coupon income is paid and the investor is forced to reinvest at a lower rate. The holder of the zero coupon bond has a guaranteed (ignoring default risk) return over the whole period.

Volatility refers to the change in the value of a bond as the market yield changes. If the yield rises, the value of the bond falls and vice versa (see section 5.7). This holds for both coupon and pure discount bonds. However, for given maturity dates, lower coupon bonds are more volatile than higher coupon bonds (see Chapter 20, section 20.3). Thus the pure discount bond is more volatile than the coupon bond.

These two factors may affect the price that investors are prepared to pay for the bond at issue and hence the required yield.

5.6 Bond yields

Two main yields are used to measure the return on a bond

- redemption yield
- flat yield.

These can both be calculated on a gross or net basis. **Gross** refers to the pre-tax situation, while **net** refers to the post-tax situation. The net redemption yield is usually published for different tax rates.

Redemption yield

The redemption yield is calculated from the total income, i.e. coupon income flow and capital or redemption value from the bond relative to the price paid. It is basically the internal rate of return (see Chapter 7).

The gross redemption yield is defined as the discount rate which equates the present value of the gross future cash flow with the price paid. Section 5.8 below discusses its derivation in detail.

Flat yield

This is also called the income yield or running yield. It is based on the annual coupon income flow only. It is calculated as

$$\frac{\textbf{Annual income}}{\textbf{Current price}} \times 100 \qquad\qquad (5.1)$$

The gross flat yield is calculated using the gross coupon income, while the net flat yield uses the coupon income net of the appropriate tax deduction.

The flat yield is comparable to the dividend yield on equity.

5.7 Pricing a bond

This section deals with the pricing of a bond at a coupon date, i.e. just after a coupon has been paid and the next one is not due until one period (year) from now. Chapter 20, section 20.1, discusses pricing between coupon dates.

Pricing a coupon and redemption bond at a coupon date

Example 5.3

Suppose the following are the parameters of the bond:

- Purchase date 1 March 2004
- Redemption date 1 March 2014
- Annual coupon is 8% of nominal value
- Nominal and redemption value is €1,000
- Annual coupon payments start on 1 March 2005.

The cash flow from the bond is as follows:

Table 5.1 Cash flow from bond

Date	Cash flow €
01/03/04	Purchase
01/03/05	80
01/03/06	80
01/03/07	80
01/03/08	80
01/03/09	80
01/03/10	80
01/03/11	80
01/03/12	80
01/03/13	80
01/03/14	1080
Total	

The investor pays a sum of money now to generate an annual income of €80 at the end of each of the next ten years and a final payment of €1,000 in ten years' time.

How much should the investor pay?

This depends on the rate of return the investor wishes to receive. Suppose a bank deposit account was paying 8% p.a. now. The investor may wish for a 2% premium over this to reflect the fact that his/her money is tied up for ten years and to reflect reinvestment risk (see section 5.5). Thus the investor wishes for a 10% p.a. return over the ten year period. The price is derived by discounting the future cash inflow by 10% p.a. This can be calculated individually for each cash inflow or alternatively by using two financial formulae.

Calculating the present values individually produces the following:

Table 5.2 Present value of cash flow @ 10% discount rate

Date	Cash flow €	PV of cash flow €
01/03/04	Purchase	
01/03/05	80	72.73
01/03/06	80	66.12
01/03/07	80	60.11
01/03/08	80	54.64
01/03/09	80	49.67
01/03/10	80	45.16
01/03/11	80	41.05
01/03/12	80	37.32
01/03/13	80	33.93
01/03/14	1080	416.39
Total		877.11

Taking the €80 receivable on 1 March 2009 as an example, the present value can be calculated as

$$PV = \frac{80}{(1.10)^5} = 49.67$$

or by using the present value tables contained in the Appendix

$$PV = 80 \times 0.6209 = 49.67$$

Alternatively the following formula can be used

$$PV = Pt \left(\frac{1 - (1 + r)^{-n}}{r} \right) + \frac{\text{Redemption value}}{(1 + r)^n} \qquad (5.2)$$

where PV = present value (price)
     Pt = annual coupon payment
      r = interest rate per annum
     n = number of payment periods

The first part of this formula is the present value of an ordinary simple annuity and the second part is a discounted value of a future receipt.

Using 10% p.a. as the required return, the fair price to pay is €877.11. If the investor pays more than this, then the return is less than 10% p.a. If the investor pays less than this, the return is above 10% p.a.

Pricing a zero-coupon bond at a coupon date

Example 5.4

Since a zero-coupon bond does not pay any regular interest income to the holder, the pricing formula is simply the second part of 5.2 above.

$$PV = \frac{\text{Redemption value}}{(1 + r)^n} \qquad (5.3)$$

where   PV = present value (price)
         r = interest rate per annum
         n = number of years to redemption.

Suppose a bond has a redemption value of €1,000 and a redemption date of 1 March 2011. Today's date is 1 March 2004. The yield on similar bonds in the market is 6% p.a. Find the price of the bond.

$$PV = \frac{€1,000}{(1.06)^7} = €665.06$$

Pricing a perpetual bond at a coupon date

Since a perpetual bond does not pay any final redemption value, the price is simply the present value of the infinite series of coupon payments, i.e. the first part of 5.2 above with $n = \infty$

$$PV = Pt\ \frac{1 - (1 + r)^{-n}}{r}$$

but since n is infinite, this collapses to

$$PV = \frac{Pt}{r} \qquad (5.4)$$

where   PV = present value
         Pt = annual coupon payment
         r = interest rate per annum.

Example 5.5

A perpetual bond pays an annual coupon of 5% of a nominal value of €1,000. The yield in the market for such investments is 7% p.a. The next coupon is due one year from today. Find the price of the bond.

$$PV = \frac{€50}{0.07} = €714.29$$

5.8 Deriving the gross redemption yield from the price

The gross redemption yield was defined in section 5.6 as **the discount rate which equates the present value of the gross future cash flow with the price paid**. What does this mean?

A price is paid today for a succession of receipts in the future. Conceptually, this price could be regarded as a series of different payments to buy each separate future receipt, i.e. some part of the price is to buy next year's coupon payment, some part is to buy the following year's coupon etc. The fair price to pay for each future receipt is its present value discounted at the required rate of return. Putting this the other way round, if the price is quoted on the market for a series of payments in the future, then the return the investor receives is the discount rate which makes the sum of the present value of the future receipts equal to the price quoted.

This can be calculated through a process of trial and error. The future cash flow is discounted at different rates until two discount rates produce answers either side of the price. Since the answer will be approximated between these two rates, the nearer they are, the more accurate the answer will be. All examples in this chapter (and in Chapter 20) approximate the answer to one place of decimals using the technique of linear interpolation between two discount rates which are one percentage point apart.

Example 5.6

Suppose the bond referred to in example 5.3 above is selling at a price of €800. What is the GRY on the bond?

Solution
The future cash flow is discounted at varying rates, until two answers, one above €800 and the other below €800 are found, using discount rates which are one percentage point apart.

Following trial and error, discount rates of 11% and 12% produce present values of €823.32 and €773.99 respectively (see Table 5.3 below).
Note: When using trial discount rates, if the present value calculated is above the target price (in this example €800), then the discount rate should be increased in order to reduce the present value. The opposite applies if the present value calculated is below the target price.

Table 5.3 Solving for the gross redemption yield

| | Discount rate 12% | | | Discount rate 11% | |
Date	Cash flow	PV of cash flow	Date	Cash flow	PV of cash flow
01/03/04			01/03/04		
01/03/05	80	71.43	01/03/05	80	72.07
01/03/06	80	63.78	01/03/06	80	64.93
01/03/07	80	56.94	01/03/07	80	58.50
01/03/08	80	50.84	01/03/08	80	52.70
01/03/09	80	45.39	01/03/09	80	47.48
01/03/10	80	40.53	01/03/10	80	42.77
01/03/11	80	36.19	01/03/11	80	38.53
01/03/12	80	32.31	01/03/12	80	34.71
01/03/13	80	28.85	01/03/13	80	31.27
01/03/14	1080	347.73	01/03/14	1080	380.36
Total		773.99	Total		823.32

Note that the present values can be calculated individually as shown above or using 5.2 above, i.e.

$$PV = 80 \left(\frac{1 - (1.11)^{-10}}{0.11} \right) + \frac{1,000}{(1.11)^{10}} = 823.32$$

and similarly for 12%.

The answer to the first part of the formula above can be got from the annuity tables in the Appendix, with r = 11% and n = 10 years. The answer to the second part can be got from the discount tables in the Appendix, with r = 11% and n = 10 years.

These answers can be interpreted as follows:

If an investor paid a price of €773.99 for the bond she would be getting a gross redemption yield of 12%, while if she paid €823.32 she would be getting a gross redemption yield of 11%. **Clearly the higher the price paid, the lower is the yield and vice versa.** In this example, the price paid is €800, so the investor is getting a yield somewhere between 11% and 12%. The answer can be approximated using linear interpolation.

Figure 5.4 Calculating a bond yield using linear interpolation

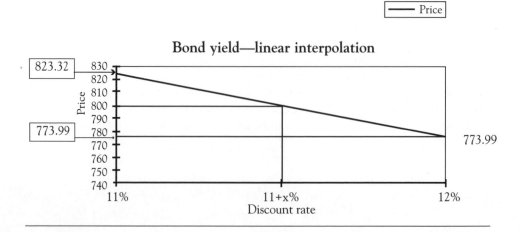

The technique of linear interpolation assumes that the price of the bond falls in a linear fashion as the GRY is increased. While the true relationship is non-linear, the assumption of linearity is a reasonable approximation for small changes in the GRY.

A one percentage point rise in the GRY from 11% causes the bond price to fall by €49.33 (823.32 – 773.99). What fraction of a 1 per cent increase in the GRY from 11% would cause the price to fall by €23.32 (823.32 – 800)? This is calculated as follows:

Discount rate	Price
11%	823.32
11 + x%	800.00
12%	773.99

$$\frac{x}{1} = \frac{23.32}{49.33} = 0.47 \cong 0.5$$

where x = fractional interest rate increase required to decrease price by 23.32 at this point.

Therefore GRY is estimated at 11 + 0.5%, i.e. 11.5%

5.9 Calculating the net redemption yield from the gross redemption yield

The gross redemption yield is the most often used and published measure of bond returns. Many investors are subject to tax on the coupon income from government bonds and so the net redemption yield is a more relevant measure.

It is important to note that the net redemption yield **is not** simply equal to the gross redemption yield × (1 – tax rate).

Example 5.7

Suppose the bond referred to in example 5.6 is currently selling at a gross redemption yield of 11%. What is the net redemption yield to a 22% taxpayer?

Solution
The price is first calculated using 5.2 above.
Price @ GRY of 11% = €823.32

The net redemption yield is found by equating the present value of the future net receipts from the bond with this price of €823.32. This is done, as before, through a process of trial and error, i.e. the future net cash flow is discounted at varying rates until two answers, one above €823.32 and the other below €823.32 are found, using discount rates which are one percentage point apart.

The net cash flow from the bond is €80 per annum *less* tax at 22%, i.e. €80 – (0.22 × €80) or 0.78 × €80 = €62.4 for 10 years *plus* €1,000 at the end of the tenth year. This is shown in Table 5.4 below.

Following trial and error, discount rates of 8% and 9% produce present values of €881.90 and €822.88 respectively (see Table 5.4 below).

Table 5.4 Solving for the net redemption yield

Date	Discount rate 9% Cash flow	PV of cash flow	Date	Discount rate 8% Cash flow	PV of cash flow
01/03/04	€	€	01/03/04	€	€
01/03/05	62.40	57.25	01/03/05	62.40	57.78
01/03/06	62.40	52.52	01/03/06	62.40	53.50
01/03/07	62.40	48.18	01/03/07	62.40	49.54
01/03/08	62.40	44.21	01/03/08	62.40	45.87
01/03/09	62.40	40.56	01/03/09	62.40	42.47
01/03/10	62.40	37.21	01/03/10	62.40	39.32
01/03/11	62.40	34.13	01/03/11	62.40	36.41
01/03/12	62.40	31.32	01/03/12	62.40	33.71
01/03/13	62.40	28.73	01/03/13	62.40	31.22
01/03/14	1062.40	448.77	01/03/14	1062.40	492.10
Total		822.88	Total		881.90

Note: There may be a small rounding error in the totals as totals are calculated from 5.2, rather than as the sum of the entries in the columns.

Note that the present values can be calculated individually as shown above or using 5.2 above, i.e.

$$PV = 62.4 \left(\frac{1 - (1.09)^{-10}}{0.09} \right) + \frac{1000}{(1.09)^{10}} = 822.88$$

and similarly for 8%.

The answer to the first part of the formula above can be got from the annuity tables in the Appendix, with r = 9% and n = 10 years. The answer to the second part can be got from the discount tables in the Appendix, with r = 9% and n = 10 years.

These answers can be interpreted as follows:

If an investor paid a price of €822.88 for the bond she would be getting a net redemption yield of 9%, while if she paid €881.90 she would be getting a net redemption yield of 8%. **Clearly the higher the price paid, the lower is the yield and vice versa.**

In this example, the price paid is €823.32 so the investor is getting a yield somewhere between 8% and 9%, but very close to 9%. The answer can be approximated using linear interpolation, or by a small iteration from 9%. Both of these approximations are shown below.

A one percentage point rise in the GRY from 8% causes the bond price to fall by €59.02 (881.90 − 822.88). What fraction of a 1 per cent increase in the GRY from 8% would cause the price to fall by €58.58 (881.90 − 823.32)? This is calculated as follows:

Discount rate	Price €
8%	881.90
8 + x%	823.32
9%	822.88

$$\frac{x}{1} = \frac{58.58}{59.02} = 0.99 \cong 1$$

where x = fractional interest rate increase required to decrease price by 58.58 at this point.

Therefore NRY to a 22% taxpayer is estimated at 8 + 1%, i.e. 9%

   This answer could also have been found by observing that the answer is clearly very close to 9% and testing whether a discount rate of 8.9% (one decimal place lower) would produce a more accurate answer. This can be calculated from 5.2 with r = 0.089

$$PV = 62.4 \left(\frac{1 - (1.089)^{-10}}{0.089} \right) + \frac{1,000}{(1.089)^{10}} = 828.54$$

A discount rate of 9% gives an answer much nearer the correct price and so is the estimated net redemption yield to a 22% taxpayer.

Example 5.8

A government bond with face value of €100 has eight more years to run. It pays an annual coupon of 10% on 1 March and has just paid this year's coupon. The redemption value is tax free, but the coupon income is subject to tax at the holder's marginal rate. It is currently selling at a gross redemption yield of 7% p.a. Calculate the net redemption yield on the bond to a 21% taxpayer.

Solution
The price must first be calculated using 5.2.

   Price @ GRY of 7% = 117.91

   The net cash flow from the bond is €10 per annum *less* tax at 21%, i.e. €10 – (0.21 × €10) or 0.79 × €10 = €7.90 for 8 years *plus* €100 at the end of the eighth year. This is shown in Table 5.5 below.

   Following trial and error, discount rates of 6% and 5% produce present values of €111.80 and €118.74 respectively (see Table 5. 5 below).

Table 5.5 Solving for the net redemption yield

| Date | Discount rate 6% | | Date | Discount rate 5% | |
	Cash flow	PV of cash flow		Cash flow	PV of cash flow
01/03/04			01/03/04		
01/03/05	7.90	7.45	01/03/05	7.90	7.52
01/03/06	7.90	7.03	01/03/06	7.90	7.17
01/03/07	7.90	6.63	01/03/07	7.90	6.82
01/03/08	7.90	6.26	01/03/08	7.90	6.50
01/03/09	7.90	5.90	01/03/09	7.90	6.19
01/03/10	7.90	5.57	01/03/10	7.90	5.90
01/03/11	7.90	5.25	01/03/11	7.90	5.61
01/03/12	107.90	67.70	01/03/12	107.90	73.03
Total		111.80	Total		118.74

Note: There may be a small rounding error in the totals as totals are calculated from 5.2, rather than as the sum of the entries in the columns.

Note that the present values can be calculated individually as shown above or using 5.2 above, i.e.

$$PV = 7.90 \left[\frac{1 - (1.05)^{-8}}{0.05} \right] + \frac{100}{(1.05)^8} = 118.74$$

and similarly for 6%.

The answer to the first part of the formula above can be got from the annuity tables in the Appendix, with r = 5% and n = 8 years. The answer to the second part can be got from the discount tables in the Appendix, with r = 5% and n = 8 years.

These answers can be interpreted as follows:

If an investor paid a price of €111.80 for the bond s/he would be getting a net redemption yield of 6%, while if s/he paid €118.74 s/he would be getting a net redemption yield of 5%. **As before, the higher the price paid, the lower the yield, and vice versa.**

In this example, the price paid is €117.91 so the investor is getting a yield somewhere between 5% and 6%. The answer can be approximated using linear interpolation.

A one percentage point rise in the GRY from 5% causes the bond price to fall by €6.94 (118.74 – 111.80). What fraction of a 1 per cent increase in the GRY from 5% would cause the price to fall by €0.83 (118.74 – 117.91)? This is calculated as follows:

Discount rate	Price
5%	118.74
5+x%	117.91
6%	111.80

$$\frac{x}{1} = \frac{0.83}{6.94} = 0.12 \cong 0.1$$

where x = fractional interest rate increase required to decrease price by 0.83 at this point.

Therefore NRY to a 21% taxpayer is estimated at 5 + 0.1%, i.e. 5.1%.

Thus if two investors, one tax exempt and the other liable to taxation on the coupon income from the bond at a rate of 21%, pay €117.91 for the bond, the first is receiving a (gross) redemption yield of 7% while the second is receiving a (net) redemption yield of 5.1%.

5.10 Calculating the net redemption yield at different tax rates

Example 5.9

A government bond with face value and redemption value of €100 has ten years to run. It pays a gross annual coupon of 9% on 1 September each year. Today's date is 1 September 2004. It has just paid the annual coupon. The redemption value is tax free, but the coupon income is subject to tax at the holder's marginal rate. It is currently selling at a net redemption yield of 8% to a taxpayer @ a tax rate of 44%. Calculate the net redemption yield on the bond to a taxpayer @ a tax rate of 21%.

Solution
First find the current price, using 5.2. Note that the coupon income is €9 *less* tax at 44% = €5.04

$$PV = 5.04 \left(\frac{1 - (1.08)^{-10}}{0.08} \right) + \frac{100}{(1.08)^{10}} = 80.14$$

Price @ NRY of 8% (@ tax rate of 44%) = 80.14

The student should observe that if two investors are paying the same price for a bond but one faces a higher taxation rate than the other, then the net redemption yield will be higher for the lower taxpayer. Therefore the answer in this case must be above 8%.

The coupon income to the second investor is €9 *less* tax at 21% = €7.11

The net cash flow from the bond is €9 per annum *less* tax at 21%, i.e. €9 – (0.21 × €9) or 0.79 × €9 = €7.11 for 10 years *plus* €100 at the end of the eighth year. This is shown in Table 5.6 below.

Following trial and error, discount rates of 11% and 10% produce present values of €77.09 and €82.24 respectively (see Table 5.6 below).

Table 5.6 Solving for the net redemption yield

Date	Discount rate 11% Cash flow	PV of cash flow	Date	Discount rate 10% Cash flow	PV of cash flow
01/09/04			01/09/04		
01/09/05	7.11	6.41	01/09/05	7.11	6.46
01/09/06	7.11	5.77	01/09/06	7.11	5.88
01/09/07	7.11	5.20	01/09/07	7.11	5.34
01/09/08	7.11	4.68	01/09/08	7.11	4.86
01/09/09	7.11	4.22	01/09/09	7.11	4.41
01/09/10	7.11	3.80	01/09/10	7.11	4.01
01/09/11	7.11	3.42	01/09/11	7.11	3.65
01/09/12	7.11	3.09	01/09/12	7.11	3.32
01/09/13	7.11	2.78	01/09/13	7.11	3.02
01/09/14	107.11	37.72	01/09/14	107.11	41.30
Total		77.09	Total		82.24

Note: There may be a small rounding error in the totals as totals are calculated from 5.2, rather than as the sum of the entries in the columns.

Note that the present values can be calculated individually as shown above, or using 5.2 above, i.e.

$$PV = 7.11 \left(\frac{1 - (1.10)^{-10}}{0.10} \right) + \frac{100}{(1.10)^{10}} = 82.24$$

and similarly for 11%.

The answer to the first part of the formula above can be got from the annuity tables in the Appendix, with r = 10% and n = 10 years. The answer to the second part can be got from the discount tables in the Appendix, with r = 10% and n = 10 years.

These answers can be interpreted as follows:

If an investor paid a price of €77.09 for the bond s/he would be getting a net redemption yield of 11%, while if s/he paid €82.24 s/he would be getting a net redemption yield of 10%. As before, **the higher the price paid, the lower is the yield, and vice versa**.

In this example, the price paid is €80.14 so the investor is getting a yield somewhere between 10% and 11%. The answer can be approximated using linear interpolation.

A one percentage point rise in the GRY from 10% causes the bond price to fall by €5.15 (82.24 − 77.09). What fraction of a 1 per cent increase in the GRY from 10% would cause the price to fall by €2.10 (82.24 − 80.14)? This is calculated as follows:

Discount rate	Price
10%	82.24
10 + x%	80.14
11%	77.09

$$\frac{x}{1} = \frac{2.10}{5.15} = 0.41 \cong 0.4$$

where x = fractional interest rate increase required to decrease the price by €2.10 at this point.

Therefore NRY to a 21% taxpayer is estimated at 10 + 0.4%, i.e. 10.4%.

Thus if two investors, one liable to taxation on the coupon income from the bond at a rate of 44% and the other liable to taxation on the coupon income from the bond at a rate of 21%, pay €80.14 for the bond, the first is receiving a (net) redemption yield of 8% while the second is receiving a (net) redemption yield of 10.4%.

5.11 Calculating the gross and net income yield

As pointed out in section 5.6 the terms **income yield**, **running yield** and **flat yield** are used interchangeably. This yield is based on the annual coupon income flow only. It is calculated as

$$\frac{\textbf{Annual income}}{\textbf{Current price}} \times \textbf{100} \tag{5.5}$$

The gross income yield is calculated using the gross coupon income, while the net income yield uses the coupon income net of the appropriate tax deduction.

It is similar in concept to the dividend yield on equity.

Example 5.10

Taking the parameters of the bond in example 5.3, i.e.

- Purchase date 1 March 2004
- Redemption date 1 March 2014
- Annual coupon is 8% of nominal value
- Nominal and redemption value is €1,000
- Annual coupon payments start on 1 March 2005
- Coupon income is subject to tax at the holder's marginal rate
- Redemption value is tax free.

Suppose the bond is selling for a price of €900. Calculate

(a) the gross income yield
(b) the net income yield to a 21% taxpayer
(c) the net income yield to a 44% taxpayer.

Solution
Using 5.1
(a) The gross annual coupon is €80.

$$\text{Gross income yield} = \frac{80}{900} \times 100 = 8.89\%$$

(b) The net annual coupon is €80 *less* tax at 21% = €63.20

$$\text{Net income yield} = \frac{63.20}{900} \times 100 = 7.02\%$$
(@ 21% tax)

(c) The net annual coupon is €80 *less* tax at 44% = €44.80

$$\text{Net income yield} = \frac{44.80}{900} \times 100 = 4.98\%$$
(@ 44% tax)

Note that the net income yield = gross income yield (1 − tax rate).

SUMMARY

- A bond is a paper asset, where the issuer agrees to pay the purchaser a sum or sums of money at a specific time(s) in the future.
- Fixed interest bonds and fixed redemption dated bonds are the principal generic types of bond.
- A discount bond is sold for less than its redemption value.
- In a discount bond, the annual coupon payment is typically below the going market rate at the time of issue.
- In a zero coupon bond, the only return to the investor is in the form of a capital gain at redemption.
- A callable bond will normally be 'called' as early as possible if the coupon rate on the bond is above the current market rate.
- The gross redemption yield is the main yield used to compare bonds.
- The gross redemption yield is defined as the discount rate which equates the present value of the future income stream with the price paid.
- The flat yield on a bond is comparable to the dividend yield on equity.
- Bonds are priced by discounting the future cash flow at the appropriate discount rate.

QUESTIONS

1.◆ A government bond with face value of €100 has eight more years to run. It pays an annual coupon of 12% and has just paid this year's coupon. The redemption value is tax free, but the coupon income is subject to tax at the holder's marginal rate. It is currently selling at a gross redemption yield of 9% p.a. Calculate the net redemption yield on the bond to a 24% taxpayer. (Answer to one place of decimals.)

2.◆ A government bond with face value of €100 has six years to run. It pays an annual coupon of 9% on 1 September each year to the holder of the bond at the close of trading on 31 August in that year. It has just paid the annual coupon. The redemption value is tax free, but the coupon income is subject to tax at the holder's marginal rate. It is currently selling at a net redemption yield of 8% to a taxpayer @ a tax rate of 48%. Calculate the net redemption yield on the bond to a taxpayer at a tax rate of 26%.

3.♦ A government bond with face value of €100 has eight more years to run. It pays an annual coupon of 9% and has just paid this year's coupon. The redemption value is tax free, but the coupon income is subject to tax at the holder's marginal rate. It is currently selling at a net redemption yield of 5% p.a. to a 44% taxpayer. Calculate
   (a) the gross income yield on the bond.
   (b) the net income yield on the bond to a 22% taxpayer.

4. A government bond with face value of €100 has nine years to run. It pays an annual coupon of 8% and has just paid this year's coupon. The redemption value is tax free, but the coupon income is subject to tax at the holder's marginal rate. It is currently selling at a net redemption yield of 6% to a taxpayer at a tax rate of 44%.
   (a) Calculate the net redemption yield on the bond to a taxpayer at a tax rate of 22%.
   (b) Using the same information as in (a) above, calculate the gross income yield on the bond.

5. A government bond with face value of €100 has twelve more years to run. It pays an annual coupon of 8% and has just paid this year's coupon. The redemption value is tax free, but the coupon income is subject to tax at the holder's marginal rate. It is currently selling at a gross redemption yield of 12% p.a. Calculate the net redemption yield on the bond to a 26% taxpayer. (Answer to one place of decimals.)

6. A government bond with face value of €100 has ten more years to run. It pays an annual coupon of 12% and has just paid this year's coupon. The redemption value is tax free, but the coupon income is subject to tax at the holder's marginal rate. It is currently selling at a gross redemption yield of 10% p.a. Calculate the net redemption yield on the bond to a 26% taxpayer. (Answer to one place of decimals.)

7. Explain the relationship between price and yield.
8. Define gross redemption yield.
9. Define net redemption yield.
10. Explain what is meant by a discount bond. Why might it be attractive to an issuer?
11. Explain what is meant by a stepped-interest bond. Why might it be attractive to an issuer?
12. Explain what is meant by an irredeemable bond.
13. Explain what is meant by the flat yield on a bond. Why is it a relevant measure?

6
Share and Company Valuations

CHAPTER OBJECTIVES

At the end of this chapter, the student will be able to calculate the price of common stock using:

1. the zero growth dividend formula
2. the constant growth formula
3. the non-constant growth formula

and be able to:

4. calculate the value of common stock using the P/E ratio
5. calculate the value of common stock using balance sheet methods
6. understand how to value companies using the free cash flow method

INTRODUCTION

In Chapter 4 we discussed the concept of the time value of money—how to value future cash. In the previous chapter, we described bond values as the present value of future interest payments plus the present value of bonds at maturity. Similarly we value common stocks in the same way as we value other assets by using the discounted cash flow formula.

6.1 Share value and cash flow

The cash flow to a holder of a common share is a stream of dividends:

Value of share = P_O = Present value (PV) of expected future dividends   (6.1)

Imagine that you purchase a share today for €2 and you expect to sell it in one year's time for €3. You also expect to receive a dividend of 20 cents over the next year. Therefore, the rate of return (r) you expect to receive from holding this share is 60%:

$$r = \frac{P_1 - P_o + D_1}{P_o}$$

$$= \frac{€3 - €2 + €0.2}{€2} = 60\%$$

where P_1 = price of share at end of the first period
  P_0 = current price of the share
  D_1 = expected dividend at the end of the first period.

Therefore, the expected return on the share is the dividend received *plus* the expected gain in the price of the share, divided by the original price.

Similarly, if you were given the expected rate of return of a security of similar risk, you can predict the current price:

$$P_0 = \frac{D_1 + P_1}{1 + r} = \frac{3.2}{1.6} = €2$$

But what determines the price of the share at the end of the year (P_1)?

How much will you receive in one year's time when you sell the share? The answer of course depends on what dividends any future investor will expect to receive from this share. Therefore the price of a share in one year's time will be the present value of expected future dividends received on that share during year 2 *plus* the expected share price at the end of year 2. The price of the share at the end of year 2 will be the expected dividends received from that share during year 3 *plus* the expected share price at the end of year 3 and so on. Therefore, the current value of a share is the present value of the future dividend stream as shown in equation 6.1. This is the generalised dividend valuation model or the **going concern** assumption model. Provided a company does not go into liquidation or is consequently acquired by another company, common shares can last for ever. We don't have to worry about terminal value. As we move further into the future the present value of cash flows approaches zero. Therefore, today's price can be expressed as shown in equation 6.1.

Example 6.1 Share valuation

Suppose you are considering the purchase of CRH shares which are currently trading at €19 a share and which will pay 19 cents in dividends a year. Security analysts expect the share to trade at €29 in one year's time. Will you buy the share at this price? To make a decision you will need to calculate the present values of expected future cash flows, which consist of the dividend payments and the expected share price in one year's time. However, before you can do this you will need to know what the required rate of return is on equity of similar risk. Suppose the rate of return you require to compensate for the risk involved in investing in this type of share is 10%.

Solution
The value of the share today is the expected value of the future cash flows:

$$PV = P_0 = \frac{D_1}{(1 + k_e)} + \frac{P_1}{(1 + k_e)} = \frac{0.19}{1.1} + \frac{29}{1.1} = €26.5$$

where PV = present value

    P_0 = intrinsic or theoretical value of the share

    D_1 = dividend received during the year

    K_e = the required rate of return on equity capital.

Alternatively, the total rate of return is

$$\frac{29.0 - 19.0 + 0.19}{19.0} = 53.6\%$$

This is a much greater return than you require.

    Therefore you would choose to buy it because the present value of the shares is €26.5 which is greater than the current value of €19. You believe the share is undervalued. You believe it is worth €26 whereas it is selling for €19. As far as you are concerned CRH shares offer a higher rate of return than similar securities of similar risk. However, this may be just how **you** feel about risk and return. Other investors may not be as optimistic about the future cash flows and they may therefore place a **higher risk** on them, which require **a higher rate of return thus lowering the market price**.

6.1.1 *What if a company never pays a dividend?*

Equation 6.1 says that the current value of a share is equal to the present value of the expected future dividend stream. But what if a company has an official policy of never paying dividends and in addition has no liquidation value. Does this share have a value? Think what would happen if you tried to sell this share. No rational investor would buy it. The company would be taking in all of this money from investors without ever giving any of it back. Therefore it has no value. This type of security doesn't exist. What we generally mean when we say that companies don't pay dividends is that they **currently** don't pay dividends. A buyer of this type of share will expect the company to pay dividends **someday**. Companies that currently don't pay dividends are called growth stocks because their value emanates from capital gains. At the time of writing Elan Corporation and Ryanair are examples. Other companies are known as income shares because their value derives from dividend income. With growth shares, investors are happy to forgo current income for future capital gains. The share price of growth stocks will increase because the date of the expected dividend payment gets closer.

    There are also companies that pay irregular dividends, i.e. the dividends can be different every year. In the following section, we examine share valuation based on different assumptions regarding dividend growth.

6.2 Zero growth

What is the value of a share in a company where dividends are expected to remain constant, i.e. zero growth? Here $D_1 = D_2 = D_3 \ldots$ etc. The value of the share is the constant dividend divided by the required rate of return:

$$P_0 = \frac{D_1}{(1+ke)} + \frac{D_2}{(1+ke)^2} + \frac{D_3}{(1+ke)^3} + \dots \frac{D}{(1+ke)\infty}$$

Therefore, because the dividend is always the same the value of a zero growth stock is a perpetuity. The constant dividend is divided by the required rate of return on equity.

Example 6.2 Valuing zero growth stocks

$$P_0 = \frac{D}{ke}$$

What is the value of a share that pays a constant dividend of €4 if the required rate of return is 10%?

Solution
Using equation 6.1

$$P_0 = \frac{4}{0.1} = €40$$

Therefore we would expect to sell the share for €40.

6.3 Constant growth stocks

Remember that dividends are paid out of earnings. In turn, earnings will be determined by the margin that companies make on their sales that in turn will be influenced by the growth rate in the economy. This will vary from company to company but, on average, dividend growth will continue at roughly the same rate of growth as nominal GDP. Companies may have an explicit goal of a constant growth in dividends.[1] Therefore if a company has just paid a dividend and if that dividend grows at a constant rate (g), then the next dividend will be

$$D_1 = D_0(1+g)$$

where D_1 = next dividend to be paid
$\quad\quad D_0$ = dividend just paid
$\quad\quad g$ = constant growth rate.

If g is constant, equation 6.1 can be modified to:

$$P_0 = \frac{D_0(1+g)}{(1+ke)} + \frac{D_0(1+g)^2}{(1+ke)^2} + \frac{D_0(1+g)^3}{(1+ke)^3} + \dots \frac{D_0(1+g)\infty}{(1+ke)^\infty} \quad\quad (6.2)$$

Provided the growth rate is less than the discount rate we can rearrange the above equation (6.2) as

$$P_0 = \frac{D_0\,(1+g)}{1+ke} \Rightarrow \frac{D_1}{ke-g} \tag{6.3}$$

where $\Rightarrow$ means 'is the same as'.

This is **Gordon's growth model.**[2]

Note that if the growth rate is greater than the discount rate the present values of the expected dividend stream will get larger and larger. This would give us a share price that is infinite, and since no share price is infinite, it would not make sense for the growth rate g to be larger than the discount rate K_e. We discuss this in more detail in section 6.3.1 below.

Example 6.3 Constant growth stock

Pioneer Company Ltd has just paid a dividend of €2 per share and dividends at the company are expected to grow at a steady rate of 7% per annum. What is the present value of the share if the required rate of return is 12%?

Solution

First, we find the expected value of the dividend at the end of the first year, D_1.

$$D_1 = D_0\,(1+g)$$
$$= €2\,(1+.07)$$
$$= €2.14$$

Remember that the dividend just paid of €2 (D_0) is **only** used to determine D_1 because the value of a share is the present value of expected **future** dividends.

We can now use equation 6.3 to find the expected price (present value) of the share P_0.

$$P_0 = \frac{€2.14}{(0.12-0.07)} = €42.8$$

6.3.1 Points to remember about the dividend growth rate g

- In Chapter 12, we will discuss dividend policy in more detail but for now you should understand that for strategic reasons companies may pursue a constant dividend growth rate.
- For equation 6.3 to hold, it is necessary for K_e to be greater than g. If it were the case that the growth rate g was greater than the cost of equity K_e, the present value of the dividend stream would become infinite. No share has an infinite price. When K_e is greater than g the PV of each dividend $D_0\,(1+g)/1+K_e$ gets smaller and smaller while the euro amount of each dividend $D_0\,(1+g)$ gets bigger and bigger. If g is greater than K_e, the PV of successive dividend payments would get progressively bigger and this just would not make sense. Note that it is however possible that some companies,

in the initial stage of their development, can have supernormal growth rates and this can lead to g being greater than K_e.

• The longer-term growth rate can also be estimated by looking at the dividend payout ratio, which is the ratio of dividends to earnings per share (EPS).

Example 6.4 Estimating dividend growth rates

(a) Using the dividend payout ratio
Consider a company that pays 60% of net earnings in cash dividends, i.e.

$$\text{Payout ratio} = \frac{\text{Dividends}}{\text{Earnings per share}} = 60\%$$

This means that it retains 40% of earnings for reinvestment purposes.[3] The **reinvestment ratio** is

$$1 - \frac{\text{Dividends}}{\text{EPS}} = 1 - 0.6 = 0.4$$

Suppose the return on equity (ROE) is 12%, i.e.

$$\text{ROE} = \frac{\text{EPS}}{\text{Equity}} = 12\%$$

If the ROE is 12% and the company reinvests 40% of earnings then the company's equity will increase by 4.8%

$$= (0.12)\,(0.4) = 4.8\%$$

Therefore, if the company follows a constant dividend policy, dividends will grow at 4.8%, i.e.

$$\text{Growth rate } g = (\text{Reinvestment ratio})(\text{ROE}) = (0.4)(0.12) = 4.8\%$$

(b) Using past changes in dividends to forecast future dividends
The dividends (pence per share) paid by the AIB Group between 1993 and 1997 were:

Year	Dividends
1992	12.7
1993	14.3
1994	16.8
1995	19
1996	20.1

The average growth rate is found using the equation

$$g = \sqrt[n]{\frac{\text{FV}}{\text{PV}}} - 1 \qquad\qquad (6.4)$$

where PV = earliest accruing dividend
  FV = most recent dividend
  n = number of intervals between the dividend payments — in this case four.

Therefore, assuming a required rate of return of 15%, AIB's dividend growth rate from 1993 to 1997 is

$$g = \sqrt[4]{\frac{€20.1}{€12.7}} - 1$$

$$g = \sqrt[4]{1.58} - 1$$

$$g = 1.12 - 1 = 0.121 = 12.1\%$$

To find the expected current value of AIB stock if dividends grow at a constant rate of 12.1% a year and where the most recent paid dividend is £0.21 and the expected return is 15%:

$$P_0 = \frac{D_0 (1 + g)}{(ke - g)}$$

$$P_0 = \frac{£.21(1 + 0.121)}{(.15 - 0.1221)}$$

$$P_0 = £8.1$$

Therefore, the expected value of AIB stock is £8.10 **if** the assumptions made are correct.

Note however that it is not advisable to use the constant growth formula for stocks that have high current growth rates because it is unlikely to be sustained.

6.4 Non-constant or supernormal growth

In the last section, we saw how companies settle down at some stage of their life cycle and tend to grow at a constant rate. In the initial start-up phase, some companies grow at above average growth rates and then begin to level off. At the time of writing, Ryanair is in this initial phase. Revenues are expected to grow from £40m in 1992 to £220m in the year 2000. However, as more and more airlines enter the **no frills** airline market, the growth rate will begin to fall off. In addition, some companies may experience a particular period when the dividend stream is either very high or very low due to either a successful investment expansion programme or an economic recession. In addition, some companies have a competitive advantage because of effective barriers of entry to the industry in which they operate. For example, the estimated cost of building a new wafer fabrication plant at Intel is huge, which effectively makes it very difficult for would be competitors to enter the microchip industry.

To illustrate a company that goes through different phases of growth we use the following example.

Example 6.4 Non-constant growth

Currach Eanach plc has just paid a dividend of 12 cents per share. Because of favourable economic conditions and a rapid expansion programme, dividends are expected to grow at an annual rate of 15% for the next three years. After the third year, company sales and earnings will fall off and dividends are expected to grow at 8% per annum. The company's required rate of return is 10%. Find the value of Currach Eanach's shares.

Solution
To find the value of a non-constant growth share such as Currach Eanach's we take the following steps:

1. Determine the present value of the dividends during the non-constant growth phase.
2. Find the constant growth rate and use it to find the present value of the dividend stream (including the price of the shares at the end of the non-constant growth phase) after the non-constant growth phase.
3. Add the present values got in steps 1 and 2 to find the theoretical value of the share.

1. Find the expected dividends during the three years of supernormal growth.
   (a) First dividend $D_1 = 12(1 + 0.15) = 13.8^4$
   (b) Second dividend $D_2 = D_1 (1 + g) = 13.8(1.15) = 15.8$
   (c) Third dividend $D_3 = D_2 (1 + g) = 15.87(1.15) = 18.25$.
2. The present value of the stream of dividends during the constant growth phase is got using Gordon's growth model which gives us the share price at the end of the **third** period. The fourth year dividends are then discounted back **one time period** to the third year. The third year price is then discounted back to year zero and this is added to the present value of the dividends received from the first three years to find the theoretical current price. First, find the dividend for the fourth year:

$$D_4 = D_3 (1 + .08) = (\text{€}.1825) (1.08) = \text{€}.1971$$

The price of the share the investor would expect to receive at the end of the non-constant growth period P_3 is

$$P_3 = \frac{D4}{ke - g} = \frac{\text{€}.1971}{0.02} = \text{€}9.85$$

In other words the value of the share at the end of year 3 is €9.85.[5]

Figure 6.1 Finding the value of a supernormal growth stock

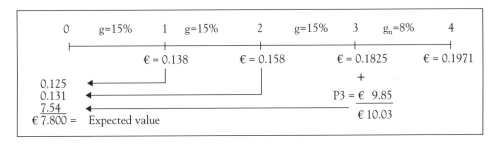

Now discount €9.85 + the third year dividend of €0.1825 = €10.03 back three periods to find its present value.

Finally, the sum of the present values provides us with an estimate of the current expected value of the stock. This is €7.8 and is illustrated in Figure 6.1.

6.5 Price earnings method

The dividend valuation models (DVMs) are the most rigorous means of valuing stocks. The difficulty is that it is not always easy to come up with the relevant information on, for example, growth rates and discount rates.

In Chapter 11 we introduce various stock market ratios. We will see how, using the P/E ratio, the market values €1 in earnings. If a company's earnings per share is 10 cents and the share price is €2, investors are prepared to pay 20 times historic earnings for the share. This is the historic price earnings ratio (PER):

$$PER = \frac{Current\ market\ price\ of\ share}{EPS} \qquad (6.5)$$

Box 6.1 P/E ratio for Waterford Wedgwood and comparable companies

	P/E 1997	P/E 1998	P/E 1999
Waterford Wedgwood	**21.9**	**17.2**	**14.3**
Royal Dalton (UK)	10.1	9.6	8.7
Mikasa (US)	11.0	13.1	9.9
Gucci (US)	19.7	18.7	16.7
Hermes (France)	32.2	29.4	26.4
LVMH (France)	26.3	23.2	20.6
Rosenthal (Germany)	—	47.4	22.0

Source: *Irish Equity Market Forecast*, Davy Equity Research, July 1998

Firms in the same industry are expected to have similar P/E ratios in the long run. We can estimate the value of a company's shares using the P/E ratio.

Example 6.5 P/E valuations of selected Irish companies

	EPS (p)	P/E 1999	Market valuation (per share in pence)
Smurfit	24.7 (15/5/1999)	8.8	217.4
Waterford Wedgwood	7.2 (10/7/1999)	14.3	102.3
Independent Newspapers	25 (10/7/1999)	14.1	352.5

Average forecast P/E ratio for 1999   Source: *Irish Equity Market Forecast*, July 1998

In the late 1990s, there were significant increases in share prices that resulted in market valuations breaching historic norms. In July 1998 for example the market traded at 18.9 times current earnings compared to a ten year average of 14.1 times.[6] We will talk more about market valuations in Chapter 11.

6.5.1 How to interpret P/E ratios

- High PE ratios may signify that investors place a low risk on these shares and are therefore willing to pay a higher price for them.
- High PE ratios may indicate high growth prospects.
- High PEs may indicate that the company has had poor financial results but investors expect the company to improve its performance.
- The weakness of using industry average PE ratios is that firm specific factors, which might lead to a company's PE ratio being above or below the industry average, are ignored.
- The financial pages of quality newspapers give the PEs of quoted companies. However, these are based on historic earnings. It would be more useful from an investor's point of view if future earnings were used in the calculation. Instead of using a historic PE ratio we can use a prospective PER (price earnings ratio) which includes next year's expected earnings:

Recall the dividend growth model.

$$P_0 = \frac{D}{Ke - g}$$

Divide both sides by next year's earnings E_1

$$\frac{P_0}{E_1} = \frac{\dfrac{D_1}{E_1}}{ke - g}$$

Here the PE multiple rises if g rises, and falls if K_e increases. $\dfrac{D_1}{E_1}$ is the payout ratio. If this rises, less earnings are reinvested in the firm and so g will fall. Therefore, the PER may not increase.

Example 6.6 Valuation using the prospective PER

Murphy Engineering Ltd's required rate of return is 12%. The company reinvests 60% of its earnings. Next year the company expects dividends to grow by 5%. What PE multiple would you attach to this share?

Solution

$$\frac{P_0}{E_1} = \frac{D_1/E_1}{ke - g} = \frac{0.4}{0.07} = 5.7 \text{ times}$$

Now if the growth rate falls to 3% and the required rate of return increases to 14% the prospective PER becomes

$$\frac{0.4}{0.14 - 0.03} = 3.6 \text{ times}$$

PE ratios are difficult to interpret because of the difficulty of comparing the earnings of different companies. For example, different methods of calculating depreciating and valuing stock will lead to different profits figures.[7]

6.6 Valuation using the balance sheet

A balance sheet is a list of a company's assets and liabilities. We can apply two methods to value a business using a balance sheet — **the net asset value and liquidation value**.

6.6.1 Net asset value (NAV)

This is sometimes referred to as a company's **net worth** or **shareholders' funds**. NAV is simply calculated by adding up the company's assets and deducting all liabilities. For example the NAV of Ryanair Holdings plc for 1999 as shown in their balance sheet is €250,964,000.

To find the book values per share simply divide the NAV by the number of shares.

$$\textbf{Book value per share} = \frac{\textbf{NAV}}{\textbf{Number of shares issued}} \qquad (6.6)$$

The company had 164,759,808 shares in issue on 31 March 1999. Therefore the book value per share is €250,964,000/164,759,808 = €1.52.

The market values not only the company's net assets but also the income flow derived from these assets and also other intangible assets not included in the balance sheet such as brand names, management quality etc. For this reason net asset values act as a starting point **only** in the overall valuation process.

6.6.2 Liquidation value

Liquidation values are based on market (realisable) values and not book values. Liquidation values are based on what the assets would realistically make on the open market. **The liquidation value of a liability is the money it takes to pay off that liability**.

Example 6.7 *Liquidation value*

ABC Ltd's liquidation values are as follows (€000)

Freehold property	100
Fixed asset value@	
70% of book value	20
Current assets valued @	
80% of book value	150
Total asset value	270
Less Current liabilities	200
Loans	50
Total liabilities	250
Net assets	20

Assuming 100 shares, the liquidation value per share is 20/100 = 20c.

6.7 Valuing the entire company using free cash flows

Some companies don't currently pay dividends. Elan and Ryanair (at the time of writing) are examples of Irish plcs that haven't paid dividends in their history. On an international scale, Microsoft is another example. In addition, some companies are private, which means they do not have a market value for their shares. Cash flow valuation methods are a means of valuing such companies. Remember cash is king. While companies can **enhance** and **manipulate** profits (see Chapter 10) this is not possible to do with reported cash flow. The wealth of a shareholder depends on the company's ability to generate cash flow, or more precisely **free cash flow**. You will recall from Chapter 2 that free cash flow is what is left for shareholders after all the necessary investments (to sustain the company) have been made in total operating capital.

Example 6.8 *Company valuation using free cash flow*

The financial statements of Brandon Ltd for 2001 (actual) to 2005 (projected) are given in Tables 6.1 and 6.2.

Table 6.1 Profit and loss account (actual and projected) for Brandon Ltd 2001–2005

	Profit and loss account				
	Actual		Projected		
	2001 €m	2002 €m	2003 €m	2004 €m	2005 €m
Turnover	1,662.8	2,258.8	2,381.8	2,450.6	2,638.8
PBIT	74.2	84.6	95.4	90.8	92.2
Interest	(24.2)	(26.2)	(26.4)	(26.6)	(19.2)
PBT	50	58.4	69	64.2	73
Taxation	7.5	8.8	10.35	9.6	10.9
PAT	42.5	49.6	58.65	54.6	62.1

Table 6.2 Balance sheet (actual and projected) for Brandon Ltd

	Actual		Projected		
	2001	2002	2003	2004	2005
	€m	€m	€m	€m	€m
Fixed assets	398.6	463	456.8	452.2	486
Current assets					
Stock	126.6	124.8	140.8	147.6	157
Debtors	227.2	254.0	259.8	252.8	255.8
Marketable securities	9.8	11.4	10.4	10.2	8.8
Cash	49.8	116	117.6	166.2	124.8
	413.4	506.2	528.6	576.8	546.4
Current liabilities					
Creditors	192.36	339.8	292.68	290.08	288.96
Accruals	128.28	84.2	122.32	124.32	123.8
	320.64	424	415	414.4	412.76
NWC	92.77	82.2	113.6	162.4	133.64
Total NA	491.36	545.2	570.4	614.6	619.64
Financed by					
Long-term debt	204.8	260.6	256.4	263.8	106.2
Share capital	244.1	234.6	279	296.8	453.2
Retained earnings	42.46	50.	35	54	60.24
	491.36	545.2	570.4	614.6	619.64

Table 6.3 Calculating Brandon's expected future free cash flow

	Actual		Projected		
	2001 €m	2002 €m	2003 €m	2004 €m	2005€m
Note 1 Operating net fixed assets	398.6	463	456.8	452.2	486
Note 2 Operating net working capital	82.96	70.8	103.2	152.4	124.84
Note 3 Total net operating capital required	481.56	533.8	560	604.4	610.84
Note 4 Total net new investment in operating capital		52.24	26.2	44.4	6.44
Note 5 Net operating profit after taxes (NOPAT) = PBIT (1 – Tax rate)	63.07	71.9	81.09	77.18	78.37
Note 5 Less total net new investment in operating capital		52.24	26.2	44.4	6.44
Note 6 Free cash flow		19.66	54.89	32.74	71.93

Note 1: Net fixed assets as per balance sheet.

Note 2: Remember from Chapter 2 that net operating working capital = (Stock + Debtors + Cash) *minus* (Creditors + Accruals). In other words, net operating working capital is operating current assets *less* operating current liabilities. Therefore, for Brandon Ltd we leave out marketable securities. These are **financial assets** and are not part of the operating requirements.

Note 3: This is the sum of net operating fixed assets and net operating working capital.

Note 4: This is the net addition to operating assets. So for example for 2002 the net addition to operating assets is €533.8 *less* €481.56.

Note 5: This is net operating profit after tax. The tax rate is 15%, therefore for 2002 the PBIT $(1 - \text{tax rate}) = €84.6(1 - 0.15) = €71.9m$. This is operating profit after taxes (NOPAT).

Note 6: This is NOPAT *less* the net investment in total operating capital. So while in 2002 the company has projected €71.9m in net operating profit after taxes, it will invest €52.24m in operating capital. This leaves €19.66m in free cash flow for shareholders. Value added economics suggests that performance-related bonuses and pay be related to **free cash flow** and not on accounting measures of profit.

Turnover at Brandon is expected to grow at a non-constant growth rate up to 2005. After 2005 a constant growth rate of 8% is expected. The company's required rate of return is 10%. We can calculate the company's value using the free cash flow calculated in Table 6.3.

The value of a business is the present value of the free cash flow up to the horizon period (H) *plus* the present value at the horizon period.

The horizon value refers to the first year of constant growth, where the NPV of growth opportunities is zero.[8] The horizon value is the value of operations at the end of the forecast period. It is what the company's operating assets are worth at the end of the forecast period. The horizon period is **the time** when the firm enters into **competitive equilibrium**. Attempts to expand sales will meet with fierce competition from competitors who have **caught up** in terms of efficiency in the market place. The horizon period is the time when the competition catches up.

Up to this point, the present value of investment opportunities is greater than the cost of capital. This is the **growth stage** of the business cycle. When more and more businesses enter the industry and when the industry becomes more efficient and competitive, the present value of investment opportunities becomes zero.

The following steps are taken:

1. Calculate the free cash flow. Remember from Chapter 2 that free cash flow is net operating profit after tax *minus* net investment in operating capital.
2. Find the present values of the free cash flows for the non-constant growth period—up to 2005.
3. Use the constant growth formula to calculate the horizon value (H) at the end of 2005. Next, calculate the present values of all subsequent years back to 2005. Then the total year 2005 value is discounted back to the year 2001 to find its present value.
4. Finally summing the present value of the free cash flow during the non-constant growth period *plus* the present value of the horizon value gets the value of the firm.

The overall market value of the company is derived as follows:
(a) The value of the company at the horizon period

$$V_H = PV = \frac{FCF_H\,(1 + g)}{ke - g} \tag{6.7}$$

where V_H = horizon value
   FCF_H = free cash flow at horizon period

Therefore the value of the operation at the end of 2005 is

$$V_H = PV = \frac{FCF\,(1 + g)}{Ke - g} = \frac{€71.93\,(1.08)}{0.1 - 0.08} = \frac{€77.7}{0.02} = €3,885m$$

This is what Brandon would expect to receive if it sold its operations at the end of 2005. In addition, the total cash flow at the end of 2005 is the sum of the expected cash flow at the end of 2005 *plus* the expected value of operations at the end of 2005:

$$€71.93m + €3,885m = €3,956.93$$

(b) The present value of the FCF for the non-constant growth periods are

Year	FCF	Discount	PV
2002	19.66	1.1	€17.87
2003	54.89	$(1.1)^2$	€45.36
2004	32.74	$(1.1)^3$	€24.59
Total PV			€87.82

(c) Present value of horizon period

$$\frac{€3,956.93}{(1.1)^4} = €2,702.58$$

(d) Therefore the total value of FCF and the total value of operations as at 2001 is

$$\begin{bmatrix} \text{Total present value of} \\ \text{operations }_{2001} \end{bmatrix} = \begin{bmatrix} \text{Present value of non-constant} \\ \text{growth period} \end{bmatrix} + \begin{bmatrix} \text{Present value of} \\ \text{horizon period} \end{bmatrix}$$

This is

$$[€2,790.4] = [€87.82] + [2,702.58]$$

Figure 6.2 illustrates these figures using a PV time line.

Figure 6.2 Valuation of whole company using free cash flows and non-constant growth rates

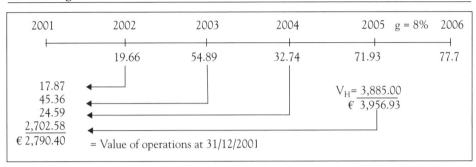

The total value of any company is the value of its operating assets *plus* the value of its non-operating assets.

$$\text{Total value of operations} = \begin{bmatrix} \text{Value of operating} \\ \text{activities} \end{bmatrix} + \begin{bmatrix} \text{Value of non-operating} \\ \text{activities} \end{bmatrix} \quad (6.8)$$

The value of Brandon's non-operating assets at the end of 2001 is €9.8m (i.e. Brandon's marketable securities) and the value of its operating activities is €2,790.4m. Therefore the overall value of Brandon Ltd as at the end of 2001 is

$$\text{Total value of operations} = [€2,790.4m] + [€9.8m] = €2,800.2m$$

Remember, a company will finance its operations with equity or debt, or a combination of both. Therefore the total value of operations *minus* the value of the company's debt must equal the value of the company's equity.

Deducting the total value of the company's debt, i.e., €204.8m, we get the market value of its equity as at the end of 2001. This is the total value of operations *less* the total value of debt:

Market value of equity = Total value of operations – Total value of debt (6.9)

For Brandon Ltd this is

$$\text{Market value of equity} = €2,800.2m - €204.8m = €2,595.4m$$

The **book value of equity** at the end of 2001 is €286.56m which represents the shareholders' actual investment in the company. By deducting this from the market value of equity, we get the **market value added**. This is the value added to shareholders' investments by management and employees. Table 6.4 gives a summary of the valuations for Brandon Ltd.

Market value added = Market value of equity – Book value of equity (6.10)

Therefore, Brandon's market value added is

Market value added		Market value of equity		Book value of equity
€2,308.84m	=	€2,595.40m	−	€286.56m

Table 6.4 Valuation summary of Brandon Ltd as at 31/12/2001 (€m)

Present value of FCFs for non-constant growth period	87.82
Plus	
Total present value of FCFs for constant growth period (i.e. horizon value)	2,702.58
Equals	
Present value of operating activities	2,790.4
Plus	
Value of non-operating activities	9.8
Total value of operations	2,800.2
Less	
Value of debt	204.8
Equals	
Market value of equity	2,595.4
Less	
Shareholders' investment	286.56
Equals	
Market value added	2,308.84

6.8 Standard valuation methods and hi-tech stocks

For a while in 2000 dot.com stocks became a password to instant financial success (see Box 6.2). What do the standard valuation methods tell us about the valuation of hi-tech stocks?

Box 6.2 Flocking to the dot.com party

Dot.com has become a password to instant success in Western equity markets. Since the arrival of Netscape on the market five years ago, the market has been flooded with new technology stocks that have fundamentally distorted market performance.

In 1998/99, for instance, the value of Internet stocks soared 400 per cent against just short of 20 per cent of the more traditional US indices—the Dow Jones and the Standard and Poor's 500.

That explains the rush by more traditional media companies and others to reinvent themselves as dot.com. In Ireland, two dramatic examples have been Independent News and Media, whose shares have jumped 36% from €7.96 to €10.80 in the 10 days since it announced the provision of Internet access via television to cable customers, and Fyffes, whose business-to-business web service has seen the share shake off the blues which dogged it for so long and rise from €1.65 to €3.85. This week BskyB showed even newish

→

media companies are not immune to the need to upgrade on technology. Announcing an interim loss of €61.5 million sterling compared with a profit of €53.2 million in the previous year, its stock surged by more than 20 per cent on the day to record highs.

Why? Quite simple. The market could not have cared less what the results said once the company announced it was to invest £250 million sterling to boost its presence online.

The same strategy has already bolstered the fortunes of two other media giants—Reuters and Pearson.

If only turning a profit were so easy.

Business Briefing, *The Irish Times*, 12 February 2000

As we have seen in this chapter the value of a share is the expected value of the future dividends received from that share as in the equation 6.1:

$$P_0 = \frac{D_1}{(1 + ke)} + \frac{D_2}{(1 + ke)^2} + \frac{D_3}{(1 + ke)^3} + \ldots \frac{D}{(1 + ke)\infty}$$

If, according to equation 6.1, an investor concludes that the stock's price exceeds a reasonable valuation but goes ahead and buys it anyway, the investor would be following the bigger fool theory—you believe that the stock is overpriced but you also believe that there is a bigger fool out there who will buy the share at an even higher price from you when you decide to sell.

There have been many examples of the bigger fool theory down through the ages.[9] More recently, the stock market crash of 1987 was preceded, among other reasons, by the bigger fool theory. At the beginning of March 2000 over €5 billion was wiped off the value of Ireland's quoted hi-tech stocks. The biggest losers were Baltimore Technologies who suffered a drop in market capitalisation of €2.86 billion. Other Irish hi-tech stocks that were hit badly included Riverdeep, Trintech and Iona. This fall-out in Internet and dotcom stocks was mirrored in the US.

The bigger fool theory describes speculative investments and doesn't fit with the dividend valuation models (DVMs) described earlier. Unrealistic expectations are applied to valuations. Many of these so called new economy stocks are valued on unrealistic assessments of sales growth—not on free cash flow or even profits. (See Box 6.3.)

Box 6.3 Don't be last one left with fool's stock

Can I pose a few questions? Are we in a bubble? Is the bubble bursting? The answer to each of these questions must be yes. As an interested observer there is no doubt in my mind that: (a) the stock market is still in a bubble despite recent corrections; (b) Irish house prices are in a bubble; and (c) the Irish economy is demonstrating many of the characteristics of a bubble. . . . Even some of the most risk friendly speculators must shudder at some of the valuations now being applied to assets . . .

The price of a share is equal to the present value of the sum of all future expectations. Bubbles happen when unrealistic expectations are applied to valuations.

$\longrightarrow$

I do not understand the current valuation model that values a company only on a multiple of sales. Don't worry about profit or return on investment.

This so called enterprise valuation model simply won't work. One example illustrates the madness of current expectations. A recent successful stock market launch in Britain resulted in a market value that could only be justified by either of the following:

- Annual sales growth of 65% at a 25% margin or
- Annual sales growth of 50% with a 40% net margin.

What are the chances of either occurring? None whatsoever. A quick look at almost all the Irish tech stock valuations should cause you to ponder. In fact, it should cause you to head for the door. . . .

Bubbles do not have to explode. Like a slow puncture, markets can decline over time. Rallies are followed by declines with subsequent peaks usually lower.

Is this what is happening? I believe it is. It is now old fashioned to think that investment must earn a return. Any venture in bricks, clicks or intellectual property rights must cover the cost of the investment and make a margin to cover profit. Profit for many seems an outdated concept. Business ventures must make a profit otherwise capital will flow to other areas. Does that make sense? It should because that's what happens.

How can you have billion dollar values on companies with small sales, no profits and only vague hopes of making profits in the future? The answer is 'the greater fool theory'. Almost every buyer of bubble stocks cares little about the business or its prospects. They expect to sell on their shares at a higher price. Buyers believe there is a greater fool out there willing to pay a higher price to buy shares, which they in turn can sell on.

As long as the 'pass the parcel' games continue, the markets can rise. Day trading[10] is grist to this mill.

Look at today's business pages; look at the valuations placed on certain new economy companies. The future is obvious—share prices will fall. Most new economy ventures will fall. Investors will lose their money. The few that succeed will be the Ges, Exxons and IBMs of the future.

Extracted from an article written by John Teeling, chairman of Cooley Distilleries as well as a member of oil and mineral resource companies *The Irish Times*, 19 May 2000

SUMMARY

- Valuing common stock is more difficult than valuing bonds because (a) cash flows are not explicit, (b) it is difficult to find an appropriate rate of return and (c) a common share's life is for ever.
- The value of a common stock is the present value of the future dividend stream.
- A zero growth stock suggests that future dividends are constant, i.e. $D_1 = D_2 = D_3$ etc.
- The value of a constant growth stock is

$$Po = D_1 (1 + g)/(ke - g) = D_1/ke - g$$

- Companies go through different phases during their business cycle from initial accelerated growth to moderate growth and finally no growth. These phases signify different dividend growths. Summing the discounted values of dividends at each stage of growth gets the market price of such a stock. This is the supernormal growth model.
- The PER is used to measure companies that don't have a market price.
- NAV is a measure of a company's book value. This is total assets *less* total liabilities, which is the company's net worth or shareholders' funds.
- Liquidation value is used to value assets below their book value or assets with poor earnings capacity.
- The cash flow valuation model is used to value companies that don't pay dividends.

QUESTIONS

1. Why is valuing common shares more difficult than valuing bonds?
2. Why is liquidation value more dependable than book value?
3.♦ The value of a common share depends on expected dividends. Why therefor can't companies increase shareholder value by simply increasing dividends?
4. Do share values reflect the long-term performance or short-term performance of a company?
5. In the dividend valuation model (DVM), why is the cost of equity assumed to be greater than the growth in dividends g? Illustrate your answer diagrammatically.
6. Why is g (growth in dividends) in DVM assumed to be constant?
7. Is there any value in a share that will never pay a dividend?
8. How do share prices reach their equilibrium position?
9.♦ The following is an estimate of dividends that will be paid on a particular share: year 1 = €1, year 2 = €1.5, year 3 = €2. It is expected that after this dividends will grow at a constant rate of 4% p.a. The company's cost of capital is 8%. Calculate: (a) the current price of the share P_0, (b) the price of the share in one year's time at P_1, (c) the capital gain between P_0 and P_1, (d) the dividend yield at P_0, and (e) draw a time line valuation of the shares.
10. Boherbawn Investments Ltd's current share price is €30. It has just paid a dividend of €2 per share. The company is now stabilised and it expects dividends to grow at a constant rate into the future. The company's cost of capital is 10% and it is expected to remain at that level. Calculate Boherbawn's expected stock price in four years' time.
11. Bolton Ltd shares are selling for €50 per share. The next dividend payment is due in one year's time and this is expected to be €2 per share and the expected share price in one year's time is €60. Calculate the shareholders' expected rate of return?
12. What does a negative dividend mean?
13. 'The value of stocks is determined by dividend income and not by capital gains.' Evaluate this statement.
14.♦ The end of year dividend on common stock of Mountjoy Ltd is expected to be €5 per share and the shares are expected to sell for €60 per share. Calculate the current share price if the expected rate of return is 10%.
15. Garbh Eoin Quarrying Ltd has just paid a €5 per share dividend to its common shareholders. There have been some concerns about financial irregularities in addition

to environmental concerns associated with the company. Because of this, the dividend growth rate is expected to be just 3%. Calculate the expected value of the price of Garbh Eoin shares, if its cost of capital is 15%. Would you buy a stock whose share price was expected to decline?

16. ♦ You are considering the following three investment opportunities. Stock A provides dividends of €5 per share forever. Stock B is expected to provide a dividend of €6 next year. Dividend growth is expected to be 5% per annum thereafter. Stock C will pay a dividend of €2 next year and dividend growth is expected to be 15% for the following 4 years and zero thereafter. The cost of capital is 8% for each share. Which share is the most valuable?

17. Flybynight Airlines is experiencing rapid growth with dividends expected to grow by 12% during the next two years, 14% in year 3, and at a constant rate of 5% thereafter. Flybynight has just paid a dividend of €1.20 per share. The market capitalisation rate is 10%. Calculate the value of stock today.

18. ♦ Yesteryear has just paid a dividend of €3 per share. The company doesn't expect to be able to continue the payout and it expects to reduce the payout by 10% next year and thereafter. The company's cost of capital is 14%. Calculate the share price.

19. ♦ Elm Co., a drugs manufacturing company, has never paid a dividend. The company has a cost of capital of 12% and a free cash flow of €200,000. The FCF is expected to grow at a constant rate of 5%. The company has debentures of €500,000. You are required to calculate the overall value of the firm.

NOTES

1. This is discussed in Chapter 12.
2. M.J. Gordon and E. Shapiro, 'Capital Equipment Analysis: The Required Rate of Profit', *Management Science*, 3 October 1956.
3. We discuss earnings per share (EPS) in detail in Chapter 11, but for the moment remember that EPS is profit for ordinary shareholders divided by the number of ordinary shares and ranking for dividend.
4. Note that D_0 is 12 cents and it is only used to estimate D_1. D_0 has already been paid and does not therefore enter the equation because we are dealing with the present values of **future** cash flows.
5. €9.85 is a year 3 cash flow because this is the expected price of the share at the end of year 3.
6. Source: *Irish Equity Market Forecasts*, Davy Research, July 1998.
7. Creative forms of accounting will be discussed in Chapter 10.
8. This general definition is used by Brealey and Myers in *Principles of Corporate Finance*, 6th ed. Chapter 4, 'The Common Value of Stock', deals with the meaning of the **horizon period**.
9. See John Kenneth Galbraith, *A Short History of Financial Euphoria*, Whittle Books.
10. Day trading is the practice of buying and selling securities on the same day.

Part 3

Strategic Investment
Decisions

7
Investment Appraisal

CHAPTER OBJECTIVES

At the end of this chapter the student should be able to

1. understand the drawbacks and attractions of the techniques available to appraise capital investment projects
2. appreciate why discounted cash flow methods are preferred to payback and accounting rate of return
3. understand why net present value is preferred to internal rate of return from an academic point of view
4. have an awareness of the empirical evidence of the techniques used in practice
5. understand the concept of capital rationing and the use of the profitability index
6. know when to use nominal discount rates and real discount rates on cash flow projections
7. incorporate risk into the investment appraisal decision
8. know how to deal with taxation liabilities and benefits and unequal project lives.

INTRODUCTION

From an investor's perspective, investment can be defined as any application of funds, which is intended to provide a return by way of interest, dividend or capital appreciation; whereas viewed from a business perspective, it is an outlay of cash now, in return for cash inflows over future periods. The allocation of funds among alternative investment projects is a crucial decision for a company. Investment opportunities often involve major funding and influence the future profitability of the company. A capital investment project is a proposed investment in a long-term asset. Examples include the purchase of new buildings and equipment, expenditure on research and development programmes, asset replacement decisions etc.

Investment appraisal or capital budgeting techniques are used to evaluate proposed projects and in this chapter we will look at the payback period, the discounted payback period, the accounting rate of return, the net present value, the profitability index and the internal rate of return. After assessing the techniques available we will look at their application and the impact of inflation, taxation and risk.

Before looking at the various techniques available it is important to look at the capital budgeting process and this can be divided into five stages.

1. **Identification**. This involves searching for possible projects that the company could undertake and the initial screening of such projects to identify likely candidates. Factors such as the amount of expenditure involved, associated risks, strategic fit and management competence in the business area would all be looked at before the short-listed projects would qualify for further analysis.
2. **Estimating cash flows.** This stage requires estimates of projected cash flows related to the project and would involve forecasts of many variables such as demand, price, variable cost, fixed cost, depreciation charges allowable, corporate tax rates etc.
3. **Evaluation**. At this stage the various appraisal techniques are used in the evaluation process.
4. **Selection**. This process involves decision-making for the selection committee based on information on the level of risk inherent in the project, the finance available, the appraisal technique used and the type of project.
5. **Post-audit**. The last stage is an important one and reviews the performance of the projects adopted. Cash flow variances are assessed based on actual versus forecasted. This continuous monitoring of projects determines if they should be continued or abandoned by the company.

Projects that were rejected previously can be reassessed, to see if they are now viable. This could be based on more favourable economic conditions prevailing or less capital rationing etc.

The quantitative assessment of projects is just the culmination of the process of identifying possible projects. The company should formulate a strategic plan to identify the direction in which the company needs to go, in terms of products, markets, financing etc. to best generate profitable investment opportunities. This process requires considerable management talent.

In this chapter we will concentrate on the appraisal techniques involved and how they are applied to projected cash flow forecasts, starting with payback.

7.1 Payback

The payback period is the time that it takes cash inflows from an investment project to equal cash outflows and is usually expressed in years. When deciding between two or more competing projects, the usual decision is to accept the one with the shorter payback. Companies who have a target payback would reject a project unless its payback period is less than a target number of years.

Example 7.1 Payback

A company is faced with two mutually exclusive projects with the following forecasted cash flows (€).

	Project A Cash flow	Project A Cumulative	Project B Cash flow	Project B Cumulative
Year 0	(60,000)	(60,000)	(60,000)	(60,000)
Year 1	20,000	(40,000)	50,000	(10,000)
Year 2	50,000	10,000	20,000	10,000
Year 3	40,000	50,000	10,000	20,000
Year 4	50,000	100,000	5,000	25,000
Payback		1.8 years		1.5 years

The payback period for both project A and project B are less than two years.
Payback for A occurs in 1 + 40/50 = 1.8 years and for B in 1 + 10/20 = 1.5 years.

- The first weakness in this technique is that it does not take into account the time value of money. In our example above, most of project B is paid back in year 1, while in the case of A it is delayed until year 2.
- The second weakness is that cash inflow beyond the payback period is ignored altogether and in the example above project A has substantial cash inflows after year 2.
- A final weakness relates to the selection of the payback duration, which can be an arbitrary decision without theoretical foundation.

Payback however has one critical advantage over more sophisticated techniques.

- It is easy to calculate, understand and communicate.
- Payback has an implicit assumption that the risks of cash flow forecasts are directly related to the length of time into the future. If funds are limited there is an advantage to receiving returns earlier and the payback method focuses on the early years.
- Finally the payback method is one of the most common initial methods of investment appraisal in use. It is not, however, often used exclusively but is rather used as a screening method or in conjunction with other techniques.

7.2 Accounting rate of return (ARR)

ARR is also known as the **return on capital employed (ROCE)**, or **return on investment (ROI)** and expresses the profits from a project as a percentage of the capital cost. The decision rule is that if the ARR of the project is greater than the company target rate, then the project is acceptable. The ratio can be calculated a number of ways with the most common method having the following definition.

$$ARR = \frac{\text{Average annual profit}}{\text{Initial capital cost}} \times 100\% \qquad (7.1)$$

Profit is based on profit before interest and tax after depreciation. If we use project A above and assume a depreciation charge of €15,000 per annum, then average annual profit is (5 + 35 + 25 + 35)/4 in €000s, i.e. €25,000.

$$\text{ARR} = \frac{\text{\texteuro}25{,}000}{\text{\texteuro}60{,}000} \times 100\% = 41.67\%$$

Another measure of ARR is $\qquad \dfrac{\textbf{Average annual profit}}{\textbf{Average capital invested}} \times 100 \qquad$ (7.2)

Here the ARR is $\dfrac{\text{\texteuro}25{,}000}{\text{\texteuro}30{,}000} \times 100\% = 83.33\%$

If a scrap value exists at the end of the project, then the average capital invested becomes (initial outlay + scrap value)/2, if straight line depreciation is used.

- The different definitions that exist for profits and assets are a weakness of ARR and may tempt management to manipulate the technique to suit their purposes.
- It fails to take account of the timing of cash flows within the project's life and again the cut-off or hurdle rate is an arbitrary decision. ARR is not based on cash, but on accounting profit, and profit figures are not as transparent as cash flow.

However the ARR technique is easy to calculate, managers are familiar with this form of profitability measure and, unlike the payback method, it looks at the full life of the investment.

Both payback and ARR suffer a major weakness in not taking into account the time value of money, the effect of which can be stated as the following general rule: **There is a time preference for receiving the same sum of money sooner rather than later. Conversely, there is a time preference for paying the same sum of money later rather than sooner.**

Discounted cash flow (DCF) is an investment appraisal technique which takes into account the time value of money and the cash flows over the entire life of the project. Discounting is the reverse of compounding which is a concept based on finding the future value of a sum of money invested at a given rate of return for a number of years. Although covered in Chapter 4, a quick recap using the following example illustrates the technique.

Example 7.2 Discounting

If you invest €10,000 at 10% for four years, what will the future value of the investment be worth?

Answer

$$\text{FV} = \text{PV} \ (1 + r)^n \qquad (7.3)$$

where FV is the future value, PV is the present value, r is the rate of return and n is the number of years or time periods.

In this case the future value = €10,000 $(1 + 0.1)^4$ = €10,000 × 1.4641 = €14,641 where 1.4641 is the compound factor.

The basic principle of discounting is finding the present value of a future sum of money if a certain rate is available. Using the last example try to find the present value of €14,641 in four years' time when rates are 10% per annum.

In this case the **present value = FV $(1 + r)^{-n}$** or $\dfrac{FV}{(1 + r)^n}$ $\hspace{2cm}$ (7.4)

and instead of a compound factor we have a discount factor of $(1 + 0.10)^{-4}$ = 0.6830 to four decimals. These discount factors are easily found in the discount tables provided at the end of the book.

Present value = €14,641 $(1 + 0.1)^{-4}$ = €14,641 × 0.6830 = €10,000 approximately.

Two of the most important measures of investment appraisal using DCF techniques are the net present value (NPV) and internal rate of return (IRR).

7.3 Net present value (NPV)

The NPV method works out the present values of all cash inflows and outflows of an investment at a given target rate of return or cost of capital, and then works out a net total. A positive NPV indicates that an investment is expected to give a return in excess of the cost of capital and will therefore lead to an increase in shareholder wealth. Cost of capital, put simply, is the opportunity cost of funds used to finance the project. **Projects with a positive NPV are deemed acceptable or viable.** Projects that exhibit a negative NPV are considered to be unacceptable.

Example 7.3 Net present value

Find the NPV of the following cash flows if the company's target rate of return is 19%.

Year	Cash flow
0	(€20,000)
1	€6,000
2	€6,000
3	€6,000
4	€6,000

Answer

1 Year (n)	2 Cash flow	3 Discount factor	2 x 3 Present value
0	(€20,000)	$(1 + 0.19)^0 = 1.000$	(€20,000)
1	€6,000	$(1 + 0.19)^{-1} = 0.8403$	€5,041.8
2	€6,000	$(1 + 0.19)^{-2} = 0.7062$	€4,237.2
3	€6,000	$(1 + 0.19)^{-3} = 0.5934$	€3,560.4
4	€6,000	$(1 + 0.19)^{-4} = 0.4987$	€2,992.2
		net present value =	(€4,168.4)

The net present value is negative with a value of (€4,168.4).

The present value of the outflow exceeds the present value of the inflows resulting in a negative NPV of €4,168.4. The project is not viable, as the return on the €20,000 is less than 19%.

If a company has a choice of projects which are mutually exclusive (only one can be chosen), then **the project with the highest NPV should be chosen**.

An annuity is a constant cash flow over a number of time periods. In the example above the cash inflows are in annuity form and instead of using a separate discount factor for each cash inflow, a compound factor or an annuity factor can be used. The formula for an annuity factor (also known as a cumulative present value factor) is

$$\text{Annuity discount factor} = \frac{1 - (1 + r)^{-n}}{r} \qquad (7.5)$$

where r is the discount rate and n is the number of time periods.

If the annuity is a perpetuity, i.e. a constant cash flow that lasts for ever, the discount factor tends in the limit to r^{-n}.

$$\text{Perpetuity discount factor} = 1/r \text{ or } r^{-n} \qquad (7.6)$$

In the example above the cash flows can be rewritten as:

Year	Cash flow	Discount factor	Present value
0	(€20,000)	1.000	(€20,000)
1 to 4	€6,000	$\dfrac{1 - (1 + 0.19)^{-4}}{0.19} = 2.639$	
			€15,832
		Net present value (€4,168)	

The net present value method has been criticised on the basis that:

- it is not as easily understood as payback or ARR.
- a more fundamental criticism relates to the discount factor used. The company's cost of capital is normally used as a basis for the discount factor. The company's cost of capital may be difficult to find and what discount factor is appropriate can also be a complex decision (see Chapter 8) and may change over the life of the project.

However, points in favour of the NPV are that

- the NPV takes into account the time value of money and the level of risk associated with the cash flows explicitly.
- it is expressed in today's money terms.
- the NPV uses cash flow rather than accounting profits over the entire life of the project.

Because of these advantages NPV is the academically preferred method of investment appraisal.

7.4 Internal rate of return (IRR)

This is an alternative to the NPV method of investment appraisal. The NPV method determines whether the investment earns a positive or negative NPV when discounted at the company's target rate of return. If the NPV is zero, the return for the project is the same as the discount factor and this is what the IRR method tries to find. The IRR method tries to find the discount factor that gives an NPV of zero, i.e. it tries to find the rate of return on an investment.

The decision rule is, **if the IRR exceeds the company's target rate of return, then the project is viable**. The IRR method, also known as the DCF yield method, involves finding two NPVs at two discount rates and then using a linear interpolation technique to find an approximate IRR. The process is illustrated in the following example.

Example 7.4 Internal rate of return

Estimate the IRR for the following project:

Year	Cash flow	Discount factor 12%	Present value €
0	(€75,000)	1.000	(€75,000)
1	€20.000	0.893	€17,860
2	€30,000	0.797	€23,910
3	€50,000	0.712	€35,600
		Net present value = €2,370	

The positive NPV indicates that the return on this investment is greater than the discount rate (12%), so the IRR of this project must be greater than 12%. Now let us try a higher discount rate, 14% for example.

0	(€75,000)	1.000	(€75,000)
1	€20.000	0.877	€17,540
2	€30,000	0.769	€23,070
3	€50,000	0.675	€33,750
		Net present value = (€640)	

The negative NPV indicates that the IRR is lower than the discount rate (14%) and so the IRR must be between 12% and 14%.

There is an interpolation formula based on the two discount rates and the two NPVs found that gives an approximate value of the IRR.

Internal rate of return approximation

$$a + \frac{A}{(A - B)} \times (b - a) \% \qquad (7.7)$$

where
a = lower discount rate   A = NPV at the lower discount rate
b = higher discount rate   B = NPV at the higher discount rate

In the example above a =12%, b = 14%, A = €2370 and B = (€640).

$$\text{IRR} = 12\% + \frac{2{,}370}{(2{,}370 + 640)} \times (14 - 12)\% = 13.6\%$$

If this IRR is above the company's target rate of return, the project will be accepted.

The interpolation formula assumes a linear relationship between the discount rate and the NPV. In calculating the two values for NPV, the closer they are to the actual IRR, the more accurate the interpolation approximation becomes. If the two discount factors used lead to negative NPVs or result in two positive NPVs, the interpolation formula will still work.

It is important to remember that the IRR calculated using the interpolation formula is only an approximation of the true IRR.

The following diagram illustrates this fact.

Figure 7.1 IRR as an approximation

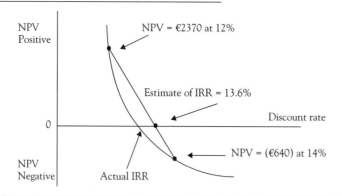

The diagram above shows that the IRR calculated using two discount factors and associated NPVs gives only an approximate value of the true IRR. The interpolation technique is a linear approximation whereas the relationship is in fact curve-like. A statistical computer package or spreadsheet package can easily perform the calculations necessary to get an accurate NPV or IRR.

Below is an extract from an Excel spreadsheet showing how to input cash flows relating to a project to find the NPV. The example is of a four year project with a discount factor of 15%.

Table 7.1 Spread sheet calculation of NPV

1	A	B
2	Year	Cash flow
3		€
4	0	–100,000
5	1	60,000
6	2	80,000
7	3	40,000
8	4	30,000
9		
10	NPV	56,119

The cell with the solution (B10) contains the formula = NPV(15%, B5:B8) + B4.

In Excel the package assumes that the first cash flow occurs at the end of time 1 and so time 0 cash flows have to be added (or subtracted) outside the brackets. The time 0 cash flow is not discounted because it occurs now.

Spreadsheets take out all the hard work associated with DCF calculations.

The same investment example can be used to show how easy it is to calculate the IRR of a project. In Excel all you do is input = IRR (B4:B8) into cell B10 and the result is given immediately.

Table 7.2 Spreadsheet calculation of IRR

	A	B
1		
2	Year	Cash flow
3		€
4	0	−100,000
5	1	60,000
6	2	80,000
7	3	40,000
8	4	30,000
9		
10	IRR	44.48%

Spreadsheets can be used to carry out all sorts of financial calculations such as annuities, mortgages etc.

Like the NPV method the IRR considers both the magnitude and the timing of the project's cash flows over the entire life of the project. Additionally the IRR is measured as a percentage, which is easy to understand. There are however serious disadvantages concerning the IRR method.

(a) It ignores the relative size or scale of investments. Both of the following investments have an IRR or DCF yield of 18%.

	Project A	Project B
Cost in year 0	(€3.5 million)	(€350,000)
Cash inflow years 1–6	€1 million	€100,000

Project A is ten times as big and more profitable, but on the basis of an IRR of 18% they are both equal.

(b) More than one IRR may result if the cash flows from projects are 'not conventional'. Most projects have conventional cash flows that consist of an initial negative cash flow followed by positive cash flows in later time periods. If negative cash flows arise in later time periods then multiple IRRs may occur.

The following cash flows are non-conventional and give two values (7% and 35%) for IRR.

Year	Cash flow
0	(€1.9 million)
1	€4.59 million
2	(€2.735 million)

There will be as many IRR rates as there are changes in the direction of cash flows.

(c) The IRR cannot accommodate changes in the discount rate over the life of the project whereas the NPV method can and this again is another reason why the NPV is the preferred method of investment appraisal.

(d) The **IRR method should not be used to assess mutually exclusive projects**, as the IRR assumes the rate at which funds generated by the projects can be reinvested is the same IRR. This is an unrealistic assumption in many cases. NPV assumes reinvestment can occur at the company's cost of capital, which is a more realistic assumption. When mutually exclusive projects are available the IRR of the **incremental cash flows** can be used to decide which project to accept.

Example 7.5 Incremental cash flow

Two mutually exclusive projects have the following cash flow forecasts

Year	Project A	Project B
0	(€10,200)	(€35,250)
1	€6,000	€18,000
2	€5,000	€15,000
3	€3,000	€15,000

At a cost of capital of 16%, the NPV for project A is €610, and for project B is €1,026. However the IRR for project A is 20% and only 18% for project B. Using NPV criteria project B would be chosen and using IRR criteria project A would be chosen. However to make a rational decision it is necessary to calculate the **incremental cash flows** and discount these at the company's cost of capital.

The incremental cash flows are

Year	Project A	Project B	Incremental cash flow
0	(€10,200)	(€35,250)	(€25,050)
1	€6,000	€18,000	€12,000
2	€5,000	€15,000	€10,000
3	€3,000	€15,000	€12,000

The NPV of the incremental cash flows at 16% is €416, which means it is worth investing the extra amount involved in project B to get the extra benefit.

In this example the IRR of the incremental cash flows is over 17%, which again indicates that project B is preferred.

When projects are mutually exclusive, the NPV is a better criteria for making investment decisions and the simple decision rule is to accept the project with the highest NPV.

If the IRR method of investment appraisal is used, then you must also find the IRR of the incremental cash flows to make the correct evaluation.

7.5 Discounted payback

This is probably a good time to look at payback again and address one of the shortcomings associated with it. The payback evaluation technique can be modified, by discounting cash flows at the company's cost of capital, to give a discounted payback time frame. Consider the payback example 7.1 again and assume a discount factor of 10%. The discounted payback period is longer for project A, reflecting the fact that the significant cash inflows are more distant, whereas the non-discounted payback was under two years. The discounted payback has the same advantages and disadvantages as before, except that the weakness associated of failing to take into account the time value of money is now addressed.

Year	Project A €	PV @ 10% DF	Project B €	PV @ 10% DF
0	(60,000)	(60,000)	(60,000)	(60,000)
1	20,000	18,182	50,000	45,456
2	50,000	41,322	20,000	16,529
3	40,000	30,053*	10,000	7,513
4	50,000	34,151	5,000	3,415
Discounted payback		2.017 years		1.88 years

Project A has now more than a two year discounted payback.* The discounted payback is found by adding up the present values until the initial investment is recovered. In the case of project A, the first two years' present values do not add to €60,000, i.e. €60,000 – (€18,182 + €41,322) = €596. The payback occurs in 2 + 596/30,053 = 2.017 years.

7.6 Profitability index and capital rationing

When a company has insufficient funds available for investment in projects with a positive NPV, the company is said to be in a capital-rationing situation.

- If the limitation on available funds is external to the firm, this is called **hard capital rationing**, for example the inability of the company to obtain funds from existing shareholders or financial markets.
- If the restriction is internally imposed, this is known as **soft capital rationing**.

When this occurs absolute NPV cannot be used to rank the better projects, because a project with a large NPV would be ranked ahead of a combination of smaller projects, which together would collectively offer a higher NPV. A more appropriate technique to adopt here is the profitability index, which shows NPV per €1 of scarce capital.

The profitability index assumes that projects cannot be deferred to a subsequent time. Projects are divisible (portions of projects can be undertaken) and capital is rationed in the initial period only. The index shows how much is received in present value terms per € invested.

$$\text{Profitability index} = \frac{\textbf{Present value of future cash flow}}{\textbf{Value of initial investment}} \qquad (7.8)$$

If there is no capital rationing, then all projects with a ratio greater than one should be accepted. This is consistent with a positive NPV.

- If capital rationing exists and projects are **divisible**, then projects should be ranked according to their profitability index. Those projects with the **highest ranking** should be undertaken before those with a lower ranking, until the available funds are depleted.
- If the projects are **not divisible**, then the projects should be looked at differently. The selection of projects should be based on the combination of projects giving the highest NPV within the budget available.

Example 7.6 Profitability index

A company has maximum funds available of €1,500 and the following projects are to be considered:

Project	A	B	C	D
Initial cost €	(500)	(600)	(700)	(800)
PV future cash flow €	1,100	1,300	1,500	1,550
NPV €	600	700	800	750
Profitability index	2.2	2.17	2.14	1.94
Ranking by NPV	4	3	1	2
Ranking by PI	1	2	3	4

If we assume that investments are divisible, then the optimum investment is all of projects A and B and 57% (i.e. 400/700) of project C. The combined investment of €1,500 is made up of €500 in A, €600 in B and €400 in part of project C.

The total NPV is €1,757, which is better than just C and D with a total NPV of €1,550.

However, if the projects are not divisible, then the optimum choice would be projects C and D as they would give the highest total NPV and use up all available capital.

The above capital rationing examples assume that funds are limited initially for a **single period** only. If this is not the case, the problem becomes more complex and involves the application of **multiple-period** linear programming techniques.

Multiple-period capital rationing implies that funds are limited over a number of years and the company may be faced with a choice of investments. Linear programming is a technique for solving such problems.

Example 7.7 Multiple-period capital rationing

Suppose a company is considering four investment projects and has a required rate of return of 12%. The cost commitments and NPVs associated with the four projects are as follows (all figures are in € millions)

Time	Project 1	Project 2	Project 3	Project 4
0	(22)	(17)	(8)	(3)
1	(10)	(4)	(2)	(3)
2	(10)	(7)	(3)	(5)
3	(12)	(7)	(8)	(6)
NPV	22.44	11.1	16.45	24.39

If we assume the company has €15 million, €14 million, €16 million and €20 million available in each of the next four years, the following linear programming model can be formulated.

Let a = the number of units of project 1 that are accepted
    b = the number of units of project 2 that are accepted
    c = the number of units of project 3 that are accepted
    d = the number of units of project 4 that are accepted.

Maximise $22.44a + 11.1b + 16.45c + 24.39d$ (in NPV)
Subject to: $22a + 17b + 8c + 3d \leq 15$
               $10a + 4b + 2c + 3d \leq 14$
               $10a + 7b + 3c + 5d \leq 16$
               $12a + 7b + 8c + 6d \leq 20$

where a, b, c and d satisfy the non-negativity constraint.

The solution to this problem using the simplex procedure is a = 0, b = 0, c = 0.1818 and d = 3.0909. This means, do not invest in project 1 or 2, invest in 0.1818 of a unit in project 3 and 3.0909 units of project d. The NPV that corresponds to this solution is $(16.45)(0.1818) + (24.39)(3.0909) =$ €78.378 million. If the restrictive assumptions of projects being divisible and undertaken more than once are relaxed, the solution to this problem becomes more complicated and is beyond the scope of this text.

7.7 Relevant and irrelevant costs

We are now in a position to apply the techniques learned, but before applying these, it is important to look at the cash flows that are relevant to the appraisal. The concept of cash flow is critical. The real cost to a business of any new project is the actual net amount of cash that flows out of the business as a result of the investment decision. The real return is the actual amount of cash which is earned for the business from the project during its life. The cash flows to be considered are those which arise as a consequence of a decision. It therefore follows that any costs incurred in the past, or any committed costs, which will be incurred regardless of whether or not a project is undertaken, are **irrelevant** items and should be **excluded**. Examples of items to exclude are as follows:

- **Depreciation**: is a purely accounting expense; it is not a cash flow. It represents an accounting regulation whereby the cost of a capital asset is charged to profit as it is being used up, not as it is being paid for. This is not a cash flow and any depreciation charges should be excluded from calculations. So if profit figures after depreciation are given, the profit needs to be increased by adding back the depreciation charge.
- **Apportioned fixed costs**: production costs may include an apportionment of a factory or other fixed costs using some standard basis for absorption. These should be excluded as they do not arise directly from the project, i.e. they are not relevant. Fixed costs may appear in cash flow calculations only if it is known that they will increase directly as a result of accepting the project.
- **Interest payments**: in most cases it can be assumed that the cost of interest has already been taken into account in the discounting process as the discount factor should reflect the cost of funds for the company.
- **Book value of assets**: these are not cash flows and fall into the same category as depreciation.
- **Sunk costs**: these are costs already incurred and should be ignored, as they are not affected by and do not vary with the investment decision about to be undertaken.

The **relevant costs** and benefits required for decision-making are only those that will be affected by the decision. These are the future cash flows, which will differ between the various alternatives being considered. These **differential or incremental cash flows** should be taken into account and cash flows that are the same for all alternatives are irrelevant. Relevant costs include:

- **Incremental working capital** related to the project such as increased/decreased levels of stock, debtors and trade creditors which represent a cash outflow must be included in the investment appraisal. At the end of the project these levels will fall and any investment in working capital will be recovered and this cash flow must be accounted for.
- The **opportunity cost** of using an asset for one purpose rather than another. For example using raw materials, already available in stock, in the new project, which could have been used elsewhere.

In cash flow calculations the various cash flows are assumed to occur at the end of the time period in which they arise. For example, if revenues are earned or costs incurred throughout the course of a year, they are assumed to occur at the end of the year in question. Making this assumption of treating cash flows later than they actually occur introduces a bias which tends to understate the NPV, as future cash flows tend to be inflows. If cash flows occur at the beginning of a year, they are assumed to occur at the end of the previous year. However using a spreadsheet package, there is nothing difficult in timing the cash flows in intervals of months, weeks or days.

Example 7.8 *Investment appraisal application*

Scribes plc has over the past four years spent €3 million on the development of a new silicon chip and is now considering whether to manufacture this silicon chip. An initial investment of €5 million in plant and machinery will be needed at the end of December 2000. Additional working capital of €2.1 million will be required when production starts in January 2001. Sales and selling prices are expected to be as follows:

Year	2001	2002	2003	2004	2005
Sales (€000)	100	100	100	80	80
Price per unit €	120	120	120	100	90

The company depreciates plant and machinery over five years, using the straight-line method and assumes a zero scrap value. Variable costs per unit are expected to be €65. Fixed costs, including depreciation, are €3 million per year. Assume all revenues and costs occur at the end of the year in question.

(a) Calculate the cash flows relevant to a decision to manufacture the silicon chips, assuming it is now December 2000.

Answer
Option 1: The €3 million already invested in the development of the silicon chip is an irrelevant cost. The cash outflow at the end of 2000 is €7.1 million. This is made up of €5 million in plant and machinery and €2.1 million in working capital. The recovery of working capital of €2.1 million is entered as a cash inflow at the end of 2005. Fixed costs are €3 million *less* a depreciation charge of €1 million per annum over the five years. The contribution for each year is (price – variable cost)(sales units). In the case of 2001 the contribution is (€120 – €65)(100,000) = €5,500,000. (All figures in €000)

Year	2000	2001	2002	2003	2004	2005
Total contribution	0	5,500	5,500	5,500	2,800	2,000
Less fixed costs		(2,000)	(2,000)	(2,000)	(2,000)	(2,000)
Profit		3,500	3,500	3,500	800	0
Plant and equipment	(5,000)					
Working capital	(2,100)					2,100
Net cash flow	(7,100)	3,500	3,500	3,500	800	2,100

Developing the example above further, suppose Scribes plc has a second option for this silicon chip project.

Option 2: Sell the know-how associated with the development of the silicon chip for a royalty of €10 per unit to another company. If this second option is taken, then the company will not manufacture the chips itself. Assume the anticipated sales are the same as above. The company discounts projects at the WACC, which is 12%. Assume all revenues and costs occur at the end of the year in question.

(b) Calculate the net present value of each option.

Answer

Option 1

Year	Cash flow (€000)	Discount factor 12%	Present value (€000)
0	(7,100)	1.000	(7,100)
1	3,500	0.893	3,126
2	3,500	0.797	2,790
3	3,500	0.712	2,492
4	800	0.636	509
5	2,100	0.567	1,191
		Net present value =	€3,008

The NPV of the net cash flows above at 12% is €3.008 million.

Net cash flow for option 2 is just sales in units at €10 per unit. There is no initial investment in plant and machinery and no working capital necessary.

Year	2000	2001	2002	2003	2004	2005
Total royalty (€000)	0	1,000	1,000	1,000	800	800

The present value of these cash inflows at 12% is €3.364 million. The option with the higher present value is option 2.

7.8 Inflation and investment appraisal

Inflation generally alters the cash flows associated with projects by reducing the real value of future cash flows and increasing their uncertainty. There are two approaches appropriate to dealing with inflation.

1. Adjust future cash flows to reflect inflationary impact to find the nominal or money values and discount these nominal values at the nominal cost of capital.
2. Deflate the nominal cash flows by the inflation rate to express cash flows in real terms (adjusted for inflation) and discount these real cash flows at the real cost of capital.

The real cost of capital (r) is the nominal amount adjusted for inflation using the following formula:

$$r = \frac{(1 + m)}{(1 + i)} - 1 \qquad (7.9)$$

where m and i are the money and inflation rates respectively.

Example 7.9 *Inflation and investment*

A project has the following cash flows before allowing for inflation

Year	Real cash flow (€m)
0	(7.5)
1	3.3
2	2.42
3	5.32

The discount rate including an allowance for inflation of 5% per annum is 15.5%. Evaluate the project using the NPV criteria.

Answer
Using nominal values the future cash flows need to be inflated by 5% per annum and then discounted by 15.5% to give an NPV of €1.5 million.
   If we are using real values we need to calculate the real discount rate.

$$r = \frac{(1 + 0.155)}{(1 + 0.05)} - 1 = 0.1 \text{ and so r} = 10\%$$

The real cash flows above are then discounted at 10% to give an NPV of €1.5 million. The result is the same in both cases and the project is viable.
   Inflation affects costs and revenues differently and this must be taken into account. This is much more easily dealt with using nominal cash flows and discount rates. In a survey carried out by Drury, Braund, Osborne and Tayles on 260 UK manufacturing firms, the majority of companies did not account for inflation appropriately in the investment appraisal process and often got misleading results.

7.9 Taxation and investment appraisal

Taxation plays an important part in any investment decision. Estimates must be made of the benefits and liabilities that arise as a result of corporate taxation. The corporate tax system allows companies to write off capital expenditure by means of capital allowances. The capital expenditure is written off against taxable profits, thus reducing tax payable and increasing cash inflow. The rules of the writing-down allowances are dictated by government, vary from country to country and change over time. Apart from capital expenditure allowances, relief for revenue expenditure includes cost of materials, wages, production overheads etc.

The rate of corporation tax also varies. In Ireland corporate taxation has been decreasing over recent years with the government's stated objective being to reduce it to 12.5% by 2003. Tax relief for interest payments should be incorporated into the cost of capital discount factor and should not therefore be included in the cash flow forecasts.

Box 7.1 Investment in mobile phone licences

The bids of more than €50 billion for the next generation of German mobile phone licences are already having a damaging impact on world stock market prices. The valuations being attached have not been calculated on the basis of any recognised criteria. There has been no evidence that the assets have been properly valued, that discounted cash flow projections have been employed or that even subjective models of future consumer behaviour have been used to forecast profit, loss and cash flow.

Instead the licences have been bought almost on instinct. It is a huge gamble, perhaps the biggest gamble in the history of capitalism, and it has been a feature of several markets in recent weeks and months: London, Amsterdam and Frankfurt. It is as if conventional means of assessing risk have been thrown out the window.

Editorial, *Sunday Business Post*, 27 August 2000

The Irish corporate tax system

An Irish resident company is chargeable to corporation tax on its worldwide profits and capital gains. It must pay its tax liability six months after the end of the accounting period within which the taxable profits arise. The standard rates of Irish corporation tax are as follows:

Period	Rate
1 January 2000 to 31 December 2000	24%
1 January 2001 to 31 December 2001	20%
1 January 2002 to 31 December 2002	16%
1 January 2003 onwards	12.5%

There is also a higher rate of corporation tax of 25% which applies to the following income:

- Income from developing land (excluding construction operations, taxed at rates above) and income derived from dealing in residential land (taxed at effective rate of 20%)
- Income from mining activities and petroleum activities
- Rental income
- Untaxed interest and income from foreign property.

Capital gains are taxable at 20% on disposals made after 3 December 1997.

Capital allowances

In computing company profits no relief is given for depreciation on fixed assets. Instead, the company is given a tax deduction known as a capital allowance over several years (depending on the 'tax life' of the asset) until the cost of the asset is fully allowed.

The current rates of **annual writing-down allowances** for the main categories of assets are as follows:

Expenditure on	Plant and machinery	Industrial buildings	Hotels	Farm buildings
Annual allowance	20%	4%	15%	15%

Accelerated allowances are available in respect of expenditure incurred on the construction or refurbishment of **industrial** and **commercial** buildings (as defined by the Tax Acts) in certain renewal incentive areas. The term 'accelerated' simply means that the allowances can be claimed more quickly than for buildings in non-designated/incentive areas, as can be seen from the following chart:

Area period	Qualifying	Comments	Rates for investment in industrial/commercial buildings
Qualifying urban renewal areas	1/8/98 to 31/12/2002		Maximum relief 100%: Lessor: 1st year 25% *plus* 4% p.a. thereafter Owner occupier: 50% *plus* 4% p.a. thereafter
Qualifying rural renewal areas	to 31/12/2002		Maximum relief 100%: Lessor: 1st year . 25% *plus* 4% p.a. thereafter Owner occupier: 50% *plus* 4% p.a. thereafter
Park and ride facilities	1/7/99 to 30/6/2003		Maximum relief 100%: Lessor: 1st year 50% *plus* 4% p.a. thereafter Owner occupier 100%
Multi-storey car parks	1 /7/95 to 30/6/98	For car parks outside Dublin & Cork extended to 31/12/2002 provided 15% of exp. incurred before 1/9/00	Maximum relief 50%: Lessor: 1st year 25% *plus* 2% p.a. thereafter Owner occupier: 50%
Childcare facilities	Post 1/12/99		Maximum relief 100%: Lessor: 1st year 50% *plus* 4% p.a. thereafter Owner occupier: 100%

Note: The lessor/landlord gets an initial or first year allowance at a fixed rate, which has to be claimed in the first year of letting (whether or not there is sufficient income to shelter), otherwise it is forfeited.

The owner-occupier can claim **free depreciation** which allows him/her to claim an allowance up to a maximum stated percentage of the qualifying expenditure. This allows the taxpayer to match the allowances claimed to the income being sheltered, thus using the allowances more tax efficiently.

Example 7.10 Taxation and inflation

Scobie plc is an Irish company specialising in the production of electric drills and has just developed a new model. The company is considering the purchase of new plant and machinery for €20 million to produce the new model of electric drill over the next five years. At the end of year 5 the plant and machinery will have a zero scrap value.

If production were to commence, 200,000 drills per annum will be produced and sold over the next five years at a price of €200 per drill. Budgeted operating costs are €140 per drill. Corporation tax in Ireland is currently 24% in 2000, and will be 20% in 2001, 16% in 2002 and 12.5% from 2003 onwards. There is a one year delay in the payment of taxation to the tax authorities. Capital allowances in Ireland are 15% per annum on a straight-line basis over the life of the plant and machinery, which in this case is taken to be five years. (The rate of capital allowances on plant and machinery is now 20% (Finance Bill 2001)). The company requires a money rate of return of 15.5% per annum and inflation is expected to be at 5% per annum over the next five years. Operating cash flows can be assumed to take place at year-ends.

Evaluate this project using the NPV technique with the information available above.

Answer
The net cash flow per unit is €200 – €140 = €60.

Therefore total net cash flow before taxation = €60 (200,000) = €12 million, but with an inflation allowance, rising by 5% each year as follows:

Year 1	€12 million (1.05)	€12.6 million
Year 2	€12.6 million (1.05)	€13.23 million
Year 3	€13.23 million (1.05)	€13.89 million
Year 4	€13.89 million (1.05)	€14.59 million
Year 5	€14.59 million (1.05)	€15.32 million

The capital allowances are €20 million (0.15) = €3 million.

The €3 million capital allowance occurs in each of the first four years and the balancing allowance will be €8 million in the fifth year, i.e. €20 million – €12 million = €8 million.

Taxable profit and tax liability (€ millions) are given in the following table:

Year	Net cash flow	Capital allow.	Taxable profit	Tax rate	Tax
1	12.6	3	9.6	24%	2.304
2	13.23	3	10.23	20%	2.046
3	13.89	3	10.89	16%	1.743
4	14.59	3	11.59	12.5%	1.448
5	15.32	8	7.32	12.5%	0.914

The net present value of the investment (€m) is as follows:

Year	0	1	2	3	4	5	6
Plant & equipment	(20)						
Operating cash flows		12.6	13.23	13.89	14.59	15.32	
Taxation			(2.304)	(2.046)	(1.743)	(1.448)	(0.914)
Net cash flow	(20)	12.6	10.926	11.846	12.843	13.867	(0.914)
Discount at 15.5% (df)	1.000	0.866	0.750	0.650	0.562	0.487	0.421
Present value	(20)	10.909	8.190	7.688	7.217	6.746	(0.385)

The NPV is €20.37 million and the project is therefore viable.

7.10 Empirical evidence of appraisal techniques

The empirical literature relating to investment evaluation techniques used in business is extensive and the following is a brief summary of the main findings.

1. The payback is the most popular technique used as it focuses on liquidity.
2. The IRR technique is the most commonly used DCF method as it is the most easily understood.
3. Companies prefer to use a combination of payback and DCF.
4. The use of qualitative judgment is an important complement to the quantitative techniques available (section 7.14).
5. The ARR is still very popular despite its limitations.

7.11 Risk and project appraisal

Management does not have precise forecasts about the future cash flows related to a particular project and a certain level of risk exists in all forecasting. Risk describes a situation where there is more than one possible outcome in the future. Risk, however, also implies a likelihood or probability associated with each potential outcome. Risk should not be confused with uncertainty, which implies that it is not possible to assign such probabilities. The risk associated with investment appraisal is business risk, not financial risk, which is dealt with in Chapters 3 and 8. There are **six common methods** used to adjust the project appraisal technique and incorporate some form of risk assessment.

1. **The discounted payback method**: is one way of incorporating risk into the investment appraisal. Since this has already been discussed, the focus will be on the remaining five methods.
2. **Risk adjusted discount rate**: This method handles the riskiness of a project by adjusting the cost of capital or discount rate and using the new rate as the required rate of return on the project. The advantages associated with this technique are:

- It is easy to understand.
- Different rates can be applied to different projects exhibiting different risk profiles.

- It adjusts for the timing of cash flows, while simultaneously incorporating risk into the analysis.

The disadvantage mainly concerns the arbitrary/subjective nature of the adjustment process

Example 7.11 Adjusting the discount rate

Refer back to example 7.4 in which an IRR was calculated.

Year	Cash flow
0	(€75,000)
1	€20.000
2	€30,000
3	€50,000

The NPV at a discount rate of 12% was a positive score of €2,370 and the project is therefore viable if the company's required rate of return is 12%. Risk could be incorporated into the decision-making process by adjusting the discount rate, for example increasing the discount rate to incorporate a safety cushion for risk. By adding 2% to reflect risk and again appraising the project using the NPV criteria, the result is a negative score of (€640) and the company would therefore reject this project.

The capital asset pricing model can be used to calculate the risk-adjusted discount rate (see Chapter 9).

3. **Certainty equivalents**: This method takes into account the riskiness of a project by adjusting (multiplying) the expected cash flows by a factor known as the certainty equivalent (CE) coefficient. The CE coefficient has a value between 0 and 1 and the more risky a cash flow, the lower will be the CE coefficient. More distant cash flows tend to exhibit greater degrees of uncertainty and therefore attract lower CEs. The technique has the advantage of

- adjusting for both the timing and the risk associated with expected future cash flows.
- It also adjusts for risk by modifying separately the net cash flow for each period and incorporates the decision-maker's utility preference with respect to risk directly.

The major disadvantage of this method lies with the estimation of the CEs, which may be arbitrary scores displaying the decision-maker's bias.

Example 7.12 Certainty equivalent

Using example 7.4 again

Year	Cash flow	CE score	Adjusted cash flow
0	(€75,000)	1	(€75,000)
1	€20.000	0.9	€18,000
2	€30,000	0.8	€24,000
3	€50,000	0.7	€35,000

The cash flows are then discounted at the company's target rate of return and if the NPV is still positive the project is accepted.

4. **Sensitivity analysis:** This is a procedure which measures the impact that a change in one or more input variables may have on the investment appraisal. It asks by what percentage could an assumption or parameter change for the worse before there would be an NPV of zero. For example input variables such as initial investment, price per unit, variable cost per unit, corporate tax rates, the discount rate etc. could be altered to identify new NPVs. Sensitivity analysis is useful in identifying the variables which, if changed, have the greatest impact on the NPV or IRR of a project. It is also useful in monitoring marginally accepted investment projects, in order to determine whether they should be continued or terminated. The difficulties associated with sensitivity analysis are identifying precisely the relationships between variables and the NPV, and the final decision is again a subjective one.

Example 7.13 Sensitivity analysis

Dugeen plc is considering a project with the following cash flows:

Year	Initial cost	Running cost	Savings
0	(€7,000)		
1		(€2,000)	€6,000
2		(2,500)	€7,000

Measure the sensitivity of the project to changes in the levels of expected costs and savings if the company's cost of capital is 8%.

Answer

Year	DF at 8%	PV of initial	PV of running	PV of savings	PV net c/f
0	1.000	(€7,000)			(7,000)
1	0.926		(€1,852)	€5,556	€3,704
2	0.857		(€2,143)	€5,999	€3,856
Total		(€7,000)	(€3,995)	€11,555	€560

The project has a positive NPV and is viable. The changes in the cash flows necessary to have an NPV of zero are as follows:

The initial cost would need to increase by €560/€7,000 or 8%, the running costs would need to increase by €560/€3,995 or 14% and the savings would have to fall by €560/€11,555 or 4.8%. The savings are the most sensitive variable.

5. **Probability distributions and decision trees**: When considering an investment decision it may be possible to make several predictions about alternative future outcomes and to assign probabilities to them. This approach generates a probability distribution of NPVs from the yearly probability distributions of net cash flows. In its simplest form these alternatives would include optimistic, most likely and pessimistic estimates. Statistical measures of expected value (return) and standard deviation (risk) can then be used to identify the expected NPV of a project and the probability of a negative NPV of a project (see Chapter 9).

A decision tree is a graphical method of showing all the possible outcomes that may result from a particular situation and their probabilities of occurrence.

The probability distribution approach specifies a risk profile associated with a project in a quantifiable fashion, helping to identify the expected value of NPV and the probability of a negative NPV. However it is not easy to understand. It is difficult to estimate probability distributions accurately, and again, subjective estimates may be biased towards the personal opinion of the decision-maker. Decision trees facilitate the process by giving a visual dimension to the decision-maker.

Example 7.14 Probability and expected values

Find the expected value of the NPV of the following project, which has an initial investment of €11,000 and the company's cost of capital is 15%.

The cash flows and probability estimates for the project are given below.

Outcome	Probability	Year 1	Year 2	Year 3	Year 4
Optimistic	0.3	€5,000	€6,000	€4,500	€5,000
Most likely	0.5	€3,500	€4,000	€3,800	€4,500
Pessimistic	0.2	€3,200	€3,600	€3,100	€4,000
Expected value		€3,890	€4,520	€3,870	€4,550

The expected values of the cash flows are given in the final row of the table above. For example the expected value in year 1 is found by multiplying the cash flows by their associated probabilities and adding the results $(0.3)(€5,000) + (0.5)(€3,500) + (0.2)(€3,200) = €3,890$.

The NPV is found by discounting each of these expected cash flows as follows:

$$NPV = -11,000 + (3,890)(0.870) + (4,520)(0.756) + (3,870)(0.658) + (4,550)(0.572)$$
$$= €950$$

6. **Simulation**: This is a risk analysis method that involves utilising predetermined probability distributions and random numbers to estimate, using a computer, a distribution

of possible NPVs. The approach requires the construction of a probability distribution for each factor affecting net cash flows. Then using a computer, a random observation from each probability distribution is selected and a net cash flow is created. These random net cash flows are then used to estimate a distribution of possible NPVs. This distribution is then analysed using statistical information of expected value and standard deviation to determine whether or not to accept the project. The technique is a sophisticated one but does not give clear investment advice. The rational investment decision would be to accept projects with the highest expected return and lowest risk. It does not offer a decision rule to indicate whether a project's expected NPV is sufficient to compensate for its risk as measured by the standard deviation of the distribution of possible NPVs.

7.12 Empirical evidence of risk assessment

There have been several empirical studies carried out to ascertain evidence on the risk assessment methods used in practice. There has been a positive trend developing, in the adoption of risk evaluation techniques, facilitated in no small way by the availability of financial software packages. The most common method used is sensitivity analysis, followed by the risk-adjusted discount rate and the adjusted payback method.

7.13 Asset replacement with unequal lives

If a company has a choice between two machines with different asset lives, then it would be a mistake to simply choose one machine on the basis of net present value alone without considering the time scales of the investments. When choosing between mutually exclusive projects with unequal lives, an investment appraisal technique that is often used is the equivalent annual cost method.

$$\text{Equivalent annual cost (EAC)} = \frac{\text{Present value cost over one replacement cycle}}{\text{Annuity factor for that cycle}} \quad (7.10)$$

Example 7.15 Unequal lives

A company has a choice between two machines with unequal lives and the following cash outflows:

Year	Machine A	Machine B
0	(€60,000)	(€75,000)
1	(€15,000)	(€10,000)
2	(€15,000)	(€10,000)
3	(€15,000)	(€10,000)
4		(€10,000)
Present value at 12%	(€96,030)	(€105,370)

The cumulative present value factor (annuity factor) for three years at 12% is 2.402 and 3.037 for four years.

Machine A: EAC = €96,030/2.402 = €39,979
Machine B: EAC = €105,370/3.037 = €34,695

The machine with the lowest equivalent annual cost should be chosen and machine B in this example is the better choice.

7.14 Qualitative factors

It is not always easy to quantify the benefits of a project in monetary terms. A company may invest in improved safety facilities for its employees or improving the recreational facilities available to employees. Company policies of this nature have a cost that is quantifiable, but the resulting benefits may be difficult to put a figure on. A **cost benefit analysis** can be carried out on these types of projects. This type of analysis includes a wider range of factors than would be involved in the traditional investment appraisal. Cost benefit analysis was applied on the ring road in Dublin with qualitative factors such as travel time saved and reduction in gridlock assessed as benefits. It is important to be aware of projects that may be a lot more difficult to appraise due to the nature of the extra qualitative variables involved.

Other forms of corporate investment may be undertaken for strategic reasons without any quantifiable appraisal used. The introduction of advanced manufacturing techniques forced companies to change their production techniques to achieve manufacturing excellence This led to reduced labour costs, defective production, delivery times and inventory levels as well as improved quality and greater flexibility due to **economies of scope**. Economies of scope is the potential for low-cost production of high-variety and low-volume products

The development of the Internet and dot.com companies in the past few years has added a new dimension to business and investment appraisal. The development of a website became not so much a choice for a company, but a necessary strategy for survival and growth. Internet online business is growing at a rapid pace and right across all business sectors new ways of doing business are emerging, new markets are opening and new opportunities are coming on stream. This type of investment decision does not lend itself to traditional investment appraisal techniques, as the benefits associated with developing Internet business, although very real, are difficult to quantify.

7.15 Conclusion

In this chapter methods of investment appraisal were assessed with the net present value technique considered the soundest academically. The problems associated with inflation, taxation, capital rationing, unequal project lives and incorporating risk into the investment appraisal were all discussed.

Empirical evidence indicates a difference in preferences between the academic world and the real world. Successful investments usually rest more on quality management in the earlier stages of the decision-making process rather than the pure quantitative stages of the appraisal level. Issues of human communication, enthusiasm and commitment are vital components in the successful company.

SUMMARY

- Investment appraisal techniques include payback, accounting rate of return, net present value, internal rate of return and discounted payback.
- Each of these techniques has advantages and disadvantages.
- Empirical evidence suggests that payback is the most commonly used technique, usually in conjunction with other techniques. Academics prefer NPV.
- In a single period capital rationing situation the profitability index provides a ranking of investments assuming investments are divisible, non-deferrable and non-repeatable.
- Only relevant cash flows should be included in the appraisal of an investment.
- Inflation, taxation and risk should be accounted for in the appraisal.
- Asset replacement with unequal lives decisions can be accommodated applying the equivalent annual cost method.
- Sometimes investments are made for strategic reasons, which do not lend themselves to traditional investment appraisal techniques.

QUESTIONS

1. The ARR method has weaknesses, but is still a popular technique. Explain.
2. What is the difference between soft and hard capital rationing?
3. What is the equivalent annual cost method and where is it useful?
4. Explain the difference between risk and uncertainty.
5.♦ A company is considering four projects at present and the following information is available:

Project A: This would involve an initial outlay of €20,000 and a further outlay of €20,000 after one year. Cash profits thereafter would be as follows:

Year 2	€15,000
Year 3	€12,000
Years 4–8	€8,000.

Project B: This is a long-term project, involving an initial outlay of €32,000 and annual cash profits of €4,500 in perpetuity.

Project C: This would involve an initial outlay of €50,000 on equipment and €15,000 on working capital. The investment in working capital would be increased to €21,000 at the end of the first year. Annual cash profits would be €18,000 per annum for five years, at the end of which time the investment in working capital would be recovered.

Project D: This involves an initial outlay of €20,000 and annual cash profits as follows:

Years 1 to 5	€5,000
Years 6 to 10	€4,000
Years 11 to infinity	€3,000.

The company discounts all projects of ten years' duration or less at a cost of capital of 12% and all other projects at a cost of 15%. Calculate the net present value of each project and comment on the results you have found.

6. A labour-saving machine costs €60,000 and will save €24,000 per annum at current wage rates. The machine is expected to have a three year life and a zero scrap value. The company discounts all investment projects at 10%. Calculate the project's NPV if there is no inflation.

   Calculate the project's NPV if general inflation in wage rates is 15% per annum.

7. Scribes plc is considering buying a new machine and has two mutually exclusive projects available to it. The following data is available to assess this investment project:

	A	B
Cost (immediate outlay)	€93,000	€60,000
	Expected annual net profit (loss)	
Year 1	€29,000	€18,000
Year 2	(€1,000)	(€2,000)
Year 3	€9,000	€8,000

The company discounts all projects at its weighted average cost of capital of 10%. In calculating net profit the company uses the straight-line method of depreciation and both machines have a zero residual value.

Calculate for each project the payback period, the net present value, and comment on your results.

8.♦ KD plc is a company which has just received a quotation of €44,700 for the installation of insulation in its office building during December 2000. The following information is available to assist in the evaluation of this project.

   The fuel bill for 2000 is expected to be €100,000. Fuel prices are expected to increase by 5% per year.

   The insulation is expected to save 10% of the fuel bill.

   The company is moving premises in six years' time and because of the uncertainties involved, the company has decided to ignore any effect of the improvement on the sale value of the building.

   The company discounts all projects at its weighted average cost of capital of 14%. Assume that all cash flows arise at the end of the year in which they occur.

   Calculate the payback period, the net present value and the approximate internal rate of return for the project and make a recommendation based on your results.

9. Explain four techniques of investment appraisal and comment on the strengths and weaknesses of each method.

10. You have been asked by a client, Paul White, who is the prospective purchaser of a new car, to write a report on the following four financing options available to him:
    (a) €10,500 cash now.
    (b) three consecutive annual payments of €4,000, with the first one now (discount factor 12% p.a.).

(c) €1,200 deposit now, and 35 monthly payments of €300, the first one in exactly one month from now (discount factor = 1% per month).

(d) 36 monthly payments of €330, the first one now (discount factor = 1% per month).

Using the criteria of net present value, evaluate these four methods and in your report identify the most economical method of paying for the car. Use discount formular, not discount tables to calculate the discount factors required.

11. Manual plc is considering the introduction of semi-automatic or fully automatic equipment in its production process. At present (2000) annual cash outflows are €185,000 and annual cash inflows are €225,000 and will remain as such until the end of 2005.

The following estimates are the future likely cash flows resulting from the use of the new equipment. All equipment would need replacing in 2005, the cost of capital is 10% and all cash flows are in €000s.

	Semi-automatic	Fully automatic
2000	–50	–150
2001	0	–50
2002	+60	+50
2003	+100	+150
2004	+100	+200
2005	+100	+200

Evaluate the three options using the NPV criteria.

12. ♦ An Irish multinational corporation with a strong export trade to the United States is considering the development of a subsidiary there. All relevant information follows:

(a) The initial investment is $40 million and the existing spot rate is €1 = $1.05. In addition $20 million is needed for working capital at the start of the project which will be recovered at the end of the project.

(b) The price, demand and variable cost are as follows:

Year	Price	Demand	Variable cost
1	$500	40,000	$30
2	$511	50,000	$35
3	$530	60,000	$40

(c) The fixed costs are estimated to be $6 million per year.

(d) The exchange rate of the dollar is expected to be $1.07 at the end of year 1, $1.09 at the end of year 2 and $1.11 at the end of year 3.

(e) The American Government will impose corporation tax of 30% on income. The Irish Government will allow a tax credit on remitted earnings and will not impose any additional taxes.

(f) All cash flows received by the subsidiary are to be sent to the parent at the end of each year.

(g) The plant and machinery are depreciated over eight years using the straight-line method, i.e. $5 million per year.

(h) At the end of three years the subsidiary is to be sold and the parent company expects to receive $60 million (including working capital) net of all taxes.

If the company requires a 20% rate of return, determine whether the project is viable using net present value technique.

13. An Irish multinational is thinking of expanding its subsidiary in the US. The following projections and relevant data have been compiled for the analysis:
Initial investment $9.5 million now. Current exchange rate €1 = $1.05.
Cash profits $3 million per year for the first year increasing by 10% per annum over the following 4 years.
US corporation tax 30%.
Irish corporation tax is 30%, but given the rate of tax in the US a double taxation agreement exists between the two countries and there is no tax in Ireland for remitted earnings from subsidiaries.
Required rate of return 12%.
Forecasted exchange rate starting at the end of year 1:

	Year 1	Year 2	Year 3	Year 4	Year 5
€1 =	$1.05	$1.05	$1.00	$1.00	$0.95

Find the net present value of this project from both the subsidiary and the Irish parent company's perspective and comment on your results.

14. A company is considering which of two mutually exclusive projects it should undertake. Relevant cash flow projections are as follows:

Year	Project A	Project B
0	(€200,000)	(€200,000)
1	€35,000	€218,000
2	€80,000	€10,000
3	€90,000	€10,000
4	€75,000	€4,000
5	€20,000	€3,000

(a) If the company target rate of return is 10%, what is the net present value of each project?
(b) Find the internal rate of return and recommend which of the two projects should be undertaken.

15.♦ Scribes plc has two courses of action open to it
(a) Sell the company for an offer of €200 million. This offer was received today informally for the company's shares.
(b) Continue with existing operations and no further capital investment, with projected financial data for the next five years including inflation as follows:

Projected cash flows (€ millions)					
Year	1	2	3	4	5
Sales	260	275	255	215	185
Variable costs	150	160	145	125	105
Fixed costs	45	45	45	45	45
Depreciation charge	40	30	25	20	10

Tax may be assumed to be payable in the year that the income arises and the tax rate is expected to remain at 24% for the duration of the project. Projections continue on an annuity basis after year 5, for a further 5 years, based on the results in year 5. The company has 50 million shares with a market value of €3.50 each. The company discounts all future cash flows at a weighted average cost of capital of 13%.

Calculate the present value of the cash flow projections above and make a recommendation.

16.♦ A company has to replace a number of machines and is faced with a choice between machine A with a life of 12 years and machine B with a life of 6 years. If machine B is used it will be replaced at the end of 6 years by another of the same type. The pattern of maintenance and running costs differs between the two types of machine and relevant data is shown below.

	Machine A	Machine B
Purchase price	€19,000	€13,000
Trade-in value	€3,000	€3,000
Annual repair costs	€2,000	€2,600
Overhaul costs	€4,000 end of year 8	€2,000 end of year 4
Financing costs	10% p.a.	10% p.a.

Calculate the equivalent annual cost of using either machine and make a recommendation.

17. Charlie Browne plc is considering the installation of new machinery in its production line. The existing machinery was bought three years ago for €27,000 and is being depreciated straight line over a ten year period at €2,500 per annum. The current market value of its old machinery is €6,000. The new machinery has a lifespan of seven years but using it would improve current production capacity. The machinery will cost €175,000 and will have a scrap value at the end of seven years of €5,000.

Information on the two pieces of machinery is as follows:

	New machinery	Existing machinery
Annual running costs	€1,700	€2,200
Annual production capacity	150,000	130,000
Variable costs per unit	€0.75	€0.90
Fixed overhead absorption rate per unit	€0.80	€0.92

Any increase in output is not expected to affect the current selling price of €2 per unit. The company target rate of return/cost of capital is 10% and corporate tax can be ignored.

Calculate the payback period, net present value and internal rate of return on an incremental basis.

18. Gobshy plc is considering if it should invest in a project costing €40,000 now. Expected sales from the project are as follows:

Probability	Sales volume (units)
0.10	2,000
0.25	6,000
0.40	8,000
0.15	10,000
0.10	14,000

Once sales are established at a certain volume in the first year, they will continue at the same volume in later years. The unit price will be €10 and the unit variable cost will be €5. Additional fixed costs will be €20,000. The project will have a life of six years, after which the equipment will be sold for €3,000. The company's cost of capital is 10%.

(a) What is the expected value of the NPV of this project?

(b) Assuming the cost of the equipment and scrap value are correct, calculate the minimum annual volume of sales required the get an NPV of zero.

APPENDIX 7 ADJUSTED PRESENT VALUE TECHNIQUE

An alternative approach to investment appraisal to the net present value technique is the adjusted present value (APV). This is an application of Modigliani and Miller propositions, which are explained in Chapter 8. The difference between the APV and NPV methods is that the APV tries to show explicitly the financial side effect of how an investment is financed. The APV suggests that the NPV of a project can be increased or decreased by the side effects of financing. The finance of a major project may change the risk profile of the existing capital structure, in which case the APV method is more appropriate.

The APV technique is applied by taking NPV as a first stage (called the base case NPV). This is evaluating the project as if it were totally financed by equity. Then the APV is introduced at a second stage by making adjustments to the base case NPV to allow for the side effects of the intended method of financing.

Method: (a) Evaluate the project as if all equity financed.

(b) Adjust for the method of finance used.

$$APV = NPV \text{ (discounted at } K_u) + DT - \text{Issue costs etc.}$$

The end result is the same as using the net present value technique, but more information is obtained because the APV shows the financial side effects explicitly.

Example
An Irish company is about to invest €1.9 million on new machinery, which will provide cost savings of €300,000 per annum indefinitely. The company is currently all equity financed with a cost of capital of 16%. The company proposes to finance the project with irredeemable debt with a 9% coupon rate. The costs of issue, which are not tax deductible, are 5% of the gross proceeds. Corporate tax is at 24%. Find the adjusted present value of the investment.

Answer

(a) Base case NPV = (€300,000/0.16) – €1.9 million = – €25,000
(b) Now adjust the base case to reflect the finance used.
     Amount raised €1.9 million/0.95 = €2 million
     Tax benefit = €2 million × 0.24 = €480,000
     Issue cost = €2 million – €1.9 million = €100,000

Finally the APV = €480,000 – €100,000 – €25,000 = €355,000 and the project is viable.

8
The Cost of Capital and Capital Structure

CHAPTER OBJECTIVES

At the end of this chapter the student should be able to

1. calculate the cost of the different sources of finance available to a company
2. understand why sources of finance are weighted using market values in calculating the weighted average cost of capital
3. appreciate the problems associated with WACC calculation in practice
4. understand the concept of financial gearing and capital structure
5. describe the traditional and Modigliani/Miller approaches to capital structure
6. understand the practical considerations and influences on the optimal capital structure debate.

INTRODUCTION

The cost of capital for a company represents the cost of the different sources of finance that a company uses, and thereby the **minimum** required rate of return on company investments. When a company uses investment appraisal techniques such as net present value, its cost of capital should be used as a minimum guide to the discount rate. The purpose of this chapter is to explain how to calculate the costs of the different sources of finance used by a company and in working out an overall average cost, to weight them according to their relative importance.

Capital structure relates to the various combinations of the different sources of finance that a company uses. The concept of an optimal capital structure is an ideal mix of finance with the lowest cost of capital, i.e. the lowest overall rate of return that needs to be paid on funds provided. If the cost of capital is low then the discounted value of future cash flows generated by the company is high, resulting in a high overall value for the company. If a company raises capital by the cheapest and most efficient means, the cost of capital will be minimised and the company value is maximised.

8.1 Cost of different sources of finance

Companies are rarely financed by just one source of capital and in the main tend to use a mixture of both debt and equity capital. In this section we consider each of the different sources of long-term finance available to a company and how to calculate their cost.

8.2 Equity

Equity capital can be raised by issuing new shares or by using the retained earnings of a company. Although retained earnings do not have any servicing costs, they have an opportunity cost equivalent to the ongoing cost of equity, since if these funds were returned to the shareholders they could make good use of these funds by investing in other firms and obtaining a return.

The fundamental theory of share values states that the market price of a share should reflect its future income stream discounted at the shareholders' cost of equity (K_e).

$$P_0 = d/(1 + K_e) + d/(1 + K_e)^2 + d/(1 + K_e)^3 \ldots \ldots \text{in perpetuity}$$

The sum of the discount factors tends in the limit to the finite progression $1/K_e$

This implies in the limit

$$P_0 = d/K_e \qquad \text{or} \qquad K_e = d/P_0 \qquad (8.1)$$

i.e. the dividend yield, where P_0 is the market price of the share ex dividend and 'd' is a constant dividend in perpetuity. The share price ex dividend implies the current dividend has been paid out and is not reflected in the current share price.

Like all theoretical models the theory is based on several assumptions:

1. New funds are invested in projects with similar business risk to existing operations.
2. There is no change in the capital structure of the company.
3. Shareholders have perfect information about future dividends etc.

Example 8.1 Cost of equity

A company has in issue equity with a current price ex dividend of €3. Dividends recently paid were 45c per share and this is expected to remain constant in perpetuity. What is the cost of equity capital?

$$K_e = d/P_0 = 45c/300c = 15\%$$

Dividend growth model (Gordon's)

Shareholders will normally expect dividends to increase over the years and not to remain constant in perpetuity.

Myron Gordon developed the model to reflect dividend growth over time.

$$P_0 = d(1 + g)/(1 + K_e) + d(1 + g)^2/(1 + K_e)^2 + d(1 + g)^3/(1 + Ke)^3 \ldots \ldots \text{in perpetuity}$$

$$\text{This can be reduced to } P_0 = \frac{d(1 + g)}{(Ke - g)} \qquad \text{(see proof in Appendix 8A)}$$

$$\text{This implies} \qquad K_e = \frac{d\,(1 + g)}{P_0} + g \qquad \text{or} \qquad K_e = \frac{d_1}{P_0} + g \qquad (8.2)$$

where K_e is the cost of equity
   d is the current dividend (to be paid shortly or just paid)
   g is the annual growth rate
   d_1 is next year's dividend
   P_0 is the market price of the share ex dividend.

Example 8.2 Dividend growth formula

A company has in issue equity with a current price ex dividend of €9. Dividends recently paid were 45c per share and this is expected to rise by 10% per annum. What is the cost of equity capital?

Answer

$$Ke = \frac{45c(1 + 0.10)}{900c} + 0.10 = 0.155 \text{ or } 15.5\%$$

If past performance of dividends indicates growth over a number of years, it may be necessary to work out the annual growth rate before finding the cost of equity.

Example 8.3 Dividend growth rate and cost of equity

An Irish company has issued share capital of 3 million shares with a current market value of €3.27 per share cumulative of dividend. An annual dividend of €810,000 is due for payment shortly, on 31 December 2000. Over the past five years dividends (€000) have been as follows:

Year	1996	1997	1998	1999	2000
Div.	620	680	740	740	810

Find the cost of equity as of 1 January 2001.

Answer
The five years' figures indicate four years' growth from the base year, and the annual growth rate is calculated as follows:

Four years compounded is $810/620 = 1.3065 = (1 + g)^4$

By getting the fourth root of either side this implies $(1.3065)^{1/4} - 1 = g = 0.069$ or 6.9% per annum.
   The current dividend is €810,000/3,000,000 = 27c and so

$$Ke = \frac{27c(1.069)}{300c} + 0.069 = 0.165 \text{ or } 16.5\% \text{ approximately.}$$

The capital asset pricing model is an alternative model to find the cost of equity, based on market risk and this is discussed in Chapter 9.

8.3 Debt

Preference shares are often included in the debt capital of the company because they have a prior charge on the company returns. Dividends on preference shares, like ordinary share dividends, are distributed out of after-tax earnings. Preference shares are irredeemable with a constant dividend based on a percentage of the nominal value of the share. This implies the cost of preference shares is given by the expression

$$Kp = d/P_0 \qquad\qquad (8.3)$$

where Kp is the cost of preference shares, like the basic equity model above.

Example 8.4 Cost of preference shares

A company has in issue 8% preference shares with a nominal value of €1. The shares are currently trading at 50p ex dividend. What is the cost of preference shares?

Answer
In this case the K_p = 8c/50c = 16%

There are two types of securitised debt, irredeemable and redeemable (also known as dated debt) debentures. In the case of interest-bearing securities, the interest payments are an allowable deduction for the purposes of taxation. This reduces the after-tax cost of the debt.

   If the debentures are irredeemable and the corporate tax rate is T, then the cost of debt (Kd) after tax is

$$K_d = \frac{\text{Int}(1 - T)}{P_0} \qquad\qquad (8.4)$$

where K_d is the cost of irredeemable debt after tax
         Int is the interest to be paid annually
         P_0 is the market price of the debenture ex interest.

The cost of irredeemable debt represents the cost of continuing to use the finance rather than redeem the security at its current market price ex interest.

   If a debenture is redeemable at some time in the future, you must find an internal rate of return on the after-tax cash flows in order to get its true cost. The interest payable is tax deductible, but the capital repayment or redemption value is not. Here again the internal rate of return (IRR) represents the cost of continuing to use the finance rather than redeem the security at the current market price.

Example 8.5 Cost of redeemable debt

A company has 8% securitised debenture stock (nominal value €100) on which the interest is to be paid annually on 31 December. The stock is due for redemption at par on 1 January 2004. The market price of the debenture at 28 December 2000 is €103 cumulative of interest.

(a) What is the cost of debt capital?
(b) What is the cost of debenture stock if the rate of corporation tax is 24%?

Answer
(a) If this were irredeemable debt the cost (pre-tax) would be = €8/€95 = 8.42%
     After tax the cost of the debentures is €8 (1 − 0.24)/€95 = 6.4%
     As it is redeemable, work out an IRR on the after-tax cash flows.

	Year	Cash flow €	Cash flow after tax @ 24%
31/12/00	0	(95)*	(95)
31/12/01	1	8	6.08
31/12/02	2	8	6.08
31/12/03	3	8	6.08
01/12/04	3	100*	100

* The model is based on ex-interest market value and the debenture being redeemable at par, i.e. the same as nominal value.

If you are calculating the IRR manually and not using a spreadsheet package then a good initial discount factor to use in calculating an initial net present value is
(a) Work out the irredeemable cost and (b) adjust it by the annualised capital gain or loss.

$$(a) \quad \frac{\text{Interest}}{\text{Price ex interest } P_0} \quad + \quad (b) \quad \frac{(\text{Redeemable value} - P_0)/\text{years to maturity}}{\text{Price ex interest } (P_0)}$$

$$\frac{€8}{€95} \quad + \quad \frac{(€100 - €95)/3}{€95} \quad = \quad 0.1 \text{ or } 10\% \text{ approximately}$$

i.e. a good initial discount factor to use is approximately 10% pre tax.

Post tax uses the same procedure, i.e. €6.08/€95 + €1.67/€95 = 8.16% or initial discount factor approximately 8%.

Using a spreadsheet package like Excel, the IRR generated is 10.01% before tax and 8.02% after tax.

Other sources of funds include floating rate loans or fixed-rate bank loans, convertible debenture, eurobonds (see Appendix 8B) and overdrafts. Overdrafts are not normally a source of capital in a company, unless the overdraft is a long-term facility.

If the finance raised involves interest payments, you must allow for its tax deductibility. If for example the interest rate is variable on a loan, base the cost on the current interest rate after tax. This is only appropriate if the company is in a non-tax exhaustion position, i.e. it has taxable profits against which to set its interest payments.

Example 8.6 Cost of convertible debenture

A company has convertible debenture stock at an 8% coupon or interest rate, with a market value of €106 per cent. An interest payment has been made recently. The debentures will be convertible into equity shares at a rate of 40 shares per €100 nominal stock in three years' time. The shares are expected to have a market value of €3.50 each at that time, and all the debenture holders are expected to convert their debentures.

(a) What is the cost of capital to the company for the convertible debentures?
(b) What is the cost of capital to the company if corporation tax is at the rate of 24%? Assume that tax savings occur in the same year that the interest payments arise.

Answer

Using an Excel spreadsheet format, the initial cash flow is the market value of the debenture ex interest, i.e. €106.

The final year cash flow is based on the future market value of conversion into equity, i.e. €3.50(40) = €140.

Year	Cash flow before tax (€)	After tax @ 24%
0	−106	−106
1	8	6.08
2	8	6.08
3	8	6.08
3	140	140
Internal rate of return	(a) = 16.64%	(b) = 14.98%

8.4 General comment

Equity finance represents the highest risk category of finance to investors (and tends to be the highest cost of finance to a company), as it is at the bottom of the creditor hierarchy should a company go into liquidation. Preference shares should cost less because they are paid dividends before ordinary share dividend (less risk) and rank higher in a liquidation situation. Debts are further up the creditor ladder than equity or preference shares implying a lower cost again. This lower cost is more pronounced if the debt is secured and if rates of corporate tax are high.

8.5 Weighted average cost of capital (WACC)

Having looked at different sources of finance, it is now necessary to work out the overall cost of capital. In reality companies are rarely financed by any one particular source of finance, and use a mixture of debt and equity. It seems appropriate, therefore, to calculate an average cost of finance. To reflect the extent of each source, a weight should be attached to each separate type of finance.

The weighting of each source of finance should be based on **market values**, as book values are of doubtful economic significance. Book values are historical and rarely reflect the current required return of providers of finance. In the case of a company using only equity and irredeemable debt, the following formula expresses the overall cost of finance for a company.

$$\text{WACC} = \frac{E}{D + E} (Ke) + \frac{D(1 - T)}{D + E} (Kd) \qquad (8.5)$$

where E and D represent the market values of equity and debt.

The equation can be expanded according to the number of different sources of finance. This WACC reflects the minimum target rate of return for the company on its investment.

The major assumptions behind the WACC discussed above are:

1. That companies continue to invest in projects of a standard level of business risk to existing operations.
2. New funds are raised in the same proportion as its existing capital structure and financial risk.
3. The project is small relative to the overall size of the company.

The major criticisms are:

(a) New investments could involve different business risks.
(b) New sources of finance may change the capital structure.
(c) Floating rate debt is difficult to incorporate into the WACC.

WACC is not a static concept, as over time the market value of the securities and the cost of the various sources of finance will change. Companies should recalculate their WACC regularly to reflect any significant changes. This implies that WACC is both difficult to calculate and to apply in investment appraisal.

8.6 Practical problems in calculating WACC

There are a number of problems in calculating the WACC in practice.

1. Which model should be used to find the cost of equity? One could use either the dividend valuation model or the capital asset pricing model, both of which rely on different assumptions.
2. The market values of both debt and equity may be hard to find, as for example there may not be a continuous trading market and some forms of debt may not trade at all.
3. Many forms of debt exist, and company accounts may not always state the interest they are paying, or the maturity date. Debt may have split redemption dates or be in foreign currency form.
4. Convertible debt and floating rate debt are difficult to cost and there is the question of whether short-term debt should be included.

Example 8.7　Weighted average cost of capital

The directors of a company are considering the feasibility of issuing 12% debentures at par to raise €1,000,000 for an investment to broaden their product range. The new plant is expected to produce a return of €240,000 per year indefinitely before tax and interest charges.

The company's existing capital structure is:

Issued ordinary shares (€0.50 nominal)	€3 million
Issued 5% preference shares (€1 nominal)	€6 million.

The current market value of ordinary and preference shares is €2 and €0.80 respectively (ex dividend).

The company's current earnings before corporation tax of 50% are €3,840,000 per year. Earnings have been constant for the last number of years and are always fully distributed.

(a) Calculate the current weighted average cost of capital (WACC).
(b) If there are no changes in the cost of equity or preference capital, what would you expect the market value of the ordinary shares and WACC to be after the issue of the debentures?

Answer (a)

Market value of equity = 6,000,000 × €2 = €12,000,000
Market value of preference shares = 6,000,000 × €0.80 = €4,800,000

To find the cost of equity, you need to find the dividend available.

Annual pre-tax profit	€3,840,000
Less tax at 50%	€1,920,000
Profit after tax	€1,920,000
Less preference dividend	€300,000
Available to equity	€1,620,000

Cost of equity = Dividend available/market value of shares
         = €1,620,000/€12,000,000 = 13.5%

Cost of preference shares = €300,000/€4,800,000 = 6.25%

$$\text{WACC} = \frac{€12\text{million}}{€16.8\text{million}} \times 13.5\% \quad + \quad \frac{€4.8\text{million}}{€16.8\text{million}} \times 6.25\% \quad = 11.43\%$$

This is the current WACC and the minimum target rate of return for the company, providing it stays in the same line of business and maintains its present capital structure.

Answer (b)

New pre-tax profit	€4,080,000
Less debenture interest	€120,000
Profit before tax	€3,960,000
Less tax at 50%	€1,980,000
After tax	€1,980,000
Less preference dividend	€300,000
Available to equity	€1,680,000

If the cost of equity is constant at 13.5%, the market value can be calculated as follows:

Dividend available

Cost of equity

= €1,680,000/13.5% = €12,444,444 giving a share value of approximately €2.07 per share.

Cost of new debentures = 12%(1 – 0.5) = 6%

$$WACC = \frac{€12.44m}{€18.244} \times 13.5\% + \frac{€4.8m}{€18.244m} \times 6.25\% + \frac{€1m}{€18.244m} \times 6\% = 11.18\%$$

The answer assumes Ke, Kp and the market value of preference shares remain constant. This is an unrealistic assumption, as the issue of debt increases the financial risk of the shareholders. This idea of increasing cost of equity because of financial risk is a core element in the capital structure debate, which is now introduced.

8.7 Capital structure

Before discussing the concept of an optimal capital structure we need to explain the term **financial gearing**. Gearing refers to the amount of debt finance versus equity finance that a company has in its capital structure. As in the case of the WACC, it is based on market values rather than book values. A company's gearing can be measured using a number of ratios, for example

$$\text{Gearing ratio} = \frac{\text{Market value of debt}}{\text{Market value of debt + Market value of equity}}$$

Another measure of financial risk is interest cover

$$= \frac{\text{Profit before interest and taxation}}{\text{Interest}}$$

A high level of gearing creates financial risk and this risk is borne by the ordinary shareholders. For equity holders, financial risk is evident in the variability of earnings after deducting payments to holders of debt capital. The higher the gearing, the greater the amount of interest payments and the less the proportion of earnings available to equity, leading to a perceived financial risk for ordinary shareholders. This financial risk requires a reward in the form of a risk premium and is reflected in a higher cost of equity. At very high levels of gearing a company may get into difficulty meeting its interest commitments and may face the risk of bankruptcy. If gearing levels are going to affect the cost of equity then it follows that a company's gearing could have a bearing on its WACC.

Be careful not to mix up operational gearing and financial gearing. Operational gearing represents the relationship of the fixed cost to the total cost of an operating unit. Both forms of gearing have a common feature in that an increase in either—i.e. higher fixed cost or higher debt—reduces the earnings available to shareholders and therefore increases their risk (see Chapter 3).

8.8 Theories on gearing

There has been a lot of academic literature on the subject of whether an ideal capital structure exists, and the theory can be summarised with the following two major models.

Both theories are based on the following assumptions:

1. All earnings are paid out in interest and dividends and are constant in perpetuity.
2. The gearing of a company can change by issuing debt for equity or issuing equity for debt.
3. No transaction costs exist in buying or selling shares.
4. No taxes exist, either personal or corporate.
5. Business risk is constant over time.
6. Companies can only issue irredeemable debt finance or ordinary equity shares.
7. Shareholders have perfect knowledge of all information.

8.9 The traditional approach to capital structure

The proposition here is that an optimal capital structure exists and that a company can increase its market value by using the best mix of equity and debt.

The WACC is saucer shaped and thus an ideal capital structure exists. Selecting a particular method of financing projects is therefore important.

Figure 8.1 Traditional theory of gearing

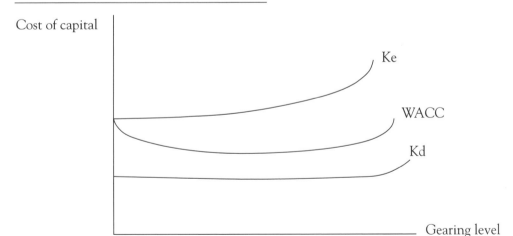

The cost of equity rises as debt increases (financial risk). The cost of debt remains unchanged up to a certain level of gearing and then increases. The WACC does not remain constant, but rather falls initially as the proportion of debt capital increases, and then begins to increase as the rising cost of equity (and possibly debt because of default risk) becomes more significant. The implication is that an optimal level of gearing does exist and is found where the WACC is at a minimum.

Example 8.8 Traditional view illustrated

Suppose a company is all equity financed with Ke =20% (= WACC). Now suppose it introduces debt capital (Kd = 10%) and its debt to equity ratio is 3:7. If the cost of equity rises because of perceived financial risk to 22%, what is the new WACC?

Answer

WACC = 7/10(22%) + 3/10(10%) = 18.4%. The WACC has been lowered with the introduction of debt.

Now suppose the company increases the proportion of debt to give a debt to equity ratio of 1:1. If the cost of equity now rises to 28%, what is the WACC?

In this case the WACC = $^1/_2$(28%) + $^1/_2$(10%) = 19% and so the WACC has started to rise again, indicating that the gearing is above the optimal level.

The traditional view has no underlying theory to show how much the cost of equity would rise due to increases in gearing, or how the cost of debt should rise because of default risk. It is purely a descriptive theory.

8.10 The net operating income approach of Modigliani and Miller

The proposition put forward by Modigliani and Miller (M & M) flew in the face of the traditional model. Their seminal paper in 1958 proposed that, for a given operating or business risk, the WACC remains unchanged at all levels of gearing, implying that no optimal capital structure exists and that how a company was financed was irrelevant.

The simple idea is that how something is financed is irrelevant. For example, if you purchase a house through a bank loan or savings, the value of the house is based on the income it can generate. How the house was financed has no impact on its resale value.

Figure 8.2 Modigliani and Miller theory of gearing without tax

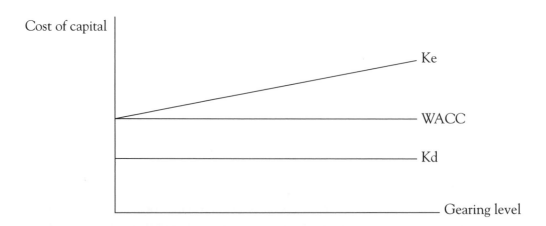

Here the cost of debt Kd remains unchanged as the level of gearing rises. The WACC is unchanged as gearing levels change. As gearing increases, the cost of equity Ke increases in such a way as to exactly offset the greater proportion of cheaper debt capital.

As the WACC remains constant, this implies the method of financing projects is irrelevant. M & M came to this conclusion based on the assumptions above, but added an extra assumption that capital markets are perfect, i.e. bankruptcy costs were zero.

Their starting point was that if two firms had similar operating and business risk, and similar earnings, then they must have the same overall value and the same WACC.

Proposition 1: Market value of the firm is independent of capital structure

$$Vg = Vu \qquad (8.6)$$

Proposition 2: Cost of equity in a geared firm is higher than that of an ungeared firm

$$Kg = Ku + \text{Premium for financial risk}$$

$$\mathbf{Kg = Ku + (Ku - Kd)\ D/E} \qquad (8.7)$$

Unlike the traditional view, this second proposition allows a way of computing the increase in the cost of equity resulting from an increase in gearing.

Vg is the value of the geared company
Vu is the value of the ungeared company
Kg is the cost of equity of the geared company
Ku is the cost of equity of the ungeared company
Kd is the cost of debt pre-tax
D and E are the market values of debt and equity respectively.

M & M developed a defence of their approach based on investor arbitrage, i.e. switching through buying/selling shares between companies. In this arbitrage process, however, investors would substitute personal gearing for corporate gearing and continue to do so, selling shares in one company and buying shares in another, until the market value of each firm is equal.

M & M argued that two companies identical in every respect except their capital structure should not have different costs of capital and therefore market valuations.

The argument is best illustrated with an example.

Example 8.9 Modigliani and Miller's theory illustrated

Suppose we have two companies A and B who are identical in every respect except for the way in which they are financed. Both are in the same risk class and have the same operating characteristics. However A is all equity financed and B has €40,000 worth of irredeemable debt at 8% interest included in its capital structure. Both companies have the same annual earnings before tax of €20,000 and these earnings are assumed to be constant in perpetuity. The cost of equity is higher in B to reflect the financial risk associated with debt capital.

The market value of both companies is as follows:

	Company A	Company B
1. Annual earnings (PBIT)	€20,000	€20,000
2. *Less* interest	—	€3,200
3. Available to equity (and distributed)	€20,000	€16,800
4. Cost of equity	13.5%	14%
5. Market value of equity (3/4)	€148,148	120,000
6. Market value of debt	—	€40,000
7. Market value of company (5 + 6)	€148,148	€160,000
8. WACC (PBIT/Market value)	13.5%	12.5%
9. Gearing ratio D/(D + E)	0%	25%

As you can see the above conforms to the traditional model, in that the two companies have different market values purely because they have different capital structures. Modigliani and Miller believed this was a short-term disequilibrium and could not last, because investors in company B could improve their return by switching companies.

If we assume an investor owns 10% of company B and receives 10% of the dividends, i.e. €1,680, the **arbitrage process** would occur as follows:

1. Sell shares in B for €12,000 (10% of €120,000)
2. Borrow €4,000 at 8%. By doing this, the investor is replicating personal gearing for the corporate gearing that exists in B (10% of €40,000). The annual interest cost is €320.
3. Invest the €16,000 in company A.

The annual return will now be

$$\frac{€16,000}{€148,148} (€20,000) \text{ } less \text{ interest of } €320 = (€ \text{ } 2,160 - €320) = €1,840$$

This is an improvement of (€1,840 – €1,680) = €160

Investors will continue to practise arbitrage, buying A shares and increasing their value (excess demand), selling B shares and depressing their value (excess supply), until the market values of the two companies are the same, and no further opportunity for arbitrage exists.

Since both the market values and the earnings in both are the same, it follows that the WACC is the same despite the difference in gearing.

Example 8.10 Modigliani and Miller and cost of equity

Crumlin is an all equity company with a 16% cost of equity. Kimmage is similar to Crumlin in all respects, except that it is a geared company financed by €1,000,000 of 5% debentures with a current market price of €50 per cent ex interest. Kimmage also has one million ordinary shares with a current market value of €1.50 ex dividend. Using the propositions of M & M, what is the cost of equity in Kimmage and what is its WACC?

Answer
Here Kd = €5/€50 = 10%, D = €500,000 and E = €1,500,000

$$K_g = K_u + (K_u - K_d)\, D/E = 16\% + (16\% - 10\%)\, \frac{€500{,}000}{€1{,}500{,}000} = 18\%$$

The company has a total market value of €2 million made up of $^1/_4$ debt and $^3/_4$ equity.

$$\text{WACC} = {}^1/_4 \times 10\% + {}^3/_4 \times 18\% = 16\%$$

Here as gearing is introduced, the cost of equity rises, but in such a way as to maintain the same WACC.

The weaknesses associated with M & M are as follows:

1. It is impossible in practice to find identical firms with different financial structures to empirically test the model.
2. The cost of borrowing tends to be higher for an individual than for a company.
3. Transaction costs can impede the arbitrage process.
4. It ignores taxation, particularly corporate taxation.
5. Earnings may be retained in practice.
6. It ignores growth and possible changes from year to year.
7. Investors are not necessarily rational and may not use arbitrage to maximise return.
8. In company A above, the investors' stake is €16,000, not €12,000.

Modigliani and Miller ignored the possibility of bankruptcy and its costs and so at high levels of gearing their theory may not be valid.

8.11 Modigliani and Miller with taxation

In M & M's second paper on capital structure in 1963 the earlier model was amended by recognising the existence of corporate taxation. Because interest is an allowable deduction for the purposes of corporate tax, the more debt a company takes on, the more of their profits the company will shield against tax. The after-tax cost of debt capital is cheaper than equity finance, and therefore the WACC will fall as debt capital is introduced. Based on this theory the balance shifts in favour of debt capital and the implication is that companies should borrow as much as possible.

Figure 8.3 Modigliani and Miller theory of gearing with tax

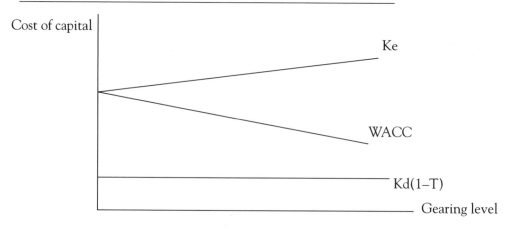

T is the rate of corporation tax.
M & M adjusted their formulae to allow for taxes

Proposition 1. $\qquad$ **Vg = Vu + DT** $\qquad$ (8.8)

Proposition 2. $\qquad$ **Kg = Ku + (1 – T)(Ku – Kd) D/E** $\qquad$ (8.9)

This implies that the WACC continues to fall up to 100% gearing levels and by implication

$$Vg > Vu \qquad [by \ DT]$$

Consider example 8.10 on capital structure and assume a corporate tax rate of 20%. The propositions above would imply that the WACC should be less than the 16% found previously.

Here Kd after tax = €5(1 – 0.2)/€50 = 8%, D = €500,000 and E = €1,500,000

$$Kg = 16\% + (1 - 0.2)(16\% - 10\%) \ \frac{€500,000}{€1,500,000} = 17.6 \ \%$$

$$WACC = {}^{1}/_{4} \times 8\% + {}^{3}/_{4} \times 17.6\% = 15.2\%, \text{ i.e. WACC is reduced.}$$

If we were to increase gearing and switch the proportions so that the company was 75% debt financed the result would be a further reduction in the WACC.

$$Kg = 16\% + (1 - 0.2)(16\% - 10\%) \ \frac{€1,500,000}{€500,000} = 30.4\%$$

WACC = ${}^{3}/_{4} \times 8\% + {}^{1}/_{4} \times 30.4\% = 13.6\%$, i.e. the higher the gearing, the lower the WACC.

There is an alternative formula to find the WACC without having to find the cost of equity in the geared company.

$$\text{WACC} = \text{Ku}\left[1 - \frac{\text{DT}}{\text{E} + \text{D}}\right] \qquad (8.10)$$

Take the example of Kimmage and Crumlin with tax at 20%.

$$\text{WACC} = 16\% \left[1 - \frac{€500{,}000\ (0.2)}{€1{,}500{,}000 + €500{,}000} = 15.2\%\right]$$

Modigliani and Miller argued that since the WACC falls as gearing rises, and the value of the company rises as WACC falls, the value of a geared company will always be higher than that of an ungeared company. The difference in value is based on the amount of debt-associated tax saving of the geared company (DT).

The positive tax effects of debt finance will be exhausted however where there is an insufficient tax liability to use the tax relief that is available (tax exhaustion). M & M defended their model using the arbitrage process. However in substituting personal gearing for corporate gearing you must allow for tax relief on corporate debt (see question 16).

Taking the earlier example of company A and company B, let us assume tax at 20% and adjust personal gearing for tax relief. In this case the investor should borrow €4,000 $(1 - 0.2) = €3{,}200$.

Companies do not follow all-debt policies, which indicates the existence of factors that undermine the tax advantages of debt finance, the most obvious being the risk of bankruptcy.

This is the risk of interest rate charges actually putting the company into liquidation and, from the shareholders' point of view, the possibility of losing the value of their initial investment, due to the position they occupy in the creditors' hierarchy.

M & M's second model ignored the market imperfection associated with bankruptcy costs. In reality there is a possibility of a company defaulting on its interest payments at high gearing levels. The costs of bankruptcy include the cost of paying lenders higher rates of interest to compensate for higher risk, the cost of employing lawyers and accountants to manage the liquidation process, and the cost of having to sell off assets below their market value. By combining the tax shield advantage of gearing with the bankruptcy costs associated with high gearing, the concept of an optimal capital structure appears again. The problem of tax exhaustion mentioned earlier is another reason why companies might try to avoid very high gearing levels.

8.12 Pecking order theory

This theory first, introduced by Donaldson (1960) and developed further by Myers (1984), suggests that financial managers **do not pursue an optimal capital structure** but that funds are raised along the line of least resistance. Consequently funds are raised in the following order:

1. **Internally generated**: This is the easiest to raise (retained earnings), with very little external scrutiny. Retained earnings are limited by the amount of cash generated from operations, and by the need to pay a dividend.
2. **Debt capital**: If insufficient funds are available from retained earnings etc. to finance new projects, various forms of debt are introduced due to low issue costs. This source of funds is limited by the company's gearing position, the probability of financial distress and the limit on borrowing imposed by lenders in restrictive covenants.
3. **Equity**: This is the last resort source of external finance, due to higher issue costs and the increased disclosure of information.

Myers suggested the order of preference relates to a form of asymmetry of information between a company and the markets. For example, suppose a company needs finance for a new project that the market undervalues. The management, with their inside information about this project, will want to finance the project through retained earnings so that, when the market finally sees the true value of the project, existing shareholders will benefit. If the retained earnings are insufficient, the management will issue debt finance in preference to equity finance, as they consider the equity to be undervalued

The consequence of this theory is that profitable companies borrow the least, as they have no need for external funds and not because they desire low gearing levels which was in sharp contrast to the idea of an optimal capital structure. Baskin also found a negative correlation between high profit levels and gearing.

8.13 Practical factors that influence a company's capital structure

1. **Tax rates**: The higher the level of corporate taxes, the more tax efficient and attractive debt capital becomes. If, however, the company becomes tax exhausted, they will not be as attracted to higher gearing levels.
2. **Asset base**: Companies with high levels of tangible assets will find it easier to take on debt, since they are in a better position to offer security in the event of bankruptcy than companies with a high level of intangible assets. The nature of the asset base has been shown empirically to affect the capital structure.
3. **Cash flow volatility**: A company with a stable cash flow can service debt capital more easily than a company with a volatile cash flow. The greater the potential variability in the projected cash flows, the more difficult it will be for a company to take on high debt levels.
4. **Interest rate levels**: Debt capital issues are attractive when interest rates are low. When interest rates are high it will be relatively expensive to attract investors in a debt issue.
5. **Stock market performance**: Where a bull market exists, with high share values, it may be attractive to issue equity as a smaller number of shares generate the finance needed.
6. **Articles of association**: This indicates what types of finance are authorised or what covenants are applicable and there may be a clause in the articles of association which restricts the ability of the company to borrow.

7. **Foreign currency operations**: A company may want to obtain finance in a foreign currency and service the capital out of their foreign currency earnings in order to minimise foreign currency exposure.

8. **Issue costs**: Debt tends to have a cheaper issuance cost than equity and no issue is needed in the caze of retained earnings.

9. **Management preference**: Retained earnings are often preferred over debt and equity issues. This is partly due to the transaction cost involved in raising the finance, but also due to the balance of ownership and control.

10. **Industry norms**: Substantial deviations from the industry norm may send the wrong signal to investors.

11. **Agency effects**: Agency problems may restrict the level of debt in a company. Agency costs arise from ensuring the agents (company management) act in the best interests of the providers of debt. For example, covenants may be placed on loans to restrict the level of dividend payments to prevent the capital base being run down, thereby increasing the risk to the lenders.

Many of these factors can have a huge impact on how a company is financed.

Box 8.1 Kerry Group and gearing levels

Kerry Group is likely to sell on a sizeable part of Bush Boak Allen (BBA) if its anticipated $1 billion bid for the business is successful, according to analysts in Dublin. One reason is that $1 billion of debt would increase Kerry's net debt to almost €1.5 billion and increase its gearing from over 100 per cent to almost 300 per cent.

Sunday Business Post, May 2000

8.14 The debate

The traditional and Modigliani and Miller theories of capital structure should be viewed as a starting point for appreciating the problems faced by a company in determining its appropriate capital structure. Debt attracts tax relief but high levels of debt can cause financial distress in a company and a financial manager must try to balance these opposing effects. The traditional model suggests an ideal capital structure exists, but gives no analytical mechanism for finding it.

In their first paper Modigliani and Miller suggested that capital structure was irrelevant, but then adjusted their model to show that with market imperfections, such as taxation and bankruptcy risk, a company should use debt capital, but avoid extremely high levels of gearing (they lead to a higher WACC).

When you look at the practical factors that a company would take on board in deciding their capital structure, it seems likely that there is a range of capital structures that could minimise WACC, rather than one optimal capital structure. Empirical research has failed to identify any unique capital structure applicable to any industry or company type. Hamada found that announcements of increased gearing levels were associated with equity value increases and reductions in gearing tend to have an adverse effect on share values. Homaifar, Zeitz and Benkato found that gearing levels tend to be higher in firms exposed to higher levels of corporate tax and that the larger the company, the higher the gearing level. Most companies are attracted to some level of gearing, but very high levels of gearing are rarely seen. The evidence seems to suggest that Modigliani and Miller are correct up to a point and that WACC falls as cheaper debt capital is introduced, but beyond which, by increasing gearing towards a 100 per cent level, the WACC begins to rise again.

Companies should perhaps pursue sensible levels of gearing, i.e. use the tax advantages of debt capital but avoid levels of debt that could cause problems of bankruptcy.

SUMMARY

- The cost of capital for a company is a fundamental determinant of its market value, as it is the basis for the discount rate in investment appraisal methods such as net present value.
- The cost of equity can be calculated based on dividend models, or risk using the capital asset pricing model.
- The cost of debt capital must be adjusted to take into account the tax deductibility of interest payments.
- The costs of individual sources of finance must be weighted according to market value if possible.
- The WACC is appropriate for appraising investments if the company's capital structure remains stable and the business risk associated is similar to existing company operations.
- Theories of capital structure include the traditional, Modigliani/Miller (pre and post corporate tax) and Donaldson's pecking order models.
- Empirical evidence suggest many practical factors influence capital structure and that the existence of an optimal capital structure is open to debate.

QUESTIONS

1. Are retained earnings a free source of finance?
2. Define capital gearing and what is meant by, a highly geared company?
3. Describe the traditional viewpoint on capital structure and its relationship with cost of capital.
4. What are the difficulties associated with finding the cost of capital in a private company?
5.♦ A convertible 8% loan stock of Tower plc currently trades at €140 per €100 nominal.
    The stock may be converted in five years' time at fifty ordinary shares per €100 of nominal stock.
    The present price of ordinary shares is €2.20 and is expected to grow by 5% per annum over the next five years.
   (a) What is the cost of the convertible loan stock?
   (b) What is the cost of capital to the company if corporation tax is at the rate of 24%? Assume that tax savings occur in the same year that the interest payments arise.

6.♦ A company has annual earnings before interest and tax of €15 million. These earnings are expected to remain constant. The market price of the company's ordinary shares is

86 cents per share cumulative of dividend and €105.5 per debenture ex interest. An interim dividend of six cents per share has been declared.

Corporation tax is at the rate of 24% and all available earnings are distributed as dividends.

The long-term capital structure of the firm is as follows:

Ordinary shares (25 cents par value)	€12.5 million
16% debentures 31/12/03 nominal €100	€23.697 million

Calculate the cost of capital of the company assuming it is now 31 December 2000.

7. The following is an extract from the balance sheet of a company:

	€000
Ordinary shares of 50c each	5,200
Reserves	4,850
9% preference shares of €1 each	4,500
14% debentures	5,000
Total long-term funds	19,550

The ordinary shares are quoted at 80c ex dividend. The dividend just paid was 4c and will grow thereafter at 12% per annum indefinitely. The preference shares are quoted at 72c (cum dividend) and the debentures are quoted at €100 ex interest (irredeemable). Corporation tax is at 24%. Find the weighted average cost of capital of the company.

8.♦ Doarunner plc is an all equity company with an equilibrium market value of €32.5 million and a cost of capital of 18% per year. The company proposes to repurchase €5 million of equity and replace it with 13% irredeemable loan stock. Doarunner's earnings before interest and tax are expected to be constant for the foreseeable future. Corporate tax is at a rate of 24%. All profits are paid out as dividends.

Using the assumptions of Modigliani and Miller explain and demonstrate how this change of capital structure will affect (a) the market value (b) the cost of equity and (c) the WACC of Doarunner plc.

9. Atack and Mariner are two companies operating in the same industry and have identical net operating incomes, which the stock market regards as being subject to the same degree of business risk. Atack is financed entirely by equity, its share capital consisting of 10 million 50c shares with a market price of €4.80 per share (ex dividend). The cost of equity of Atack is 16%. Mariner is financed by a combination of €10,000,000 12% irredeemable debenture stock (market price €120%) and 15 million €1 ordinary shares. The market price of Atack's shares and Mariner's debentures are considered to be in equilibrium. Using the Modigliani-Miller propositions calculate:

(a) the equilibrium market price of Mariner's shares.
(b) the equilibrium cost of equity for Mariner.
(c) the weighted average cost of capital of Mariner.

Assume: (i) no taxation and (ii) corporation tax at 24%, and make separate calculations for each assumption.

10. The government has just announced that corporation tax is to be reduced from 24% per year to 20% per year and the directors of your company wish to know the likely effect of this change on the company's share price and cost of capital.

    The company's current capital structure is

	€m
Ordinary shares (50c par value)	30
Share premium	48
Other reserves	62
Shareholders' equity	140
10% debentures (irredeemable)	40
	180

The company's shares are trading at €3.20 ex dividend, and the debentures at €125 ex interest. The company's current cost of equity is 14% and the tax cut is expected to increase the net present value of the company's operating cash flows by €15 million. Assume that the cost of debt and the market price of debt do not change as a result of this tax change.

(a) Estimate the company's current weighted average cost of capital.
(b) Using M & M's theory of capital structure (with tax), find the expected share price after the tax change.
(c) What is the company's expected weighted average cost of capital after the tax change?

11. Comment briefly on the practical factors which a company may take into account when determining capital structure.

12. The company's current authorised share capital consists of 4 million ordinary shares, each with a nominal value of 25c. During the past five years the number of shares in issue has remained constant at three million and the market price per share at present is €1.35 ex div. The company pays only one dividend per year and for the last five years dividends per share have been as follows:

Year	1996	1997	1998	1999	2000
Dividend	10.0c	10.8c	11.6c	13.6c	13.6c

The company has in issue €800,000 of 8% debentures redeemable at par on 31 December 2003. The current market price of these debentures is €82.5 ex interest and the interest is payable in one amount each year on 31 December.

The company also has a €900,000 bank loan repayable on 31 December 2003. The rate of interest on this loan is variable, at 1.5% above the bank's base rate, which is currently 5%. Coporation tax is 20%.

(a) Calculate the weighted average cost of capital (WACC) for the company as at 1 January 2000.
(b) What assumptions are involved if the WACC calculated above is used as a discount rate in evaluating investment projects.

13.◆(Ref. Appendix 8B) An Irish multinational company has $100 million of eurobonds issued at 6%, and redeemable at par in three years' time. The eurobond issue has a nominal value of $1,000 and is currently trading at $900 ex interest. The current rate of exchange is €1 = $1.10. The corporation tax rate is 24%.

(a) What is the cost of capital to the company if the exchange rate remains stable?
(b) What is the cost of capital if the dollar is expected to appreciate by 15% per annum?
(c) What is the cost of capital if the dollar is expected to depreciate by 5% per annum?
(d) What is the current market value of the eurobond issue in Euros?

14. Scobie plc is trying to decide on its cost of capital to use as a discount factor in investment appraisal. It has in issue 2.3 million ordinary shares each with a market value of €3.20 cumulative of dividend. The ordinary dividend due in two days' time will be €560,000 and dividends are expected to increase by 4% per annum. It has €3 million of 9% debentures (€100 nominal value) which are redeemable at par in three years' time and have a current market value of €105% ex interest. It also has a Swiss franc loan of SF4 million due for repayment one year from now, the rate of interest is fixed at 6% and payable one year from now when the exchange rate is expected to be equal to the present rate of SF2.4 = €1. The rate of corporation tax is 20%.

(a) Calculate the weighted average cost of capital (WACC) for Scobie.
(b) If the company were to increase the amount of debentures in issue, comment on how it would affect the WACC.

15. Scribes plc is a food and drinks company with 15 million shares in its capital structure. The current share price is €2.75 ex dividend.

Year	1996	1997	1998	1999	2000
Div. per share (c)	24	28	32	35	38

Scribes plc also has the following debt in its capital structure as at 31 December 2000. All interest has just been paid.

Type	Book value	Market value per €100	Redemption value
7% irredeemable	€10 million	€70	–
5% redeemable 31 Dec. 2008	€5 million	€80	par

Find the cost of each type of finance and the weighted average cost of capital for Scribes plc. Under what circumstances is it not appropriate to use the WACC as a target rate of return in investment appraisal?

16. Alpha and Beta are two companies in the electronics industry. The companies have the same business risk and are almost identical in all respects except for their capital structures and market valuations. The capital structure of Alpha is entirely equity financed with 80 million shares with a market value of €1.40 per share. Beta has 25 million shares with a share value of €4 each and €25 million of 12% irredeemable debentures currently valued at par.

Annual earnings before interest and taxation are €25 million. Corporation tax is at 20%.

If you owned 4% of the equity of Alpha and you agreed with the theories of Modigliani and Miller, explain what action you would take to improve your financial position and calculate the financial improvement.

17.♦ The board of directors of a company is considering whether to alter the company's capital structure. The board is proposing to issue €5 million of new debentures at par, and to use the funds to repurchase ordinary shares. A summary of the company's current balance sheet as at today, 16 December 2000, is shown below.

	(€000)
Fixed assets (net)	24,500
Current assets	12,300
Less current liabilities	(8,600)
	28,200
Financed by:	
25c ordinary shares	4,500
Reserves	14,325
	18,825
5% debentures redeemable at par in 10 years	9,375
	28,200

The company's ordinary share price is €1.67 ex dividend, and the dividend is expected to be constant at 28.5c per year in the future. The debentures are currently priced at €80 ex interest. The price of the ordinary shares and debentures are not expected to change as a result of the proposed issue of new debentures. Issue costs and transaction costs may be assumed to be zero.

(a) Calculate the current weighted average cost of capital (WACC):
   (i) if the company does not expect to pay corporate taxes; and
   (ii) if the company pays tax at a rate of 24%.
(b) Evaluate the likely effect on the WACC if the company restructures its capital and the rate of corporate tax is 24%.

APPENDIX 8A Dividend Growth Model Proof

Equation 1:

$$P_0 = d(1+g)/(1+K_e) + d(1+g)^2/(1+K_e)^2 + d(1+g)^3/(1+K_e)^3 + \ldots d(1+g)^n/(1+K_e)^n$$

For the series above to converge and be finite, discounting must more than compensate for the growth in dividends. Therefore Ke must be greater than g.

If equation 1 is multiplied by $(1+g)/(1+K_e)$ the result is equation 2.

Equation 2:

$$P_0(1+g)/(1+K_e) = d(1+g)^2/(1+K_e)^2 + d(1+g)^3/(1+K_e)^3 + \ldots d(1+g)^{n+1}/(1+K_e)^{n+1}$$

Subtract equation 2 from equation 1 to get the following

$$P_0 - \frac{P_0(1+g)}{(1+Ke)} = \frac{d(1+g)}{(1+Ke)} - \frac{d(1+g)^{n+1}}{(1+Ke)^{n+1}}$$

If Ke is greater than g, then the right term above $\dfrac{d(1+g)^{n+1}}{(1+Ke)^{n+1}}$ approaches zero as n approaches infinity.

Therefore the equation simplifies to $\quad P_0 - \dfrac{P_0(1+g)}{(1+Ke)} = \dfrac{d(1+g)}{(1+Ke)}$

Multiply both sides by $(1+Ke)$ and solve for P_0

$$P_0(1+Ke) - Po(1+g) = d(1+g)$$
$$P_0[1+Ke-(1+g)] = d(1+g)$$
$$P_0(Ke-g) = d(1+g)$$

to give us $\qquad P_0 = \dfrac{d(1+g)}{Ke-g}$

And re-arranging this expression gives us the cost of equity formula

$$Ke = \frac{d(1+g)}{P_0} + g$$

APPENDIX 8B Cost of International Source of Finance

Small and medium-sized companies and other small enterprises are usually limited to their domestic markets in their search for sources of finance. Large companies and multinationals have access to a wide range of international sources. The international money markets relate to short and medium sources, and include the eurocurrency market (not to be confused with the euro). The international capital markets relate to long-term sources of finance and include the eurobond market.

When an Irish company borrows in a foreign currency from an Irish bank, the loan is known as a eurocurrency loan.

The eurocurrency markets involve the depositing of funds with a bank outside the country of origin of the funds, and the bank re-lending these funds for a short term, which is typically three months.

A **eurobond** is one which is issued in a capital market, denominated in a currency which often differs from that of the country of issue, and is sold internationally. Eurobonds are long-term loans raised by international companies or other institutions in several countries at the same time. Eurobonds can be sold by one bondholder to another, i.e. a secondary market exists. The term of a eurobond issue is typically 10 to 15 years. Eurobonds would only be used by a company to raise large sums of money (above €10 million) and are very suitable for an organisation with an excellent credit rating, such as a successful multinational company. The interest rate on the bond may be fixed or variable. A variable bond is called a floating rate note. Many variable rate issues guarantee the bondholder a minimum interest rate, even if the market rates fall below this level (drop-lock floating rate bonds). Other variants are zero coupon (deep discount) bonds, convertibles and multi-currency used to reduce the risks of currency movements.

Example of eurobond cost

Greenbacks plc, an Irish company, has $40 million of eurobonds issued at 10% and redeemable at par in four years' time. The eurobond issue has a nominal value of $1,000 and is currently trading at $800 ex interest. The current rate of exchange is €1 = $1.

(a) What is the cost of capital to the company if the exchange rate remains stable?
(b) What is the cost of capital if the dollar is expected to appreciate by 10% per annum (ignore taxation)?

Answer

The cash flows need to be identified from the company point of view.

The current dollar market value is $800 and each year the interest payment in dollars is 10% of the nominal value ($1,000) or $100. At the end of year 4, there is an interest payment and also the redemption value of $1,000 or $1,100.

The exchange rate is currently €1 = $1 and as the dollar appreciates by 10% each year, the exchange rate in year 1 is $1/1.10 = $0.909, the exchange rate in year 2 is $0.909/1.10 = $0.826 etc.

The solution to the IRR is calculated on an Excel spreadsheet as follows.

Year	$ cash flow	€ cash flow	Exchange rate	€ cash flow
0	– 800	– 800	1.000	– 800
1	100	100	0.909	110
2	100	100	0.826	121
3	100	100	0.751	133.1
4	1,100	1,100	0.683	1,610.51
		(a) 17.34%	(b) IRR = 29.07%	

The cost of the eurobond increases dramatically due to the appreciation of the dollar.

9
Portfolio Theory and the Capital Asset Pricing Model

CHAPTER OBJECTIVES

At the end of this chapter the student should be able to:

1. calculate two asset portfolio expected returns and standard deviations from discrete probability distributions
2. understand the impact of covariance and correlation on portfolio selection
3. identify efficient portfolios using indifference curves and the capital market line
4. understand systematic and unsystematic risk and the capital asset pricing model
5. calculate the required rate of return of a security using the capital asset pricing model and risk-adjusted discount rates for use in investment appraisal
6. have an awareness of empirical research on the reliability of the capital asset pricing model in practice.

INTRODUCTION

One of the earliest theories associated with efficient investment was that of Charles H. Dow, known as Dow theory. Dow, who was the editor of the *Wall Street Journal*, started to compile daily averages of share prices in 1897. Even today the Dow Jones index is one of the best-known stock market performance indices in the world.

The birth of modern portfolio theory began with an article written by Harry Markowitz in 1952. A portfolio is a collection of two or more assets, and the idea of identifying portfolios which give the highest return for a given level of risk was developed by Markowitz. In this chapter we will focus on financial securities such as ordinary shares in companies, but the fundamental techniques have a wider application in areas associated with reducing corporate risk by having a diversity of projects in a company or producing a product range instead of just one product etc.

The chapter is broken down into three sections: the basic statistical analysis of risk and return; the application of Markowitz's theory using indifference analysis; and finally considering the capital asset pricing model (CAPM) developed by William Sharpe in 1963, which gives us a way of valuing securities according to their level of risk. In the final section of this chapter CAPM will be applied to find an appropriate cost of capital for a company and to identify a project specific discount rate which focuses on risk explicitly.

9.1 Risk and return

The portfolio mantra is **maximise return and minimise risk** and in this section we will look at the statistical measures of risk (standard deviation/variance) and return (average). Both of these measures will be based on discrete probabilities. The expected return, variance and standard deviation of security a are given by the following.

$$\text{Expected value (EV)} = \sum Pa = \bar{a} \tag{9.1}$$

$$\text{Variance } (\sigma^2_a) = \sum P(a - \bar{a})^2 \tag{9.2}$$

$$\text{Standard deviation } (\sigma_a) = \sqrt{\sigma_a^2} \tag{9.3}$$

where P is the probability of the various outcomes and a is the associated outcome

Example 9.1

Securities A and B have the following returns and associated probabilities:

Probability (P)	Return for A	Return for B
0.1	15%	10%
0.8	25%	30%
0.1	35%	50%

Probability (P)	Return for A	Pa
0.1	15%	1.5%
0.8	25%	20%
0.1	35%	3.5%
	Expected value of return $\sum Pa$ = 25%	

The expected return on security A is 25%.

The expected return of security B is (0.1)(10%) + (0.8)(30%) + (0.1)(50%) = 30%.

On the basis of expected values, investment B offers, on average, a higher return, but in choosing B the level of risk is ignored. The definition of risk that is often used in finance literature is based on the variability of return from the expected value. Statistical measures of variability are the variance or standard deviation of returns. The variance of return is the weighted sum of squared deviations from the expected return.

Squaring deviations ensures that positive and negative deviations from the expected value contribute equally to the measure of variability regardless of sign.

The variance formula is $\sum P (a - \bar{a})^2$ and the standard deviation is the square root of the variance.

The variance of the expected return for each security is as follows:

Probability (P)	Return for A	Mean deviation $(a - \bar{a})$	$P(a - \bar{a})^2$
0.1	15%	−10	0.1(100)
0.8	25%	0	0.8(0)
0.1	35%	10	0.1(100)
		Variance $\Sigma P(a - \bar{a})^2 =$	20%

The variance is 20% and the standard deviation of A $(\sigma_a) = \sqrt{20\%} = 4.472\%$

$$\sigma^2_b = (0.1)(10 - 30)^2 + (0.8)(30 - 30)^2 + (0.1)(50 - 30)^2 = 80\%$$
$$\text{and } \sigma_b = \sqrt{80} = 8.944\%$$

The variability score for B is larger, indicating a higher degree of risk.

If these investments are mutually exclusive, i.e. only one can be chosen, then a better measure of risk is the coefficient of variation (CV)

$$CV = \sigma / EV \qquad (9.4)$$

This risk measure takes on board the relative values of both expected value and variability.

$$CV \text{ of } A = 4.472/25 = 0.17888; \text{ and for } B = 8.944/30 = 0.29813$$

B has the higher risk measure and therefore the higher risk.

In financial markets it has been observed that the returns on securities have a normal distribution and therefore there is an equal probability of returns being above or below the expected value (mean). Because of this the variance becomes a very strong measure of risk.

9.2 Covariance and correlation

In the previous examples the investor was confined to choosing either A or B. If we now assume investments can be combined into a two asset portfolio, by combining the above investments in a portfolio, with 50% invested in A and 50% invested in B, the average return will be

$$(0.5)(25\%) + (0.5)(30\%) = 27.5\%$$

However, when you combine investments into a portfolio it is important to look at more than the individual variance factors of the two securities. It is necessary to quantify the extent to which the two securities move up or down together, and this is measured by their covariance.

The covariance of A and B is

$$Cov_{ab} = \Sigma P(a - \bar{a})(b - \bar{b}) \qquad (9.5)$$

Using the example above the covariance of A and B is found as follows

Probability	a	b	$a - \bar{a}$	$b - \bar{b}$	$P(a - \bar{a})(b - \bar{b})$
0.1	15%	10%	−10	−20	0.1(−10)(−20)
0.8	25%	30%	0	0	0.8(0)(0)
0.1	35%	50%	10	20	0.1(10)(20)
				Covariance =	40

A positive covariance indicates that the returns of the two securities move in the same direction. If the result were negative, it would imply the returns were moving in opposite directions. The problem with covariances is that it is difficult to compare them with each other, as their magnitude does not tell the full story. However if they are used as an input into the correlation formula, results are then comparable as the correlation coefficient scale has a strictly limited range from −1 to +1.

The correlation coefficient for A and B is

$$r_{ab} = \frac{Cov_{ab}}{\sigma_a \, \sigma_b} \tag{9.6}$$

In the example above $\qquad r_{ab} = \dfrac{40}{(4.472)(8.944)} = +1$

This is an example of perfect positive correlation and indicates that the returns of the two securities rise and fall together. Correlation can only take on values from +1 to −1.

- A positive result means returns tend to move together.
- A negative result means returns tend to move in opposite directions (the most extreme example being a value of −1).
- If the correlation coefficient has a value of zero, then the securities are independent and have no relationship with each other.

When a portfolio is made up of just two assets, then the expression for the variance of the portfolio is given by

$$\sigma^2_{a+b} = \sigma^2_a W_1^2 + \sigma^2_b W_2^2 + 2W_1 W_2 r_{ab} \sigma_a \sigma_b \tag{9.7}$$

where W_1 and W_2 are the weighted proportions invested in A and B. This is a formula that on first sight sent students for a strong cup of coffee! The most important part of the formula is the value of the correlation coefficient r_{ab}.

If the previous example is used with an equal investment in A and B (i.e. W_1 and W_2 = 0.5) and we change the value of r_{ab} from +1 to 0 to −1, the following results are obtained

If r_{ab} = +1 then σ^2_{a+b} = (20)(0.5)² + (80)(0.5)² + 2(0.5)(0.5)(1)(4.472)(8.944) = 45%
$$\sigma_{a+b} = \sqrt{45\%} = 6.71\%$$

If r_{ab} = 0 then σ^2_{a+b} = (20)(0.5)² + (80)(0.5)² + 2(0.5)(0.5)(0)(4.472)(8.944) = 25%
$$\sigma_{a+b} = \sqrt{25\%} = 5\%$$

If r_{ab} = –1 then σ^2_{a+b} = (20)(0.5)² + (80)(0.5)² + 2(0.5)(0.5) (–1)(4.472)(8.944) = 5%
$$\sigma_{a+b} = \sqrt{5\%} = 2.24\%$$

From the results it can be seen that the variability is highest when there is perfect positive correlation, lower when there is none, and lowest when there is perfect negative correlation. The implication is fairly obvious. Investors should try and avoid positively correlated securities.

9.3 Markowitz and modern portfolio theory

Indifference curves

The attitudes of investors to risk can be shown graphically with indifference (utility) curves. While investor attitudes to risk may differ, they do act rationally and are not prepared to expose themselves to higher levels of risk without the possibility of higher returns. Along any curve there is an equal level of utility available to the investor. The usual trade-off between risk and return occurs. The indifference curve slopes upwards at an increasing rate because of the increasing rate of marginal substitution, i.e. by taking on more risk units, progressively larger units of return are required to compensate the investor and keep utility constant.

Figure 9.1 Indifference curves

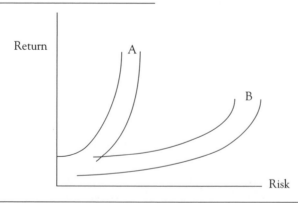

The graph shows two different types of investor. In the diagram investor A is risk averse and demands greater compensation in the form of increased return for a relatively small increase in risk. Investor B is not as conservative and more open to taking risks for a relatively smaller compensation. This difference in attitude to risk is reflected in the slopes of the two curves.

Having looked at investor preferences, Markowitz turned his attention to the availability of investments that existed in the real world. Earlier it was shown that by diversifying and avoiding positively correlated investments, risk levels are reduced. Markowitz studied combinations of many shares in different portfolios and found an egg-shaped cluster of portfolios (known as the envelope curve). While investors could position themselves anywhere inside the cluster of possible portfolios, it was evident that some of them were more efficient than others.

A portfolio is mean-variance efficient if it offers the maximum return for a given level of risk, or the minimum risk for a given level of return. The most efficient portfolios lie on the portfolio efficiency frontier, as can be seen on the curve AB in the diagram below. Markowitz developed a technique called quadratic programming to find this efficient frontier. If the indifference curve map of an individual is superimposed on the envelope curve, the optimum portfolio is found where the highest indifference curve touches the efficient frontier at a tangent (portfolio M).

Figure 9.2 Market portfolio position M

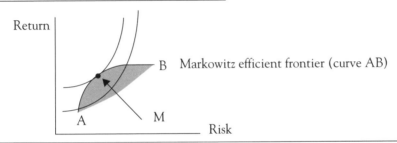

Portfolio M contains a proportion of all the securities on the market, i.e. shares, bonds, gold, property and rare paintings etc. Clearly no individual can hold the market portfolio, but a good approximation might be the FT100, the Standard & Poors 500 or the FTSE Actuaries All-Share Index which contains about 900 shares.

James Tobin extended Markowitz's analysis in 1958 by including risk-free securities into any portfolio. If risk-free securities (Rf) are introduced, such as post office savings or government gilts, then the efficient set of portfolios can become a straight line. This line is known as the **capital market line** (CML) and it supersedes the old efficient frontier. This line is found by pivoting a line clockwise from Rf on the Y-axis, until it reaches a point of tangency with the efficient frontier at M.

Figure 9.3 Capital market line and efficient portfolios

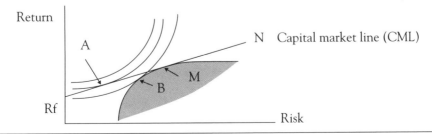

Portfolio M represents the optimal combination of risky securities. The capital market line (CML) is the line joining the points Rf, M and N. Investors will vary their attitudes to risk but will all find their optimal return/risk combination somewhere on the line joining these two investments. The investor only deals in portfolio M or Rf.

The major assumption behind the CML is that investors can borrow and lend at the risk-free rate of return. Investors can now move along the CML by splitting their investment between risk-free assets and the market portfolio M.

Without the existence of risk-free securities the investor in the diagram above would locate at point B, but because they are available the investor is located at point A.

Portfolio A represents the investor's preference for a larger proportion of total investment in risk-free assets than in the market portfolio M, and this is an example of a person who is somewhat risk averse, i.e. the position of portfolio A is closer to Rf than M.

If the investor likes to take a risk, then portfolios such as N are available. In this case the investor borrows at the risk-free rate and has more than 100% of his/her investment in portfolio M.

9.4 The equation of the capital market line (CML)

The formula for the CML is expressed by a general linear equation of the form $y = a + bx$ where a is the risk-free rate of return and b represents the increase in the return as the risk increases, i.e. the slope of the risk/return line.

Figure 9.4 Capital market line

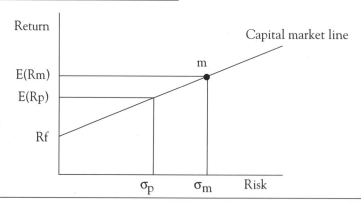

R_f = risk-free rate of return
$E(R_m)$ = the expected return for the market portfolio
$E(R_p)$ = the expected return for any portfolio on the CML
σ_m = the risk (standard deviation) of returns in portfolio M
σ_p = the risk (standard deviation) of returns in any portfolio on the CML.

The slope of the CML can be expressed as

$$\frac{(E(R_m) - R_f)}{\sigma_m} \qquad (9.8)$$

This slope indicates the change in return due to a change in risk in moving from Rf to M and this represents the extent to which the required returns from a portfolio should exceed the risk-free rate of return, to compensate the investors for risk.

The equation of the CML can be expressed as

$$E(R_p) = R_f + \frac{(E(R_m) - R_f)\sigma_p}{\sigma_m} \qquad (9.9)$$

The expression additional to the risk-free rate represents the risk premium the investor requires as compensation for accepting portfolio risk. This risk premium includes both business risk and financial risk. This equation forms the basis of the capital asset pricing model.

9.5 Practical problems in applying portfolio theory

In trying to apply portfolio theory in practice, the following problems exist:

1. Investors cannot borrow at the risk-free rate.
2. Identification of the market portfolio M involves finding out returns and risks for all investments, which is more or less impossible in practice.
3. The market portfolio is not static over time.
4. The transaction costs associated with constructing M would be too expensive for a small investor.
5. The techniques rely on past data to predict future risk and return, complicated calculations and the generation of indifference curves for individual utility preferences.

Some of the problems mentioned above can be overcome by investing in unit trusts or stock exchange index tracker funds as a proxy for the ideal market portfolio M.

While the Markowitz model provides a relatively simple solution for investment criteria in the two-asset case, it becomes much more complicated when the number of assets becomes larger. The calculation of covariances in combinations of two is based on $(N^2 - N)/2$ where N is the number of securities. In the case of a portfolio of 100 securities, it is necessary to calculate $(100^2 - 100)/2 = 4,950$ covariances. These difficult calculations, although relatively easy with a computer today, stimulated other approaches to investment management. The capital asset pricing model (CAPM) was one such new approach developed by William Sharpe in 1964.

Both Sharpe and Markowitz were awarded the Nobel prize for Economics in 1990. Before explaining the CAPM it is important to understand the difference between systematic and unsystematic risk.

9.6 Systematic and unsystematic risk

The total risk of an investment can be broken down into systematic and unsystematic risk. Unsystematic risk, which is also known as diversifiable or specific risk, is that part of risk that can be eliminated by holding a well-diversified portfolio. Examples of unsystematic risks include the nature of the business a company is involved in (oil exploration or food retailing), operational risk, financial risk and industrial relations problems which exist within the company etc. The risk associated with an asset that cannot be eliminated by diversification is systematic risk (also known as non-diversifiable or market risk). Systematic risk relates to the market and the economy as a whole and its impact on investment, for example, the impact which interest rate changes, inflation changes, taxation changes or exchange rate changes have on a company.

Figure 9.5 Systematic and unsystematic risk

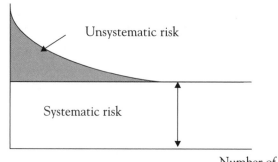

Solnick (1974) found that a substantial reduction in the risk of a portfolio occurred as the number of different shares held in a portfolio approached 20. After that the reduction in risk was quite modest. The systematic risk associated with any security will vary and the CAPM tries to determine a fair price for an individual security by measuring its systematic risk. Systematic risk must be accepted by any investor, unless investment is entirely focused on risk-free opportunities. In return for accepting systematic risk, an investor will expect to earn a return which is higher than the return on risk-free investment. The influence of CAPM on the world of finance has been enormous over the past 30 years. Its far-reaching consequences changed the way portfolios were constructed for pension and insurance funds around the world. It has given the world of finance an alternative method of calculating the cost of capital for a firm and the required rate of return on projects.

9.7 The capital asset pricing model

This economic model is based on a set of assumptions:

1. All unsystematic risk is eliminated as the investor holds a well-diversified portfolio of securities.
2. Investors can borrow and lend at the risk-free rate.
3. Investors act rationally and try to maximise utility.
4. There is perfect information available in the market to investors.
5. Capital markets are perfectly competitive.

Sharpe's basic observation was that shares tend to move with the market, and that there was a linear relationship between the market as a whole and any individual security.

A statistical analysis of historical returns from an individual security and from the average market return would indicate if such a linear relationship exists. A series of comparative figures could be prepared over time of the return of a company's shares and the average return of the market as a whole. The results can be drawn on a scatter diagram and, using regression analysis, a line of best fit could be drawn. This line is called the characteristic line and the slope of this line is the share's beta (β), which indicates the sensitivity of the share's return to the return on the market.

Figure 9.6 Security characteristic line

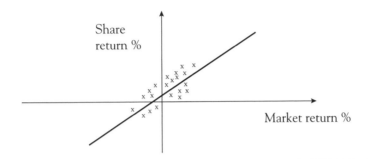

From the diagram, the return from the share and the return from the market tend to move together, i.e. they are positively correlated. The return from the share may be higher or lower than the market return and this is because the systematic risk of the individual share differs from that of the market.

CAPM tries to measure this individual systematic risk, known as beta (β). The most popular way of calculating beta is to observe the historical relationship between returns and assume that the covariance will persist into the future. This is called ex-post analysis. A share's beta factor is the measure of the volatility of its returns relative to the market. The beta factor of the market as a whole is 1.0. A company's beta factor is simply a yardstick against which the risk of other companies can be measured. Beta is calculated as the ratio of the covariance of an individual security's return with the return of the market (Cov_{jm}) and the variance of the market (σ^2_m).

$$\beta_j = \text{Cov}_{jm}/\sigma^2_m \tag{9.10}$$

This ratio is easily calculated using the regression statistics on a spreadsheet. The CAPM assumes that unsystematic risk can be cancelled out by diversification. The CAPM also uses the principle that returns on shares in the market are expected to be higher than the returns of risk-free investments. The difference between the market return and risk-free return is called the excess return. The capital asset pricing model can be stated as follows:

$$E(R_j) = R_f + [E(R_m) - R_f]\beta_j \tag{9.11}$$

This is also known as the equation for the security market line.

R_f = risk-free rate of return, $E(R_m)$ = the expected return for the market portfolio $E(R_j)$ = the expected return for share j and β_j is the beta coefficient for share j.

In the equation the systematic risk as measured by β_j is compared with the risk and return of the market and the risk-free rate of return to calculate a required return of share j and hence a fair price for share j.

The risk-free rate can be approximated by taking the return on short-term government bonds or post office savings. The return for the market is difficult to calculate and is usually approximated by using stock exchange indices as a representation of the market.

The excess return or market risk premium of $(E(R_m) - R_f)$ has traditionally been estimated by academics at between 8% and 9% on an arithmetic average basis.

Example 9.2 CAPM *formula application*

Company A has a share beta of 1.5. The risk-free rate is 4% and the expected market return is 12%. What is the expected return of company A's share?

Answer

Expected return = 4% + (12% – 4%) × 1.5 = 16% . This also represents the cost of equity.

If the company has a policy of paying a constant dividend of 10p, what is the theoretical share price?

Answer

From the dividend valuation model Ke = div/Po or Po = div/Ke.

This implies the share price = 10p/0.16 = 62.5p in theory.

9.8 CAPM and portfolios

Just as an individual security has a beta factor, so too has a portfolio of securities. The beta factor of a portfolio is the weighted average of the beta factors of the securities that make up a portfolio.

Example 9.2 CAPM *and portfolios*

A portfolio consisting of four securities has information as follows:

Security	No. of shares	Beta	Share price
A	60.000	1.16	€4.29
B	80,000	1.28	€2.92
C	100,000	0.90	€2.17
D	125,000	1.50	€3.14

The current market rate of return is 15% per annum and the risk-free rate is 6%.
Find the overall portfolio beta and the expected return for the portfolio.

Answer

Market value	Beta	Market value x beta
€257,400	1.16	298,584
€233,600	1.28	299,008
€217,000	0.90	195,300
€392,500	1.50	588,750
€1,100,500		1,381,642

Beta as a whole = 1,381,642/1,100,500 = 1.26
Expected return on the portfolio = 6% + 1.26(15% – 6%) = 17.34%

A beta value of 1.0 is the yardstick against which all share betas are measured.

- If a share has a beta value greater than 1.0, it will be classified as an aggressive share. In a bull market it would rise faster than the market average and in a bear market it would fall more than the market average.
- If a share has a beta value less than 1.0, it will be classified as a defensive share. In a bull market it would rise more slowly than the market average and in a bear market it would fall less than the market average.
- A beta value of 1.0 would simply follow the market.

This information could be used by investors to identify portfolio selection to suit their risk profile or possibly to identify shares that were incorrectly priced on the basis of beta level and returns.

9.9 Gearing and beta

The gearing of a company will affect the risk of the equity. If a company is geared its financial risk will be higher than a company that is all equity financed (Chapter 8). This financial risk is an element of systematic risk and should be reflected in the beta value of a company's shares if that company is geared. The beta value of a geared company will be higher than the beta of a company that is identical in every respect except that it is an ungeared company. This is because of the extra financial risk involved. The mathematical expression to show the relationship between geared and ungeared betas is as follows:

$$\beta a = \beta e \left[\frac{E}{E + D(1 - T)} \right] + \beta d \left[\frac{D(1 - T)}{E + D(1 - T)} \right] \quad (9.12)$$

where βa is the asset beta or beta of an ungeared company, βe is the equity beta of a similar company that is geared, and βd is the beta of the debt in the geared company (sometimes considered risk free).

D is the market value of the debt capital. E is the market value of the equity. T is the rate of corporation tax.

The formula above is an expression of the company's asset beta or all equity beta as a weighted average of its equity and debt betas. If the assumption is made that companies do not default on their interest payments, and the beta of debt can be assumed to be zero, then the formula is simplified somewhat.

In this case the formula reduces to

$$\beta a = \beta e \left[\frac{E}{E+D(1-T)} \right] \qquad (9.13)$$

From the formula a company's equity beta will always be greater than its asset beta (ungeared beta), unless a company is all equity financed. This ties in with the Modigliani and Miller formulae in Chapter 8. The asset beta measures purely business risk as the finance is in all equity form and no financial risk exists.

The formula above can be used to estimate the beta of an unquoted company by adjusting the beta of a quoted company in the same industry with similar operating characteristics.

Example 9.3 Gearing and beta

Company X is an all equity company that has just gone public and insufficient data is available at the moment about its own equity performance to calculate the company's equity beta. Company X is essentially a mobile phone sales company and a similar type of company (company Y) has a published beta of 1.15. Company Y has a capital structure at market value of 30% debt and 70% equity. Estimate the beta for company X. Corporate tax rate 24%.

Assume the beta of debt is zero.

Answer

$$\beta a = \beta e \left[\frac{E}{E + D(1-T)} \right]$$

$$\beta a = \frac{1.15\,(70)}{70 + 30(1-.24)} = 0.87$$

The above beta estimate could then be used to find the cost of equity in company X. If company X were a geared company, the same formula could be used to adjust 0.87 to reflect the financial risk associated with the level of debt capital in the company.

Example 9.4 Gearing and beta

If company X has a capital structure made up of 60% equity and 40% debt, what would be the geared beta for company X?

Answer
The ungeared beta for company X is 0.87, so this must now be re-geared to reflect the new capital structure

$$\beta a = \beta e \left[\frac{E}{E + D(1 - T)} \right]$$

$$0.87 = \text{beta of geared} \quad \times \quad \frac{60}{60 + 40(1 - 0.24)}$$

Calculating for beta, the result is $\beta e = 1.31$

In this case the beta has increased to reflect the increased financial risk.

There are problems associated with calculating beta factors using data about other companies:

1. It is difficult to find companies with identical operating characteristics.
2. Estimates of beta values are based on a statistical analysis of past data which may not be accurate.
3. Estimates using one company's data may differ from estimates using that of other companies.
4. Debt capital may not be risk free.

9.10 CAPM and WACC

The CAPM can be used instead of the dividend valuation model to establish an equity cost of capital.

$$Ke_j = E(R_j) = R_f + [E(R_m) - R_f] \beta_j$$

where Ke_j = cost of equity capital in company j.

Example 9.5 CAPM and WACC

Scobie plc is financed by €3 million of equity and €1 million of irredeemable debt capital. The debt capital has a coupon rate of 6% before tax and is considered risk free. The beta value of the company's equity is 1.25, the market return is expected to be 15% and the rate of corporation tax is 24%.

Answer
Ke = 6% + (15% − 6%) 1.25 = 17.25% using CAPM
Kd = 6%(1 − 0.24) = 4.56% the after-tax cost
WACC = $^3/_4$ (17.25%) + $^1/_4$ (4.56%) = 14.08%

The WACC above would be an appropriate discount rate to use in the appraisal of projects with the same systematic risk as Scobie's current investments.

If a company plans to invest in a diversification project outside its normal business expertise, the investment will involve different levels of systematic risk. The company's existing WACC would not be an appropriate discount factor to apply in investment appraisal. A discount rate should be calculated which is specific to the new project, and which takes into account both the project's systematic risk and the company's gearing level (financial risk). This is a three stage process:

1. Obtain published information on the beta values of companies in the industry into which the company is planning to diversify.
2. Adjust these beta values to reflect the company's capital structure.
3. Use CAPM to find the cost of equity and the WACC.

Example 9.6 Diversification discount rate

Using the example of Scobie plc above, assume the following situation occurs. The company is now proposing to invest in a project which would involve diversification into a new industry, and the following information is available about a company in this industry. The company has a beta of 1.59 and a debt/equity ratio of 1:2 based on market values. Find an appropriate discount rate to appraise this new investment.

Answer

First adjust the beta

$$\beta a = \beta e \left[\frac{E}{E + D(1-T)} \right]$$

$$= \frac{1.59\,(2)}{2 + 1(1 - 0.24)} = 1.15$$

This is equivalent to the ungeared beta of the other company.

The next step is to gear this all equity beta to Scobie's capital structure.

$$\beta a = \beta e \left[\frac{E}{E + D(1-T)} \right]$$

$$1.15 = \frac{\beta e\,(3)}{3 + 1(1 - 0.24)}$$

$1.15 = 0.7979\,\beta e$ and therefore $\beta e = 1.44$. This is the geared beta of Scobie plc.

We can now get a project specific cost of equity using CAPM.

$Ke = 6\% + (15\% - 6\%)\,1.44 = 18.96\%$
$Kd = 6\%(1 - .24) = 4.56\%$

Finally

$WACC = 3/4\,(18.96\%) + 1/4(4.56\%) = 15.36\%$

The application of CAPM in finding a target rate of return specific to individual projects is that it can be used to compare projects of all the different risk classes. It is therefore superior to an NPV approach, which uses only one discount factor for all projects, regardless of risk.

While the application of the CAPM may lead to better investment decisions, practical problems exist:

1. Companies may have difficulty identifying surrogate companies with similar systematic risk characteristics. Many companies have diversified activities rather than a specific area related to the project being appraised.
2. Capital structures measured by market values may be difficult to ascertain.
3. CAPM is a single period model, usually one year, whereas the duration of projects tends to be over a number of years.
4. CAPM assumes that all investors are mean variance efficient.

9.11 General comment

There has been great debate on the validity of CAPM and a lot of empirical research has been carried out. Much of this research has focused on beta and its stability over time. While empirical evidence on individual betas has been inconclusive, there is general agreement that the betas of shares display high levels of stability over time. The idea behind such portfolio betas being stable is based on the actual changes in individual betas tending to cancel each other out to some degree. Tests have also been carried out on the security market line using regression analysis, the most celebrated being the work done by Fama and Macbeth (1973). Their work suggested a linear relationship does exist between risk and return. However the CAPM and systematic risk measures do not fully explain the expected returns of individual securities.

Roll (1977) suggested that it was impossible to empirically test the CAPM, as the true market portfolio cannot be ascertained. The stock exchange indices are a poor substitute for the market, as they fail to include all possible investments (bonds, foreign currency, property, antiques etc.). The consequence of this leaves CAPM difficult to prove or disprove.

CAPM is seen as a very useful model. However critics believe that the relationship between risk and return is more complex than the linear model assumed by Sharpe. One model that could replace the CAPM is the arbitrage pricing model (APM) developed by Stephen Ross.

9.12 Arbitrage pricing model (APM)

Instead of looking for a single factor which influences the return on each security, the APM assumes that the return is based on a number of independent factors (a form of multiple regression analysis). The actual return on any security is of the form

Return = a + b1 factor 1 + b2 factor 2 + b3 factor 3 + b4 factor 4 + etc.

The factors involved in the APM were not identified by Ross in his original paper. He also suggested some securities were considered more sensitive to some factors than others. Further research done by Roll, Ross and Chen showed that there were four dominant factors:

1. the level of industrial activity
2. the rate of inflation
3. the spread between short-term and long-term interest rates
4. the spread between the yield of low and high-risk corporate bonds.

The disadvantage of this form of analysis is its relative complexity and although the problem of finding the market portfolio is avoided, you now have to identify the sensitivities of the factors involved.

CAPM however remains the standard model used by investment practitioners and no other model has improved on its usefulness in explaining risk return relationships.

SUMMARY

- Investment risk and return can be measured by standard deviation and expected value statistics.
- When combining investments in a two asset portfolio, the key determinant of risk is the level of correlation that exists between the investments.
- Markowitz's portfolio theory provides a framework to identify the most efficient portfolio of risky and risk-free investments.
- The risk of an investment can be broken down into systematic and unsystematic risk.
- Unsystematic risk can be eliminated by holding a well-diversified number of investments.
- The CAPM tries to measure systematic risk (beta factor) assuming a linear relationship between an individual share's returns and those of the market.
- The beta factor for a share reflects both business and financial risk and a discount rate can be found using CAPM for appraising a project which reflects its risk.
- Empirical tests neither prove nor disprove the validity of the CAPM, but it does provide a good understanding of the relationship between systematic risk and the required rate of return of investments.

QUESTIONS

1. Explain the term expected value, standard deviation and correlation and comment on their application in portfolio theory.
2. What is the Capital Market Line?
3. What is the difference between systematic and unsystematic risk?
4. What is the beta factor of a share and how can it help an investor choose what shares to invest in?
5. Has diversification at a company level any value to a company's ordinary shareholders?
6. Explain why the asset beta of a company is less than the equity beta, unless a company is all-equity financed?

7. You have identified two quoted shares which you believe will exhibit negative correlation in their possible returns over the next year as follows:

Economic state	Probability	High stool	Low stool
A	0.30	25%	14%
B	0.45	22%	18%
C	0.25	12%	20%

(a) Calculate the expected return, variance and standard deviation of each security.
(b) Calculate the covariance between the two securities and the correlation coefficient.
(c) Construct a portfolio consisting of 70% by value of High stool and 30% Low stool. Calculate the expected return, variance and standard deviation of the portfolio.

8.♦ Three possible investments have been identified by a company. The company wants to invest an equal sum in two of these investments and the following information is available:

	M	N	O
Expected return	15%	18%	17%
Standard deviation	2.4%	6.2%	4.3%
Covariance of returns			
M & N 12.2%			
M & O 8.1%			
N & O − 4.5%			

(a) Estimate the correlation coefficient between each of the three possible portfolio combinations and explain the implications of these coefficients for portfolio risk.
(b) Which of the three possible combinations would you consider the most efficient on the basis of mean-variance efficiency?

9. An investor has €800,000 to invest for a year, on which she is seeking a return of at least 16%. She has identified the following possible non-divisible investments.

Project	Investment needed	Percentage return mean	Standard deviation
1	€500,000	14%	3%
2	€300,000	17%	4%
3	€500,000	20%	8%
4	€500,000	24%	7%

Unused cash of €100,000 or more can be invested in the money market (MM) to earn a mean return of 14% and a standard deviation of 3%.

Correlation coefficients between the returns on various investments have been estimated as follows:

	Market	MM	Projects 1	2	3	4
Market	1	0.8	0.7	0.7	0.8	0.8
MM	0.8	1	0.4	0.4	0.5	0.5
Project 2	0.7	0.4	0.7	1	0.6	0.5

Advise this person using portfolio theory on the most efficient use of the €800,000, assuming that all of the funds must be invested for one year.

10. Company A is trying to decide on a discount factor to use in a new investment appraisal which is a diversification project. Company A has a debt to equity ratio based on market values of 3:5.

Company B, operating in the same industry into which A is entering, has a debt to equity ratio based on market values of 1:2. Company B has a beta coefficient of equity capital of 1.7.

The corporate debt of company A is risk free, the rate of return is 11% (before tax) and the expected market return is 16%. Corporation tax is 20%.

Calculate an appropriate discount rate for company A.

11.♦ The following information relates to Manu plc, a manufacturing company (all figures in €000s):

Financial information for year ending 31 December

Balance sheet	1996	1997	1998	1999	2000
Shares (50c)	4,000	4,000	4,000	4,000	4,000
10% debentures	1,000	1,000	1,000	1,000	1,000
P & L account					
Profit	1,080	1,208	836	1,478	1,720
Tax (50%)	540	604	418	739	860
After-tax	540	604	418	739	860
Dividend paid	280	308	336	378	410

The current market value of the shares is €1.13 ex dividend, while the irredeemable debentures are quoted at €82.50 per €100 ex interest.

The company's equity beta has been calculated at 1.4 and the current risk-free rate is 10%. Analysts forecast a 15% per annum return on the stock exchange index over the next few years.

(a) Estimate the cost of equity using both the dividend valuation model and the capital asset pricing model.

(b) Estimate the weighted average cost of capital using both models.

12. Company A is trying to decide on a discount factor to use in a new investment appraisal.

A competitor, company B operating in the same industry into which A is entering, has a debt to equity ratio based on market values of 1:3.

Company B has a published equity beta of 1.2 and this is unlikely to change in the foreseeable future. Company B has a debt beta of 0.2.

The risk-free rate of return is 8%. The expected market return is 13%. Company A has 5 million shares (trading at €2 ex interest) in issue and a €2 million bank loan which is considered risk-free.

Calculate an appropriate discount rate for company A.

13. The directors of a company are considering whether to alter the company's capital structure. They are proposing to issue €5 million of new debentures at par, and to use the funds to repurchase ordinary shares.

A summary of the company's current balance sheet as at today, 16 December 1996, is shown below:

	(€000)
Fixed assets (net)	24,500
Current assets	12,300
Less current liabilities	(8,600)
	28,200
25p ordinary shares	4,500
Reserves	14,325
	18,825
5% debentures redeemable at par	9,375
in ten years' time	28,200

The company's ordinary share price is €1.67 ex dividend. The risk-free rate of interest is 5.5% and the estimated market return is 15%. The company's equity beta is estimated to be 1.24.

The debentures are currently priced at €80 ex interest. The price of the ordinary shares or debentures are not expected to change as a result of the proposed issue of new debentures.

Issue costs and transaction costs may be assumed to be zero.

(a) Calculate the current weighted average cost of capital (WACC) if the company pays corporation tax at a rate of 20%.

(b) Evaluate the likely effect on the WACC if the company restructures its capital structure.

14. Spondulix plc is a company which has two divisions, X and Y, and they account for one-third and two-thirds respectively of the company's total market value.

The following information is available:

Spondulix balance sheet extract 31 December 2000

	(€000)
Fixed assets	5,000
Current assets	4,600
Current liabilities	(4,250)
Creditors	
Three year loan	(700)
14% bond redeemable at par 2009	(2,000)
Ordinary shares 10p	1,200

The bonds are currently priced at €129 ex interest and the current share price ex dividend at 53c.

The company has an overall beta (β) of 1.25. The overall beta of other firms in the same industry as division Y is 1.35, with an industry average market-weighted debt to equity ratio gearing of 50% : 50%.

The risk-free rate of return is 6% and the expected market return is 12%. The rate of corporation tax is 24% and debt is considered risk free.

(a) Use the capital asset pricing model to find the cost of equity in both X and Y.
(b) Calculate a discount rate (weighted average cost of capital) for both the X and Y divisions.

15. Company A has one project lasting one year. Company B has three projects lasting one year and in different industries. The net cash flows and beta factors associated with the projects are:

	(€000)	Beta factor
Company A	200	1.2
Company B		
Project 1	50	1.5
Project 2	50	1.5
Project 3	100	0.9

The market rate of return is 10% and the risk-free rate of interest is 5%.

(a) Calculate the total present value of the projects undertaken by company A and company B.
(b) Determine the overall beta value of company B assuming all projects are undertaken.
(c) Based on the information, discuss which company is likely to be valued more highly by an investor.

16.♦ A company has a capital structure made up of €14 million of 10% irredeemable debt capital with a market value at par and 20 million shares with a market value of 92c. The corporate tax is 20%.

   The company's equity beta has a value of 1.25. The real risk-free rate (i.e. excluding inflation) of return is 4% and the real market return is 10%. The expected inflation rate is expected to be 5% per annum for the next five years. The company wants to discount its projected cash flows (including inflation) at its weighted average cost of capital. Find an appropriate discount rate for the company.

17.♦ Cabbage plc is an engineering company which has just announced its final results for the year ended 31 December 2000. Earnings per share (EPS) and dividends per share (DPS) for the past five years have been as follows:

Year	1996	1997	1998	1999	2000
EPS in cents	61	64	71	73	76
DPS in cents	38	40	41	42	44

The board of directors believes that the annual growth rate in dividends will be consistent with the average growth rate in dividends above. Cabbage's beta factor is 1.4, the risk-free rate of return is 7% and the market return is expected to be 15% for the next year.

(a) Use the capital asset pricing model and Gordon's growth model to calculate the share price (€) that might be expected.
(b) Give reasons why the share price might react differently.

18. McGurk plc is about to invest an equal sum of money in each of two companies from a choice of three available. The companies are in different industries and the data on risk and return over the past six years is given below:

Company	Average annual returns	Standard deviation of return
Groucho	11%	17%
Harpo	20%	29%
Zippo	14%	21%

The correlation coefficient between returns is as follows:

Groucho and Harpo   0.00
Groucho and Zippo   0.40
Harpo and Zippo   0.62

Estimate which of the portfolios is the most efficient.

19. The management of Wrinkles plc want to estimate their firm's equity beta. Wrinkles has had a stock market quotation for only three months and the financial manager feels it would be inappropriate to estimate beta from the actual share price behaviour over such a short period.

Instead, she has suggested using equity betas of other companies operating in the same industry and with the same operating characteristics as Wrinkles.

Three companies have been identified as having operations in the same industry. However, only one company, Mariner, operates exclusively in the same industry as Wrinkles. The other two have some dissimilar activities in addition to those which are the same as Wrinkles. Wrinkles is financed entirely by equity. The tax rate is 20% and all debt capital is considered risk free.

Details of the three companies are as follows:

(a) Mariner plc has an observed equity beta of 1.14. The capital structure at market values is 60% equity and 40% debt.

(b) Roomtack plc has an observed equity beta of 1.12. It is estimated that 30% of the current market value of Roomtack is caused by risky growth opportunities, which have an estimated equity beta of 2. The growth opportunities are reflected in the observed beta. Roomtack's other activities are the same as Wrinkles and it is financed entirely by equity.

(c) Shak plc has an observed equity beta of 1.15 and has two divisions, East and West. East's operating characteristics are considered identical to those of Wrinkles. Those of West are considered to be 50% more risky than those of Wrinkles. In terms of market value East is estimated as being twice as valuable as West. The capital structure of Shak at market values is 75% equity and 25% debt.

    (i) Make three estimates of the equity beta of Wrinkles based on the information provided for Mariner, Roomtack and Shak.

    (ii) Why would the estimated beta of Wrinkles, when eventually determined from observed share price movements, differ from the values derived from the approach employed above?

Part 4

Long-term Financial Planning

10
Financial Forecasting and Planning

CHAPTER OBJECTIVES

At the end of this chapter the student should be able to:

1. understand the importance of financial forecasting and planning
2. construct pro-forma income statements and balance sheets
3. discuss the weaknesses of accounting-based management
4. understand how shareholder wealth is maximised via the maximisation of free cash flows
5. evaluate the valuation of an entire company using free cash flows
6. understand the concepts of economic value added and market value added.

INTRODUCTION

The primary objective of financial management is maximising shareholder value. Wealth creation occurs when investments generate returns that are greater than the cost of capital used for the investments. The first step in the management process of maximising shareholder value is a coherent corporate plan. This will include the short-term, medium-term and long-term objectives of the firm. Financial planning involves the conversion of the corporate plan into quantitative terms. The financial plan will involve projected financial statements (pro forma) that analyse the effect the corporate plan will have on projected profits. A strategic corporate plan ensures:

1. Money needed for investment purposes will be available. This will include money needed for fixed assets, stock, debtors, research and development etc. Raising funds will take time. A financial plan will estimate the future financial needs and will therefore provide the necessary time for management to source the required finance.
2. Financial plans can be used to forecast free cash flows (FCF). If the cash flows arising from the business plans are insufficient to cover dividend payments, increases in net working capital and fixed assets (i.e. negative FCF), then management must reappraise its capital structure by borrowing or issuing additional shares.
3. Financial planning will allow for unexpected changes in economic conditions in which the plan is based. Forecasting is important because business decisions are based on forecasts of expected and unexpected situations that a business will be exposed to in the future. Sensitivity analysis deals with unexpected events occurring by factoring in

different scenarios like changes in interest rates, currency fluctuations and domestic or international demand side shocks to the economy. Failure to anticipate future events can have devastating effects on company performance.

This chapter looks at two approaches to financial forecasting and planning. The first approach is based on traditional accounting information. We refer to this as **accounting-based management.** We follow this with a look at the weaknesses of accounting-based management as a financial planning tool.

The second approach emphasises that the essence of financial planning is to maximise shareholder value. This approach to financial planning is called **value-based management**, and it is used to overcome the weaknesses of accounting-based management.

10.1 Financial forecasting

Financial forecasting involves making projections about future events. This begins with the budgeting process which identifies the assets that are required and what revenues will be generated from the use of these assets. Chapter 7 has analysed how capital budgets are prepared and how they are accepted or rejected. In this chapter we examine how a budget, once accepted, is implemented. Remember budgets are plans that have been converted into quantitative terms. **Capital budgets** cover investments in fixed assets. **Operating budgets** are those that deal with day-to-day activities. The principal operating budget is the sales budget.

10.1.1 The financial planning process

Financial planning is designed to ensure that companies meet their investment objectives. The process begins with the sales forecast. Because all other budgets will depend on the volume of activity in sales, the sales budget is the most important budget of all.

Sales forecasts

The projected financial forecasts (pro forma statements) require accurate sales forecasts. However, forecasting sales is difficult. The following factors will need to be considered:

- Economic conditions. Economic factors such as inflation, interest rates and growth rates in GDP will impact on the market in which the firm sells its product.
- Production capacity. The forecasted sales figure may be constrained because of a lack of production capacity.
- Estimating the number of customers who will not pay their debts.
- Estimating the effect sales projections will have on cash balances. As we will see later on in the chapter, it is possible to run out of cash during periods of high sales growth as it is during periods of low sales growth.
- Competition. Identifying the level of competition in the market may have the effect of making sensible projections out of crazy sales forecasts. Allied to this should be a realistic assessment of anticipated market share the firm expects to achieve.

- Advertising campaigns and terms of credit also affect sales and these will be imputed in the sales forecast.

Getting the sales forecast accurate is crucial. An overly optimistic forecast will mean too much investment in fixed assets and inventory and high storage costs.

Underestimating demand for the product will mean losing customers and market share. The consequences will lower share prices and lower shareholder value.

Forecasting sales — historical average growth rates

Before discussing how companies forecast sales growth, it is important to note that growth in itself should not be an appropriate corporate goal. Consider a company whose sales growth is rapid. In order to expand production to meet demand, the company invests additional cash in plant and equipment. Still unable to meet the additional demand, over-utilisation of its plant and equipment will result in failure and break-down. In their efforts to expand production, more cash is invested in stock, raw materials and accounts receivable. Soon the company runs out of cash and it goes into liquidation. The good news in all of this is that demand for the company product is high and this is reflected in the sales growth forecast. The bad news is that poor financial planning failed to identify the increased financial needs required to fund the sales growth. Consequently, **an important aspect of financial planning is to ensure that a firm does not run out of cash**.

10.2 Financial forecasting—pro forma statements

10.2.1 The per cent of sales method

Once the sales forecast has been completed, we must then forecast the effect the forecasted growth in sales will have on the balance sheet and income statement. In other words, we must construct a pro forma profit and loss account and balance sheet. The financial planning model we describe here is the per cent of sales method. The items on the profit and loss account and balance sheet are divided into two groups—**those that vary directly with sales and those that do not.** We will then be able to measure the amount of additional financing the company needs to support the increase in sales.

Using the per cent of sales approach, the following steps are taken:

1. Forecast the estimated sales.
2. Calculate as a percentage of current sales each item on the profit and loss account and balance sheet that varies with sales.

Example 10.1 Pro forma statement using the per cent of sales approach

The profit and loss account of Parnell Ltd is as shown in Table 10.1.

Table 10.1 Parnell Ltd profit and loss account for year end 2000

Turnover	€5,000
Operating costs (70% of sales)	€3,500
Profit before tax (PBT)	€1,500
Tax (20%)	€300
Profit after tax (PAT)	€1,200
Dividends	€300
Retained earnings (RE)	€900

Parnell Ltd has projected an increase in sales of 20% for the next twelve months. Therefore anticipated sales will be €5,000 × 1.2 = €6,000. If costs remain at 70% of sales, we forecast costs at €6,000 × 0.7 = €4,200. We will also assume that Parnell Ltd will maintain a constant dividend payout ratio of 25%, i.e. €300/€1,200

$$\text{Dividend payout ratio} = \frac{\text{Ordinary dividends}}{\text{Profit after tax}} \tag{10.1}$$

Therefore the percentage of retained earnings to profit after tax is 75% or €900/€1,200 **This is the retention ratio.**

$$\text{Retention ratio} = \frac{\text{Retained earnings}}{\text{Profit after tax}} \tag{10.2}$$

The pro forma profit and loss account of Parnell Ltd is shown in Table 10.2.

Table 10.2 Parnell Ltd pro forma profit and loss account for year end 2001

Sales	€6,000
Costs	€4,200
Profit before tax (PBT)	€1,800
Tax (20%)	€360
Profit after tax (PAT)	€1,440
Dividends	€360
Retained earnings	€1,080

Note that this is a simplified example and we have lumped all costs including depreciation and interest payments together in a single figure. We will relax this assumption in a more detailed example later on in the chapter.

10.3 Pro forma balance sheet

To prepare a pro forma balance sheet we take each item on the balance sheet and decide which items vary directly with sales and those that don't.

The balance sheet of Parnell Ltd is given in Table 10.3.

Table 10.3 Parnell Ltd balance sheet for year end 2000

Fixed assets	€7,200	(144% of sales) note 1
Current assets		
Stock	€2,400	(48% of sales) note 2
Debtors	€1,760	(35.2% of sales) note 3
Cash	€640	(12.8% of sales) note 4
	€4,800	(2.4 x) note 5
Less current liabilities		
Creditors	€1,200	(24% of sales) note 6
Short-term loan	€400	note 7
	€1,600	
Net working capital	€3,200	
Net total assets	€10,400	
Financed by		
Debentures	€3,200	
Ordinary share capital	€2,200	
Retained earnings	€5,000	
	€10,400	

Note 1: This is €5,000 × 1.44 = €7,200. The assumption here is that the company is operating at full capacity, i.e. no excess capacity. Therefore any increase in sales will require additional investment in fixed assets. We will relax the full capacity assumption in the next section to allow for expansion in sales without additional investment in fixed assets. Note that even if plant and machinery is operating at full capacity, it may be possible to expand production by running additional shifts or by increasing the speed of use of existing machinery.

Note 2: It is reasonable to assume that as sales increase the company will require more stock to support the increase in sales. For Parnell Ltd the ratio of stock to sales is

$$\frac{€2,400}{€5,000} = 48\%$$

We will discuss stock management in Chapter 14, but assuming no change in inventory management, the forecasted stock for the year 2001 is €6,000 × 0.48 = €2,880.

Note 3: Debtors/accounts receivable
These are assumed to change proportionately with sales. Parnell's 2000 debtors to sales percentage is

$$\frac{€1,760}{€5,000} = 35.2\%$$

Therefore the forecasted debtors figure for the year 2001 is €2,112 (€6,000 × 0.352).

Note 4: The amount of cash needed to support the level of sales is expected to remain at the year 2000 level, which is

$$\frac{€640}{€5,000} = 12.8\%$$

Therefore Parnell forecasts a cash balance of €768 (€6,000 × 0.128) for the year 2001.

Note 5: Parnell has total assets of €7,200 (fixed assets) *plus* €4,800 (current assets) = €12,000. The total assets to sales ratio is therefore

$$\frac{€12,000}{€5,000} = 2.4 \text{ x} \quad (x = times)$$

So Parnell currently needs €2.4 in total assets to generate €1 in sales. This is referred to as the **capital intensity ratio**.

$$\textbf{Capital intensity ratio} = \frac{\textbf{Total assets}}{\textbf{Sales}} \qquad \textbf{(10.3)}$$

Note 6: Of course to increase total asset investments to meet an increase in sales requires an increase in funds to finance this increase in investment. Therefore, on the 'financed by' section of the balance sheet we will show accounts payable varying with sales. As the volume of sales increases, the company will place more orders for materials with its suppliers. Therefore, accounts payable will change with sales. So part of the increase in investments in total assets would be financed 'spontaneously' with increases in accounts payable. Items in the balance sheet that increase spontaneously with increases in sales are called **spontaneously generated funds**. In 2000 accounts payable as a percentage of sales is

$$\frac{€1,200}{€5,000} = 24\%$$

Therefore we project Parnell's accounts payable in 2000 to be €1,440 (€6,000 × 0.24).

Note 7: Short-term loans, debentures and ordinary share capital will not vary spontaneously with sales. These are decisions taken by company management. Retained earnings will not vary spontaneously with sales, but it will change with sales. It will depend on profit after tax and the dividend payout ratio adopted by management.

We can now construct Parnell's pro forma balance sheet for the year 2000 based on the projections we have already discussed. This is shown in Table 10.4.

10.4 Additional financial needs (AFN)

The AFN are the additional funds the company needs if the increase in assets required to finance the increase in sales is greater than the spontaneously generated funds produced from the sales increase. Parnell requires an additional €1,440 in fixed asset investment *plus* an additional €960 in current assets for a total additional financial requirement of €2,400.

Part of this would come from spontaneous increases in accounts receivable of €240 and part from the profit after tax that is not paid out as dividends, i.e. retained earnings of €1,080. Therefore Parnell Ltd will require additional financing of €1,080:

Increase in total assets (€2,400) = increase in creditors (€240) *plus* increase in retained earnings (€1,080) *plus* AFN (€1,080).

The AFN figure of €1,080 is what makes the balance sheet balance.

10.4.1 Financing the AFN

The benefit of financial planning models is that it allows management to investigate the various options it has. For example, Parnell could plan to raise the AFN of €1,080 by additional borrowing or by issuing additional shares. On the other hand, Parnell may have a policy of not borrowing any additional funds and not issuing any additional equity. In this case, the forecasted 20% increase in sales will not be feasible and planned growth is scrapped. In the next section on value-based management we will discuss the effect of growth on key financial ratios. For example, Parnell's net working capital in 2000 was €3,200 (€4,800 – €1,600). The projections based on a 20% growth rate show the current assets will increase by €960 and current liabilities will increase by €240. This means it can raise an additional €720 (€960 – €240) in short-term loans and maintain its net working capital of €3,200 (€5,760 – €2,560). The remaining additional funds required of €360 (€1,080 – €720) can be financed as management sees fit.

Table 10.4 Parnell Ltd pro forma balance sheet 2000

	2001	Change from 2000
Fixed assets	€8,640	€1,440
Current assets		
Stock	€2,880	€480
Debtors	€2,112	€352
Cash	€768	€128
	€5,760	€960
Total assets	€14,400	€2,400
Financed by		
Current liabilities		
Creditors	€1,440	€240
Short-term loan	€400	——
	€1,840	€240
Working capital	€3,920	€720
Net total assets	€12,560	
Long-term loans	€3,200	——
Share capital	€2,200	
Retained earnings	€6,080	€1,080
	€13,320	
AFN	€1,080	€1,080
	€14,400	

10.4.2 *Capacity utilisation*

In formulating the pro forma statements we assumed that Parnell Ltd was operating at full capacity and therefore any increases in sales growth was followed by an increase in fixed assets. However some companies may, because of economies of scale, build excess capacity. Therefore any increase in sales and production can be accomplished without additions to fixed assets. If the capital intensity ratio is low, sales can increase without much additional external capital. A high capital intensity ratio will mean that additions to production output will lead to high levels of external finance.

10.5 AFN—the equation approach

As we have seen, pro forma statements are used to forecast capital requirements. The equation approach is a simpler method and can be used if the **ratios are expected to remain constant** and if a rough measure of capital requirements is required. The following formula is used to forecast the additional financial needs:

$$\text{AFN} = \frac{A}{S_0} \, \Delta S - \frac{L}{S_0} \, \Delta S - [NS_1(1-d)] \qquad (10.4)$$

where AFN = additional funds needed

$\quad$ A= assets that are linked directly to sales

$\quad S_0$ = sales during the last year (in Parnell's case, 2000)

$\quad \Delta S$ = change in sales, i.e. projected sales for 2001 *minus* previous year's sales 2000

$\quad$ L = liabilities that change spontaneously with sales

$NS_1(1-d)$ = increase in retained earnings where N net margin = the net profit divided by sales or profit per €1 of sales. d is the dividend payout ratio

$\quad S_1$ = sales in the projected period (2001)

Applying this equation to Parnell Ltd, we find the AFN as

$$\text{AFN} = \frac{€12,000}{€5,000} \; €1,000 - \frac{€1,200}{€5,000} \; €1,000 - [0.24 \times €6,000 \times (1-0.25)]$$

$$= (€2,400 - €240) - (€1,080) = €1,080$$

We get the same answer using the equation approach as we did the tableau method. However we can't assume that this will always be the case. The formula method assumes that

1. assets increase in proportion to sales.
2. liabilities such as accounts payable will grow at the same rate to sales. However a change in a company's credit policy may alter this.
3. the net profit margin remains the same as sales grow. This would be unlikely.

10.6 Lumpy assets

In some industries, growth can only be accommodated by large discrete increases in fixed assets. An increase in capacity can only happen in lumpy increases in assets. This is illustrated in Figure 10.1. We assume that the minimum and most economically efficient investment in fixed assets is €1,400m. This produces enough output to generate sales of €1,000m. To increase sales beyond this point would require a total investment in plant of €2,100m. So any small increase in sales beyond the €1,000m mark will require a large financial investment.

Figure 10.1 Lumpy assets

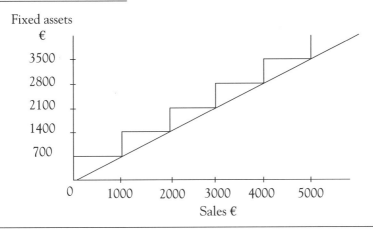

10.7 Maximum internal growth rates

What is the growth rate a firm can achieve without recourse to external funds?

This is the growth rate in sales that can be achieved with internal financing only and where the AFN is zero. Algebraically this is computed as

$$\text{Internal growth rate} = \frac{\text{ROA}(1-d)}{1 - \text{ROA}(1-d)} \qquad (10.5)$$

where

ROA = return on assets (in Parnell's case this is profit after tax of €1,200 divided by total assets of €12,000=10%
d = dividend payout ratio (for Parnell this is the dividends of €300 divided by the profit after-tax figure €1,200 which is = 25%).

This results in an internal growth rate of

$$\frac{0.10(1-0.25)}{1-0.10(1-0.25)} = \frac{0.075}{0.925} = 8.1\%$$

Therefore Parnell Ltd can grow at 8.1% per annum without requiring external finance.

10.8 Maximum sustainable growth rate

This is the growth rate that can be achieved without recourse to additional external equity financing while keeping a constant debt to equity ratio. We will discuss the reasons why companies might want to avoid selling additional equity shares in Chapter 11. The principal reasons are the costs involved and the existing shareholders may not want to share the profits of the company with new shareholders. Why companies will want to maintain a particular debt/equity relationship has been discussed in Chapter 8. The algebraic formula to ascertain this sustainable growth rate is

$$\text{Sustainable growth rate} = \frac{\text{ROE}(1-d)}{1-\text{ROE}(1-d)} \qquad (10.6)$$

where ROE = return on equity (for Parnell this is PAT of €1,200 divided by equity of €7,200 which is 16.6%) and $(1-d)$ is the retention ratio.

Therefore Parnell's sustainable growth rate is

$$\frac{0.166(1-0.25)}{1-0.166(1-0.25)} = \frac{0.1245}{0.8755} = 14.2\,\%$$

Therefore, Parnell can grow at 14.2% without issuing additional equity.

Of course, growth rates will attract more companies into the industry, forcing growth rates down. Therefore the long-term sustainable growth rate will be affected by economic factors. For example

- An increase in the profit margin will increase the return on equity and therefore increase the sustainable growth rate.
- Total asset efficiency: the more sales generated per €1 of assets, the higher the return on equity and therefore the higher the sustainable growth.
- Financial gearing: a higher proportion of debt relative to equity in the firm's capital structure reduces the need for equity and therefore increases the sustainable growth rate.
- Dividend policy: a reduction in the dividend payout increases retained earnings and therefore the greater the maximum sustainable growth rate.

Finally, **if actual growth exceeds the sustainable growth rate, the company will run short of cash**. If growth exceeds the sustainable growth rate, the company must increase its profit margin, increase its asset efficiency (i.e. generate more sales per €1 of assets), increase its gearing, increase the retention ratio (i.e. keep more earnings for reinvestment), or it will have to sell new equity shares.

Example 10.2 Sustainable growth rates

A company has the following characteristics:

1. Total assets = €100
2. Total equity = 60%

3. Total debt = 40%
4. Debt to equity ratio of 0.66
5. An dividend payout ratio of 35%
6. An asset turnover ratio of 1.3
7. A net profit margin of 4%.

The company wants to expand its sales growth beyond its sustainable level to 12%. Calculate:

(a) the sustainable growth rate.
(b) the increase in the net profit margin necessary to fund the increase in the sustainable growth level to 12%.

Solution
(a) First, we calculate the return on equity. Remember in Chapter 3, on financial statement analysis, we defined the ROE, using the Du Pont formula, as

$$\text{ROE} = \text{Net profit margin} \times \text{asset turnover} \times \text{equity multiplier}$$
$$\text{ROE} = \quad 4\% \quad \times \quad 1.3 \quad \times \quad 1.66$$
$$\text{ROE} = 8.63\%$$

(Note the equity multiplier can be calculated as 1+ the debt equity ratio).[1]

The dividend payout ratio d is 35%. Therefore the sustainable growth rate is

$$\text{Sustainable growth rate} = \frac{\text{ROE}(1-d)}{1-\text{ROE}(1-d)}$$

$$= \frac{0.0863(1-0.35)}{1-0.0863(1-0.35)}$$

$$= \frac{0.0561}{0.94} = 5.9\%$$

(b) If the proposed growth rate is 12%, we can solve for the new profit margin necessary to make this happen. Let's call the new profit margin X. Therefore

$$12\% = \frac{(X)(1.3)(1.66)(0.65)}{[1-(X)(1.3)(1.66)(0.65)]}$$
$$x = 10.7\%$$

10.9 Weaknesses of accounting-based management

The primary purpose of any financial plan is to determine whether the plan maximises shareholder value. The problem with the approach we have adopted above (i.e. accounting-based management) is that it is based on accounting concepts (e.g. profits, balance sheets, earnings per share etc.) and this approach can fail to maximise shareholder value. In particular the **accounts-based management approach ignores some basic aspects of firm value, i.e. incremental cash flow, risk and timing (i.e. present values).**

Example 10.3 Earnings quality

Growth in earnings per share may not take account of the increased investment needed to achieve the EPS growth.

Two companies, A and B, may achieve the same 20% increase in earnings. Based on accounting information, both companies give the same value. However let's suppose that company B was much more generous in granting credit to its customers. This helped them achieve the sales necessary to generate a 20% increase in earnings. In other words, company B invested more than company A, yet both achieved the same increase in earnings. Company B will have a higher debtors figure in its balance sheet than company A, and it will have spent more cash to support this higher debtors figure. Current assets will be higher in B's balance sheet, but its profit and loss account will not contain any additional cost for the increased cash outflow.

From a value-based management perspective, company A has created more value for its shareholders because it has generated more cash flow.

Table 10.5 Comparison of A and B—earnings and cash flow

	Company A (€000)		Company B (€000)	
Year	1	2	1	2
Profits	100	120	100	120
Increase in debtors	0	5	0	30
Cash flow	100	115	100	90
% change		15%		(10%)

Even though both companies see a 20% increase in earnings, company A is creating more shareholder value because it is generating more cash flow.

It is not wise to rely on accounts-based management. It is all very well for management to say that they have achieved a 20% increase in after-tax profits. What shareholders want is a maximisation of wealth. For example, a 20% increase in sales is only good news for the shareholders if the increase in investments required to boost sales have a **positive net present value**. This would happen only if the return on investment is greater than the cost of capital (which includes opportunity cost, i.e. the cost of equity capital).

10.9.1 What's wrong with accounting-based management?

In any introductory course to financial accounting, the **bottom line** figure or net profit is calculated by taking the annual revenues for operations and deducting the costs used up in generating this revenue.[2] The earnings figure calculated is divided by the weighted average number of shares outstanding to give earnings per share, which is then used as a company valuation measure.[3] Earnings per share determine the economic health of a company.

However relying on earnings-based management can result in a reduction in shareholder wealth rather than what should be the main objective of financial management, which is the **enhancement of shareholder value**. Accounting-based management can lead to the destruction of shareholder value because of distortions and manipulation of accounting methods. The first is the problem of revenue recognition:

(a) **Trade loading**: refers to the practice of pulling next year's deliveries into the last period of the current accounting year. With long-term contracts, revenues can span different accounting periods and turnover becomes more difficult to determine. The problem is when to recognise turnover on the company's profit and loss account. This is usually done as a percentage on completion basis. There are different methods used in calculating the percentage completion and this will give different turnover figures.

(b) **Charging costs**: There are two kinds of costs: invoiced costs (actual costs that require an invoice, e.g. rent and rates etc.) and paper costs that do not require an invoice, e.g. bad debts and depreciation. Calculating paper charges requires a lot of judgment and this can result in charges being made that alter profits. For example, interest payments can be capitalised, i.e. charged to the balance sheet and not to the profit and loss account. The capitalisation of interest payments has the effect of improving profit and asset values. Furthermore, changing depreciation policy can result in profit manipulation. For example, extending the life of an asset reduces the depreciation charge and boosts profits. Similarly, increasing residual values will lower the depreciation charge. In addition, firms will differ in the treatment of research and development costs. Cross-company comparisons are difficult because some companies will write off the research and development expenditure against profits and consequently have lower asset values than companies that do not write off the research and development expenditure.

(c) **Stock valuation**: Changing the method of stock valuation can have important effects on reported profits.

(d) **Provisions**: Markets don't like surprises. They prefer a non-volatile growth in profits. Announcing a profit figure this year of €100m suggests that the market will expect €110m next year. If the market expects, say, €90m in profits this year, should the company report the actual profit figure of €110m? There's a tendency for companies to make large provisions in good years and low provisions in bad years. The effect will be to smooth out profits over the years.

(e) **Risk**: Earnings-based management doesn't take into account the risk inherent in different investment projects. For example, the manager whose objective is to increase earnings will select projects that offer the highest expected profits, even though the same projects may have a higher risk. In order to adequately compare two companies, A and B, that show the same growth and earnings per share, and therefore on an earnings basis would appear to offer the same attractiveness, it would be necessary to consider the levels of investment needed to generate that growth. The company that has invested more in terms of working capital and/or fixed assets will generate less shareholder value. For example, if company A has had to provide longer payment periods to its customers in order to boost sales than company B, then it will cost A more to support higher debtors. Company A may also have to invest more in stock and fixed assets in order to increase sales. Consequently the higher investment in working capital and fixed assets is shown in the balance sheet, but the additional costs are not shown in the profit and loss account. Company B will be generating more in cash flow and therefore more shareholder value than company A.

(f) **Short termism**: It is clear therefore that focusing on accounting-based management can lead to short termism. Concentrating on reported operating profit and balance sheet figures for capital invested can be worthless in calculating shareholder value. Judging the performance of management by looking at accounting rates of return can lead to management decisions which result in reductions in shareholder value. For example, an investment in plant and machinery that would lead to financial gain in the long term could be postponed because it may lead to a fall in the accounting rates of return in the short term. This is because it raises the denominator in the accounting rate of return calculation. This is what happens if managers are judged based on accounting rates return. In the long term, however, such an investment could raise shareholder value.

(g) **Agency theory**: In Chapter 1 we introduced the student to agency costs. Managers can claim benefits from the company and in doing so can reduce shareholder value. These could include using expensive company cars where a smaller inexpensive car would do, taking Wednesday afternoon off for golf, and anything else that is essentially for the managers' pleasure but does not increase shareholder value.

10.10 How is shareholder wealth maximised?

From the preceding discussion we can conclude that rather than maximising profits the objective of management should be to maximise shareholder value.

In essence, shareholder wealth is maximised by maximising share prices. A shareholder's wealth is the number of shares held by that shareholder multiplied by the share price. A shareholder, in order to increase her wealth, will want an increase in share prices. In Chapter 6 we saw how the valuation of a share depends on:

- the ability of the company (more precisely the ability of the company's assets) to generate cash flows.
- when the cash flows are received—cash flows received sooner are better because they can be reinvested or paid out as dividends.
- the firm's risk—if a firm's risk falls, investors will, all else being equal, pay a higher price per share for cash flows that are more certain than for a share whose cash flows are risky.

Therefore, the key to creating shareholder value is to increase the cash flows and get them into the company as quickly as possible and by minimising the riskiness of the cash flows.

10.10.1 Free cash flow

More specifically, the way for managers to maximise shareholder value is to increase their **free cash flows**. This is why free cash flow is the most important determinant of shareholder value. Free cash flow is what is available for distribution to the shareholders after the company has made all the reinvestment in working capital and fixed assets necessary to maintain the business. In other words, having made a provision for depreciation to cover the annual cost of **existing** assets, expanding companies will make **further** investments in working capital and fixed assets. That is, they make a **net**

investment. If the company's net earnings are greater than net investment, the free cash flow is positive. If net earnings are less than net investment, then free cash flows are negative. Focusing on cash flow, which is more difficult to manipulate than accounting profits, makes cross-border comparisons of companies easier. Different countries can have different ways of dealing with depreciation, valuations of assets etc. A classic example was provided by Daimler-Benz, which became the first German firm to list its shares on the New York Stock Exchange. Under German accounting rules, it reported a $372 million profit. However, under American accounting rules it had losses of $1.1 billion.[4] (We have discussed how to calculate free cash flow in Chapter 2.)

10.10.2 Company valuations using free cash flows[5]

We can therefore use free cash flows to value the entire company. **Value is created when the rate of return on capital invested is greater than the cost of that capital, i.e. the required rate of return**. The difference between actual rates of return and required rates of return is the **investment spread**. If the actual rates of return is greater than the required rates return, the investment spread is positive. So, for example, if ABC Ltd invests €1m which requires a rate of return of 10% and the actual return is 15%, then the value of ABC Ltd would have increased by €50,000, i.e. €1m × (15% − 10%). If the investment spread is positive, then value is created. If the investment spread is negative, then value is diminished. Positive investment spreads signify **growth stocks**. Examples of growth stocks include (at the time of writing) companies such as Elan, Microsoft and Amazon.com. However at some time in the future growth stocks will settle into **competitive equilibrium**. As more companies enter the industry and competition becomes intense, the scope for investment spread and hence supernormal growth will evaporate. The time when this occurs is referred to as the **horizon** or **terminal** period where subsequent growth or value creation opportunities are zero. The positive performance spread will evaporate and rates will return to minimum acceptable levels. General Motors, for example, was the Microsoft of the 1960s—a supernormal growth stock. Competition eventually forced it into competitive equilibrium, so that it has now settled into a state of steady growth. Intel currently enjoys a sort of competitive advantage in that the costs of entry into the industry are excessive— it can cost an excessive amount to build a wafer fabrication plant. As long as this competitive advantage remains, Intel will remain a growth stock, other things being equal.

When companies reach this stage of their life cycle and where opportunities for further growth are zero, this period is called the **horizon period**. In the following example, we will see how a company, which goes through these different stages of growth, can be valued.

Example 10.4 Valuation based on free cash flow

Table 10.6 gives the summarised balance sheet and summarised profit and loss account for Extra Value Ltd.

Table 10.6 Summarised balance sheet for Extra Value Ltd

(Actual and projected)

Year	Actual 2001	Projected 2002	2003	2004	2005
Net fixed assets	140	150	180	185	190
Marketable securities	30	35	40	40	45
Net operating working capital	100	120	140	145	150
	270	305	360	370	385
Financed by:					
Debentures	130	145	180	180	190
Equity	140	160	180	190	195
	270	305	360	370	385

Summarised profit and loss account for Extra Value Ltd

(Actual and projected)

	Actual 2001	2002	Projected 2003	2004	2005
Net sales	1000	1220	1427	1529	1574
Operating costs	872	1068	1248	1339	1378
Depreciation	28	30	36	37	38
PBIT	100	122	143	153	158
less interest	5	6	7	8	8
PBT	95	116	136	145	150
Tax (25%)	23.75	29	34	36.25	37.5
PAT	71.25	87	102	108.75	112.5
Dividends	—	—	—	65.25	67.5
Retained earnings	71.25	87	102	43.5	45
Number of shares	50	50	50	50	50

The horizon for Extra Value is after 2005 and sales are expected to grow at a constant rate of 2% afterwards.

Table 10.7 Calculation of free cash flows

	Actual	Projected			
Year	2001	2002	2003	2004	2005
NO PAT = (PBIT)(1–tax rate)	75	91.5	107.25	114.75	118.5
less Incremental investment in fixed capital		10	30	5	5
less Incremental investment in operating working capital		20	20	5	5
FCF		61.5	57.25	104.75	108.5

An alternative method of calculating free cash flows is to use gross investment in operating fixed assets and deducting depreciation from fixed assets:

	2001	2002	2003	2004	2005
NOPAT	75	91.5	107.3	114.8	118.5
plus Depreciation	28	30	36	37	38
Operating cash flow	103	121.5	143.3	151.8	156.3
less Gross investment in fixed assets		(40)	(66)	(42)	(43)
less Increase in operating working capital		(20)	(20)	(5)	(5)
Free cash flow		61.5	57.3	104.8	108.5

Table 10.7 shows the calculation of free cash flows. In 2002, for example, Extra Value Ltd would generate €91.5m in after-tax operating profit and it would invest a further €30m in additional assets. Therefore the free cash flows for 2002 are €91.5 *minus* €30 = €61.5.

Process for finding corporate valuation

1. Find the present value of the expected free cash flows for each year within the horizon period. Extra Value's cost of capital is 12%.

$$PV = \frac{61.5}{1.12} + \frac{57.25}{(1.12)^2} + \frac{104.75}{(1.12)^3} + \frac{108.5}{(1.12)^4} = €244.6m$$

2. Calculate the present value of the free cash flows after the horizon period.
   Because growth is expected to be constant after 2005, we can use the constant growth formula to calculate the value of operations as at the end of 2005. First, we can use the free cash flow for 2005 to find the free cash flow for 2006.

$$FCF_{2006} = FCF_{2005}(1 + g)$$
$$= €108.5(1 + 0.02)$$
$$= €110.67$$

Therefore the value of operations at the end of 2005 is

$$\frac{€110.67}{0.12 - 0.02} = €1,106.7$$

We now discount the year 5 value back to the present to get the present value:

$$\frac{€1215.2}{(1.12)^4} = €772.3$$

3. The sum of the present values got in 1 and 2 is €947.9m. This represents the current value (2001) of its operating assets. This is illustrated in Figure 10.2.

Figure 10.2 Valuation of whole company using free cash flows and non-constant growth rates

4. The total value of the company is the value of its operating assets *plus* the value of its non-operating assets, in Extra Value's case marketable investments of €30m. Therefore Extra Value's total valuation at the end of 2001 is €947.6m + €30m = €977.6m.

5. The value of equity (i.e. shareholders' value) is the value of operations *less* debt. This is:

Total value of operations (€977.6m) *less* value debt (€130m) = €847.6m

Summary (€millions)	
Value of operation assets	€947.6
Value of non-operating assets	€30
Total value of operations	€977.6
less value of debt	€130
equals value of equity	€847.6

One of the benefits of value-based management (projecting financial statements into the future), in addition to giving us a current valuation of the business, is that it allows us to identify ways of increasing shareholder value. Furthermore we can compare the pro forma statements and the financial plan to see if the targets set out in a financial plan are met. For example, the value of shareholders' funds is €847.6m. There are 50 million shares outstanding, which means that the value of a single share is €16.96. If the current market price is greater than €16.96, it would clearly not be acceptable. Management will therefore have to make adjustments to and *revise their financial plan*. They could start by improving the company's actual financial ratios (profitability, acid management, expenses, debtors collection periods, payment periods) that are lagging behind some benchmark like the industry average. The company may have higher costs to sales ratios, and below average accounts receivable to sales and stock to sales ratios. The company will need to revise its financial plan to minimise its investments in working capital so that it can increase its overall return on assets. It could possibly do this by scrapping low-profit products and lowering operating costs. It might need to be more aggressive in cutting the debtors collection period and in reducing the stock to sales ratio. The overall effect will be to increase the NOPAT and improve the net operating working capital. The result will be an improvement in free cash flows. This of course would have the effect of improving company and shareholder value. Therefore, the benefit of value-based management is that it helps increase shareholder value.

10.11 Economic value added (EVA)

Another way to assess the economic performance (value creation) of management and the company is **economic value added**. This focuses on 'adjusted accounting information' rather than cash flows. While some top executives' bonus packages are based on share price performance, earnings per share and other accounting measures are also important, particularly for divisional and lower level management. As discussed earlier, focusing on accounting measures as a performance yardstick has obvious drawbacks. Managers whose compensation packages depend on end of term profits can manipulate short-term earnings at the expense of creating longer-term difficulties. Earnings-based bonus payments can result in managers offering huge discounts which require employees working overtime to produce and distribute extra product (trade loading). These practices consume vast amounts of extra capital (for warehousing, additional working capital etc.) and the extra costs do not appear on the income statement. Economic value added attempts to prevent this type of problem. Whereas traditional profit and loss accounts only deduct the cost of debt capital to arrive at the bottom line, economic value added deducts the cost of all capital (including the cost of equity capital) to arrive at the bottom line figure. For example if a company has invested €100m in capital and its cost of capital is 10%, its required rate of return is €10m. If the company's actual rate of return is €30m, its EVA is €20m. The company will have enhanced shareholder value by €20m. If the company's actual return is €5m, its EVA is *minus* €5m and it will have diminished shareholder value by €5m. The formula for economic value added is

$$\text{Economic value added (EVA)} = \text{NOPAT} - \text{WACC}$$
$$= \text{PBIT}(1 - T) - \begin{bmatrix} \text{Adjusted} \\ \text{invested} \\ \text{capital} \end{bmatrix} \begin{bmatrix} \text{After-tax} \\ \text{cost of} \\ \text{capital} \end{bmatrix} \quad (10.7)$$

where WACC = weighted average cost of capital

T = tax rate

Alternatively,

$$\text{Economic value added (EVA)} = \begin{bmatrix} \text{Adjusted} \\ \text{operating profits} \\ \text{after tax} \end{bmatrix} - \begin{bmatrix} \begin{pmatrix} \text{Adjusted} \\ \text{invested} \\ \text{capital} \end{pmatrix} (\text{WACC}) \end{bmatrix} \quad (10.8)$$

Example 10.5 Economic value added calculation

Using the data from the income statement and the balance sheet we can calculate Extra Value Ltd's economic value added.

Table 10.8 Extra Value Ltd's economic value added calculation

PBIT	€100
Tax rate	25%
NOPAT	€75
Invested operating capital	€240
WACC	12%
Cost of capital	€28.8
EVA = NOPAT *less* WACC	€46.2

In calculating economic value added, we use the term **adjusted** in describing capital invested and adjusted operating profits after tax. The term 'adjusted' is used because, according to Stern Stewart, the arbiters of EVA, over 160 adjustments may need to be made to the accounting data before calculating economic value added. The main adjustment is to include a cost for equity supplied capital. Equity capital has a cost called **opportunity cost** because shareholders give up the opportunity of investing funds elsewhere and receiving a more favourable rate of return. The rate of return they could receive, if they invested the capital elsewhere in companies of similar risk, is the cost of equity capital. While the cost of equity capital is the main difference between economic value added and accounting profit, there are other adjustments needed to accounting earnings before calculating economic value added. The following is a list of some of the most common adjustments:

- Goodwill: If it is the practice of a company to write off goodwill to the profit and loss account, then it should be added back to shareholders' funds when calculating economic value added. This is because the goodwill payment represents what the acquisition is actually worth. Therefore, in calculating EVA, the current period's goodwill amortisation is added back to net operating profit after tax (NOPAT) and goodwill amortised in past years is added back to capital.
- Research and development costs: Again, if the practice is to write off research and development costs to the profit and loss account then these should also be treated as an asset and added back to shareholders' funds. This is because the research and development is obviously an investment in future products and will generate future cash flows. Accounting rules state that all research and development costs should be

immediately deducted from earnings. For companies that spend a lot of money on research and development, such as high-tech pharmaceutical companies, this treatment reduces one of their most valuable assets to nothing. The economic value added treatment is to capitalise research and development costs. This of course is the correct treatment for such a valuable asset.

- Minority interests:[6] Since all capital is working in the company, regardless of where it comes from, minority interests and total debt are added to shareholders' funds.

- Expenses and revenues: Many companies spend money on marketing in order to enter new markets, gain new market share and establish brand names. Following the deregulation of the telecommunications market in Ireland, emerging companies spend a lot of money on winning customers, which is an investment that will lead to future profitability. However accounting rules state that these expenses must be written off and deducted from earnings. Economic value added companies capitalise customer acquisition costs and amortise them over the appropriate period.

- Depreciation: With economic value added the capital charge for depreciation declines in line with the depreciation value of the asset. So companies using the straight-line method of depreciation, which has the same capital charge each year, will have to make the appropriate adjustment under economic value added. The effect of EVA adjustment however is to make old assets look cheap and new assets look expensive, and managers may therefore be reluctant to replace old equipment with new.

- Taxes: For the purpose of calculating EVA (and consequently NOPAT) companies should only deduct the cash taxes they pay. Deferred taxes that were deducted from earnings in the past should be taken out of the liability section of the balance sheet and added to shareholders' funds for calculating cost of capital.

- Passive investments: Passive investments such as marketable securities are deducted from capital because they are not used in the operating activities of the company. The income from these investments should be subtracted from the net operating profit after tax (NOPAT). In addition, any form of free capital (e.g. accrued wages, trade creditors) should be subtracted from capital.

Box 10.1 EVA and performance pay

Economic value added can be used to determine value creation at all levels and divisions as well as for the company as a whole.

Research in Britain and the US suggests there is little correlation between performance and chief executive salaries . . . A key performance criterion centres on shareholder value. Capitalism proposes share price as an anchor indicator for other types of performance measures, especially profitability.

Profitability, in turn, is deemed to result from superior management decisions and practices. If share price is a good proxy for performance, it should be tightly correlated to profitability and management behaviour. Unfortunately, a link up among these criteria is not apparent. In the present bull market, relatively mediocre profitability performers have enjoyed rising share prices. The tenuous link between profit and share price highlights the tendency to speculation and the astronomical price/earnings ratios of some companies. Often companies are valued not for their intrinsic value creation,

$\longrightarrow$

through products and services to customers, but on the fervent hope that they will attract a takeover bid, especially if in a trendy industry, viz. many Internet and biotechnology companies have never posted a profit. Why was Telecom so oversubscribed?

An increasingly accepted performance criterion is economic value added (EVA). This measure seeks to assess the intrinsic value created by the company rather than merely its 'paper' value. EVA subtracts cost of capital from after tax profit. Cost of capital includes interest paid, dividends and the cost of equity through capital gains to shareholders.

Published EVA figures for Irish and UK companies in 1997 show that of the 20 Irish listed companies, eight had negative EVAs, while 141 of 200 UK companies had negative EVAs. According to Stern Stewart, the arbiters of EVA, these companies would be better off if they were taken over or if they installed new management.

Extracted from an article by Dr Eleanor O'Higgins (UCD) titled 'Spotlight on pay-for-performance system'

The Irish Times, 20 October 1999

10.12 Market value added

One of the problems with EVA is that it tells us nothing about how current management strategies are likely to affect future shareholder value. To resolve this problem, Stern Stewart have come up with market value added (MVA), which deducts the total equity capital supplied by shareholders from the market value of its shares. Increasing EVA will increase the share price (other things being equal) and MVA will therefore increase because of an increase in share price.

$$
\begin{aligned}
\text{Market value added (MVA)} &= \begin{bmatrix} \text{Market value} \\ \text{of equity} \end{bmatrix} - \begin{bmatrix} \text{Equity capital supplied} \\ \text{by shareholders} \end{bmatrix} \\
&= \begin{bmatrix} \text{Number of shares} \\ \text{outstanding} \end{bmatrix} \begin{bmatrix} \text{Share} \\ \text{price} \end{bmatrix} - \begin{bmatrix} \text{Total common} \\ \text{equity} \end{bmatrix}
\end{aligned}
\tag{10.9}
$$

Since the primary objective of companies is the maximisation of shareholders' wealth, MVA is the definitive measure of wealth and wealth creation. Market value added is the difference between the capital invested by shareholders and the market value of that capital at today's market price. It is therefore a measure of how the company has enhanced or diminished shareholder value. As an illustration, the market value of Kingspan on 10 September 2000 was €496.4m, while shareholders had invested only €81.8m. Therefore, Kingspan had a market value added of €496.4m *less* €81.8m = €414.6m.

MVA is risk adjusted because the market automatically incorporates judgments on risk into stock prices. Therefore we can use MVA to compare different companies in different industries and countries. The company with the highest MVA is the one that has created most wealth for its shareholders. If we think of a company as a whole series of investment projects, then MVA is equivalent to the company's net present value (NPV). MVA is the difference between gross market value and the cumulative capital investment. This is the net present value. However we cannot use accounting book values to estimate MVA.

Accounting rules tend to understate the amount of capital a company has invested. Various adjustments have to be made similar to those discussed under EVA, for example adding back research and development costs and goodwill to shareholders' funds.

EVA shows the value added during a given year, whereas MVA shows the value added over the company's entire existence. Unlike EVA, there is no MVA for business units, divisions or subsidiaries. Therefore, unlike EVA, MVA cannot be used to assess annual internal performance.

SUMMARY

- Financial planning involves the conversion of the corporate plan into quantitative terms. This will involve projected financial statements that show the effect the corporate plan has on corporate profits.
- Financial forecasting begins with the budgeting process, which identifies the assets that are required and the revenues that will be generated from the use of these assets.
- The sales budget is the most important budget of all, because all other budgets will depend on the volume of sales activity.
- One method used to assess the effect the forecasted growth in sales has on the income statement and balance sheet is the 'per cent of sales method'. Here items on the profit and loss account and balance sheet are divided into two groups — those that vary directly with sales and those that do not.
- Additional finance needs (AFN) are the additional funds the company needs if the increase in assets required to finance the increase in sales is greater than the spontaneously generated funds produced from the sales increase.
- The equation approach is another method used to estimate the AFN.
- The maximum internal growth rate is the growth the firm can achieve without recourse to external funds.
- The maximum sustainable growth rate is the rate that can be achieved without recourse to additional equity financing, while keeping a constant debt:equity ratio.
- The weakness of accounting-based management is that it is based on accounting concepts and this approach can fail to maximise shareholder value.
- The objective of financial management is to maximise shareholder value rather than maximising profits.
- Specifically, shareholder value is maximised by maximising the company's free cash flows (FCF). FCF is the most important determinant of shareholder value. Free cash flow is what is available for distribution to shareholders and lenders after the company has made all the reinvestment in working capital and fixed assets necessary to maintain the business.
- Shareholder value is created when the actual rate of return is greater than the required rate of return (positive investment spread). Shareholder value is destroyed when the actual rate of return is less than the required rate of return (negative investment spread).
- Economic value added focuses on adjusted accounting information rather than cash flows. EVA is defined as NOPAT *minus* WACC.
- Market value added is the market value of equity *minus* the capital supplied by shareholders.

QUESTIONS

1. Describe pro forma financial statements and explain the use of pro forma statements in creating shareholder value. Why is forecasting necessary?
2. Explain the term 'competitive advantage period'. Is it possible to have positive NPV where it has no competitive advantage?
3. Outline the deficiencies in accounting-based management as a performance measure.
4. ✦ Companies can grow too fast. Explain.
5. Explain the terms 'maximum internal growth rate' and 'maximum sustainable growth rates'.
6. Financial plans have qualitative and quantitative inputs. Explain.
7. The sales forecast is the most important input in financial plans. Why?
8. Explain the terms 'spontaneously generated funds' and 'AFN'.
9. What is value-based management?
10. ✦ The following are the summarised financial statements of XYZ Ltd for the year ended 2000:

Profit & loss account	
Turnover	€20,000
Costs	€16,000
Profit before tax	€4,000
Tax (20%)	€800
Profit after tax	€3,200
Dividends	€500
Retained earnings	€2,700

Balance sheet	
Assets	€140,000
Financed by	
debt	€28,000
Equity	€112,000
	€140,000

Sales for the year are expected to be €23,000. Calculate the additional financial needs based on the following assumptions:

(a) The company wishes to maintain a constant payout ratio.
(b) Both assets and costs are directly proportional to sales.

11. The following is a list of assets and liabilities of Coolroe Ltd and its profit and loss account for year end 2001.

Assets	
Fixed assets	€6,000
Current assets	€1,050
Total assets	€7,050
Liabilities	
Creditors	€300
Short-term loans	€60
Debentures	€4,500
Ord. shareholders' funds	€900
Retained earnings	€1,290

Sales for the year were €3,000 and they are expected to grow by 50% during 2001 and operating costs should increase at the same rate. The net profit margin is 14.8% and the company has a policy of paying out 50% of its profit for ordinary shareholders. The company can expand its sales to grow without further investment in fixed assets. Net current assets should increase at the same rate as sales.

Calculate the additional finance needs using balance sheet method.

12. ♦ Explain how the capital intensity ratio affects the AFN.

13. What are the weaknesses in using the AFN formula in forecasting financial requirements?

14. ♦ The following is the balance sheet of Clashmore Ltd for the year ended 2000:

Fixed assets	€100,00
Current assets	€75,00
Total	€175,000
Financed by	
Creditors	€10,000
Short-term loans	€5,000
Ord. shares	€160,000
	€175,000

All of the company's profit for ordinary shareholders is paid out as dividends and the company has excess capacity. Sales for 2000 were €175,000 with a net income of €35,000. Sales for 2001 are expected to be €350,000. Calculate the AFN for 2001. Assume that the short-term debt is paid off during the year.

15. Sales for Ring Ltd last year were €1m. The ratio of required assets to sales is 2:1. The ratio of liabilities that change spontaneously with sales is 0.6:1. The payout ratio is 50% and the profit margin is 12%. What is the maximum growth rate that Ring Ltd can expect to accomplish without having recourse to non-spontaneous external capital?

16. Dunmore Enterprises is currently not paying dividends. Sales for the year just gone were €20m. Current assets are €4m and current liabilities are €0.6m. Sales are forecasted to increase by 20% next year. What are the additional finance needs (AFN) if the profit margin is 7%?

17. Portlaw Technologies Ltd—summarised income statement and balance sheet

Profit & loss acc. for year ended 31 Dec. 2000		Balance sheet		
		Fixed assets (net book value)		€176,400
		Current assets		
		Debtors	€90,720	
Turnover	€504,000	Stocks	€126,000	
Operating costs	€454,160	Cash	€15,120	
PBIT	€4,9840			€231,840
Interest	€7,840			€408,240
PBT	€42,000	less Current liabilities		
Tax (20%)	€8,400	Creditors	€60,480	
PAT	€33,600	Prepayments	€40,320	
Dividends (40%)	€13,440	Short-term loans	€29,400	
Retained earnings	€20,160			€130,200
		Total net assets		€278,040
		Financed by		
		Debentures		€49,000
		Ord. shareholder funds		€49,000
		Retained earnings		€180,040
				€278,040

Using the percentage of sales method prepare a pro forma balance sheet and income statement for December 2001 basing your answer on the following assumptions:

(a) Sales are expected to grow by 20% during 2001.
(b) Assets, spontaneous liabilities and operating costs are expected to increase by the same percentage as sales.
(c) The company is operating at full capacity.
(d) The company has decided to borrow any additional finance as short-term debt.
(e) Interest rates on short-term debt is 5%.
(f) You should incorporate any financing feedbacks into your answer.

18. From the following information calculate (a) the return on equity and (b) the sustainable growth rate.

Net profit	€16,500
Profit margin	8%
Debt:equity ratio	50%
Capital intensity ratio	70%
Dividends	€5,000

19. ♦ A firm has been operating successfully (it thinks) and wants to maintain its growth rate of 10% per annum. The ratio of total assets to sales is 170% and it has a net profit margin of 5%. Its total assets are financed with 40% debt in its capital structure. Advise the company on its growth rate.

NOTES

1. Remember that the equity multiplier is

$$\frac{\text{Total assets}}{\text{Total equity}} = \frac{1}{0.6} = 1.66$$

The debt: equity ratio is:
$$\frac{0.4}{0.6} = 0.66$$

Therefore
$$1 + 0.66 = 1.66 = \text{Equity multiplier}$$

2. This is the accruals concept underlying financial accounting.
3. Investment ratios are discussed in Chapter 11.
4. This particular fact was extracted from an article titled 'A Star to Sail by', *The Economist*, 2 August 1997.
5. There are different methods of calculating free cash flow. The method used here is that used by Brigham, Gapenski and Ehrhardt, op. cit.
6. When companies consolidate subsidiaries that are not wholly owned, some of the profits shown on the profit and loss account do not belong to the shareholders. That part of the profits that does not belong to the parent company's shareholders is shown as minority interests.

11
Raising Equity Finance

CHAPTER OBJECTIVES

At the end of this chapter the student will be able to:

1. outline the features of common shares
2. understand primary markets, secondary markets and initial public offerings (IPOs)
3. explain the concept of underpricing
4. understand different methods of issuing shares
5. analyse venture capital as a source of long-term funds
6. understand the different stock market indices and why Irish companies get listed on more than one exchange
7. understand the trading systems and the regulation of the Irish Stock Exchange
8. calculate various stock market ratios
9. gain an appreciation of the concept of the 'efficient market hypothesis'.

INTRODUCTION

Companies raise new equity capital in the market all the time. In Chapter 6 we discussed share valuation techniques. In this chapter we look at equity capital as a source of long-term finance. This includes why firms sell shares and the methods used in selling shares, the impact of issues of shares on the price of shares and different theories relating to market efficiency.

11.1 Ordinary shares and shareholder rights

Ordinary shares or common stocks are shares that have a claim to the financial success of the company and have no preferential treatment in terms of dividends or in cases of bankruptcy. The owners of these shares have control over the company along with the right to vote at company meetings and elect company directors. They have the right to either accept or reject company strategic moves such as company merger plans or other major capital investment decisions. In the area of voting rights, the rule is one share, one vote. Therefore, a shareholder with 100 shares can cast 100 votes. Shareholders must receive as much information as is sensible and must receive a copy of the company's annual report. Common shareholders have the right to purchase any new shares (in proportion to their existing holding) issued by the company. This is called the **pre-emption right.** This right is enshrined under the Irish

Company's Amendment Act 1983. This enables existing shareholders to maintain control. For example if new shares issued were purchased by management, control of the company would be seized by management away from the shareholders. In addition, the pre-emption right works to protect shareholders from a dilution in their wealth. Suppose for example there are 100 shares in issue and each share has a market value of €10 giving a market capitalisation of €1,000. If the company issues an additional 100 shares at €5 per share, the new market capitalisation will be €1,500 giving a share price of €7.50. Therefore, the existing shareholders will have suffered a 25% dilution in their shares. Effectively the new share issue has transferred wealth away from the existing shareholders to the new shareholders.

Shareholders do not receive any interest on their shares, and they have no legal right to any return on their investment. However, once all other costs have been paid, e.g. interest on debt, taxes to the government and payments made to other creditors, common stockholders have the right to whatever is left over—if anything. This may be paid out to the shareholders as a dividend or it may be reinvested in the company at the discretion of the company's directors.

Furthermore, shareholders do not have the right to take their money out of the company. If they want to 'liquidate' their investment, they can do so by selling their shares to other investors who may want to buy them. Remember that shares do not have a fixed price. The price of a share is determined in the market place by supply and demand. Liquidity refers to the ability to convert assets into cash at short notice. Even if companies are doing very well, investors are unlikely to commit their money to shares in that company if they believe they will not be able to liquidate (sell for cash) their shares.

Many companies continue to exist as successful private firms and have no desire to go public. Indeed some of Ireland's biggest companies are private, e.g. Dunnes Stores and Clery's. Furthermore, there have been many notable examples of companies that **delisted** and went from being public companies back to being private. Examples of these include James Crean and Clondalkin.

11.2 Primary markets, secondary markets and initial public offerings (IPOs)

Some companies are **privately owned**. This means that the shares in these companies are not traded. They are owned by the family members who own the company or perhaps by the managers of the company. When the shares of a company are actively traded, they are called **publicly owned** companies. The shares of large companies are listed on **organised security exchanges** like the ISEQ or FTSE. These shares are said to be **listed**. Shares of smaller companies are not listed on organised exchanges. They trade in the over-the-counter market (OTC market) and are said to be **unlisted**. We will explain more about the various markets later on in the chapter.

11.2.1 Advantages and disadvantages of selling shares in the company to the public (going public)

Advantages
- Liquidity: Privately owned firms do not have a ready market for their shares. Selling shares to raise cash is difficult and it is even more difficult to establish a fair price for the shares. Publicly owned firms do not have these liquidity problems.

- Valuation: It establishes a market valuation of a firm.
- No obligation to pay dividends: Corporations do not have an obligation to pay a dividend on the shares. Interest on debt must be paid.
- Debt: equity ratio: If a company's debt:equity ratio is too high, borrowing more may be too expensive. Companies may see equity financing as the cheaper option. It would also bring the debt:equity ratio down to more acceptable levels. This could facilitate further borrowing in the future.
- Status: Listed companies will get an amount of free advertising and being listed gives a certain amount of prestige.

Disadvantages
- Issuing new stock means sharing power and profits with new shareholders.
- Flotation costs: Fees paid to bankers, lawyers and advisers are very high. Flotation costs associated with equity issues are higher than the costs associated with debt issues.
- Signalling: Selling shares may send the wrong signal to the market. We discuss this in a later section.
- Cost of reporting: Quarterly and annual reporting is expensive.
- Disclosure: Privately held firms can operate in such a way as to pay high salaries and show favouritism in promoting employees (nepotism). These are more difficult to do when the company is public. In addition, operating data must be reported in annual reports which become available to competitors.
- Stock price: The market may not be putting a fair price on the company's shares. Indeed this is one of the reasons cited why companies delist and revert back to being private concerns. An example is Clondalkin plc, discussed in Chapter 19.

When a publicly owned firm wishes to raise new finance, it can do so by selling securities (shares and bonds) to investors. This is the **primary market**. When the owners of these shares wish to liquidate or sell these shares to other investors, they do so in the **secondary market**. The secondary market is where shareholders sell their shares to other investors. When privately held firms wish to **go public** to raise equity capital by selling shares to the public, we refer to this as an **initial public offering**. IPOs also describe the privatisation programmes of governments around the world, where government-owned utilities such as telecommunications are **sold off** to the public. Examples include Telecom Éireann (now Eircom), Deutsche Telecom (Germany), Nippon Telephone and Telegraph (NTT, Japan) and British Telecom. Going public provides companies with an immediate market valuation of their company. Employees are usually offered share options. We discuss share options later in the chapter.

11.3 Initial public offerings and underpricing

IPOs generate many headlines particularly in the areas of the so called new economy stocks and government privatisations. New economy stocks are described as technology or dot.com stocks.

If IPOs are oversubscribed, the share price will go up on the first day of trading. The investment bankers who deal with the issue will usually favour the large institutional investors like pension funds that will get the bulk of the shares. The smaller investor will usually have to wait until the after market to buy up shares after they have been initially sold. The **after market** is defined as the period after the issue is sold to the public. The problem is, as evidence shows, that IPOs tend to underperform the market in the long run.[1] IPOs are costly if the shares are issued at a price below their true value. Investors who buy these shares gain at the expense of the original shareholders. This is true for a government-owned utility (the taxpayer loses out) as it is for a privately owned firm (the existing shareholders lose out). This is called the **cost of underpricing**. On the other hand, it can also be costly if the shares are priced too high, because the issue may be unsuccessful. Another reason for underpricing is what economists call the **winner's curse**. If you buy a house at an auction, you could say that you have won. You beat off all the others to buy the house. However, it could be that everybody else in the auction room thought that the house was overpriced. It seems that you have overpaid. The same reasoning applies to stock issues. If you apply for every IPO you will have no difficulty getting whatever stock you apply for in companies whose stock is overpriced (that nobody else wants). However, in issues that are underpriced you will only get a fraction of what you want. It would be better therefore if you apply for IPOs that are underpriced. So underpricing will counteract the winner's curse. Thus if you are offered all the shares you want, it is more than likely that the issue is overpriced and smart investors will stay away. This is seen as a rationale for underpricing. (See Box 11.1.)

Underpricing of IPOs occurs in all countries.[2] In America the average age of IPO companies is about seven years, whereas in continental Europe it is about 50 years. Research by American economists Roger Ibbotson, Jody L. Sindelar and Jay R. Ritter[3] shows significant underpricing of IPOs from 1960 to 1998. Only five of the 36 periods witnessed overpricing. Between 1960 and 1992, the average underpricing of IPOs was 15%. Interestingly, the number of IPOs tended to increase around the same time as the underpricing. This is because underpricing signals high returns to investors and companies react to the positive sentiment among investors by going public. However the research also shows that much of the underpricing occurs in companies that are high-risk, very young companies with low sales growth. Underpricing is necessary therefore to attract investors for these types of companies.

Box 11.1 IPOs and the winner's curse

Sean and Mary are both investors. Two IPOs are coming on the market, company X and company Y. Mary is a smart investor and considers company X to be overpriced and company Y to be underpriced. Sean on the other hand considers that share prices tend to rise after an initial issue of shares. He therefore invests in all IPOs. Because company Y is underpriced, the issue will be oversubscribed and neither Sean nor Mary will get all the shares they wanted. However, because Mary, the smart one, correctly considered company X to be overpriced, she did not invest any of her money in company X shares. Therefore Sean gets all the shares he asked for in company X. Therefore the moral of the story is that if you are offered all of the shares you wanted, it is likely that the IPO is overpriced and the smart investor will stay away. Therefore, you should only subscribe for shares in IPOs that are underpriced. Avoiding the winner's curse is a rationale for underpricing.

In addition to the cost of underpricing, there are administrative costs which involve legal, financial and underwriter costs. **Underwriters** perform three functions: (a) they provide advice to the company; (b) they buy the new issue of shares; and (c) they resell the shares to the public. They make their money on the spread. This means that they buy the shares from the company at a price below which they resell them to the public.

11.4 Ways of selling common shares

There are five ways of raising cash through the sale of common stock. These are:

1. through a public offering to the general public.
2. through a private placement or a stock exchange placing of shares to a single investor or a small group of investors.
3. through a rights issue to existing shareholders in proportion to their existing holdings of shares.
4. through stock purchase plans to employees.

11.4.1 Going public

This is mainly used for larger companies where shares are offered to institutional investors and the public.

Prospectus and underwriting

The prospectus or the listing particulars are critical to the success of any new listing. It serves the requirements of the stock exchange and it acts as a marketing instrument that will raise the awareness of the company. A summary of the listing requirements is given in section 11.6.

Methods used in public issues of shares

(a) Bookbuilding: Most issues in the US are priced using the bookbuilding procedure. Investors indicate to the underwriters how much of the stock they wish to buy and indicate the maximum price they wish to pay. Others will indicate that they just want to invest a certain amount of money regardless of the price of the issue. So, for example, they may say that they will take $10,000 of shares. This is used by the underwriters to give an estimate of the issue price. They will also take into consideration the share price of similar companies in the same industry and will, in addition, undertake discounted cash flow analysis.

(b) Fixed Price: Companies undergoing IPOs in the UK do so on a fixed price basis or by auction. The selling price is fixed and the number of shares to be issued is advertised. If the issue is overpriced, not all the shares on offer will be sold and the underwriters will buy the shares that were not sold. If the issue is underpriced and oversubscribed, each investor will get a proportion of the shares s/he applied for. As explained earlier, the fixed price offer leaves investors open to the winner's curse.

(c) Auction: With an auction system, investors are invited to submit their bids on the number of securities they want to buy and how much they are prepared to pay for them. The securities are then issued to the highest bidders. Unlike the bookbuilding system used in the US, the bids made under an auction system are binding. The auction system can bypass the underwriters because there are no unsold securities, unless of course the seller imposes a minimum bid price, in which case underwriters could be used to buy any securities that remain unsold at this minimum price. There are two types of auctions—**discriminatory price** and **uniform price**. An example will illustrate.

Example 11.1 Issuing securities and auctions

Suppose that 5 million securities are being issued by auction. Suppose that three investors apply for the issue. Investor A applies for 2 million securities and is willing to pay €100 each. Investor B wants 3 million securities at €90 each and investor C has applied for 1 million securities at €80 each.

Investors A and B are the winners. Investor C loses out and gets no allocation. If the auction was a discriminatory auction, the total proceeds would be €470m, i.e. (€100 × 2m) + (€90 × 3m) = €470m. On the other hand if the auction was a uniform auction, the total proceeds would be €450m, i.e. (€90 × 2m) + (€90 × 3m) = €450m. Under a discriminatory price auction the investors are required to pay whatever price they bid, while under a uniform price system all investors will pay the lowest winning bid, in this example €90 bid by investor B.

Box 11.2 A note on auctions and the winner's curse

In example 11.1 the uniform price system yielded lower proceeds than the discriminatory price system. However, there is a hidden cost here, which we have not imputed. It seems that the uniform price auction acts as an insurance against the winner's curse. Under uniform pricing the issue is less likely to be overpriced. In the example, investor B pays €90 per security, whereas investor A pays €100 per security. The discriminatory price leaves investors exposed to the winner's curse. If investors recognise this, then the proceeds from a uniform price issue could possibly yield more. In fact, some government bond issues in the US have switched from discriminatory pricing to uniform pricing.

Share issues and the effect on share price

There have been some famous examples of share price fluctuations and collapses following IPOs down through the years. One of the most memorable of recent times is the flotation of the Internet stock, lastminute.com. (See box 11.3.)

Supply and demand analysis indicates that a share issue (an increase in supply) will depress share price. However, evidence suggests that share prices do not fall **in proportion** to the size of the stock issue. There are other factors at work. Share issues send signals (information) to the market about the company's intentions. If the prospects for the company are good, it will not want to share the fruits of future successes with new shareholders. For this reason the issue will not be seen as a favourable development by investors and the share price will fall when the announcement of the issue is made. Effectively what happens is that investors see the issue as being risky and consequently assign a higher cost of capital to the company's shares to compensate for the higher risk and the share price falls. Similarly, companies are more likely to issue shares when they believe their shares are overvalued. This information feeds into the market and investors mark down the price the shares are offered at because of this information. In other words, if companies have discretion when to issue shares, they are more likely to do so when it is advantageous to them, i.e. when the shares are overvalued. This doesn't fool the market and prices drop. However, it appears that the market is not as efficient as we might like to think it is. Studies conducted by Loughran and Ritter[4] have shown that for both IPOs and issues from established companies, share prices have underperformed, in terms of average returns, than portfolios of similar stocks by a significant margin. This can be to the tune of 30% over a five year period.

Box 11.3 How to sink flotation opportunity

If somebody ever gets around to writing a worthy paper on how not to float a company on the stock market, the shambles of the recent lastminute.com flotation is sure to be one of the case histories. Quite simply this is a company that was floated on little more than dot.com hype.

But for the moment, let's forget whether this online corner sweetie shop should have been floated in the first place. Let's look instead at how the flotation turned sour with lastminute.com now left with a veritable army of small shareholders who are seriously cheesed off.

First, punters were so sure of the dot.com revolution that 189,000 of them signed up with lastminute.com to make sure that they qualified for an allocation for the website's shares.

The promoters—obviously convinced democrats—decided that everybody would get the same allocation and this meant that the punters ended up with a grand total of just €235 worth of shares each.

They should be thankful that €235 was all they got given the way lastminute.com shares have tanked in the past couple of weeks. From a float price of 380p sterling and a post-float high of 555p, the shares this week have been trading below 200p. The words 'bubble' and 'burst' spring to mind.

And then to make matters even worse, the company's registrars IRG were forced to issue a cringing apology to investors for mistakes which led to mistakes in getting share certificates to investors. Bit of a problem this—no certificate meant that punters couldn't take advantage of the very brief jump in the shares and may now be left with lastminute.com shares worth half what they paid for them.

Problem number two came when some refund cheques sent to punters who didn't get their full allocation bounced! In a statement IRG said: 'IRG wish to emphasise that these errors did not result from lastminute.com and wishes to apologise.' Indeed.

The Irish Times, 7 April 2000

Setting the price of shares in publicly quoted firms

For companies that are already publicly owned, the new issue share price will be based on the existing market price of the share. Investment bankers will usually quote a price below the last price quoted on the day before the issue. Like IPOs, seasoned issues tend to be followed by a decline in the share price. The reasons are similar to those discussed above for IPOs. First, there is the information signalling reason. Managers will try to fool the market by issuing shares when they believe that the share price is overvalued. The market anticipates this and marks the prices of the share down. Secondly, the market might take the view that if the company is so confident about the future, why would it want to let new shareholders share in the rewards. Existing shareholders could have all the gain and the company could finance its expansion plans by issuing debt.

Maintaining a secondary market in shares of small companies

The market for **blue chip** companies such as Smurfit, Bank of Ireland, AIB, Cement Roadstone Holdings, Intel etc. is liquid. Buyers and sellers of these shares are easily matched. The transactions volume of such securities is high, which makes it easier for these shares to be bought and sold. This creates liquidity.

However smaller companies have fewer transactions and it is therefore more difficult to match buyers and sellers. This does not mean that the market for such shares is illiquid. These shares usually trade in the **over-the-counter market**. The investment bankers or dealers will usually agree to **make a market** in such stocks to keep them liquid. They do this by holding an inventory of such stock and when a buyer surfaces the shares are pulled from the inventory and sold over-the-counter—hence the term 'over the counter'. Therefore, an active secondary market is maintained in such securities.

Table 11.1 Summary of costs of public offerings

Spread: The difference between the price the issuer receives and the offer price. This is the spread, the fee charged by the underwriter.

Expenses: These include legal fees, costs of filing the issue, and administrative and management time spent on the issue.

Underpricing: the losses that arise from selling stock below their intrinsic or true value.

Abnormal returns: On the announcement of the issue, the price of existing stock falls in relation to overall stock market or other similar companies.

11.4.2 Private placements

This is the most frequently used method in Ireland of bringing a new company to listing. In a private placement, securities are sold to a single investor or a small group of investors. These are usually institutional investors like insurance companies or pension funds. Private placements have the main advantage in that they can avoid the costs of selling securities to investment bankers, which can be very significant. One of the drawbacks of the private placement of equity is its liquidity. Investors will find it difficult to resell the investment. **A stock exchange placing** is the process by which the company gets a stockbroking firm to sell shares to its various clients. Another example of a private placement is the process of firms taking out equity holdings in other companies. This might be a company in which it has a stake, e.g. a supplier or a company in which there is a joint venture in operation. For example, Eircom have taken out a number of joint ventures with companies aimed at supplying services to Eircom. These joint ventures centre on Eircom's **access network** which links customers to telephone exchanges. Fiat and General Motors, in September 2000, announced a $2.4 billion joint venture alliance aimed at reducing the two car makers' costs.

11.4.3 Rights issues

Earlier in the chapter, we described **pre-emptive rights** which gives existing shareholders the right to purchase any additional issue of stock in proportion to their existing shareholding in the company. We also illustrated how pre-emptive rights help to prevent the dilution of existing shareholder wealth. More formally, a rights issue allows shareholders the **right** to purchase a certain number of shares for a specified price within a specified period. If the current shareholders do not wish to exercise their rights, they can sell their rights in the market.

The number of rights needed to buy one new share

To illustrate the procedure of a rights issue we take the following example. Suppose that Decies Ltd needs to raise an additional €4m to finance further expansion and it plans to raise this capital from a rights issue. It has 4,000,000 shares outstanding, each with a current market price of €10. Decies has set the price of the subscription at €5 per share. How many rights are needed to purchase one new share? The company will have to issue an additional 800,000 shares (€4m/€5 = 800,000 shares). Therefore the number of rights needed to purchase one new share is 5 (old shares/new shares = 4,000,000/800,000 = 5). This is a 1 for 5 rights issue. To buy one new share the shareholder will need to give up 5 rights *plus* the price of the new share of €5.

The value of each right

Existing shareholders have the right to purchase a share that has a current market value of €10 for €5. This right therefore has value. What is this value? Suppose that a shareholder owns 100 shares. The value of her existing holding is €1,000 (number of shares × price per share = 100 × €10 = €1,000). The rights issue gives this shareholder who has 100 shares the rights to purchase 20 new shares for €5 each. If the shareholder exercises her rights and buys the new shares, she will now have 120 shares. Her total investment in the company will now be €1,000 + €100 = €1,100. Therefore the price per share is now €1,100/120 = €9.17 per share. The difference between the old share price of €10 and the new share price of €9.17 is the value of one right, that is €10 − €9.17 = €0.83. The old shares carry a right to subscribe for new shares. Therefore the difference between the old share price and the new share price must be equal to the value of one right, i.e. €0.83. The old shares are called **cum-rights** shares and the new shares are called **ex-rights** shares. We can confirm this as the correct price of a right by imagining an investor who has no shares in the company and wishes to get some. She can do so by buying 5 rights at a cost of €0.83 and then exercising her rights by investing another €5 to buy the share. Her total investment will be €9.15 (allowing for rounding errors), which is what we calculated to be the ex-rights price.

Theoretical ex-rights price

The price of the share after the rights issue, or the ex-rights price of the share in the above example, is €9.17. The ex-rights price is below the market price of the share before the issue was announced and above the price the rights were offered at. If the rate of return on the new funds is the same as that on the existing capital of the company, the ex-rights price can be calculated using the following equation:

$$\text{TXRP} = P_0 \frac{N_0}{N} + P_n \frac{N_n}{N} \qquad (11.1)$$

where
TXRP = theoretical ex-rights price
P_0 = original price of share
N_0 = original number of shares
N_n = number of new shares
P_n = price of new shares being issued
N = total number of shares in issue following the rights issue.

Therefore:
$$\text{TXRP} = €10 \ \frac{100}{120} + €5 \ \frac{20}{120} = €9.17$$

The value of a right can be got using the equation

$$\text{Value of a right} = \left[\frac{\left(\begin{array}{l}\text{Ex-rights} \\ \text{price}\end{array}\right) - \text{Rights price}}{\begin{array}{l}\text{Number of rights needed} \\ \text{to buy one new share}\end{array}} \right] \qquad (11.2)$$

$$\frac{€9.17 - €5}{5} = 83 \text{ cents}$$

The actual ex-rights price of the share will depend on the reaction of the market to the rights issue. If the rights issue is seen in a positive light and investors are sure that the proceeds from the issue will be invested in positive net present value projects, the market price may not drop, if at all. The result could be an overall gain in shareholder value. If on the other hand the market views the rights issue in negative terms and if investors expect the proceeds from the issue to be used to simply repay some outstanding debt, for example, then the price will fall more than that predicted by the theoretical ex-rights price.

Rights issues and the effect on shareholders' wealth

Suppose that Decies Ltd offered a 1 for 10 rights issue instead of a 1 for 5 rights issue. The new issue price will be €2.50 instead of €5. In other words, it issues twice the number of shares at half the price. Therefore, to raise €4m it will need to issue 1,600,000 shares (€4m/€2.50). The theoretical ex-rights price of the share will be €7.86, i.e. €10 (4m/5.6m) + €2.50(1.6m/5.6). The value of the right in this case is the cum-rights price €10 *less* the ex-rights price €7.86 = €2.14.

A shareholder can exercise her rights or sell them on the open market. In either of these two cases, the shareholder's wealth is not affected. In the Decies example our investor who had 100 shares had shareholder value of €1,000, i.e. 100 shares × €10 each. After exercising her rights she has 120 shares and her wealth is €1,100. In other words she buys 20 extra shares at €5 each for a total additional investment of €100. Her wealth increases by the amount of her investment. Therefore, she is neither better nor worse off. This is explained in Table 11.2.

Table 11.2 Effect of rights issue on shareholder wealth

Number of shares	Original value	New value	Gain/loss
100	€1,000	€917	− €83
20	€100	€183	+ €83
120	€1,100	€1,100	—

The shareholder's gain from the discount price is offset by the fall in the market price of the share. The shareholder receives rights (which have value) and these rights are offset by the fall in the market price of the share.

Instead of exercising her rights, the investor could sell her rights. If she sells her rights she will receive €83 (100 × €0.83). She will then have her original 100 shares at the ex-rights price of €9.17 each or €917. So the cash received from selling her rights of €83 *plus* the new market value of her holding of €917 is €1,000 which is exactly the value of her holding before the rights issue. She will not make or lose any money.

Note that it is not possible to underprice a rights issue. As long as the issue price is greater than zero and less than the market price, it is irrelevant what the subscription price is. It is irrelevant because there is no transfer of wealth from the existing shareholders and it does not affect existing shareholders' claims on the assets of the company.

If for some reason the shareholder fails to exercise her rights, her percentage holding in the company falls and suffers a loss because of the fall in the market value of the shares. This failure to exercise valuable rights is probably due to lack of knowledge of the issue or indifference. Stock exchange rules permit companies to sell any rights that are not taken up and the proceeds to be distributed to the shareholders concerned.

11.4.4 Employee stock ownership plans

These are stock option plans that allow employees to purchase shares on favourable terms. This provides employees with a stake in the performance of the company and as a result, if the company does well, the share price increases and the stock options increase in value. See Box 11.4 and Box 11.5 for a very succinct definition of the terms and the different ways of obtaining shares.

Box 11.4 Defining the terms of financial participation

Profit Sharing: involves employees receiving a proportion of their income from profits. Share-based profit sharing involves allocating shares to employees based on profits.

Employee share ownership: This refers to the arrangements that provide for the broadly based ownership of shares by employees in their own firm. It may involve employee share ownership plans (ESOPs), where shares are held for employees in a trust, or it may consist of reserving a proportion of company shares for employees, which are offered at privileged terms and limited to a worker's period of employment.

Gainsharing: is a group incentive scheme in which employees receive a bonus related to the performance of the group. This may be based on cost savings or productivity improvements within a production line or sales team, for example.

Formal gainsharing plans have been used in the US since the 1930s. Research is under way into the potential of some form of gainsharing in the public sector.

Clare O'Dea, *The Irish Times*, 9 June 2000

Box 11.5 Variety of ways to get a share

Approved profit sharing schemes (APSS)

Incentives to promote approved profit sharing schemes were first introduced in 1982. Employees in a company may be given shares worth up to €12,697 in that company per annum tax free. In the 1999 Finance Act, the €12,697 annual limit was increased to €38,000 on a once off conditional basis. To qualify, shares must have been held in the Employee Share Ownership Trust (ESOT) for 10 years.

Employee share ownership plans (ESOPs)
First introduced in 1997, the basic idea of an ESOP is that a trust acquires shares in the company for the benefit of employees. They are being introduced mainly in commercial State enterprises undergoing privatisation.

Save-as-you-earn (SAYE) share option schemes
Under this scheme, employees agree to save for a fixed time and are given the option to buy shares at a predetermined discount price. At the end of the savings period employees can: (a) take their savings and a tax-free bonus or (b) avail of the option to purchase the shares at the initial fixed price.

    Gains depend on the share price performance and profits made on the exercise of the share option are subject to capital gains tax on disposal rather than income tax.

→

To date (April 2000) 28 SAYE schemes have been approved by the Revenue Commissioners and there are 30 applications awaiting a decision.

Tax relief
An employee may claim full tax relief on shares purchased in his or her employer's company up to a lifetime of €6,337. The shares must be retained for a minimum of three years.

Tax relief can be claimed on the interest on loans taken out to purchase shares in an employer's company. Tax relief can also be claimed on loans made by employees to a company that is not publicly quoted.

Clare O'Dea, *The Irish Times*, 9 June 2000

11.5 Venture capital

Venture capital is **zero-stage financing** or financing for start-up, often high-risk ventures. If you have a good idea for a business venture but have no money and no assets to your name, you might think of going to a bank to get some capital to get started. Not all banks however are willing to help fund a new venture that doesn't have any equity capital of its own. You may need to look at other individuals or firms that specialise in this type of financing. Some venture capitalists specialise in **seed capital**. This is referred to as **initial stage financing**. Other venture capitalists will specialise in **secondary financing** or **mezzanine finance** (the floor above the ground floor).

In addition, companies such as Intel have made venture capital investments in Irish technology companies such as Baltimore Technologies, Iona Technologies, Enba and International Financial Services. Because 75% of Irish IT output is exported, companies like Intel are looking at a much greater market. Intel has a global investment technology fund of circa $5 billion. Much of this is invested in European technology companies in an effort to stimulate demand for PC and communications products.

Venture capital companies take an equity holding in companies that can be anything up to 40%. They seek investment opportunities in companies that have the potential for high rates of return. They do not seek security on their investment, so if the venture fails they lose their investment. Venture capitalists may have seats on the board of directors and may even appoint members to operational management. This along with the high equity holding in the company makes venture capital very expensive. The venture capitalists will also add their arrangement fees, which could be as high as 2.5%, and similar amounts will be incurred for legal and professional fees. In Ireland and in other countries the fastest growing companies in terms of employment and profitability have a venture capital shareholder. In Ireland, venture capital is also used for acquisition, mergers and management buy-outs. At the time of writing, venture capital from Irish venture capitalists comes to about €253m with individual investments ranging from €250,000 to about €6m. Venture capitalists will exit the company when they feel it is the right time to do so and when they feel they can get an adequate return. From the client's point of view it is important to know how and under what circumstances the venture capitalist will exit the company.

Because of the rapid economic growth from 1995 to 2000, the venture capital market is likely to provide a nursery for new companies entering the Irish Stock Exchange. This would seem to be an appropriate exit mechanism for venture capital investments. In addition to Irish venture capital funds, there are a considerable number of British venture capital funds in operation in Ireland.

The most important first step in seeking venture capital is the **business plan**. We discussed financial planning in Chapter 10, which is part of the overall business plan. In addition to the financial aspects of the plan it will be important for the budding entrepreneur to show the venture capitalists that he has the managerial ability to propel the business forward.

Table 11.3 Comparison of average annual growth rates % (1991–1995)

	Venture backed companies	FT-Extel top 500 European companies
Employment	15	2
Share capitalisation	36	15
Sales revenue	35	14
Pre-tax profits	25	17
Fixed assets	27	11
Long-term debt	14	13

Source: Baker, Peter, 'Economic Impact of Venture Capital in Europe', *Strategic Development Options for Ireland's Capital Markets in a Comparative Context.*

11.5.1 Venture capital markets and economic growth

Research has found an important link between venture capital and economic growth.[5] A study by the European Venture Capital Association (EVCA) shows that between 1991 and 1995 employment increased by 15% per annum in companies funded by venture capital, compared to just 2% for the top 500 largest companies. The jobs created in venture capital companies were shown to be high-quality jobs. A study by the National Venture Capital Association (NVCA) found that the number of scientists, engineers and managers employed in venture capital companies was 61%, compared to 15% for the US labour force. This would indicate that innovative companies tend to employ highly skilled and professional workers with consequent higher pay scales. In addition, a study by Cognotec found that between 1995 and 1996 young venture capital-backed companies called **gazelles** accounted for 80% of job growth, even though they represented just 3% of the firm population.

Box 11.6 Venture capitalists finance only six out of every 1,000 business plans received annually and fewer than 10% of funded start-ups go public

Taking their company public with visions of untold wealth is the dream of many Internet entrepreneurs. However not all Internet companies have succeeded in even getting to the public stage. For every success story, there are nine times as many failures.

Breakfastnetwork.com, which organises breakfast meetings for the Silicon Valley community in New York, had a get-together last week for entrepreneurs and venture capitalists to talk about how to take an Internet company public and the pitfalls to watch out for along the way. Several of the panellists who spoke were entrepreneurs whose ideas paid off.

Ms Rosalind Rosnick, chief executive officer and chairman of Netcreations, an opt-in e-mail marketing company, said when she and her partner set up the business all they had was $1,000 and their two computers. They decided not to accept any money from Internet venture capitalists, but instead financed their business by securing a bank credit line with her house.

'We wanted to run our own show', she said. As recently as two years ago, Ms Rosnick was offered $2 million for a 20% stake in Netcreations. She refused, and since going public, her company is now worth $800 million, of which she owns 75%. In general, founder CEOs can expect their stock to be worth about $6.5 million if a company succeeds in going public.

There are two reasons people take their companies public, said Mr Bruce Strzelczyk, a partner and co-chair of the Internet/New Media Group at Richard A. Eisner & Co., a venture capital firm. 'People go public for the valuation of their company', he said. 'Secondly, the market votes on a public company everyday. So you can create a more valuable company by responding to market conditions.'

On average venture capitalists finance only six out of every 1,000 business plans received each year and it is thought that fewer than 10% of funded start-ups actually go public.

Mr Strzelczyk said when planning to do an IPO, companies have to raise capital. 'These venture capital rounds are onerous. People typically lose if they miss one of these steps. They need to tell their story about where the Internet is going and what their role is. They should never stop evaluating their position either privately or publicly.'

He said the CEO's job was to craft a good account of the start-up's story. When a company is trying to raise venture capital financing, 'your job is to convince', he said. This contrasts with the IPO rounds, 'when your primary objective is to communicate to investors'.

Mr Scott Kurnit, chief executive officer and founder of About.com, a company that provides a network of guides to help people navigate around the Internet, advised taking six months to raise money and accept more money than is needed. 'Always have cash and raise more cash', he said. 'While the IPO can be a gruelling process, go the distance.'

Mr Ron Bloom, chief strategic officer of Think New Ideas, an Internet company, said a new company needs to hire a professional management team who'll take the company public. 'Take two years to plan and make it an eight month plan. Question and refine everything about your business and do not sleep until you find partners who share your vision.'

Extract from 'Wired On Friday—From New York', Carol Power,
The Irish Times, 3 March 2000

11.6 Stock markets

Earlier in the chapter we distinguished between primary and secondary markets. The most important secondary market is the stock market. The stock market determines the share prices of individual shares and since it is the primary goal of financial management to maximise shareholder wealth, knowledge of how the stock market works is important.

We have already seen that stock markets are divided into two types: (a) the organised and (b) the over-the-counter market.

(a) **Organised markets**: have a physical existence and location, their own building and an elected board of governors. There are organised stock exchanges around the world. In Ireland there is the Irish Stock Exchange (ISE), in London there is the London Stock Exchange (LSE) and in New York there is the New York Stock Exchange (NYSE).

The Irish Stock Exchange

Companies seeking a listing of their securities on the Irish Stock Exchange may do so on the official list, the developing companies market or exploration securities market. The official list is the main market for listed companies and Irish Government bonds. The developing companies market is for new and developing companies. The exploration securities market is confined to exploration and mineral companies.

Eligibility requirements for admission to the official list

There are basic minimum requirements for companies that apply to have their shares admitted to the official list:

- Incorporation: The company must be organised and be operating in conformity with its own articles of association.
- Three year record: The company must have been independently carrying on its main revenue-earning activity for at least three years.
- Audited accounts: This three year record must be supported by published audited accounts with unqualified audit reports.
- Profits and assets: There are no minimum profitability or net asset requirements.
- Directors: The board of directors and senior management must have appropriate expertise and experience for the management of the business.
- Controlling shareholders: The company must be capable of carrying on its business independently of any shareholder which controls 30% or more of the company's voting rights or which is able to control the board.
- Conflicts of interests: The company must ensure that all the directors are free from any conflicts between their duties to the company and any other interests or responsibilities.
- Working capital: The company must confirm that it has sufficient working capital for at least the next twelve months from the date of the prospectus.
- Free transfer of shares: Shares must be freely transferable.
- Shares in hands of the public: At least 25% of shares must be held outside the hands of the directors, major shareholders owning more than 5% of the company's shares, or

the trustees of any employee share scheme or pension fund established for the benefit of directors or employees of the issue.

(b) **The over-the-counter market:** The over-the-counter market does not have a physical location. It is a market driven by computer screens and telecommunications. For shares that are new, or traded infrequently, some means of maintaining liquidity in these shares is necessary. This is achieved by dealers who keep an inventory of these stocks and when an order comes in, they simply sell the security over the counter. The brokers who deal in such securities are said to be **market makers** in these securities. The over-the-counter market today is a generic term incorporating the market makers and the computer-driven electronic trading system which brings investors and dealers together. Dealers will quote **bid** prices and **ask** prices over the computer screen for whatever stocks they are making a market in. The bid price is the price the dealer will pay for the stock, or the price they are willing to buy the stock. The ask price is the price the dealer will sell the stock. The difference between the bid and the ask price is the **spread** and it constitutes the dealer's profit. When a dealer finds that her inventory levels in a particular stock are rising, she will lower both her bid price and her ask price. As a result investors will be more likely to buy and less likely to sell the stock. On the other hand if the dealer's inventory of a security is falling, she can raise both the bid price and the ask price. This will encourage more selling and less buying. The supply and demand for a particular security determines its price. The NASDAQ computer system is an example of an over-the-counter market. NASDAQ stands for National Association of Securities Dealers Automated Quotation System. It was first introduced in 1971 and, in terms of the number of companies listed, is bigger than the New York Stock Exchange. The OTC market consists of stocks that generally have less trading volume than companies listed on organised exchanges. There used to be a tendency for NASDAQ companies to move from the NASDAQ to the organised exchanges whenever they became large enough. However, companies like Microsoft and Intel, which are huge international companies, have remained on the NASDAQ. There are a number of Irish companies listed on the NASDAQ, such as Baltimore Technologies, Iona, Riverdeep and Elan Corporation. There is a European equivalent to the NASDAQ called the EASDAQ or the European Association of Securities Dealers Automated Quotation, which raises finance for fast growing high-tech firms. It is possible to list on both the NASDAQ and the EASDAQ. In London there is the Alternative Investment Market (AIM), in Germany the Neuer Market, in France the Nouveau Marché and the DCM in Dublin, all designed to generate finance for small developing companies.

11.7 Stock market indices

A stock market index shows the weighted average price of shares making up the index. It is a summary of what is happening to a group of similar shares. So, for example, the ISEQ is a summary of what is happening to the share prices of the 91 companies listed on the Dublin Stock Exchange. Indices are useful because they allow the investor to see what is happening to an individual share compared to the index as a whole. For example, it is possible for the share price of an individual stock to fall on a particular day when the index for all the companies quoted on the index goes up. In other words, a share can do badly compared to the rest of the market. Stock market indices are **benchmarks** that allow individual shares to be compared to a market index. The characteristics of some of the better-known indices are given below:

11.7.1 ISEQ

The Irish Stock Exchange Quotation (ISEQ) is a broad based index representing all publicly quoted companies. Companies that are large and relatively safe are referred to as blue chip companies. The index is weighted in such a way that a change in the largest capitalisation stocks will have a bigger impact on the index than a change in smaller capitalisation stocks. In other words, a 1% change in Smurfit will have a greater impact on the index than a 1% change in Abbey plc.

The Irish equity market had a market capitalisation of €56.6 billion at the end of June 1999.[6] Irish institutional investors are the largest investors in the Irish equity market, holding some 60% of the equity of quoted Irish companies. From Table 11.4 note that the bulk of overseas investment in the Irish stock market comes from UK and US investors. This is a result of the process of internationalisation with domestic funds rebalancing their portfolios following the removal of exchange controls in 1989 and international funds adopting positions in Irish equities. However, over the next few years investment from euro zone investors is expected to grow strongly because of the strength of the Irish economy and privatisations.[7]

The Irish equity market is dominated by five companies (AIB, Eircom, Bank of Ireland, Elan and CRH). These account for 65% of the total equity market capitalisation.[8] The two main banks between them account for nearly 30% of the Irish index. Lower interest rates as a result of a single currency and greater competition in the domestic banking sector from foreign competition have had a negative impact on financial stocks, which therefore affected the market as a whole.

Table 11.4 Shareholding structure of selected Irish quoted companies (estimates, percentages, H1, 1998)

	Domestic institutional	Domestic private	UK institutional	US institutional	Other
AIB	43	6	19	30	2
Anglo Irish Bank	35	3	50	10	2
Bank of Ireland	47	7	24	16	6
Hibernian	52	5	3	–	40
CRH	42	12	46		
Independent	30	5	12	16	42
Smurfit	46	7	11	23	13
Waterford	40	12	15	1	32
Glanbia	22	15	5	2	56
Fyffes	59	12	5	2	56
Greencore	53	3	25	15	4
Golden Vale	42	57	–	–	1
IAWS	39	2	5	2	52
Kerry	28	25	2	5	41

Source: 'Internationalisation Well Under Way', John Clarke, in *The Irish Stock Market, Finance* 1998 (taken from 'Strategic Development Options For Ireland's Capital Markets In a Comparative Context', Peter Bacon & Associates.

Membership of the stock exchange has been beneficial to companies such as Kerry and Ryanair. Kerry was initially quoted on the USM (unlisted securities market) in October 1986 with a market capitalisation of £9.175m. By July 1999 it was a member of the full list, the number of shares in issue had risen ten fold from 18.3m to 172.05m, the share price had risen from 50p to 849p and as a result the market capitalisation had reached €1,850m. Ryanair was on the official list in 1997 with a market capitalisation of £522.5m (€662.23). Two years later its share price had doubled, giving a market capitalisation of €1,646.4m.

11.7.2 FTSE 100

The 'footsie' 100 is based on the largest (in terms of market capitalisation) 100 companies listed on the UK Stock Market. The market capitalisation of companies on the footsie is usually greater than Stg £1.8bn.

The London Stock Exchange and the Deutsche Börse had planned to merge in May 2000 to form the iX international exchange. Combined, the two would have more than half of Europe's trading in blue chip stocks and over 56% of Europe's derivatives trading.[9] However (at the time of writing) this proposed merger seems to have failed.

Nevertheless, a merger of some description is likely and, along with the other merger forming the Euronext (discussed below), Europe's stock exchanges are likely to be transformed because it is likely that exchanges currently outside these two will eventually join them.

11.7.3 Dow Jones

The Dow Jones Industrial Average index (DJIA) (after Charles H. Dow who created the index) is an index composed of 30 blue chip industrial companies. The editors of the *Wall Street Journal* select the companies that make up the index. The difficulty is the index is narrowly based (only 30 companies). Most broader based indices (e.g. the NASDAQ) give a better indication of the overall performance of the market. Other international benchmark indices include the Japanese Nikkei 225 index, the German Dax, the Hong Kong Hang Seng index and the French CAC-40.

The growth in online trading[10] is expected to account for nearly half of all equity trades in the US by the end of 2000, and along with the expansion of after-hours trading is changing the structure of the US equity market. It is possible that the two main markets, the NYSE and the NASDAQ might merge sometime in the future in an effort to combat these changes.[11]

11.7.4 FTSE all-share index

This is the UK's broadest based index and therefore the most accurate in assessing the performance of the market because it comprises 900 companies. In addition to the overall market index, the index is also subdivided into sectors such as media, engineering, retail etc. This allows you to compare companies that are similar and in the same industry. An entire industry can be doing very poorly while the rest of the market can be flying high.

11.7.5 Euronext

The stock exchanges of Paris, Amsterdam and Brussels merged in March 2000 to create Euronext and it represented the first formal step towards a single European stock market. The Euronext provides for a common trading platform, common settlement system and clearance and a common rule book. A consolidation of European bourses is developing to provide greater liquidity and lower transaction costs to combat increasing competition from online trading and by the competition expected from the arrival of the NASDAQ in Europe.[12]

11.8 Listing on more than one exchange

Many Irish companies are listed not just on the Irish Stock Exchange but also on the London stock market and in New York on the NASDAQ. The Smurfit group, Baltimore Technologies, CRH and Iona are some examples. High-tech companies such as Iona and Baltimore are better understood and more highly valued in the US[13] and get a better price on a major market like the NASDAQ. In Ireland's case, the domestic market is too small and companies such as Smurfit have no choice but to seek a quote on larger markets such as London and the NASDAQ. Instead of issuing shares in the US, companies outside the US issue American Depository Receipts (ADRs), which are claims on their shares. ADRs are administered by American banks. They trade on US stock exchanges. So, for example, Smurfit plc with trading shares in foreign countries is indicative of the globalisation of the international economy. ADRs have become a means whereby foreign companies tap into the capital markets of the US. The number of ADRs has grown from 836 in 1990 to 1,350 in 1997.[14]

Furthermore, the advent of EMU has meant that institutional investors such as pension fund managers have taken advantage of the abolition of exchange rate controls and the single currency to invest in overseas markets. The consequence of this has been to depress the overall ISEQ index.

11.8.1 Representation in international benchmarks

A number of Irish stocks figure prominently among the largest in the EMU sector. CRH is ranked second in terms of market capitalisation of the euro zone building materials companies. Eight of Ireland's leading companies are ranked within the top 15 in their individual sectors, and Ireland's top companies are represented in several European benchmarks.[15]

Table 11.5 Market cap rankings of largest Irish stocks in EMU sector

	Sector	Market capitalisation ranking
CRH	Building materials	2
Smurfit	Paper/packaging	3
Elan	Pharmaceuticals	3
Kerry	Food	5
Irish Life	Life assurance	5
Ryanair	Transport	5
AIB	Banks	12
Bank of Ireland	Banks	14

Source: NCB, taken from the Bacon Report

Table 11.6 Representation of Irish stocks in major European indices

FTSE Eurotop 100	None
FTSE Eurotop 300	AIB, Bank of Ireland, CRH
MSCI index (Morgan Stanley)	AIB, CRH, Irish Life, Smurfit, Irish Permanent, Irish Independent Ryanair, Waterford Wedgwood, Fyffes, DCC, Jurys, ICG
DJ Eurostoxx	AIB, Bank of Ireland, Elan, CRH, Irish Life, Kerry, Independent Newspapers, Greencore, Smurfit, Waterford Wedgwood, Fyffes
DJ Eurostoxx 50	None

Source: Bacon Report

11.9 Regulation

The Irish Stock Exchange operates a system of self-regulation in the supervision and the operation of the stock market. Ultimate responsibility for the supervision of the stock market is placed with the Central Bank. The stock exchange was given day-to-day authority over the securities market. The exchange has to produce rules that ensure fairness in the market but at the same time does not prevent or restrict competition any more than is necessary to protect investors. The exchange has responsibility for the regulation of listed companies and their disclosure requirements.

11.10 Trading system

The order driven system is how trading in equities in Ireland is conducted and this is how most stock exchanges in the world operate. When a stockbroker receives a buy or sell order from an investor, the broker will try to match the investor with another investor with whom to trade. When a broker receives an order, s/he will try to match the order to one of his/her own clients. For example, if a broker receives an order from an investor to sell a security the broker will see if one of their own clients wishes to buy the security. This is an in-house deal and the transaction is known as a **put-through**. Obviously there are restrictions on brokers who want to conduct such a trade, and permission is required from the exchange to do so.

Alternatively, the order is put on a central system and a deal is done where a buyer and seller are matched. In addition, most Irish securities are traded on the London market, and the Irish broker may contact his/her London counterparts to conduct a trade. All deals must be reported to the exchange and this information is then made available to all other market participants. After the deal has been struck, the settlement must take place, which transfers the ownership of shares from seller to buyer. **CREST** is the real time settlement system for Irish and UK shares. Investors normally pay for shares five days after the transaction is completed. The previous system was known as the talisman system and it involved a long paper-chase between investors, brokers, company registrars and the exchange's talisman. The CREST system is electronic and paperless.

11.10.1 Introduction of electronic trading system

On 6 June 2000 the Irish Stock Exchange changed over to electronic trading. This allows Irish stockbrokers to offer online Internet trading facilities to customers. Trading is conducted via a screen-based system. This allows brokers to execute buy and sell orders more quickly and this helps improve liquidity. The introduction of electronic trading will allow brokers to bring in execution-only online dealing services, which means that customers will have a choice in how they deal with brokers.[16]

11.11 Types of securities traded on the Irish Stock Exchange

There are five types of securities traded on the Irish Stock Exchange:

1. Domestic Irish ordinary shares issued by Irish companies.
2. Overseas equities issued by non-Irish companies.

3. Irish Government bonds which pay regular interest payments and repayment of the fixed sum at a given date in the future.
4. Bonds or fixed interest stocks issued by companies or local authorities.
5. Investment funds that invest in portfolios of investments based on spreading risk. (See Chapter 18.)

Figure 11.1 Securities sold on the Irish Stock Exchange

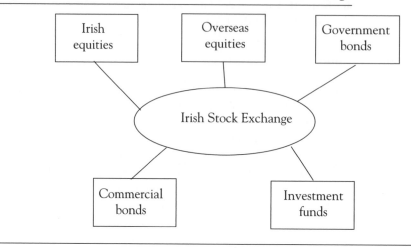

11.12 Stock market ratios

Companies can find it useful to calculate ratios that bring together data from the stock market and from the company's accounts. The following ratios are the most useful.

11.12.1 Dividend yield

As we discuss in more detail in Chapter 12 the overall rate of return on a stock is made up of two components—an annual income in the form of a dividend payment and a capital gain in the form of a rise in the share price. The expected dividend payment as a percentage of the current share price is the dividend yield.

$$\text{Dividend yield} = \frac{\text{Dividend per share}}{\text{Market price of share}} \times 100 \qquad (11.3)$$

Yield is inversely related to price and a rising price will mean a falling yield. A low dividend yield could mean that investors are satisfied with a low rate of return as they can look forward to higher dividends in the future and capital growth in the value of their shares. On the other hand, a low dividend yield could mean the company is in trouble and is unable to pay worthwhile dividends.

In order to compare the dividend yield with the return from other investments (debentures, gilts etc.), the dividend yield needs to be calculated on a gross basis. This is done by adding back the tax credit to the net dividend.

Example 11.2 Calculating dividend yield

XRH Ltd has just paid out a net dividend of 20 cents per share. The current market price of the share is €7. The basic rate of income tax is 22%. Therefore the gross dividend yield is:

$$\frac{20c \times 100}{78} = 26 \text{ cents}$$

Therefore the dividend yield is $\quad \dfrac{0.26 \times 100}{€7} = 3.7\%$.

11.12.2 Earnings per share

We have discussed earnings per share in other chapters, particularly in terms of the limitations of EPS as an investment ratio. For example in Chapter 10 we saw how the quality of earnings reported is not always reliable and therefore has limitations as a ratio in its own accord and as the denominator in the calculation of the P/E ratio. However the EPS is always shown in the accounts of publicly quoted firms and is the subject of the Statement of Standard Accounting Practice, number 3 (SSAP 3). Earnings per share is defined as: 'the profit in pence attributable to each equity share, based on the profit (or, in the case of a group, the consolidated profit) of the period after tax, minority interests and extraordinary items, and after deducting preference dividends and other appropriations in respect of preference shares, divided by the number of equity shares in issue and ranking for dividend in respect of the period.'

Therefore, earnings per share are defined as earnings divided by the number of shares. Earnings are defined as profit available to equity shareholders, which are profits after taxation, minority interests, preference dividends and extraordinary items. The number of shares is based on those in issue and ranking for dividend during the period.

$$\textbf{Earnings per share} = \frac{\textbf{Profit available for equity shareholders}}{\textbf{Equity shares issued and ranking for dividend}} \qquad (11.4)$$

The point of SSAP 3 is to standardise the calculation of EPS. It deals with **basic earnings per share** and **fully diluted earnings per share**.

Basic earnings per share

In calculating the basic earnings per share, we use a weighted average number of shares, having taken into account any new shares issued during the year.

Shares can be issued:

(a) at their full market value
(b) as a bonus issue for no consideration
(c) at a discount in a rights issue, and
(d) in exchange for shares in a subsidiary.

Example 11.3 shows the calculation of basic EPS assuming no change in the company's capital. Here EPS are earnings available for ordinary shareholders divided by the number of shares.

Example 11.3 Calculation of basic EPS assuming no change in capital

	2000 (€000)	1999 (€000)
Portlaw Ltd share capital 1 January		
1,000,000 Preference shares of €1 each	1,000	1,000
6,000,000 Ordinary shares of 20 cents each	1,200	1,200
	2,200	2,200
Profit after tax	600	500
Preference dividends	100	100
Earnings for ordinary shareholders	500	400
Number of ordinary shares	6,000	6,000
EPS	8.33 cents	6.67 cents

Example 11.4 below shows the calculation of basic earnings per share after an issue of ordinary shares at full market price. If shares are issued during the year, the number of shares in the calculation of EPS must be adjusted to reflect the fact that this new capital is generating a return (in terms of earnings) for only part of the year. In other words, we use **a weighted average** share capital in the denominator of the EPS calculation.

Example 11.4 Calculation of basic EPS assuming an issue of shares at full market price

Assuming that Portlaw Ltd issued an additional 1m ordinary shares at full market price on 1/10/ 2000

	2000 (€000)	1999 (€000)
Profit after tax	600	500
Preference dividends	100	100
Profit for ordinary shareholders	500	400
Weighted average number of shares		
6,000,000 shares for 9 months (6m x 9/12)	4,500	
7,000,000 for 3 months (7m x 3/12)	1,750	
	6,250	6,000
Earnings per share	8 cents	6.7 cents
500/6,250 for 2000 and 400/6,000 for 1999		

Calculation of EPS following a bonus issue of shares

A bonus issue of shares is an issue of shares to existing shareholders free of charge. Because the company is not raising any new capital, the new shares issued do not generate a matching increase in revenue. For a bonus issue, no weighting of shares is necessary. All that is necessary is that the number of shares for the previous year is adjusted so that the EPS figures remain comparable.

Example 11.5 Calculations of EPS following a bonus issue

Portlaw Ltd, instead of issuing shares at full market price on 1/10/2000, gives the shareholders a bonus issue on the same date. The terms of the bonus issue is one new share for every five shares already held.

	2000 €000	1999 €000
Profit after tax	600	500
Preference dividends	100	100
	500	400
Number of shares		
at 1 January	6,000	6,000
Bonus issue	1,200	1,200
	7,200	7,200
Earnings per share	6.9 cents	5.5 cents
500/7,200 for 2000 and 400/7,200 for 1999		

Calculation of EPS following a rights issue

Earlier on in this chapter we discussed rights issues which are issues of shares to existing shareholders in proportion to their existing shareholding in the company at a discount to the prevailing market price of the share. A rights issue can be separated into a cash issue at full market price *plus* a bonus issue. To calculate the EPS, the features of the cash issue and the bonus issue must be used. SSAP 3 recommends the following approach for the adjustments necessary to calculate the EPS after a rights issue.

1. Calculate the theoretical ex-rights price of the share and divide it by the market price of the share cum-rights on the last day the shares were quoted cum-rights. This adjusts the previous year's EPS for the effects of the bonus issue in the rights.

$$\frac{\textbf{Theoretical ex-rights price}}{\textbf{Cum-rights price of shares on last day of quotation cum-rights}} \qquad (11.5)$$

2. The number of shares before the issue is multiplied by the fraction of the year which has passed before the date of the issue to give a weighted average share of capital and by the fraction

$$\frac{\text{Cum-rights price of share on last day of quotation cum-rights}}{\text{Theoretical ex-rights price}} \tag{11.6}$$

This is the adjustment for the pre-rights share capital.

Example 11.6 Calculation of EPS following a rights issue

On 1 April 2000, Portlaw Ltd made a 1 for 5 rights issue at 50 cents per share. The market price of the share cum-rights is €1.

	2000 €000	1999 €000
Profit after tax	600	500
Preference shares	100	100
Profit for ordinary shareholders	500	400

1. Calculate the theoretical ex-rights price.

   5 shares @ €1 *plus* 1 share @ 50 cents = 6 shares = €5.50
   Therefore TXRP = €5.50/6 = 92 cents

2. Calculate the EPS for 2000.

   Number of shares before issue = 6,000,000. Number of shares issued = 1,200,000.
   6m × 3/12 × €1/€0.92 = 1,630,434

   plus   7.2m × 9/12 = 5,400,000

   Therefore, the weighted average number of shares = 1,630,434 + 5,400,000 = 7,030,434

   $$\text{EPS} = €500,000/7,030,434 = 7.1 \text{ cents}$$

3. Calculate the EPS for 1999
   Portlaw Ltd's EPS before the rights issue in 1999 was 6.7 cents. Taking the rights issue into consideration the 1999 EPS is €0.92/€1 × 6.7 = 6.16 cents.

11.12.3 Fully diluted earnings per share

The EPS of a company can be diluted in the future if it has:

(a) convertible debentures or preference shares convertible into equity shares,
(b) warrants or options which provide the holder with the right to subscribe for equity shares, or

(c)   a separate class of equity share which doesn't rank for dividend at present but will at some future date.

Fully diluted EPS is calculated by assuming that **all** possible ordinary shares were in issue from the first day of the accounting period under consideration. The number of shares in issue will increase but these new shares will not generate any new income. Fully diluted EPS is calculated so that the impact of this dilution is shown in the current period.

Example 11.7   Calculating fully diluted earnings per share

The following information is available for Molleran's Ltd for the year ended 31/12/2001

Profit after tax and preference dividend	€100,000
Number of ordinary shares already in issue	300,000

In addition, Molleran's Ltd has €100,000 10% convertible loan stock in issue. These give the holders of this convertible loan stock the right to convert this stock into equity shares. The conversion rights are

Date	Price per share
30/5/2001	€1.20
30/5/2002	€1.30
30/5/2003	€1.40
30/5/2004	€1.50

Calculate the fully diluted earnings per share for 31/12/ 2001. Assume a corporation tax of 15%.

Remember, when calculating fully diluted earnings per share we assume that all of the convertible loan stock was converted at the beginning of the accounting period. If this was the case then we will need to add back to the profit after tax figure the interest savings that would arise.

Profit after tax and preference dividend		€100,000
Add back interest payment that would have arisen if the loan stock had been converted	€10,000	
less tax (15%)	€1,500	€8,500
		€108,500

The fully diluted EPS is calculated at the end of year 2001. The next conversion will occur on 30/5/2002. Therefore the number of shares to be converted in calculating the fully diluted earnings per share for the end of year 2001 is €100,000/€1.30 = 76,923 shares. The number of shares already in issue is 300,000. Therefore we assume that there are 376,923 shares in issue on 1/1/2001. The fully diluted earnings per share is €108,500/376,923 = 28.8 cents.

11.13 Warrants

Warrants are securities that give the holder the right to buy shares at a fixed price over a certain period. Warrants are sometimes called **equity sweetners** or **kickers**. They are typically issued with loans or bonds because they make the bond more attractive to the lenders. Warrants cause the number of shares issued to increase. The profit after tax figure is then distributed over a larger number of shares, thus causing a dilution in the EPS. Fully diluted EPS is therefore lower than basic EPS because the numerator in the fully diluted EPS equation is larger.

Warrants give rise to additional future capital, unlike the conversion process in the previous example where loan capital was converted into equity capital. Therefore, if we assume that warrants were exercised during the period, we must have some way of estimating the rate of return on this additional capital. SSAP 3 requires that when warrants are used, the diluted EPS should be calculated on the assumptions that (a) earnings from the period be adjusted, assuming that the proceeds of the subscription were invested in 2.5% consolidated war bonds (consols), and (b) the maximum number of shares are issued under the terms of the warrants.

Example 11.8 Exercising warrants

Glaxis Ltd has 150,000 shares already in issue and has warrants which entitle the holders to subscribe for an additional 100,000 shares in the company. The warrants can be exercised after 31/12 at €1.50 per share. The price of 2.5% consolidated stock on 1/1/2000 was €50. Glaxis has just earned profit after tax of €70,000. The tax rate is 15%.

Subscription income received = 100,000 × €1.50 = €150,000. The yield on 2.5% consolidated stock is 2.5 × 100/50 = 5%. Therefore, we assume that the subscription from exercising the warrants is invested in consols yielding 5%. This is €150,000 × .05 = €7,500 *less* tax (15%) = €6,375.

Therefore the total earnings for calculating the fully diluted earnings per share is €76,375. The total number of shares for calculating fully diluted earnings per share is 250,000.

Therefore the fully diluted earnings per share is €76,376/250,000 = 31 cents.

If the dilution is 5% less than the basic EPS, it need not be disclosed.

11.14 Headline EPS

The Institute of Investment Managers and Research (IIMR) has introduced its own version of earnings per share, which it describes as 'headline EPS'. This measure adjusts standard EPS to eliminate capital items only, rather than exceptional items. FRS 3 required calculation of EPS **after** extraordinary items instead of **before** extraordinary items, which was the case prior to 1992 when FRS 3 was published. The following is a guideline for the calculation of headline EPS:

Exclude

- profits and losses from the sale or termination of operations, both continuing and discontinued.
- profits and losses from the sale of fixed assets.

- permanent diminutions in the value of fixed assets.
- exceptional profits and losses on the reorganisation or redemption of long-term debt.
- any impact of goodwill.
- extraordinary items net of tax.

Include

- all trading profits and losses.
- trading results of discontinued or acquired operations as reported.
- any costs incurred in relation to profits or losses on sale or termination of operation.
- any costs of a fundamental reorganisation or restructuring having a material effect on the nature of the reporting entity's operations.

Example 11.9 Calculating headline EPS

The basic EPS reported for Westwood Ltd is 9 cents for the year 2000 and 8 cents for the year 2001. The total weighted average number of ordinary shares in issue during year 2000 is 300,000,000 and 299,000,000 in 2001. The following adjustments were made to calculate headline EPS:

	2001 Cents per share	2000 Cents per share
Basic EPS	9	8
(Profit) on sale of discontinued operations	—	(0.20)
(Profit)/loss on sale of fixed assets	(0.20)	0.1
Investments written off		0.3
Headline EPS	8.8	8.2

11.15 Earnings yield

This is the earnings per share divided by the market price per share.

$$\text{Earnings yield} = \frac{\text{EPS}}{\text{Market price of share}} \qquad (11.7)$$

For example, the annual reports of *Independent News and Media* show an EPS of €0.25 in 1998 and an average share price in 1998 of €3.45.[17] This gives an earnings yield of 7.2%.

In general, a low earnings yield would indicate that the company has good growth prospects. A high yield would indicate that investors believe that the share is risky and are unsure about the future prospects of the company.

11.16 Price/earnings ratio

This is the market price of the share divided by the EPS.

$$\text{P/E ratio} = \frac{\text{Market price of share}}{\text{EPS}} \qquad (11.8)$$

It is a measure of the time needed to recover the purchase price, assuming that earnings per share remain constant. It is the inverse of the earnings yield.

Example 11.10 Calculating the P/E ratio

The market price of a share (ex-dividend) is €5. The company's most recent EPS figure is 50 cents. Therefore the P/E ratio is €5/€0.50 = 10 times.

This means that the market is valuing the current earnings of the company at a multiple of 10. Therefore, if the company is currently earning net profits of €1m on a P/E basis, the market value of the company is €10m. Therefore a high P/E ratio would suggest that investors are optimistic about the growth prospects of the company with a low risk. We discuss P/E ratios in more detail in Chapter 10.

11.17 Dividend cover

Dividend cover is defined as

$$\text{Dividend cover} = \frac{\text{EPS}}{\text{Dividend per share}} \qquad (11.9)$$

Alternatively,

$$\text{Dividend cover} = \frac{\text{Profit for ordinary shareholders}}{\text{Actual dividends paid to shareholders}} \qquad (11.10)$$

Profits available for distribution (i.e. PAT and preference dividends)/Actual dividends paid to shareholders.

Management may decide not to pay out all after-tax earnings in the form of a dividend. Some of the earnings may be reinvested in the company. A high cover may mean that dividends can continue to be paid even if earnings drop. In this way, it is a measure of the riskiness of the investment.

Furthermore, the dividend cover will show how much of the company's profits are being retained (retention ratio) for further investment. Therefore, for example, a dividend cover of 5 will mean that 80% of the company's profits are being retained.

For example, the dividend per share of Independent News and Media plc in 1998 was €0.11 and the EPS was given as €0.25. Therefore the dividend cover was 2.27 times.

11.18 The efficient market hypothesis

The efficient market hypothesis (EMH) deals with the extent to which share prices reflect all available information about the company and the economy. The market share price reflects the true underlying intrinsic value of the share. If all information is reflected in the market price of the share, then it is impossible for any investor to consistently outperform the market. When an investor buys a stock she gets exactly what she pays for and investors and companies who sell shares get exactly what they are worth. The difference between the market value of the investment and its cost is zero. Therefore all investments in the market have zero net present values. Note that because no investor or analyst is better informed than the market, the quest for mispriced stocks is futile. The **rationale for market efficiency** is competition among investors. Investors cannot consistently beat the market because stock markets are extremely competitive. For example, if it was the case that it became well known that companies that reinvested all their after-tax earnings did particularly well, more and more investors would buy stocks in these companies, forcing up the price of these stocks and eliminating any excess profits that were being made. Stocks that are mispriced will become fewer and fewer because of competition. The market will become increasingly efficient. The EMH says that trying to find patterns in stock prices or trying to find 'winners' is a waste of time. The possibility of making excess profits in the stock markets is as rare as finding a sum of money on the street. If a sum of money is lost it will be picked up by somebody very quickly. In the very same way an opportunity to make excess profits will be taken up quickly, so that no such opportunity will exist for long.

11.18.1 Forms of market efficiency

It is generally understood that there are **three** forms of market efficiency. Markets are either **weak form efficient**, **semi-strong form efficient** or **strong form efficient**. The distinction between these three forms of market efficiency depends on the level of information incorporated into the stock price.

Weak form efficiency

If markets were weak form efficient, then all historical information would be reflected in the stock price. It is not possible to make excess returns by using historical information, such as company reports, past prices, or any other information that is readily available on the company. Investors would not be able to benefit from this type of information because it is readily available and doesn't cost very much. Selecting stocks based on historical information would be of no use to investors. The fact that a share price might have risen for the past four days, for example, doesn't give us any information about how the stock price will perform on the fifth day. Analysts who plot past price movements are called chartists. If you believe that weak form efficiency exists, then you believe that chartists are wasting their time. For example, if a chartist finds a pattern which shows that if a stock price falls for three consecutive days and then rises by 5% on the fourth day, investors could make money by buying stocks that fall for three consecutive days. However, no investor would sell a stock that had fallen for three consecutive days if she thinks that it will rise in price the following day. In fact, if the share price is €10 on the third day and if it is expected to rise by 5% on the fourth day, the share price would probably rise to €10.50 on the third day, which will eliminate any opportunity for excess profits.

Semi-strong form efficiency

Could any public information be used to earn excess returns? Markets are said to be semi-strong form efficient if no excess returns can be made using public available information. The semi-strong form of the EMH indicates that market prices reflect all publicly available information. Excess returns cannot be earned by looking at annual reports or any other published data because all such information, good or bad, would have been incorporated into the share price when the information became available. However, any information that is not made available to the public such as that held by company insiders (e.g. directors) can be used to earn excess returns under semi-strong form efficiency. In addition, stock prices will be affected by information that becomes available if the information is different to what was expected. For example, if the company reports a 10% increase in after-tax earnings, the share price won't be affected by this news if that is what the market was expecting. On the other hand, if the market was expecting an earnings increase of an amount greater than 10%, then the share price will drop and the share price will rise if the increase in earnings was greater than 10%.

Strong form efficiency

In strong form efficient markets, **all** information, public and private, is reflected in the share price. Incorporating all private information would seem to be difficult. Some information like a company's sales figures may only be known to the directors of the company. If this information is not divulged, then it doesn't seem possible for the market to incorporate this information into the share price. It might be possible to observe if there was any buying or selling of company shares by insiders acting on privately held information. Remember that some forms of insider trading are illegal (see Chapter on takeovers). If a strong form of market efficiency exists, even insider information cannot be used to earn excess returns.

Empirical tests

Empirical research suggests that stock markets are highly efficient in weak form, moderately efficient in semi-strong form, but the strong form efficient market does not hold and excess returns can be made by insider held information.

SUMMARY

- Ordinary shareholders have a claim on the financial success of the company but have no preferential treatment in terms of dividends or in cases of bankruptcy.
- The pre-emption right gives shareholders the right to purchase any new shares, in proportion to their existing holding, issued by the company.
- The shares of privately owned companies are not traded. When the shares of companies are traded, they are publicly owned companies.
- The **primary market** is where publicly owned firms raise finance by selling shares.
- The **secondary market** is the market where the owners of shares sell their shares to other investors.

- An initial public offering (IPO) occurs when a privately owned firm goes public for the first time. It also refers to the privatisation programme of governments.
- IPOs are costly if priced below their true value. This is the cost of underpricing.
- Underpricing avoids the winner's curse.
- There are five ways of raising cash through selling shares: (a) public offering, (b) through a private placing, (c) through a stock exchange placing of shares, (d) through a rights issue, (e) through stock purchase plans to employees.
- Share issues tend to depress share prices. This is partly due to the increased supply of shares and due to signalling, or the information sent to the market about the company's intentions.
- Venture capital is zero stage financing or financing for start-up, often high-risk ventures.
- Stock markets are divided into organised exchanges and over-the-counter markets.
- A stock market index is a summary of what is happening to a group of similar shares.
- The order driven system is how trading in equities in Ireland is conducted.
- Warrants are securities that give the holder the right to buy shares at a fixed price over a certain period.
- The efficient market hypothesis states that share prices reflect all available information about the company and the economy. The rationale for market efficiency is competition among investors.

QUESTIONS

1. What are the characteristics of ordinary shares?
2. Distinguish between privately owned and publicly owned companies.
3. What are the advantages and disadvantages of selling shares to the public?
4. Distinguish between the primary and secondary capital markets.
5. ♦ Explain IPOs and why they are usually underpriced.
6. Distinguish between the bookbuilding, fixed-price and auction method of issuing shares. Under what circumstances can uniform pricing lead to higher proceeds than discriminatory pricing?
7. What is the difference between organised stock markets and over-the-counter markets?
8. Why do companies list on more than one exchange?
9. What types of securities are listed on the Irish stock exchange?
10. Distinguish between strong form, semi-strong form and weak form efficient markets.
11. ♦ It has been consistently shown that the returns from shares outperform the return from bonds. Why is it that investors hold bonds for long periods?
12. Can a market be both semi strong form efficient and weak form efficient at the same time?
13. ♦ If the market is strong form efficient, what happens when investors try to outperform the market?
14. A company's share is selling at €100 and it has an exercise price of €70 per share. The warrant gives the holder the right to buy five shares at the exercise price. What is the exercise value of the warrant?
15. Crehana Ltd has paid an annual dividend to its shareholders of €1.50 per share. The share price at the start of the year was €20 and the current share price €25. Calculate: (a) the dividend yield, (b) the capital gains yield and (c) the total return.

16.♦ The sales director of a company has just put together figures with unexpected but positive sales growth. Could the sales director profit by buying shares in the company before the information becomes public? To what form of market efficiency does this refer?

17. Distinguish between value stocks and growth stocks.

18. If you read some of the advertisements in the newspapers, you will be told that some fund managers outperform the average market performance. Does this make market efficiency theory invalid?

19. What effect do you think the elimination of the pre-emptive right would have on the ability of a company to raise new capital? Do you think that in terms of ownership and control, pre-emptive rights are critically important to shareholders of very large publicly owned firms?

20.♦ Brandon Ltd needs to raise an additional €15m in equity capital. The current market price of Brandon's Shares is €10 each. They have decided to employ the expertise of underwriters who inform the company that they must price the issue at 20% below the current market price. The underwriters will receive 3% of the price the Shares are issued at and additional costs of the issue to the company amount to €20,000. Calculate the number of Shares the company must issue to raise the capital it needs and cover all its costs.

21 Qwelly Quarrepus Ltd has 300,000 shares in issue at €55 each. The company is proposing a rights issue of 50,000 new shares at €45 each.
(a) What is the new market capitalisation?
(b) How many rights are needed to purchase one new share?
(c) What is the theoretical ex-right price of the share?
(d) What is the value of a right?

22 Tinhallow Ltd needs an additional €10m to finance new investments. It is proposing to sell new Shares at an offer price of €15 per Share. The underwriters of the issue charges a 6% spread. How many shares will need to be sold by Timhallow Ltd?

23 ABC Ltd has decided on a rights issue. The current price of the share is €20 and there are 3 million shares in issue. The company has decided that the ex rights price will be €17 per share. The rights issue would raise €35 million. At what price can existing shareholders subscribe for additional Shares?

NOTES

1. 'The market's problem with the pricing of IPOs', R.G. Ibbotson, J. Sindelar and J.R. Ritter, *The Journal of Applied Corporate Finance* 7, Spring 1994.
2. 'IPO underpricing around the World', J.R. Ritter in *Fundamentals of Corporate Finance*, 5th ed., Ross, Westerfield and Jordan.
3. G.f. note 1.
4. R. Loughran and J. Ritter, 'The New Issues Puzzle', *Journal of Finance* 50, 1995.
5. Bacon Report p. 9.
6. Bacon Report p. 69.
7. Bacon Report p. 73
8. Bacon Report p. 70
9. 'Cheap accessible cross-border trading possible after merger', Margaret Doyle (of the *Economist*), from *The Irish Times*, 5 May 2000.

10. Online trading is share trading via the Internet.
11. 'Wall Street echoes to clamour for change in markets', from *The Irish Times*, 10 March 2000 (*Financial Times* Service).
12. 'Irish exchange faces new challenge from Euronext', Mary Canniffe, *The Irish Times*, 24 March 2000.
13. 'Foreign Firms Flock to US for IPOs', M.R. Seist, the *Wall Street Journal*, 23 June 1995.
14. '101 Trends every investor should know about the Global Economy', J.P. Quinlan and K.L. Stevens, CB.
15. 'Strategic Development Options for Ireland's Capital Markets in a Comparative Context', Peter Bacon & Associates, Economic Consultants, Oct. 1999.
16. 'Exchange to switch to electronic trading tomorrow', Mary Canniffe, *The Irish Times*, 5 June 2000.
17. For simplicity, this average price is got by taking the high and low price for the year and dividing by 2.

12
Dividend Policy

CHAPTER OBJECTIVES

At the end of this chapter, you should be able to:

- understand what dividends are
- know the sequence of events in dividend payments
- know why companies need to have a dividend policy
- analyse the controversy about dividend policy. Does dividend policy affect shareholder value?
- understand how companies determine the level of dividends paid out at any one time
- assess the alternatives to cash dividends.

INTRODUCTION

Dividends are cash payments out of profits to shareholders and are therefore a major cash outlay for many corporations. How much of the company's retained earnings (profit for ordinary shareholders) will be paid to shareholders (if any) and how much will be ploughed back into the company's investment plans? This is the **dividend policy** decision. What is of greater importance is the effect this policy decision will have on shareholder wealth. We will explore this question later on in the chapter. However, why is it necessary to have a planned dividend policy at all? The answer is that shareholders don't like surprises. Companies are reluctant to pay out substantial cash dividends if they know that they cannot repeat it the following year. If shareholders don't get the dividend they expect, they can react by selling their shares and driving down the share price. Therefore companies try to plan their dividend payouts and by doing so help stabilise share prices.

In addition, dividend policy can impact on companies' investment plans. If a company has a high dividend payout policy, then any investment plans the company has earmarked to be financed by retained earnings may have to be put on hold. Therefore, dividend policy must be taken into account along with the company's investment and capital expenditure decisions.

12.1 Dividend payments sequence

Irish public limited companies usually pay dividends twice a year every six months. An **interim** dividend is paid relating to the first six months of trading, followed by a **final** dividend after the end of the financial year. Dividends are usually expressed as (a) dividends per share (euro per share), (b) dividend yield (see Chapter 11) dividends as a percentage of the market price) or as (c) the dividend payout, which is dividends as a percentage of earnings.

Table 12.1 Kerry Group consolidated profit and loss account 1997 (extract)

Profit after taxation and attributable to ordinary shareholders	£64,632
Dividends: paid (interim)	£2,392
proposed	£4,817

(Note that the word 'proposed' is used which means that the directors are proposing a final dividend but it is up to the shareholders at the group's AGM to decide whether it should be paid or not.)

The dividend payout is 11.2%.

The board of directors decides when the company will pay a dividend. The following is the sequence of events leading up to the actual payment.

1. *Declaration date*: on this date the board declares a dividend to be paid on a certain date in the future.
2. *Date of record*: When shares are sold it takes time to process the paper work and to record the change of ownership. This is the date the holder of the share must be on record in order to receive a dividend.
3. *Ex-dividend date*: Because it takes time to process the buying and selling of shares and to make sure that the dividends go to the right people, the stock exchange establishes an ex-dividend date. This is generally four working days before the date of record. This means that if you buy a share before this date you are entitled to the dividend—the share is said to **trade with dividend** or **cum dividend**. Investors who buy the share on or after this date will not be entitled to the dividend—the share will trade **ex-dividend**. The ex-dividend date is important for two reasons: (a) it determines who is entitled to the dividend and (b) the value of the share will fall by roughly the amount of the dividend. Therefore, if a share has a market value of Report €5 cum dividend and if a €1 dividend is declared on that share, then the ex-dividend price will fall to roughly €4. Because dividends are taxed as income, the actual ex-dividend price of the share will be influenced by the individual investor's marginal tax rates.
4. *Payment date*: The cheques are posted to the investors.

We should note, however, that this process is likely to become much simpler because of technological developments, particularly with the electronic transfer of funds.

12.2 The dividend policy debate

In the opening chapter of this book, we said that the overriding consideration of financial management is to maximise shareholder value. In this section we will set out to evaluate the effect dividend policy has on shareholder wealth. **Remember that the dividend policy** decision is whether to pay out cash now or invest the cash and pay it out later. How much of the company's retained earnings should be paid out now (if any) and how much should be reinvested? What effect does this decision have on shareholder value? There are essentially three schools of thought in answer to this question. The first states that dividend policy has no effect on shareholder value. This is the **irrelevancy** argument and was first developed by Franco Modigliani and Robert Miller. The second school suggests that an increase in dividend payout ratio increases shareholder value—the **bird in the hand** theory. The third school of thought states that an increase in dividend payout ratio reduces shareholder value—the **tax differential** theory. The main arguments are outlined below along with some real world resolutions to the debate.

12.2.1 The irrelevancy argument in perfect capital markets

The value of a firm is determined by the earning power of its assets, not how these earnings are distributed. You can slice a cake into many pieces but it doesn't change the size of the cake. Similarly, a company's dividend policy has no effect on the price of a company's shares and no effect on the overall value of the firm. Modligiani and Miller (MM) assumes perfect capital markets (see Chapter 8) and ignores taxes and commission costs.

Example 12.1 Irrelevance of dividend policy

Boyvale Ltd has the following capital structure:	
Balance sheet (market values)	€
Fixed assets	600,000
Cash	400,000
	1,000,000
Financed by:	
100,000 ordinary shares	1,000,000

The market value of Boyvale shares is 1,000,000/€100,000 = €10. The company has decided to pay the €400,000 as a cash dividend, or €400,000/100,000 shares = €4 per share. Ignoring taxes, commission costs and other market imperfections, does this policy decision affect shareholder value?

After paying out the cash dividend each share is worth €600,000/100,000 shares = €6 per share. Therefore the share price has fallen but the value of the shareholders' holdings hasn't changed. A shareholder with 100 shares before the dividend payment was worth 100 × €10 = €1,000. After the dividend payment her worth is now 100 × €6 = €600. However, she also has €4 cash dividend per share which is worth 100 × €4 = €400. So her total wealth is now €600 + €400 = €1,000. To further illustrate, MM's irrelevancy argument understands that any shareholder can create his/her own **home-made dividend**. Suppose, for example, that Boyvale decided not to pay a dividend. Our shareholder in the above example could, if she desired, sell 40 of her 100 shares at €10 per share in order to generate €400 in cash. Her overall wealth won't have changed because she now has €400 in cash *plus* €600 in shares, giving her a total value of €1,000.

The criticism of MM is that their assumptions are unrealistic. However, remember that the validity of a theory is determined by its ability to predict and explain, and not in the realism of its assumptions. In particular, they assumed perfect capital markets, rational investors, and no taxes and commission costs. The next two theories try to incorporate these real world factors.

Example 12.2 The dividend irrelevancy argument and present value

MM assumed no risk. Assume that the interest rate or the rate at which cash can be invested is 5%. Now assume that the company has €20,000 available to pay out in cash dividends to its shareholders. Alternatively, it can reinvest the €20,000 in the company. If it pays out the €20,000 as a cash dividend today, the present value of this option is €20,000. If it reinvests the €20,000 for 3 years it produces a capital gain of €20,000 $(1.05)^3$ = €23,152. This has a present value of €20,000. Therefore the firm's policy decision of high payout versus low payout gives the same present value.

12.2.2 The bird in the hand theory

This theory states that investors prefer to receive dividends now (a bird in the hand), instead of having company earnings invested in the firm in the expectation of future capital gains (two in the bush). Dividends are in the hand while capital gains are in the bush. There is a certainty about cash dividends, whereas there is an uncertainty about capital gains. The risk attached to capital gains is greater than the risk attached to near dividends. Therefore we can conclude that high payout ratios reduce risk and therefore reduce the cost of equity.[1] Consequently, companies with high payout ratios will be more popular and will therefore have higher share prices and higher company valuations. Furthermore, issuing new shares to increase dividends will incur commission and flotation costs, which will have the effect of lowering share value.

This is different to MM. The critical conclusion of the bird in the hand theory is that dividend policy affects company risk and therefore the cost of equity. For MM, the cost of equity is independent of dividend policy, and company risk (and therefore investors' required rate of return) depends on the company's operational cash flows that depend on the company's investment and borrowing policies and not on dividend policy. Proponents of MM would say that while it is true that cash dividends are less risky, this is so because the cash is in the bank. The investor could achieve a similar outcome if she sold some shares and put the money in the bank.

12.2.3 Tax differential theory

Irish tax laws are such that tax rates on dividend income are higher than the tax rates on capital gains. This would be the case in most countries. Shareholders should prefer capital gains to dividends because most investors would have unused capital gains allowances, while our personal allowances are usually used up. The tax rate in Ireland on capital gains is 20%, whereas dividend income will be taxed at rates according to the individual investor's marginal tax rate, which is greater than 20%. Depending on marginal tax rates, this could be 22% or 44% (at the time of writing). From a tax point of view it would make sense for a company to plough back its earnings into the business where subsequent earnings growth would lead to higher share prices (capital gains) which would be subject to lower capital gains tax. Company dividend policy should be for low dividend payouts, which will result in lower taxes, and investors will therefore be willing to pay more for low payout shares. Note that, according to this theory, a low payout will lower the risk and consequently lower the cost of equity.

12.3 Resolutions to the dividend controversy

12.3.1 The information (signalling) content of dividends

There is a lot of empirical evidence to suggest that share prices rise when dividends are **unexpectedly increased** and fall when they are **unexpectedly reduced**. This would suggest that high payouts are best. However MM argued that share prices change because of the **information content** of dividends and not because of changes in dividend payout ratios per se. In other words, a dividend cut is a **signal** that management is not confident about the future and that current dividends cannot be maintained. The risk attached to expected future dividends rises, the cost of equity rises and the share price falls. In addition, an unexpected increase in dividends is a signal from management that it is confident about the future prospects of the company and that current dividends can be maintained. This reduces the risk attached to expected future dividend payments, the cost of equity is reduced and share values rise. Briefly, we can be sceptical about the quality of the earnings reported by the company, unless these earnings are backed up by appropriate dividends.

12.3.2 Clientele effect

There are also real world examples of investors attracted to particular companies because of their dividend policy. This clientele effect suggests that young investors, for example, will prefer shares that grow in value from capital gains and that they will sacrifice current income in the form of cash dividends for future capital gains. Therefore they look for companies that retain earnings and with low dividend payouts. Similarly, other groups, e.g. retired pensioners, will seek out companies with high payout policies because they may prefer current income.

Therefore companies with a low payout policy will attract certain groups and companies with a high payout will attract other groups. A change in dividend policy attracts a different clientele. The supply and demand for high payout shares will determine the share's equilibrium price. If demand for these shares exceeds the supply, the share price will rise. Low dividend payout companies will then be enticed to switch their dividend policy to a high payout until the dividend market is in equilibrium and all the clientele are satisfied. As long as there are enough high dividend payout companies to satisfy high yield investors, a company cannot increase its share price by increasing its dividend.

12.4 Dividends as a residual of profits

Having examined the theoretical approaches to dividend policy and looked at some empirical evidence, we can now look at how companies decide on the actual dividends they pay to their shareholders.

In principle, companies should reinvest retained earnings in projects as long as these projects give a rate of return greater than the company's cost of capital, i.e. a positive net present value. In other words, dividends should not be the main focus of attention, but what should be of primary consideration is the amount of retained earnings available for profitable investment opportunities. Earnings should not be retained unless the company can earn a rate of return greater than shareholders can get for themselves by reinvesting their dividends in investments of equal risk. However, companies adopting this policy must make sure that they maintain their optimal capital structure (Chapter 8) by adding an appropriate amount of borrowed funds to their equity. Otherwise they would have an inappropriate amount of equity, which would therefore increase the cost of capital and lower the share price.

Example 12.3 Residual dividend theory

Hexel Construction Ltd has just earned profits after tax of €1m. The company's cost of capital is 10% and its optimal debt: equity ratio is 40%. The company's investment managers have listed three projects, all with yield rates greater than the company's cost of capital.

Project	Cost (€)
A	100,000
B	150,000
C	300,000

The total finance required for all three projects is therefore €550,000. To maintain its optimal debt: equity ratio of 40%, it will need to borrow €220,000, i.e 40%. Therefore the amount of residual profits is €670,000 (i.e. €1m *minus* €330,000), and this is what is paid to shareholders as a cash dividend.

Table 12.2 Residual dividend policy—Hexel Construction

Total finance required	€550,000
Capital structure	40% debt and 60% equity
Borrowings	40% × €550,000 = €220,000
Equity investment	60% × €550.000 = €330,000
Total earnings	€1,000,000
Dividends	€1,000,000 *less* €330,000 = €670,000

By following the residual dividend theory the amount of dividends paid out can be expressed as

$$\text{Dividends} = \left(\begin{array}{c}\text{Profit for ordinary}\\ \text{shareholders}\end{array}\right) - \left(\begin{array}{c}\text{Retained earnings}\\ \text{required to finance}\\ \text{new projects}\end{array}\right)$$

$$= \left(\begin{array}{c}\text{Profit for ordinary}\\ \text{shareholders}\end{array}\right) - \left[\left(\begin{array}{c}\text{Percentage of equity}\\ \text{in the capital structure}\end{array}\right)\left(\begin{array}{c}\text{Total finance}\\ \text{required}\end{array}\right)\right]$$

In the above example the dividends paid = €1,000,000 *less* (60% × €550,000) = €670,000

12.5 Dividend stability

The residual policy, if adopted, could result in unstable dividends. In years when earnings are high and profitable investment opportunities are low, then dividends will be high. When earnings are low and profitable investments are high, then dividends may be zero. However, shareholders may prefer stable cash dividends. As we have already seen, cutting dividends may send the wrong signal to the market about the future prospects of the firm and share prices may drop. An optimal dividend policy is about balancing the needs of shareholders against the need for internal sources of finance. With this in mind, public companies tend to adopt a policy of **stable dividends**. In other words, most publicly quoted companies do not follow the **residual dividend approach** to dividend policy.

12.6 Summary of factors when firms decide on dividend policy

The long-run policy of firms is to decide on a percentage of earnings that they will pay out of earnings—their target payout ratio. This is done after considering the following factors:

(a) Avoid cutting dividends.
(b) Don't reject positive NPV projects so as to pay a dividend.
(c) Avoid issuing new equity to pay a dividend.
(d) In deciding what dividend to pay, the company should maintain its target debt:equity ratio.

12.7 Factors influencing dividend policy

Directors of companies are not free to decide on whatever dividends they wish to pay out. There are certain restrictions placed on them by external and internal forces:

- **Providers of debt capital**: People and institutions that loan money to a company will expect to be paid interest on their loans out of the cash tank of the company. This is the same cash tank from which shareholders expect to be paid cash dividends. Therefore before investors provide loans to companies, they may place restrictions on excessive cash dividends.
- **Legal restrictions**: Companies cannot pay dividends out of legal capital, which is defined as the par value of existing shares. This means that companies can only pay dividends from retained earnings, i.e. accumulated profits. Companies that make losses in any particular year can still pay dividends, provided it comes out of profits retained

from previous years. This gives some protection to creditors by preventing shareholders withdrawing capital originally provided by shareholders. If this rule did not exist, any company who got into financial difficulties could liquidate their assets and distribute the proceeds to their shareholders leaving their creditors (debt providers) in the lurch.

- **Shortage of cash**: Dividends are paid out of cash and any shortage of cash may mean that dividends are not paid. However, if a company has a planned dividend policy and if shareholders expect a dividend payment, a shortage of cash may lead to higher company borrowing.
- **Investment opportunities**: A company's dividend payout ratio will depend on its investment plans. If a company has profitable investment plans, it will tend towards a low payout ratio. Conversely, if profitable investment opportunities are scarce, it will normally have a high payout ratio.
- **Cost of issuing new equity shares**: Companies can finance their investments from (a) retained earnings, (b) issuing new shares and/or (c) borrowing. If the cost of issuing new shares (commission costs, flotation costs etc.) is higher than the cost of retained earnings (see Chapter 8), this will favour a low dividend payout.
- **Ownership and control**: Directors may be concerned about losing control of their company and they may be reluctant to issue new shares to finance their investment plans. Therefore they depend on retained earnings as a source of finance and consequently opt for a low dividend payout.

12.8 Alternatives to cash dividends

12.8.1 Share or scrip dividends

This is a payment to existing shareholders which dilutes the value of each outstanding share. Share dividends are usually expressed as a percentage. For example a 20% scrip dividend would mean that all existing shareholders would receive one new share for every five shares they already hold.

Example 12.4 Share dividends

The balance sheet of Dodgy Ltd is as follows:	
Balance sheet (extract)	€000
Net assets	6,000
Financed by	
Share capital	
100,000 @ €1 per share	100
Share premium account	900
Retained earnings	5,000
	6,000

The company announces a 20% share dividend. The principal use of the share premium account is to pay bonus share issues. In all 20,000 new shares are issued to existing shareholders. The balance sheet after the scrip dividend shows the share premium account reduced by €20,000. No cash has changed hands. The overall financial effect is nil. The overall value of the firm is unaffected although it is cut into a further 20,000 pieces. The book value of the shares will however fall because there are more shares in issue.

Dodgy Ltd balance sheet (after scrip issue)	
	€000
Net assets	6,000
Financed by	
Share capital 120,000 @ 1 each	120
Share premium a/c	880
Retained earnings	5,000
	6,000
Book value of the shares before scrip dividend	6,000,000/100,000 = €60
Book value of the shares after the issue	6,000,000/120,000 = €50

When shareholders receive a share dividend, they can either hold on to them or sell them for cash. This opens up the possibility for the shareholder of making a profit. **An enhanced scrip dividend** is where the shares offered are worth more than the cash dividend (see Box 12.1). **Special dividends** are the same as normal dividends but are usually bigger and paid on a once-off basis.

Box 12.1 AIB shareholders stand to gain on scrip dividend

AIB shareholders have the opportunity to make an immediate tax-free profit if they opt to take AIB shares instead of cash for their half-year dividend. The weakness of AIB shares in the middle of the month has meant that the scrip dividend will be offered to shareholders at €11.85 (£9.33) per share—the average price for the five days leading up to 17 August ex-dividend date. But since the ex-dividend date, AIB shares have recovered strongly and although they lost five cents yesterday, they still closed on €12.65 (£9.96), 80 cents higher than the price at which new shares will be issued to shareholders under the scrip dividend. That presumably should ensure a good take-up.

Source: Brendan McGrath, Markets Editor, *The Irish Times*, 28 August 1999

12.8.2 Share splits

These are similar to share dividends in that they both increase the number of shares outstanding and neither increases the overall value of equity outstanding. The difference is that while share dividends are issued instead of a cash dividend, share splits are used to bring share prices into what is believed by management to be a **realistic trading range**. Companies may find that their share price has grown to such a high price that demand for their share has fallen. To correct this and to bring the share into a more popular trading range, the company can **split its stock**.[2] This is usually expressed as a ratio, e.g. a 3 for 1 share split indicates that three new shares will be issued for every one share already in issue.

12.8.3 Share repurchases

A company can pay cash to its shareholders in either of two ways:

- cash dividend, or
- share repurchase.

A company that has a large amount of unwanted cash (i.e. after paying a cash dividend and after all profitable projects have been identified) will see its debt:equity ratio change in favour of high cost equity. This increases the overall cost of capital. To avoid this the company will give back this cash to its shareholders by buying back some of their shares. This is a share repurchase.

A share repurchase reduces the number of shares outstanding but doesn't affect the company's earnings. Therefore earnings per share (EPS) rises. However, the P/E ratio is not affected because the share price follows exactly the rise in the EPS. Therefore share repurchase has no effect on company value.

Example 12.5 Share repurchase

XYZ Ltd expects to earn €2m in the current year. The company has 1,000,000 shares outstanding, which have a current market price of €10. It is proposing to pay out €1m to its shareholders by way of a share repurchase. It will buy back the shares at a 10% premium to the current market price, i.e. at €11. This means that it will buy back 1,000,000/€11 = 90,909 shares.

The EPS before the repurchase = €2,000,000/1,000,000 = €2
The P/E ratio = €10/€2 = 5
The EPS after repurchasing = €2,000,000/909,091 = €2.2
The expected price after repurchase = (EPS) x (P/E) = €2.2 x 5 = €11
The market value of the company before the share repurchase was 1,000,000 shares x €10 = €10,000,000
In addition, the market value of the company after the share repurchase is 90,9091 x €11 = €10,000,000.

The actual impact of share repurchases on P/E ratios depends on the market's reaction to the buy-back. If it views the share repurchase as positive, then the P/E ratio may rise. On the other hand if it views it unfavourably, then the P/E ratio may fall. (See Box 12.2.)

Features of a share buy-back

- A share repurchase may act as a signal to the market that the shares are undervalued and that the company sees its own shares as a good investment.

- A buy-back may also be seen as an indication by management that it is not prepared to use shareholders' money on wasteful investments.
- There may be an excess supply of shares on the market so a share repurchase can keep the share price solid. When share prices went into free fall in October 1987 (black Monday, 19th), many large American corporations announced share buy-backs, which helped to slow down the drop in prices.
- A share buy-back is treated as a capital gain by the individual shareholder and will therefore receive more favourable tax treatment than if the shareholder received a cash dividend.
- Shares that are bought back from shareholders are held as **treasury shares**.
- Share buy-backs cost the company and shareholders money. (See Box 12.2.)

Box 12.2 Who wins in a share buy-back?

When companies go into the market and buy back shares, there are usually mixed feelings.

Is it a sign that the company simply doesn't have any ideas on how to spend excess money? Or more positively, is it a genuine mechanism to put some money back into shareholders' pockets while simultaneously boosting earnings per share?

Whatever the benefits for shareholders, when shares are bought or sold there is one sure-fire winner—the brokers who handle the deal.

Bank of Ireland's broking subsidiary Davy and London broking blueblood Cazenove handled the bank's recent €342 million buy-back of 52 million shares. How much did all this realise for Davy and Cazenove in terms of fees and commissions?

That's hard to gauge as fund managers are notoriously coy about telling people like 'Current Account' what sort of arrangement they have with stockbrokers.

But even a commission of 0.5% would have given Davy and Cazenove commission of €1.7million on shares they bought from institutions for Bank of Ireland—not to mention the fee they would have negotiated with the bank itself to handle the buy-back.

'Current Account—An inside track on Business',
The Irish Times, 9 May 1999

Box 12.3 Buying back shares reveals a poverty of ideas

Share buy-backs are rarely questioned. They should be. Those who advocate them are usually devoid of appropriate alternatives, or incapable of tackling the core problems.

Ardagh, the glassmaker, is the latest to try to justify its planned offer to buy back up to 2.5 million of its shares. Why? To help support the share price that had fallen sharply as investors moved out of small or mid-capitalisation companies.

The company believes it is undervalued based on its dividend and earnings yields .
. . .

This raises a very basic question: is it a corporation's function to influence the share price? Corporations may argue that it is not a device to alter share price, but it is. By taking shares out of circulation, there are fewer to trade, so technically that should be a share support mechanism.

⟶

It is really a cop out, however. Share prices are weak because a sufficient number of investors do not want the shares. They do not want them because the companies are not performing, or because they are in an unacceptable sector, or because of question marks over the future.

The heady pursuit into, or hasty retreat out of, tiny untried IT companies proves that size is not the only consideration.

In addition, at the end of the day share buy-backs tend to be sticking plaster jobs. In time, they peel away because they do not deal with the root problems. In some cases, the benefits from the mechanism can be very short term.

Take Bank of Ireland, for example. Last July it received sanction from its shareholders to buy back up to ten per cent of its shares. The opportunity came the following September when the shares fell by 11 per cent in just two days following speculation that other British banks might follow Bank of Scotland into the Irish market and offer further financial products that compete with the Irish banks.

So Bank of Ireland weighed into the market and bought 5% in two tranches: 47.3 million at €8.45 per share and 4.7 million at €8.15 per share. While there was an initial recovery, the share price fell to close just 55 cents up on the day at €8.15 but still well below the €9 at which the shares were traded a week before.

Since then, the shares fell to a low of €6.65 and now stand at €7.65. Clearly Bank of Ireland's share buy-back exercise was a failure. It also proved costly. The costs (including dealing) amounted to €562 million. These have eaten into the surplus capital, estimated by Goodbody Stockbrokers at €1.1 billion at March 2000. In addition, it could have cancelled the shares when it made the purchase: instead, it decided to hold them as treasury stock. . . .

Another company, Greencore, the food group, concerned about the weak share price, is looking at options including another share buy-back. This is surprising considering that the last one—in 1998—backfired. The timing was wrong, as the share price was marginally above the offer price of 482.5 cents per share. It offered to buy 10 million shares for £18.6 million. The shares now languish at 308 cents. . . .

At a time of low interest rates, share buy-backs can enhance earnings. However, available cash, or higher borrowings, should be used to grow the business and not affect the share price.

Bill Murdoch, *The Irish Times*, 17 April 2000

SUMMARY

- Dividend policy is a decision taken by management to determine what proportion of a company's earnings is paid out to shareholders over time.
- In a world of no taxes and other imperfections, dividend policy is irrelevant and makes no difference to shareholder wealth.
- Income tax paid on dividends and flotation costs of new issue favour a low dividend payout and therefore increasing dividend payouts will lower shareholder value.
- The bird in the hand theory states that cash dividends are less risky than future potential capital gains. Therefore, high payouts can raise shareholder value.

- The information content of dividends and the clientele effect suggests that there are some groups of investors who prefer a high payout and others that prefer a low payout. Therefore, dividend policy will be determined by the financial needs of shareholders.
- The theoretical approach as to what is the optimal dividend policy is inconclusive. Empirically the fact that companies pay substantial dividends can be seen as evidence that that is what shareholders want.
- The residual dividend theory suggests that the amount of earnings retained within the firm is important and the amount paid as dividends should not be the principal issue.
- There are certain restrictions placed on the directors of companies when it comes to paying dividends.
- A scrip dividend occurs when shareholders receive additional shares in proportion to their existing holdings instead of a normal cash dividend.
- A company with excess cash can give it back to shareholders via a share repurchase. These may have a tax advantage over cash dividends.

QUESTIONS

1. Explain dividend irrelevance theory; bird in the hand theory; tax differential theory.
2. Define optimal dividend policy.
3. Would it be rational for a company to pay out dividends and issue new equity during the same year?
4. What effect do scrip dividends have on the market price of a share? Would it increase the market value of the firm?
5. How might clientele effects influence dividend policy?
6. Can a change in a company's dividend policy send a signal to shareholders? Explain.
7. 'Dividends are important but dividend policy is irrelevant.' Discuss.
8. James Ltd has just issued its annual report, which showed a profit for ordinary shareholders of €100, 000. It has declared a dividend of €20,000. Calculate the payout ratio.
9. ✦ Is it sensible to have a residual dividend policy?
10. ✦ A company has 100,000 shares in issue and pays an €8 per share as a cash dividend. The company's profit after tax and after all preference dividends have been paid is €2,000,000. It has a P/E ratio of 10. Calculate the (i) Share price; (ii) payout ratio.
11. ✦ Murphy Construction Ltd has just announced end of year profits after tax of €100,000. The company maintains a debt:equity ratio of 60% debt and 40% equity. It follows a residual dividend policy. The company has positive NPV projects for the coming financial year of €200,000.
    (a) How much can Murphy spend on capital projects while maintaining its capital structure?
    (b) How much will Murphy pay in dividends?
12. Decies Ltd has a capital structure consisting of 60% debt and 40% equity. Its capital budget is €3.6m and the company estimates that its earnings for the year will be €1.8m. Calculate the company's payout ratio if it follows a residual dividend policy.
13. ✦ How can dividend policy be irrelevant if share prices rise following an increase in dividend payments?
14. Divine Ltd has a cost of capital of 10%. The company is to pay a current year dividend of 20 cents, but in two years time the company is to close down. It will

distribute the proceeds of liquidation via a cash dividend. The proceeds of the sale are expected to be €1m. In addition, there will be 100,000 shares outstanding. Calculate:

   (a) the current share price

   (b) the amount received in dividends in each of the two years if you would prefer to receive the same amount in both years. Assume that you own 1% of the shares. (Home-made dividend). Ignore taxes.

15. If dividends attract more tax than capital gains, why pay any dividends at all?

16. The Athlone company paid a dividend of 80 cents a share which was an increase of 10% over the last year's pre-split dividend. The dividend just paid of 80 cents was after a 4-for-1 stock split. Calculate the dividand per share for last year.

17. Why would a firm decide to pay a scrip dividend instead of a cash dividend? Explain the difference between a share dividend and a share split.

18.✦ The balance sheet of Garbh Eoin Ltd is as follows:

Balance sheet (market values as at 6/5/20000	
Fixed assets	200,000
Cash	30,000
	230,000
Financed by	
10,000 shares	230,000

The company has declared a dividend of €3 per share and the shares go ex-dividend on 7/5/2000. Calculate the value of the shares on 7/5/2000. Ignore taxes.

19. Alternatively, suppose the company in question 18 decided to repurchase €12,000 worth of shares. Ignoring taxation, show how the effect of a repurchase is the same as a cash dividend.

20. Use the concept of present value to explain the 'bird-in-the-hand' theory.

NOTES

1. Recall from Chapter 6 the constant share growth valuation model: $P = D/K - g$ and therefore $K = D/P + g$. So K is reduced because investors value €1 of dividends (D/P, the dividend yield is less risky) more than €1 of capital gains (the g component).

2. There is little empirical evidence to support the notion that shares trade within an optimum trading range. However, there is a belief that the market value of companies will suffer if their shares do not trade within this range. If the share price is above the upper limit of this range, demand for these shares will fall, the share price will fall and consequently the market value of the firm. For example, if the top of the trading range is 100, a doubling of the number of shares will halve the price of the shares to 50, leaving the overall market value of the firm unaffected. However, because of the lower price additional demand might shift the price above 50, thereby increasing the overall market value of the firm.

Part 5

Short-term Financial Planning

13
Working Capital and Cash Management

CHAPTER OBJECTIVES

By the end of this chapter the student should be able to:

(a) understand what is meant by working capital policy and the working capital cycle
(b) estimate how much should be invested in current assets
(c) understand the connection between working capital and sales
(d) distinguish between liquidity and profitability
(e) understand the concept of overtrading
(f) appreciate the concept of zero working capital and the connection between economic value added (EVA) and working capital
(g) understand the notion of a minimum cash balance
(h) calculate the operating and cash cycles
(i) calculate float
(j) understand the Baumol model as a theoretical model in estimating optimum cash balances
(k) develop a cash flow forecast.

INTRODUCTION

Ask any financial manager about the amount of time they spend on making sure they have the right amount of current assets and they would tell you that it is quite a lot, in particular, making sure they have sufficient cash at the end of each month/quarter to pay the bills. In earlier chapters we discussed long-term financial decisions, dividend policy, investment appraisal, long-term financial planning and capital structure decisions. Yet, even if we get all of the long-term financial decisions correct, the company can be knocked out and put into liquidation by not having enough cash to pay current bills.

Working capital policy is a firm's policy regarding the levels of investment in working capital and how this investment should be financed. In this chapter we discuss the first of these issues, namely, how much should be in current asset holdings. Chapter 15 looks at how current asset holdings are financed.

13.1 The cash flow cycle

Figure 13.1 illustrates the working capital cycle for a typical manufacturing firm. Cash comes into the business initially in the form of shareholders' funds and debt capital.

Investments are made in the form of raw material inventories, which are combined with labour and other direct costs of production to produce work-in-progress and finished goods. These finished goods are then sold or held as stock until sold. They are sold as cash sales (in which case the money goes directly back into the cash tank of the business) or on credit (in which case the stock is converted into debtors). Having enough cash in the cash tank of the business is necessary to pay the creditors, interest on loans to the bank and other providers of debt capital, dividends to shareholders and tax to the government. A fall-off in demand for the product or an unnecessary build-up in raw materials would mean that cash will be tied up in stock of finished goods. This is cash which would not come back into the cash tank of the business. The same result would occur if there is an increase in account receivables (debtors). The result will be a shortage of cash to meet the bills that have to be paid. A liquidity crisis develops. Increasing the amount of borrowings would improve the cash position, but this will exacerbate the problem in the long term. The real problem is releasing the cash tied up in stock and debtors. In other words minimising the amount of cash tied up in working capital will not only enhance company liquidity, it will also increase the overall return on investment (see example 13.1).

Figure 13.1 Working capital cycle and cash flows

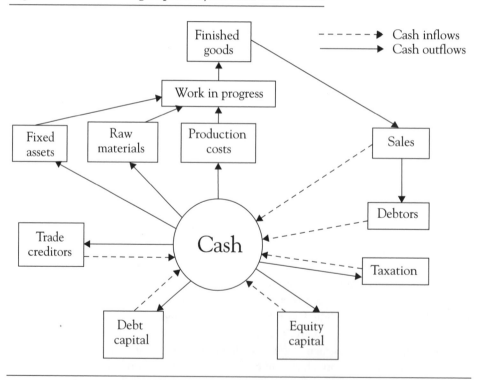

Example 13.1 Minimising investment in working capital

Two companies A and B have invested the same in fixed assets. However, company B has managed to achieve a higher return on capital because it manages to minimise the amount of cash tied up in working capital.

	Company A	Company B
Fixed assets	€400,000	€400,000
Net current assets	€200,000	€100,000
Total capital employed	€600,000	€500,000
Operating profit	€100,000	€100,000
Return on capital employed	16.7%	20%

13.2 Working capital definitions

Gross working capital: refers to investment in current assets. Current assets are those that can be converted into cash in a relatively short period (usually a year). Current assets include cash, debtors and stock.

Net working capital: is current assets *less* current liabilities.

For example, the consolidated balance sheet of Golden Vale Ltd (1998) gives current assets of £152,236,000 and current liabilities of £128,190,000. It therefore reported a net working capital figure of £24,046,000.

13.2.1 Investments in current assets

How much should be invested in current assets? The answer depends on sales. How much should be carried in current assets to support a given level of sales? Figure 13.2 illustrates the different policies regarding investment in current assets. The top line, or the line with the steepest slope, illustrates a **relaxed** approach where large amounts of cash, near cash balances and higher stock levels are held, and where sales are made on generous credit terms (i.e. long debtors payment periods). Where there is uncertainty about future sales, a relaxed approach is appropriate. Here, a company will need to keep extra holdings of stocks (safety stocks) and a minimum cash balance to meet likely variations to what might be expected and therefore avoid production stoppages.

In an environment of **certainty**, where sales, creditors and debtors payment periods are known for certain, firms would only need to hold minimal investments in current assets. This is an **aggressive** policy towards management of investments in current assets. Firms would only need to hold minimum cash and stock and would operate tight credit policies. This policy would provide the highest return on invested capital (see example 13.1 above), but it would also have the highest risk because of the possibility of losing sales. **Operating risk** is low when a company has high holdings in current assets because there is less danger of running short. However, there are opportunity costs and storage costs in holding excessive working capital. The opportunity costs arise because firms must use cash to purchase raw materials. Cash comes from either equity capital or debt capital or a combination of both and, as we know, capital has a cost.

Figure 13.2 Current asset investment policies

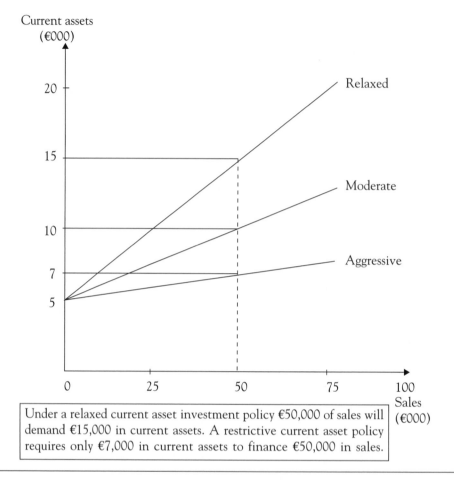

Under a relaxed current asset investment policy €50,000 of sales will demand €15,000 in current assets. A restrictive current asset policy requires only €7,000 in current assets to finance €50,000 in sales.

13.3 Working capital investment and sales

The sales activity a company undertakes will impact on its working capital requirements. In other words, while expansion in sales is good news, the bad news is that the company will require additional working capital to finance the increase in sales. This will be in the form of a rise in raw materials, finished goods and higher debtors to support the increase in sales. Additional working capital will therefore be required to finance the increase in sales. If the additional working capital is not forthcoming, the company is in a situation called **overtrading**. Overtrading occurs when the business experiences an increase in the level of activity in the working capital area of the business, but has insufficient working capital to finance the increased level of activity. Another word for overtrading is under-capitalisation. In other words, the company may have had insufficient start-up equity capital to support the level of activity in terms of cash and in terms of supporting additional borrowing capacity. Therefore, if there isn't enough equity capital there may not be sufficient debt capital forthcoming. To avoid overtrading (illiquidity) is to make sure that increases in sales are matched by increases in the necessary working capital to finance the increase in sales. To rectify an overtrading situation, the company will need to:

(a) increase the capital base in equity capital or organise additional borrowing
(b) minimise the investments in current assets, e.g. by lowering stock or debtor levels
(c) If it is not possible to either increase the capital base or reduce investments in working capital, then the only solution will be to cut back on sales.

Therefore, it is possible for a company to double sales and profits and still go out of business because of a lack of liquidity. This highlights the possibility that profitable companies can go out of business because of insufficient liquid assets. It illustrates the very important distinction between profitability and liquidity.

13.4 Zero working capital

Some companies (e.g. General Electric in the US) have a policy of zero working capital. Advocates of zero working capital claim that it leads to greater efficiency, generates cash and speeds up production. Zero working capital is defined as

Zero working capital = Stocks + Receivables + Payables   (13.1)

Reducing working capital (towards zero) as a percentage of sales increases the cash flow and lowers inventories. In other words, releasing cash tied up in stocks or receivables or by increasing payables leads to increased cash flow. As stated earlier, capital has a cost, so reducing the capital tied up in working capital improves profitability because of the savings in capital costs. Because working capital is reduced, companies are consequently forced to speed up production and delivery times (which helps improve sales) and capital tied up in excessive warehousing can be released by selling it off.

The key to zero working capital is **demand based management** or **demand flow management**. What this means is that the company only produces **after** it has received an order, while still being able to meet customer delivery time. As soon as the product is made, it is delivered immediately. There is no warehousing and no storage costs. Therefore a movement towards zero working capital improves efficiency, leads to higher profitability and improves cash flow.

13.5 Economic value added (EVA) and working capital

The concept of economic value added has been discussed in previous chapters. EVA can be defined as

Sales *less* Operating costs *less* Capital costs = EVA

In other words, after the operating profit figure is calculated, an additional deduction is charged. This additional deduction is for the cost of capital. Therefore by minimising the amount of capital tied up in stock, debtors or cash holdings, more cash will become available which can then be used to buy back shares or pay off debt. The effect of those two policies will be to reduce capital and the cost of financing, thus raising economic value added.

13.6 Cash management

Having cash balances can be a waste of money, particularly if the cash balances themselves earn little or no interest. Still, most companies hold some cash balances to 'grease' the wheels of business. The objective of cash management is to keep the amount invested in cash to a minimum, while keeping enough cash to keep the firm operating as efficiently as possible. In other words, cash is needed to pay for raw materials, to buy fixed assets, to pay taxes and dividends etc.

13.6.1 Factors affecting the size of the minimum cash balance

The size of the minimum cash balances a firm should hold depends on:

1. The need to meet unexpected cash needs.
    Some of the cash that comes into the business will need to be held to grease the wheels. The rest of the cash will be invested in interest-bearing securities that will generate more income for the firm. The amount of cash held will depend on the opportunity cost of holding cash, i.e. the interest rate, and on the speed at which cash can be obtained. If the opportunity cost is zero (i.e. the cost of borrowing money is zero) and if cash can be obtained at very short notice, then it would not be necessary for a firm (or an individual for that matter) to hold any cash. All the cash that comes into the firm would be immediately invested in income-generating investment.

    However, because borrowing money has a cost (interest rate) and because it takes time, firms must maintain some 'cash on hand'. The more expensive it is to borrow (the higher the interest rate), the more cash the firm needs to keep.
2. The company's need to maintain its credit rating by lenders and trade creditors.
3. The ability to take advantage of trade discounts that become available for cash payments.
4. Business risk: Cash flows can be volatile. For instance, in times of recession sales will be weak, as will cash flows, because companies pay their bills more slowly. Similarly, the unexpected emergence of such things as industrial relations difficulties and strikes will mean that cash must be at hand when it is needed.

13.6.2 Operating cycles and cash cycles

To illustrate the concept of working capital management we can look at the **operating cycle** and **cash cycle**. Let us look at the following simple example.

Example 13.2 The operating and cash cycle

Curraghmore Ltd has decided to buy €500,000 worth of inventories on credit. It pays the bill for these 40 days later. Forty-two days later (i.e. on day 82) the inventory is sold for €700,000. The customer will not pay until 50 days later. The effect of these events on the cash cycle can be summarised as follows:

Day	Decision	Effect on cash cycle
0	Buy stock	0
40	Pay for stock	(€500,000)
82	Sell stock	0
132	Receive payment	+ €700,000

From the time stock is acquired to the time payment is received takes 132 days. This is called the **operating cycle**. The operating cycle can be divided into two parts. The first is the **inventory period**—the time it takes to acquire and sell the stock. This is, in this example, 82 days. The second part is the **debtor collection** period—the time it takes to collect the payment for the goods sold. This is 50 days in our example. Therefore the operating cycle of 132 days is

Operating cycle = Inventory period + Debtors collection period   (13.2)

Operating cycle = Inventory period + Debtors collection period
132 Days   =   82 days   +   50 days

13.6.3 The cash conversion cycle

In the above example, the problem for Curraghmore Ltd from a cash flow point of view is that it pays out cash 40 days after it has bought the inventory (payment period), but it doesn't receive any cash flow until day 132. Therefore Curraghmore Ltd will have to find some way of arranging to finance €500,000 for 92 days (132–40). This is the **cash cycle** period. Equation 13.3 shows the cash cycle and Figure 13.3 illustrates the connection between the operating cycle, the cash conversion cycle, the debtors collection period and the inventory period.

$$\begin{pmatrix} \text{Cash cycle} \\ \text{period} \end{pmatrix} = \begin{pmatrix} \text{Stock} \\ \text{conversion} \\ \text{period} \end{pmatrix} + \begin{pmatrix} \text{Debtors} \\ \text{conversion} \\ \text{period} \end{pmatrix} - \begin{pmatrix} \text{Creditors} \\ \text{payment} \\ \text{period} \end{pmatrix} \qquad (13.3)$$

(92 days)   =   (82 days)   +   (50 days)   −   (40 days)

Figure 13.3 The operating cycle and the cash conversion cycle

Example 13.2 Calculating the cash conversion cycle

The example above is straightforward and simple. Usually however we will have to calculate the cash conversion cycle from the information given in the financial statements. The following example extracts information from the annual report of the Kerry Group 1997:

Table 13.1 Kerry Group 1997 extracts from annual report

	Closing €	Opening €	Average €
Stock	155,681	142,358	149,110
Debtors	155,761	143,750	149,756
Creditors	215,618	185,322	200,470

Cost of goods sold was €965,905 and sales were €1,344,129.

To calculate the cash conversion cycle for the Kerry Group for 1997 we must first calculate the inventory or stock period.

The inventory or stock period is the average time it takes to convert raw materials into finished goods and then to sell the goods. For the Kerry Group in 1997 the average stocks €149,110 and €965,905 was spent on stocks (cost of goods sold). Therefore stock was turned over $\frac{€965,905}{€149,110}$ = 6.5 times. Therefore stock was bought and sold 6.5 times during the year.

Therefore, on average, stock was held for $\frac{365}{6.5}$ = 56 days in warehouses before being sold.

Next, we calculate the debtor collection period. This is the average length of time required to convert debtors into cash, that is, the average length of time it takes debtors to pay. The average debtors figure is €149,756. The average debtors turnover figure is got by dividing credit sales by average debtors.

$$\frac{\text{Credit sales}}{\text{Average debtors}} = \frac{€1,344,129}{€149,756} = 9 \text{ times}$$

The average collection period is

$$\frac{\text{Debtors}}{\text{Sales}} \times 365 = \frac{€149,756}{€1,344,129} \times 365 = 41 \text{ days}$$

Therefore it took, on average, 41 days for customers to pay.

The next step in the process of calculating the cash conversion cycle for the Kerry Group for 1997 is to calculate the creditors payment period. This ratio might be more accurately referred to as the payables deferral period because it is the length of time between the purchase of materials and labour and the payment for them. In other words, it is the number of days it takes to pay for materials and labour. Average payables is €200,470 and the cost of goods sold (COGS) is €965,905, which means that the payables turnover is

$$\frac{\text{COGS}}{\text{Average payables}} = \frac{€965,905}{€200,470} = 4.8 \text{ times}$$

The payables period is

$$\frac{\text{Average payables}}{\text{COGS}} \times 365 = \frac{€200,470}{€965,905} \times 365 = 76 \text{ days}$$

So, on average, it took the Kerry Group 76 days to pay their creditors.

Finally, the cash conversion cycle is the length of time between the firm's cash payments and its cash receipts from sales. This can be interpreted as the average length of time one euro is tied up in current assets. The cash conversion cycle for the Kerry Group for 1997 is 21 days. In other words, it takes 56 days from the time it buys its raw materials to the time it converts them to finished goods and sells them. It takes 41 days to collect the cash from the sales. However, it takes 76 days before the raw materials are paid for. This gives a cash conversion cycle of 21 days, which is the number of days' finance it needs for its operations. The longer the cash cycle, the more expensive it is, because cash is tied up longer in the cycle. Remember, cash is supplied by shareholders or debt holders and it therefore has a cost. Cutting the cash conversion cycle would therefore be less expensive (in terms of the cost of capital) and more profitable.

13.7 Shortening the cash cycle

It follows therefore that shortening the cash cycle can improve profitability and liquidity and, as we have already discussed, it can enhance economic value added. Therefore management should aim to minimise the cash cycle (without hurting operational activities). It can do this by:

(a) shortening the stock period. This can be accomplished by speeding up the production and selling process.
(b) improving its credit control by getting cash in more quickly from debtors.
(c) slowing down the payment period.

13.8 Reasons for holding cash

John Maynard Keynes in his work, *The Theory of Employment Interest and Money*, outlined three reasons why cash holdings are necessary:

(a) The transactions motive
It is necessary to hold cash balances to pay debts that are due to be paid, such as wages, creditors, dividends, taxes etc. Cash inflows from sales should be sufficient to cover cash outflows to pay debts. If inflows are greater than outflows, the balance is reinvested in the business or returned to shareholders in the form of dividends. However cash inflows and cash outflows are not always synchronised in the sense that inflows are not always sufficient to meet the cash outflows and some **buffer** cash level is needed. (We discuss cash synchronisation later on in the chapter.)

(b) The precautionary motive
Cash inflows and outflows are unpredictable. Firms need to keep some cash in reserve for unforeseen events. The cash balances are called **precautionary balances**. Banks may also require their customers to maintain minimum cash balances with the bank. These are called **compensating balances.**

(c) The speculative motive
This motive for holding cash allows the individual to take advantage of any profitable bargain purchases that might arise from time to time. However this motive for holding cash can be accomplished (and generally is in business today) by having spare borrowing capacity and/or portfolios of liquid or **near** liquid (cash) balances such as commercial paper (discussed in Chapter 15) or marketable securities.

13.9 Cash management control

Most business is conducted by large firms operating both nationally and internationally. Some of these global companies operate in Ireland, e.g. Dell, Intel, IBM. Having sales and manufacturing points around the globe means that they can have thousands of bank accounts. In some of these accounts, inflows may be greater than outflows, and in others there will be net outflows. Having excess cash in some accounts imposes an opportunity cost because they will be earning rates of return lower than they could if invested elsewhere, e.g. in short-term securities. On the other hand, accounts with net outflows will cost them interest. Cash management of these firms will necessitate transferring funds to where they are needed and investing excess cash immediately. In addition, many payments are made out of central funds such as dividends and taxes, and a system must be in place to transfer funds to central HQ when needed. In Ireland, **repatriation** of profits in 1999 came to almost €20bn which amounted to 18% of GDP.

Cash flow synchronisation is one method used to control cash flows. By equating cash inflows to cash outflows, firms can be sure of holding their minimum cash balances. Companies such as the ESB and Eircom try to achieve this synchronisation by billing their customers on a regular basis (every two months).

13.10 Cheque clearing system

Delays in the cheque clearing system can work to the advantage of firms. **Float** occurs because of delays in the bank clearing system. The time that lapses between writing a cheque and when it clears is called the float. Technically, it is the difference between a firm's (or individual's) cheque book balance and the firm's (or individual's) balance in the bank's books.

Disbursement float is when the float works in the firm's favour. When a firm signs a cheque, it credits the amount in the firm's own cash account in its own cash book. However, it can be days before it appears as a debit in the firm's account in the bank's books. The effect of disbursement float is to increase the firm's balance in the bank's books relative to the balance in the firm's own books.

Collection float is when the float works against the firm. It is the delay between the time of receiving a cheque and when the bank credits the firm with the amount. When a firm receives a cheque, it is immediately debited in the cash account of the firm's books, but it can be days before it clears as a credit in the company's account in the bank's books. Collection float reduces the firm's balance in the bank's books relative to the firm's balance in the firm's books.

Net float

Net float is the sum of the disbursement float and the collection float. A company that has to pay bills should be concerned with its balance in the bank rather than with its balance in its own books. It's what's in the bank that pays the bills. So net float is the difference between the firm's book cash balance and the firm's available cash balance in the bank.

Net float = Available cash balance in bank – Firm's book cash balance   (13.4)

Example 13.3 Calculating float

A firm pays out an average €20,000 per day in cheques. It takes about four days for these cheques to clear. At the same time suppose the firm receives an average of €20,000 from customers and it takes two days to clear these cheques. The disbursement float is €80,000, that is, the bank will show €80,000 more than will be in the firm's own records. The collection float is €40,000, that is, there will be €40,000 less available in the bank than what appears in the company's books. Therefore the net float is

Net float = Disbursement float (€80,000) + Collection float (−€40,000) = €40,000

Taking the time to manage float can be very profitable. For example, if a company has daily sales of €1m, by accelerating the collection of cheques from customers by just one day, and if the daily interest rate is .0003%, profits could increase by €300 a day or €109,500 a year. Ireland's public electric utility, the Electricity Supply Board (ESB), ran a very successful advertising campaign with a prize draw for customers who paid their bills on time.

13.11 Computing the optimum cash balances

Next, we discuss a theoretical model to compute the optimum cash balances. The theoretical model we will look at is the **Baumol model**. The main assumptions underlying this model are:

1. The firm's consumption of cash is steady and predictable.
2. Both cash outflows and cash inflows occur at steady predictable rates.

For example, suppose that Dunmore Ltd has a weekly cash outflow of €500,000 and a weekly cash inflow of €400,000, leaving it with a net cash flow of minus €100,000. Note that negative cash flows are not unusual for companies that are going through the expansionary phase of their business cycle.

Suppose also that Dunmore Ltd has an initial cash balance of €400,000. Given the initial assumptions of this model, we can conclude that it will take four weeks for this initial cash balance to drop to zero. This is illustrated in Figure 13.4.

Figure 13.4 Cash balances using the BAT model

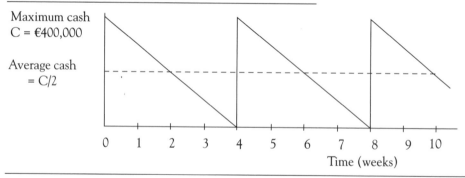

Therefore, at the end of week 4 the firm will have to sell some short-term liquid assets or borrow to replenish its cash balances. If the initial cash balance was higher than €400,000, then it would take a longer period of time before it would be necessary to either borrow or sell short-term liquid assets to replenish the cash balance. Conversely, if the initial cash balance was lower than €400,000, there would be a shorter period before it would be necessary to replenish the cash balance.

Borrowing cash or selling securities to replenish cash balances will incur transaction costs, and the more frequently it needs to replenish its cash balances, the higher the total transaction costs. Therefore the larger the cash balances, the lower the transaction costs. On the other hand, holding cash balances has a cost—opportunity cost. Holding cash balances earns no income. The opportunity cost of holding cash balances is the income (interest) foregone. Therefore, the higher the cash balances, the greater the opportunity cost incurred. This scenario is depicted in Figure 13.5. Note how the transactions costs are high when the firm has to raise more cash to replenish a cash balance. In addition, the opportunity cost curve increases with the size of the cash balance because holding cash does not provide a rate of return.

Figure 13.5 Determining the optimum cash balance

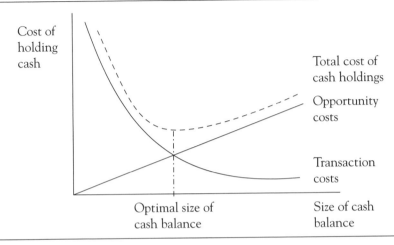

The total cost of holding cash balances is therefore

$$\textbf{Total cost = Opportunity cost + Transactions costs} \qquad (13.5)$$

where

Opportunity costs = $\left(\begin{array}{c} \text{Average cash} \\ \text{balance} \end{array} \right) \times \left(\begin{array}{c} \text{Interest} \\ \text{rate (r)} \end{array} \right)$

Average cash balances = $\dfrac{\text{Maximum cash balance (Q)}}{2} = \dfrac{Q}{2}$

Transactions costs = $\left(\begin{array}{c} \text{Number of} \\ \text{transactions} \end{array} \right) \times \left(\begin{array}{c} \text{Cost per} \\ \text{transaction (C)} \end{array} \right)$

and

The number of transactions = $\dfrac{\begin{array}{c}\text{Total amount of net new}\\ \text{transactions needed for the year (N)}\end{array}}{\text{Maximum cash balance (Q)}}$

Therefore

$$\textbf{Total cost} = \dfrac{Q}{2}\,\textbf{(R)} + \dfrac{N}{Q}\,\textbf{(C)} \qquad (13.6)$$

By differentiating equation 13.6 with respect to Q we can calculate the optimum cash balance (Q*). (To calculate the optimal cash balance equation, differentiate equation 13.6 with respect to Q. Set the derivative equal to zero, and solve for Q = Q*.)

$$Q^* = \sqrt{\frac{2CN}{R}}$$

Suppose in our example the transaction cost for Dunmore Ltd of selling €100,000 of securities or borrowing €100,000 is €300, and if holding costs or opportunity costs (interest forgone) of holding cash is 5%, then the optimum cash balance Q* is

(Remember that €100,000 is required each week. Therefore N in the equation = 52.)

$$Q^* = \sqrt{\frac{2 \times €300 \times €5,200,000}{0.05}} = €249,800$$

So the company should replenish its cash balances when they reach zero to the tune of €249,800.

The main weakness of the BAT model is that it doesn't allow for uncertainty and seasonal fluctuations in cash disbursements and collections. The student should be aware however that the Baumol model, and indeed other optimal cash balance models, is not generally used in practice. In reality, financial managers use experience in judging their optimal cash balance. Nevertheless the theoretical models do provide an insight into the reasoning behind optimal cash balances. The Baumol model illustrated that the higher the interest rate, the lower the target cash balance. Secondly, the higher the order cost, the higher will be the target balance.

13.12 Cash budgets

In Chapter 10 we investigated long-term financial planning and pro forma statements. In this chapter we discuss short-term financial planning. As we have seen, it is necessary for firms to know when they will have cash surpluses and cash deficits. Knowing when these deficits and surpluses occur will allow the firm to know when they will need to replenish their cash stock or invest their surpluses.

One way of estimating cash balances is the **cash budget**. This is a detailed plan estimating cash inflows and cash outflows on a weekly, monthly or quarterly basis.

13.12.1 Developing a cash flow forecast

The first step in a cash flow forecast is to ascertain the likely cash inflows. The cash inflow forecast will depend crucially on the sales budget. In our chapter on long-term financial planning, we said that the sales budget was the most important budget to get right because the accuracy of all other budgets will depend on the accuracy of the sales budget. The sales budget is equally as crucial in short-term financial planning. The **GIGO** effect rules, i.e. **garbage in, garbage out**. If the input into any forecast is garbage, then the output will be garbage. Therefore accuracy in sales forecasting is essential in cash flow forecasting.

In developing a cash flow forecast, the following steps are taken:

Step 1: Estimating the anticipated cash inflow

Table 13.2 Decies Engineering Ltd projected sales forecast

Nov. 2000	€20,000	May 2001	€30,000	Oct. 2001	€25,000
Dec. 2000	€21,000	Jun. 2001	€32,000	Nov. 2001	€22,000
Jan. 2001	€19,000	July 2001	€34,000	Dec. 2001	€21,000
Feb. 2001	€22,000	Aug. 2001	€31,000	Jan. 2002	€20,000
Mar. 2001	€24,000	Sept. 2001	€28,000	Feb. 2002	€19,000
Apr. 2001	€27,000				

All of Decies sales are on credit (i.e. no cash sales). From past experience 20% of debtors will pay their bills at the end of the first month of sale, 50% will pay their account in the month following the sale, and 30% will pay two months after the sale. So, for example, the cash collections for January are as shown in Table 13.3.

Table 13.3 Cash collections for January 2001 (Decies Ltd)

20% of January sales	=	€3,800
50% of December sales	=	€10,500
30% of November sales	=	€6,000
Total	=	€20,300

The cash inflow forecast is presented in Table 13.4.

Step 2: The next step in generating a cash budget is to forecast the cash outflows. The cost of raw materials is 25% of sales. The raw materials are purchased two months prior to the sale of the finished product and will be paid for in full one month after the purchase. For example, the purchase of raw materials for March sales will be made in January and paid for in February. All purchases are on credit. There are no cash purchases. Additional cash outflows are as follows:

- Production expenses are equal to 30% of sales.
- Sales, general and administrative expenses of €4,000 are paid each month.
- Fixed interest charges of €500 are paid at the end of each quarter.
- Taxation of €8,000 for 2001 is paid at the end of each quarter.

Table 13.4 Cash inflow forecast for Decies Ltd 2001 (€000)

	Jan	Feb	Mar	Apr	May	June	July	Aug	Sept	Oct	Nov	Dec
20% in month of sale	3,800	4,400	4,800	5,400	6,000	6,400	6,800	6,200	5,600	5,000	4,400	4,200
50% one month after sale	10,500	9,500	11,000	12,000	13,500	15,000	16,000	17,000	15,500	14,000	12,500	11,000
30% two months after sale	6,000	6,300	5,700	6,600	7,200	8,100	10,000	9,600	10,200	9,300	8,400	7,500
Total cash inflows	20,300	20,200	21,500	24,000	26,700	29,500	32,800	32,800	31,300	28,300	25,100	22,700

Table 13.5 Cash outflow for Decies Ltd 2001 (€000)

	Jan	Feb	Mar	Apr	May	June	July	Aug	Sep	Oct	Nov	Dec
Cost of raw materials	5,500	6,000	6,750	7,500	8,000	8,500	7,750	7,000	6,250	5,500	5,250	5,000
Production costs	5,700	6,600	7,200	8,100	9,000	9,600	10,200	9,300	8,400	7,500	6,600	6,300
Sales, general & admin.	4,000	4,000	4,000	4,000	4,000	4,000	4,000	4,000	4,000	4,000	4,000	4,000
Interest charges			500			500			500			500
Tax			2,000			2,000			2,000			2,000
Total cash outflow	15,200	16,600	20,450	19,600	21,000	24,600	21,950	20,300	21,150	17,000	15,850	17,800

Table 13.6 Cash inflows and outflows and net cash flows 2001 (€000)

	Jan	Feb	Mar	Apr	May	June	July	Aug	Sep	Oct	Nov	Dec
Total cash inflow	20,300	20,200	21,500	24,000	26,700	29,500	32,800	32,800	31,300	28,300	25,100	22,700
Total cash outflow	15,200	16,600	20,450	19,600	21,000	24,600	21,950	20,300	21,150	17,000	15,850	17,800
Net cash flow	5,100	3,600	1,050	4,400	5,700	4,900	10,850	12,500	10,150	11,300	9,250	4,900

Table 13.7 Decies cumulative cash flow 2001 (€000)

	Jan	Feb	Mar	Apr	May	June	July	Aug	Sep	Oct	Nov	Dec
Opening cash balance	20,000	25,100	28,700	29,750	34,150	39,850	44,750	55,600	68,100	78,250	89,550	98,800
Net cash inflow (outflow)	5,100	3,600	1,050	4,400	5,700	4,900	10,850	12,500	10,150	11,300	9,250	4,900

Table 13.8 12 month cash flow summary for Decies Ltd 2001 (€000)

	Jan	Feb	Mar	Apr	May	June	July	Aug	Sep	Oct	Nov	Dec
20% in month of sale	3,800	4,400	4,800	5,400	6,000	6,400	6,800	6,200	5,600	5,000	4,400	4,200
50% one month after sale	10,500	9,500	11,000	12,000	13,500	15,000	16,000	17,000	15,500	14,000	12,500	11,000
30% two months after sale	6,000	6,300	5,700	6,600	7,200	8,100	10,000	9,600	10,200	9,300	8,400	7,500
Total cash inflows	20,300	20,200	21,500	24,000	26,700	29,500	32,800	32,800	31,300	28,300	25,100	22,700
Cost of raw materials	5,500	6,000	6,750	7,500	8,000	8,500	7,750	7,000	6,250	5,500	5,250	5,000
Production costs	5,700	6,600	7,200	8,100	9,000	9,600	10,200	9,300	8,400	7,500	6,600	6,300
Sales, general & admin.	4,000	4,000	4,000	4,000	4,000	4,000	4,000	4,000	4,000	4,000	4,000	4,000
Interest charges			500			500			500			500
Tax			2,000			2,000			2,000			2,000
Total cash outflow	15,200	16,600	20,450	19,600	21,000	24,600	21,950	20,300	21,150	17,000	15,880	17,800
Total cash inflow	20,300	20,200	21,500	24,000	26,700	29,500	32,800	32,800	31,300	28,300	25,100	22,700
Total cash outflow	15,200	16,600	20,450	19,600	21,000	24,600	21,950	20,300	21,150	17,000	15,880	17,800
Net cash flow	5,100	3,600	1,050	4,400	5,700	4,900	10,850	12,500	10,150	11,300	9,250	4,900
Opening cash balance	20,000	25,100	28,700	29,750	34,150	39,850	44,750	55,600	68,100	78,250	89,550	98,770
Net cash inflow (outflow)	5,100	3,600	1,050	4,400	5,700	4,900	10,850	12,500	10,150	11,300	9,220	4,900
Cumulative cash flow	21,100	28,700	29,750	34,150	39,850	44,750	55,600	68,100	98,250	89,550	98,770	103,670

The cash outflow forecast is presented in Table 13.5.

Step 3: Calculate the net cash flow. For each month, subtract the cash outflow from the cash inflow. This gives the net cash flow for each month. This is presented in Table 13.6.

Step 4: Calculate the cumulative cash flow. For this example assume an opening cash flow of €20,000 for Decies Ltd on 1 January 2001. This opening cash balance is added to the net cash flow for January to give the cumulative cash figure for January. The cumulative cash figure then becomes the opening cash position for the next period. Decies Ltd's cumulative cash flow is shown in Table 13.7.

Step 5: Combine steps 1 to 4 to form a complete cash budget, Table 13.8.

In the next chapter we will look at the decision of firms to extend credit to customers. This will have costs and benefits for the firm.

SUMMARY

- Working capital policy is a firm's policy regarding the levels of investments in working capital and how these investments should be financed.
- The cash flow cycle illustrates how cash moves through the business.
- Gross working capital refers to investments in current assets, including cash, debtors and stock.
- Net working capital is current assets *less* current liabilities.
- The level of investments in current assets depends on the level of sales. A relaxed approach to investments in current assets is one where there is uncertainty about future sales and where there are large amounts of investments in current assets. Where a degree of certainty exists about future sales, an aggressive approach is appropriate where the firm keeps minimum investments in current assets.
- Overtrading occurs when the business experiences an increase in the level of activity but has insufficient working capital to finance the increase in sales activity.
- Minimising the amount of capital tied up in working capital can reduce the cost of capital and therefore increase economic value added.
- The operating cycle is the time between acquiring the stock of raw materials to getting paid for the sale of finished goods.
- The inventory period is the time it takes to acquire and sell the stock.
- The debtors collection period is the time it takes to collect payment for the goods sold.
- The cash conversion cycle is equal to the stock conversion period *plus* the debtors collection period *minus* the creditors payments period
- Float occurs because of delays in the bank's clearing system. Disbursement float is when the firm's account in the bank has not been debited with cheques paid out by the firm and credited in the firm's books. Collection float is when the bank has not yet credited cheques lodged to the firm's bank account. Net float is the difference between the two.
- The BAT model determines the amount of cash a firm should hold so that the total costs of holding cash is minimised.
- A cash budget is a detailed plan estimating cash inflows and cash outflows on a monthly, weekly or quarterly basis.

QUESTIONS

1. Explain each of the following:
   (a) working capital
   (b) net working capital
   (c) disbursement float
   (d) collection float
   (e) net float
   (f) cash conversion cycle
   (g) target cash balance.
2. Some firms will have longer operating and cash cycles than other firms. Explain.
3. What are the motives for holding cash balances?
4. How does a firm reach the optimal level of current assets?
5. Consider ways in which a firm can increase its liquidity.
6. 'Managing float can be profitable.' Explain
7. Explain the terms (a) relaxed current asset investment policy, and (b) restricted current asset investment policy.
8. Why is it that working capital policy requires a firm to balance liquidity and profitability?
9. Aggressive working capital policy has low cost but is highly risky. Why?
10. ♦The following is the summary information provided from the accounts of Comeragh Ltd for the year ended 31 December 2000:

Stock (opening)	€5,000
Stock (closing)	€5,700
Debtors (opening)	€4,300
Debtors (closing)	€4,000
Creditors (opening)	€2,000
Creditors (closing)	€2,200

Sales for the year came to €20,000 and the cost of goods was €16,000. Calculate and illustrate (a) the cash cycle and (b) the operating cycle.

11. Brickies Ltd has a stock conversion period of 60 days, a debtors collection period of 30 days and a creditors payment period of 25 days. Calculate the firm's cash conversion cycle.

12. Using the BAT model, calculate the target cash balance from the following information:

Total cash required	€300,000
Opportunity cost	10%
Ordering costs	€150

What is the opportunity cost of holding the average cash balance?

13. Pontoon Ltd has a cash need of €30,000 per annum. On average its daily cash balance is €200. The trading cost of obtaining cash is €10 every time the cash needs to be replaced.

The annual interest rate is 9%. Calculate the opportunity cost and the total cost. Minimise total cost.

14. You have an original bank balance of €1,000. You then start writing cheques totalling €500 that have not yet cleared the banking system. What is your net float?

15.◆ A company has €2,000,000 in marketable securities which give a rate of return of 3%. It costs €1000 to convert these marketable securities to cash. Annual cash disbursements come to €30m. Using the BAT model, calculate the optimal conversion amount.

16. A firm signs cheques totalling €10,000 each day. The cheques take five days to clear. The firm also receives €7,000 in cheques which take on average two days to convert to cash. Calculate the net float.

17. Why is net disbursement float more desirable than net collection float?

18.◆ Suppose that on 1 September you buy a new computer scanner costing €200 and you write a cheque for this amount. Because you are a student your parents send you a cheque for €100 to help you pay for the scanner. You receive the cheque on 3 February. Suppose it takes seven days for your cheque to clear and five days for your parents' cheque to clear. Before any of the above events occur, you have €100 in your bank account. Calculate the net float on 5 February and your available balance on 7 February.

19. Is it possible to hold too much cash?

20.◆ (a) Using the following information calculate (i) the target cash balance using the BAT model and (ii) the total cost of holding cash.
    Annual interest rate = 10%
    Fixed order costs = €50
    Total cash needed = €30,000.
   (b) What factors are likely to affect a firm's target cash balance?
   (c) How would synchronisation of a firm's cash inflows and cash outflows affect a firm's target cash balance?

21. Ebont Ltd has a debt to asset ratio of 40%. Fixed assets are €1,000,000. The company is considering two alternative working capital policies: 30% or 50% of sales. Projected sales are estimated at €5m and profit before interest and tax is expected to be 12%. The company's cost of debt is 7% and corporation tax is 20%. From a shareholder's point of view what is the **optimum** current asset policy?

22.◆ A large retail outlet has €1m in cash. The cash will not be needed for 24 hours. The annual rate of interest is 8%. What do you think the company should do—hold on to the cash or invest it?

23. You are the treasurer of a company that has a large amount of excess cash. You are required to put a report together outlining the various options available to the company as to what to do with this cash.

24. From the following information draw up the cash budget for Tiffy Ltd. It has a 60 day collection period and it has a minimum cash balance requirement of €100.

	Sales	Opening debtors	Cash outflow	Opening cash balance
First quarter	€200	€350	€220	€50
Second quarter	€250		€240	
Third quarter	€270		€280	
Fourth quarter	€150		€200	

25. The following sales information is given for Widgets Ltd (€000):

2000		2001												2002	
Nov	Dec	Jan	Feb	Mar	Apr	May	Jun	Jly	Aug	Sept	Oct	Nov	Dec	Jan	Feb
200	150	140	150	160	170	200	230	250	200	180	160	150	130	120	120

There are no cash sales. The assumption is that 10% of sales will be paid for in the month of sale, 80% will be pay the amount due in the month after the sale, and the final 10% will pay their bills two months after the sale. The cost of raw material is 20% of sales. The raw material for each month's production will be ordered the month before (i.e. the raw material for January's production is ordered in December). Monthly sales of finished product are made the previous month (i.e. the sale of finished product in February is manufactured in January). Purchases of raw material are paid for in the month after purchase. The following expenses are also incurred and paid for during the month incurred:

(a) Sales and marketing expenses 10% of sales
(b) Production expenses 85% of sales
(c) General expenses €10,000 per month.

An interim dividend of €40,000 is paid in May. A final dividend of €60,000 is paid in December. Interest on loans amounts to €20,000 annually and is paid at the end of each quarter.

Calculate Widget Ltd's net cash flow for the year ended 31 December.

14
Inventory and Credit Management

CHAPTER OBJECTIVES

At the end of this chapter the student should be able to:

1. understand and calculate the optimum inventory level
2. appreciate the inventory management techniques of just-in-time and out-sourcing
3. understand how optimum inventory management can enhance economic value added (EVA)
4. assess the components of credit policy
5. determine the optimum credit policy
6. understand ways of monitoring accounts receivables
7. evaluate a proposed change in credit policy.

INTRODUCTION

Inventories consist of raw materials, work-in-progress and finished goods. All businesses carry inventories of one kind or another. The amount of inventory held at any one point in time will depend on factors such as the production cycle (how long it takes to produce the product). For example, a company that makes fresh cream cakes will have a low inventory relative to sales than, say, a DIY retailer who will carry a vast amount of inventory to satisfy a wide-ranging customer base. Manufacturers of Boeing 737s will have proportionally higher inventory levels than food retail outlets.

14.1 Optimum inventory levels

The objective of inventory management is to determine what level of inventory will maximise shareholder value. This will be settled by a trade-off in the costs of holding low inventories against the cost of having high inventory levels.

Higher inventory levels result in:

- higher storage costs (e.g. rent, insurance etc., cost of obsolescence and damage)
- higher opportunity costs because of the lost interest in cash tied up in stocks.

Lower inventory levels result in:

- higher reordering costs, e.g. administration costs such as employee time and the processing of each order whenever an order is made
- shortage costs—'stock-outs' occur when a firm runs out of raw materials, which results in loss of sales, profits and the reputation of the firm.

14.1.1 Inventory and sales

Minimising the cost of inventory (having the lowest cost of inventory) may not lead to the optimum inventory level because more stock on display can boost sales. Therefore, more stock might mean more sales. Consequently, **the optimum inventory level is a matter of balancing the costs and benefits of various inventory levels.**

14.2 The economic order quantity (EOQ)

This is the most popular approach in estimating the optimum inventory level. The EOQ is illustrated in Figure 14.1. The costs of holding stocks are expressed on the vertical axis and the order size in units is expressed on the horizontal axis. Holding costs (carrying costs) increase and reordering costs decrease as stock levels rise. The total costs of holding inventory are the sum of carrying costs and reordering costs. The total cost curve in Figure 14.1 is u-shaped and is the summation of the carrying costs line and the restocking line. The optimum size of the stock order corresponds to the minimum point of the total cost of holding inventory curve.

Figure 14.1   The economic order quantity (EOQ)

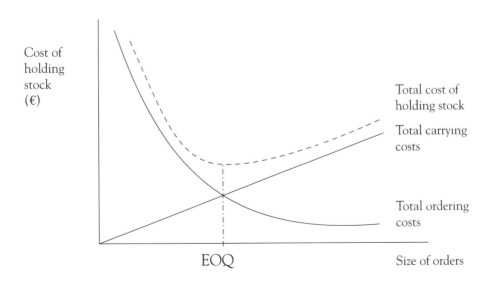

14.2.1 Developing the EOQ model

Suppose that Lismore Ltd sells 20,000 units a month and reorders new inventory once a month. Each time the firm makes an order, it will be for 20,000 units. Assume that it is sold off at a steady rate until it is zero. At this point the firm restocks back to the optimum level. If the firm starts off with 20,000 units of stock and annual sales amount to 240,000 units, or about 4,616 units a week, after four weeks all stock will be sold and the firm will restock by ordering 20,000 units to bring the stock level back up to the optimum level. This is illustrated in Figure 14.2. We can see that the process exhibits a *sawtooth pattern* for stock holdings. The firm always starts with 20,000 units and ends up with zero. The average stock therefore is 10,000 units. The average investment in inventories depends on the size of each order made and, of course, on how often the order is made. For example, by placing an order once a month average investment in inventories will be much smaller than if one order a year was placed. Similarly, average investment in inventory will be much smaller if orders are placed every week rather than every month.

Figure 14.2 Stock position for Lismore Ltd

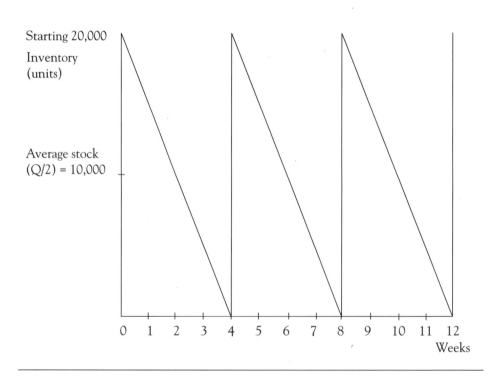

14.2.2 Computing the EOQ model

Carrying costs tend to rise in direct proportion to the average inventory carried. In our example, the firm sells 240,000 units each year (TS) and places orders N times per year.

Therefore
$$\frac{TS}{N} = \text{the number of units purchased with each order}$$

The average inventory A will be in our example

$$A = \frac{TS}{N} \div 2 \tag{14.1}$$

where: $N = 12$
$TS = 240{,}000$

Therefore, the inventory is steadily drawn down from 20,000 units to zero and the average inventory is

$$A = \frac{TS}{2N} = \frac{240{,}000}{(2)(12)} = 10{,}000 \text{ units}$$

Total carrying costs (TCC)

Now consider the cost of inventory and the cost of holding the inventory. Suppose that the cost of purchasing and holding stock for Lismore Ltd is as follows:

Stock price per unit	= €3 (€3 x 10,000 = €30,000)
Taxes, insurance and general storage costs	= €3,000
Depreciation of inventory	= €600
Cost of capital (5%)	= €1,500 (5% x €30,000)
Total carrying cost (TCC)	= €5,100

We can see that average inventory is €30,000. This will need to be financed, and if the cost of short-term debt is 5%, then the cost of financing is €30,000 × 0.05 = €1,500

So the total cost (TCC) of €30,000 of average stock is €5,100, or 17%

The total carrying cost is equal to the percentage carrying cost (defined as X%) times the price per unit times the average number of units:

$$TCC = (X\%) \times (€P) \times (A)$$

For Lismore this is TCC = 0.17 × (€3 × 10,000) = €5,100

Total reorder costs

Assume that reorder costs are fixed, in other words, every time an order is made there are fixed costs incurred. For example, the administrative costs incurred in placing an order (telephone calls, paper work etc.) are generally fixed so that they don't vary with the size of the order. We refer to these fixed costs with the letter F. Therefore the total reorder costs (TRC) will be the number of orders made per year (N) times the fixed costs per order:

$$TRC = (F)(N) \qquad\qquad (14.2)$$

In equation 14.1 we defined the average inventory (A) as being equal to

$$A = \frac{TS}{N} \div 2$$

We can rearrange equation 14.1 to become $\;N = \dfrac{TS}{2A}$

By substituting equation 14.1 into equation 14.2 we get

$$TRC = F\left(\frac{TS}{2A}\right)$$

Suppose that Lismore Ltd has fixed restocking costs (F) of €100. We have already established that N = 12 (i.e. 12 orders per year), average inventory (A) is 10,000 units, and sales for the year (TS) = 240,000 units. Therefore the total restocking costs are

$$TRC = €100 \left(\frac{240,000}{20,000}\right) = €100\,(12) = €1,200$$

The total cost

The total costs incurred in holding inventory is the sum of the total reorder costs and the total carrying costs:

Total costs (TC) = Total carrying costs (TCC) + Total reordering costs (TRC)

or $\qquad\qquad\qquad\qquad$ TC = TCC + TRC

$$(X)(P)(A) + F\left(\frac{TS}{2A}\right)$$

Our objective therefore is to find the value (Q) of the restocking which minimises this cost. For Lismore Ltd we have already established the following:

Purchase price per unit of stock (P)			= €3
Carrying costs as a percentage of average inventory value (X%)			= 17%
Fixed costs of placing an order (F)			= €100
Annual sales in units (TS)			= 240,000

Table 14.1 calculates the total cost for different reordering quantities.

Table 14.1

Reordering quantity Q	Holding costs $(X)(P)(A)$	+	Reordering costs $F\,(TS/2A)$	=	Total costs $TC\ (€)$
3,000	765	+	8,000	=	8,765
4,500	1,148	+	5,333	=	6,481
6,000	1,530	+	4,000	=	5,530
7,500	1,913	+	3,200	=	5,113
9,000	2,295	+	2,667	=	4,962
9,700	**2,474**	**+**	**2,474**	**=**	**4,948**
10,000	2,550	+	2,400	=	4,950
12,000	3,060	+	2,000	=	5,060
13,500	3,443	+	1,778	=	5,221
15,000	3,825	+	1,600	=	5,425

For example, when the reordering quantity is 6,000 units, the holding costs are €1,530. Here A or average inventory is 6,000/2 = 3,000 units. At €3 per unit (P = €3) and with X = 17%, we get €1,530.

We can read from the figures that the economic order quantity (EOQ) is that which gives the lowest total cost, i.e. 9,700 units. This is the optimum quantity to be ordered when an order is made. We can see this from Figure 14.3. Note that, diagrammatically, the EOQ is where the total inventory cost curve is at a minimum. This corresponds to the point where the total carrying costs line and the total ordering costs line intersect, i.e. where the total carrying costs and the total ordering costs are the same. This is at a carrying cost and a reordering cost of €2,474. We can verify this algebraically by equating the carrying costs and the reordering costs and then solving for the optimum reordering level Q.

Figure 14.3 The economic order quantity (EOQ) for Lismore Ltd

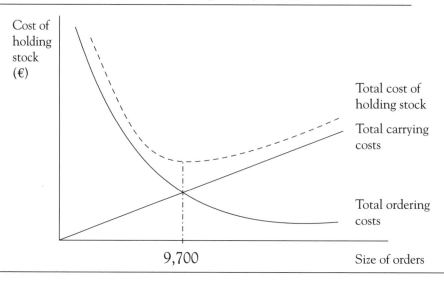

So, by putting carrying costs = reorder costs we get

$$(X)\,(P)\,(\frac{Q}{2}) = (F)\,(\frac{TS}{Q})\qquad(14.3)$$

Remember that average inventory is $A = \dfrac{Q}{2}$

The point where the total inventory cost is minimised is the economic order quantity. The EOQ formula is found by differentiating equation 14.3 with respect to Q, and setting the derivative equal to zero.

Therefore $\dfrac{d(TC)}{dQ} = \dfrac{(X)(P)}{2} = \dfrac{(F)(TS)}{Q^2} = 0$

Now solving for Q $\dfrac{(X)(P)}{2} = \dfrac{(F)(TS)}{Q^2}$

$$Q^2 = \dfrac{2(F)(TS)}{(X)(P)}$$

$$Q = EOQ = \sqrt{\dfrac{2(F)(TS)}{(X)(P)}}\qquad(14.4)$$

For Lismore Ltd we have

$$Q = EOQ = \sqrt{\dfrac{2(100)(240,000)}{(0.17)(€3)}} = \sqrt{94,117,647} = 9,700 \text{ units}$$

Therefore, for Lismore, the reorder quantity is 9,700 units.

14.3 Safety stocks and the EOQ model

To make the EOQ model more realistic some of the assumptions underlying the model are relaxed. For example the EOQ model assumes that the company will allow stock levels to run down to zero before it reorders. Allowing stocks to drop to zero before reordering may not be something that firms wish to do because it runs the risk of **stock outs** and the consequent problems of lost sales and customers.

Figure 14.4 illustrates the concept of safety stocks. Safety stocks are the minimum level of stocks that a firm holds. Suppose, for example, that Lismore Ltd sets a safety stock level of 1,000 units so that it initially orders 10,700 units (EOQ of 9,700 units + safety stock of 1,000 units). The consequence of this is that the firm does not run its stock down to zero. Furthermore, because it can take days or even weeks to get stock delivered, a firm will usually place an order **before** the minimum stock levels are reached. Suppose that Lismore uses 1,000 units while it is waiting for the delivery of new stock. Then the company will reorder its EOQ whenever stock levels reach 2000 units (safety stock of 1,000 units + 1,000 units delivery time). Not having safety stocks can be problematic (see Box 14.1).

Figure 14.4 Safety stocks and reorder points

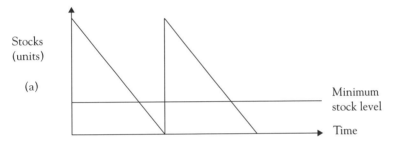

(a) The firm reorders when the stock level reaches the minimum level.

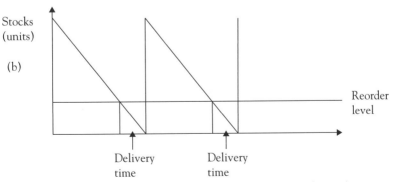

(b) If there are delays in delivery time, the firm reorders when the stock
     level reaches the reorder level.

Figure 14.4 (cont.)

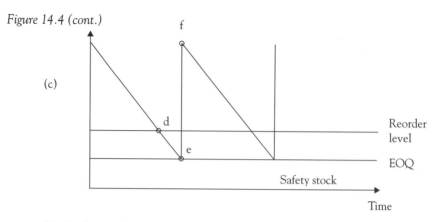

(c)

(c) Combined safety and reorder levels: when stock falls to point d an order
is placed which allows for delivery time. The new stock arrives when the
inventory has fallen to e. The new stock brings the total inventory back to f.

14.4 Just in time (JIT) inventory and out-sourcing

In addition to the theoretical EOQ model, there are other inventory control systems. JIT
is a Japanese system of stock delivery that was adopted particularly by large US
manufacturing firms in the 1980s, such as General Motors, Hewlett Packard and Intel.
Under this system, production is designed so that stocks of raw materials and parts are
delivered to the factory just as they are required. The purpose of JIT is to increase the stock
turnover levels and, typically, firms using JIT have higher stock turnover ratios.

Out-sourcing is a system of buying components instead of making the components in-
house. Car manufacturing companies around the world use out-sourcing as a means of
keeping stock levels, and consequently carrying costs, down.

E-commerce now has the capability of changing the way inventory is managed. There
are inventory management advantages of having a web business (see Box 14.1).

Box 14.1 Direct PC sellers pay the price for efficiency

Just when you baulk at the seemingly endless headlong rush to embrace new technologies
and efficiencies, along comes something to restore your faith in the simpler life.

Most recently Dell and Gateway, which between them, employ 5,000 people in Ireland,
announced they would fail to meet analysts expectations on profits. The alerts by the two
largest direct sellers of computers took on added significance alongside the absence of such
warnings by Hewlett-Packard and Compaq—whose Irish work force total 4,000—which
sell the bulk of their output by more traditional network of dealers.

The cause of their troubles? Efficiency, according to at least one analyst.

Basically, the direct sellers have made a virtue of building PCs to order and holding tiny
inventories, sufficient to last only three days. Problems arise in getting a sufficient supply
of processors and chips to meet accelerating demand.

This meant that, at Dell for instance, it was taking up to 25 days to process an order
from arrival to delivery, compared with the more usual seven to 10 days. Tut, tut.

Dominic Coyle, *The Irish Times*, May 1999

Box 14.2 Irish Express Cargo moves into virtual market

While freight forwarding was once simply a delivery business, the advent of e-commerce means that Irish freight companies are moving into providing a physical infrastructure for a virtual market.

One such company is Irish Express Cargo (IEC). They decided to look at adding value along the supply chain as customer demands grew in tandem with developments in technology and the rise in the use of the Internet...

A major development has been a pan European contract which it has with Hewlett-Packard to handle the product logistics for Hewlett Packard's e-commerce European shopping Village . . .

IEC's success has been based on providing key information to its clients about the flow of their goods from the manufacturing to supply and consumption stage.

By taking partners in different countries and concentrating on managing the flow of products, IEC has become the largest provider of supply chain management in Europe . . .

Demand from consumers for companies' products varies widely even from week to week. What IEC offers to clients such as Dell, Gateway, Compaq and Hewlett Packard is a system where they can see at any time what is happening with the products they ordered or supplied, the demand for the products, the numbers being manufactured anywhere in the world.

As technology changes, it makes products more time-sensitive, and so time taken to bring goods to the market becomes even more important.

The advantage of IEC's system is that it reduces inventory to a minimum and avoids fully finished products being outdated by new technology.

Rory Kelleher, *The Irish Times*, 30 January 2001

14.4.1 *Materials requirements planning (MRP)*

The principal idea behind MRP is that it is designed to work backwards. The first item that is estimated is the stock of finished goods. Once this is set, it is then possible to determine the level of work-in-progress stock necessary to meet the requirements for the finished goods. Finally, once the stock levels for work-in-progress are set, it is possible to determine the stock requirements for raw materials that are needed for the work-in-progress.

14.5 Managing accounts receivables

Managing accounts receivables is not just a matter of calculating the average number of days it is taking customers to pay their bills. Granting credit can bring benefits to firms in the form of increased sales. Nevertheless it also carries costs in the form of increased risk of bad debts and the actual cost of carrying receivables. The amount of trade credit granted will therefore be a trade-off between the benefits and costs associated with granting credit.

14.5.1 Establishing a credit policy

A company's credit policy consists of the following factors:

Credit period: This is the length of time customers have before payment is made. This can vary between 30 and 120 days. In granting credit, a customer's (i.e. the buyer's) stock period and credit period will be considered. The stock period or the inventory period is the length of time it takes to buy the raw materials, to turning them into finished goods for sale. The debtors cycle or accounts receivable cycle is the amount of time it takes to collect on the sale. As we discussed in the previous chapter, the stock period *plus* the inventory period is the operating cycle. The longer the buyer's operating cycle, the longer the credit period the buyer will look for. The credit period granted to the buyer helps finance part of the buyer's operating cycle. Consequently, if the credit period granted to a buyer is longer than the buyer's stock period, the supplier ends up financing part of the buyer's capital needs.

If a cash discount is offered, the credit period will have two components—the **net credit period** and the **cash discount period**. The net credit period is the length of time the customer has to pay, and the cash discount period is the length of time for which the cash discount is available.

For example the terms of sale of 2/10 net 60 means that the customer has 60 days from the invoice date to pay the amount due in full. However if payment is made in full within 10 days, a 2% cash discount is given. Therefore, if an order for €100 is made and if the terms of sale are 2/10 net 60, the customer has the option of paying €100 (1 − 0.02) = €98 in 10 days or paying the full amount of €100 in 60 days. To see why the discount is important, we can calculate the cost to the customer of **not paying** within 10 days. Effectively, the customer obtains a 50 day loan for 2% of the amount due. This is a loan at a cost of 2% for 50 days. This means the customer is paying €2 to borrow €98 for 50 days. The effective cost of the loan is €2/€98 = 2.041% and as the 2% is for 50 days there are 365/50 = 7.3 discount periods in the year.[1] Therefore the annual percentage rate (APR) is given by the equation

$$\text{APR} = \left[1 + \left(\frac{R}{N} \right)^n \right] - 1$$

where R = quoted rate of interest
N = number of discount periods

Therefore
$$\text{APR} = \left[1 + \left(\frac{.149}{7.3} \right)^{7.3} \right] - 1$$

$$= 15.89\%$$

This is also the cost to the seller of the discount allowed to the customer. The cash discount is an inducement given by the seller to speed up its cash collections. From the customer's point of view it is a source of short-term money (with a high cost).

Credit standards: Once a company has decided to offer credit to a customer, it then becomes imperative to find out the credit worthiness of the customer. This involves assessing the financial strength of the customer. What all companies that extend credit will want to find out is which customers are likely to turn out as a bad debt and which of them they will find difficulty in getting money from. **Credit quality** refers to the probability of a customer not paying his/her debts. A company will need to get access to the financial statements of potential customers. Acceptable minimum standards in terms of financial ratios (discussed in Chapter 3) can be used to accept or reject a customer's request for credit. Banks will sometimes provide information on the credit worthiness of firms. In addition, there are some organisations that sell information on the credit worthiness and credit history of firms, the best known being Dun & Bradstreet. Obviously the most readily available information about a customer is the customer's own payment history with the firm.

Profitability of credit sales: Granting credit will have costs — cash discounts and the cost of having more debtors tied up in current assets. If the cash discount **is** availed of by most customers, the company takes in less cash, and this is costly for the company, particularly if it is not accompanied by increased sales revenues. If the cash discount **is not** availed of by most customers, the customer ends up paying more, and consequently more cash is taken in by the company. Forgoing the discount will work to the advantage of the seller. The additional costs incurred in granting trade credit can be offset by the increased revenues in granting credit. If the revenues are greater than the costs, then granting trade credit can be profitable. For example, General Motors offers credit to customers to buy cars. Computer companies adopt a similar approach. Granting trade credit can be very profitable and some of these companies have established very profitable subsidiaries, e.g. Ford Finance.

Cost of debt: An increase in accounts receivable (debtors) must somehow be financed. Therefore the cost of short-term finance must be a factor in a company's credit policy.

The Five C's of credit: In deciding to whom the company should advance credit, a classic approach is to consider the five C's:

(a) Character—the ability of customers to pay their bills
(b) Capital—customer's financial capital and liquidity
(c) Conditions—the business environment and business risk of the customer
(d) Collateral—the valuation of the assets that could be sold if the customer does not pay
(e) Capacity—Does the customer have the ability to pay?

Credit scoring: This method works by awarding points to customers based on the information provided on their credit worthiness. Points are awarded on different criteria, e.g. the five C's, net profit history, number of years in business, shareholders' funds, market valuation of fixed assets etc. Scoring could be 10 (excellent) down to 1 (very bad). The company might have a cut-off score below which they will refuse credit.

14.6 The optimum credit policy

The optimum credit policy for a company is where the **net cost of receivables** is at a minimum. Remember **the cost of granting credit**:

(a) increased risk of bad debts
(b) cost of administration due to increased credit, i.e. increased staff costs of analysing customers, sending out bills etc.
(d) cost of holding increased amounts of current assets
(d) cost of cash discounts allowed.

All of these costs will increase with the extension of credit granted. This is illustrated in Figure 14.5 as an upward-sloping line. On the other hand, if the firm restricts credit to its customers, sales may be lost with a consequent reduction in profit. Therefore restricting credit has an opportunity cost. The opportunity cost is the lost sales because of refusing credit. Opportunity costs decline as more credit is granted. The net total cost curve combines the carrying costs of advancing credit with the additional income from advancing credit. The point where the carrying cost curve and the opportunity cost curve intersect is the point of optimum credit. By extending credit beyond this level, the total carrying costs exceed the additional net cash flow from increased sales. Below this level the firm is losing out on increased profit.

Figure 14.5 The optimum level of credit

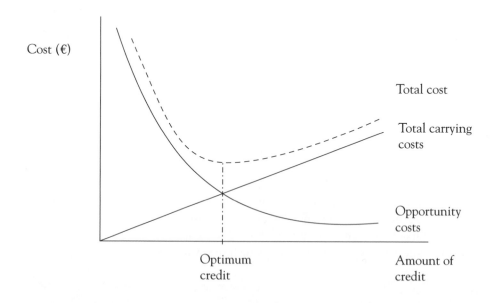

14.7 Monitoring accounts receivable

The accruals concept in accounting implies that as soon as a sale is made for cash or on credit, it is included as an income in calculating profit. Even though the cash from the sale may not have been received, profits will increase and share prices will probably increase. Shareholders should have some idea of a company's accounts receivable policy. Is the company selling goods or services to weak customers just to boost sales and reported profits? An analysis of the accounts receivable will help the shareholder in this regard.

14.7.1 Debtors collection period

For example, the average debtors collection period (DCP) is the number of days, on average, it takes to collect the payment due from customers. Suppose for example that ABC Ltd makes 100,000 bicycles a year which are sold to bicycle shops for €1,000 each. The terms of sale are 2/10 net 40. In other words, if ABC Ltd receives payment within 10 days they give a 2% discount, otherwise the payment is to be paid in full within 40 days. Furthermore, suppose that 60% of the customers take advantage of the discount and the other 40% do not avail of the discount and pay on day 40. The debtors collection period (DCP) is

$$DCP = 0.6(10 \text{ days}) + 0.4(40 \text{ days}) = 22 \text{ days}$$

ABC's average daily sales (ADS) is

$$ADS = \frac{100,000 \times €1,000}{365} = €173,973$$

Therefore at any one point during the year the amount of debtors outstanding would be

$$Debtors = (ADS)(DCP) = (€273,973)(22) = €6,027,406$$

14.7.2 Ageing schedule

This is another policy firms have in monitoring the quality of a firm's debtors. An ageing schedule is a break-down of the amounts due from debtors arranged by due dates. An example is given in Table 14.2

Table 14.2 Ageing schedule of debtors

Age of account	Amount	Number of customers
0 to 10 days	€100,000	100
11 to 30 days	€80,000	70
31 to 49 days	€40,000	30
50 to 70 days	€20,000	15
Over 70 days	€5,000	4

If, for example, the terms of trade were 2/10 net 30, 49 customers need watching, while 19 of these need particular attention.

14.7.3 The payment pattern approach to monitoring accounts receivable[2]

The main reason for monitoring debtors is to see if there is a change in the pattern of payment being received. It may be that debtors are paying more slowly and the quality of these accounts may be declining. The debtors collection period (DCP) and the ageing schedule of debtors are useful tools in analysing accounts receivable. However, seasonal fluctuations in sales can distort the information provided in the DCP figures. If there are seasonal fluctuations, the DCP and the ageing schedule will change with the seasonal fluctuations in sales, **even though there are no changes in customer payment behaviour.**

Example 14.1 Payment pattern approach to monitoring accounts receivable

Fews Ltd, which commenced operations in January 2000, manufactures garden tools. Table 14.3 gives the company's credit sales details for the year 2000. Note the seasonal variation in sales with the summer months having the highest level of sales. The payment pattern of Fews' customers is as follows: 20% pay in the month of sale, 40% pay in the month following the sale, 30% pay in the second month following the sale and 10% pay in the third month. Therefore at the end of January the debtors figure will be €80, i.e. 0.8(€100) = €80.

At the end of February the debtors figure will be 120, i.e. 40% of January sales and 80% of February sales:

$$\text{Debtors for February} = 0.4\ (\text{€}100) + 0.8(100) = \text{€}120$$

In March the debtors figure will be

$$\text{Debtors for March} = (0.1)(\text{€}100) + (0.4)(\text{€}100) + (0.8)(\text{€}100) = \text{€}130, \text{ and so on.}$$

Table 14.3

Month	Credit sales (€000)	Debtors at the end of the month	ADS— quarterly (€000)	DCP (quarterly) (days)	ADS (yearly) (€000)	DCP (yearly) (days)
(1)	(2)	(3)	(4)	(5)	(6)	(7)
Jan.	100	80				
Feb.	100	120				
Mar.	100	130	3.3	40	3.3	40
Apr.	100	130				
May	120	146				
Jun.	150	178	4.0	44	3.7	48
July	190	224			$\longrightarrow$	

Table 14.3 (cont.)

Month	Credit sales (€000)	Debtors at the end of the month	ADS— quarterly (€000)	DCP (quarterly) (days)	ADS (yearly) (€000)	DCP (yearly) (days)
(1)	(2)	(3)	(4)	(5)	(6)	(7)
Aug.	180	235				
Sept.	130	195	5.5	36	4.3	45
Oct.	100	150				
Nov.	100	133				
Dec.	100	130	3.3	39	4.1	32

Columns 4 and 5 give the average daily sales (ADS) and the debtors collection period (DCP). So, for example, at the end of March the average daily sales is (€100 + €100 + €100)/91 = €3,300 and the DCP is €130/3.3 = 40 days.

Columns 6 and 7 give the DCP and the ADS on an annual basis. For example, at the end of June the ADS = €670/182 = €3,682 and the DCP = €178/€3.7 = 48 days. The main point here is that **seasonal variations in sales cause the DCP to change even though there is no variation in customer payment pattern. Therefore using the debtors collection period as a tool in monitoring receivables is not reliable enough when there are seasonal variations in sales**.

Introducing the payment pattern approach deals with this problem. Using this approach, **variations in the constant payment pattern would be revealed**. The amount of each month's sales remaining unpaid at the end of each quarter is divided by that month's sales to give a debtors to sales ratio for each month. For example, at the end of March (first quarter) €10,000 of January sales remain unpaid which is 10%. Therefore at the end of March 10% of January sales have still to be paid. Also at the end of the first quarter 40% or €40,000 of February sales remain unpaid and 80% (€80,000) of March sales remain unpaid. Therefore the total debtors to sales ratio, or the total uncollected sum, at the end of the first quarter is 130%. This is illustrated in Table 14.4.

We can see that despite the variation in sales throughout the year, the payment pattern does not change. The benefit of the payment pattern approach is that any variation in the payment pattern of customers can be immediately highlighted and shown as a change in the debtors to sales ratio at the end of each month. For example, a slowing down in the payments of customers in the first quarter will be detected in the figures shown in Table 14.5. Because of the slow-down in collections, the total amount of debtors to sales percentage or the total amount of outstanding balances rises from 130% to 175%. Therefore management should take note of the decline in the quality of debts.

Table 14.4

Quarter (€000)	Credit sales	Debtors at the end of quarter (€000)	Debtors as a % of sales
Jan.	100	10	10%
Feb.	100	40	40%
Mar.	100	<u>80</u>	<u>80%</u>
		130	130%
Apr.	100	10	10%
May	120	48	40%
June	150	<u>120</u>	<u>80%</u>
		178	130%
July	190	19	10%
Aug.	180	72	80%
Sept.	130	<u>104</u>	<u>80%</u>
		195	130%
Oct.	100	10	10%
Nov.	100	40	40%
Dec.	100	<u>80</u>	<u>80%</u>
		130	130%

Table 14.5

Quarter 1	Credit sales	Debtors (€000)	Debtors as % of sales
Jan.	100	15	15%
Feb.	100	60	60%
Mar.	100	<u>100</u>	<u>100%</u>
		175	175%

14.8 The cost-benefit of a proposed change in credit policy

What effect will a proposed change in a company's credit policy have on the company's profitability? To evaluate a change in credit policy, consider the case of Nixus Ltd that manufactures computer games. Their current sales policy is to sell for cash only. Nevertheless, they are evaluating the effect on profitability of selling on credit on terms of net 45 days. The current price per package (P) is €100. The variable cost of production (Vc) is €40 and it sells 150 units (Q) per month. Lexus believes that selling on credit will boost sales to 170 units per month (Q*). In addition, when a firm grants credit it must finance the resulting debtors. Therefore a company's cost of short-term finance is a factor to be considered in evaluating its new credit policy. Suppose that the required rate of return (r) is 12% per annum or 1% per month. Should Lexus switch to a new credit policy?

Write down what variables we know: $P = €100$
$$Vc = €40$$
$$Q = 150$$
$$Q^* = 170$$

Therefore current monthly sales are $P \times Q = €15,000$

Variable cost per unit per month is $Vc = €40 \times 150 = €6,000$

Therefore, the current policy of cash only gives a cash flow of

$$(P - Vc)Q = (€100 - €40)(150) = €9,000$$

A switch to 45 days' credit will mean monthly sales of

$$(P)\,(Q^*) = (€100)\,(170) = €17,000$$

The monthly variable cost will be $(Vc)\,(Q^*) = (€40)\,(170) = €6,800$

Therefore the monthly cash flow under the new policy will be

$$(P - Vc)\,(Q^*) = (€100 - €40)\,(170) = €10,200$$

Therefore the incremental cash flow of a change in policy is

Cash flow under new policy – Cash flow under old policy = Incremental cash flow   **(14.5)**
    €10,200   €9,000   €1,200

Therefore the present value (PV) of this future incremental cash flow is

$$PV = (P - Vc)\,(Q^* - Q) \div r$$

$$PV = (€100 - €40)\,(170 - 150) \div 0.01$$

$$= \frac{€60 \times 20}{0.01} = \frac{1,200}{0.01} = €120,000$$

The costs of the new credit policy are:

(a) increased variable cost (Vc) of producing $(Q^* - Q)$ additional units, and
(b) the sales income that would have been collected under the current policy will not now be collected for one month. Therefore the total cost of the switch in credit policy is

$$PQ + Vc\,(Q^* - Q) = 15,000 + 800 = €15,800$$

Therefore the NPV of the change in credit policy is

$$- [(PQ + Vc \, (Q^* - Q))] + [(P - Vc) \, (Q^* - Q)] \div r$$

$$NPV = - €15,800 + €120,000 = €104,200$$

This says that the cost of switching is €15,800 and the benefit of the proposed switch is €1,200 per month in perpetuity which is €120,000. Therefore there is a clear advantage in switching to a new credit policy.

SUMMARY

- Optimum inventory is the level of inventory that will maximise shareholder value. This is the result of a trade-off between the cost of holding low inventory levels against the cost of having high inventory levels. The optimum inventory levels are a matter of balancing the costs and benefits of various inventory levels.
- The economic order quantity (EOQ) is the most popular approach in establishing the optimum inventory levels.
- The total carrying costs of holding inventory include the stock price per unit, taxes, insurance, general storage costs, depreciation of inventory and the opportunity cost of investing in stock.
- Restocking costs are the fixed costs incurred when placing an order, e.g. paper work, telephone calls.
- The total cost of holding inventory is the sum of the total carrying costs and the total reordering costs.
- Safety stocks are the minimum level of stocks that a firm holds.
- Just-In-Time (JIT) is a system of production where stocks of raw materials are delivered to the factory just as they are needed.
- Out-sourcing is a system of buying components instead of making the components in-house.
- Minimising the amount of inventory tied up in working capital will enhance economic value added.
- Granting credit can increase the level of sales, but it will also have additional costs in the form of increased bad debt risk, and the cost of carrying receivables. The optimum credit policy will therefore be a trade-off between the costs and benefits associated with granting credit.
- The credit period is the amount of time customers have before payment is made.
- The credit terms of 2/10 net 60 means that customers have 60 days from the time the invoice is received to pay the amount due in full. If payment is made within 10 days, a 2% cash discount is received.
- Credit quality refers to the probability that customers will not pay their bills.
- The five C's of credit are character, capital, conditions, collateral and capacity.
- Credit scoring is a method of awarding points to customers based on the information provided on their credit worthiness.
- The main reason for monitoring receivables is to see if there is a change in the pattern of payment being received. Using the payment pattern approach to monitoring debtors, variations in the constant payment pattern would be revealed.

QUESTIONS

1. Define JIT inventory systems. Explain how JIT inventory impacts on EVA.
2. Define ACP.
3. Explain the following terms: carrying costs; reorder costs; ageing schedule; EOQ; EOQ Range.
4. XYZ Ltd is about to switch to a new credit policy. The current policy is cash only. The new policy will offer credit for 30 days. The current interest rate is 1.5% per month. Under the new policy, sales are expected to increase by 10% from 500 units per month to 550 units per month. The price per unit is €100 and the variable cost per unit is €60. Should the switch be made?
5.♦ The following information is given for Garravoone Ltd:

   Credit sales = €2m
   Credit control expenses (debt control expenses) = €20,000 p.a.
   Average collection period (ACP) = 40 days
   Bad debts = 1%.

   The company is now considering easing its credit policy such that sales will increase to €2.3m, bad debts will rise to 1.5% and the ACP will be 50 days. Debt collection expenses will fall to €12,000. If the company's cost of funds is 10% and variable costs amount to 75% of sales, is the firm's new policy worthwhile? (Assume tax of 20%)
6. Windgap Ltd, manufacturer of garden tools, has a variable cost per unit of €10 and a sales price of €15. A customer is looking for a 40 day credit period to buy 1,500 units. You believe there is a 12% chance of default. The required rate of return on a 40 day credit period is 2%. Should credit be given to this customer?
7.♦ Explain the costs involved in carrying debtors, and what are the costs and benefits of granting trade credit?
8. Describe the five C's of credit.
9. Explain the payment pattern approach to assessing debtor quality.
10. A company always accepts trade credit because it wants to avoid borrowing and never takes a trade discount. The terms of credit are 2/10 net 30. The company's cost of debt is 12%. Should the company accept the discounts?
11. X Ltd begins each period with 100 units of stock. At the end of each period, the stock is depleted and reordered. The carrying cost per unit per annum is €5. The company sells 5,000 units a year, and the restocking cost is €30 per order. Calculate:

    (a) total carrying costs, and
    (b) total restocking costs.
    (c) EOQ

12.♦ Beginning inventory is €200,000 and closing inventory is €20,000. Carrying costs per unit is 20 cents. Calculate the total carrying costs.
13. Syntax Ltd sells 5,000 personal computers per annum. Order costs per PC are €1 and holding costs are 20 cents each. What is the EOQ?
14. Plastics Ltd has 200 units of raw materials in stock at the beginning of each week. The annual carrying cost per head is €20 and the fixed costs are €15. Calculate:

(a) the restocking costs

(b) total carrying costs

(c) the economic order quantity.

15. Fiddler Ltd sells 4,000 fiddles annually. It has a safety stock of 50 fiddles. The cost of each fiddle to the firm is €40. Carrying costs are 15% and ordering cost is €10. Calculate:

(a) the EOQ

(b) the maximum inventory of Fiddles Ltd.

16. Flybynight Production, when operating at full capacity, sells 1,000 electronic devices each week. As soon as this happens it orders another 1,000 electronic devices. The company has established that the fixed order cost amounts to €600 and the carrying cost per device is €10. Comment on the company's inventory policy.

17.♦ If carrying costs are €2m per year and restocking costs are €1m per year, what advice would you give to the company?

18. The following information is available for Carrick Ltd:

Carrick Ltd	Industry average
Credit terms = net 60 days	Credit terms = net 30 days
Average collection period = 70 days	Not available

Credit sales for Carrick Ltd amount to €3m. The management of Carrick is concerned about its credit policy. It has estimated that by changing its credit policy to the industry average of 30 days will lead to a reduction in sales to €2.5m. However, the ACP will, as a result of this change, fall to 36 days. Carrick's variable costs come to 75% of sales and short-term debt finance is 10%. Assuming a tax rate of 20%, should Carrick change its credit policy?

19.♦ Sportiris Ltd sells 100,000 football kits per annum. Each kit costs the company €10 and the cost of placing an order is €30. Inventory carrying costs are 15% and the company has an optimal safety stock of 599 kits. Calculate:

(a) the EOQ.

(b) the number of times the company must order each year.

(c) the maximum inventory of football kits.

20. How will an increase in inflation, interest rates and competition affect average inventory holdings?

NOTES

1. We will discuss effective and annual percentage rates of interest in the next chapter.
2. A very comprehensive treatment of this area is covered in: Brigham, Gapenski, Ehrhardt, 'Working Capital Management' in *Financial Management—Theory and Practice*, 9th ed. Chapter 23.

15
Short-term Sources of Finance

CHAPTER OBJECTIVES

Having studied this chapter the student will be able to:

1. understand the difference between the **hedging approach**, the **aggressive approach** and the **prudent approach** to financing current assets
2. to appreciate the various sources of short-term finance available to business
3. calculate annual percentage rates (APR)
4. assess the cost of different types of bank loans.

INTRODUCTION

Many factors affect the level of investment in current assets. It will of course depend on the nature of the business. The working capital requirements of a manufacturing business will differ to that of a service company. Companies that have seasonal variations in sales will have different working capital requirements to a company that has the same monthly production levels throughout the year. Construction companies generally will have high working capital requirements during the spring and summer months, and companies that supply construction companies, generally, will tend to follow the construction companies' pattern of working capital. Although possible (see Chapter 13), it is unlikely for working capital to fall to zero. This is because companies tend to have a minimum requirement of stock, cash and debtors and this is maintained over time. This minimum requirement of investment in current assets is called **permanent current assets** (see Figures 15.1 and 15.1A). These current assets are held even during periods of slow demand for the company's product. As the level of sales fluctuates over the business cycle, the level of stock, accounts receivable and cash will also fluctuate. These are referred to as **temporary current assets**. The way in which permanent and temporary current assets are financed is hugely important. Notice from Figure 15.1 how the fixed asset line rises gradually over time. This reflects the increased investment in fixed assets necessary to fund the increase in business activity over time.

Figure 15.1 The build-up of current assets over time

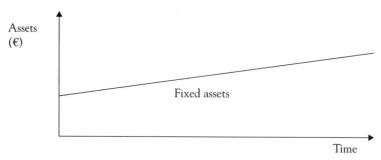

(a) The fixed asset line rises gradually over time as the firm expands

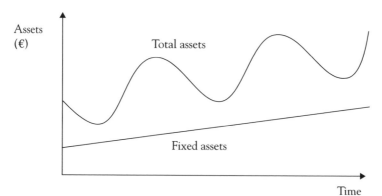

(b) Adding net current assets (current assets *less* current liabilities) to fixed
    assets. Because of the seasonal variations in sales this total asset line is
    seen fluctuating over time. The total asset line reflects the total funds
    required to finance the business at any point in time.

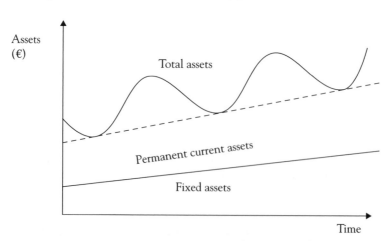

(c) The area between the fixed asset line and the line that is tangential to the
    valley points of the total assets line represents permanent net current
    assets.

Figure 15.1A The build-up of current assets over time

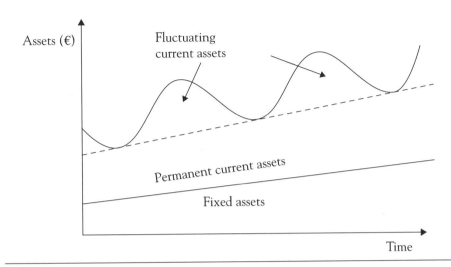

15.1 Financing permanent and temporary current assets

15.1.1 Hedging or matching approach

One system of financing current assets is known as the **hedging** or **matching** approach. It is important that the maturity of the assets is **matched** with the maturity of the liability (debt) used to finance them. Short-term finance should be used to finance short-term assets, medium-term finance should be used to finance medium-term assets, and long-term finance should be used to finance long-term assets. It makes sense therefore to finance short-term assets with short-term debt because short-term assets can be converted into cash in the near term. For example, if stock is to be sold in 40 days, a 40 day loan should be used to finance it. Fixed assets, like buildings, should be financed by, say, a 30 year mortgage. Figure 15.2 illustrates the hedging approach. Note that only the short-term requirement is financed by short-term debt. This is represented by the fluctuations at the top of the diagram. The **permanent** portion is financed by a mixture of long-term debt, equity, medium-term and revolving finance.

Figure 15.2 Hedging approach to current asset financing

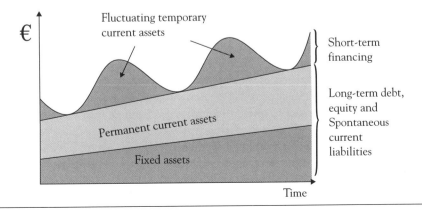

15.1.2 The aggressive approach

Matching the maturity of assets to the maturity of debt is all very cosy in theory. However some companies adopt a much more aggressive approach to financing. This stems from the fact that short-term debt is usually cheaper than long-term debt (see section 15.2 on the features of short-term finance). Consequently firms will try to take advantage of this and borrow more short term. In other words, some companies will try to finance their fixed assets with long-term debt and part of their **permanent** current assets with short-term debt. However, short-term debt carries higher financial risk because of the short space of time in which the debt must be repaid. Many businesses have gone into liquidation because of this approach. The risk is increased because, while long-term interest rates tend to be relatively stable, short-term interest rates can be more volatile, and companies can be caught up in sharp rises in short-term rates. Furthermore, any downturn in economic activity and demand will result in companies being unable to meet their debt repayments. This aggressive approach to financing is illustrated in Figure 15.3. The dotted line represents a proportion of permanent current assets that are financed by short-term sources of finance. The dashed line could be below (more aggressive) or above (less aggressive) where it is shown in the diagram. If the dashed line was on the fixed asset line, it would mean that all of the permanent current assets were financed by short-term debt.

Figure 15.3 Aggressive approach to financing current assets

15.1.3 The prudent approach

This is a very cautious approach. Here permanent capital is used to finance not only the permanent assets but also part of the fluctuating needs. Only the very top fluctuations, as depicted in Figure 15.4, are financed by short-term debt. However, part of the fluctuation in current assets is financed by **buffer** liquidity in the form of near cash balances such as marketable securities. This means that the company meets part of its seasonal requirements by **hoarding** liquidity, perhaps in the form of marketable securities. The firm uses a small amount of short-term finance to finance **peak** requirements.

Figure 15.4 Prudent approach to financing current assets

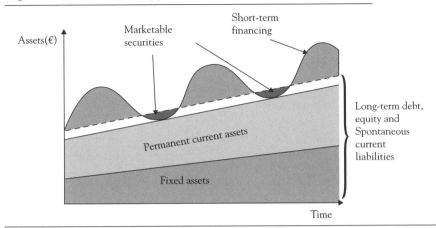

15.2 Features of short-term finance

Relative costs of short-term and long-term debt

The aggressive approach uses the most short-term finance, while the prudent approach uses the least amount of short-term finance. The costs of short-term loans are often cheaper than long-term loans. There are a number of reasons for this:

1. Long-term investments are riskier than short-term investments. It is more difficult to predict how well a company will be doing in 20 years' time than it is to predict how well it will be doing next year.
2. The **liquidity preference theory** suggests that borrowers (who are assumed to be risk averse) prefer to make long-term loans, while lenders prefer to make short-term loans. Therefore borrowers must pay a premium to lenders to entice them to make long-term loans.
3. **Pure expectations theory** holds that interest rates will reflect expected rates of inflation. The interest rate charged on long-term loans would be the average of the interest rates expected throughout each period that the loans span. For example, if interest rates are expected to be 10% over the next twelve months, and 15% over the following twelve months, the 2 year interest will be 12.5% (10% + 15%) = 25%/2. If inflation is expected to increase over the coming years, interest rates in the long term will be higher.

Example 15.1 Interest rates using pure expectations theory

Inflation is expected to increase over the next few years. The financial institutions estimate that annual interest rates will be as follows:

Year	Expected annual interest rate	Expected average annual interest rate
2001	7%	7%
2002	9%	8%
2003	11%	9%
2004	13%	10%

If inflation is expected to increase, long-term interest rates will increase.

On the other hand, long-term rates are more stable. Short-term loans can be riskier than long-term loans because of the risk of increases in short-term interest rates. This makes short-term debt riskier than long-term debt. For example, short-term interest rates in Ireland in 1976 reached 17%.

Flexibility

In terms of flexibility, short-term debt is more flexible. Flexibility is particularly useful if business activity is seasonal. Some months the firm will borrow to finance additional short-term working capital needs, while for other months its borrowing requirements may be nil.

In general, short-term credit is less restrictive than long-term loan agreements, which may contain provisions on how the funds are used.

Furthermore, lenders will insist on an extensive research into the company before advancing long-term loans. Note, however, that small firms do not usually have access to long-term finance—so, in this respect, choice is limited.

15.3   The cost of bank loans

Interest rates vary for different types of borrower. If the risk profile of the borrower is high, the interest rate charged will be correspondingly high. Interest rates can be either fixed or floating.

15.3.1   Fixed-interest rate loans

Interest rates can be fixed for short or long periods, e.g. for 3 months or 10 years. The cost of a fixed-rate loan will depend on:

- the time period for which the funds are required
- the variable interest rate and the forecast for the likely movement in variable rates.

However, the borrower will not benefit if interest rates fall over time. If the borrower wishes to pay off the fixed-rate loan before maturity, s/he is likely to incur penalties.

15.3.2   Variable-interest rate loans

Variable rate simply means that the interest rate the borrower pays will vary in accordance with the rates being paid on the wholesale money markets. The interest rate charged will depend on ECB interest rate policy and on general economic conditions.

15.3.3 Annual percentage rate

Consumer legislation in Ireland requires all financial loan products to include the APR.

Quoted interest rates are the rates expressed as the payment made for each period covering the loan. The effective annual interest rate, or the annual percentage rate (APR), is the interest rate expressed as if it was compounded once a year. For example, if a rate is quoted at 6% compounded semi-annually, it implies that it pays 3% every six months. However, this 3% every six months is not the same as 6% per annum. Investing €1 at 6% you will receive €1.06 in 12 months' time. If you invest €1 at 3% every six months, then what you end up with is €1.03 (€1 × 0.03) after six months, *plus* 3% on 3 cents which is 0.09 cents. Therefore, what you receive after 12 months is 6.09%. Here the 6% is the quoted interest rate, and the 6.09% is the APR.

To convert quoted rates to annual percentage rates proceed as follows:

1. Take the quoted rate and divide it by the number of periods for which the interest is compounded.
2. Add 1 to your answer.
3. Raise the answer to the number of times the interest is compounded.
4. Subtract 1.

These steps are summarised as follows:

$$APR = \left[1 + \left(\frac{R}{N}\right)\right]^n - 1$$

where R = quoted interest rate
      N = number of times the interest is compounded.

Example 15.2 Calculating annual percentage rate (APR)

You are offered a loan at 10% compounded on a monthly basis. What is the annual percentage rate?

Solution

$$APR = \left[1 + \left(\frac{0.1}{12}\right)\right]^{12} - 1 = 10.47\%$$

Example 15.3 Calculating annual percentage rate (APR)

Suppose that a credit card company requires monthly payments and quotes a rate of 18%. This implies that monthly payments will be 0.18 /12 = 1.5% per month. The effective annual rate (APR) will be

$$APR = \left[1 + \left(\frac{0.18}{12}\right)\right]^{12} - 1 = 19.6\%$$

Therefore, the actual interest rate paid is 19.6%.

15.3.4 Interest only loans

Interest is paid by the borrower each period and the original amount of the loan is repaid in the future. This type of repayment schedule is called an interest only loan. For example, a loan of €10,000 at 6% for four years would require an interest payment of €600 at the end of the first three years *plus* €10,600 at the end of the fourth year. Here the interest is paid once a year. If the interest is paid over a number of periods during the year, then the interest payments per period are calculated as follows:

1. Find the interest rate per day. This is got by taking the nominal interest (the quoted) rate and dividing it by the number of days in the year:

$$\frac{\text{Nominal rate}}{365} = \frac{0.06}{365} = 0.00016438356$$

2. The daily rate is then multiplied by the number of days in the period to give the rate per period. For example, if interest is paid monthly (31 days), then the monthly interest payment is

$$(31)\,(0.00016438356)\,(€10,000) = €50.96$$

Incidentally, the more frequently interest has to be paid, the higher the effective interest rate. The reader can satisfy him/herself that this is the case by calculating the effective annual rate in the above example on a quarterly, monthly, weekly and daily basis. You could also compound it on an hourly basis.

Example 15.4 Annual percentage rates and frequent compounding
Money is placed on deposit that has a quoted rate of 6%. Calculate the APR on a quarterly, monthly, weekly, daily, hourly and minute basis.

Solution
The APR is as follows:

$$APR = \left[1 + \left(\frac{R}{N}\right)\right]^{n} - 1$$

Period	Compounding times	APR (%)
Quarter	4	6.136355%
Monthly	12	6.167781
Weekly	52	6.179981
Daily	365	6.183131
Hourly	8,760	6.183632
Minute	525,600	6.183651

The APR keeps getting larger, but as we increase the compounding periods, the difference gets very small.

15.3.5 Pure discount loan

With a pure discount loan, the borrower receives the money today and repays a lump sum at some date in the future. **The principal and the interest are lumped into one payment.** This is the same as an interest only loan if there was just one period. For example, a 6% pure discount loan would require the borrower to repay €106 at the end of one year for every €100 borrowed.

15.3.6 Discount interest loans

With a discount interest loan, the bank deducts the interest (or discounts the loan) in advance. For example, borrowing €10,000 for one year at 6% on a discount basis means that you only get the use of €9,400, i.e. €10,000 *minus* (€10,000 × 0.06). The face value of the loan is €10,000, but you only receive €9,600. The funds received are equal to

$$\text{Funds received} = \text{Face value of loan } (1 - \text{Nominal interest rate}).$$

Therefore the face value of the loan is

$$\frac{\text{Funds received}}{1 - \text{Nominal interest rate}}$$

Therefore if you actually need the use of €10,000, with a discount interest loan, you will need to borrow

$$\text{Face value} = \frac{€10,000}{1 - 0.06} = €10,638$$

15.4 Sources of short-term finance

Having discussed financing permanent and temporary current assets, we turn our attention to various sources of short-term finance.

15.4.1 Bank overdrafts

Subject to authorised limitations, bank overdrafts allow customers to withdraw more funds from their current account than they have deposited. Individual banks have their own regulations for the use of overdraft facilities.

Features of bank overdrafts
- Repayable on demand. Users of bank overdrafts should bear this in mind. This adds to the risk of using overdrafts as a source of funds. Consequently bank overdrafts should only be used for specific short-term needs. For example, because retailers peak around the Christmas period, bank overdrafts are suitable to pay for Christmas stocks. The Christmas period will usually generate enough cash to repay the overdraft after Christmas. When a loan is used to finance assets that will generate enough cash to repay the loan, we refer to such loans as **self-liquidating loans.**

- An upper limit is put on the overdraft facility and it is allowed to fluctuate within that limit. If the limit is exceeded, penalties will be imposed.
- There is no obligation on banks to renew an overdraft facility.
- Generally, banks will look at balance sheet data over some historical period before granting overdraft facilities.
- Because it is repayable on demand, the financial risk from the bank's point of view is low. This makes it one of the cheapest sources of finance available.
- The actual cost of overdrafts will depend on the prime or base rate of the bank. Overdrafts will be priced at a cost above the prime rate depending on whatever risk the bank attaches to the borrower.
- There is often a requirement that businesses maintain compensating balances, which is usually a credit balance in another account. The effect of having **compensating balances** is to raise the effective interest rate charged to the borrower. For example, if a company needs €8,000 to pay creditors and if the bank requires a 20% compensating balance, how much must the company borrow? The company must borrow the amount that leaves €8,000 after it takes out the 20% compensating balance. Therefore the company must borrow €10,000 for the use of €8000, i.e. €8,000/0.8. The interest paid on €10,000 at 5% is €500. However, since we are only getting €8,000, the effective interest rate is €500/€8,000 = 6.25%. In other words, we are paying 5 cents interest on every 80 cents that we have borrowed. We do not have the use of the 20 cents that is tied up in the compensating balance, i.e. 0.05/0.80 = 6.25%.
- Security in the loan is generally not required. If security is required, it is generally in the form of a mortgage or lien, which of course restricts management from pledging that asset for further finance (unless it gets the bank's permission). However, by having a good relationship with the bank and providing all relevant information is submitted, then security will generally not be asked for.
- Interest is charged on the amount outstanding each day.
- There are transaction fees which can be expensive.

15.4.2 Short-term loans

Short-term loans are provided for specific purposes and repayable by agreed amounts within 12 months. The main features of short-term loans are:

- Short-term loans are for specific purposes and if the terms of the contract are adhered to, it cannot be withdrawn prior to maturity. This makes short-term loans more disciplined than bank overdrafts.
- Term loans are priced at a margin above that of the Euribor. This is usually 1.5% to 3% depending on the risk profile of the borrower.
- A facility to repay the loan early may be available. Repayments can be structured in such a way as to coincide with a time when a company has sufficient cash flow.
- Loans will be interest only or amortised. If interest only, interest is paid only during the life of the loan and the principal is paid at maturity of the loan. **Amortised** means that part of the principal is repaid on each of the repayment dates (sometimes called instalment loans). If repayment is made in one full lump sum, it is called a **bullet loan**.

- Short-term loans are usually secured against some collateral or asset. This prevents the borrower from using the same assets to guarantee other finance.
- Loans borrowed at a fixed rate will be costly if variable rates begin to decline.

15.4.3 Accruals

Income taxes deducted from payrolls, pay-related social insurance and VAT on sales are usually paid on a fortnightly and monthly basis. The company's balance sheet will show some accrued taxes. Similarly, wages are usually paid on a weekly or monthly basis and therefore the balance sheet can show an amount for wages due. Accruals are seen as a spontaneous source of finance, that is, they tend to increase spontaneously as the firm expands its level of sales. Accruals are also a **free** source of short-term finance because no interest is paid on them. Other types of accrued expenses include telephone charges and electricity expenses.

15.4.4 Accounts receivable (debtors)

Next to cash, accounts receivable can be the most liquid asset. Banks can grant loans to companies using receivables as security. In this sense, debtors are collateral for sources of finance, rather than as a source of finance per se. The default risk stays with the borrower. In other words, the bank has recourse to the borrower even if the accounts receivable do not materialise.

15.4.5 Factoring

Factoring is the total sale of a firm's accounts receivable to a financial institution or bank (called a factor). With **recourse factoring**, the risk of bad debts is borne by the business and not by the factor. With **non-recourse factoring**, the risk of the bad debt is borne by the factor. The factoring company takes full control over the debts and advances anything up to 80% of the book value of the debtors to the company. The remaining amount will be given over to the business when the debtor pays (this is after the factor has received his fees, costs, interest and the loan advanced). This type of finance increases spontaneously as the business expands. However, the downside is that it usually costs more than the cost of bank overdrafts.

The cost of factoring can be high. The interest charge can be as high as Euribor plus a margin depending on a customer's risk profile, plus a charge for bad debt risk and a service charge. For companies that have a high quantity of invoices but where each is for a small amount, administrative costs involved could be very high. Furthermore, factoring may be seen as weakening the position in the eyes of creditors who might therefore refuse to sell on credit to the firm.

Finally, when we use a credit card to buy or sell goods, the sellers of these goods are in fact factoring receivables (debtors). The seller receives the amount due, less the fee, the next working day and the buyer of the goods gets usually 30 days to remit the amount due to the credit card company.

Example 15.5 The cost of factoring

Maggie Ltd has made sales of cakes in the past year of €600,000. At the end of the year it has an average debtors figure of €40,000. As a source of finance, Maggie has used a factoring company to factor its accounts receivable. It sells its debtors for 98 cents in the euro. It needs to know what the effective rate of interest is on this source of funds.

Debtors are turned over, on average, €600,000/€40,000 = 15 times a year with an average debtors collection period of 365/15 = 24 days. Maggie receives finance of 98 cents and pays 2 cents in interest on the loan. Therefore the interest rate is 0.02/0.98 = 2.04% per 24 days.

On an annual basis, this is 2.04% × 15 = 30.6%. The annual percentage rate is

$$APR = 1.0204^{15} - 1 = 35\%$$

15.4.6 Invoice discounting

Invoice discounting occurs when a borrower submits or sells selected invoices to a lender. Depending on the risk profile of the borrower, the lender will provide up to 80% of the face value of the invoices. It is estimated that some €114m is advanced through invoice discounting in Ireland, and the business is growing at an annual rate of about 25%. It is estimated that about 600 enterprises accounting for about €1.26 billion of turnover between them are using the facility in the year 2000.[1] The business collects the amount of the invoices and pays the full amount to the lender. The lender will keep whatever amount was advanced plus any interest due on the advanced amount, and give whatever is left back to the business. In invoice discounting, the business decides on the invoices to be sold. An application for invoice discounting can be made through the bank. The cost of invoicing is the bank's cost of funds plus a margin depending on the risk of the customer. The total cost has two elements: the actual cost and a service or administration charge.[2] This actual cost is slightly higher than normal overdraft rates to AA customers, i.e. small and medium enterprises (SMEs). The administration cost is charged as a percentage of the debts purchased, which is usually 0.5% or less. Other important requirements are for a good spread of clean debts. The information the bank needs from the enterprise will include the following:

(a) details of new sales raised
(b) monthly debtor age analysis, which highlights problem accounts.

Like full factoring, the level of financing available will increase as the level of business activity increases. Consequently, business expansion can be financed by increased sales rather than by issuing more and dearer equity. Like recourse factoring, the risk of bad debts is still borne by the business.

Comparing invoice discounting and factoring

Legally, invoice discounting and factoring are the same: each is a financial facility offered through the purchase of debt. The principal differences between the two are as follows:

1. Under invoice discounting, the responsibility for credit management and sales administration remains firmly with the enterprise. In contrast, factoring is for enterprises whose credit management and administration systems are **inadequate**. With factoring, the factoring company (the bank) takes a very active role in the enterprise's credit control function by sending out **reminders** and statements to debtors. The factoring company receives payment from the debtor directly.
2. Invoice discounting has taken over from factoring as the main source of debtor finance. Factoring had become known as a **last chance finance**, and it was often seen in a negative light when the bank got involved in the credit control and administration of the enterprise. In contrast, debtors are not aware of the involvement of banks in invoice discounting because the banks keep a discreet distance in the background.

Box 15.1 Case study[3]

A Dublin-based enterprise, specialising since 1990 in the manufacture and distribution of industrial materials to aid the transport of large consignments, decided in favour of further expansion in 1992 to take advantage of certain opportunities. However, its bankers could not extend any more facilities, as it had no additional security to offer. With demand increasing, for want of working capital the company had to stretch its creditors to the point where the constant supply of materials was threatened. Yet the account for 1992 showed after-tax profit of £27,000 on sales worth £2.1 million in a business employing 18 people.

Eventually, realising that its fastest growing asset was its debtors, the enterprise used this to secure fresh working capital. Under an invoice discounting arrangement, £300,000 was raised against debtors of £500,000, and this revolving facility allowed growth to continue. By the end of 1994, both after-tax profit and turnover had virtually doubled to £52,000 and £4m respectively. A regional depot to co-ordinate national distribution and a subsidiary company to control exports had been established, and a total of 28 were employed. At the same time the discounting facility had increased to £600,000, reflecting the way in which increased sales were converted into cash without having to wait for payment.

15.4.7 Bills of exchange

A **bill of exchange** is a contract that enables a buyer to postpone payment for a period of up to 130 days. A post-dated cheque is an example. Another example is when the government borrows money by selling **government bonds**—it promises to repay the loan at some stage in the future. **Commercial bills of exchange** are bills of exchange issued by commercial organisations. When goods are sold, the seller draws up a legal document that shows the indebtedness of the buyer. The buyer accepts a bill of exchange by signing it and by writing **accepted** across it. This means that the buyer agrees to pay the amount due at some date in the future. The seller will either hold the bill to maturity or discount it at a bank, and so get immediate cash. In the latter case, if the bill is discounted at a bank, the bank will pay an amount that is lower than would be received by the customer if held to maturity.

Figure 15.5 Bill of exchange: sequence of events

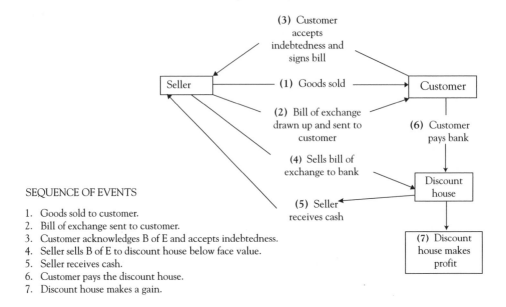

SEQUENCE OF EVENTS

1. Goods sold to customer.
2. Bill of exchange sent to customer.
3. Customer acknowledges B of E and accepts indebtedness.
4. Seller sells B of E to discount house below face value.
5. Seller receives cash.
6. Customer pays the discount house.
7. Discount house makes a gain.

Example 15.6 Discounting bills of exchange

A bill of exchange commits a customer to pay €100,000 in 90 days' time. It is immediately sold to a bank for €95,000. At maturity, i.e. after 90 days, the bank realises a profit of €5,000 on an asset of €95,000. This is a rate of return (interest rate) of 5.26%. This is equivalent to an effective annual percentage rate of

$$(1.0526)^4 - 1 = 22.8\%$$

The result of this process is:

1. The customer receives 90 days' credit.
2. The seller makes a sale and gets cash to the amount of 95% of the amount due.
3. The bank gets a rate of return equivalent to 22.8% per annum. If this is greater than the bank's own cost of capital, the bank will have made a gain.

Acceptance credits are a sort of formal line of credit agreed between the bank and the customer. In a sense, therefore, they are similar to bills of exchange. The company (which needs cash) draws up an acceptance credit document agreeing to pay a sum of money at some date in the future. Once the acceptance credit is drawn up, it is then sent to the bank. The bank accepts, and a commission is paid to the bank. The bank accepts a promise made by the company that it will pay a sum of money at some future date. The company will then sell the acceptance credit to another bank or discount house. The company therefore receives the cash it needs. The bank pays the discount house that bought the acceptance credit the sum due. Finally, the company then pays the bank the accepted amount of money due.

Figure 15.6 Acceptance credits: sequence of events

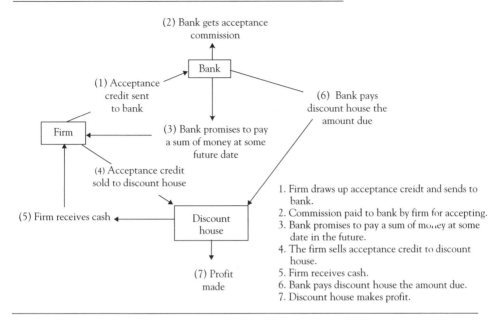

(2) Bank gets acceptance commission

Bank

(1) Acceptance credit sent to bank

(6) Bank pays discount house the amount due

Firm

(3) Bank promises to pay a sum of money at some future date

(4) Acceptance credit sold to discount house

(5) Firm receives cash

Discount house

(7) Profit made

1. Firm draws up acceptance creidt and sends to bank.
2. Commission paid to bank by firm for accepting.
3. Bank promises to pay a sum of money at some date in the future.
4. The firm sells acceptance credit to discount house.
5. Firm receives cash.
6. Bank pays discount house the amount due.
7. Discount house makes profit.

15.4.8 Commercial paper

The main function of banks is to act as intermediaries between lenders and borrowers. The bank profits by charging a higher rate of interest to borrowers than it gives to depositors. Sometimes, however, large well-known companies can bypass the bank and lend directly to borrowers. This type of lending is known as commercial paper. Therefore commercial paper is a sort of unsecured promissory note or IOU issued by large firms and sold to other firms via the money market. The maturity of commercial paper can be up to six months. The interest rate on commercial paper fluctuates with supply and demand conditions in the money market. Issuers can normally issue commercial paper at Euribor + 0.15%. This makes it cheaper than term loans. The principal disadvantage of commercial paper is that if a firm (the debtor) runs into short-term financial difficulties, it will get very little sympathy because of the impersonal nature of the commercial paper market. Banks tend to be more helpful to good customers in times of need. However, the benefit of commercial paper is that it allows businesses to tap into a wider source of finance. The most common type of commercial paper in the Irish market is government guaranteed notes issued by semi-state bodies and bank guaranteed notes issued by major Irish companies. Bank guarantees for commercial finance are off balance sheet contingent liabilities and do not need the same amount of capital backing as traditional bank loans. This allows the bank to offer cheaper funding to the borrower.

15.4.9 Predetermined expense financing

Certain business expenses such as corporation tax, insurance, audit fees and income tax can be discharged by financial institutions and repaid by the business over a period of 6 to 11 months.

15.4.10 Inventory financing

A popular method of short-term finance is inventory financing. Generally, stock is regarded as a liquid asset. Loans (or **stock loans**) are advanced by financial institutions (mainly by commercial finance companies) with inventory used as collateral. The main features of inventory financing are:

Collateral can be in the form of a **blanket lien** which provides the lending institution with a lien against all the borrower's stock. However, the borrower is free to sell the inventory, which effectively reduces the lien that a lender had at the start of the agreement.

Another instrument of security used in inventory financing is the **trust receipt**. The borrower signs a trust receipt for the stock. The stock is held in trust for the lender. The lender has specific legal control over these items of stock. The goods are held on the borrower's premises on the lender's behalf. Income from the sale of these goods is transferred to the lender. In order to verify the trust receipt, the lender will have to send somebody to the borrower's premises from time to time to verify that the specific items of stock are correct and still on the premises. Automobile dealers can be ideal users of trust receipt financing. However, it is possible for the dealer to sell cars under trust receipt and use the money for purposes other than remitting it to the lender. Further difficulties arise if the borrower has different locations spread over a wide geographical location.

To overcome some of the difficulties of trust receipt financing, **warehouse receipt** financing uses inventory that is under the physical and legal possession of the lender. Unlike the trust receipt the inventory is now in the control of the lender. A **terminal warehousing** agreement is where the stock is stored on the lender's premises and a third party is used to monitor and manage the inventory. A **field warehousing** agreement is where the inventory is stored on the borrower's premises, which is monitored by a third party. Once the loan is being repaid, the lender authorises the third party to release the appropriate amount of inventory held.

The cost of this type of financing is high and the cost of the third party has to be paid for by the borrower. Consequently only large firms use it.

SUMMARY

- Permanent current assets are those that are held even when the demand for the company's product is slow.
- Temporary current assets are those that fluctuate over the business cycle.
- It is important that the maturity of assets is matched by the maturity of liabilities used to finance those assets. This is the hedging approach to financing. For example, if stock is expected to be sold in 40 days, then a 40 day loan should be used to finance it.
- The aggressive approach to financing stems from the fact that short-term finance is usually cheaper than long-term finance. Some firms will therefore try to finance part of their permanent current assets with short-term debt. This is the aggressive approach to financing current assets.
- Bank overdrafts allow customers to withdraw more funds from their accounts than they have deposited.

- Short-term loans are for specific purposes and are repayable by agreed amounts within 12 months.
- Accruals in the form of income taxes deducted from payrolls, PRSI and VAT on sales, wages etc. are seen as a spontaneous source of short-term finance.
- Banks can grant short-term loans to companies and use accounts receivable as a form of security.
- Invoice discounting is where the borrower submits or sells selected invoices to a lender.
- Factoring is the total sale of a firm's accounts receivable to a financial institution or bank (called a factor). Recourse factoring occurs when the risk of bad debts is borne by the business and not by the factor. With non-recourse factoring the risk of the bad debt is borne by the factoring company.
- A bill of exchange is a contract that enables the buyer to postpone payment for a period of up to 80 days.
- Commercial paper is lending by large well-known companies directly to borrowers. The maturity of this form of loan is usually six months.
- Inventory financing is advancing loans with stock used as collateral.
- The annual percentage rate of interest (APR) is the interest charged per period multiplied by the number of periods in the year.
- Bank loans can be in the form of interest only loans and discount interest loans.

QUESTIONS

1. Explain the following:
   (a) Permanent and temporary current assets
   (b) Current asset financing policies
   (c) Self-liquidating loans
   (d) Bank overdrafts
   (e) Accruals
   (f) Commercial paper
   (g) Compensating balances
   (h) Interest only loans
   (i) Instalment loans
   (j) Pure discount loans.
2. Why is matching the maturities of assets and liabilities so important? What are the benefits of such an approach? What is the downside to such an approach?
3. ◆ Why do you think bank loans are potentially more significant to small firms rather than large firms?
4. Quick-Build, a builders providers company, has approached its bank with a view to borrowing €100,000 for one year. The bank has provided the following options:
   (a) 10% per annum on a simple interest loan. No compensating balances are required. Interest is paid at the end of the year.
   (b) A simple interest loan @ 7% per annum with interest due at the end of the year. However, under this deal the bank requires a compensating balance of 15%.
   Calculate the effective annual percentage rate of interest under each proposal.

5. You require a loan of €20,000 for one week. The rate of interest quoted is 10% per annum. The nature of the loan is a discount interest loan. The bank also requires a 12% compensating balance. Calculate the effective annual percentage rate of interest.

6.♦ (a) Explain the trade off between liquidity and profitability.

   (b) Distinguish between the conservative, aggressive and matching approach to financing working capital

7. A company adopts a prudent approach to the financing of its assets. An inspection of the company's balance sheet shows that it has permanent current assets of €50,000 and fixed assets of €190,000. It is also shown that the company's temporary current assets fluctuate about €20,000 every month. How should the company finance these assets, assuming that it maintains its prudent policy of financing? Considering the cost element of different types of financing, which policy would provide the most return for shareholders?

8. Companies that have aggressive working capital policies are considered to have higher risk. Why?

9. A company has total assets of €1,000,000 and permanent current assets of €200,000. Its fixed assets amount to €500,000. If the company follows the matching or hedging approach to financing, how much should the firm invest in current assets?

10. The following is information obtained from the accounts of Milo Ltd:

	Aggressive	Prudent (or conservative)
Temporary current assets	€150	€150
Permanent current assets	€150	€150
Fixed assets	€700	€700
	€1,000	€1,000
Current liabilities	€260	€35
Long-term liabilities	€300	€380
Common equity	€440	€585
	€1,000	€1,000

Using the above information, show how working capital policies affect accounting ratios. What are the main conclusions you can draw from the ratios?

NOTES

1. *Bank Brief*—Irish banks' information service, issue no. 9.
2. *Bank Brief*—Irish banks' information service, issue no. 9.
3. This case study is extracted from the above issue of *Bank Brief*.

Part 6

The Investment Market

16
Investment Market Structures and Operation

CHAPTER OBJECTIVES

At the end of this chapter the student will:

1. understand the structure and operation of the Irish bond market
2. understand the structure and operation of the Irish pension fund industry
3. understand the structure and operation of the unit-linked fund industry
4. understand the concept of a unit-linked fund
5. understand the attractiveness of unit-linked funds to small investors
6. be aware of the different types of unit-linked funds
7. have a broad overview of the scale of the unit-fund industry
8. understand the concept of a pension fund
9. be able to distinguish between defined benefit and defined contribution pension schemes
10. understand the key investment objectives, criteria and management approaches of pension funds
11. have a broad overview of the scale of the pension fund industry.

INTRODUCTION

The bulk of the Irish bond market is in government issued bonds, with a relatively small market in non-government bonds. This chapter deals with the structure and operation of the Irish bond market.

The chapter also gives the student an overview of the unit-linked and pension fund industries in Ireland. These are two of the mechanisms through which many investors will access the equity and bond markets described in earlier chapters in this book.

Part 1. The Irish Bond Market

16.1 Size and structure of the Irish bond market

The total nominal value of issued Irish Government bonds at €21.8 billion is about one-sixth the size of the Irish equity market in terms of market capitalisation. While there are nineteen fixed-interest bonds currently traded on the market, the bulk of the value is in just five bonds which each have an issued value in excess of €2 billion and between them account for a total issue of almost €21.5 billion or over 95% of the total market. The full list of government stock currently in issue is given in Appendix 3 at the back of this book. There is no variable rate stock in the market at present.

These five bonds are all treasury bonds, i.e. bonds issued by the National Treasury Management Agency (NTMA) since its inception in 1990, and denoted by the prefix TRY. There are four other smaller treasury bonds. These bonds differ from the other bonds traded, i.e. those with the prefixes DEV (development), EXC (exchequer), GOV (government) and CAP (capital) in that the coupon is paid annually, whereas with the other bonds half of the stated coupon is paid twice yearly at six month intervals.

Eighteen of the bonds are bullet issues, i.e. single date, while there is one dual-dated bond. The longest bond matures in the year 2016. The bulk of value, 83% is concentrated in the short to medium (up to 10 years) range. Less than 20% are in long-term bonds.

The coupons range from 2.75% to 14.75%.

Gross redemption yields currently range from about 4.75% at the short end to 5.3% at the long end of the market.

16.2 National Treasury Management Agency (NTMA)

The NTMA was established by the Irish Government in 1990 to manage the country's national debt, which at the time stood at about 95% of GDP. The principal objective of the NTMA is to manage the national debt and government funding programmes in a cost-effective manner and to achieve savings in debt servicing. It is responsible for both the domestic and foreign elements of the funding programme.

Since its inception, the agency has made a number of changes to the operation of the bond market. These include:

- new issues which are now on an annual coupon basis. The semi-annual payment is being phased out as these bonds are redeemed or repurchased.
- benchmark stocks which have been established by concentrating funding in these bonds and encouraging **switching** into them from smaller issues.
- a new market-making system which has been established.
- primary dealers who have been appointed.

16.3 Benchmark stocks

The NTMA has designated benchmark bonds with maturities of approximately 1, 4, 9 and 15 years. The current benchmark bonds are:

- 6.5% TRY 2001
- 2.75% TRY 2002
- 3.5% TRY 2005
- 4% TRY 2010
- 4.6% TRY 2016.

16.4 Market-making

In 1995 the NTMA established a system of market-making. Under this system, designated primary dealers were appointed and are obliged to quote bid and offer prices for eight nominated bonds. The current market makers are:

- ABN AMRO, Dublin and Amsterdam
- AIB Capital Markets, Dublin
- Credit Agricole Indosuez, Paris
- Davy Stockbrokers, Dublin
- Deutsche Bank, Frankfurt
- NCB Stockbrokers, Dublin.

A primary dealer is obliged to continuously display bid and offer prices electronically in benchmark bonds.

Where the primary dealer is part of a larger organisation involved in buying and selling bonds for treasury or fund management purposes, the two functions must be entirely separate and 'Chinese walls' must be maintained.

Primary dealers have exclusive access to the NTMA's tap issues and have access in a non-competitive auction situation to 20% of the amount sold in the normal monthly auction.

16.5 Taxation

There is no tax withheld on Irish Government bonds. Coupons are paid gross but are liable to tax at the appropriate rate for the particular holder, i.e. the marginal income tax rate for an individual, the corporation tax rate for companies etc. There is no tax on the redemption value if held to the redemption date, but otherwise the asset may give rise to a capital gains tax liability for some classes of investors.

The tax treatment of bonds clearly has an implication for the pricing of bonds. Because coupon income is taxed, lower coupon stocks are subject to less tax than higher coupon ones and therefore tend to trade at a premium to higher coupon stocks. The income flow from low coupon bonds is based more on the redemption value, which is tax free, whereas with higher coupon stocks taxable coupon income accounts for a greater part of the income flow.

The longer end of the market tends to attract pension fund investment and since pension funds are not subject to tax on the coupon income, taxation is less important in this maturity range. It is important where higher rate taxpayers are dominant or significant in the market, since they will tend to pay a premium for low coupon stock.

16.6 Tracking of the bond market

Most of the major stockbroking firms publish indices of the Irish bond market on a restricted basis to their clients. These are generally broken into indices for short, mediums and longs together with an overall index of the market. These indices are normally based on total return, i.e. capital growth (or decline) plus a notional reinvestment of the coupon income into the maturity range from which it has come. Indices are also available for capital and income separately.

The Irish bond market has recently been included in a number of international bond indices as follows:

- Salomom Smith Barney—World Government Bond Index
- Lehman Brothers—Global Bond Index
- Merrill Lynch—Global Government Bond Index II
- J.P. Morgan—Irish Government Bond Index
- Bloomberg/EFFAS—Government Bond Index.

16.7 Membership of economic and monetary union

Ireland's membership of the EMU has removed the currency risk associated with Irish bonds in the past for investors from elsewhere in the euro zone. This also works the other way round in that bonds issued elsewhere in the euro zone are now more accessible to risk-averse Irish investors.

A further implication of membership of EMU is that the yield differential *vis-à-vis* the major European bond markets, principally Germany, has been significantly reduced and now represents a liquidity (and credit) premium rather than primarily an exchange risk premium.

16.8 Participants in the market

Approximately 55% of Irish bonds (by value) is held by domestic institutions and other investors, with the remainder held by overseas investors. The main domestic investors in the bond market are insurance/assurance companies, banks and pension funds. Foreign players comprise a wide range of investors, including both euro zone and also non euro-based investors from the UK and the US.

Table 16.1 shows the break-down of Irish bond holdings at the end of 1999.

Table 16.1 Value of Irish bonds held—end 1999

Investor	Euro million	% of total
Insurance companies	6,400	30.4
Banks and building societies	5,010	23.8
Pension funds	2,300	10.9
Unit & investment trusts	300	1.4
Other domestic inc. personal sector, charities etc.	2,630	12.5
Overseas investors	4,390	20.9
Total	21,030	100.0

Source: NTMA

16.9 Non-government bonds

The corporate bond market is small in comparison to the government bond market and relatively underdeveloped compared to other countries. About two-thirds are issued by the European Investment Bank or state companies (e.g. HFA, ESB, ACC) and are thus regarded as relatively low risk, but normally trade at a small yield premium to government stock. The remainder are issued by domestic financial institutions.

16.10 Recent performance of the Irish Government bond market

Given the degree of integration between international financial markets and the free flow of capital between countries, bond markets are influenced by both domestic and international issues. In addition, the establishment of Economic and Monetary Union (EMU) and the launching of the euro have effectively meant that bond markets throughout the euro area constitute a single entity. The differential which existed in the past between, say, Irish and German bond yields was primarily due to the perceived riskiness of the IR£ relative to the Dm and the interest rate differential in the respective money markets. The (much smaller) differential which exists now is largely related to liquidity conditions in the two markets and any perceived credit risk. Exchange rate risk is still a live issue for investors from outside Euroland, e.g. UK and US investors. This is a double-edged sword in that, for Irish institutions and other investors considering investment outside the euro area, there remains some element of risk.

This section tracks the movement in the Irish bond market over the first quarter of 2000 in order to show the pattern of price and yield movements. A ten year bond is used to represent the market.

Table 16.2 shows the movement in the price and yield of the 4% TRY 2010 bond.

Table 16.2 Price and yield of 4% 2010 bond

Date	Price €	Change Yield %	Price €	Yield bps[1]
14/01/00	86.75	5.74	− 0.15	2
21/01/00	86.00	5.86	− 0.75	12
28/01/00	86.00	5.86	0.00	0
04/02/00	86.90	5.73	0.90	− 13
11/02/00	86.30	5.82	− 0.60	9
18/02/00	86.40	5.81	0.10	− 1
25/02/00	87.45	5.66	1.05	− 15
03/03/00	87.20	5.70	− 0.25	4
10/03/00	87.95	5.59	0.75	− 11
16/03/00	88.25	5.55	0.30	− 4
24/03/00	88.90	5.48	0.65	− 7
31/03/00	89.00	5.45	0.10	− 3
07/04/00	89.15	5.43	0.15	− 2
14/04/00	88.85	5.48	− 0.30	5
21/04/00	88.75	5.50	− 0.10	2

Source: AIB capital markets.

A number of issues should initially be observed about the bond price and its relationship with the yield:

- The price of the bond is quite variable, changing in 14 of the 15 weeks.
- The trend in the price changes direction six times over the period.

The graphs below show the above more clearly.

Figure 16.1 Price and yield of 4% TRY 2010 bond mid-January–mid-April 2000

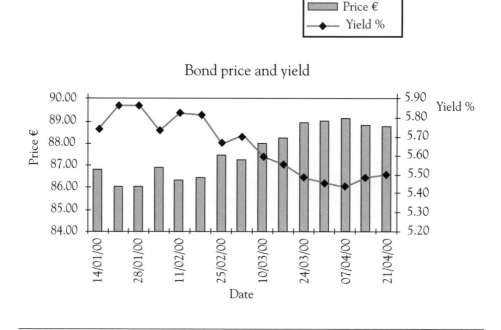

Figure 16.2 Price of 4% TRY 2010 bond mid-January–mid-April 2000

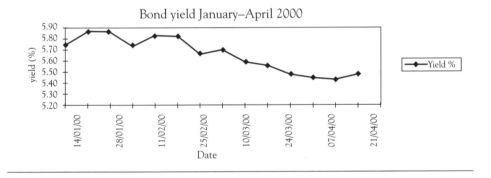

Bond price January–April 2000

Figure 16.3 Price of 4% TRY 2010 bond mid-January–mid-April 2000

Bond yield January–April 2000

Part 2. The Irish Unit-linked Fund Industry

16.11 Definition of a unit-linked fund

A unit-linked fund is an investment vehicle where the investor takes a stake in a pooled investment and **owns** the assets of the fund in proportion to the percentage of the overall number of units held. Unit-linked funds and unit trusts are, from the investor's point of view, practically the same and no distinction is made here.

16.12 Types of funds

There are many different types of funds available to the investor largely based on the asset category in which the bulk of the assets are held. The following are the principal categories at present. There are no precise definitions for these categories, but funds are allocated to each category based on the proportion of assets held and the risk stance of the fund.

Equity

- General equity
- Specialist equity
- International equity.

Fixed interest

These funds invest primarily in government gilts or other fixed-interest bonds. They are generally low-risk funds. There is a small amount invested in index-linked funds, but these have become less important given the low levels of inflation throughout the 1990s.

Guaranteed

These funds operate by providing a guarantee to the investor that the capital value of the investment will remain intact for a specific period. The fund manager achieves this by placing a proportion of the fund into (risk-free) fixed-interest stock which will have a maturity value equal to the amount invested, e.g. if the redemption yield on gilts is 5% and the timespan of the guarantee is one year, then the fund manager would invest 100/(1.05) = 95.24% of the amount invested into gilts. This leaves only 4.76% of the investment amount to be placed in other income-earning assets.

Cash

These funds are generally low risk, but typically low return as they are invested in money markets and short-dated government stocks. They can be used as a short-term repository for spare cash, perhaps while the investor makes up his/her mind about which sector to commit to. The issue of bid/offer spread (see section 16.14) must be taken into account however. Most companies allow **switching** between funds which will get over this problem.

Property

The investments are normally made in prime property in the retail, office and industrial sectors. Unlike the UK, where funds could have a geographical as well as a sectoral spread, Irish investments are predominantly located in Dublin and to a smaller extent in Cork. This limits the potential for locational diversification. Many funds, however, invest in the UK property market. Property tends to be a popular asset in times of high inflation due to its historical record of outpacing the rate of inflation. **Bricks and mortar** still retain a certain comfort factor for investors.

Mixed/managed funds

These are funds which have a spread across the main asset types. The level of risk will vary across different funds. The higher risk funds will tend to be heavily weighted towards equity and high risk equity for the most aggressive funds. This category includes:

- Cautiously managed
- Managed growth
- Aggressively managed (mainly equity).

16.13 Attractions for the small investor

Unit-linked funds are particularly attractive for the small investor. The main advantages for such an investor are:

- They offer a mechanism for the small investor to build a personal diversified portfolio without the time or capital commitment which would normally be required.
- The risk may be spread over a wide range of asset types in the key sectors of the market and across geographical areas.
- They are professionally managed.
- A competitive environment encourages fund managers to perform. This however does have the drawback that it can encourage **short-termism** in relation to performance, i.e. fund managers become more concerned with making short-term gains perhaps at the expense of longer-term growth in the fund. Tactics can become more important than strategy.
- Regular **league tables** of competing funds are available allowing the investor to make comparisons.
- Most assets have a daily or at least weekly valuation. However, with property-based funds, prices may move slowly due to the periodic valuations of the underlying assets.
- They generally offer a good degree of liquidity. This is particularly important in relation to property-based funds, since the underlying asset itself is highly illiquid.
- Units can be bought or sold, but it is generally not profitable to do so over a short period. This is due to the 'spread' between the bid and offer prices, which could be as high as 5% in certain cases. The spread will vary depending on the length of time the unit is held and may be waived as a loyalty bonus if the units are held for a specific period.

16.14 Bid and offer prices

The offer price is the price at which units are sold by the fund manager, while the bid price is the price at which the fund manager will buy units back from the unit holders. The pricing structure reflects the value of the underlying assets in the fund and is based on the notional figure for establishing or realising the entire fund, tempered by the manager's pricing policy.

16.15 Market size and structure of the Irish unit fund industry

There were over 330 funds in Ireland at the end of 1999, up from just over 200 in 1990. The break-down of these into the principal asset types is shown in Table 16.3.

Table 16.3 Irish unit-linked industry by fund type

Asset	No.	% by no.	Value	% by value €m
Equity[2]	193	58.1	4,888.8	82.0
Cash	41	12.3	145.5	2.4
Cautiously mgd.	11	3.3	69.2	1.2
Fixed interest	31	9.3	404.4	6.8
Guaranteed	23	6.9	146.1	2.5
Property	28	8.4	306.5	5.1
Other	5	1.5	—	—
Total	332	100.0	5,960.4	100.0

Source: MoneyMate Database, The Software Vineyard, Dublin

It is clear from table 16.3 that equity is the dominant asset type, accounting for over 80% of the industry by value. Since equity funds account for under 60% of the industry by number, this indicates that on average equity funds are larger than other types. There are a large number of cash funds, but they account for only 2.4% of the value of the industry.

The fund returns are normally measured, for comparative purposes, on an offer-to-offer basis, i.e. the bid-offer spread is ignored for this purpose. This information is readily available and is widely published. It is not reproduced here. Investors will often choose on the basis of the available information on fund performance. Chapter 18 discusses the analysis of fund performance which goes beyond return only and examines the importance of the level of risk inherent in each fund.

Part 3. Pension Fund Structure and Management

16.16 Market size and structure

The Irish Association of Pension Funds (IAPF) undertakes an annual survey of pension fund investment in Ireland. The most recent survey relates to end 1999. The key results are presented below.

16.17 Annual survey of pension fund investment in Ireland

Asset distribution

The total assets of Irish pension funds at end 1999 amounted to €48.5 billion, equivalent to over 55% of GDP and almost 65% of GNP. This is up almost 24% on 1998. This growth of 24% is made up of

- inflow of contributions
- plus earnings on existing assets
- less payments made from fund.

The growth in asset value is primarily due to investment return.

The share of Irish assets held was down by 15 percentage points. Other key highlights were:

- exposure to Irish equity decreased by over 5 percentage points
- exposure to international equity was up by over 12 percentage points
- the above is partly due to a switch into European equity, following the introduction of the euro and the consequent removal of the exchange rate risk in the Eurozone, but also due to growth in value elsewhere due partly to the weakness of the euro
- fixed interest now accounts for a little over 24% down from almost 40% in the early 1990s
- cash and other short-term investments increased only slightly indicating that funds are generally fully invested
- property holdings fell by over 1 percentage point and now account for less than 5% of total value.

Returns

Overall returns averaged 24% with Japanese equity leading the way with a return of over 100%, albeit from a low base. North American equity returned 42% while European equity also delivered an excellent return at 36%.

16.18 Types of funds

The funds are divided into three types:

- segregated funds
- unit-linked funds
- insured asset schemes.

The IAPF surveys show the break-down of funds into these types over the past 5 years.

Table 16.4 Distribution of pension funds by fund type 1993–99

Investment management vehicle	% distribution			
	end	end	end	end
	1993	1996	1998	1999
Segregated assets[3]	58	59	57	56.4
Unit-linked assets	29	31	31	33.2
Insured assets[4]	13	10	12	10.4
Total	100	100	100	100

Source: Irish Association of Pension Funds—*Annual Investment Survey 1999*

16.19 Defined benefit schemes

A defined benefit scheme is where the value of the pension is known in the sense that it is normally based on the finishing salary or average salary over the last few years of work. The pension is normally equal to a fraction of the finishing salary based on the number of years' membership, e.g. one-eightieth of the finishing salary for each year of service up to a maximum of 40 years, which produces a maximum pension equal to half the finishing salary; one-sixtieth of the finishing salary for each year of service up to a maximum of 40 years which produces a maximum pension equal to two-thirds of the finishing salary. In this instance any shortfall in investment performance is made up by the employer whose liabilities are generally linked to wage inflation. It is normal that the pension is then index-linked to some benchmark, e.g. the consumer price index, the rate of wage inflation in the economy or the rate of wage increase in the company.

16.20 Defined contribution schemes

A defined contribution scheme is where the value of the pension is not known with any certainty and is not related to final salary. Instead, its value depends on the investment performance over the period of contributions. If a shortfall occurs in the sense that the built-up value of the pension fund is insufficient to support the required level of pension payments, then the pension scheme member (the employee) will have to make additional contributions to increase the value of the fund.

16.21 Investment objectives and management

Like any investment fund the objective is to find an acceptable trade-off between return and risk.

The return requirement is informed by the extent to which liabilities are linked to inflation. This is in turn determined by:

- the age profile of the membership
- whether it is a defined benefit or defined contribution scheme.

The attitude to risk is largely a function of the maturity match of assets and liabilities, i.e. if the liabilities are primarily long term, then the fund manager may be prepared to take on greater risk, e.g. high-risk equity; whereas if the fund has reached a stage where net outflows will start to occur in a few years' time, then the manager may be risk averse and attempt to consolidate gains already made by investing in low-risk assets such as short-dated bonds.

The need for a satisfactory liquidity position is normally a key objective for investment funds. However it may be less important for pension funds, especially **younger** ones, given the long-term nature of the liability structure and also because of the more predictable pattern of outflows.

Diversification both across and between markets is an important strategic objective. The increasing investment overseas by Irish pension funds is partly due to their desire to reap the diversification benefits of investing in these markets, but also because of the somewhat limited opportunities that exist in the Irish equity market.

There are normally three levels of management:

- long-term **strategic** asset management
- short-term **tactical** asset allocation
- **stock** selection.

Strategic allocation

This refers to the allocation between asset types considered appropriate for a fund over the long term. Clearly for a pension fund this is a critical issue. The most important decision is how to establish the appropriate allocation of assets. There are a number of approaches to this:

- devising a benchmark portfolio
- relate asset distribution to liabilities
- mirror other funds.

Tactical allocation

This refers to the short-term deviations from the strategic allocation in an attempt to enhance return. It is predicated on a view of short-term risk and return prospects. The key question is: how wide a range around the strategic weights should tactical allocation cover? It should be narrow if transaction costs are high and timing skills are poor.

Stock selection

This refers to the process of attempting to identify and invest in winners.

16.22 Performance measurement

Performance measurement is important for a number of reasons, including:

- the competitive nature of the pension fund industry
- the need for members of defined contribution schemes to track the ongoing value of the fund
- the need for employers who run defined benefit schemes to track the ongoing value of the fund.

While it is useful as a medium/long-term monitoring device, there is a danger of over-emphasis on comparison, especially with peer groups. This gives rise to the problem of short-termism, i.e. where fund managers are forced to deliver short-term gains through tactical management. This carries the danger of a movement away from the strategic focus of the fund.

SUMMARY

- The Irish bond market is mainly comprised of government-issued bonds.
- The National Treasury Management Agency (NTMA) is responsible for overseeing the operation of the Irish bond market.
- The NTMA has designated five benchmark bonds.
- Six companies operate as primary dealers or market-makers in the Irish bond market.
- The Irish bond market is now included in a number of international bond indices.
- Overseas investors hold over 45% of the value of Irish bonds.
- Unit-linked funds have certain attractions for small investors.
- Bid-offer spreads can be as high as 5%.
- Fund performance is normally measured on an offer-to-offer basis.
- Over 80% of the unit-fund industry by value is in equity funds.
- Total assets of Irish pension funds accounted for over 55% of GDP at the end of 1999.
- In a defined benefit scheme, the onus is on the employer to make up any shortfall in investment performance.
- In a defined contribution scheme, the value of the pension payable depends on the investment performance of the fund.
- Investment objectives and management are determined by the age profile of the membership and whether the fund is a defined benefit or defined contribution scheme.

QUESTIONS

1. Describe the recent changes made to the operation of the Irish bond market by the NTMA.
2. Describe two principal implications for the Irish bond market of Ireland's participation in EMU.
3. What are the principal attractions of a unit-linked fund for the small investor?
4. What is the distinction between bid and offer prices?
5. Distinguish between a defined benefit and defined contribution pension scheme.
6. What is meant by tactical asset allocation?

NOTES

1. Basic points. A basis point is one-hundredth of a percentage point.
2. Equity here refers to those funds with over 50% of the assets invested in equity and includes aggressively managed and managed growth funds.
3. Mainly occupational pension schemes.
4. Mainly annuities through life offices.

Part 7

Special Topics in Finance and Investment

17
Risk Management

CHAPTER OBJECTIVES

At the end of this chapter the student should be able to:

1. understand the nature of interest and exchange rate risks
2. appreciate the difference between internal and external risk management techniques
3. understand the types of financial derivatives available
4. have the ability to select appropriate risk management techniques
5. appreciate the benefits and costs associated with risk management techniques.

INTRODUCTION

There are many aspects to a business that involve risk. When a company invests in a project there will be an element of business risk and when a company uses debt finance in its capital structure there is financial risk to the equity holders. Here we look at other types of risk that can affect the profitability of a business. These are risks relating to movements in currency exchange rates and interest rates.

Risk management describes the policies which a company may adopt and the techniques the company may use to manage these risks. The action a company takes to manage these risks is known as **hedging**. In this chapter we look at the kinds of currency and interest rate risks that companies face and then consider the techniques available to manage these risks. We first look at techniques that are internal to the company, and then look at external techniques available, some of which are quite topical, such as the development of financial derivatives.

Box 17.1 Majority of Irish exports outside euro zone

In 1999 Irish exporters sold €28.3 billion worth of products to the euro zone (42% of all exports). By comparison, 22% of exports went to Britain (including Northern Ireland) which continues to be Ireland's largest single market. The United States, the second largest market, took 15% of total exports.

Sunday Business Post, May 2000

17.1 Currency risk

Prior to 1971 the world had a relatively fixed exchange rate system. In August of that year, the Bretton Woods regime collapsed and the major currencies of the world began, for the first time, to float against each other. This floating exchange rate between two currencies is determined primarily by supply and demand in the foreign exchange markets (Appendix 17 A). This floating rate system and the accompanying growth in world trade over the past thirty years has led to the increasing importance of risk management in currency exposure.

Exposure means being open to or vulnerable to risk.

The following different types of currency risk can be identified.

1. **Transaction exposure**: This is the risk of adverse exchange rate movements occurring in the course of normal international trade. When international trade occurs, a company either pays or receives foreign currency at some future date. The amount of local currency paid or received in these foreign currency transactions may change due to floating exchange rates.

2. **Translation exposure**: This is the risk that the company will make exchange losses when the accounting results of its foreign subsidiaries are translated into the multinational home currency. Suppose an Irish company buys a subsidiary in the US for $20 million when the exchange rate is €1 = $1 and the following year the subsidiary is still valued at $20 million but the exchange rate has moved to €1 =$1.10. In this example, on consolidation of the company accounts, the asset value of the subsidiary will be reduced in the balance sheet.

   The cost of the subsidiary was $20 million/1.0 = €20 million. Its value in the following year has fallen to $20 million/1.1 = €18.18 million which is a loss of €1.82 million.

3. **Economic exposure**: This refers to the risk of long-term movements in exchange rates undermining the competitiveness of a company. It is quite different to transaction or translation exposure in that the company may not even be involved in international trade at all. Suppose an Irish company was supplying frozen pizzas to the local supermarkets in the domestic market and the euro appreciates against sterling. This may lead to import substitution from similar type companies in the UK. Irish supermarkets would find that the local currency has increased buying power in sterling and may begin to source frozen pizzas in the UK. So even though the Irish supplier does not operate internationally, he still has economic exposure to currency movements.

In Ireland exchange rates are quoted indirectly, i.e. the number of foreign currency units per €. A direct quotation is the value of one foreign currency unit in terms of the euro. In the case of the euro versus the Swiss franc a **direct quotation** would be of the form €0.40 = SF1 and an **indirect quotation** would be quoted as €1 = SF2.5. The tradition in Ireland is to quote currencies indirectly.

The **spot rat**e refers to the rate of exchange today and a **forward rate** refers to the rate available from a bank in the future. Banks expect to make a profit from selling and buying currency and this is achieved by quoting a different rate for selling and buying foreign currency.

Example 17.1 Bid and offer rates

The rate of exchange for the dollar versus the euro is as follows:
spot €1 = 1.0251 – 1.0252.
The lower rate is called the **offer rate** and is the rate at which the bank
will sell dollars, €1 = $1.0251.
The higher rate is called the **bid rate** and is the rate at which the bank
will buy dollars, €1 = $1.0252.
The difference between the two spot rates is known as the **spread**.

17.2 Interest rate risk

The most obvious form of interest rate risk is that of a company with high levels of
variable or floating-rate debt. However interest rate risk can affect companies in many
ways and has consequences whether a company is cash rich or cash poor. The incidence
of interest rate exposure can impact on corporate performance in the following ways:

1. Companies with floating-rate debt are exposed to interest rates rising.
2. Companies with fixed-rate debt are exposed to interest rates falling.
3. Companies with cash deposits at fixed rates are exposed to interest rates rising.
4. Companies with cash deposits at floating rates are exposed to interest rates falling.

Even where companies have matching assets and liabilities at floating rates, more subtle
forms of exposure exist:

(a) The deposits/loans attached may not be determined using the same basis (e.g. one is
linked to Euribor and the other to Libor). It is unlikely that both floating rates will
move perfectly in tandem and this is known as **basis risk**.
(b) Asset rates may be revised on a three monthly basis, while liability rates are revised
on a six monthly basis. This is called **gap exposure**. Both of these forms of exposure
are outside the scope of this text.

Whether a company is exposed to foreign currency or interest rate risk, it is important to
keep the scale of the risk in mind.

**Where the magnitude of the risk is immaterial in comparison to the company's
overall cash flows, one option is to do nothing and to accept the effects of any
exchange/interest rate movements that occur.**

17.3 Risk management techniques

Before looking at the various techniques applicable to exchange rate and interest rate risk
management, it is useful to split the techniques into internal and external. **Internal risk
management** relates to the way a company structures its assets and liabilities.

Foreign currency risk can be managed internally as follows:

1. **Invoicing in domestic currency**: One way of avoiding exchange risk is for an exporter to invoice the foreign customer in his domestic currency, or for an importer to arrange with his foreign supplier to be invoiced in his domestic currency.

2. **Matching**: A company can reduce its foreign exchange transactions exposure by matching receipts and payments in each foreign currency in which it has exposure. The process of matching is made simpler by having foreign currency accounts with a bank. Foreign currency drafts can then be deposited or cheques drawn through the same account.

   Translation exposure can also be reduced. For example, a company purchasing foreign assets can borrow in a foreign currency to finance such assets and service the loans with the foreign currency revenues received.

3. **Netting**: Although not technically a method of managing exchange risk, netting is used by multinational corporations to reduce transaction costs in foreign currency dealing. Many multinationals engage in intra-group trading (trading between subsidiaries based in different countries) denominated in different currencies. The procedure for netting is usually co-ordinated by the company's own central treasury, which establishes a common currency and the exchange rates to use for netting purposes. The advantage of netting (known as **multilateral netting** if more than two subsidiaries are involved) is that currency purchase and selling costs, including commission and the bid/offer spread between selling and buying rates, and money transmission costs are reduced.

4. **Lead and lagged payments**: Lead payments are payments in advance and would be used by a company that was afraid of a foreign debt becoming expensive due to a currency appreciation. By paying in advance the company hopes to avoid the increased costs of buying the currency later. However by paying in advance of the due date the company is giving up a credit facility which would have an implied cost. A lagged payment is a payment delayed beyond its due date. If a company believed a currency was weakening over time, it might delay the payment as long as possible to avail of the favourable foreign exchange rate movement. Again there may be a cost associated with a loss of goodwill/credit rating on the international markets.

Internal risk management methods used for interest rates include:

1. **Mix of fixed to variable rates**: Too much fixed-rate debt creates a problem when interest rates fall and too much variable-rate debt leads to higher costs when interest rates increase. A company should try to balance these two extremes.

2. **Matching**: Companies can internally match their assets and liabilities when they both have a common interest rate. For example, a financial institution could match interest received from borrowers with interest paid to depositors

3. **Maturity mix**: It is important not to have too much debt becoming repayable within a short period, as this can lead to difficulties if rates are high on the renegotiation of these debts. It may be a better policy to stagger the debt roll-over on a longer time horizon.

17.4 External risk management

Because internal techniques are dealt with inside the company, they are likely to involve lower costs. In some cases these methods can substantially reduce exposure. However they cannot eliminate exposure. We will now look at external techniques available, beginning with **forward contracts** and **money market operations** and then the more recent techniques, known collectively as the **derivatives markets**. The subject of derivatives has received a lot of publicity in the past decade, much of it negative. Examples of a few of the more famous disasters are listed in Appendix 17B.

17.5 Forwards

Forward contracts exist for both currency and interest rate risk.

A **forward exchange contract (FEC)** is an immediately firm and binding contract between a bank and its customer for the purchase or sale of a fixed quantity of foreign currency, at a fixed rate of exchange and for performance at a future time. FECs are traded on an over-the-counter (OTC) market and can be tailor made with respect to maturity and size. There may be an initial small arrangement fee, but they give the company certainty about the amount of local currency involved. While a forward contract protects against unfavourable movements in exchange rates, the binding nature of the contract means the company forgoes any potential benefit from favourable currency movements.

The date for performance of the contract can be fixed (**fixed FEC**) or can have an option facility (**option FEC**). The latter type of contract means that the customer has the option to call for performance of the contract at any time between two dates.

Example 17.2 Forward rates

An Irish exporter needs to purchase $1 million in three months' time to pay for imported goods from the US and the rates the bank quotes are as follows:

€1 =	Offer	Bid
$ Spot rates	1.0211	1.0221
$ Two month forward	1.0231	–1.0237
$ Three month forward	1.0242	–1.0249

What will it cost the company to use a forward exchange contract?

Answer
The bank's three month forward offer rate is 1.0242.

The exporter will pay $1 million/1.0242 = €976,371.80 for the required dollars.

Suppose the exporter was unsure whether the dollars were needed in two or three months. In this case the exporter can arrange an option forward exchange contract covering this time frame.

Here the bank will pick the rate that best suits itself over the option period, i.e. 1.0231, and the customer has the option of going through with the purchase at any time during the option period. The cost in euros to the exporter is $1 million/1.0231 = €977,421.56.

The forward rate is the spot rate on the day the forward exchange contract is made plus or minus the interest differential for the period of the contract. **It is not a forecast!** It is however likely that the difference in interest rates in the two economies is likely to have an impact on future exchange rate movements, i.e. currencies with high interest rates are likely to depreciate in value against currencies with low interest rates.

The difference between spot and forward rates reflects differences in interest rates. If this were not so, then investors holding the currency with the lower interest rate would switch to the currency with the higher rate, ensuring they would not lose on returning to the original currency by fixing the exchange rate in advance at the forward rate.

If enough investors acted in this way (arbitrage dealings), forces of supply and demand would lead to a change in the forward rate to prevent such risk-free profit-making.

There is an implied interest rate in the cost of forward cover.

The approximate cost (annualised) of forward cover is

$$\frac{(\text{Spot rate} - \text{Forward rate}) \times 12 \times 100\%}{\text{Number of months' cover taken} \times \text{Spot rate}} \tag{17.1}$$

Example 17.3 Cost of forward cover

Using the spot and three month forward rate in the previous example, the cost of forward cover, based on the offer rates, is calculated as follows:

$$\frac{(1.0211 - 1.0242)12 \times 100}{3 \times 1.0211} = -1.214\%$$

The negative value means it is cheaper to buy dollars forward than at the spot rate.

This 1.214% is the interest differential between the dollar and euro zone. Here the rate of interest is higher in the US by over 1%. Offer and bid differentials are usually averaged in calculating the cost of forward cover.

Forward rates can also be quoted, using the last example, as follows:

€ =	Offer	Bid
$ Spot rates	1.0211	1.0221
$ Two month forward	0.20c–0.16c dis.	
$ Three month forward	0.31c–0.28c dis.	

In the example above the dollar was at a **discount** (dis.) to the euro in the future, meaning it was cheaper and the interest rates were lower in the euro zone than in the US. To get the forward rate, discounts are added (the three month forward adjustment to the spot rate is 0.31 cent or $0.0031). If a currency is more expensive in the future, it is said to be at a **premium** (pm) and premiums are subtracted.

Example 17.4 Forward exchange contract

Dodgy-Tabs plc operating from London sells shoes to Italy. A shipment has just been made to a major Italian customer, invoiced in Italian lire, payable in three months' time. The amount due is 56 million lire.

Exchange rate LIRE /Sterling £			£1 =
	spot		2,320 – 2,322
	3 months forward		15 – 23L dis.
Interest rates:		Bid	Offer
	Sterling £	6%	8.75%
	Lire L	9.25%	12%

(a) Show how a forward exchange contract would operate in this example.
(b) How would your advice differ, if at all, were Dodgy-Tabs to make a payment of 30 million lire to an Italian supplier in three months' time?
(c) What is the cost of forward cover for Dodgy-Tabs?

Answer
In this example the UK trader is afraid that the lire will weaken over time and the trader will receive less sterling for the lire in the future. By entering into a forward exchange contract the trader will know in advance how much sterling will be received in three months' time.

(a) First work out the forward rate = 2,322 + 23 = 2345. Dodgv-Tabs agrees to sell L56 million to the bank at an agreed rate of 2,345.
L56 million/2,345 = €23,880.60. This is the value in three months' time.
(b) The company could match the L30 million payment and take out an FEC for the L26 million remaining.
L26 million/2,345 = £11,087.42.
(c) The annualised cost of forward cover is negative as the lire is at a discount to sterling. It is calculated as an average of the bid and offer rates.

$$\frac{2,320 - 2,335}{2,320} \times \frac{12 \text{ months}}{3 \text{ months}} \times 100\% = -2.586\%$$

and

$$\frac{2,322 - 2,345}{2,322} \times \frac{12 \text{ months}}{3 \text{ months}} \times 100\% = -3.962\%$$

The average of the two scores of the cost of forward cover = − 3.274%. By entering into a forward contract the company is locking into a lower value of the lire and is losing about 3.3%, which is the interest rate differential in the two economies.

Money market operations

The connection between interest rates, spot rates and forward rates allows the possibility for an alternative hedging technique. This technique is sometimes called a **synthetic forward** or a **money market hedge**. There are a few steps involved in the operation of this type of hedge. Suppose an exporter has a foreign currency receipt in the future. The procedure is as follows:

1. Borrow an appropriate amount of foreign currency now.
2. Convert the foreign currency to local currency now.
3. Place this local currency on deposit (optional step).
4. When the foreign currency is received, repay the foreign currency loan.

Example 17.5 Money market hedge

Consider the information in example 17.4 above and compare the FEC to a money market operation.

Answer

1. Borrow an amount of lire that will leave the exporter owing exactly L56 million in three months' time. Since the annual rate for borrowing lire is 12%, the quarterly rate is 3%.
   So borrow L56 million/1.03 = L54.369 million now.
2. Convert at today's bid rate (i.e. sell the lire back to the bank) = L54.369 million/2,322 = £23,414.70.
   This is the amount of sterling available to the exporter today, whereas the FEC value is in three months' time.
3. To make a direct comparison in the same timeframe as the FEC the £23,414.70 can be placed on deposit at the bid rate in the UK. The annual deposit rate in sterling is 6% and so the quarterly rate is 1.5%. If this sterling amount is placed on deposit for three months, the equivalent amount in three months' time is £23,414.70(1.015) = £23,766.
4. When the L56 million is received, repay the foreign currency loan.

In this situation the FEC is better at £23,880.60 by a small amount.

The steps involved in a money market operation for a foreign currency payment (cash outflow) is as follows:

1. Buy foreign currency today (spot).
2. Place this foreign currency on deposit.
3. When payment is due, pay from the deposit account.
4. Buying the currency spot in step 1 may involve borrowing locally if the company is short of funds.

Example 17.6 Comparison of FEC and money market operation

Again using example 17.4, but this time assume Dodgy-Tabs plc has to pay L56 million in three months' time. In this situation the trader is afraid that the lire will strengthen over time and will cost more in sterling in the future.

Compare a forward exchange contract with a money market operation.

Answer

(a) First work out the forward rate = 2,320 + 15 = 2,335.
    L56 million/2,335 = £23,982.87 payment in three months' time using a forward exchange contract.

(b) Using a money market operation the company would deposit lire for three months at the bid rate. The annual bid rate for lire is 9.25% and so the quarterly rate is 2.3125%.

The company could buy 56 million/1.023125 = L54,734,270 today and place it on deposit for three months.

This deposit will grow to L56 million in three months' time.

The cost of buying the lire today is L54,734,270/2,320 = £23,592.36 at the spot rate.

Again to make this directly comparable, assume Dodgy-Tabs has to borrow the sterling to buy the lire. The borrowing rate for three months is 8.75%/4 = 2.1875%.

The cost in three months' time is £23,592.36 (1.021875) = £24,108.44. In this example the FEC is better.

Forward rate agreement (FRA)

A forward rate agreement (FRA) is a contract to borrow or lend money in the future at an interest rate that is agreed today. FRAs are traded on the OTC market so maturity dates and periods can be tailored to the company's requirements. Here again interest rates are quoted on a bid/offer basis, so that a quote of 6.50 – 6.40 means a company can fix a borrowing rate at 6.5% and fix a deposit rate at 6.4%. The rate agreed is based on a notional amount starting on a date in the future and lasting for a specified period (for example, a 3 x 6 means the FRA starts in three months and lasts for 3 months).

The FRA can be arranged with a separate institution as a separate transaction to the company's original exposure. The overall effect of an FRA is that, regardless of the actual rate in the future, the company will know in advance what interest is effectively involved, based on a simple compensation mechanism and this compensation occurs at the start of the period of the notional deposit or borrowing. The company will lend/borrow at actual interest rates, and a compensating mechanism between the company and the bank will adjust the effective rates to the agreed amount.

This is illustrated with an example.

Example 17.7 Forward rate agreement

It is now 1 June and Gazaybo plc uses certificates of deposit (CDs) for its short-term investment. The company currently holds €2 million worth of CDs which mature in three months' time. The company treasurer intends to replace these CDs when they mature by buying further CDs with three months' maturity, and is afraid that interest rates will fall before the investment is renewed.

The treasurer decides to hedge against a reduction in interest rates by using a forward rate agreement (FRA) which fixes the rate at 6%.

Indicate what outcomes will occur and calculate the resulting payments if on the settlement date the three month CD rate has moved to (a) 4% and (b) 9%.

Answer

(a) If the rate is 4% the company will receive interest of €2 million × 4% × $^1/_4$ = €20,000.
The bank compensates the company for the difference between 4% and 6% for the three month period.
The amount of interest differential = €2 million × (6% − 4%) × $^1/_4$ = €10,000.
The settlement date is at the start of the notional deposit and the sum involved is discounted at the prevailing interest rate
= €10,000 × 1/(1 + 0.04/4) = €9,901
When this is added to the actual 4% received on deposit, the result is an effective interest rate of 6%.

(b) If the rate is 9% the company will receive interest of €2 million × 9% × $^1/_4$ = €45,000.
Here the company compensates the bank for the difference between 9% and 6% for the three month period.
The amount of interest differential = €2 million × (9% − 6%) × $^1/_4$ = €15,000
The settlement date is at the start and the sum involved is discounted at the prevailing interest rate.
= €15,000 × 1/(1 + 0.09/4) = €14,670 and this is subtracted from the actual 9% received over the next three months.
The overall effect of the FRA is that, regardless of the actual rate of interest, the company will receive interest at 6%. The effect is analogous to forward exchange contracts. When using an FRA the company is protected against adverse movements but cannot benefit from favourable movements.
When a company is operating an FRA for a borrowing exposure, then the compensation mechanism works in the opposite way. If rates go above the FRA rate the bank compensates the company, and if rates go below the FRA rate the company compensates the bank.

17.6 Futures

Derivatives, like futures, allow producers, traders and speculators to bet on future price fluctuations in order to speculate on or protect themselves from, unexpected changes in market prices. There have been a few famous financial disasters associated with futures (Appendix 17B).

A **future** is a standardised contract, covering the sale or purchase of a set quantity of a specific commodity, financial instrument or foreign currency at a set future date, at a price agreed between two parties. The contracts are binding to both parties. Currency futures are traded on a number of futures exchanges around the globe, the most important being the Chicago Mercantile Exchange. FINEX, which is connected to the New York Cotton Exchange, operates out of the International Financial Services Centre in Dublin and trades mainly in currency futures.

Currency futures have the following characteristics:

1. Not all currencies are traded and the major currencies available are £, ¥, € and SF. All contracts are priced in dollars.
2. Each currency has a specific contract size: €62,500; ¥12.5 million; €125,000; SF125,000.
3. The contract price is the price at which contracts can be bought or sold. This price is determined by trading on the floor of a futures exchange.
4. Settlement dates for futures contracts are at the end of March, June, September and December. The maximum cover available is up to 9 months ahead.
5. The minimum price movement is called a **tick** and it is based on the 4th decimal place of the currency quotation or 0.01% cent per unit of the contract size, e.g. $0.9881 = €1.
    In the case of a euro contract, the tick value is $125,000 \times 0.01\% = \$12.50$.
    The value of a tick depends on the contract size and these vary according to the currency involved. In the case of the yen the tick movement is per 100 yen as in example 17.10 below.
6. When you buy or sell a contract a deposit known as an **initial margin** is paid which is a small percentage of the total value of the contract. The market is highly regulated and on a daily basis a **variation margin** is received or paid, depending on the price movement of the futures contract and the position you have taken with a futures contract.

If a trader is afraid of an adverse currency movement, then the trader should take a futures position (i.e. buy or sell futures) that will result in a profit if the spot exchange rate moves against the company. This should compensate the company for the loss it incurs from the adverse movement in the spot rate. It is not necessarily a perfect hedge, as will be seen with an example.

Example 17.8 Currency future

Shades plc, a US company, wants to hedge an appreciation in the € against the $ and owes €125,000 in one month. The current futures price is 0.9245 $/€. Tick value for a € contract is $0.01% of 125,000 or $12.50. Show how a currency futures hedge would operate. Ignore the margin requirements.

Answer

As the company is afraid of the euro strengthening and the cost rising in dollars, the company should take a position to buy at the current strike price.

   The company should buy one € contract @ 0.9245 now and when payment is due sell one € contract.

   Assume the € strengthens and the futures price in one month's time has moved to 0.9370.

   To realise a futures gain or loss the futures trader must **close-out** (make an opposite trade) the futures position. In this example the trader should sell one euro future in one month's time.

   The profit in this case is calculated as follows:
(Number of contracts)(Number of ticks)(Tick value)

$$\text{No. of ticks} = \frac{0.9370 - 0.9245}{0.01} = 125 \text{ ticks}$$

The profit is therefore 1 contract × 125 ticks × $12.50 = $1,562.50

The company will, in one month's time, pay its debt buying the €125,000 at the prevailing spot rate at that time and as the euro has strengthened, the company will incur an extra cost.

The futures profit can then be set off against the loss the company will make when the company buys the € in the spot market.

The prices in the futures market do not necessarily move exactly in line with the spot market, which means futures contracts will not necessarily provide a perfect hedge. This is known as **basis risk**.

The exposure may not equate to an exact number of contracts, which again makes a perfect hedge unlikely.

Settlement date

Currency futures are available for a period of up to 9 months. This implies there is a choice of date relating to the futures contract needed. To hedge currency receipts and payments, a futures contract must have a settlement date **after** the date that the actual currency is needed. Usually the best hedge is achieved by selecting the contract which matures next **after** the actual cash is needed.

Example 17.9 Currency futures

Sterling futures: contract size £62,500; price in $ per £.

| Sep 1.5552 | Dec 1.5556 | Mar 1.5564 |

A British company will receive $2 million on 13 December and wants to hedge this exposure using currency futures. Show how a futures hedge would operate.

Answer

1. The appropriate futures date in this example is the December contract.
2. To find the number of contracts, the dollars are transferred to sterling and then multiples of £62,500. $2,000,000/1.5556 = £1.285,678 and dividing by 62,500 = 20.57 or 21 contracts approximately.
3. Today buy 21 sterling contracts at $1.5556 and close out on 13 December by selling 21 contracts.

If the dollar weakens, there will be a profit on the futures position, which will help compensate the loss in the value of the dollar cash inflow.

If the dollar strengthens, then there will be a loss on the futures position, but the company will receive more sterling for the dollar inflow.

Transactions not involving $

As the major currency futures are priced against the dollar, when a company is not exposed to a future dollar cash flow, the company needs to deal in more than one type of contract.

This complication makes the use of the currency futures markets much more complex than the use of forward markets and contributes to their lack of popularity.

Example 17.10 Futures and exposure not in dollars

A British company has purchased steel from Japan and needs to pay for this in yen (¥) in 90 days' time.

It can hedge this by buying Japanese yen futures.

However, on the futures market yen are bought with dollars. The company therefore needs to sell sterling futures (to get dollars) and buy yen futures (with dollars).

In 90 days it will close out by buying sterling futures and selling yen futures.

Suppose a UK company needs to buy ¥100 million in 90 days' time. Japanese yen futures are trading at $0.8106 per 100 yen and the sterling future is trading at $1.6250 per pound. Show how currency futures can be used to hedge the company's position.

Answer

Contract sizes are ¥12.5 million and £62,500.
The number of yen futures is ¥100 million/¥12.5 million = 8 contracts.
The UK company should buy 8 yen futures contracts.

$$\text{Buy 8 contracts (¥)} = \frac{8 \times 12.5\text{m} \times \$0.8106}{100} = \$810,600$$

This amount of dollars needs to be covered using sterling futures.
This is then converted at the sterling futures price, i.e. $810,600/1.6250 = £498,831.
This implies the number of sterling contracts is £498,831/62,500 = 7.98 rounded to 8 contracts.
The company should therefore sell 8 sterling futures.
Therefore the futures position to take is: buy 8 yen and sell 8 sterling now, and in 90 days sell 8 yen and buy 8 sterling contracts.

Interest rate futures

Interest rate futures offer a means of hedging against interest rate risk. If a company wishes to use an interest rate futures contract as a hedge against interest rate risk, the idea is to take a futures position that will result in a profit if the interest rate moves against the firm. This should compensate the firm for the loss it incurs from the adverse movement in the interest rate.

Short-term interest rate futures are notional fixed-term deposits, usually for three month periods starting at a specified time in the future. The outlay to buy/sell futures only involves a small initial deposit (margin) and so a company can hedge large exposures with a small outlay. The pricing of an interest rate futures contract is determined by prevailing interest rates and the price is quoted at a discount to 100. For example, if the rate is 8%, it is quoted as (100 – 8) = 92.00, and if the rate falls to 6.6%, the price is quoted as 93.40.

This implies that if a company is afraid of a rate rise, and therefore a falling futures price, it should sell contracts, and if a company is afraid of a rate fall, it should buy contracts. Many different types of contract exist, e.g. 3 month sterling.

This is a notional contract of £500,000 in size, with the minimum price movement known as one tick or 0.01% (0.0001) of the contract size. A full 1% move is equivalent to 100 ticks. The tick value for a 3 month sterling interest rate future is (£500,000) $(^1/_4)(0.01\%) = £12.50$.

Example 17.11   Interest rate future

In three months' time (June) a UK company will need to borrow £10 million for a six month period.

Current interest rates for such a loan are 8% per annum. The company treasurer expects interest rates to rise over the next three months. Three month sterling futures of £500,000 are available, with June futures priced at 92.50.

Show how a futures hedge would operate if interest rates rise by 2% and the futures price moves by 1.8%.

Answer

The number of contracts involved is £10 million/£500,000 = 20 contracts, but since cover is needed for six months and the contracts are for a notional 3 month period, the number of contracts is doubled to 40.

The company should sell 40 contracts at 92.50 and then **close out** the position when the futures price has moved in three months' time.

In this case the 1.8% move is a value of 90.70 (92.50 − 1.80), so buy 40 contracts at 90.70.

The futures profit is (92.50 − 90.70)/0.0001 = 180 ticks.

The profit is 180 ticks at £12.50 and 40 contracts = $180 \times £12.50 \times 40 = £90,000$

This £90,000 profit helps compensate for the increased cost of the loan.

The actual cost of the loan increases by $(2\%)(£10 \text{ million})(^1/_2) = £100,000$

The company actually pays $(10\%)(£10 \text{ million})(^1/_2) = £500,000$ *less* the profit on the futures market of £90,000 = £410,000

In this case there is 90% hedge efficiency, i.e. 90% of the potential increase in cost is covered.

The major interest rate futures available are in $, £, ¥, € and SF. Contract sizes: $1 million, £500,000; ¥100 million; €1 million; SF1 million.

These are all three month notional contract sizes, with a tick movement of 0.01%. The standardised nature of the contract size is a limitation of their use, as they cannot always be matched with specific interest rate exposures. There is also **basis risk** in that the price movement of the futures contract may not move in tandem with the underlying interest rate move.

17.7   Options

Currency and interest rate options are agreements giving the holder the right, **but not the obligation**, to buy or sell foreign currency at a stated rate of exchange, or borrow or lend at a specific interest rate, at some time in the future. They give the holder flexibility to take advantage of favourable movements in exchange rates or interest rates. Buying an option involves a cost, known as a **premium**. Options come in two forms, namely **over the counter (OTC)** and **exchange traded**.

Currency options OTCs

The main purpose of a currency option is to reduce exposure to adverse currency movements, while allowing the holder to profit from favourable currency movements. They are particularly useful where there is uncertainty about foreign currency receipts or payments, either in timing or amount.

A **call** option is an option to buy currency and a **put** option is an option to sell currency. Puts and calls can be subdivided into **American** and **European** options. The former can be exercised at any time up to their expiry date. The latter can be exercised only on the expiry date. The **exercise price** under the terms of the option contract is the stated rate of exchange.

Example 17.12 *OTC currency option*

Suppose the current spot offer rate is €1 = $1.02 and an Irish company has an outflow of $100,000 in three months' time. The company arranges an OTC call option contract to buy dollars from its bank at an exercise price of $1.02 for a premium of €1,000. The OTC contract will be tailor made to suit the company and should the company exercise the option, because the spot rate turns out to be less than $1.02, the Irish company will pay 100,000/1.02 = €98,039.22 *plus* the premium of €1,000 = €99,039.22.

If the exercise (strike) price is $1.02, the option is said to be **at the money**.

If the exercise price were less favourable to the company (€1 = $1.01), the option is **out of the money.**

If the exercise price is more favourable (€1 = $1.03), the option is **in the money**.

Example 17.13 *OTC currency option*

An Irish engineering company is tendering for a contract to build a bridge in Switzerland. The company costs the construction project at €18.5 million and tenders a bid at €20 million. The expected profit is therefore €1.5 million.

However the bid must be priced in Swiss francs. The current exchange rate is €1 = SF1.6 and so the company prices the bid at SF32 million. The contract is awarded in 6 months' time and assume, for simplicity, that the revenue of SF32 million is received up front, if the company is successful with its bid.

This is a classic example of uncertainty with regard to a possible foreign currency receipt. In this example it would be inappropriate to enter into a forward exchange contract, as this is a binding obligation and if the tender is unsuccessful, the company could be faced with an expensive close-out. The company would have to buy the currency at the spot rate in six months' time and sell it to the bank under the terms of the FEC.

Assume the company buys an OTC put option contract at the money (€1 = SF1.6) and the premium is €400,000.

There are four possible situations that could occur.

(a) The tender is unsuccessful and the Swiss franc strengthens. Abandon the option and lose €400,000.
(b) The tender is unsuccessful and the Swiss franc weakens. The company should buy SF36 million at the spot rate and sell it to the bank under the terms of the option.
(c) The tender is successful and the Swiss franc weakens. The company will have successfully covered this risk. Exercise the option.
(d) The tender is successful and the Swiss franc strengthens. The company should abandon the option and sell the SF32 million on the spot market and improve its profit on the construction project.

The currency option gives the company a lot of flexibility. However, the downside is the cost of the premium, which is an up-front payment.

Exchange traded options

These are standardised (like futures) with respect to the amount of currency and maturity dates. They are available only in certain currencies and are traded on an options exchange. The most important currency options are those on the Chicago Mercantile Exchange and the Philadelphia Stock Exchange.

The major currencies available are £, ¥, € and SF and all contracts are priced in dollars. Contract size: £31,250; ¥6.25million; €62,500; SF62,500. The following example illustrates their usage.

Example 17.14 Traded currency option

Stark plc is a UK-based company and expects to receive $6 million in September (3 months' time). The company wants to use currency options to hedge its position. Since it needs to buy pounds using dollars, the company can buy September sterling **call** options. The price of these are quoted on the Philadelphia Stock Exchange as follows:

Sterling £31,250 contracts	September calls	
	Exercise price	Cents per £
	$1.450/£	5.70
	$1.500/£	1.45

The current spot rate $/£ is 1.4850 – 1.4900

Show how currency options could be used at a strike price of $1.450/£.

Answer

The UK company first needs to identify the number of contracts involved.
At $1.450 the company would buy $6 million/1.45 = £4,137,931

This amount of sterling is then divided by £31,250 to give 132.41 or approximately 132 contracts.

The contracts will cover $132 \times 31{,}250 \times 1.45 = \$5{,}981{,}250$ and the remaining $18,750 will be sold at the spot rate.

The premium cost here is 5.7 cents per £ or $31{,}250 \times 132 \times 5.7$ cents $= \$235{,}125$

This will cost $\$235{,}125/1.4850 = £158{,}333$ at spot rate.

The company policy will then be:

(a) If the spot rate is above 1.45, the option will be exercised and the net outcome will be: $\$5{,}981{,}250/1.45$ *less* $£158{,}333 = £3{,}966{,}667$, and extra dollars ($18,750) need to be sold at the spot rate in three months' time.

(b) If the September spot rate is less than $1.45, the option would not be exercised and the dollars received would be sold on the spot market.

For example, if the spot rate is $1.35 the net outcome would have been as follows:

$6 million/1.35 *less* $£158{,}333 = £4{,}286{,}111$ receipt.

In the OTC and exchange traded examples above, the companies involved faced foreign currency cash inflows. The fear in both cases was that the foreign currencies would weaken. The companies were in effect buying an upper limit on the exchange rate. This is known as a **cap**. If the foreign currencies were cash outflows, the fear would have been that the currencies would strengthen and therefore give a lower amount of foreign currency. In this case a lower limit option can be bought called a **floor**.

Figure 17.1 Cap floor and collar

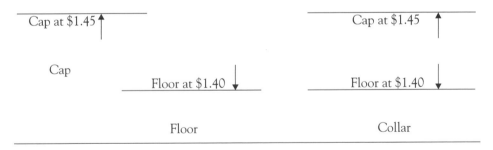

Caps and floors can be combined to produce what is known as a collar. The idea behind a collar is to reduce the cost of the premium by sacrificing some of the potential gains. A collar involves buying a call and selling a put or buying a put and selling a call.

Example 17.15 OTC currency collar

A company in Ireland has to pay £300,000 sterling in three months' time and is afraid that sterling will strengthen over that time. It decides to use an OTC option contract to cover its exposure. The current exchange rate is €1 = £0.65 sterling and the company arranges with its bank an OTC call at €1 = £0.64 for the purchase of £300,000 sterling in three months' time. The bank charges a premium of 3 cents per £ giving a premium cost of $300{,}000 \times €0.03 = €9{,}000$.

The company considers the premium to be too expensive and to reduce the cost of the premium it writes a put at £0.67, for which the bank agrees to pay a premium of 2 cents per £. The company is telling the bank that if the rate goes above £0.67, the company will still accept £0.67 per euro.

The company is now guaranteed to operate between £0.64 and £0.67. In this case the company has sacrificed some of the potential gains beyond €1 = £0.67, but has reduced the cost of the premium to $300,000 \times €0.01 = €3,000$.

The net premium in a collar depends on the exercise prices for both call and put. A **zero cost collar** is possible and both options in a collar are for the same amount of foreign currency.

The factors that will determine the option premium include the current spot rate, the exercise price, the volatility of the exchange rate (measured as a standard deviation), the time duration to expiry and the interest rate differential between the currencies.

Interest rate options

These again can be subdivided into OTCs and exchange traded. Interest rate options grant the buyer the right but **not the obligation** to deal at an agreed rate of interest (strike rate) at a future maturity date. The term **interest rate guarantee (IRG)** is used for an option for a single period of up to one year. Tailor-made OTCs can be purchased from the major banks, with specific values, periods of maturity and rates of agreed interest. The cost of the option involves the up-front payment of a premium, as in currency options.

An interest rate **cap** is an option which sets an interest rate ceiling. A **floor** is an option which sets a lower limit to interest rates. A **collar** is an arrangement involving a cap and a floor.

Example 17.16 OTC interest rate option

Cabbage plc is an Irish company needing to borrow €10 million in three months' time for a period of six months. The current rate of interest for company borrowings is 5.5% and the company treasurer wants to avoid rates above 7%. The treasurer buys a cap at 7% from her bank for a premium of 0.25% of the size of the loan. The premium is thought to be too expensive (€25,000) and so the treasurer sells a floor at 6% to the bank for a premium for 0.2%.

The company now knows that if rates go above 7% the company will only pay 7%. However, if rates are below 6%, the company will have to pay 6%, because the company has sacrificed the potential gain of reduced rates below 6%. The net cost of the premium is much reduced, however, at 0.05% of the amount borrowed (€5,000), and the company knows its cost of borrowing will be between 6% and 7%.

Exchange-traded interest rate options are available as options on interest rate futures. They give the buyer the right to buy (call) or sell (put) a futures contract on or before the expiry of the option at a specified price.

Example 17.17 Traded interest rate option

If we use example 17.11 in which a UK company, in March, needs to borrow £10 million in three months' time for a period of six months and an extract from the *Financial Times* on June short sterling options is as follows:

Strike price	Calls	Puts	premium based on points of 1%
92.50	0.05	0.10	
93.00	0.02	0.35	

Since the company is afraid of a rise in interest rates, the futures position to take is to sell now (June puts) and buy back at a lower futures price if rates rise.

The premium is set at points of 1%, so the put futures price of 92.50 has a premium cost of 0.10 (of 1%) to sell contracts. As explained earlier, the number of contracts is 40 and in buying 40 put options the premium involved is £500,000 × 0.10/100 × 40 = £20,000.

If interest rates rise by 2% and the futures price falls by 1.8%, the company will exercise its right to sell the futures at 92.50 and buy them at 90.70 (answer 17.11).

The profit is £90,000 *less* the premium cost of £20,000 and this will help compensate the company for the increased cost of borrowing.

The company will actually pay £10 million × 10% × $^1/_2$ *less* the futures profit of £70,000 = £430,000.

If the interest rate falls and the futures price rises, the company will abandon its put options. It will have a reduced cost of borrowing but will have lost the premium of £20,000.

17.8 Swaps

This is an arrangement whereby two organisations contractually agree to exchange payments on different terms, for example, in different currencies or different interest rates. The currency swap market was developed in the 1980s. Companies often found they could borrow one currency relatively cheaply while the currency they needed was relatively expensive. By finding a counterparty in the opposite position, they could get together and arrange a swap in which both companies would be better off. Swaps are used extensively by large companies and banks to capitalise on their comparative advantages in different debt markets.

Currency swaps usually involve an initial exchange of principal, a periodic exchange of interest payments during the life of the swap, and finally a re-exchange of principal at the end of the term of the swap. They are traded on the OTC market on terms that are negotiated individually by the counterparties to the swap.

Example 17.18 Currency swap

A US multinational company needs a €100 million loan to finance a new subsidiary in Ireland. It has been offered a dollar loan from its bank at 6% and a euro loan at 7.5%. The company has identified through a merchant bank an Irish multinational company which needs to raise $105 million to finance a major expansion in the US.

The Irish company has been offered a dollar loan at 6.5% and a euro loan at 6.7%. All the interest rates are fixed rates (fixed to fixed rate swap).

The two companies agree to raise five year loans for the amounts mentioned in their respective home currencies to obtain the most favourable rates. They sign a currency swap contract at an exchange rate of €1 = $1.05, in which each company agrees to hand over the proceeds of the loans.

In this simplistic example they both receive the currency they need, but at more favourable rates. The US company pays a rate of 6.7%, not 7.5%, and the Irish company pays 6% and not 6.5%. The merchant bank mentioned above would receive a fee for its services, which would reduce some of the interest savings.

Swaps are flexible since they can be arranged in any size, and are reversible. The transaction costs are low, only amounting to legal fees, since there is no premium to be paid. Liability on the principal is not transferred in a swap and the parties are liable to counterparty risk (if one party defaults on the agreement to pay interest, the original borrower remains liable to the lender). Currency swaps can be fixed to fixed rate (see example above), fixed to floating rate and floating to floating rate.

Interest rate swaps are transactions that exploit different interest rates in different markets for borrowing, to reduce interest costs for either fixed or floating rate loans. An interest rate swap is an arrangement whereby two companies swap interest rate commitments with each other. A company which has debt at a fixed rate of interest can make a swap so that it ends up paying interest at a variable rate and vice versa. The parties to the swap retain their obligations to the original lenders. This means the parties must accept counterparty risk.

Example 17.19 Interest rate swap

Company A has a good credit rating and can borrow at a fixed rate of 11% or at a variable rate equal to Euribor. It wants to borrow at a variable rate.

Company B is a company with a lower credit rating and it wants to borrow at a fixed rate. Company B can borrow at a fixed rate of 12.5% or at a variable rate of Euribor *plus* 0.5%.

Without a swap company A would borrow at Euribor and company B would borrow at 12.5%.

Show what benefit is available to both companies (arbitrage opportunity) if they engage in a swap arrangement.

Answer

In this example the arbitrage opportunity can be identified as follows:

	A	B	Difference
Fixed	11%	12.5%	1.5%
Floating	Euribor	Euribor + 0.5%	0.5%
Difference in differences or arbitrage opportunity			1%

This represents the potential gain which can be made out of a swap arrangement.

Each company must borrow at the rate in which it has comparative advantage (fixed rate for A and floating rate for B). There are an infinite number of swap arrangements that can occur, depending on the negotiating skills of the respective treasurers.

Suggested swap

With a swap A borrows at 11% fixed and B at Euribor + 0.5%

Both companies have agreed a swap in which A will pay B a variable interest rate of Euribor and B will pay A a fixed interest rate of 11.5%. Evaluate whether both companies can benefit from the proposed swap.

Answer

1. A will pay (11% to the bank), (Euribor), in the swap and receive 11.5% under the terms of the swap.

$$(11\%) + (\text{Euribor}) + 11.5\% = (\text{Euribor} - 0.5\%)$$

Without a swap A would have borrowed at a variable rate of Euribor and so the cost is reduced by 0.5%.

2. B will pay (Euribor + 0.5%) to the bank, (11.5%) in the swap and receive Euribor in the swap.

$$(\text{Euribor} + 0.5\%) + (11.5\%) + \text{Euribor} = 12\%$$

Without a swap the fixed rate would have been 12.5% and again the cost is reduced by 0.5%

To determine the terms of the swap above the following pro forma can be used to move from the original interest paid to the desired result.

	Company A	Company B
Pays to the bank	(11%)	(Euribor + 0.5%)
Pays in the swap		
Receives in the swap		
Net interest cost	(Euribor – 0.5%)	(12%)

By entering any figure into any slot of the pro forma the other figures must automatically balance out.

Here is one of many possible solutions.

	Company A	Company B
Pays to the bank	(11%)	(Euribor + 0.5%)
Pays in the swap	(Euribor + 0.5%)	(12%)
Receives in the swap	12%	Euribor + 0.5%
Net interest cost	(Euribor – 0.5%)	(12%)

A major advantage of swaps over other derivatives such as traded options, forwards and futures is that they can be used to lock into interest and exchange rates for much longer periods of time.

17.9 Swaptions

Many hybrid derivatives now exist and one of the most popular is the swaption. As the name suggests, they are a combination of an option and a swap. They give the holder the option to become involved in a swap. For example, a company might buy an OTC swaption from its bank, giving it the right, but not the obligation, to enter into an interest rate swap with the bank at or before a specified time in the future. A European style swaption is exercisable only on the maturity date, whereas the American style swaption is exercisable on any day during the exercise period.

Example 17.20 Swaption

Today is 1 January 2001 and your company has a variable rate loan of €2 million which is due for renewal on 31 June 2004. The current rate of interest is 7% and the company is afraid that rates will rise in the near future. The bank the company deals with has offered an American style swaption as follows:

Interest rate 7.75%. Exercise period 1 July 2001 to 31 December 2001. Maturity date is 30 June 2001.

Premium is €40,000. Under what circumstances would your company gain from exercising the swaption?

Answer

This swaption would be exercised if the interest rate rose above 7.75% in the next six months. The cost over the remaining three years is €2 million × 7.75% × 3 + €40,000 = €505,000.

This represents an effective rate of €505,000/3/€2 million = 8.417%

The average rate of interest would have to exceed 8.417% over the next three years for the swaption to be beneficial. If the interest rate falls over the maturity period, the swaption would not be exercised and the company would take advantage of the lower interest rate. The premium is lost, however, and should be viewed as the price paid for the possibility of taking advantage of lower interest rates.

17.10 The Irish experience of the OTC market

Box 7.2 Foreign currency products used by Irish corporates

Product	Usage	Features
Foreign exchange forward contracts	The most common form of FX cover used in Ireland— used widely by all customers covering forward	It allows for certainty of exchange rates and leaves management to concentrate on other aspects of the business besides FX.
Participating forward**	Used regularly	There is **full** protection from adverse movements, with **some** opportunity for gains, without paying a premium up front. $\longrightarrow$

Box 7.2 *cont.*

| Zero-cost cylinder | Used regularly | There is potential benefit by surrendering some protection, without paying a premium up front. |
| Currency options | Used Infrequently* | It provides full protection/insurance and allows the freedom to benefit fully from favourable market movements, but a premium must be paid up-front. |

* Currency options are not very popular with Irish corporates for the following reasons:

- A premium must be paid up front.
- It may be written into the company's articles that options may not be dealt as part of the treasury policy.
- At board of management level there is quite often resistance due to lack of understanding.

** A participating forward involves buying a currency option for part of your exposure and a forward exchange contract for the rest.

Box 17.3 Interest rate products used by Irish corporates

Product	Usage	Features
Interest rate swap (IRS)	The most widely used way of managing interest rates	Gives full protection from movements in interest rates. They are very flexible in terms of repayments.
Forward rate agreement (FRA)	Widely used	Fixes an interest rate now for the loan to be taken out in the future. Allows protection against rising rates and allows planning of cash flows.
Interest rate cap/floor	Widely used	Full protection from adverse rate movements but freedom to benefit fully from favourable movements. A premium must be paid either up front or over the life of the contract.
Interest rate collar (zero-cost)	Widely used	Reduces the cost of interest rate protection and gives full protection from adverse interest rate movements while surrendering some potential benefit of favourable rate movements. No premium to be paid, hence zero cost. $\longrightarrow$

Box 7.3 *cont.*

Product	Usage	Features
Swaption	Used infrequently	Full protection from adverse movements and freedom to benefit from favourable movements. The swaption can be negotiated with any bank. A premium must be paid.
Interest rate guarantee (FRA option)	Not used very often	Full protection from adverse movements and freedom to benefit from favourable movements. A premium must be paid.
Source: Allied Irish Banks, May 2000		

17.11 Issues arising

Companies should have a clear strategy concerning how much foreign currency and interest rate risk they are prepared to take. A highly risk-averse or defensive strategy of hedging all transactions is expensive in terms of commission costs, but recognises that floating rates are very unpredictable and can cause major losses. When formulating hedging strategies, it is important for companies to be clear about their objectives, to identify and quantify exposures and select appropriate risk management techniques. A sensible strategy to adopt may be to hedge as much as possible using internal hedging techniques and cover any remaining exposures with appropriate external techniques. Bank-created products or OTCs may be more suitable for smaller companies as they are likely to lack the experience and knowledge associated with traded derivatives.

Risk management introduces greater certainty to the exchange and interest rates that companies face and while recent derivative disasters have occurred, they stemmed from their misuse and lack of understanding rather than fundamental problems with the instruments themselves.

SUMMARY

- Both foreign currency and interest rate risks need to be managed in a company.
- Exchange rate risks include transaction, economic and translation exposure.
- Interest rate risks face companies with cash surpluses and borrowings.
- Companies should form policies to manage these risks internally as much as possible.
- External techniques include forwards, futures, options, swaps and swaptions.
- Companies should specify hedging objectives, quantify exposures and select appropriate hedging techniques.

QUESTIONS

1. What is transaction exposure to foreign currency movements?
2. What is the difference between a forward exchange contract and forward rate agreement?
3. Describe techniques available to reduce foreign exchange risk?
4. What is the difference between an OTC option and a traded option?
5. Describe four techniques available to hedge interest rate risk?
6. ◆ An Irish company has bought goods from a US supplier and must pay $10 million for them in three months' time. The company's finance director wishes to hedge against the foreign exchange risk and has asked you to help out. Assume that the company needs to borrow to make any payments (cash poor).

   You are asked to assess three methods:

   (a) forward exchange markets
   (b) money market and
   (c) lead payments.

   The following annual interest rates and exchange rates are currently available:

US dollar rates		Euro rates		$/€ exchange rate	
Bid	Offer	Bid	Offer	Spot	1.0625 – 1.0635
7%	8%	3%	4%	3 months forward	1.10 – 1.05c dis.

   Ignoring commission costs, consider the three methods available. What is the cost of forward cover?
7. An Irish company is to receive $10 million from a US importer in three months' time. The company's finance director wishes to hedge against the foreign exchange risk and has asked you to help out. You are asked to assess a forward exchange market and a money market hedge with the information in question 6 above.
8. ◆ Assume it is now 1 January and your company is arranging a six month €6 million loan at an interest rate based on 6 months Euribor to commence in 6 months' time on 1 July. You want to hedge against an increase in interest on this loan by using an FRA. So on 1 January you buy a 6 × 12 FRA from a bank at 9%.

   Calculate the amount payable by the company or the bank if on the settlement date, which is 1 July, the six months Euribor has moved to 13% or 7%.
9. ◆ A group of companies controlled from the USA has subsidiaries in the UK, Italy and France.

   At 17 February inter-company indebtedness is as follows:

Debtor	Creditor	Amount
UK	Italy	L240 million
UK	Switzerland	SF480,000
Switzerland	Italy	L180 million
Italy	UK	£74,000
Italy	Switzerland	SF375,000

The central treasury of the American MNC uses the following exchange rates for netting off inter-company imbalances:

$$\$1 = L1,680 = £0.68 = SF1.88$$

Calculate the net payments to be made between the subsidiaries after netting off the imbalances.

10. An Irish company has bought goods from a US supplier, and must pay $1 million for them in three months' time. The company's finance director wishes to hedge against the foreign exchange risk and has asked you to help out. You are asked to assess the use of futures contracts and forward exchange contracts.

    € futures are currently priced at $1.0600 with a contract size of €125,000 and tick value of $12.50.

	$/€
Spot	0.8625 – 0.8635
3 months forward	0.80 – 0.75c pm

Compare a forward exchange contract as against a futures contract. Assess both methods if, with hindsight, the spot turns out to be 0.9450 – 0.9460 and the futures price has moved to 0.9400.

11. An Irish company, Dosh plc, trades with several countries. Much of this trade involves credit. Today is 1 June 2001 and the following data relates to existing future trade:

	Date	Receive	Pay
Australia	1/9/01	A$120,000	£40,000
Japan	1/9/01	¥400million	¥320million
France	1/9/01	F1 million	Nil

Exchange rates versus the £ Irish			
Spot	$2.1400–2.1425	¥128.5–129.3	F8.32894
3 month	2–2.5c dis	1–1.5¥ dis.	F8.32894

Interest rates	Offer	Bid
Ireland	6%	5%
Australia	8%	7%
Japan	9%	8%
France	6%	5%

Find the Irish £ position on 1/9/01 using forward exchange contracts and the international money markets.

12. If the above trades were reversed as follows:

	Date	Pay	Receive
Australia	1/9/01	A$120,000	£40,000
Japan	1/9/01	¥400million	¥320million
France	1/9/01	F1 million	Nil

Find the Irish £ position on 1/9/01 using forward exchange contracts and the international money markets.

13. On 1 March, an Irish company, Cabbage plc, purchased goods from Switzerland and the US.

Payment for the Swiss goods costing SF850,000 is due in 6 months' time, while the payment of $320,000 for the American goods is due in 3 months.

Market information		
Exchange rates	$/€	SF/€
Spot	1.0480 – 1.4510	1.0840 – 1.0844
3 month fwd	1.0542 – 1.0572	1.0744 – 1.0749
6 month fwd	1.0604 – 1.0635	1.0649 – 1.0652
Interest rates		
Per annum rates	Offer rate	Bid rate
Ireland	7%	5%
US	9.5%	7.5%
Swiss	6%	4%

Assess the use of forward contracts, money market operations and lead payment in these trades.

14. Spondulix plc, an Irish company, will have a cash outflow of $900,000 in three months. You are asked to assess the use of futures contracts as a means of hedging exchange rate risk.

Euro futures contracts are currently priced at $1.1000 with a contract size of €125,000 and tick value of $12.50.

$/€ exchange rate

Spot   1.0900 – 1.0910

How should the hedge operate? Evaluate the effect of the risk management policy, if after three months € futures are trading at $1.0500 and the spot rate has moved to

Spot (in 3 months) 1.0450 – 1.0460

15. Scobie plc is a US company which imports goods from Germany. Scobie is due to pay €260,000 in 30 days' time and is afraid the € will strengthen during this time. It wants to use currency futures to hedge its position.

The spot rate today is 0.9221 $/€ and the € futures contract rate is 0.9247 $/€.

In 30 days' time the spot rate is 0.9351 $/€ and the futures price has moved to 0.9367 $/€.

How should the hedge operate and evaluate the effect of the risk management policy?

16. An English importer has to pay $6 million in September (6 months' time). The company wants to use currency options to hedge its position. Since it needs to buy dollars using pounds, the company can buy September sterling put options. The price of these are quoted on the Philadelphia Stock Exchange as follows:

    Sterling £31,250 contracts—September puts

Exercise price	Cents per £	
$1.500/£	1.45	The current spot rate is 1.4850 – 1.4900

Show how currency options could be used at a strike price of $1.500/£.

17. An Irish company has a payment of $2.8 million to make in three months' time on 1 September. The current exchange rates are as follows:

Spot Euro/$	1.0610 – 1.0661
3 months forward	1.0656 – 1.0715

The company can borrow at 7% and is currently in overdraft.

Euro market traded options prices (125,000 euro contract size) in the US are as follows:

Exercise price ($/€)	June contracts		September contracts	
	Calls	Puts	Puts	Calls
0.938	0.560	1.205	1.015	1.570

The option premia are in cents per euro and are payable up front.

Compare a forward exchange contract to an options hedge strategy and comment on your findings if the spot rate on 1 September is $1= £1.100.

18. It is 1 June and Dropkick plc, operating out of London, needs to borrow £6 million in three months' time for a period of six months. For the type of loan finance which Dropkick would use, the rate of interest is currently 13% per year and the treasurer is unwilling to pay a higher rate. The treasurer is considering interest rate futures and interest rate guarantees as risk management techniques. The current price of three-month futures is 87.25 (contract size £500,000 and tick value 0.01% of the contract size).

    Interest rate guarantees can be purchased at 13% for a premium of 0.25% of the size of the loan to be guaranteed.

    Calculate the effect of using the futures market or interest rate guarantees under the following situations:

    (a) if interest rates increase by 2% and the futures price moves by 2%
    (b) if interest rates increase by 2% and the futures price moves by 1.75%
    (c) if interest rates fall by1.5% and the futures price moves by 1.25%.

The time value of money, taxation and the margin requirements can be ignored.

19.◆ In three months' time (June) an Irish-based company will need to invest €20 million for a six month period.

Current interest rates for such deposits are 8% per annum. The company treasurer expects interest rates to fall over the next three months.

Three month futures €1,000,000 points of 100% are available, with June futures priced at 92.50.

Show how a futures hedge would operate, if interest rates rise by 2% and the futures price moves by 2%.

20.◆ Two companies are considering entering into a swap agreement with each other. Their corresponding borrowing rates are as follows:

	Floating rate	Fixed rate
Company X	Euribor	12%
Company Y	Euribor + 0.3%	13.5%

Company X wants a floating rate loan of €10 million, while company Y wants a fixed rate loan of €10 million.

At what rate will company A (floating) and company Y (fixed) pay, if they engage in a swap agreement, with the benefits of the swap split equally between them? Suggest a swap arrangement.

21. Walsh Power plc has €20 million borrowed at a floating rate of Euribor + 0.75%, with a three month roll-over. The company treasurer has decided to look at alternative techniques for hedging this exposure. The four alternatives available to the company are as follows:

(a) Buy a cap at 10% for a premium of 1% per annum.
(b) Buy a collar between 8% and 10% for 0.25% per annum.
(c) The company bank has offered a forward rate agreement at 10% interest.
(d) Do not hedge the exposure.

Show the effective interest rate paid in the next quarter if the Euribor moves to 6.25%, 8.25% or 10.25%.

APPENDIX 17A Theories of Exchange rate determination

There are many factors which influence a currency's exchange rate, such as a country's balance of payments position, government policy carried out by central banks, the activity of speculators and the comparative differences in inflation rates and interest rates in trading countries. Both inflation and interest rate differentials have formal theories attached.

Purchasing power parity (PPP) theory predicts that the exchange rate of a foreign currency depends on the relative purchasing power of each currency in its own country and that spot exchange rates will move over time according to relative price changes (inflation rates). Countries with relatively high inflation rates tend to depreciate over time.

Purchasing power parity can be expressed in the following formula

$$\text{Future rate of \$/£} = \text{Spot rate \$/£} \times \frac{(1 + \text{US inflation rate})}{(1 + \text{UK inflation rate})}$$

Example

Suppose the spot rate is £1 = \$1.5 and inflation in the US and the UK are expected to be 10% and 5% respectively over the next year. What is the expected spot rate next year using PPP theory?

Answer

Expected spot rate $= 1.50 \times \frac{(1.10)}{(1.05)} = 1.5714$ or £1 = \$1.5714 next year, i.e. the dollar is weaker.

Interest rate parity (international Fisher effect) links the foreign exchange markets and the international money markets. Currencies with relatively higher interest rates than their trading partners are expected to depreciate, and hence the high interest rates are seen by foreign investors as a compensating payment for future currency depreciation. The international Fisher effect shows how differences in interest rates indicate the difference between the spot rate and the forward rate as follows:

$$\text{Forward rate of \$/£} = \text{Spot rate \$/£} \times \frac{(1 + \text{nominal US interest rate})}{(1 + \text{nominal UK interest rate})}$$

If the same example above is used and the differential rates relate to nominal interest rates instead of inflation rates, the result will be a forward rate of £1 = \$1.5714.

APPENDIX 17B Risk Management Disasters and VAR analysis

There have been a number of high-profile risk management disasters in the 1990s. Among these were:

1. Metallgesellschaft. A subsidiary built up large positions in oil futures and the resulting fall in oil prices lead to massive losses (\$1.3 billion).
2. Baring's bank. The infamous Nick Leeson, a trader working out of Baring's subsidiary in Singapore, built up a huge unauthorised position in futures and options. The bank lost \$1.3 billion.
3. Daiwa bank. Toshihide Iguchi, a bond trader, lost \$1.1 billion over an eleven year period.
4. Sumitoma Corporation. Yasuo Hamanaka, a copper trader, lost \$1.8 billion over a ten year period on unauthorised trades.

Risk management is one of the most important topics in the finance world and quantifying risk is an important function of the financial manager. These examples invariably reflect poor control systems and one of the more recent developments has been **value at risk (VAR)** analysis. In the past decade the value at risk system was developed to help quantify such risks. A survey by the New York University Stern School of Business found that 60% of pension funds used value at risk (Linsmeier and Pearson, 1996), and the use of VAR is continuing to grow among financial institutions and large companies.

Value at risk is the maximum amount that a company can lose over some target period — the maximum likely loss. So VAR refers to a particular amount of money, the maximum amount a company is likely to lose over a period, at a given level of confidence. There is a VAR estimation procedure, a numerical or statistical procedure to produce VAR figures. VAR has its roots in the portfolio theory developed by Markowitz in the 1950s, but is applicable across a range of different corporate exposures. These exposures include investment decisions, hedging decisions, managing portfolios, credit risk, liquidity risk, operational risk and strategic risk management.

One of the problems with VAR analysis is that it attempts to forecast future losses using past data, i.e. it assumes the past is replicated in the future. If there is a major disturbance like a stock market collapse, losses may be much greater than VAR would predict. VAR models, like all models, are based on assumptions that may not be valid in certain circumstances. The important point of the criticism is to be aware of the limitations of any system when interpreting results.

A detailed look at the value at risk techniques is outside the scope of this textbook, but those who need to study this area further can read the references.

Linsmeier, T., Pearson N., *Risk Measurement: An Introduction to Value at Risk*, Mimeo, University of Illinois at Urbana-Champaign 1996.

Dowd, K., *Beyond Value at Risk. The New Science of Risk Management*, Wiley, 1998.

18
Portfolio Performance taking account of Risk

CHAPTER OBJECTIVES

At the end of this chapter the student should:

1. understand the importance of taking explicit account of risk in portfolio selection, performance and evaluation
2. understand the concept of **safety-first** criteria as they relate to portfolio selection
3. understand and be able to apply numerically the three safety-first criteria detailed in this chapter, viz. Roy, Kataoka and Telser
4. understand the concept of **risk-adjusted** portfolio return measures
5. understand and be able to apply numerically the four risk-adjusted portfolio performance evaluations detailed in this chapter, viz. Sharpe, Treynor, Jensen and the differential (total risk) return measure.

INTRODUCTION

Investment selection and performance evaluation tends to focus primarily on return only, i.e. investors base their perception of the attractiveness of different funds/portfolios on the level of return achieved over, say, a three to five year period. The level of risk inherent in a portfolio is often addressed by the potential investor through the advertised risk stance of the fund, e.g. a risk-averse investor may choose a capital-guaranteed fund or a low-risk equity fund, while a risk-taking investor may opt for an aggressively managed equity fund.

This chapter deals with a number of approaches to investment evaluation and fund selection which specifically and explicitly address the issue of risk.

Two specific approaches are dealt with:

- Safety-first investment criteria, and
- Risk-adjusted return measures.

18.1 Safety-first investment selection criteria

Suppose the following return information on fund performance over a thirty year period is available for three funds—no other information is available:

Fund	A	B	C
Average annual return (%)	8	10	13

If you were investing in one fund, which one would you choose?

Most investors would choose fund C since, on average, it has paid the highest return over the past 30 years.

Now suppose that information is also available on the standard deviation of returns.

Fund	A	B	C
Average annual return (%)	8	10	13
Standard deviation (%)	4	9	15

Which fund would you now choose?

The answer is no longer as clear cut. Different investors would choose different funds reflecting their attitude to risk.

Safety-first investment selection criteria may assist investors in making a choice as to the most desirable fund to invest in.

The basis of this approach to investment selection is to attempt to limit the risk of unacceptable or unsatisfactory out-turns.

Clearly the investor cannot control the return on an investment, but may be anxious to avoid a disaster or avoid making losses. Investors may give primacy to the avoidance of unsatisfactory out-turns over and above expected returns.

Take a simple example. Suppose a family has a stock of wealth of £100,000 which it can invest in order to earn a return, but has no other income. The family requires an absolute minimum of £7,000 each year to live on. A 7% return on its investment will meet its minimum requirement. A return above 7% is a bonus and will allow it to do many more things like take a holiday, decorate the house etc. Nowhere, however, is it guaranteed a 7% return. The family is most concerned with avoiding disaster and less concerned with the potential for extra returns. It therefore wishes to invest in a fund that is **least likely** to underperform its minimum requirement, i.e. achieve a 7% return.

There are three main approaches to safety-first investment selection, each called after the author who devised the approach. These are:

- Roy
- Kataoka
- Telser.

The basis of each of the approaches, together with a numerical example, is given below. Further examples are given at the end of the chapter.

Note: In order to keep the mathematics simple, it is assumed that the portfolio returns are normally distributed. An alternative approach where this condition is not met is suggested.

Roy's criterion

The basis of this approach is to minimise the probability that the portfolio return is below some specified lower limit, i.e.

$$\text{Minimise prob. } (R_p < R_l) \qquad\qquad 18.1$$

where
R_p = the portfolio return, and
R_l = the lower limit or lowest acceptable return.

The best portfolio is the one that has the lowest probability of producing a return below the specified level R_l.

Here the investor **subjectively** selects a lower acceptable return R_l, say, 7%, below which she does not want the portfolio return to go. The criterion then **objectively** selects the preferred portfolio on the basis that it has the least chance of falling below R_l.

Note: Since the lower limit is a subjective choice by the investor, different investors will choose different lower limits and Roy's criterion will select a different preferred portfolio for each investor.

Assuming that the distribution of portfolio returns is normal, then the best portfolio is the one where R_l is the maximum number of standard deviations below the mean.

Figure 18.1 Distribution of portfolio returns

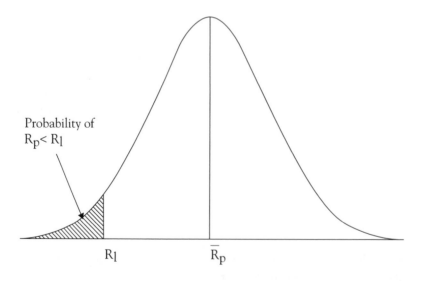

Probability of
$R_p < R_l$

R_l $\overline{R}_p$

The best portfolio is one where $R_p - R_l$ = maximum number of standard deviations (σ)

Example 18.1 Roy's safety-first criterion

Let 5% be the minimum desired return.

Fund	A	B	C
Mean return	10	14	17
Standard deviation (σ)	5	4	8

What Roy's criterion establishes is the probability of getting a return below the lower limit (in this case 5%) based on the historical mean and standard deviation of the returns from the portfolio. In the case of fund C, for example, the mean return is 17% and the standard deviation is 8%. To get a return of 5% means falling 12 percentage points (17 − 5) below the mean. This is 1.5 standard deviations below the mean. The probability of this occurring in a normal distribution can be read off from the standard normal distribution table provided in the Appendix and is 7.7%. The results for all three funds are shown below.

Fund	A	B	C
Mean return	10	14	17
Standard deviation (σ)	5	4	8
Difference from 5% (σ)	−1	−2.25	−1.5
Probability of return <5%	16%	1.2%	7.7%

A has a 16% chance of delivering a return of 5% or less (i.e. about once in six years), B has a 1.2% chance of such a return (about once in over 80 years), while C has a 7.7% chance (once in 13 years). Therefore B is the preferred portfolio.

As discussed above, different investors may set different lower limits.

Example 18.2 Roy's safety-first criterion

Let 12% be the minimum desired return and repeat the analysis above.

Fund	A	B	C
Mean return	10	14	17
Standard deviation (σ)	5	4	8
Difference from 12% (σ)	+0.4	−0.5	−0.625
Probability of return <12%	65.5%	30.9%	26.6%

Here C has the least chance of delivering a return below 5% (little over once every 4 years) compared to A (about 2 years in 3) and B (little less than once in 3 years) and so C is the preferred portfolio.[1]

Kataoka's criterion

The basis of this approach is to maximise the lower limit subject to the probability that the portfolio return, being less than the lower limit, is not greater than some specified value.

Unlike Roy's criterion, where the investor specifies a minimum acceptable **return** level, in Kataoka's criterion, the **subjective** input by the investor is in the form of an acceptable **risk** level. In other words, the investor accepts that in a certain percentage of the time (investment periods) the return will fall below some level, let's call it a **floor**. He is prepared to accept that once in, say, every twenty periods (5% of the time) or once in every 15 periods (7% of the time) the return will fall below the floor. Each fund will have a different floor below which it falls, say, 7% of the time. The **objective** selection criterion is then to identify the fund which produces the highest floor.

Let α = specified risk level

Criterion is

Maximise R_l
Subject to probability $(R_p < R_l) \leq \alpha$ 18.2

The subjective selection is α, i.e. a risk level acceptable to the investor.

Objective criterion is to select the portfolio with the highest possible lower value (floor) satisfying the constraint.

Let α = 5%. This means that the investor is prepared to accept a 1 in 20 chance of falling below some floor level.

Once again assuming that the returns from the portfolio are normally distributed, a number can be derived below which the return from the fund will fall only 5% of the time (and by definition above which the return will lie 95% of the time). From the standard normal distribution tables it can be seen that the bottom 5% of the distribution (5% in the left-hand tail of the distribution) occurs at 1.645 standard deviations below the mean. This holds for all normal distributions. Thus the value of R_l can be calculated for each fund as 1.645 standard deviations below the mean, i.e.

$$R_l = \overline{R}_p - 1.645\sigma$$

Figure 18.2 Distribution of portfolio returns

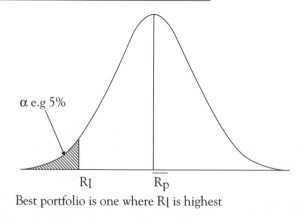

α e.g 5%

R_l   R̄_p
Best portfolio is one where R_l is highest

The objective then is to select the portfolio which allows the highest value of R_l.

Example 18.3 *Kataoka's safety-first criterion*

Using the same data as in example 18.1 above and letting $\alpha = 5\%$

Portfolio		A	B	C
$\overline{R_p}$		10	14	17
σp		5	4	8
R_l (Note 2)	=	1.78	7.42	3.84

The results indicate that 5% of the time fund A will fall below 1.78% return, fund B will fall below 7.42%, while fund C will fall below 3.84%. Since fund B produces the highest floor, it is the preferred portfolio.

Example 18.4 *Kataoka's safety-first criterion*

Suppose α was set at 25%. The relevant figure from the normal distribution tables which cuts off the bottom 25% is 0.67. Therefore R_l is equal to $R_p - 0.67\sigma$.

Portfolio		A	B	C
$\overline{R_p}$		10	14	17
σ_p		5	4	8
R_l (Note 3)	=	6.65	11.32	11.64

The results now indicate that 25% of the time fund A will fall below 6.65%, fund B will fall below 11.32%, while fund C will fall below 11.64%. Since fund C produces the highest floor, it is the preferred portfolio.

The reader should be clear regarding a critical difference between Roy's and Kataoka's criteria. In the case of Roy, the investor **subjectively** selects a minimum **return** percentage and objectively selects the preferred portfolio on the basis of the lowest risk of not meeting this desired return. In the case of Kataoka, the investor **subjectively** selects an 'acceptable' **risk** percentage and objectively selects the preferred portfolio on the basis of the **highest minimum return** consistent with this risk level.

Telser's criterion

The basis of this approach is to revert back to the intuitively appealing criteria of selecting the portfolio with the highest average return, provided it obeys a safety constraint. The constraint is effectively a combination of Roy and Kataoka $\Rightarrow$ that the probability of a return below some floor is not greater than some specified level.

Criterion is

$$\text{Maximise } \overline{R}_p$$

$$\text{Subject to probability } (R_p < R_l) \leq \alpha \qquad\qquad 18.3$$

Here there are two subjective decisions
⇒ Choice of acceptable risk level = α
⇒ Choice of acceptable lower limit = R_l

The **objective** criterion is to select that portfolio with the highest expected return satisfying the constraint. The constraint effectively operates as a filter. Only those funds meeting the constraint qualify for consideration. Of those that qualify, the preferred portfolio is simply the one which has delivered the highest average return in the past.

Example 18.5 Telser's safety-first criterion

Using the same data as in example 18.1 above, let R_l = 3% (minimum desired return), and α = 5% (acceptable risk level).

Fund	A	B	C
Mean return	10	14	17
Standard deviation (σ)	5	4	8
Difference from 3% (σ)	– 1.4	– 2.75	– 1.75
Probability of return < 3%	8.08%	0.3%	4.01%
Obeys constraint?	No	Yes	Yes

Fund A fails the constraint since it has a greater than 5% (8.08%) chance of falling below a 3% return in any period. Both funds B and C meet the constraint. While fund C is 13 times more likely than fund B to fall below a 3% return (once in 25 periods, compared to once in 330 periods), it falls within the acceptable risk tolerance level and it therefore qualifies for consideration. Of the qualifying funds (here B and C), fund C has the highest average return and is therefore the preferred portfolio.

Example 18.6 Telser's safety-first criterion

Now let R_l = 4% (minimum desired return), and let α = 5% (acceptable risk level).

Fund	A	B	C
Mean return	10	14	17
Standard deviation (σ)	5	4	8
Difference from 4% (σ)	–1.2	–2.5	–1.62
Probability of return <4%	11.5%	0.6%	5.25%
Obeys constraint?	No	Yes	No

Now only fund B meets the constraint and is chosen ahead of fund C (which fails the constraint) despite the fact that it has a lower average return. Fund B is therefore the preferred portfolio.[4]

Summary of the three approaches

The key differences between the approaches are

- Roy's approach gives primacy to keeping the risk of **bad** out-turns to a minimum, where 'bad' is determined by the investor.
- Kataoka's approach is to explicitly recognise and quantify what is an acceptable risk level and then to select on the basis of the portfolio having the highest 'worst' out-turn consistent with the risk level.
- Telser's approach is to revert to the intuitively appealing selection criteria of highest average return, but forcing adherence to a constraint that sets both an explicit level of risk and a worst out-turn.

Non-normally distributed returns

In the case where returns are not normally distributed, the investor could attempt to determine the functional form of the distribution and adapt the analysis above to fit the distribution. Alternatively the investor could have recourse to Tychebyshev's inequality,[5] which offers an approach which is independent of the functional form of the distribution but is much weaker or less convincing in terms of the results. A simple alternative utilising the logic of each of the three criteria is offered here.

Roy's criterion: The basis of the suggested approach is simply to count the number of returns which have fallen below the specified lower limit and to express these as a percentage of the total. The fund with the lowest percentage falling below the lower limit is the preferred fund.

Kataoka's criterion: Once again an acceptable risk level is chosen, say 10%. Each fund's returns are ranked and the return on the fund just above the bottom 10% represents the target lower limit. The fund with the highest lower limit is the preferred fund.

Telser's criterion: A lower limit and an acceptable risk level are specified. Following the approach in Roy's criterion set out above, the percentage falling below the lower limit is calculated. If this percentage is lower than the specified risk level, then the fund qualifies for consideration. The fund with the highest average return from among the qualifying funds is the preferred one.

18.2 Risk-adjusted return measures

Performance evaluation and analysis based only on return achieved is somewhat crude and limited. Evaluation techniques tend to be primarily concerned with comparing the return on one portfolio with the return on some other portfolio. This could be with a benchmark fund, e.g. an appropriate mixed asset fund for the type of investor, the performance of competitor funds or with market indices such as the ISEQ for an Irish equity fund, the FTSE 100 for a UK equity fund, the index of the Irish bond market for a fixed-interest fund etc. This however is unsatisfactory if one wishes to reflect the level of risk carried by the fund manager. Comparisons should be made between portfolios of similar risk levels or, if different risk levels exist, then comparisons can be made by developing an explicit risk/return trade-off.

The measures set out below address the issue of the level of return achieved for the amount of risk taken. There are two broad approaches, one which measures the return per unit of risk taken and the other which measures the **differential** return on a fund, where differential refers to the additional (positive or negative) return compared to that which would have been achieved by following a naive investment strategy.[6]

Return per unit of risk measures

There are two measures of this type differing in their definition of risk, and therefore in the type of fund to which they are most applicable. These are

- the Sharpe measure and
- the Treynor measure.

Measures of risk

The two measures of risk used are

- Total risk: normally measured by standard deviation of returns and is denoted by σp.
- Non-diversifiable risk: normally measured by the β coefficient of the fund/portfolio.

The Sharpe measure

This is sometimes referred to as the excess return to variability measure and is measured by the formula

$$\frac{(R_p - R_f)}{\sigma p}$$
18.4

where
R_p = the return on the portfolio
R_f = the return on the risk-free asset
σ_p = the standard deviation of the portfolio returns.

The logic of the measure is quite straightforward. Every fund should expect to earn a return of the risk-free rate plus something more. How much more depends on the level of risk taken. The ratio allows an analysis as to whether the amount of return over and above the risk-free rate (excess return) is sufficient to compensate for the additional risk taken.

Example 18.7 The Sharpe measure

The risk-free rate of return was 5% p.a. over a certain period of time. Fund A had an average return of 12% and a standard deviation of 6%, while fund B had an average return of 15% and a standard deviation of 9% over the same period. This says that fund A earned a return 7 percentage points above the risk-free asset by taking on a risk level of 6% while fund B earned a return 10 percentage points above the risk-free asset by taking on a risk level of 9%.

The Sharpe measure for the two funds is

Fund A
$$\frac{12-5}{6} = 1.17$$

Fund B
$$\frac{15-5}{9} = 1.11$$

Fund A earned 1.17% return for each 1% of risk carried, while fund B earned 1.11% return for each 1% of risk carried. While fund A is paying a lower return on average than fund B, it is delivering a greater return for the level of risk attached and is therefore the preferred fund.

The Sharpe measure is appropriate if a large percentage of one's total investment is invested in a single fund and therefore total risk is the relevant measure.

The Treynor measure

This measures the excess return to non-diversifiable risk and is measured by the formula

$$\frac{(R_a - R_f)}{\beta_a}$$
   18.5

where
R_a = the return on an individual asset/portfolio
R_f = the return on the risk-free asset
β_a = the risk of the asset as measured by the β value of the asset/portfolio.

The logic is broadly similar to that of Sharpe except that the Treynor measure is more appropriate to the analysis of a well-diversified portfolio or an individual stock.

Example 18.8 The Treynor measure

The risk-free rate of return was 5% p.a. over a certain period of time. The market average return was 11% p.a. Fund A had an average return of 12% and a β of 1.2, while fund B had an average return of 15% and a β of 0.8 over the same period.

The market average return was 6% p.a. above the risk-free rate. Fund A earned a return 7 percentage points above the risk-free asset by taking on a risk level which was 120% of the market average, while fund B earned a return 10 percentage points above the risk-free asset by taking on a risk level which was 80% of the market average.

The Treynor measure for the two funds and the market average is

Market average
$$\frac{11-5}{1} = 6$$

Fund A
$$\frac{12-5}{1.2} = 5.83$$

Fund B
$$\frac{15-5}{0.8} = 12.5$$

Since the market portfolio has a β value of 1, any fund carrying a greater risk than the market average (β > 1) should have an excess return higher than the market average, and any fund carrying lesser risk than the market average (β < 1) should have an excess return lower than the market average. Fund A earned an excess return of 5.83% when the risk level is neutralised to the market average, while fund B earned an excess return of 12.5% when the risk level is neutralised to the market average. Fund A is therefore paying an excess return lower than the market average and lower than fund B, while fund B is paying an excess return greater than the market average when account is taken of the risk inherent in each fund. Fund B is therefore the preferred fund.

Differential return measures

There are two measures of this type, differing in their definition of risk and therefore in the type of fund to which they are most applicable. These are

- differential return (total risk) measure, and
- the Jensen (β risk) measure.

The basis of this approach is the assumption that the investor has an alternative investment strategy of investing in a combination of the market portfolio and borrowing/lending at the risk-free rate, i.e. the investor can choose a risk level through a combination of the risk-free asset and the market portfolio—**the naive strategy**. The investor through, say, stock selection, may receive a return which differs from that which would have been achieved by the naive strategy. This differential return can be calculated and analysed to determine the fund manager's stock-picking ability.

As shown in Chapter 9, all combinations of the market portfolio and the risk-free asset lie on a straight line intercepting the return axis at the risk-free rate.

Figure 18.3 Differential return measures

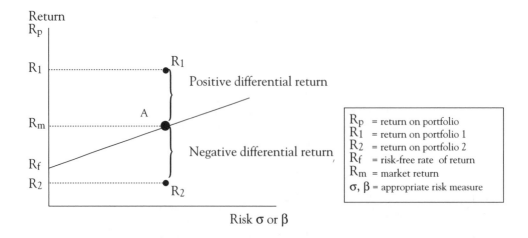

Any portfolio with a return above the line has achieved a positive differential, while any fund with a return below the line has achieved a negative differential. This relationship can be drawn with risk measured by either total risk or β risk (the CAPM).

Differential return (total risk) measure

The slope of the line connecting the market portfolio and the risk-free rate is

$$\frac{E(R_m) - R_f}{\sigma_m} \qquad\qquad 18.6$$

where
$E(R_m)$ = the expected return on the market portfolio
R_f = the return on the risk-free asset
σ_m = the standard deviation of the returns on the market.

The equation of the line is: $E(R_i) = R_f + ((E(R_m) - R_f)/\sigma_m) * \sigma_i$

where
$E(R_i)$ = the expected return on an individual asset/portfolio
σ_i = the standard deviation of the returns on an individual asset/portfolio.

This can be rewritten: $E(R_i) = R_f + (E(R_m) - R_f) \times \dfrac{\sigma_i}{\sigma_m}$

This form of the equation allows the ratio of the total risk of the asset/portfolio to the total risk of the market to be explicitly recognised.

Example 18.9 The differential return (total risk) measure

The risk-free rate of return was 5% p.a. over a certain period of time. The market average return was 10% p.a. and the standard deviation of market returns was 7%, while fund A had an average return of 13% and a standard deviation of 9% over the same period.

The expected return on fund A is $5 + (10 - 5) \times \dfrac{9}{7} = 11.43\%$

The actual return on fund A was 13%
    The differential return is therefore 13% – 11.43% = 1.57%
    Fund A has therefore achieved a return of 1.57% above that which could have been achieved by simply borrowing at the risk-free rate and investing in the market portfolio.

The Jensen measure

This is sometimes referred to as **Jensen's alpha** and is broadly similar to the previous measure except that the measure of risk used is β rather than total risk.
    The formula for calculating the expected return on a fund is the CAPM.

$$E(R_i) = R_f + \beta_i (E(R_m) - R_f) \qquad\qquad 18.7$$

Example 18.10 The Jensen measure

The risk-free rate of return was 5% p.a. over a certain period of time. The market average return was 11% p.a., while fund A had an average return of 12% and a β of 1.2 over the same period.

The expected return on fund A is

$$5 + 1.2(11 - 5) = 12.2\%$$

The actual return on fund A was 12%.

The differential return is therefore $12\% - 12.2\% = -0.2\%$.

Fund A has therefore achieved a return 0.2% below that which could have been achieved by simply borrowing at the risk-free rate and investing in the market portfolio.

SUMMARY

- This chapter has set out two approaches to portfolio performance evaluation and selection when account is explicitly taken of risk. They are safety-first investment criteria and risk-adjusted return measures.
- There are three main approaches to safety-first investment selection.
- Roy's criterion is to select a minimum return level and minimise the risk of failing to reach this.
- Kataoka's criterion is to specifically accept a risk level and select the portfolio which offers the highest minimum return (floor) consistent with that risk level.
- Telser's criterion is to revert to the intuitively appealing selection criterion of highest average return, but forcing adherence to a constraint while recognising both a risk level and a minimum desired return level.
- The chapter also deals with the issue of risk-adjusted portfolio return analysis. Four measures are discussed:
  - (a) the Sharpe measure
  - (b) the Treyner measure
  - (c) the differential return to total risk measure
  - (d) the Jensen measure.
- The Sharpe and Treyner measures neutralise the risk across different portfolios and compare the adjusted return. The measures differ in their concept of risk, with Sharpe using total risk and Treyner using β risk.
- The other two measures compare the return achieved to that achievable through a naive investment strategy. The differential return may be positive or negative. The measures differ in their concept of risk, the first using total risk and the Jensen measure using β risk, i.e. the CAPM.

QUESTIONS

1.◆ The table below shows the average return on three unit-linked funds over a thirty year period together with the standard deviation of returns:

Fund	A	B	C
Average return (%)	13	17	21
Standard deviation (%)	5	9	12

Adopting a **safety-first** approach to the investment selection, which of the funds would be chosen by an investor adopting:

(a) Roy's criterion (lower acceptable return, R_L = 7%)

(b) Kataoka's criterion (risk level, α = 13%)

(c) Telser's criterion (R_L = 7%, α = 13%)?

2.♦ The table below shows the average return on three unit-linked funds over a forty year period together with the standard deviation of returns:

Fund	A	B	C
Average return (%)	12	15	20
Standard deviation (%)	4	7	10

Adopting a **safety-first** approach to the investment selection, which is the most desirable fund, under

- Roy's criterion (lower acceptable return, R_L = 5%)
- Kataoka's criterion (risk level, α = 8%)
- Telser's criterion (R_L = 5%, α = 8%)?

3. The table below shows the average annual return on three unit-linked funds over a 35 year period together with the standard deviation of returns:

Fund	A	B	C
Average annual return (%)	13	17	19
Standard deviation of return (%)	5	8	10

Which of the funds would be chosen by an investor adopting

(a) Roy's criterion (lower acceptable return, R_L = 6%)

(b) Kataoka's criterion (α = 10%)

(c) Telser's criterion (R_L = 6%, α = 10%)?

4.♦ The risk-free rate of return was 4% p.a. over a certain period of time. Fund A had an average return of 11% and a standard deviation of 5%, while fund B had an average return of 14% and a standard deviation of 7% over the same period. Calculate the Sharpe measure for the two funds and indicate which fund would be preferred on this measure

5.♦ The risk-free rate of return was 6% p.a. over a certain period of time. The market average return was 9% p.a. Fund A had an average return of 13% and a β of 1.4, while fund B had an average return of 14% and a β of 1.2 over the same period. Calculate the Treynor measure for the market and for the two funds and indicate which fund would be preferred on this measure.

6.♦ The risk-free rate of return was 6% p.a. over a certain period of time. The market average return was 11% p.a. and the standard deviation of market returns was 5%.

Fund A had an average return of 16% and a standard deviation of 8% over the same period, while fund B had an average return of 9% and a standard deviation of 6% over the same period. Calculate the differential return (total risk) measure for the two funds and indicate which fund would be preferred.

7.◆ The risk-free rate of return was 7% p.a. over a certain period of time. The market average return was 10% p.a. Fund A had an average return of 11% and a β of 1.4 over the same period, while fund B had an average return of 13% and a β of 1.6 over the same period. Calculate the Jensen measure for the two funds and indicate which fund would be preferred.

8. Explain clearly the basis of the three safety-first approaches shown below, indicating the key differences between them:
   (a) Roy's criterion
   (b) Kataoka's criterion
   (c) Telser's criterion.

9. Discuss the main approaches to risk-adjusted portfolio performance, indicating the differences between the various measures.

NOTES

1. In the case of A, the mean return is 10%. Therefore the lower limit lies to the right of the mean and the probability of achieving a return below 12% is greater than 50%.
2. R_l is calculated as $R_l = R_p - 1.645\sigma_p$
3. R_l is calculated as $R_l = R_p - 0.67\sigma_p$
4. The mathematics used in Telser is the same as that used in Roy. The difference is that in Roy it is the fund with the lowest probability of falling below the minimum acceptable return which is chosen, while in Telser it is the fund with the highest average return so long as the calculated probability is not greater than the specified risk tolerance level.
5. This is discussed in most advanced statistics or investment textbooks. See, for example, Elton and Gruber.
6. A naive investment strategy is one where the investor invests in a combination of the risk-free asset and the market portfolio.

19
Mergers and Acquisitions

CHAPTER OBJECTIVES

At the end of this chapter the student will be able to:

1. distinguish between the different types of takeover
2. understand how mergers/acquisitions are grouped
3. understand the rationale for mergers
4. analyse mergers.

INTRODUCTION

Merger activity in Ireland in 1999 was at an all time high with Irish companies spending almost €4.1 billion on domestic and overseas acquisitions. The value of merger activity in Ireland in 1998 was €5.7 billion, but this included the €2.8 billion merger of Irish Life and Irish Permanent.[1] Irish companies, such as the Kerry Group, Jefferson Smurfit, CRH and Waterford Wedgwood, have become significant international businesses because of merger and acquisition activity. At the time of writing, CRH have 14 development teams operating throughout the Americas and Europe assessing potential acquisition targets. According to its annual report (2000), it spent €931 million on more than 30 acquisitions in the first half of 2000. In 1999 the company spent €1.4 billion on more than 40 acquisitions. At the end of 2000, CRH planned to issue 19.57 million new shares, or about 5% of the group's ordinary share capital, to raise €380 million to fund further acquisitions. Table 19.1 gives the 1999 top ten acquisitions by Irish companies.

From a legal point of view, mergers are different to acquisitions. A merger is a combination of two separate companies, which merge into a new entity via the exchange of shares. An acquisition is where one company acquires shares in another company for cash and the acquired company loses its identity. Mergers fall into different categories, but whatever the category they generate lots of interest, controversy and lots of money for many people involved. This chapter sets out to explain some of the main issues involved.

Table 19.1 1999 Top ten acquisitions

Buyer	Target	IR£m
1. MBO	Cantrell & Cochrane	575
2. AIB	80% stake in Bank Zacondi	443
3. CRH	Finnsemenetti Oy & Lohja	327
4. MBO	Clondalkin	303
5. Ardagh	Rockware	280
6. CRH	Thompson-McCully	262
7. Jury's	Doyle's Hotels	240
8. Integrity Holdings	Jyris	165
9. Esat Telecom	PostGem/Ireland On Line	115
10. Aerfi	Indigo Aviation	110

Source: Chapman Flood Mazars — CFM Capital Acquisitions Surveys

19.1 Legal forms of acquisition

When one group of shareholders takes control from another group of shareholders, it is referred to as a takeover. A takeover can be accomplished by:

1. acquisition or merger
2. proxy contests, or
3. going private transaction.

19.1.1 Merger or acquisition

For one company to acquire another there are three legal mechanisms available:

(a) The merger or complete consolidation of one company by another
A merger is the complete assimilation of one company by another. The **bidder**, or the acquiring firm, acquires all the assets and liabilities of the acquired firm. The bidder retains its name and the acquired firm will no longer exist after the merger. A consolidation is exactly the same as a merger except that neither the acquiring firm nor the acquired firm will legally exist after the consolidation. An entirely new firm will be created with a new name and a new identity. The main disadvantage of a merger/consolidation is that it must get the approval of usually two-thirds of the shareholders of each firm, which may not be easily obtained.

(b) Acquisition of shares
The acquiring firm can buy up a firm's voting shares with a combination of cash, stock etc. A public statement made by the acquiring company to the shareholders of the target firm can accomplish this. This is referred to as a **tender offer**. The offer can be withdrawn if sufficient voting shares are not acquired. In a share acquisition, no shareholder meeting is

required. The shareholders can choose to either tender their shares or not. It can be effective particularly if there is hostility on the part of the target firm's management because the bid goes directly to the shareholders and bypasses management.

(c) Acquisition of a company's assets
A company can acquire another company by effectively buying all of its assets. This will require agreement by the target firm's shareholders.

19.1.2 Proxy contests

A proxy is the right to cast somebody else's vote. A group of (usually unhappy) shareholders can gain the proxies of a sufficient number of other shareholders and through a **proxy contest** can vote in new directors and therefore gain control of the company.

19.1.3 Going private transactions

In a going private transaction all the publicly owned shares are bought by a small group of private shareholders. The small group of investors is usually the management and such transactions have become known as **management buy-outs** (MBOs). Because it is common for such transactions to be financed largely by borrowed funds, they are referred to as **leveraged buy-outs** (LBOs).

Figure 19.1 Forms of takeover

19.2 Types of mergers/acquisitions
Mergers and acquisitions are usually grouped into the following three types:

1. Horizontal
This type of merger occurs when firms in the same line of business combine, e.g. two banks combining (Lloyd's with TSB in Britain) or two retailers (Sainsbury's with Texas Homecare). Another example was the Chrysler/Daimler-Benz merger in 1998.

2. Vertical Merger

This involves the combination of firms at different stages of the production process. For example, the acquisition by an airline company of a group of travel agents would be a vertical merger.

3. Conglomerate merger

This occurs when firms that are not related to each other combine. The combination of a food producer with a car manufacturer would be an example. Sometimes the motivation for such mergers is diversification and the possibility of risk reduction. Conglomerate mergers were all the rage in the 1960s and 1970s. The 1980s were spent breaking up most of the conglomerate mergers formed in the previous two decades and the 1980s were characterised with LBOs and junk bond acquisitions. The 1990s has been characterised by strategic alliances because of the proliferation of the global economy.

19.3 Rationale for mergers

The level of merger/acquisition activity in the 1980s and 1990s has been enormous. Obviously there are reasons behind this phenomenal growth in merger activity. The following is a list of some of the motives behind the mergers.

19.3.1 *Synergy*

The idea behind this motive is that the combined entity will be greater than the sum of the parts that make up the entity. Synergy is sometimes expressed as 2 + 2 = 5. In other words, the merger will be beneficial if the combined value of the two firms will be greater than the sum of the values of the individual firms. Suppose that firm A wants to acquire firm B to form a new entity called firm C. The merger will make sense if the value of firm C (Vc) is greater than the combined value of firm A (Va) and firm B (Vb). It is important to **estimate only the incremental cash flows** that will occur from the acquisition. That is, if

$$Vc > Va + Vb$$

Therefore the difference between the combined values of the two firms and the value of the new entity (ΔV) is the net incremental gain from the merger.

$$\textbf{Net incremental gain from merger} = \Delta V = V_c - (V_a + V_b) \qquad \textbf{(19.1)}$$

If ΔV is > 0 there is synergy. If Δ < 0 there is no incremental gain and the merger does not make financial sense.

The value of firm B to firm A is the value of firm B *plus* the incremental gain ΔV. If we denote the value of firm B to firm A as Vb*, then the value of firm B to firm A is

$$\textbf{Value of firm B to firm A} = V_b{}^* = \Delta V + V_b \qquad \textbf{(19.2)}$$

To determine the financial merits of an acquisition we will therefore need to determine the incremental gains that can be made. The incremental gains are the incremental cash flows arising from the acquisition. In other words, we must determine the cash flows of the combined entity and compare them to the cash flows that the two firms generate when operating separately. We will return to this later on in the chapter.

19.3.2 Economies of scale

Synergy occurs because of economies of scale. Economies of scale begin to set in when the average cost of production falls as the firm increases in size. Reductions in average cost per unit occur because of:

(a) operating economies from rationalisation of manufacturing capacity, management, production, distribution and administration
(b) increased market power, which is one of the most important driving forces behind merger activity. A firm can acquire another firm to become a dominant player in the market. This reduces competition and leads to higher profits. This is not a socially desirable rationale for mergers and the regulatory authorities will monitor such acquisitions very carefully.
(c) differential efficiency, which occurs if the management of the acquiring firm is more efficient and it increases the efficiency to which the assets of the firm taken over are put.
(d) lower financing costs because a merged firm will generally be able to borrow funds more cheaply than the separate firms could. This is because from a lender's point of view the merged firm is less risky. As separate firms, firm A cannot guarantee firm B's debts and vice versa. If the two firms merge, the combined firm AB is less risky because one part of the business effectively guarantees the other part's debt. There is a mutual guarantee that makes the debt of the combined firm less risky.

19.3.3 Market entry

If a company decides to enter a new market, it may decide that the best way (and the most cost efficient way) to penetrate the new market is by means of an acquisition of a company already established in that market. This is referred to as **growth by acquisition**. It may be much more difficult and costly to grow into a market **organically** (by the firm's own efforts). In addition, a new entry into the market will mean more competition, which could depress prices and profits. It would make more sense therefore for the company to enter a new market by acquisition.

19.3.4 Tax advantages

In the United States, tax considerations have been a powerful consideration in mergers and acquisitions. In the US tax losses in any particular year can be used to reduce taxable profits in later years. Therefore profitable firms can acquire firms with large accumulated losses, which can be turned into a tax saving after the merger. Furthermore, mergers provide a way of minimising taxes when disposing of surplus funds. If a company has free cash flow, it can dispose of it in any one of four different ways (provided there are no internal positive net present value projects). First, it can distribute the surplus cash to the shareholders, in which case the shareholders are subject to tax liabilities. Secondly, the company can repurchase its own shares, but this incurs capital gains tax for the shareholders. Thirdly, it can invest the money in short-term marketable investments, but the rates of return are usually very low, particularly in a low interest rate environment. Finally, using the surplus funds to purchase another company will avoid all the tax considerations of dividends and share repurchase.

19.4 Company: market value and book value

Companies can be seen as acquisition targets because the market is undervaluing their shares. If the book value of a company's assets is greater than the market value of the company's shares, then the company may be seen as an acquisition target. In other words, it may be cheaper to buy existing companies than build new plants.

19.4.1 Break-up value

Break-up value is the value of each individual part of the business if they were sold off separately. If this is greater than the market value, the firm becomes an acquisition target. Buying the company and subsequently selling off the company in individual parts makes an incremental gain.

19.4.2 Managerial motives

Not all the motives for merger/acquisition activity are based on economic rationale. Many decisions are made as a result of the personal motivations of managers. These may be described as egotistical motives for mergers (empire building). The larger the firm one manages, the more prestigious it is. In addition, it can be the case than managerial salaries are based on turnover and profits. The bigger the company, the bigger the manager's salary.

19.4.3 Eliminating inefficiencies

Some companies can be undervalued because of poor management of resources, which leads to the inability to embark on ways to increase sales and improve cost to sales ratios and hence improve profits. Better management, via a takeover, can exploit the various opportunities that exist within the company. Greater efficiencies can help drive profit growth. (See Box 19.1.)

Box 19.1 Acquisitions help drive profit growth at Oakhill

Oakhill Group, the demerged printing and packaging division of James Crean, has announced a 22% increase in profit before tax and goodwill amortisation, to €3.71 million in the six months to 30 June 1999.

Most of this growth was due to a contribution from acquisitions ... 'The company is being focused on developing the organic and acquisitive growth strategies which will enhance long-term shareholder value. . . . Printing operating profits were up 14%, helped by the contribution from acquisitions.'

Extracted from *The Irish Times*, Bill Murdoch, 9 November 1999

19.4.4 *Risk arbitrage and other third party motives*

Arbitrage is the process of buying and selling the same securities in different markets at different prices and thus making a profit. Risk arbitrage is the process of buying (speculating) in securities of companies that are likely takeover targets. This is a speculative process and vast amounts of money can be made if the individuals concerned can get **in** and **out** of the market at the right time with minimum cost. There is however scope for illegal **insider trading** and some famous risk arbitrageurs, like the American Ivan Boesky, have gone to jail for such actions.

In addition, many advisers and investment bankers can make substantial fee income during the acquisition process. Advice is provided on the rules and regulations regarding takeovers, finance, defence tactics etc.

19.5 Questionable motives for mergers

There are certain financial consequences of mergers that happen regardless of whether a merger takes place or not. Sometimes these consequences are given as rational motives for mergers. We look at two of those—the effect on earnings per share and diversification.

19.5.1 *Increasing EPS*

Mergers can create an illusion of gains in the form of growth in EPS. This can lead investors to believe that the firm is financially better off than it actually is. An example will illustrate.

Rathgormac takes over Cluain Fhia. The financial position before the merger is set out in the first two columns in Table 19.2. The assumption is that the merger makes no economic gains, i.e. no additional value. Therefore, the firms are worth the same, when merged, as they are as separate units.

Rathgormac will exchange one of its shares for 1.5 shares in Cluain Fhia in a share for share exchange, i.e. (€30/€20 = 1.5). Therefore, the total number of shares issued by Rathgormac will be 133 (200/1.5).

After the merger the market value of the combined firms is the sum of the values of the two firms before the merger, i.e. €10,000. The earnings per share of the merged firms is now €1.20 (€400/333) or a 20% increase. **This is despite the fact that there is no real gain made by the merger.** However the P/E ratio falls. Why? Remember that the total market value of the merged entity is the same as the sum of the values of the two firms. This is as it should be. The market has not been fooled by the 20% increase in the EPS. Therefore the market price reflects this and therefore it does not change. Consequently the P/E ratio must fall. On the other hand, if investors see the 20% increase in earnings as an indication of real growth, the price of Rathgormac's shares will rise, as will the P/E ratio. This is **EPS growth illusion** or magic. For it to work, shareholders in both companies must get something for nothing. This is unlikely. **Companies can increase their EPS by buying companies with a lower P/E ratio than their own.** Their EPS will rise despite the fact that there is no economic gain from the merger. The management of the acquiring firm will promise higher earnings through better management and greater operational efficiencies. If the market believes this, then it will still place a high P/E ratio on the acquiring firm. In other words, the value of the acquiring firm goes up and shareholders are happy. But these shareholders have been fooled. The increase in value has been achieved by an illusion of earnings growth and not by any significant managerial acrobatics or operational efficiencies. Growth in EPS has been achieved by buying a company with a lower PER. In the long run EPS will fall because you are not increasing value by implementing any operational efficiency. In other words, you cannot keep fooling investors all the time.

Table 19.1 Mergers and EPS growth illusion

	Rathgormac	Cluain Fhia	Rathgormac post-merger
EPS	€1	€1	€1.20
Price per share	€30	€20	€30
P/E ratio	30	20	25
Number of shares	200	200	333
Earnings	€200	€200	€400
Value	€6,000	€4,000	€10,000

19.5.2 Diversification

Diversification is sometimes used as a rationale for acquisitions. The argument goes as follows. Diversification reduces risk. Mergers can be seen as diversification in order to reduce risk. In other words, if income comes from a variety of sources and markets, then the cash flows will be less risky and less volatile. They achieve the same income and return **but** with lower risk. A reduction in risk is therefore a gain from the merger. Therefore investors will be prepared to pay a premium for diversified firms.

But does diversification increase value? And will investors be prepared to pay a premium for diversified firms? The answer to both these questions is no. The simple answer is that mergers don't do anything that shareholders can't do for themselves. In fact, diversification is cheaper and easier for shareholders to do themselves than it is for the company. In other words, shareholders can get all the diversification they need by buying shares in as many companies as they want. Therefore they will not be prepared to pay a premium for a share in a merged company just for the benefit of diversification—they can achieve the benefits of diversification more easily and more cheaply themselves.

19.6 Merger gains and costs

An economic incremental gain is made when the two firms are worth more together than they are apart. From equation 19.1, we learned that an economic gain is made when the combined value of firm A and firm B is greater than the sum of the value of firm A and firm B:[2]

$$\text{Incremental gain} = \Delta V = V_c - (V_a + V_b)$$

where
V_a = value of firm A
V_b = value of firm B
V_c = combined value of firm A and firm B.

Also, the value of firm B to firm A is

$$V_b{}^* = V_b + \Delta V$$

where
$V_b{}^*$ = value of firm B to firm A.

The net present value to A of a merger with B is the difference between the gains from the merger and the costs incurred. In other words

$$NPV = V_b{}^* - Cost \qquad (19.3)$$

The merger should go ahead if the NPV is positive.

19.6.1 Cash acquisitions

Suppose that firm A has a value of €300 and firm B has a market value of €100. A merger between the two would allow an incremental value (gain) of €100. Therefore

$$\Delta V = €100$$
$$V_a = €300$$
$$V_b = €100$$

Suppose that a sale is agreed and firm A agrees to buy firm B for €175 cash. The €175 cash paid is the cost of the acquisition. This means that firm A agrees to pay a premium of €75 (€175 – €100) for firm B.

Note that the overall merger gain ΔV is €100 and the shareholders of firm B have amassed €75 of this.

Therefore, if the overall gain from the merger is €100 and firm B's shareholders receive €75 of this, then the incremental gain to firm A's shareholders is €25. In other words, the value of firm B to firm A is

$$V_b{}^* = \Delta V + V_b = €200$$

Therefore if firm A pays €175 in cash to acquire firm B, the NPV of the cash acquisition is

$$NPV = V_b{}^* - cost$$
$$= €200 – €175 = €25$$

Therefore the acquisition is profitable.

Suppose that the number of shares in issue after the merger is 20. After the merger the value of the merged entity is the pre-merger value of firm A €300 *plus* the NPV of €25 = €325. Therefore the value of each share outstanding is €325/20 = €16.25. This represents a gain of €1.25.

19.6.2 *Stock acquisition*

With cash payments the shareholders in the target company receive cash payments and they are no longer part of the new company. The cost of the acquisition is the cash paid to pay off the shareholders in the target company.

If the merger is in the form of a share for share exchange, then no cash changes hands. The shareholders of the target company remain as shareholders of the newly formed merged company. The value of the merger will simply be the sum of the pre-merger values of firm A and firm B *plus* the incremental value or the gains from the merger:

$$V_c = V_a + V_b + \Delta V$$
$$€300 + €100 + €100 = €500$$

Example 19.1 Mergers via stock acquisitions

The cost of the acquisition for firm A is €175 worth of firm A stock. If the price of firm A shares is €15, firm A will give up €175/€15 = 11.7 shares. The number of shares in issue after the merger is now 20 + 11.7 = 31.7 shares, giving each share a value of €500/31.7 = €15.77.

How much does the merger cost firm A? Firm A gave €175 worth of its shares to firm B's shareholders. Firm B's shareholders now have 11.7 shares in the new company after the merger. These shares are now valued at €15.77 each. Therefore the gain to B's shareholders is 11.7 × €15.77 = €185. The gain for B's shareholders is a loss to the shareholders in firm A. The overall value of firm B to firm A we estimated to be €200. The cost of the acquisition is €185. Firm A must give €185 of the overall gain to the shareholders of firm B. Therefore the NPV of the merger is

$$NPV = V_b{}^* - Cost$$
$$= €200 - €185 = €15$$

19.6.3 *Comparing cash and stock acquisitions*

In the above example, firm B shareholders share in the NPV of the merger because they become shareholders in the new company. With the cash acquisition, firm A shareholders get to keep all of the NPV. **In a share for share exchange the cost of the merger will depend on the gains made from the acquisition.** This is because the shareholders in the target firm will become shareholders in the merged firm, and the shareholders in the acquiring firm must share the gains made from the merger with the shareholders of the target firm. Therefore, if shares are used to buy a company, the cost will usually be higher. If cash is used to finance an acquisition, the shareholders in the target firm will not benefit from the incremental gains arising from the merger. Incidentally, if firm A overvalued firm B, perhaps because it miscalculated some of firm B's strengths, and makes an offer that is too much, then firm A's shareholders will benefit from this because it will share this loss with the shareholders of Firm B if the offer is on a share for share basis. Of course this would not be the case if it were a cash offer. Finally, a cash payment will not affect the voting control of the merged entity, whereas if shares are used, control of the company after the merger may be affected.

19.7 Discounted cash flow analysis in valuing the target firm

Here we discuss a common method used in valuing a target firm.[3] To use the DCF analysis to value the target firm, it will first be necessary to estimate the incremental free cash flows that are expected to result from the merger. This is similar to the corporate valuation model we discussed in Chapter 6 and Chapter 10.

Table 19.3 shows the pro forma cash flow statement for Southside Ltd which is seen as a possible target by Northside Ltd. These are projected estimates of Southside Ltd's cash flow after any merger takes place. The cash flow includes all synergistic impacts of the merger. Southside Ltd would become a subsidiary of Northside Ltd.

Table 19.3 Pro forma statement of Southside Ltd

	2000 €m	2001 €m	2002 €m	2003 €m	2004 €m
1. Net turnover	100	120	150	160	170
2. Cost of goods sold	70	84	105	112	119
3. S, G & A expenses	10	12	15	16	17
4. Depreciation	5	5	6	6	7
5. PBIT	15	19	24	26	27
6. Interest	4	5	6	7	7
7. PBT	11	14	18	19	20
8. Taxation (20%)	2.2	2.8	3.6	3.8	4
9. PAT	8.8	11.2	14.4	15.2	16
10. + depreciation	5	5	6	6	7
11. Cash flow	13.8	16.2	20.4	21.2	23
12. *Less* earnings retained for growth	4	5	5	6	6
13. + horizon value					367
14. Net cash flow	9.8	11.2	15.4	15.2	384

The method used here to value the target firm is the **equity residual method**. The residual cash flows are what is left over for the acquiring company's shareholders.

Depreciation is added back in on line 11 to estimate the firm's cash flow. Some of the cash flows generated by Southside Ltd will be used by Southside to replace obsolete assets, and additional equity funds will be required to expand Northside's new subsidiary. Therefore some of the cash flows generated by Southside will be used to finance asset replacement and fund growth opportunities. The rest will belong to the shareholders of Northside Ltd.

In this example we have projected cash flows up to 2004, but of course we can assume that Northside will operate Southside as a subsidiary for ever. Therefore, we must estimate Southside's cash flows **beyond** 2004. From Chapter 6 we remember how to estimate this 'horizon value' using the constant growth formula. We assume that Southside's cash flows will grow at a constant rate of 8% after 2004. Note that the appropriate cost of capital to use is Southside's, which we assume to be 13%. Therefore the value of Southside at the end of 2004 (or the present value of all cash flows after 2004) is €367m:

$$V_{2004} = \frac{CF_{2005}}{K_e - g} = \frac{(€23 - €6)(1.08)}{0.13 - 0.08} = €367m$$

On line 14 are the cash flows that belong to the shareholders of Northside. These are the cash flows that Northside Ltd uses to estimate the valuation of the proposed merger. Note that we used 13% as the discount rate in estimating the value of operations at 2004. The cash flows on line 14 represent equity because they are taken after interest and taxes have been deducted. Therefore the appropriate cost of capital is the cost of equity capital rather than a general weighted cost of capital. Besides, in any acquisition process it is the owners of the company that are being bought out and not the creditors. Consequently, in merger valuations the appropriate valuation is the value of the target firm's equity. Therefore the appropriate cost of capital is the cost of equity capital.

We can use the CAPM to estimate Southside's cost of equity capital of 13%. Assume that Southside's post-merger beta doesn't change and stays at its pre-merger value of 1.5. If the risk-free rate is 7% and the market risk premium is 4%, then Southside's cost of equity capital is calculated as

$$K_e = K_f + (R_m)ß = 7\% + (4\%)1.5 = 13\%$$

Therefore the value of Southside as at the end of 2001 is the present value of expected future cash flows discounted at 13%

$$V_{2000} = \frac{9.8}{(1.13)^1} + \frac{11.2}{(1.13)^2} + \frac{15.4}{(1.13)^3} + \frac{15.2}{(1.13)^4} + \frac{367}{(1.13)^5} = €236.6m$$

This is the value of Southside to Northside at the end of 2001. This is the maximum price that Northside will pay for the acquisition.

19.8 Hostile and friendly takeovers

Having put together the analysis of the possible takeover target (e.g. the DCF analysis) and having decided on the method of payment, the management of the acquiring firm will need to decide how it is going to approach the target firm's management. If the target firm's management is receptive to the proposed merger, then a statement will be issued to the shareholders of both companies encouraging acceptance of the deal. This is a so called **friendly merger**.

However, mergers sometimes involve less than friendly transactions when the target firm resists the approaches of its suitor. If the management of the target firm, for whatever reason (maybe they feel the price being offered is too low), rejects the offer, then the acquiring firm will appeal directly to the target firm's shareholders and ask them to tender their shares for the price being offered. The management of the target firm will encourage their shareholders to reject the offer on the grounds that the price is too low. This is called a **hostile takeover** bid. One of the first stages in a hostile takeover is the **dawn raid**. This is where the acquiring firm buys up shares in the target firm with such alacrity that the acquiring firm will have built up a substantial holding of the target firm's shares before the target firm's management has time to react. Prices are usually offered at substantial premiums to the previous day's closing price.

Note that the rules governing takeovers require that any individual or company that holds a 30% stake in a company must make a mandatory bid for all the target company's shares. This is designed to prevent a predator buying the company on the cheap. Thirty per cent is a substantial holding, making it very difficult for anyone else to launch a bid. In order to avoid making a mandatory bid, many individuals or companies hold 29.9% of the shares. This is the maximum amount they can hold without making a formal bid for all the shares.

The target firm in a hostile bid may embark on a series of defensive strategies to repel the acquiring firm's advances. The various defensive tactics involved include:

1. **Press releases** and mail shots to their shareholders outlining their view. Of course this might be the self-interest of management and not in the shareholders' interests.
2. **Targeted repurchase**. The target firm purchases its own stock from a specific investor at a substantial premium. These very high premiums can be seen as a bribe to eliminate hostile bidders. In America they are referred to as **greenmail**.
3. **White knight**. This is where the target firm invites a second bid from a friendly company to compete with the hostile bidder.
4. **White squire**. This is somebody who is on the side of the target firm who will buy enough shares in the target firm to prevent the merger.
5. **Poison Pills**. This is tantamount to economic suicide in order to make a hostile takeover impossible. Poison pills can take different forms. For example, shareholders may be allowed to buy shares at a large discount should the bid be successful. These are sometimes called **share rights plans**.
6. **Golden parachutes**. This is where managers get lucrative payouts if the bid is successful. This could make the potential bid infeasible.
7. **Employee share ownership plans (ESOPs)**. Employees are given share ownership, which makes it more difficult for the bidder to take over.
8. **Crown Jewels**. Target firms will often threaten to sell off valuable company assets when faced with a hostile takeover—sometimes referred to as the **scorched earth** strategy. This might involve a lock-up which is an option granted to perhaps a white knight to purchase the crown jewels at a set price in the context of a hostile bid.
9. **Pac-man defence**. Here the target firm makes a counter bid for the hostile bidder.

19.9 Leveraged buy-outs

The two main differences between a merger and a leveraged buy-out are:

(a) Most of the purchase price is financed with debt.
(b) After the LBO, the company goes private (it is no longer traded on the stock exchange).

Where the existing management is involved, the LBO is called a management buy-out or MBO. The debt is financed by the acquired company's operations. An analysis of the cash flows of the acquired company is carried out (similar to that in Table 19.2). All earnings and cash flows will be retained in the business to pay off the debt. After a number of years the entire debt is paid off and the shareholders are left with a substantial increase in their original investment. Sometimes after the company has been made strong and profitable, the management will plan to make it public again. Substantial profits can be made from LBOs. The risks of course are very high because of the highly leveraged means of financing the LBO. But along with high risk come high returns. The most successful LBO merchants in 1980s America, Kohlberg Kravis Roberts & Co. (KKR) were reputed to have made in the region of 50% annual return on their investments in LBOs.

The first MBO of an Irish public company was the Candover-backed buy-out of Clondalkin. For a brief assessment and case study see Box 19.2.

Box 19.2 Clondalkin management buy-out set to succeed

The first management buy-out (MBO) of an Irish public company—the €385 million Candover-backed buy-out of Clondalkin—seems assured of success after more than 35% of Clondalkin's shareholders gave irrevocable acceptances to the €9.10 a share offer from Edgemeade, the vehicle for the management bid.

The total cost of the buy-out rises to €475 million when Clondalkin's debt at the end of June is taken into account.[4]

Assuming the offer succeeds, a 44-strong management team will end up owning 19% of Edgemead, with Candover putting up €122 million in equity finance for its 81% stake.

Clondalkin chairman Mr Henry Lund said that each of the executives involved in the MBO group was investing the proceeds from their Clondalkin shares and share options. He added that the management group would be investing on a roughly pro rata basis as Candover, with an unspecified discount reflecting the expertise the management group is providing to the new private company.

Despite this discount, it looks like the management group is investing in the order of €25 million for its 19% stake....

About one quarter of the cost of the buy-out and €90.6 million in assumed debt will be covered by the equity component, with a further 50% in senior debt and 25% in mezzanine finance coming from a group of banks including AIB, Warbourg Dillon Read and Lehman Brothers.

$\longrightarrow$

Clondalkin management first began exploring the possibility of a buy-out after the stock market slumped in August last year in the wake of the Asian crisis.

Unlike front-line industrial shares like CRH, which have rallied strongly since that slump, Clondalkin shares have suffered as sentimen towards small/mid-capitalisation companies turned negative.

The movement of industrial funds out of Irish stocks into European shares following the introduction of the single currency was another major factor which affected shares like Clondalkin.

Mr Lund was exasperated at the market's treatment of his company's shares, given the strength of the group's earnings over the past 15 years. 'CRH shares have risen 148% since last year's crash. We are up 48% even though our earnings growth was the same. If we had risen 148% since August last year, our shares would be at €19 now and we wouldn't be doing this.'

But the management's offer to take Clondalkin private is not cheap, with the €9.10 offer to shareholders equivalent to 12 times historic earnings per share and 7.5 times earnings before interest, tax and depreciation.

'We couldn't cheapskate this deal. There's always some scepticism about management buy-outs and Warburgh and Candover told us we had to offer a full price up front. This was a one-shot opportunity and, to be credible, we had to come up with our best offer straight away. . . .

We have sufficient facilities for bold-on acquisitions and will be able to fund acquisitions up to €100m . . . half of our growth has come through acquisitions in the past 15 years and we want to maintain that pattern. . . .

The difference between us and a stock market company is that we can take a long-term view and are not driven by six month earnings per share growth and share prices.'

Extract from *The Irish Times*, Brendan McGrath, 9 November 1999

19.9.1 Junk bonds

Up to the 1980s institutional investors such as pension funds and insurance companies generally did not tend to invest their funds in risky projects. It was very difficult for risk-taking companies to find the type of capital to fund their operations. This was all to change in the 1980s when American investment bankers such as Drexel Burnham Lambert sold the idea of high rewards compensating for the high risk. The **junk bond** industry was born. They were high-risk high-yield bonds sold to investors to fund risky companies that were in trouble, mergers and leveraged buyouts. Some of these mergers and LBOs were financed with 95% debt. Obviously the risk of not being able to generate sufficient cash flows to finance the debt was very high. Because of this there were many calls to ban the junk bond market. Many of the investments took a hammering because of their inability to generate the cash flows to repay the debt. The default risk on these bonds increased and the market dried up in the early 1990s. However, the default risk on junk bonds has now fallen and the market is healthier than previously. But don't forget that many junk bond deals were successful, such as those used by Ted Turner to finance the development of CNN.

19.10　Winners and losers

Who are the winners and losers in acquisitions and mergers? The evidence suggests that value is created, but the question is how is this added value distributed.

(a) **Shareholders**. Most empirical research suggests that the shareholders of the target firm benefit most from a merger. Firstly, the target firm's shareholders benefit if two or more firms are competing for the merger, thus pushing up the share price. Secondly, the management of the acquiring firm may be more concerned with the idea of managing a larger organisation and in return may be willing to surrender all of the added value to the shareholders of the target firm. Therefore, the evidence suggests that the added value created because of mergers is captured almost entirely by the shareholders of the target firm.
(b) **Employees**. Cost-cutting can often follow mergers in an effort to boost profits and shareholder value. Unfortunately these cost cuts can result in redundancies.
(c) **Financial institutions**. As mentioned earlier, some advisers and financial institutions benefit greatly from mergers because of the fees they receive.
(d) **Society.** The general economy will suffer from merger activity if these mergers result in monopoly power. However, the monopoly commission will monitor such mergers to see if such monopoly power develops. On the other hand, greater efficiencies and better management may result in lower prices of goods and services.

19.11　Divestitures and spin-offs

Companies can, in addition to buying other companies, sell part of their own company. This is referred to as a **divestiture**. The sale could be to another firm or a new company is created and the shares in the new company are distributed to the parent company's shareholders. This is referred to as a **spin-off**. The parent company's shareholders will become the owners of the divested division. Sometimes divestitures occur because of anti-trust legislation where the government wants to break up the company (e.g. Microsoft). AT & T paid about $8 bn for the computer group NCR in 1990. It subsequently discovered that it didn't 'fit in' (no synergy) with AT & T's core business and it was sold off. Markets generally react positively to spin-offs because management time can be devoted to managing operations that they know best. In addition, shareholders will be content in the knowledge that management will not be tempted to invest in projects in a part of the business that is doing badly.

Governments around the world are undergoing programmes of privatisation, which is an example of divestitures. At the time of writing, there are government proposals to break up CIÉ and spin off the company into its constituent parts—Dublin Bus, Bus Éireann and Iarnroid Éireann. Telecommunications, electric utilities and airlines have undergone significant worldwide privatisation.

Carve-outs are similar to spin-offs except that the shares are sold in a public offering. In other words, shares are sold to the public instead of to the existing shareholders.

SUMMARY

- A takeover can be achieved in one of three ways: (a) acquisition or merger, (b) proxy contests, or by (c) going private.
- Horizontal mergers develop when two firms in the same industry combine.
- A vertical merger occurs when a firm combines with one of its suppliers or customers.
- A conglomerate merger occurs when firms in unrelated industries combine.
- Synergy is the idea that the combined entity will be greater than the combined value of the parts that make up the entity.
- Economies of scale are a motive for mergers. Economies of scale set in when the average cost of production falls as size increases.
- Growth by acquisition may be more advantageous than organic growth.
- Growth in EPS should not be a motive for mergers.
- Merging to reduce risk by diversification does not make economic sense.
- In an acquisition paid for with stock the target firm's shareholders share in the NPV because they are now part of the merged firm. With a cash acquisition the target firm's shareholders get to keep all of the NPV.
- Discounted cash flows are a method used in evaluating a merger.
- With a leveraged buy-out most of the purchase price is financed with debt and the company goes private.

QUESTIONS

1. Define the following terms:
   (a) horizontal merger, vertical merger, conglomerate merger, friendly merger, hostile merger, target company, operating merger, financial merger.
   (b) the DCF method used to evaluate a merger.
   (c) greenmail, white knight, golden parachute, crown jewels, tender offer, shark repellants, poison pill.
   (d) leveraged buy-out.
   (e) junk bonds.
2. 'Mergers take advantage of economies of scale.' Explain.
3. Diversification is sometimes used as a rationale for mergers. Is this a correct reason for mergers?
4. Does merging to increase EPS make economic sense?
5.♦ Empirical evidence suggests that the shareholders of acquiring firms benefit very little from takeovers. Discuss some reasons for this phenomenon.
6. What are the possible difficulties that result from mergers?
7.♦ Many companies split up voluntarily. What are the main reasons?
8. Evaluate the gain and cost of a merger financed by (a) cash and (b) stock.
9. Firm A is considering the acquisition of firm B. The purchase price has been estimated at €11m. Both firms generate annual cash flows of €1m per annum into perpetuity. The management of firm A believes that synergistic benefits of €500,000 will result from the merger. The appropriate cost of capital is 10%. Should the acquisition go ahead?
10.♦ Murphy Corporation is considering the acquisition of Patterson plc. The following information is available on Patterson:

Expected dividend (year end)	€1.50 per share
Dividend growth	6%
Beta	0.8

If Murphy acquires Patterson it is expected that synergies will lead to an increase in dividend growth to 7% per annum instead of the current 6%. Furthermore, because Murphy plans additional investments in Patterson and because this investment will be financed with debt, it is estimated that Patterson's beta will increase to 1.1. The risk-free rate of interest is 7% and the market risk premium is 8%.
Calculate:
(a) Patterson's share price before the acquisition.
(b) The value of Patterson to Murphy and the possible purchase price.

11. McMurrow Airlines wants to acquire Celtic Airlines and operate it as a subsidiary. McMurrow has estimated the following post-merger information on Celtic Airlines:

	2001	2002	2003	2004
Net turnover	€800	€1,000	€1,200	€1,500
Expenses	€70	€90	€100	€120
Interest	€30	€32	€35	€40

The debt ratio of Celtic will increase after the merger therefore adding to the financial risk and consequently increasing Celtic's beta to 1.4. McMurrow also estimates that Celtic's gross profit percentage will be 30% and the new post-merger consolidated corporation tax rate will be 25%. Having completed its analysis McMurrow believes that a terminal growth rate of 6% is achievable on Celtic's cash flows after 2004.

Calculate the value of Celtic Airlines to McMurrow. (Note: use the CAPM to evaluate the appropriate cost of capital. The risk-free rate is 9% and the market risk premium is 3%.) Depreciation funds are not available to the sharelholders by McMurrow.

12. Pike Electronics wants to acquire Electric Power Ltd for €1m. Having carried out an analysis of the proposed acquisition, Pike estimates that the merger will generate incremental cash flows of €120,000 annually for about 12 years. It is also estimated that the cost of capital for this acquisition will be 10%. Should Pike Electronics acquire Electric Power?

13. Smiley wants to acquire Wiley. Both are in the same line of business and both generate annual cash flows of €100 into perpetuity. The cost of equity capital for both firms is 12%. Synergy is expected to add a total of €10 to the merged firm. Calculate the value of Wiley to Smiley.

14.♦The following information is available for two firms X and Y:

	Firm X	Firm Y
Number of shares	1,000,000	2,500,000
Share price	€50	€40
Gearing	0%	0%

X wants to acquire Y and estimates that synergy will add €1m to a merged firm. Y has agreed but wants to be paid €50 a share. Should X agree to the purchase price?

15. Kuncrete Ltd wants to acquire Concrete Ltd. Kuncrete has a market capitalisation valuation of €100m and Concrete has a market capitalisation valuation of €80m. They are both all equity firms. Kuncrete expects synergy to increase its incremental after-tax cash flows by €2m per annum into the future. Kuncrete needs advice on the possible payment mechanism of any possible deal. There are two options (a) a cash payment of €85m or (b) a share for share exchange involving 45% of Kuncrete's shares. Advise Kuncrete on the alternatives. Concrete's cost of equity is 8%.

16. Decies Ltd wishes to acquire Premier Ltd. Decies Ltd has 1,000 shares in issue with a current market price of €20, while Premier has 700 shares in issue with a current market price of €10. Decies Ltd has estimated that the value of the acquisition in terms of synergistic incremental gains would be €3,000.

   (a) If Premier wants cash of €11 per share, what is the NPV of the merger? What will the share price be after the merger?

   (b) If, on the other hand, Decies offers 10 of its shares for every 15 shares in Premier, what will the price of the share be in the merged firm? What is the NPV of the merged firm?

   (c) Under which option (cash or stock) are the shareholders better off?

NOTES

1. Figures from the *Sunday Business Post*, 27 February 2000. Derived from Chapman Flood Mazars (CFM).
2. The NPV method is used extensively in academic literature. For a more detailed description of this method, see Ross, Westerfield, Jordan, op.cit., and Brealey & Myers, op. cit.
3. Although there are a number of methods used in DCF analysis of mergers, the free cash flow and DCF method used here is the clearest and most rigorous, and is used by Brigham, Gapenski & Ehrhardt, op. cit.
4. Candover is a venture capital company.

20
A More Detailed Examination of Bond Market Investment

CHAPTER OBJECTIVES

At the end of this chapter the student should

1. understand the concept of a callable bond/dual-dated bond
2. understand the importance of price volatility in relation to fixed-interest bonds
3. understand the factors that determine price volatility
4. be able to calculate bond prices between coupon dates
5. understand the concept of the true cost of finance
6. be able to calculate the true cost of finance
7. understand the required accounting treatment for a range of capital instruments under Financial Reporting Standard 4

INTRODUCTION

This chapter builds on the material in Chapter 5 and deals with more advanced aspects of bonds.

20.1 Pricing between coupon dates

Bonds trade every day, not just on exact coupon dates. The price of a bond therefore has to reflect the time which has elapsed since the last coupon payment or, more particularly, the time until the next coupon payment. This section examines the mathematics of pricing the bond between coupon dates.

Example 20.1 Pricing between coupon dates

A government bond with face value of €100 is due for redemption on 1 July 2008. It pays an annual coupon of 15% on 1 July each year to the holder of the bond at the close of trading on 30 June in that year. The redemption value is tax free, but the coupon income is subject to tax at the holder's marginal rate. Using a net redemption yield (at 22% tax) of 8% p.a., calculate the price of the bond on

- 1 July 2005
- 30 June 2005
- 31 March 2005
- 31 December 2004
- 30 September 2004
- 1 July 2004
- 30 June 2004.

1 July 2005: The price on this date is calculated using 5.2 with the following parameters
$$Pt = 11.70 \ (\text{€}15 \ less \ \text{tax @ 22\%})$$
$$r = 0.08$$
$$n = 3$$

This gives a price of €109.54.

Note that the investor buying the bond on this day does not get the coupon payment on that date, but must wait until one year later to receive his/her first income from the bond.

30 June 2005: An investor buying the bond on this day is getting the same as the person buying it on 1 July 2005 *plus* an extra €11.70 in one day's time. Since they are both parting with their money at virtually the same time, the buyer on 30 June should pay an extra €11.70 for the bond. The price on 1 July 2005 is calculated as above and the extra coupon of €11.70 payable the next day added to it. This produces an answer of €121.24. Strictly speaking this should be discounted for one day. But this is ignored here for simplicity.

30 March 2005: An investor buying the bond on this date gets the same cash flow as the investor buying it on 30 June 2005. However, she has to part with her money three months earlier and so the price paid on this date should be lower to reflect this. Thus the price of the bond on this date should be €121.24 discounted for three months at a rate of 8% p.a. This produces a price of €118.92.

$$\text{Price } 31/03/05 = \frac{\text{Price } 30/06/05}{(1.08)^{1/4}} = \text{€}118.92$$

31 December 2004: The same logic holds in this case, except that the price must be discounted for six rather than three months. This produces a price of €116.66.

$$\text{Price } 31/12/04 = \frac{\text{Price } 30/06/05}{(1.08)^{1/2}} = \text{€}116.66$$

30 September 2004: The same logic holds in this case, except that the price must be discounted for nine rather than three months. This produces a price of €114.44.

$$\text{Price } 30/09/04 = \frac{\text{Price } 30/06/05}{(1.08)^{3/4}} = \text{€}114.44$$

30 June 2004: The price on this date can be calculated in two ways. Using the same logic as above, with the price discounted for a full year but then adding the extra coupon of €11.70 which would be paid on 1 July 2004, this produces a price of €123.95.

$$\text{Price } 30/06/04 = \frac{\text{Price } 30/06/05}{(1.08)} + €11.70 = €123.95$$

Alternatively, the price on 1 July 2004 (€112.25) can by calculated using 5.2 as before with the following parameters

$$Pt = 11.70 \ (€15 \ \textit{less} \ tax \ @ \ 22\%)$$
$$r = 0.08$$
$$n = 2$$

This gives a price of €112.25.

The extra coupon of €11.70 is then added to it as before. This produces the same answer as above i.e. €123.95.

It can be seen from these prices that the longer the period to the next coupon payment is, the cheaper the bond will be. The bond price will drop immediately after the coupon is paid and rise continuously until the next coupon date. This assumes that redemption yield remains constant.

The prices are summarised in Table 20.1.

Figure 20.1 presents a graphical analysis of the price movements.

Table 20.1 Prices between coupon dates

	€		€
30/06/04	PV = 123.95	31/03/05	PV = 118.92
01/07/04	PV = 112.25	30/06/05	PV = 121.24
30/09/04	PV = 114.44	01/07/05	PV = 109.54
31/12/04	PV = 116.66		

Figure 20.1 Bond price between coupon dates

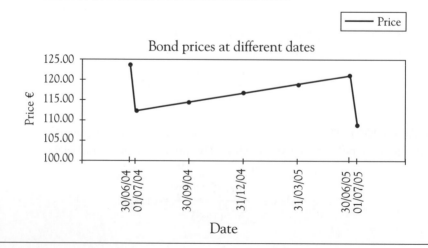

20.2 Price volatility

The general principle evident from section 5.8 above is that bond prices fall as the yield rises and vice versa. This is obviously of importance to an investor holding a portfolio of bonds. However, it would be of much greater use to know by **how much** the price of an individual bond and therefore the value of a portfolio of bonds would change for a given change in the yield. This can be estimated if the price volatility of the bond is known.

Price volatility is defined as the % change in price that occurs when the gross redemption yield changes by one percentage point.

Example 20.2 Price volatility

A government bond pays an annual coupon of 8%, has face value and redemption value of €100 and has nine years to run. It is currently selling at a gross redemption yield (GRY) of 11% p.a. Calculate the price volatility of the bond for

(a) a one percentage point fall in the GRY
(b) a one percentage point rise in the GRY.

Solution
First calculate the price at the different GRY using 5.2. This gives the following:

GRY	Price
11%	83.39
12%	78.69
10%	88.48

Volatility can be calculated as

$$\text{Price volatility} = \frac{\text{Final price}}{\text{Original price}} - 1 \times 100$$

or as

$$\text{Price volatility} = \frac{\text{Final price} - \text{Original price}}{\text{Original price}} \times 100$$

Using the figures above for a change in the GRY from 11% to 12%

$$\text{Price volatility} = \frac{78.69}{83.39} - 1 \times 100 = -5.6\%$$

or

$$\text{Price volatility} = \frac{78.69 - 83.39}{83.39} \times 100 = -5.6\%$$

Repeating the same calculation in moving between 11% and 10% GRY gives the following:

GRY	Price volatility
11% – 12%	– 5.6%
11% – 10%	6.1%

Note: The negative measure above simply reflects the fall in the price brought about by a rise in the GRY, i.e. the inverse relationship between price and GRY. A fall in the GRY, e.g. from 11% to 10%, produces a positive volatility measure.

If we re-calculate the above volatility measure from the other direction, i.e. from a GRY of 12% to a GRY of 11% and from a GRY of 10% to a GRY of 11%, we get the following:

GRY	Price volatility
12% – 11%	6.0%
10% – 11%	– 5.7%

20.3 Features of price volatility

A number of aspects of volatility should be noted. The last two features are of particular importance in that they will assist the investor in the selection of which bonds to purchase.

Price volatility is not symmetric.

In the example above, the absolute measure of price volatility is higher for a one percentage point **fall** in the GRY than for a one percentage point **rise** in the GRY, i.e. in going from a GRY of 12% to a GRY of 11%, rather than going in the opposite direction, viz. 6.0% compared to 5.6%. This is simply because, while the absolute size of the price change must be the same whichever direction it is measured from, the original price against which the % change is calculated is lower when the GRY is higher and vice versa.

Price volatility is lower, the higher the starting yield level is.

In the examples above we see that

GRY	Price volatility
11% – 12%	– 5.6%
10% – 11%	– 5.7%

This is simply because increasing the discount rate by one percentage point at a starting discount rate of 10% represents a 10% rise, whereas raising it by one percentage point at a starting rate of 11% only represents a rise of 9%. Thus the impact of a rise in the discount is lower if the starting rate is higher.

Price volatility is not linear.

Price volatility is normally defined for a one percentage change in the GRY. Thus it measures the percentage change in price brought about by a one percentage point change in the GRY. If the GRY were to move by half a percentage point, the resultant price change will not be half what it would be for a one percentage point change, or if the GRY were to move by two percentage points, the resultant price change will not be double what it would be for a one percentage point change. This is because the relationship between price and yield is convex rather than linear and so a doubling (1% – 2%) in the yield change will lead to a less than doubling in the price change, while a halving (1% – 0.5%) in the yield change will lead to more than a halving in the price change.

GRY	Change in GRY	Price volatility
11% – 12%	1%	–5.6%
11% – 11.5%	0.5%	–2.875%
11% – 13%	2%	–10.85%

These figures can be interpreted as follows:

Starting from a yield of 11%, a one percentage point rise in yield will lead to a fall in price by 5.6%, while a rise in yield of 0.5% will lead to a fall in price of 2.875% (more than half), and a rise in yield of 2% will lead to a fall in price of 10.85% (less than double).

Figure 20.2 Convexity of price volatility

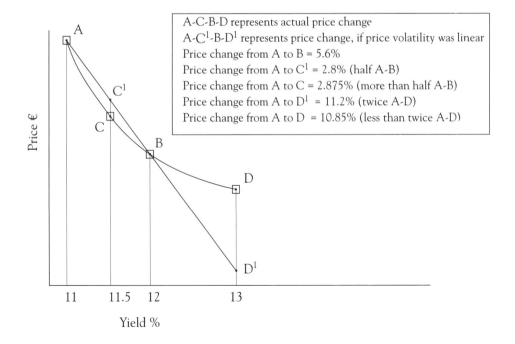

Bonds paying lower % coupons are more price volatile than those paying higher % coupons

(a) Consider two bonds A and B.

The key parameters of the bonds are as follows:

Bond	Time to maturity	Coupon %
A	5	20
B	5	2.5

(b) Suppose the current yield level is 10%.

Price of A		% of value
Coupon element	3.7907 x 20 = 75.81	45 *
Redemption element	0.6209 x 100 = 62.09	55**
Total	= 137.90	100

Price of B		% of value
Coupon element	3.7907 x 2.5 = 9.48	13.2
Redemption element	0.6209 x 100 = 62.09	86.8
Total	= 71.57	100.0

(c) Suppose the current yield level rises to 11%

Price of A		% reduction in value
Coupon element	3.6959 × 20 = 73.92	2.5
Redemption element	0.5935 × 100 = 59.35	4.4
Total	= 133.27	3.36

Price of B	% of value	
Coupon element	3.6959 × 2.5 = 9.24	2.5
Redemption element	0.6209 × 100 = 59.35	4.4
Total	= 68.59	4.16

B is more price volatile than A, 4.16% compared to 3.36%.

Note: * 3.7907 is the value of the expression $\dfrac{1 - (1.1)^{-5}}{0.1}$

This value can be read from the annuity tables at the back of the book

** 0.6209 is the value of the expression $\dfrac{1}{(1.1)^5}$

This value can be read from the discount tables in the Appendix.

(d) Explanation

Price/value is equal to the present value of the total income stream.

When discounting at 10% p.a., coupon income is discounted at varying rates from 0.9091 (1/1.1) to 0.6209 (1/(1.1)^5), see discount tables in the Appendix, while the capital value is all discounted at 0.6209.

When discounting at 11% p.a., coupon income is discounted at varying rates from 0.9009 (1/1.11) to 0.5935 (1/(1.11)^5), while the capital value is all discounted at 0.5935.

The first coupon is about 1% lower in present value terms, the second is about 2% lower etc. and the fifth is about 4.4% lower. The capital value is all of 4.4% lower.

Therefore the bond which **depends** more on the capital value (i.e. the lower coupon bond) is **harder hit** by a rise in yield to 11%, i.e. a larger chunk of its value is reduced by the full 4.4%.

Therefore the value of that bond falls more than the bond less dependent on the capital value (i.e. the higher coupon bond).

Longer-dated bonds are more price volatile than shorter-dated bonds

(i) Now consider two other bonds C and D.

Bond	Time to maturity	Coupon %
A	5	20
B	5	2.5
C	10	20
D	10	2.5

(ii) Price/value of bonds

Price/value	10% yield	11% yield
C	161.44	153.00
D	53.91	49.94

(iii) Price volatility

C	D
5.23%	7.36%

Price volatility of the 10 year bonds in both cases is substantially above the equivalent 5 year bond, i.e. C (5.23%) compared to A (3.36%), and D (7.36%) compared to B (4.16%).

(iv) Explanation
The higher volatility is due to the impact of time on the discount rate

	Capital value		Coupon income cumulative	
	5 year	10 year	5 year	10 year
Yield	Discount factor		Annuity factor	
10%	0.6209	0.3855	3.7907	6.1445
11%	0.5935	0.3522	3.6959	5.8892
% reduction	4.4	8.6	2.5	4.2

Increasing the yield by 1% (10% =>11%) reduces the present value of the total income stream, but has a proportionately greater effect on the 10 year bond both for the capital element and the cumulative coupon element.

Summary of the two key factors affecting volatility of bonds

	% Price volatility		
Coupon ⇒	20%	2.5%	Conclusion
Maturity ⇓			
5 Year	3.36	4.16	Low coupon more volatile
10 Year	5.23	7.36	Low coupon more volatile
Conclusion	Longer maturity more volatile	Longer maturity more volatile	

Therefore in selecting bonds, investors who are expecting yield levels to fall and thus prices to rise should choose long-dated, low-coupon bonds rather than short-dated, high-coupon ones, since these will experience the greatest price rise for a given fall in yields. The opposite applies if yields are expected to rise and prices are expected to fall.

20.4 Price volatility of callable bonds

Section 5.4, Chapter 5, defined a callable bond. As pointed out in that section, callable bonds will invariably be called if it makes economic sense for the issuer to do so. The corollary of this is that it is called when not in the investor's interest. Because of this, these bonds will normally trade at a higher yield to similarly dated bullet bonds. Also because of the possibility of early redemption of these bonds, the price volatility may be different to otherwise similar bullet bonds. This is particularly so when the current yield level is close to the coupon rate in the bond. An example will help to elucidate this.

Example 20.3 Price volatility of a callable bond

Two bonds *Capital* and *Development* pay an annual coupon of 11.5%, have a face value and redemption value of €100 and have two and a quarter years to run. The next coupon payment on both bonds is due in three months' time. The issuer of *development bond*, however, has the option to redeem it three months from now. Assume, for simplicity, that both bonds are selling at a gross redemption yield (GRY) of 12% p.a. Calculate the price volatility of the two bonds for a one percentage point fall in the GRY.

While the market yield is 12%, the issuer has no immediate reason to call the bond early, since to reissue would cost more than the existing coupon of 11.5%.(Note that in practice the bond might be called even if the market rate was above the coupon rate if the expectation is that it is will fall below it in the near future. This is ignored here.) Therefore the two bonds are effectively the same at this yield level and will be priced similarly. However, if the market yield were to drop to 11%, the issuer would be wise to redeem *Development* bond early. It will therefore be priced on the basis of the short date.

The price of both bonds at a 12% yield and an 11% yield can be calculated using formula 5.2 above and work out at

Price at 12% yield *Capital* bond	=	107.56
Price at 11% yield of *Capital* bond	=	109.46
Price volatility of *Capital* bond	=	1.77%

Price at 12% yield *Development* bond	=	107.56
Price at 11% yield of *Development* bond	=	108.63*
Price volatility of *Development* bond	=	0.99%

* The assumption of early redemption results in the redemption value being paid in three months' time along with the normal coupon, but with no further payments thereafter. The price is therefore calculated as

$$\text{Price} = \frac{111.50}{(1.11)^{0.25}} = 108.63$$

A number of features of the price volatility of callable bonds should be noted:

- The risk of early redemption is greater, the closer the % coupon is to current yield levels.
- The longer the option period, the greater the possibility that the stock will be redeemed early.

20.5 The yield curve

The yield curve refers to the pattern of yields on financial instruments as the time to maturity lengthens. The normal situation is that the longer the time to maturity, the higher is the required yield. This reflects the greater illiquidity of a longer bond and the greater danger of erosion of the redemption value and later interest payments due to inflation.

The typical yield curve is illustrated below.

Figure 20.3 The yield curve

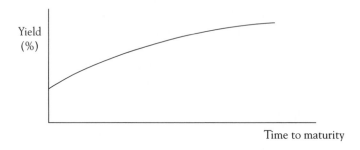

Thus an issuer will normally have to offer a higher yield on a longer bond than on a shorter one.

If the yield on longer-dated bonds is below that on shorter-dated ones, the yield curve is said to be inverted. This reflects the fact that the market expects the rate of interest to fall in the near future, thus exposing those with short-term investments to the risk of reinvesting at lower rates. In a sense they are being compensated now for a future reduction in yield. Another way to interpret this is that longer-term investors are locked in to a rate of interest and are not subject to the same risk as short-term investors. They are therefore prepared to accept a lower yield as a result.

Figure 20.4 The inverted yield curve

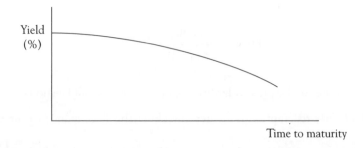

20.6 Rating

A bond issued by a National Treasury/Exchequer or which is State guaranteed is generally regarded as low risk. This bond will be the most highly rated and the issuer can thus issue it at a relatively low yield. Bonds issued by corporations will receive a rating based on the company's size, stability, reputation, track record etc. Ratings are issued by a number of established rating agencies. The highest rating of AAA, for example, represents a virtually riskless bond and the yield at issue will reflect this. The rating system of each agency is a spectrum, with the expected yield increasing as the bond moves out along the risk spectrum. A lower rating might increase the yield required by investors by, say, 50 basis points (50 one-hundredths of a percentage point, i.e. half a percentage point).

20.7 Corporate bonds

The focus up to this point has been on government issued bonds. Most of the mathematical issues are the same for corporate bonds. A key difference concerns the perceived additional risk attached to corporate bonds. This will be manifest in a higher required return for the investor and a higher cost of funds for the company. The yield margin over government stock will vary according to the rating which the company has, either explicitly or implicitly, and will be affected by factors such as

- the size of the company
- the purpose for which the money is being raised
- the existing debt structure of the company
- the guarantees attached to the bond issue etc.

One specific, technical aspect of relevance to corporate bond issues, i.e. the true cost of finance, is dealt with in the next section.

20.8 The true cost of finance

If a company issues a fixed-interest bond at par, e.g. an 8% coupon bond with a redemption value of €1,000 at a price of €1,000, then the annual cost of finance is simply equal to the coupon rate of 8%, i.e. the company carries a debt on its balance sheet of €1,000 for, say, 5 years, pays €80 interest per year and repays the debt at the end of the fifth year. In other words the annual cost of finance is the same as the interest paid.

However, if a company issues the bond at a discount or issues a stepped-interest bond, then the annual interest payment is no longer the same as the true finance cost to the company on an annual basis.

Prior to the introduction of Financial Reporting Standard 4 (FRS 4) *Capital Instruments* in 1993, companies could charge to the profit and loss account the **actual** interest paid rather than the underlying true cost of finance. This was referred to as **off-P & L a/c financing** and allowed companies to minimise the charge to the P & L a/c in the early years of the debt and to back-end load the cost of finance on the P & L a/c.

A typical example of this would be a property company developing a new shopping centre which would take two years to build. The company would have no income from the development during the construction phase and so would be in a difficult cash flow position. By back-end loading the interest payment through a stepped-interest, a zero-coupon or a discount bond, the company could structure its debt servicing to coincide with its expected cash inflow from the development.

This introduced the danger of a potential misinterpretation of a company's debt profile by investors or lenders, since it is the P & L a/c and the balance sheet, rather than the cash flow statement, which tended to receive most attention from analysts.

'The objective of FRS 4 is to ensure that financial statements provide a clear, coherent and consistent treatment of capital instruments' (FRS 4, *Capital Instruments*, Accounting Standards Board, 1993) and to present capital instruments in financial statements in a way that reflects the obligations of the user.

The basic approach is that the P & L a/c should show the cost of servicing the debt instrument at a constant rate on the carrying amount on the balance sheet. The balance sheet treatment is that an adjustment is made, where appropriate, each year to reflect the change in the carrying amount. The examples below help to explain the approach.

The standard also requires companies to treat certain types of indirect equity, such as convertible loan stock (which in the past had been regarded as deferred equity and so reduced the measured gearing ratio) as debt, until it is actually converted.

The following examples are based on the examples shown in the 'Application Notes' which accompany FRS 4. Examples are given for the following situations:

- Convertible debt with enhanced interest
- Debt issued with warrants
- Index-linked loans
- Repackaged perpetual debt
- Stepped-interest bonds.

In the cases shown below the true annual cost of finance is given. In practice this will normally be determined by trial and error. This is similar to the derivation of the gross redemption yield on a bond discussed in Chapter 5. A simple example of the derivation of the true cost of finance is given here as an introduction to the examples below.

Example 20.4 Derivation of the true cost of finance

A company funds a new development through the issue of a four year discount bond. The bonds have a nominal and redemption value of €1,000 and pay an annual interest rate as follows:

End year	% of nominal value
1	3
2	6
3	9
4	12

The bonds are issued at a price of €700.

(a) Calculate the true average annual cost of borrowing for the company over the four year period. (Answer to one place of decimals.)
(b) Verify the answer to (a) above by showing the annual finance cost, annual interest payment and the end-of-year debt position for each of the four years. (Ignore any small rounding error at the end of year 4.)

The cash flow from the bond is as follows:

End-year	1	2	3	4
Cash flow	30	60	90	1,120

The cash flow is discounted at varying rates until two rates are found which give a present value either side of €700. As before, these rates should be one percentage point apart. The true cost of finance can be approximated between these two trial rates by linear interpolation.

In the example a trial rate of 18% produces a present value of €700.97. A discount rate of 18.1% produces a present value of €698.79. The first answer of 18% is marginally more accurate and taken as the estimated true cost of finance.

The annual cash flow and debt position can be shown as follows:

End-year	Finance cost @18%	Interest paid	Debt
0			700
1	126	30	796
2	143.28	60	879.28
3	158.27	90	947.55
4	170.56	1,120	−1.89

The small positive balance at the end of year 4 is simply a rounding error as the true cost of finance is marginally above 18%.

In all of the following examples, the true annual cost of finance is given.

Convertible debt with enhanced interest

This arises where the interest on the convertible bond is due to be increased at some point in the future. It is uncertain as to whether the bond will have been converted before the interest is due to rise. FRS 4 requires that the interest for the full term of the convertible be taken into account.

Example 20.5 Convertible debt with enhanced interest

Convertible debt is issued on 1 January 2004 for €100,000 and is redeemable at the same amount on 31 December 2013. It carries interest of €8,000 a year (a nominal rate of 8%) for the first five years and then rises to €14,900 per year (a nominal rate of 14.9%). The true annual cost of finance is 10.6% (to one place of decimals).

The finance cost in the first year is 10.6% of the debt at the start of the year, i.e. €10,600 (10.6% of €100,000). The company pays €8,000 in the first year, i.e. it underpays by €2,600. This is added to the opening debt of €100,000. The debt therefore ends the year at €102,600. The finance cost in the second year is 10.6% of the balance at the start of the year, i.e. 10.6% of €102,600 = €10,875.60. The company pays €8,000, i.e. it underpays by €2,875.60. This is added to the debt at the start of that year of €102,600 to give a new debt of €105,475.60. This is repeated for each successive year. Note that the interest paid rises to €14,900 in the 6th year.

Table 20.2 Convertible debt with enhanced interest

Year end	Balance at start of year €000	Finance costs for year €000	Cash paid during year €000	Balance at end of year €000
31.12.2004	100,000.00	10,600.00	8,000	102,600.00
31.12.2005	102,600.00	10,875.60	8,000	105,475.60
31.12.2006	105,475.60	11,180.41	8,000	108,656.01
31.12.2007	108,656.01	11,517.54	8,000	112,173.55
31.12.2008	112,173.55	11,890.40	8,000	116,063.95
31.12.2009	116,063.95	12,302.78	14,900	113,466.73
31.12.2010	113,466.73	12,027.47	14,900	110,594.20
31.12.2011	110,594.20	11,722.99	14,900	107,417.18
31.12.2012	107,417.18	11,386.22	14,900	103,903.41
31.12.2013	103,903.41	11,013.76	114,900	17.17

Note: The balance at the end of the tenth year of 17.17 is simply a rounding error as the true cost of finance is slightly below 10.6%.

Debt issued with warrants

An investor who subscribes for this form of capital instrument is buying two separate investments—a bond investment and options on the company equity. The key decision in this situation is how to allocate the proceeds of the issue between the debt and the warrants. The amount attributable to the debt effectively means that, at the beginning of the term of the debt, its value is below the redemption amount by the value of the warrants.

Example 20.6 Debt issued with warrants

A company issues debt with equity warrants attached for a total of €2,200. The redemption value of the debt is €2,200 and the term is 6 years from 1 January 2004. It carries interest at 7.9% p.a. A fair value for the debt and the warrants at the time of issue is €2,000 and €200 respectively.

   The debt is initially valued at €2,000. The interest charge is 7.9% of €2,200 = €173.80. The total finance cost of the debt is the difference between the payments required by the debt which is €3,242.8 ((6 × €173.8) + €2,200) and the deemed proceeds of the debt of €2,000, i.e. €1,242.8. The true finance cost is determined to be 10% p.a.

Table 20.3 Debt issued with warrants

Year ending	Balance at start of year €000	Finance costs for year €000	Cash paid during year €000	Balance at end of year €000
31.12.2004	2,000.00	200.00	173.8	2,026.20
31.12.2005	2,026.20	202.62	173.8	2,055.02
31.12.2006	2,055.02	205.50	173.8	2,086.72
31.12.2007	2,086.72	208.67	173.8	2,121.59
31.12.2008	2,121.59	212.16	173.8	2,159.95
31.12.2009	2,159.95	216.00	2,373.8	2.15

The finance cost for the first year is 10% of the opening debt, i.e. 10% of €2,000 = €200. Since the company only pays €173.80, it underpays by €26.20 and this amount is added to the debt at the end of the first year. This process is continued for each successive year.

   Note: The balance at the end of the tenth year of €2.15 is simply a rounding error as the true cost of finance is slightly below 10%.

Deep discount bonds

The required treatment is similar to that under debt issued with warrants. Example 20.4 above has dealt with this type of instrument.

Index-linked loans

Debts may be issued or loans may be taken out where either the interest payments or the capital value may be determined by reference to an external variable or index, e.g. the interest payments are a mark-up on, say, the inter-bank rate or the capital value is linked to, say, the consumer price index.

FRS 4 requires that finance costs should only be adjusted to reflect the change in the index when they have occurred. The carrying amount of the debt is recalculated to reflect such changes and is accounted for by a change in the finance cost for the period.

Example 20.7 Index-linked loans

A loan of €1,250 is issued on 1 January 2004, on which interest at 6% (€75) is paid annually and the principal amount is repayable based on an index. The balance at the end of each year is found by multiplying the original principal amount by an index at the end of the year. The debt is repayable after 5 years. The index changes as follows:

Date	Index value
1–01–2004	100
1–12–2004	107
1–12–2005	112
1–12–2006	115
1–12–2007	125
1–12–2008	140

The interest paid in the first year was €75. The index rose by 7% in the first year, therefore the debt is adjusted to €1,337.50 (€1,250 × 1.07). The finance cost for the year is 6% interest *plus* the 7% capital adjustment, i.e. 13% of €1,250 = €162.50. The actual payment is €75 and therefore there is an underpayment of (€162.50 – €75 = €87.50). The debt is adjusted upwards by this amount, i.e. €1,250 + €87.50 = €1,337.50. This process is repeated in the subsequent years.

Table 20.4 Index-linked loans

Year ending	Balance at start of year €000	Finance costs for year €000	Cash paid during year €000	Balance at end of year €000
31.12.2004	1,250.00	162.50	75	1,337.50
31.12.2005	1,337.50	137.50	75	1,400.00
31.12.2006	1,400.00	112.50	75	1,437.50
31.12.2007	1,437.50	200.00	75	1,562.50
31.12.2008	1,562.50	262.50	1,825	0.00

Perpetual debt

In the case of perpetual debt, the issuer has neither the right nor the obligation to repay the principal amount of the debt. However, since the company carries an obligation to make interest payments, the debt should be shown on the balance sheet as the net proceeds of the issue. The P & L treatment is that the coupon payment represents the finance cost.

Repackaged perpetual debt

Occasionally perpetual debt is issued such that interest is paid at a relatively high rate for a number of years (the primary period) and subsequently no further or a nominal amount of interest is paid. It is usual that an agreement will allow the issuer to redeem the debt for a nominal amount. The finance cost is the difference between the net proceeds and the payments that the issuer is required to make, allocated at a constant rate on the carrying amount. The balance sheet treatment is to record the debt as the carrying amount.

Example 20.8 Repackaged perpetual debt

A company issues an irredeemable bond on 1 January 2004, the proceeds of which are €1,000. It carries interest at 18.75% for 8 years and no interest thereafter. In effect the interest payments discharge the debt over the period of the interest payments. The constant interest rate works out at 10% p.a.

Table 20.5 Repackaged perpetual debt

Year ending	Balance at start of year €000	Finance costs for year €000	Cash paid during year €000	Balance at end of year €000
31.12.2004	1,000.00	100.00	187.5	912.50
31.12.2005	912.50	91.25	187.5	816.25
31.12.2006	816.25	81.63	187.5	710.38
31.12.2007	710.38	71.04	187.5	593.91
31.12.2008	593.91	59.39	187.5	465.80
31.12.2009	465.80	46.58	187.5	324.88
31.12.2010	324.88	32.49	187.5	169.87
31.12.2011	169.87	16.99	187.5	−0.64

The finance cost in the first year is 10% of €1,000 = €100. Since the company pays €187.50 it is overpaying and so the debt on the balance sheet is reduced by the amount of the overpayment. The debt falls to €912.50. In the second year the finance cost is 10% of

€912.50 = €91.25. Again since the company pays €187.50 it is overpaying and so the debt is reduced on the balance sheet. This process is repeated for each successive year.

Note: The balance at the end of the tenth year of – 0.64 is simply a rounding error as the true cost of finance is slightly over 10% p.a.

Stepped-interest bonds

In this case the interest paid rises in a stepped fashion over the life of the bond (see section 5.4, Chapter 5). The payments are apportioned between a finance charge for each period (at a constant rate on the outstanding debt) and a change in the carrying amount of the debt. The carrying amount of the debt will increase in the periods where the interest payments are below the finance charge (the earlier periods) and decrease in the periods where the payments are higher than the finance costs (the later periods).

Example 20.9 Stepped-interest bond

A company funds a new development through the issue of a four year stepped-interest bond on 1 January 2004. The bonds have a nominal and redemption value of €1,000 and pay an annual interest rate as follows:

Year	% of nominal value
1	3
2	8
3	12
4	18

The bonds are issued at par, i.e. at a price of €1,000. The constant rate works out at 9.7%.

Table 20.6 Stepped-interest bonds

Year ending	Balance at start of year €000	Finance costs for year €000	Cash paid during year €000	Balance at end of year €000
31.12.2004	1,000.00	97.00	30	1,067.00
31.12.2005	1,067.00	103.50	80	1,090.50
31.12.2006	1,090.50	105.78	120	1,076.28
31.12.2007	1,076.28	104.40	1,180	0.68

The finance charge in the first year is 9.7% of €1,000 = €97. Since the company only pays €30, it underpays by €67. This is added to the debt which now becomes €1,067.50. The finance charge in the second year is 9.7% of €1,067 = €103.50. Since the company only pays €80, it underpays by €23.50. This is added to the debt, which now becomes €1,067 + €23.50 = €1,090.50. This process continues for the remaining years of the term of the bond.

Note: The balance at the end of the tenth year of 0.68 is simply a rounding error as the true cost of finance is slightly under 9.7% p.a.

SUMMARY

- Bonds may be priced off the coupon payment date by first pricing at the coupon date and then discounting for the period between the purchase date and the next coupon date.
- Bond prices rise as the coupon payment date approaches and then fall after the coupon is paid.
- Price volatility of bonds is defined as the percentage change in the price brought about by a one percentage point change in the gross redemption yield.
- Price volatility is higher for longer-dated bonds compared to shorter-dated ones.
- Price volatility is higher for bonds with lower coupons rather than those with higher coupons.
- If bond market yields are expected to fall, investors should purchase long-dated, low coupon bonds.
- Callable bonds can be expected to be redeemed as early as possible if it is in the issuer's interest to do so.
- If the market yield falls below the coupon rate on the bond, a callable bond will exhibit lower price volatility than an otherwise similar bullet issue.
- The yield curve normally slopes upwards as the time to maturity lengthens.
- The yield may be inverted if the market expects interest rates to fall in the near future.
- Under Financial Reporting Standard 4, *Capital Instruments*, companies must show the cost of servicing debt at a constant rate on the carrying amount.

QUESTIONS

1. ◆Two government bonds, Finance and Treasury, pay an annual coupon of 9.5%, have a face value and redemption value of €100 and have three years and two months to run. The next coupon payment on both bonds is due in two months' time. The government, however, has the option to redeem the Treasury bond two months from now. Both bonds are selling at a gross redemption yield (GRY) of 10% p.a. Calculate the price volatility of the two bonds for a one percentage point fall in the GRY.
2. ◆A company funds a new development through the issue of a five year discount bond. The bonds have a nominal and redemption value of €1,000 and pay an annual interest rate of 4% of nominal value. The bonds are issued at a price of €800.
   (a) Calculate the true average annual cost of borrowing for the company over the five year period.

(b) Verify the answer to (a) above by showing the annual finance cost, annual interest payment and the end-of-year debt position for each of the five years.

3. ◆(a) A government bond with face value of €100 is due for redemption on 1 July 2002. It pays an annual coupon of 12% on 1 July each year to the holder of the bond at the close of trading on 30 June in that year. The redemption value is tax free, but the coupon income is subject to tax at the holder's marginal rate. Using a net redemption yield (at 24% tax) of 7% p.a., calculate the price of the bond on

    (i)   1 July 1997
    (ii) 1 May 1997
    (iii) 25 June 1997.

(b) Using the information in (a) above, what is the gross income yield on the bond on the same three dates?

4. A company funds a new development through the issue of a six year discount bond. The bonds have a nominal and redemption value of €1,000 and pay an annual interest rate of 2% of nominal value. The bonds are issued at a price of €600.

(a) Calculate the true average annual cost of borrowing for the company over the six year period.

(b) Verify the answer to (a) above by showing the annual finance cost, annual interest payment and the end-of-year debt position for each of the six years.

5. Two bonds, Capital and Development, pay an annual coupon of 12.5%, have face value and redemption value of €100 and have two and a half years to run. The next coupon payment on both bonds is due in six months' time. The issuer of the development bond, however, has the option to redeem it six months from now. Both bonds are selling at a gross redemption yield (GRY) of 13% p.a. Calculate the price volatility of the two bonds for a one percentage point fall in the GRY.

6. (a) A government bond with face value of €100 is due for redemption on 1 June 2008. It pays an annual coupon of 8% on 1 June each year to the holder of the bond at the close of trading on 31 May in that year. The redemption value is tax free, but the coupon income is subject to tax at the holder's marginal rate. Using a net redemption yield (at 24% tax) of 6% p.a., calculate the price of the bond on

    (i)   1 June 1999
    (ii) 1 March 1999
    (iii) 31 May 2006.

(b) Using the information in (a) above, calculate the price volatility of the bond on 1 June 1999 for a 1% rise in the gross redemption yield from its current level.

7. ◆ A company intends to issue a five year bond to raise funds for a new development. It considers two alternative bonds:

Bond A would be a stepped-interest bond which would have a nominal value of €1,000 and pay an annual interest rate as shown on next page.

Bond A End year	Interest as % of nominal value
1	2
2	5
3	8
4	12
5	15

Bond A would be issued at a price of €1,000, but would have a redemption value of €1,200, i.e. it would pay a capital bonus of €200 on redemption.

Bond B would have a nominal and redemption value of €1,000 and pay an annual interest rate of 10% of nominal value. Bond B would be issued at a price of €1,000.

Using the true average annual cost of borrowing associated with each bond over the five year period, determine which of the two bonds is the cheaper from the company's point of view.

8. (a) A government bond with face value of €100 is due for redemption on 1 June 2004. It pays an annual coupon of 10% on 1 June each year to the holder of the bond at the close of trading on 31 May in that year. The redemption value is tax free, but the coupon income is subject to tax at the holder's marginal rate. Using a net redemption yield (at 26% tax) of 9% p.a., calculate the price of the bond on
     (i) 1 June 1997
     (ii) 1 May 1997
     (iii) 20 April 1997.
   (b) Using the information in (a) above, what is the gross income yield on the bond on the same three dates?

9. A company funds a new development through the issue of a five year discount bond. The bonds have a nominal and redemption value of €1,000 and pay an annual interest rate of 3% of nominal value. The bonds are issued at a price of €700.
   (a) Calculate the true average annual cost of borrowing for the company over the five year period.
   (b) Verify the answer to (a) above by showing the annual finance cost, annual interest payment and the end-of-year debt position for each of the five years. (Ignore any small rounding error at the end of year 5.)

10. (a) A government bond with face value of €100 is due for redemption on 1 June 2010. It pays an annual coupon of 9% on 1 June each year to the holder of the bond at the close of trading on 31 May in that year. The redemption value is tax free, but the coupon income is subject to tax at the holder's marginal rate. Using a net redemption yield (at 22% tax) of 8% p.a., calculate the price of the bond on
     (i) 1 June 1998
     (ii) 1 February 1998
     (iii) 15 March 1998.
   (b) Using the information in (a) above, what is the gross income yield on the bond on the same three dates?

11. A company funds a new development through the issue of a five year discount bond. The bonds have a nominal and redemption value of €1,000 and pay an annual interest rate of 5% of nominal value. The bonds are issued at a price of €750.

(a) Calculate the true average annual cost of borrowing for the company over the five year period.

(b) Verify the answer to (a) above by showing the annual finance cost, annual interest payment and the end-of-year debt position for each of the five years. (Ignore any small rounding error at the end of year 5.)

12. A government bond with face value of €100 is due for redemption on 1 July 2006. It pays an annual coupon of 7% on 1 July each year to the holder of the bond on 30 June in that year. Using a gross redemption yield of 8% p.a., calculate the price of the bond on

(a) 6 May 1999

(b) 31 January 1999

(c) 6 May 2000

(d) 1 July 2004.

13. A company funds a new development through the issue of a six year discount bond. The bonds have a nominal and redemption value of €1,000 and pay an annual interest rate of 3% of nominal value. The bonds are issued at a price of €800.

(a) Calculate the true average annual cost of borrowing for the company over the six year period.

(b) Verify the answer to (a) above by showing the annual finance cost, annual interest payment and the end-of-year debt position for each of the six years.

14. A company funds a new development through the issue of a four year discount bond. The bonds have a nominal and redemption value of €1,000 and pay an annual interest rate as follows:

End year	% of nominal value
1	0
2	5
3	10
4	15

The bonds are issued at a price of €750.

(a) Calculate the true average annual cost of borrowing for the company over the four year period (answer to one place of decimals).

(b) Verify the answer to (a) above by showing the annual finance cost, annual interest payment and the end-of-year debt position for each of the four years. (Ignore any small rounding error at the end of year 4.)

15. ◆A government bond with face value of €100 is due for redemption on 1 August 2008. It pays an annual coupon of 6% on 1 August each year to the holder of the bond on 31 July in that year.

(a) Using a gross redemption yield of 9% p.a., calculate the price of the bond on

(i) 26 May 2000

(ii) 31 January 2000

(iii) 26 August 2000

(iv) 26 May 2001

(v) 1 August 2005.

(b) (i) Explain briefly why the bond is cheaper in (a) (ii) above than in (a)(i).

(ii) Explain briefly why the bond is cheaper in (a) (iii) above than in (a)(i).

16. Two bonds, Capital and Development, pay an annual coupon of 10.5%, have face value and redemption value of €100 and have three and a quarter years to run. The next coupon payment on both bonds is due in three months' time. The issuer of the Development bond, however, has the option to redeem it three months from now. Both bonds are selling at a gross redemption yield (GRY) of 11% p.a. Calculate the price volatility of the two bonds for a one percentage point fall in the GRY.

17. A government bond with face value of €100 is due for redemption on 1 November 2005. It pays an annual coupon of 7% on 1 November each year to the holder of the bond on 31 October in that year. Using a gross redemption yield of 10% p.a., calculate the price of the bond on
    (a) 31 October 1998
    (b) 6 June 1998
    (c) 6 November 1998
    (d) 1 November 2003.

18. A government bond with face value of €100 is due for redemption on 1 September 2003. It pays an annual coupon of 9% on 1 September each year to the holder of the bond on 31 August in that year. Using a gross redemption yield of 12% p.a., calculate the price of the bond on
    (a) 6 July 1999
    (b) 30 April 1999
    (c) 6 July 1998
    (d) 1 September 2002.

19. A company funds a new development through the issue of a four year stepped-interest bond. The bonds have a nominal and redemption value of €1,000 and pay an annual interest rate as follows:

Year	% of nominal value
1	2
2	5
3	8
4	10

   The bonds are issued at a price of €750.
   (a) Calculate the true average annual cost of borrowing for the company over the four year period.
   (b) Verify the answer to (a) above by showing the annual finance cost, annual interest payment and the end-of-year debt position for each of the four years.

20. Define price volatility in relation to bonds.

21. Set out the key features of price volatility.

22. Explain why price volatility is higher for longer-dated bonds than for shorter-dated ones.

23. Explain the different price volatility exhibited by a callable bond and an otherwise similar bullet bond.

24. Explain why the yield curve may become inverted.

25. Explain what is meant by bond rating.
26. Explain what is meant by the true cost of finance.

21
Loans and Mortgages

CHAPTER OBJECTIVES

At the end of this chapter the student should be able to:

1. understand the various types of mortgage loans available
2. in particular, understand the difference between an annuity (repayment) and an endowment-linked mortgage
3. calculate the gross (monthly) payment for both the annuity and endowment-linked mortgage
4. calculate the net (monthly) payment for each year of the mortgage term for both the annuity and endowment-linked mortgage
5. calculate the outstanding balance on a loan/mortgage at any point during the term
6. construct an amortisation schedule
7. calculate the new payment on a loan if the rate of interest changes
8. understand the concept of refinancing a loan
9. calculate the cost of servicing a loan before and after refinancing
10. understand the basic criteria used by banks in assessing loan applications.

INTRODUCTION

This chapter deals with the a number of important mathematical issues in relation to loans and mortgages. It also examines the different types of mortgage packages available in Ireland, mainly focused on the residential mortgage market. Numerical examples are given for the main types and a range of examinable questions, e.g. the impact of changing rates of interest and the impact of missed or additional payments are provided at the end of the chapter. As the material in this chapter draws on material in earlier chapters, and the latter part of the chapter draws on the earlier part, the solutions to questions assume that the student has mastered this earlier material and will benefit from working through the examples with less hand-holding than earlier. Solutions are therefore not displayed in step-by-step detail in every case.

A short section examines briefly the lending criteria applied by commercial banks.

21.1 The Irish mortgage market

The residential mortgage market in Ireland was traditionally the preserve of the building societies, with only limited market presence by the commercial banks. This changed during the 1980s when the banks aggressively targeted this form of lending. The building societies responded by becoming more customer oriented. With the passing of the Building Societies Act in 1989, the distinction between the two became effectively redundant from the point of view of service provision. Access to the wholesale money markets improved the consistency of funding to the building societies and **mortgage famines** became a thing of the past.

Since then a number of the largest building societies have become public limited companies and/or merged with other financial institutions. The market has become extremely competitive both in terms of cost (interest rates) and availability of finance. There has been an explosion in the range and type of finance packages available. The potential borrower is presented with a sometimes bewildering array of mortgage products. These include

- standard annuity (repayment) mortgage
- endowment-linked mortgage
- pension mortgage
- low/slow start mortgage
- payment holidays
- lump sum payments
- fixed versus variable rate.

Each of these is described in section 21.2 below.

Coupled with the general increase in loan-to-value ratios, the net result has been that consumers have far greater access to finance than ever before both for first-time buyers and those trading up. This has, in no small way, contributed to the massive growth in residential prices in Ireland over the past five years.

21.2 Types of mortgage loans

Annuity/repayment

This is the traditional method of repaying a mortgage in which a fixed periodic payment is made for the duration of the mortgage term. The payment is made up of capital and interest, with the bulk of the payment meeting the interest charge at the beginning of the period, with only a very small capital contribution. By the end of the term the same payment is primarily being used to repay the capital debt with only a small interest component.

The interest content of the mortgage payment qualifies as a tax allowance at the standard rate of tax, (tax credit) up to a limit of £5,000 interest p.a. for first-time buyers in the first five years of the mortgage and £4,000 for other borrowers. The effect of this is shown in section 21.5 below.

Endowment-linked mortgage

With an endowment mortgage, the mortgagor only pays interest on the loan and the capital value of the loan remains constant for the duration of the term. At the same time the borrower takes out an endowment policy (effectively an investment policy). This is targeted to mature at a value which is at least as high as the loan size. The proceeds of the endowment policy are used to redeem the loan.

Up to the early 1990s these loans could be more tax efficient than the annuity mortgage since the premium on the endowment policy could also be set off against the tax liability and became very popular for a period of time. They are far less popular now due to poor investment performance in the early 1990s and the removal of the tax relief on premium payments.

This type of mortgage loan carries additional risks compared to the traditional mortgage. If the rate of interest rises during the term, the full capital value is exposed to the increased charge, whereas with the annuity mortgage some of the capital will have been paid off and the increased interest rate will be against a smaller loan balance. Clearly the opposite applies if the rate of interest falls during the mortgage term. There is also the danger (unless it is a full-cost endowment policy), if the investment returns are not high enough, that the terminal value of the policy will not reach the mortgage loan size and the borrower will have to make up the shortfall. Again this can work both ways, with the possibility of a capital bonus at the end of the term when the mortgage has been redeemed. Section 21.3 below provides a number of numerical examples.

Pension mortgage

This is similar in concept to the endowment mortgage, in that the borrower only pays interest on the mortgage loan and simultaneously contributes to a pension plan. The loan is repaid at the end of the period from the proceeds of the pension lump sum. Since pension contributions are tax allowable and the cash lump sum from a pension is tax free, this can be a tax efficient way to repay a mortgage. It is aimed primarily at the self-employed and those not in an occupational pension scheme.

New Variants

Payment holidays

Breaks in the repayments can be made, say, for up to three months for particular family needs, e.g. the birth of a child, house renovations etc. The missed payments can be dealt with by increasing the term of the mortgage or by increasing the size of the remaining payments in order to pay off the mortgage in the original timeframe. This facility may not be available if the loan is at a fixed rate. A related facility is where repayments are made 10 or 11 times a year rather than the normal 12, with the payment being missed at, say, Christmas and at summer holiday time.

Slow/low start mortgage

This is aimed at the first-time buyer, either a single person or a couple who may be trying to furnish a home at the same time as starting to pay off the mortgage. It allows for reduced payments for a period of time to give the borrower(s) some breathing space to meet other expenses. It may simply be a moratorium on capital payments, e.g. the borrower only meets the interest charge and the capital value of the loan remains the same until the payments are increased. If the payment doesn't meet the interest charge, then this will be capitalised, i.e. added to the loan size. The borrower then faces an increased payment later.

Lump sum payments

Here the borrower can make occasional lump sum payments which will reduce the capital debt and therefore reduce the interest charge on the loan. This will lead to the term of the mortgage being shortened. It is of particular benefit to individuals who may occasionally make abnormal or windfall gains, e.g. end-of-year bonuses. This type of lump sum payment facility may not be available if the mortgage is at a fixed rate of interest.

21.3 Calculating the mortgage payment

Endowment

In the case of the endowment mortgage, the payment is simply the rate of interest applied to the capital value of the loan *plus* the endowment policy premium.

Example 21.1 Calculating the mortgage payment for an endowment mortgage

A mortgage loan of €80,000 is taken out over a 15 year period. The rate of interest is 6% p.a. payable monthly and the endowment policy premium costs €300 per month. The monthly cost of servicing the mortgage is therefore

Payment to bank: €80,000 × 0.005 =	400
Endowment policy premium	300
Total	700

Note: the interest charge per month is 0.06/12 = 0.005

The endowment policy is targeted to reach a terminal value of at least €80,000 at the end of 15 years.

Example 21.2 Calculating the mortgage payment for an annuity mortgage

The cost of an annuity mortgage for the same amount as above, where the interest is charged on a reducing balance basis, can be calculated using the ordinary simple annuity formula introduced in Chapter 4. (Note: The lending institutions do not publish the precise formula for calculating the size of the periodic payment. This formula provides a close approximation where the interest is charged on reducing balance basis.)

$$\text{Loan size} = P_t \left[\frac{1 - (1 + r)^{-n}}{r} \right] \tag{21.1}$$

P_t = periodic payment
r = interest rate per compounding period
n = number of payments.

Through algebraic manipulation this can be rewritten as follows:

$$P_t = \text{Loan} \times r \times \frac{(1+r)^n}{(1+r)^n - 1} \qquad (21.2)$$

Using the figures from the example above

$$\text{€80,000} = P_t \left[\frac{1 - (1.005)^{-180}}{0.005} \right]$$

solving for P_t as shown in Chapter 4 gives a figure of €675.09

This payment is broken into interest and capital components.

In the first month the interest charge is €80,000 × 0.005 = €400

The amount available for capital payment is therefore €275.09

This will be used to reduce the capital debt which now reduces to €80,000 − €275.09 = €79,724.91.

The interest charge in the second month is €79,724.91 × 0.005 = €398.62

The amount available for capital payment in the second month is therefore €675.09 − €398.62 = €276.47

This process continues for each payment period, with the interest component declining and the capital component rising.

21.4 Amortisation schedule

The amortisation schedule shows the manner in which the debt is written down over the life of the loan. The schedule is drawn up as described above. The amortisation schedule is shown as Table 21.1 on page 482.

Using the data in example 21.2 above, it can be seen from the amortisation schedule that the interest element is declining and the capital element is rising over the course of the repayment term. The final payment is slightly smaller than the previous one since the monthy payment was rounded up to the nearest cent.

It can also be seen that the total paid over the first year can be divided into interest and capital payments. The summary shown for the first year is used in section 21.5 to determine the amount of tax relief available and the resultant net payment.

It can also be seen that the amount of capital paid in the first year can be calculated either as the sum of the capital payments column or by subtracting the outstanding balance at the end of the 12th month from the opening balance.

Outstanding balance during the term

The schedule could be completed for all 180 months. To avoid doing this, the balance at the end of the 177th month is calculated and the last three months are shown. The outstanding balance at any point in time can be calculated from either of the following two formulae:

Table 21.1 Amortisation schedule

		Loan size 80,000	Number of payments 180	Interest Rates 0.005
			payment = 675.09	

Time	Payment	Interest	Capital	Balance
0				80,000
1	675.09	400.00	275.09	79,724.91
2	675.09	398.62	276.46	79,448.45
3	675.09	397.24	277.84	79,170.61
4	675.09	395.85	279.23	78,891.38
5	675.09	394.46	280.63	78,610.75
6	675.09	393.05	282.03	78,328.72
7	675.09	391.64	283.44	78,045.28
8	675.09	390.23	284.86	77,760.42
9	675.09	388.80	286.28	77,474.13
10	675.09	387.37	287.71	77,186.42
11	675.09	385.93	289.15	76,897.27
12	675.09	384.49	290.60	76,606.67
Year 1	8101.03	4707.69	3393.33	
177				2003.88
178	675.09	10.02	665.07	1338.81
179	675.09	6.69	668.40	670.41
180	673.76	3.35	670.41	0.00

(a) Retrospective method

$$OB_k = PV(1 + r)^k - P_t\left[\frac{(1 + r)^k - 1}{r}\right] \tag{21.3}$$

where
PV = present value (loan size)
P_t = periodic payment
r = interest rate per compounding period
k = number of payments already made.

The logic of the above formula is:
• The first term represents the value that the loan would have reached if no payments had been made against it, i.e. it is the original balance compounded by the rate of interest for the relevant number of periods.
• The second term represents the value of a notional savings fund into which the payments have been lodged and which pays the same rate of interest as the charge on the loan.
• The loan balance is the difference between the two. It can be shown that where k = n, i.e. the end of the loan term, the balance is zero.

(b) Prospective method

$$OB_k = P_t \left[\frac{1 - (1 + r)^{-(n-k)}}{r} \right]$$

(21.4)

where

P_t = periodic payment

r = interest rate per compounding period

n = planned total number of payments

k = number of payments already made.

This method requires that the final payment be the same as previous payments. The logic of this formula is that the balance at any point has the same value as a loan which could be taken out at that point, to be repaid at the same rate of interest, with the same size and number of payments remaining. This is just the present value at that point of the remaining (n–k) payments. The formula is the same as the formula for the present value of an ordinary simple annuity introduced in Chapter 4.

Example 21.3 *Finding the outstanding balance using the retrospective method*

Using the data in example 21.2, find the outstanding balance at the end of the
(a) 12th month
(b) 177th month.

(a)

$$OB_{12} = 80{,}000 \, (1.005)^{12} - 675.09 \, \frac{(1.005)^{12} - 1}{0.005}$$

$$84{,}934.22 - 8{,}327.61 = 76{,}606.61$$

(b)

$$OB_{177} = 80{,}000 \, (1.005)^{177} - 675.09 \, \frac{(1.005)^{177} - 1}{0.005}$$

$$193{,}411.78 - 191{,}407.89 = 2{,}003.88$$

Example 21.4 *Finding the outstanding balance using the prospective method*

Using the data in example 21.2, find the outstanding balance at the end of the
(a) 12th month
(b) 177th month.

(a)

$$OB_{12} = 675.09 \, \frac{1 - (1.005)^{-168}}{0.005} = 76{,}607.18$$

(b)

$$OB_{177} = 675.09 \, \frac{1 - (1.005)^{-3}}{0.005} = 2{,}005.18$$

21.5 Gross versus net payments

Interest payments on mortgage loans qualify for tax relief at the standard rate (22%). The tax allowance is the amount of interest paid, subject to a maximum interest payment of £5,000 p.a. for first-time buyers in the first five years of the mortgage and a maximum of £4,000 otherwise. To introduce the concept of tax relief in a simple way, the examples below assume a first-time buyer and assume that the interest limit is set at €5,000 rather than £5,000 and is available for the full term of the mortgage.

Endowment mortgage

In the case of the endowment mortgage, assuming no change in the rate of interest, the amount of interest paid each year remains constant, therefore the tax relief remains constant and the net payment (gross payment *less* tax relief) remains constant. Using the information in example 21.1 above, this can be calculated as follows:

Annual tax relief

Interest paid: $12 \times €400 = €4,800$
Tax allowance = €4,800 (since interest is below the €5,000 limit)
Tax relief = $€4,800 \times 0.22 = €1,056$

Monthly equivalent

€1,056/12 = €88
Gross payment = €700.00 (€400 interest on loan + €300 endowment premium)
Tax relief = €88.00
Net payment = €612.00
This will remain constant for the duration of the mortgage.

Annuity mortgage

Using the information in example 21.2 above produces the results shown in table 21.2. It can be seen that the tax relief diminishes from €86.31 in the first year to €4.72 in the last year and that the net payment rises from €588.78 in the first year to €670.39 in the last year.

The working calculations are shown in the accompanying table.

Table 21.2 Mortgage payments

Loan 80,000	Term 180 months	Interest rate 0.005%	Payment 675.09
Year	Gross payment	Monthly tax relief	Net payment
1	675.09	86.31	588.78
2	675.09	82.47	592.61
3	675.09	78.40	596.69
4	675.09	74.07	601.01
5	675.09	69.48	605.61
6	675.09	64.61	610.48
7	675.09	59.43	615.66
8	675.09	53.93	621.16
9	675.09	48.10	626.98
10	675.09	41.91	633.18
11	675.09	35.33	639.75
12	675.09	28.35	646.73
13	675.09	20.94	654.15
14	675.09	13.07	662.01
15	675.09	4.72	670.37

The pattern of the gross and net payments under the two mortgage types is shown in figure 21.1 below.

Figure 21.1 Gross and net monthly mortgage payments

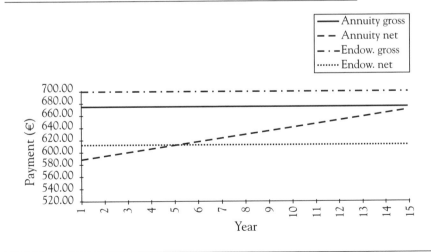

It can be seen that the net payment under the annuity mortgage rises over the course of the term. It crosses the fixed net payment under the endowment mortgage in the seventh year.

Working Calculations:

Outstanding balance	Year	Capital paid	Interest paid	Tax allowance	Tax relief	Monthly relief
80,000.00						
76,606.67	1	3,393.33	4,707.69	4,707.69	1,035.69	86.31
73,004.04	2	3,602.63	4,498.40	4,498.40	989.65	82.47
69,179.21	3	3,824.83	4,276.20	4,276.20	940.76	78.40
65,118.47	4	4,060.74	4,040.29	4,040.29	888.86	74.07
60,807.28	5	4,311.19	3,789.83	3,789.83	833.76	69.48
56,230.18	6	4,577.10	3,523.93	3,523.93	775.26	64.61
51,370.78	7	4,859.40	3,241.62	3,241.62	713.16	59.43
46,211.65	8	5,159.12	2,941.90	2,941.90	647.22	53.93
40,734.33	9	5,477.33	2,623.70	2,623.70	577.21	48.10
34,919.17	10	5,815.15	2,285.87	2,285.87	502.89	41.91
28,745.35	11	6,173.82	1,927.29	1,927.29	423.99	35.33
22,190.75	12	6,554.61	1,546.42	1,546.42	340.21	28.35
15,231.86	13	6,958.88	1,142.14	1,142.14	251.27	30.94
7,843.77	14	7,388.09	712.93	712.93	156.85	13.07
0.00	15	7,843.77	257.25	257.25	56.60	4.72

21.6 Missed payments

If payments are missed in a mortgage loan (either through default or through an agreed payment holiday), then the borrower must either increase the remaining payments or increase the term of the mortgage.

Example 21.5 Missed payments

A borrower is repaying a loan of €60,000 subject to interest at a rate of 13.2% p.a. compounded monthly with equal monthly payments over a period of ten years, the first payment one month after the loan is taken out. The payments due at the end of the 70th, 71st and 72nd months are missed.

(a) If the borrower continues with the same monthly payment as before at the end of the 73rd month, calculate the number of payments required to clear the loan.

(b) If the borrower increases the remaining payments starting at the end of the 73rd month in order to repay the loan in the same time as originally scheduled, find the size of these new payments

The parameters required to find the original payment and the outstanding balance after 69 payments are:

PV = 60,000

n = 120 months

r = 0.011 per month.

The original payment is got from 21.1 above and works out at €902.96. The outstanding balance after the payment at time 69 is made is got from 21.3 above and works out at €35,100.90.

Since the borrower makes no payments in time 70, 71 and 72, this balance will be charged interest at the rate of 1.1% per month for the next 3 months (i.e. until time 72). The balance at time 72 will therefore be €36,272.02.

Note that the interest in month 73 should not be calculated as it is taken into account in 21.1 above.

(a) The required number of payments can be calculated from 21.1 above using the following parameters. The situation is effectively treated as a new loan from this point on with an **opening** balance equal to €36,272.02

PV = 36,272.02

Pt = 902.96

r = 0.011

n = unknown number of payments to be calculated.

This produces an answer of 53.3. This can be interpreted as 53 full payments and one final smaller payment.

(b) The required payment can be calculated from 21.1 above using the following parameters:

PV = 36,272.02

r = 0.011

n = 48 (120 – 72)

Pt = unknown payment size to be calculated.

This produces an answer of €976.69.

Therefore the borrower can either stick with the existing payment of €902.96 and pay the loan off in 54 more months or increase the payment to €976.69 and pay the loan off in the term originally intended.

21.7 Additional payments

Additional payments will have the opposite effect of a missed payment, in that they will decrease the outstanding balance at any point and lead to either a shortening of the term or a decease in the remaining payments.

Example 21.6 Additional payments

A borrower is repaying a loan of €60,000 subject to interest at a rate of 13.2% p.a. compounded monthly with equal monthly payments over a period of ten years, the first payment one month after the loan is taken out. Suppose the borrower made an additional payment of €2,000 at the end of the 69th month.

(i) If the borrower continues with the same monthly payment as before, at the end of the 70th month calculate the number of payments required to clear the loan.

(ii) If the borrower reduces the remaining payments starting at the end of the 70th month in order to repay the loan in the same time as originally scheduled, find the size of these new payments.

  (i) The balance after 69 payments is known from example 21.5 and equals €35,100.09. This is now reduced by €2,000. The required number of payments can be calculated from 21.1 above using the following parameters:

    PV = 33,100.09 (35,100.09 – 2,000)

    Pt = 902.96

    r = 0.011

    n = unknown number of payments to be calculated.

    This produces an answer of 47.2. This can be interpreted as 47 full payments and one final smaller payment. This is almost 4 payments less than the original 51 remaining payments.

  (ii) This is similar to part (i) above except that the unknown factor is now the periodic payment. The required payment can be calculated from 21.1 above using the following parameters:

    PV = 33,100.09

    r = 0.011

    n = 51 (120 – 69)

    P_t = unknown payment size to be calculated.

    This produces an answer of €851.48.

Therefore the borrower can either stick with the existing payment of €902.96 and pay the loan off in 48 more months or reduce the payment to €851.48 and pay the loan off in the term originally intended.

21.8 Change in the rate of interest

All of the examples discussed so far assume that the rate of interest remains the same for the duration of the loan term. In practice this will rarely be the case and rates of interest can be expected to change a number of times over the course of a normal mortgage term, i.e. 15, 20 or 25 years. If the borrower opts for a fixed-rate loan, this will overcome the issue of changing rates, but a fixed rate would not normally be available for 15 or 20 years. The example below looks at the impact of a change in the rate of interest on both the gross and net payment for an annuity and endowment mortgage.

Example 21.7 Change in the rate of interest

You are taking out a €60,000 mortgage loan repayable over fifteen years. The local bank is quoting an interest rate of 7.2% p.a. compounded monthly on an annuity mortgage and a rate of 7.8% p.a. compounded monthly on an endowment-linked mortgage. The premium payable on the endowment policy would be €160 per month, payable at the same time as the mortgage payment. The interest content of the mortgage repayments, up to a maximum interest of €5,000 per annum, qualifies as a tax allowance at the standard rate of tax (22%). This will hold for the full term of the mortgage.

Calculate for both options:
(a) the gross monthly repayment
(b) the net monthly repayment in the first year
(c) the net monthly repayment in the twelfth year
(d) the net monthly repayment in the twelfth year if the nominal rate of interest on both options rose by 0.6% p.a. compounded monthly at the end of the eleventh year and the gross monthly repayments for the remaining four years of the mortgage term were increased to a new equal value to reflect the new interest rate.

(a) Gross payment
Annuity
The monthly payment is calculated from 21.1 above as €546.03

Endowment
The monthly payment to the bank is calculated as €60,000 × 0.0065 = €390
Add the endowment policy premium = €160
Total = €550

(b) and (c) Net payments

Interest paid (annuity)

		Year 1		Year 12
Outstanding balance	Time 0	60,000.00	Time 132	22,714.12
	Time 12	57,692.50	Time 144	17,631.65
Capital paid	Year 1	2,307.50	Year 12	5,082.52
Total paid	Year 1	6,552.36	Year 12	6,552.36
Interest paid	Year 1	4,244.84	Year 12	1,469.84

Interest paid (endowment)
Interest paid = 390 x 12 = 4,680

Tax relief annual	Annuity Y1	Annuity Y12	Endowment
Interest paid	4,244.84	1,469.84	4,680.00
Tax allowance	4,244.84	1,469.84	4,680.00
Tax relief	933.86	323.36	1,029.60
Monthly tax relief	77.82	26.95	85.80
Gross payment	546.03	546.03	550.00
Tax relief	77.82	26.95	85.80
Net payment	468.21	519.08	464.20

(d) Change in the rate of interest
The rate of interest changes at the end of the 11th year.
    Calculate the loan balance at this point.

Annuity: Outstanding balance @ time 132 using 21.3 = €22,714.12

Endowment: Balance = Original loan size = 60,000

New monthly payment
Annuity
The outstanding balance is treated conceptually like a new loan at this point. The periodic payment can be found using 21.1.

PV = 22,714.12*
r = 0.0065
n = 48
Pt = unknown payment size to be calculated.
The monthly payment works out at €555.39
* Balance at the time the new interest rate becomes operational.

Endowment
The monthly payment to the bank is calculated as €60,000 × 0.007 = €420
Add the endowment policy premium   = €160
Total   = €580

Net Payments
Interest paid (annuity)
Year 12 (€)

Outstanding balance	Time 132	22,714.12 (start of **new** loan)
	Time 144	17,679.39
Capital paid	Year 12	5,034.73
Total paid	Year 12	6,628.56
Interest paid	Year 12	1,593.83

Interest paid (endowment)
Interest paid = €420 x 12 = £5,040

Annual tax relief	Annuity Y12	Endowment
Interest paid	1,593.83	5,040.00 (>5,000)
Tax allowance	1,593.83	5,000.00
Tax relief	350.64	1,100.00
Monthly tax relief	29.22	91.67
Gross payment	552.39	580.00
Tax relief	29.22	91.67
Net payment	523.17	508.33

21.9 Refinancing loans

Borrowers are sometimes presented with opportunities to refinance existing loans, i.e. borrowing from a second financial institution and paying off the first. If the new financial package is at a lower rate of interest than the existing loan, then the borrower stands to gain. Against that, however, there may be a penalty or other charge imposed by the original lender. The borrower would then have to borrow more than is currently owed in order to redeem the existing loan. Therefore it becomes a trade-off between a higher loan balance at a lower rate of interest versus a lower loan balance at a higher rate of interest. The refinancing option is worth taking if the periodic payment required to clear the new loan is lower than the existing periodic payment or, alternatively, if sticking with the existing payment, the second loan would be paid off more quickly than the first.

Example 21.8 Refinancing a loan

Using the information in example 21.5 above, suppose the borrower is offered an alternative source of finance at the end of the fifth year at a rate of interest of 9.6% p.a., but the original bank charges an early repayment penalty of €200 *plus* the amount of interest which was paid in the previous six months. Should the borrower refinance the loan?

Calculate the balance on the loan at the time the refinancing option becomes available using 21.3 with k = 60.

Balance at time 60 = 39,506.70

The borrower needs to borrow this amount *plus* the penalty in order to redeem the loan.

Penalty	€
OB at time 60	= 39,506.70
OB at time 54	= 42,211.92
Capital paid (time 55–60)	= 2,705.22
Total paid (time 55–60)	= 5,417.76
Interest paid (time 55–60)	= 2,712.54
Penalty	= 2,712.54 + 200 = 2,912.54
Need to borrow	39,506.70 + 2,912.54 = 42,419.24

The choice is now between continuing an existing loan valued at 39,506.70 at a rate of interest of 13.2% p.a. compounded monthly or a loan of 42,419.24 at a rate of interest of 9.6% p.a. compounded monthly, each to be paid off over 5 years with monthly payments

The new periodic payment can be calculated from formula 21.1 with

PV = 42,419.24

n = 60

r = 0.008

This produces a payment of €892.96

Since 892.96 < 902.96 the borrower should refinance the loan.

21.10 Bank lending criteria

This section discusses the criteria applied by the lending institutions in assessing loans both for personal mortgages and also for commercial borrowing. The commercial lending criteria are presented in the context of lending to the property sector

Personal mortgage lending criteria

The principal lending criteria relate to

- the loan-to-value ratio (LTV)
- ratio of loan size to income (combined income) of the borrower(s)
- % of net income required to service the loan
- stability/security of borrower's income.

Loan-to-value ratio (LTV)

LTV refers to the proportion of the value of the property which the lender is prepared to lend. This may range from 75% to 90% although it can be higher. The typical figure for first-time buyers is about 90%, leaving the borrower(s) to make up the remaining 10% themselves. The LTV serves a number of purposes:

- It caps the lender's risk.
- It forces an input from the borrower's own resources.
- It acts as a buffer for the lender in a time of falling property values.
- It helps to prevent the possibility of a negative equity position for the borrower if property values fall.

If the value of the property rises, and the loan is being written down, the ratio in practice is being reduced from the start. It is a particularly important ratio from the bank's point of view if property values are at the top of a cycle at the time the loan is taken out.

Ratio of loan size to income

This is typically at a maximum of 2.5–3 times the annual earnings of the (higher earning) borrower *plus* one and a half times the earnings of the second borrower, in the case of a joint application. The purpose is to ensure that the loan is repayable from current earnings and does not represent too large a burden to the borrower. Clearly as the income of the borrower(s) increases and the loan is partially redeemed, this ratio will fall. It is thus at its maximum at the beginning of the loan period.

Percentage of net income required to service the loan

The lender will normally place a cap on the % of net income which should be used to service the loan. This is now one of the key measures of housing affordability used by lenders in Ireland and abroad (and also by local authorities in Ireland in exercising their housing provision function). It can be used to determine the maximum loan size that can be afforded by a borrower. A typical cap operated by lenders is in the range 30–35%.

Commercial lending criteria

This section is primarily concerned with the criteria used by the banks to assess commercial loan applications. It is presented in the context of the property sector. However, most of the criteria would be applicable to all sectors of the economy.

The property sector competes with other sectors of the economy for a share of the available lending from the financial institutions. Depending on the overall availability of funds, the property sector may find it more or less difficult to borrow money from the banks. In an environment of easy availability of bank finance, the financial institutions may compete to lend to property companies/projects. It is clear that, no matter how competitive the lending environment is, the banks will apply certain criteria in assessing loan applications.

General criteria

As with personal lending the banks will also apply general criteria to the assessment of loan applications by companies. These include

- trading history
- equity exposure of borrower
- security offered.

Trading history of borrower

This is concerned with the borrower's track record in relation to finishing developments on time and within the original cost.

Equity exposure of borrower

This relates to how much equity the borrower is prepared to put up and whether or not it is provided from the borrower's own resources or whether there is an outside equity involvement.

Security offered

This relates to the security being offered by the borrower, its current value and potential realisable value. It is also concerned with whether or not there is a parent company guarantee and whether the loan is of a limited or non-recourse nature. Non-recourse lending is where the lender's only recourse is to the project being funded and not to other assets of the borrower.

To these general criteria could be added the lender's overall relationship with the borrower, i.e. **relationship banking**. Relationship banking refers to the ongoing business relationship that exists between borrower and lender which has been built up over time. Relationship banking works both ways. On the one hand a lender will take a more benign view of a long-established client and so the borrower benefits in having easier, perhaps less restrictive access to funds. It does, however, confer certain obligations on the borrower, e.g. not to walk away from a failed project, to prepare realistic cash flow projections for project proposals and to inform the lender at an early stage if things start to go wrong.

Specific lending criteria

In addition to the general criteria that the lender will apply there are a number of specific, technical criteria that may be enforced. These are similar in some instances to those described for personal lending, but are reproduced here in a different context.

Loan-to-value ratio (LTV)

This is one of the key criteria used by lenders. LTV refers to the proportion of the value of the project/property which the lender is prepared to put up, e.g. if a project has an expected value of €10 million, a €6 million loan would represent an LTV of 60%. While LTVs can range to higher levels, e.g. 90%, the norm would be of the order of 70%. The gap between the LTV and 100% serves a number of purposes:

- it caps the lender's risk
- it forces an equity input
- it acts as a buffer for the lender in a time of falling property values where the property is used as collateral.

Clearly the initial valuation must be realistic from the lender's point of view or else the LTV will offer a less effective safety net. In a time of inflated property values, where the only direction that values can realistically go is downwards, the banks may be prudent in reducing the LTV in order to improve the safety factor.

In a time of easy access to funding, where the banks are competing with each other to lend money, there is a danger that the LTV will be pushed upwards. While this might appear to be positive from a property development/investment point of view, it may help to over-inflate the market and/or decrease the quality and hence increase the risk if taken.

A loan-to-cost ratio may be used for speculative projects as it may offer a better protection than LTV.

Income-to-interest cover

The income-to-interest cover refers to the ratio between the operating income generated by the project and available to service the interest payments on the loan, and the size of these interest payments, e.g. if a project generates an annual operating income of €1 million and the annual interest required on the loan is €800,000, then the income-to-interest cover is 1.25:1

Income-to-interest cover is sensitive to the LTV, i.e. as the LTV rises, the income-to-interest cover will fall. Lower cover ratios will probably be acceptable if the rate of interest is fixed.

Repayment structure

There is a wide variety of repayment structures, e.g.

- interest only with bullet payment at end of term
- regular capital and interest payment (annuity)
- interest payment with some capital payment (partial amortisation)
- deferred interest or capital payments.

Loan security

The quality of the collateral offered may affect either the availability or cost of finance. The lender will be interested in the following aspects of the security offered:

- It must be capable of being valued.
- There must be a market for the asset if the lender is forced to realise it.
- The value of the security exceeds the value of the loan and it is capable of maintaining or increasing its value.

SUMMARY

- In an annuity mortgage, the regular payment is made up of capital and interest components.
- In an annuity mortgage, the capital component rises and the interest content of the payment falls as the mortgage moves through the term.
- In an endowment mortgage, interest only is paid to the lender, with a separate payment made into an endowment policy.
- The maturity value of the endowment policy is used to redeem the mortgage.
- If the rate of interest rises, endowment mortgages are more exposed than annuity mortgages as none of the capital has been paid off.
- The opposite applies in the case of falling interest rates.
- The outstanding balance on a loan can be calculated as the discounted value of the remaining payments (the prospective method).
- It can also be calculated using the retrospective method. This method adds compound interest to the loan as if no payments have been made and then nets off the value of a notional fund into which payments have been made.
- If the rate of interest on an annuity loan rises, either the payment can be increased in order to pay off the loan in the original term, or the same payment can be continued but the term of the mortgage lengthens.
- The key lending criteria applied by banks to personal lending are:
  - percentage of net income required to service the loan
  - loan-to-value ratio
  - ratio of loan size to income.
- The key lending criteria applied by banks to commercial lending are:
  - trading history of borrower
  - equity input of borrower
  - security provided
  - loan-to-value ratio
  - loan-to-cost ratio
  - income-to-interest cover.

QUESTIONS

1.♦ Ann is due to repay a loan of €25,000 subject to interest at a rate of 9.6% p.a. compounded monthly with equal monthly payments over a period of twelve years, the first payment one month after the loan is taken out.

   (a) If the payments due at the end of the 49th, 50th and 51st months are missed, and Ann continues with the same monthly payment as before at the end of the 52nd month and the bank agrees to extend the term of the loan, show the last three lines of the amortisation schedule.

   (b) If following the missed payments as in (a) above, the rate of interest rose to 10.8% p.a. compounded monthly at the and of the 54th month, and Ann continues with the same monthly payment as before at the end of the 55th month, show the last line of the amortisation schedule.

   (c) Suppose Ann is offered an alternative source of finance at the end of the fourth year at a rate of interest of 8.4% p.a., but the original bank charges an early repayment penalty of €200 *plus* the amount of interest which would have been paid in the next six months if the loan repayment had gone ahead as usual. Should Ann refinance the loan?

2.◆ You are taking out an €80,000 mortgage loan repayable over fifteen years. The local bank is quoting an interest rate of 9% p.a. compounded monthly on an annuity mortgage and a rate of 9.6% p.a. compounded monthly on an endowment-linked mortgage. The premium payable on the endowment policy would be €220 per month, payable at the same time as the mortgage payment. The interest content of mortgage repayments (up to a maximum interest of €5,000 per annum) qualifies as a tax allowance. Tax relief can be claimed at the standard rate of tax (22%).

   Calculate for both options

   (a) the gross monthly repayment.
   (b) the net monthly repayment in the first year.
   (c) the net monthly repayment in the twelfth year.
   (d) the net monthly repayment in the twelfth year, if the nominal rate of interest on both options fell by 1.2% p.a. compounded monthly at the end of the eleventh year and the gross monthly repayments for the remaining four years of the mortgage were reduced to a new equal value to reflect the new interest rate.

3. ◆ (a) A small company is borrowing €35,000 for a period of seven years. The bank charges interest at a rate of 1.1% per month. The bank agrees to the following repayment schedule:

     (i) a payment of €1,500 at the end of each year starting one year after the loan is taken out.

     (ii) an equal payment at the end of each month, starting one month after the loan is taken out. The monthly payment would be made even in those months when the annual €1,500 payment is made.

     Show the first three and last three lines of the amortisation schedule.

   (b) Suppose the rate of interest in (a) above changed to 1.2% per month at the end of the third year, and the company increased the monthly payment to a new equal value but continued to make the annual €1,500 payment. Show the last three lines of the amortisation schedule.

4. You are taking out a €60,000 mortgage loan repayable over fifteen years. The local bank is quoting an interest rate of 7.2% p.a. compounded monthly on an annuity mortgage and a rate of 7.8% p.a. compounded monthly on an endowment-linked mortgage. The premium payable on the endowment policy would be €160 per month, payable at the same time as the mortgage payment. The interest content of mortgage repayments (up to a maximum interest of €5,000 per annum) qualifies as a tax allowance. Tax relief can be claimed at the standard rate of tax (22%).

   Calculate for both options

   (a) the gross monthly repayment.
   (b) the net monthly repayment in the first year.
   (c) the net monthly repayment in the tenth year.
   (d) the net monthly repayment in the tenth year, if the nominal rate of interest on both options rose by 0.6% p.a. compounded monthly at the end of the ninth year and the gross monthly repayments for the remaining six years of the mortgage were increased to a new equal value to reflect the new interest rate.

5. (a) A company is borrowing €50,000 for a period of twelve years. The bank charges interest at a rate of 1.2% per month. The bank agrees to the following repayment schedule:

      (i) a payment of €2,500 at the end of each year starting one year after the loan is taken out.
      (ii) an equal payment at the end of each month, starting one month after the loan is taken out. The monthly payment would be made even in those months when the annual €2,500 payment is made.

      Show the first three and last three lines of the amortisation schedule.

   (b) Suppose the rate of interest in (a) above changed to 1.1% per month at the end of the seventh year, and the company reduced the monthly payment to a new equal value but continued to make the annual €2,500 payment. Show the last three lines of the amortisation schedule.

6. Tom is due to repay a loan of €20,000 subject to interest at a rate of 13.2% p.a. compounded monthly with equal monthly payments over a period of fifteen years, the first payment one month after the loan is taken out.

   (a) If the payments due at the end of the 120th, 121st and 122nd months are missed, and Tom continues with the same monthly payment as before at the end of the 123rd month and the bank agrees to extend the term of the loan, show the last three lines of the amortisation schedule.
   (b) If following the missed payments as in (a) above, the rate of interest rose to 14.4% p.a. compounded monthly at the end of the 124th month, and Tom continues with the same monthly payment as before at the end of the 125th month, show the last line of the amortisation schedule.
   (c) Suppose Tom is offered an alternative source of finance at the end of the eighth year at a rate of interest of 12% p.a., but the original bank charges an early

repayment penalty of €200 *plus* the amount of interest which was paid in the previous three months. Should Tom refinance the loan?

7. You are taking out a €100,000 mortgage loan repayable over twenty years. The local bank is quoting an interest rate of 6% p.a. compounded monthly on an annuity mortgage and a rate of 6.6% p.a. compounded monthly on an endowment-linked mortgage. The premium payable on the endowment policy would be €180 per month, payable at the same time as the mortgage payment. The interest content of mortgage repayments (up to a maximum interest of €5,000 per annum) qualifies as a tax allowance. Tax relief can be claimed at the standard rate of tax (22%).
   Calculate for both options:

   (a) the gross monthly repayment.
   (b) the net monthly repayment in the first year.
   (c) the net monthly repayment in the fifteenth year.
   (d) the net monthly repayment in the fifteenth year, if the nominal rate of interest on both options fell by 1.2% p.a. compounded monthly at the end of the fourteenth year and the gross monthly repayments for the remaining six years of the mortgage were reduced to a new equal value to reflect the new interest rate.

8. Discuss the main lending criteria applied by banks in relation to personal mortgage lending.
9. Discuss the main lending criteria applied by banks in relation to commercial lending.
10. Distinguish between an annuity and an endowment mortgage.
11. Explain why the net (after-tax) payment in an endowment mortgage will be level for the full term (assuming interest rates do not change), whereas the net payment in an annuity mortgage will rise over the term of the mortgage.
12. Distinguish between the retrospective and prospective method for calculating the outstanding balance on a loan.
13. Discuss the new features of personal mortgages now available.

Appendix 1
Solutions to Selected End of Chapter Questions

CHAPTER 2

Question 2

NOPAT is net income if the company had no debt and had no financial assets. NOPAT is a better indicator of the operating performance because debt reduces income.

Question 7

Net working capital = Current assets – Current liabilities = €10,000 – €3,000 = €7,000.
Net worth = Total assets – Total liabilities = €40,000 – €18,000 = €22,000.

Question 9

Profit & Loss Account	
Sales	€100,000
Cost of sales	€600,000
Gross profit	€400,000
Depreciation	€12,000
PBIT	€388,000
Interest	€5,000
PBT	€383,000
Tax (15%)	€57,450
Pat	€325,550

Operating cash flow (OCF) = PBIT $(1 - T)$ + Depreciation
= €388,000 (0.85) + €1,200 = €341,800.

Question 12

(i)

Profit & Loss Account	
Sales	€1,000,000
COGS	€600,00
PBDIT	€400,000
Depreciation	€10,000
PBIT	€390,000
Interest	€3,000
PBT	€387,000
Tax	€58,050
PAT	€328,950

(ii) Operating cash flow = NOPAT + Dep = €PBIT $(1 - T)$ + Dep. = €341,500

(iii) Change in operating working capital = €6,000 – €2,500 = €3,500
Change in fixed Capital = €30,000
Gross capital expenditure = €30,000 + €10,000 = €40,000
Change in total operating capital = €40,000 + €3,500 = €43,500
Free cash flow = €341,500 - €43,500 = €298,000.

Question 13

Profit after tax (PAT) = €1m
Profit before interest and tax (PBIT) = €3m
Tax (T) = 15%
Interest = ?

Tax = €1m/1 – T = €1m/ $(1 - 0.15)$ = €176,470
Interest = PBIT – PBT = €3,000,000 – €1,176,470 = €1,823,530

PBIT	€3,000,000
Interest	€'X'
PBT	€1,176,470
Tax	€176,470
PAT	€1,000,000

CHAPTER 3

Question 2

Manufacturing companies will have much larger inventories. Service companies (e.g. financial services) will not have much stock at all since financial products are paper transactions between companies. It is important therefore in analysing accounts to look at the particular business in question.

Question 4

Effects of inflation:
 (i)   Earnings will rise without a corresponding increase in the volume of sales
 (ii) Depreciation and the book value of the assets used in generating sales will remain at historic figures. However the cost of replacing these assets are not not reflected in the depreciation charged and in the book values.
(iii) Consequently, a ratio such as earnings to total assets (ROA) will increase even though the assets are generating the same volume of sales.
(iv)   Companies whose assets have been purchased at inflated prices will have higher asset values than companies who purchased their assets earlier. Therefore, two companies with the same sales and the same physical assets will have different ROAs.

Question 8

Sales	100%
COGS	65%
Depreciation	10%
Total Operating Costs	75%
PBIT	25%
Interest	5%
PBT	20%
Tax (15%)	3%
PAT	15.5%

Question 9

(a)   (i)   Current ratio = 0.52; Acid test = 0.33
     (ii)   Stock turnover = 8.8 times
    (iii)   Debtors turnover = 14 times
     (iv)   Days sales outstanding = 26
      (v)   Cash ratio = PBIT + Depreciation / Interest = 3 times
     (vi)   Times interest earned = PBIT/Interest = 1.8 times
    (vii)   Total Debt Ratio = Total assets minus Total equity/ Total assets = 0.56.

(b) The ROE is the ratio of net profit to total equity. This is €10/€88 = 11.3.

With the Du-Pont identity, we can write the ROE as:

ROE = Profit margin x Total assets x Equity multiplier

= (€10/€126) x (€126/€204) x (€204/€88)

= 7.9 x .62 x 2.3.

= 11.35%.

Question 13

M/B ratio = market price per share/ Book value per share.

If the market price per share is greater than the book value per share, the market expects the present value of future earnings are worth more than the company's liquidation value. The difference between the future earnings' value and the liquidation value is the going concern value. The higher the M/B ratio the greater is the value based on its going concern value.

With a M/B value <1 it is sometimes assumed that the company's liquidation value is greater than its going concern value. However, we must remember that M/B ratios are accounting based values. In reality, it is likely that liquidation values will be greater than book values. The liquidation value of assets may be greater than their book values. In addition, the market value of a company's bonds can be greater than their book values.

Question 17

ROA = 11%; ROE = 16% and Net margin (NM) = 3%.

ROA = Net income/assets

Profit Margin = Net income/sales

ROE = Net margin/Equity

ROA = Profit Margin x Sales/Total assets

Net Income/Assets = (Net Income/Sales) × (Sales/Total assets)

11% = 3% x Sales/Total assets

Therefore Sales/Total assets = 3.7 times.

ROE = Profit margin × (Sales/Total assets) × (Total assets/Equity.)

Net Income/Equity = (Net income/Sales) × (Sales/Total assets) × (Total assets/Equity)

= 16% = 3% × 3.7 × Total assets/Equity

Therefore Total assets/Equity or the Equity multiplier = 1.44.

CHAPTER 4

Question 2

This question is an example of discounting a future value back to a present value.

(a) Here:

FV = €10,000

r = 1% per month

n = 84 months

PV represents the value of the fund seven years ago.

Using 4.5
$$\text{PV (7 years ago)} = \frac{€10,000}{(1.01)^{84}} = €4,335.15$$

(b) Here: FV = £10,000
r_1 = 1% per month for 48 months
r_2 = 5% per half-year for 6 half-years

Using 4.5
$$\text{PV (4 years ago)} = \frac{€10,000}{(1.01)^{48}} = €6,202.60$$

$$\text{PV (7 years ago)} = \frac{€6,202.60}{(1.05)^{6}} = €4,628.48$$

Note that the answer to part (b) is higher than to part (a). This is because the effective rate of interest in the first three years of the investment is lower in (b) than in (a), 10.25% p.a. compared to 12.68% p.a. and therefore in order to have the same amount today, (b) must start from a higher value.

The solution could also be found using annual effective rates

(a) PV
$$\text{(7 years ago)} = \frac{€10,000}{(1.126825)^{7}} = €4,335.15$$

(b) PV
$$\text{(4 years ago)} = \frac{€10,000}{(1.126825)^{4}} = €6,202.60$$

$$\text{PV (7 years ago)} = \frac{€6,202.60}{(1.1025)^{3}} = €4,628.^{48}$$

Question 6

This is an example of an ordinary simple annuity.

Here: PV = €8,000
r = 1.1% per month
n = 84 months

To calculate the amount of interest paid over the life of the loan, the periodic payment must first be calculated.

Find P_t using 4.8

$$8,000 = P_t \left[\frac{1 - (1.011)^{-84}}{0.011} \right]$$

Solve for the periodic payment as shown in example 4.15.

This produces Pt = €146.41.

Since payments are part interest and part capital (see chapter 21), the total payments made equals the total interest paid plus the total capital paid.

Total payments over course of loan term = 84 x €146.41 = €12,298.44

Subtract original loan value (capital) = €8,000.00

Interest paid = €4,298.44

Question 7

This question combines an ordinary simple annuity and a compound interest calculation.

(a) It is useful to notionally separate the initial deposit and the annuity into two different accounts.

Before the monthly payment can be calculated, the target value for the annuity must be determined. This in turn requires that the future value at time 36 of the initial deposit be determined.

This is an example of a compound interest calculation.

Here: PV = €5,000

r = 1% per month

n = 36 months

Using 4.4 the initial deposit of €5,000 will grow over 36 months to:

FV   = €5,000$(1.01)^{36}$ = €7,153.84

(time 36)

Since the target at time 36 is €15,000 and the initial deposit provides €7,153.84 of this, the annuity must provide the remaining €7,846.16. Thus:

FV = €7,846.16

r = 1% per month

n = 36 months

$$7,846.16 = P_t \left[\frac{(1.01)^{36} - 1}{0.01} \right]$$

Solve for the periodic payment as shown in example 4.13.

This produces P_t = €182.14

(b) Calculate the total value of the savings at time 30. This involves two calculations:

Compound interest
FV $\quad = \quad$ €5,000$(1.01)^{30}$ = €6,739.24
(time 30)

Annuity
$$FV = 182.14 \left[\frac{(1.01)^{30} - 1}{0.01} \right] = €6,335.72$$

Total value at time 30 = €6,739.24 + €6,335.72 = €13,074.96

This will grow through compound interest.

Here: PV = €13,074.96
        FV = €15,000.00
        r = 1% per month

To find the time required to reach the target of €15,000 use the approach as in example 4.7.

€15,000 = €13,074.96$(1.01)^n$

This produces n = 13.8

The fund will reach the target of €15,000 between 13 and 14 months after month 30. To complete the answer fully, calculate the value 13 months after month 30.

FV = €13,074.96$(1.01)^{13}$ = €14,880.52

Finally use the simple interest calculation to find the fraction of the next month required to reach the target.

PV = €14,880.52
FV = €15,000.00
r = 1% per month

Using 4.3
€15,000 = €14,880.52$(1 + (0.01) \times n)$
This produces n = 0.8 of a month. To express this in days multiply by 30, i.e. 24 days

The final answer is thus 43 months and 24 days.

(c) Calculate the total value of the savings at time 24. This involves two calculations:

Compound interest
FV $= €5,000(1.01)^{24} = €6,348.67$
(time 24)

Annuity
$$FV = 182.14\left[\frac{(1.01)^{24} - 1}{0.01}\right] = €4,912.95$$

Total value at time 24 $= €6,348.67 + €4,912.95 = €11,261.62$
This will grow through compound interest.

Here: PV $= €11,261.62$
        n $= 12$ months
        r $= 1\%$ per month

To find the value of this fund at time 36 use the approach as in example 4.6.

FV $= €11,261.62(1.01)^{12} = €12,689.88$

Since the target at time 36 is now €18,000 and the payments made to date will provide €12,689.88 of this, the annuity must provide the remaining €5,310.12. Thus:

FV $= €5,310.12$
r $= 1\%$ per month
n $= 12$ months

$$€5,310.12 = P_t\left[\frac{(1.01)^{12} - 1}{0.01}\right]$$

Solve for the periodic payment as shown in example 4.13.
This produces $P_t = €418.70$.

Question 9

This question deals with the comparison of two different payment streams by expressing both in present value terms.
(a) Calculate the PV of the payment stream and compare it to the once-off payment option of €200,000 now.
The rate of interest can either be expressed as the monthly equivalent of 14.4% p.a., i.e. 1.2% p.m. or as an annual effective rate using 4.6 above. If the monthly rate is used then the time should be expressed in months, while if the annual effective rate is used, then the time should be expressed in years.

$$PV = €100,000 + \frac{€30,000}{(1.012)^{12}} + \frac{€30,000}{(1.012)^{24}} + \frac{€30,000}{(1.012)^{36}} + \frac{€30,000}{(1.012)^{48}} + \frac{€30,000}{(1.012)^{60}}$$

This gives a value of €199,644.25. Since this is below €200,000 then the stream of payments should be chosen.

Alternatively the payment stream can be treated as an ordinary simple and the present value calculated using 4.8.

The appropriate rate of interest is the annual effective rate which from 4.6 is 15.39%.

Thus: $P_t = €30,000$
$r = 15.39\%$ p.a.
$n = 5$

PV is calculated using 4.8. This gives €99,644.25. The €100,000 is added to this to give the same value as above.

(b) Since the rate of interest changes over the 5 years, the annuity formula cannot be used. The rate of interest should be expressed in monthly/quarterly form and the number of months/quarters used to calculate the present value or alternatively, the annual effective rate for each year may be calculated and the present value found using the number of years as the appropriate time factor.

$$PV = €100,000 + \frac{€30,000}{(1.012)^{12}} + \frac{€30,000}{(1.012)^{24}} + \frac{€30,000}{(1.012)^{24}(1.013)^{12}} + \frac{€30,000}{(1.012)^{24}(1.013)^{12}(1.033)^4} + \frac{€30,000}{(1.012)^{24}(1.013)^{12}(1.033)^8}$$

This gives a value of €199,655.40. Since this is below €200,000 then the stream of payments should be chosen.

Question 15

This is an ordinary simple annuity.
Here: PV = €700,000
$P_t = €100,000$
$n = 10$

Using formula 4.8:
$$700,000 = 100,000 \left[\frac{1 - (1 + r)^{-10}}{r} \right]$$

Trial values of r are inserted into the equation above.

Using $r = 7\%$ produces PV = €702,358.15. This means that at a rate of interest of 7%, 10 annual payments of €100,000 would pay of a loan of €702,358.15. Since the loan is only €700,000, the rate of interest must be above 7%.

Using $r = 8\%$ produces PV = €671,008.14. This is below the loan size and so the required rate is below 8%.

The rate is therefore between 7% and 8%. The answer can be approximated using linear interpolation.

A one percentage point rise in r from 7% causes the present value to fall by €31,350.01 (€702,358.15 − €671,008.14). What fraction of a 1 per cent increase in r from 7% would cause the present value to fall by €2,358.15 (€702,358.15 – €700,000.00)? This is calculated as follows:

$$\frac{x}{1} = \frac{2,358.15}{31,350.01} = 0.075 \approx 0.1$$

The answer is therefore approximated as 7.1%. This can be checked by using 7.1% as the value of r in 4.8 and calculating PV. This produces PV = €699,122.97 which is €877.03 short of the given loan size. Since this is nearer to the loan size of €700,000 then when 7% was used (€702,358.15), the answer is therefore r = 7.1% correct to one place of decimals.

Question 16

This can be treated as a compound interest calculation applied to a reducing balance over the life of the loan.

  The annual effective rate for each year should initially be calculated from 4.6.

This gives:

Year	Effective rate
1	16.08%
2	12.68%
3	9.38%
4	12.55%

Time	Borrow	Interest	Repay	Balance
0	14,000			–14,000
1		2,251.20	4,000	–12,251.20
2		1,553.45	5,000	–8,804.65
3		825.88	6,000	–3,630.53
4		455.63	4,086.16	0.00

The final payment is calculated as 3,630.53 + 455.63, i.e. the amount required to clear the debt at the end of the previous year and the interest charge for the final year.

CHAPTER 5

Question 1

This can be solved as shown in example 5.7 in the text.
The price is first calculated using 5.2 above

$$PV = 12 \left[\frac{1 - (1.09)^{-8}}{0.09} \right] + \frac{100}{(1.09)^8} = 116.60$$

Price @ GRY of 9% = €116.60

The net redemption yield is found by equating the present value of the future net receipts from the bond with this price of €116.60. This is done, as before, through a process of trial and error, i.e. the future net cash flow is discounted at varying rates, until two answers, one above €116.60 and the other below €116.60 are found, discount using rates which are one percentage point apart. Remember that the net redemption yield will be less than the gross redemption yield, here less than 9% p.a.

The net cashflow from the bond is:

€12 per annum less tax at 24% i.e. €12 – (0.24 x €12) or 0.76 x €12 = €9.12 for 8 years plus €100 at the end of the eighth year.

$$116.60 = 9.12 \left[\frac{1 - (1 + r)^{-8}}{r} \right] + \frac{100}{(1. + r)^8}$$

Following trial and error, discount rates of 7% and 6% produce present values of €112.66 and €119.37 respectively.

Since the current price is €116.60, the investor is getting a yield somewhere between 6% and 7%.

The answer can be approximated using linear interpolation.

A one percentage point rise in the discount from 6% causes the bond price to fall by €6.71 (€119.37 – €112.66). What fraction of a 1 percent increase in the discount rate from 6% would cause price to fall by €2.77 (€119.37 – €116.60)? This is calculated as follows:

Discount Rate	Price
6%	119.37
6+x%	116.60
7%	112.66

$$\frac{x}{1} = \frac{2.77}{6.71} = 0.41$$

where x = fractional interest rate increase required to decrease price by €2.77 at this point. Therefore NRY to a 24% taxpayer is estimated at 6 + 0.4% i.e. 6.4%.

Question 2

This can be solved as shown in example 5.8 in the text.

The price is first calculated using 5.2 above.

The appropriate cashflow to be discounted is the net coupon at 48% tax, i.e. €9 per annum less tax at 48%, i.e. €9 – (0.48 × €9) or 0.52 × €9 = €4.68 for 6 years plus €100 at the end of the sixth year.

$$PV = 4.68 \left[\frac{1 - (1.08)^{-6}}{0.08} \right] + \frac{100}{(1.08)^6} = 84.65$$

Price @ NRY (@48% tax) of 8% = €84.65

The net redemption yield at 26% tax is found by equating the present value of the future net receipts from the bond with this price of €84.65. This is done, as before, through a process of trial and error, i.e. the future net cash flow is discounted at varying rates, until two answers, one above €84.65 and the other below €84.65 are found, discount using rates which are one percentage point apart. Remember that the net redemption yield at the lower tax rate (26%) will be higher than the net redemption yield at the higher tax rate (48%).

The net cashflow from the bond is:

€9 per annum less tax at 26% i.e. €9 – (0.26 × €9) or 0.74 × €9 = €6.66 for 6 years plus €100 at the end of the sixth year.

$$84.65 = 6.66 \left[\frac{1 - (1 + r)^{-6}}{r} \right] + \frac{100}{(1. + r)^6}$$

Following trial and error, discount rates of 11% and 10% produce present values of €81.64 and €85.45 respectively.

Since the current price is €84.65, the investor is getting a yield somewhere between 10% and 11%.

The answer can be approximated using linear interpolation,.

A one percentage point rise in the discount from 10% causes the bond price to fall by €3.81 (€85.45 – €81.64). What fraction of a 1 percent increase in the discount rate from 10% would cause price to fall by €0.80 (€85.45 – €84.65)? This is calculated as follows

Discount Rate	Price
10%	85.45
10+x%	84.65
11%	81.64

$$\frac{x}{1} = \frac{0.80}{3.81} = 0.21$$

where x = fractional interest rate increase required to decrease price by 0.80 at this point.

Therefore NRY to a 26% taxpayer is estimated at 10 + 0.2% i.e. 10.2%.

Question 3

This can be solved as shown in example 5.10 in the text.

The price is first calculated using 5.2 above.

The appropriate cashflow to be discounted is the net coupon at 44% tax, i.e. €9 per annum less tax at 44% i.e. €9 – (0.44 × €9) or 0.56 × €9 = €5.04 for 8 years plus €100 at the end of the eighth year.

$$PV = 5.04 \frac{1 - (1.05)^{-8}}{0.05} + \frac{100}{(1.05)^8} = 100.26$$

Price @ NRY (@44% tax) of 5% = €100.26
The income yields can be found using 5.1
(i) The gross annual coupon is €9

$$\text{Gross income yield} = \frac{9}{100.26} \times 100 = 8.98\%$$

(ii) The net coupon is €9 less tax at 22% = €7.02

$$\text{Net income yield} = \frac{7.02}{100.26} \times 100 = 7\%$$
(@22% tax)

CHAPTER 6

Question 3

The value of a share is the expected value of future cashflows. This does not mean that the share price can be increased simply by increasing the dividend. Shareholders are concerned about all of their dividends — dividends paid now and dividends paid in the future. Companies that pay out high dividends now will have less money to reinvest in the company and this will lower expected future dividends. This will have the effect of lowering share price.

Question 9

(a) Current price of the share: (P_o)
     €1/1.08 + €1.5/(1.08)^2 + €2/(1.08)^3 +€2.08/(8% − 4%)/1.08)^3
     P_o= €0.93 + €1.29 +€1.6 +€41.27 = €45
(b) The price of the share in one year's time: (P_1)
     = (P_1) = €1.5/(1.08) +€2/(1.08)^2 + €2.08/.04/(1.08)^2.
     = €1.38 + €1.7 + €44.6 + €48.
(c) Capital Gain:
     (€48 − €45)/€45 = 6.25%.
(d) Dividend yield
     €1/€45 = 2.2%.

Question 14

P_o = (€5 + €60)/1.1 = €59.

Question 16

P_A = Div$_1$/K$_e$ = €5/0.08 = €62.5
P_B = Div$_1$ (K$_e$ − g) = €6/(0.08 − .005) = €200.

$P_C = Div_1/(1.08) + Div_2/(1.08)^2 + Div_3/(1.08)^3 + Div_4/(1.08)^5 + Div(1.08)^5$
$+ (Div_6/.08)(1/(1.08)^5$:
$\quad €2/(1.08) + €2(1.15)/(1.08)^2 + €2.3(1.15)/(1.08)^3 + €2.64(1.15)/(1.08)^4$
$+ (€3.45/.08)(1/1.08)^5$:
$\quad = €1.85 + €1.97 + €2.11 + €2.24 + €2.37 + €29.32 = €39.85.$
Stock B is most valuable.

Question 18

$P_o = D_o (1 + g)/K_e - g) = €3(0.9)/(0.14 - 10) = €2.7/0.04 = €67.5$

Question 19

$P_o = FCF (1 + g)/(K_e - g) = €200,000 (1 + 0.05)/(0.12 - 0.05) = €3m.$
$\quad$ Value of equity = Total value of operating activities less value of debt.
$\quad €3m - €500,000 = €2.5m.$

CHAPTER 7

Question 5

(a) Payback occurs in year 5. The NPV using EXCEL is as follows:

Year	Cash flow €	Discount rate 12%	Present value
0	–20,000	1	–20,000
1	–20,000	0.893	–17,857
2	15,000	0.797	11,958
3	12,000	0.712	8,541
4 to 8	8,000	2.566	20,528
			NPV = 3,170

Project A is viable.

(b) Payback never occurs. The NPV using EXCEL is as follows:

Year	Cash flow €	Discount rate 15%	Present value
0	–32,000	1	–32,000
1 to infinity	4,500	1/0.15	30,000
			NPV = –2,000

Project B is not viable.

(c) Payback occurs in year 4. The NPV using EXCEL is as follows:

Year	Cash flow €	Discount rate 12%	Present value
0	−65,000	1	−65,000
1	−6,000	0.893	−5,357
1 to 5	18,000	3.605	64,890
5	21,000	0.567	11,907
			NPV = 6,440

Project C is viable.

(d) Payback occurs in year 4. The NPV using EXCEL is as follows:

Year	Cash flow €	Discount rate 15%	Present value
0	−20,000	1	−20,000
1 to 5	5,000	3.352	16,760
6 to 10	4,000	1.667	6,668
11 to infinity	3,000	1.648	4,944
			NPV = 8,372

Project D is viable.

Question 8

Year	Cash flow in €	Dis. rate 14%	Present value in €
0	−44,700	1	−44,700
1	10,500	0.877	9,209
2	11,025	0.769	8,478
3	11,576	0.675	7,814
4	12,155	0.592	7,196
5	12,763	0.519	6,624
6	13,401	0.456	6,111
			NPV = €731

The project is viable with a positive NPV of €731 and the payback occurs in four years. Using EXCEL the IRR is14.6%.

Question 12

Year 1 Cash flow

Total revenue =	40,000($500)	$20,000,000
Total variable cost =	40,000($30)	($1,200,000)
Fixed cost =		($6,000,000)
Depreciation =		($5,000,000)
Total expenses =	VC+FC+Dep	($12,200,000)
Before-tax earnings =	Revenue – Expenses	$7,800,000
Host tax @ 30% =		($2,340,000)
After-tax earnings =		$5,460,000
Cash flow remitted =	* Add back deprec.	$10,460,000
		expense
Exchange rate	€1 = $1.07	€9,775,701
		Net cash flow in €
Initial investment	$60 million/1.05	
Year 3 cash flow	Add $60000000	

Net cash flow

Year	Cash flow in $ millions	In € millions
0	–60	–57.142857
1	10.46	9.775701
2	13.96	12.807339
3	77.88	70.162162

NPV at 20% = €0.5 million

The project is viable.

Question 15

Year	Cash flow In € millions	Discount factor 13%	Present value
1	59	0.885	**52.22**
2	60.4	0.783	**47.29**
3	55.4	0.693	**38.39**
4	39	0.613	**23.91**
5	29	0.543	**15.75**
6 to 10	29	1.909	**55.36**

The present value of these future cash inflows is €232.92 million and since this is greater than the offer of €200 million, the offer should be rejected.

Question 16

$$\text{Equivalent annual cost (EAC)} = \frac{\text{Present value cost over one replacement cycle}}{\text{Cumulative present value factor for that cycle}}$$

Year	Cash flow Machine A	Year	Cash flow Machine B
0	(€19,000)	0	(€13, 000)
8	(€4,000)	4	(€2,000)
12	€3,000	6	€3,000
1 to 12	(€2,000)	1 to 6	(€2,600)
NPV at 10% =	(€33,540)	NPV at 10% =	(€24,016)

EAC for machine A = €33,540/6.81 = €4,925. EAC for machine B = €24,016/4.36 = €5,508

Machine A is more efficient assuming the cash flow estimates are correct. The cash flows occur at year end and machine reliability is the same for both machines.

CHAPTER 8

Question 5

The current market value of the convertible is €140 assuming it is ex-interest.

The conversion value is $(€2.20)(1.05)^5(50) = €140.39$.

The after tax interest cost is $€8(1 - 0.24) = €6.08$ and so the relevant cash flows are as follows:

Year	Cash flow before tax	Cash flow after tax
0	−€140	−€140
1	€8	€6.08
2	€8	€6.08
3	€8	€6.08
3	€140.39	€140.39
Internal rate of return =	5.8%	4.43%

Question 6

The cost of equity can be found using the constant dividend formula Ke = dividend available/market value.

Constant earnings	€15,000,000
Less interest	€3,791,520
Earnings before tax	€11,208,480
Less tax at 24%	€2,690,035
Dividend available	€8,518,445

Market value of equity = 50 million shares @ €0.80 = €40 million.
Ke = €8,518,445/€40,000,000 = 21.3%
The cost of the debentures is found as follows:

Year	Cash flow before tax	Cash flow after tax
0	−€105.5	−€105.5
1	€16	€12.16
2	€16	€12.16
3	€16	€12.16
3	€100	€100
Internal rate of return =	**13.65%**	**9.95%**

Market value of the debentures = €23.697(1.055) = €25 million.

$$\text{WACC} = \frac{€40\text{ million}(21.3\%) + €25\text{ million}(9.9\,5\%)}{€65\text{ million}} = 0.16.93 \text{ or } 16.93\%$$

Question 8

(a) Vg = Vu + DT = €32.5 + €5(0.24) = €33.7 million and market value has increased by €1.2 million.

(b) Kd = 13% D = €5 million and E = €33.7 − €5 = €28.7 million
Ke = Ku + (1 − T)(Ku − Kd)D/E = 18% + (1 − 0.24)(18% − 13%)5/28.7 = 18.66%
The cost of equity rises to reflect increased financial risk.

(c) Ke = 18.66%, Kd after tax = 13%(1 − 0.24) = 9.88%, D = €5 million and E = €28.7 million

$$\text{WACC} = \frac{18.66\%(28.7) + 9.88\%(5)}{28.7 + 5} = 0.1589 \text{ or } 15.89\%$$

The WACC falls as debt capital is introduced. It was 18%.

Question 13

The cash flows need to be identified from the company point of view.

The current dollar market value is $900 and each year the interest payment in dollars is 6% of the nominal value ($1,000) or $60. At the end of year three, there is an interest payment and also the redemption value of $1,000 or $1,060.

The exchange rate is currently €1 = $1.10.

The solution to parts (a), (b) and (c) is calculated on an EXCEL spreadsheet as follows:

(a)

Year	$ cash flow	After tax	€1 = $ Exchange rate	€ cash flow
0	−900	−900	1.10	−818.18
1	60	45.6	1.10	41.45
2	60	45.6	1.10	41.45
3	1060	1045.6	1.10	950.55
				IRR = 8.47%

(b)

Year		After tax	Exchange rate	€ cash flow
0		−900	1.100	−818.18
1		45.6	0.957	47.67
2		45.6	0.832	54.82
3		1045.6	0.723	1445.66
				IRR = 24.74%

(c)

Year		After tax in $	Exchange rate	€ cash flow
0		−900	1.100	−818.18
1		45.6	1.155	39.48
2		45.6	1.213	37.60
3		1045.6	1.273	821.12
				IRR = 3.31%

(a) The cost of the eurobond is 8.47% when the exchange rate remains stable.
(b) The cost of the eurobond increases dramatically when the dollar appreciates, to almost 25%.
(c) The cost of the eurobond issue falls to around 3% when the dollar depreciates.
(d) The current market value of the eurobond issue is 0.9 (100 million)/1.1 = €81.821 million.

Question 17

$K_e = 28.5c/167c = 17.07\%$

The debenture cash flows are as follows:

Year	Cash flow without tax effect	Cash flow after tax
0	(€80)	(€80)
1 to 10	€5	€3.80
10	€100	€100
IRR =	**7.57%**	**6.27%**

Market value of equity = €1.67 × 18 million = €30.06 million

Market value of debt = €9.375 × 0.80 = €7.5 million

$$\text{Present WACC} = \frac{30.06\,(17.07\%) + 7.5(7.57\%)}{37.56} = 15.17\%$$

$$\text{Present WACC with tax at 24\%} = \frac{30.06\,(17.07\%) + 7.5(6.27\%)}{37.56} = 14.91\%$$

(b) $\text{New WACC} = \dfrac{25.06\,(17.07\%) + 12.5(7.57\%)}{37.56} = 13.91\%$

$$\text{New WACC with tax at 24\%} = \frac{25.06\,(17.07\%) + 12.5(6.27\%)}{37.56} = 13.48\%$$

The WACC falls in both situations, due the introduction of cheaper debt capital. The reduction is more pronounced with the lower cost of the after-tax cost of debt capital. This question ignores the impact of financial risk on the cost of equity.

CHAPTER 9

Question 8

(a) The correlation coefficient $= \dfrac{\text{Covariance xy}}{\text{SDx Sdy}}$

    M and N = 12.2/(2.4)(6.2) = 0.82

    M and O = 8.1/(2.4)(4.3) = 0.78

    N and O = –4.5/(6.2)(4.3) = –0.17 the lowest risk on correlation criteria.

(b) Expected value M and N = 0.5(15%) + 0.5(18%) = 16.5%

                M and O =16% and N and O = 17.5%

    Variance M and N = $0.5^2(2.4)^2 + 0.5^2(6.2)^2 + 2(0.5)(0.5)(0.82)(2.4)(6.2) = 17.1508\%$

    Standard deviation M and N $= \sqrt{17.1508} = 4.14\%$

    Standard deviation M and O = 3.18%. Standard deviation N and O = 3.46%

    In this example portfolio M and N are inferior to portfolio N and O on both expected value and standard deviation measures. However conflicting results are found for both portfolio M and O and portfolio N and O and it is therefore difficult to say which portfolio is the most efficient.

Question 11

(a) The company has 8 million shares in issue, with the most recent dividend
= €410,000/8 million = €0.05125.
Five years figures indicate four years growth. $(1 + g)^4$ = €410,000/€280,000 fi g = 10%

Using the dividend growth model Ke = $\dfrac{€0.05125(1.10)}{€1.13}$ + 0.10 = 0.15 or 15%

Using the capital asset pricing model Ke = 10% + 1.4(15% – 10%) = 17%

(b) The market value of equity = 8 million × €1.13 = €9.04 million
The market value of debt capital = €1 × 0.825 = €0.825 million.

$$Kd = \frac{€10(1 - 0.50)}{€82.50} = 6.06\%$$

$$WACC = \frac{15\%(9.04) + 6006\%(.825)}{9.865} = 14.25\%$$

$$WACC = \frac{17\%(9.04) + 6006\%(.825)}{9.865} = 16\%$$

Question 12

Using the information from company B and the geared/ungeared formula find βa.

$$\beta a = \beta e \times \frac{E}{E+D} + \beta d \times \frac{D}{E+D}$$

$$= 1.2 \times {}^3/_4 + 0.2 \times {}^1/_4 = 0.95$$

Now adjust this to reflect the gearing of company A assuming βd = 0

βa = 0.95 = βe × 10/12 and βe = 1.14 assuming no tax.

The appropriate discount factor is based on the WACC as follows

Ke = 8% + (13% – 8%)1.14 = 13.7%

$$WACC = \frac{13.7\%(10) + 8\%(2)}{12} = 12.75\%$$

Question 16

The risk-free rate of return including inflation = 1 – 1.05 × 1.04 = 9.2%.
The market rate of return including inflation = 1 – 1.05 × 1.10 = 15.5%.

The cost of equity = 9.2% + (15.5% – 9.2%)1.25 = 17.075%

The cost of debt = 10%(1 – 0.2) = 8%

The market value of equity = 20 million × €0.92 = €18.4 million and the market value of debt = €14 million

$$\text{WACC} = \frac{17.075\%(18.4) + 8\%(14)}{32.4} = 0.1315 \text{ or } 13.15\%$$

Question 17

(a) Ke = 7% + (12% – 7%)1.4 = 14%

$$\text{Ke} = \frac{D1}{Po} + g \text{ or } Po = \frac{D1}{(Ke - g)}$$

Now find the growth rate and next year's dividend.
Dividends have grown from 38c to 44c over a four-year period, i.e. five years' figures means four years' growth (1 + g)4 = 44/38 and this implies the growth rate is 3.73%. The dividend next year is 44c(1.0373).

$$Po = \frac{44c(1.0373)}{0.14 - 0.0373} = €4.44.$$

(b) The model assumptions may be wrong (Rf, Rm, beta factor, g, Po etc.) and share prices are influenced by many factors, such as world stock markets, market sentiment, state of the national economy/industry, macroeconomic indicators (interest rates etc.).

CHAPTER 10

Question 4

It is possible for a company to grow too fast. A company's growth can be greater than the company's ability to generate the capital to fund growth. Quality may also suffer because of rapid growth. A company might decide to limit distribution or it may increase prices to slow down growth.

Question 10

XYZ Ltd Pro-Forma Profit and Loss Account 31 December 2000	
Sales	€23,000
Costs	€18,400
PBIT	€4,600
Interest	—
Tax (20%)	€920
PAT	€3680

Dividends = €552
Addition to RE = €3128

Pro-Forma Balance Sheet 31 December 2000	
Assets	€161,000
Debt	€28,000
Equity	€112,000
Addition to retained earnings	€3,128 €143,128

AFN = €161,000 – €143,128 = €17,872.

Question 12

The capital intensity ratio is the amount of assets that are required per euro of sales, i.e. A/S_0 in the AFN formula. If a firm is capital intensive (a high A/S_0 ratio), a small increase in production and output will require much additional external funds. A low capital intensity ratio will mean output and sales can grow without much additional capital.

Question 14

Pro-Forma Balance Sheet (2001) Clashmore Ltd.	
Fixed assets	€100,000
Current assets	€150,000
Total assets	€250,000
Financed by creditors	€20,000
Short term debt	€0
Equity	€160,000
	€130,000
Therefore the AFN = €70,000.	

Question 19

First, we need to discover if the current growth rate is possible.
Remember from chapter 3 that the ROE = ROA × Equity Multiplier.

> = ROA × (1+ Debt:Equity)
> 5% × 1/1.7 × (1 + 0.4) = 4.11%.

The sustainable growth rate is given as 10%.

> = 0.1 = [0.0411 (b)]/ [1 – 0.0411(b)] where 'b' is the retention ratio.
> = 0.0411(b) = 0.1 – 0.00411(b)
> = 0.03521(b) = 0.1 = 2.2 = 'b'.

Therefore the retention ratio is 2.2 and the pay-out ratio is (1 – b) = –1.2. Since the retention ratio plus the pay-out ratio must equal 1, it is impossible to have a pay-out ratio of –1.2 or minus 120%. If all earnings are retained, the dividend pay-out will be zero, which is the lowest possible pay-out.
Therefore the maximum sustainable growth rate for the firm is:

> 'g' = 0.0411/(1 – 0.0411) = 4.2%.

CHAPTER 11

Question 5

Setting the offer price is the most difficult part of an IPO. If the offer price is set too low, the issuing firm is faced with a potential loss. On the other hand, set the price too high and the issue may be unsuccessful.

Underpricing helps new shareholders get a higher rate of return on the shares they buy. Existing shareholders will experience a loss.

Much of the underpricing is concentrated on smaller and very speculative issues with little or no sales record. They must be underpriced in order to attract investors.

Another reason why IPOs have such a large initial return is because of the 'winners curse'. The only way in which the winners curse can be avoided is by 'underpricing'.

Finally, underwriters could possibly be sued if they consistently got the offer price wrong. Therefore, underpricing could be seen as an insurance against being sued.

Question 11

The only reason is that some investors are completely risk averse.

Question 13

If markets are efficient, all available information is incorporated into the share price. Therefore, in order for you to outsmart the market, you must have information that *nobody else* has. If you believe this then the market will end up outsmarting you.

Furthermore, don't try to predict what the future holds. Past price performance is no evidence of future prices. If the stock market rises for 15 days in a row, it doesn't mean that it will continue to rise.

Investors who try to find good deals can spend a lot of money buying and selling securities hoping for abnormal returns. The transactions costs alone can push up the required rate of return necessary for you just to break even. It would be wise for the investor to minimise transactions costs by investing long term.

In summary, with efficient markets, investors will, on average, earn what the market offers. When we include trading costs, these investors will loose out by the amount of the transactions costs.

Question 16

Yes. This violates strong form market efficiency, because the sales director can make a profit by using insider information.

Question 20

Proceeds per share = 8(1 − 0.03) = €7.76. This is the net proceeds per share sold. In addition, it has to pay additional expenses of €20,000. Therefore, the total number of shares it must issue is = (15m + 20,000)/€7.76 = 1,935,567.

CHAPTER 12

Question 9

Modern corporations do not follow a residual dividend policy. Some people think that cash dividends are what is 'left over' after everything else has been paid. If this were the case then a 'residual' dividend policy would lead to volatile dividend payments. This would adversely affect share prices.

Question 10

P/E ratio = 10. The earnings per share (EPS) = €2,000,000/100,000 = €20.
Therefore the P/E ratio = 10 = ?/20, which means the price of the share is €200.
Dividend pay-out ratio = Dividends/Net income
= €8 per share × 100,000 = €800,00
= €800,000/2,000,000 = 40%.

Question 11

(a) Murphy's Debt: Equity ratio is 0.6/0.4 = 1.5. By reinvesting all of its earnings, it would need to borrow €100,000 × 1.5 = €150,000 to maintain its debt: equity ratio. Therefore, it can spend €250,000 (€100,000 earnings + €150,000 borrowings) on capital projects without raising new equity. The company's planned investment is €200,000. This will be financed with 40% equity. This is €200,000 × 40% = €80,000.
(b) Profits after tax are €100,000. Therefore it can pay €100,000 = €80,000 = €20,000 in dividends.

Question 13

Dividend policy can be irrelevant even when the share price rises following an increase in dividends. The change in the price of the share is due to the change in the dividend, not in dividend policy.

Question 18

The value of equity is €230,000 and with 10,000 shares this gives a market value per share of €23. Paying a dividend of €3 per share, the price of the share, ex-dividend, will be €20 per share. Total assets decrease €30,000 (cash), and equity is now 10,000 × €20 = €200,000, i.e. fall of €30,000. Incidentally, the EPS after the dividend is the same as it is before the dividend, i.e. €2. However, the P/E ratio is €20/€2 = 10, compared to 11.5 before the dividend (€23/€2).

CHAPTER 13

Question 10

Stock Turnover = Cost of goods sold/Average stock
= €16,000/[€5,000 + €5,700/2] = €16,000/€5,350
= 2.99 times
Debtors Turnover
Sales/Average Debtors
€20,000/[€4,300 + €4,000/2]
€20,000/€4,150
= 4.8 times

Creditors turnover
= Cost of goods sold/Average creditors
= €16,000/[€2,000 + €2,200/2]
= €16,000/[€2,100] = 7.6 times.

Therefore:

Stock period = 365/2.99 = 122 days
Debtors period = 365/4.8 = 76 days
Creditors period = 365/7.6 = 48 days

Consequently, it takes 122 days to acquire and sell stock. It takes 76 days to collect the cash from debtors. The operating cycle is therefore 122 + 76 = 198 days.
The cash cycle is 198 days – 48 days = 150 days.

Question 15

$Q^* = [(2)(\text{annual cash disbursements})(\text{cost per sale of securities})/\text{interest rate}]^{.5}$.
$Q^* = [2 \times €30m \times €1,000/ 0.03]^{.5}$.
$Q^* = [€60m \times €1,000/ 0.03]^{.5}$.
$Q^* = €1,414213$.

Question 18

Net Float is the difference between the balance available at the bank and your own book balance.

The available balance will be €100, what you started with. The €200 cheque will not have cleared, and the cheque sent by your parents will not have cleared either. Your book balance on 5 February is:

€100 + €100 – €200 = €zero.

Therefore, your net float is:

€100 – €Zero = €100.

Your cheque will be presented on 7 February. So it is necessary for the available balance to be at least €200 on that date. Your parents cheque will be presented on February 8th. The available balance on 7 February is €100 – €200 = –€100. The cheque will bounce.

Question 20

(a) $Q^* = [(2 \times €30,000 \times €50)/0.1]^{.5} = €5,477.2$.
     What this means is that the initial balance should be €5,477.2. If the balance drops to zero, a further €5,477.2 should be put into cash.
     The average cash balance is:

$Q^*/2 = €5,477.2/2 = €2,738.6$.

The opportunity cost is:

$(€2,738.6)(0.1) = €2,737.8$.

In addition, there will be €30,000/€5,477 = 5.5 orders during the year. Therefore the total trading costs are:

$(5.5)(€50) = €274$.

The total costs are:
>   Opportunity costs + Trading costs
>   €2,73.8 + €274 = €5,476.6

(b) (i)   Synchronization.
 (ii) Increase in the forecast sales which leads to lower target cash balances.
 (iii) Reduce marketable securities, which would increase firm's cash balances.
 (iv) Arranging an overdraft will allow the firm to hold less cash.

Synchronisation of cash flows is a plan to keep cash balances to a minimum by improving the firm's forecasting so that cash inflows occur simultaneously with cash outflows.

Question 22

The daily interest rate is about .022 basis points. The rate of return earned on €1m per day is €1,000,000 x 0.00022 = €220. This is the opportunity cost. The order cost will usually be much less than this. Therefore, large firms will buy and sell short-term securities regularly rather than leave cash lying around.

CHAPTER 14

Question 5

Profit and Loss Account under Old and New Policies		
	OldPolicy	NewPolicy
Turnover	€2,000,000	€2,300,000
Variable Costs	€1,500,000	€1,725,000
Gross Profit	€500,000	€575,000
Cost of Carrying Debtors*	€16,437	€23,630
Credit Control Expenses	€20,000	€12,000
Bad Debts	€20,000	€23,000
Profit Before Tax	€443,563	€516,400
Tax (20%)	€88,713	€103,280
Profit After Tax	€354,850	€413,120

Therefore, the new policy will improve the profit after tax figure.
*   Cost of Carrying Debtors is the average collection period by the variable cost percentage by the cost of the funds used to carry debtors. Note the variable costs represent the costs of goods sold.

Cost of carrying debtors:
(Debtors Collection Period)(Daily Sales)(VC: Sales ratio)(Cost of Funds)
(40 days)(€5,479)(0.75)(0.1) = €16,437 = Old policy.
(50 days)(€6,301)(0.75)(0.1) = €23,630 = New policy

Question 7

The cost of debtors:
  (i)   Probability of default
  (ii) The actual cash discount
  (iii) Cost of debt
By not granting credit there is the cost of lost sales. Firms that give credit have the cost of running credit departments. This job is often factored out to outside companies.

Total carrying costs are the costs that are incurred when credit is granted. These are positively related to the amount of credit that is granted.

Opportunity costs are the sales that are lost by not granting credit. Opportunity costs decline when credit is given.

Question 12

$(0.2)(110,000) = €22,000$

Question 17

Remember an optimum inventory policy requires restocking costs to equal carrying costs. Since this is not the case, the company does not have optimum inventory. Furthermore, since carrying costs are high compared to restocking costs, the company should reduce its stock levels.

Question 19

(a) EOQ = $[2(F)(TS)/(X)(P)]^{0.5}$.
     $=[2(30)(100,000)/(0.15)(10)]^{0.5} = 2000$ units
(b) 100,000/2000 = 50 orders a year or 365/50 = 7.3 days.
(c) The maximum stock is the stock that is available immediately a new order is received is 2,000 + 599 (safety) = 2,599.

CHAPTER 15

Question 3

Larger firms generally have greater access to the financial markets in terms of issuing shares and bonds. In addition, older and more mature companies will have built up a substantial level of retained earnings over their lifetime. Smaller firms are therefore more dependent on short-term finance.

Question 6

(a) Investors who lend money to a company would prefer if the company had a healthy current ratio, i.e., a sizeable excess of current assets over current liabilities.

However, from the point of view of the company, it is wasteful if the current ratio is too high. Having money tied up in cash, stock, debtors, etc., does not provide a return. Having cash in a current account usually doesn't pay interest. Stock on hand provides no return because the company hasn't sold it. Debtors are customers who owe money to the company, which cannot be used until it is received.

On the other hand, fixed assets generate the income that earns profit, but they are not very liquid. The decision for companies is whether they should invest in long term assets that generate returns (profit), and consequently have low investments in current assets, or should they keep a high level of cash and other current assets and stay liquid.

(b) Aggressive working capital policy finances temporary current assets, possibly all of its permanent current assets and maybe some of its fixed assets with short-term debt.

If it finances its temporary current assets and most of its permanent current assets with current liabilities (short-term debt), it will have very little net working capital. In other words, there is only a small difference between liquid assets and the amount due for current liabilities. Therefore, this policy is very risky. As described in chapter 13 zero working capital results from financing all current assts with short-term debt. Negative working capital is the situation where all current assets and part of the fixed assets are financed with short-term debt.

Conservative working capital policy involves using long-term debt to finance all fixed assets, permanent current assets, and part of the temporary current assets. Only a small portion of the current assets is financed with current liabilities. The current ratio is therefore very high. This is a low risk strategy. However, because long-term funds are more expensive than short-term loans, a conservative working capital policy is expensive to the firm.

The moderate or matching approach to financing is where temporary current assets are financed with current liabilities, and all permanent current assets and fixed assets should be financed by long-term liabilities and equity. The level of net working capital is larger than under the aggressive policy and smaller than under the prudent or conservative policy. The level of risk is therefore medium.

CHAPTER 17

Question 6

Lead payment – $10,000,000/1.0625 = €9,411,765

Money market – deposit $10,000,000/1.0175 = $9,828,010 at a cost of 9,828,010/1.0625 = €9,249,892.

FEC – forward rate = 1.0625 + 0.0110 =1.0735. FEC = $10,000,000/1.0735 = €9,315,324 in three months.

To make a direct comparison discount at the cost of borrowing in euros, i.e. €9,315,324/1.01 = €9,223,093.

The FEC is the lowest cost.

The cost of forward cover $\dfrac{0.011 \times 12 \times 100}{3 \times 1.0735}$ = 4.098%.

$$\dfrac{0.0105 \times 12 \times 100}{3 \times 1.0740} = 3.911\%$$

The cost of forward cover is approximately 4% and this also reflects the difference in interest rates in the two economies.

Question 8

If Euribor has moved to 13% the bank will compensate the company as follows:
(13% – 9%) × €6 million × 1/2 = €120,000. However the compensation is paid up front on the 1 of July and this €120,000 must be discounted at the prevailing interest rate for 6 months.
€120,000 × 1/1.065 = €112,676
If Euribor has moved to 7% the company will compensate the bank as follows
(9% – 7%) × €6 million × 1/2 = €60,000. However the compensation is paid up front on the 1 of July and this €60,000 must be discounted at the prevailing interest rate for 6 months.
€60,000 × 1/1.035 = €57,971

Question 9

Multilateral netting is carried out by first changing all values into $.
L240 million/1680 = $142,857   SF480,000/1.88 = $255,319   L180 million/1680 = $107,143
£74,000/0.68 = $108,824   SF375,000/1.88 = $199,468

Then net them off in the following table:

	Paying $ U.K.	Paying $ Italy	Paying $ Swiss	Total $ receipts
U.K. Receiving $		108,924		108,824
Italy Receiving $	142,857		107,143	250,000
Swiss Receiving $	255,319	199,468		454,787
Total $ payments	(398,176)	(308,292)	(107,143)	
Total $ receipts	108,824	250,000	454,787	
Net cash flow in $	(289,352)	(58,292)	347,644	

The UK subsidiary pays the Switzerland subsidiary $289,353.
The Italian subsidiary pays the Switzerland subsidiary $26,292. Transaction costs including bid/offer spread and commissions associated with dealing in foreign currencies are reduced.

Question 19

Contract type €1 million 3-month. Exposure €20 million for 6 months, therefore the number of contracts
= (€20 million/€1 million)2 = 40 contracts.
Company fears a fall in interest rates over the next three months. A fall in interest rates leads to a rise in futures prices. Therefore the company should buy contracts today.

Today   Buy 40 contracts at 92.50
In three months   Sell 40 contracts at 90.50

The loss on the hedge is 2% or 200 ticks per contract. Tick value = €1 million (0.01%)(1/4) = €25
Futures loss = 40(200)(€25) = €200,000
Interest received after 6 months = €20 million (10%)(1/2) – €200,000 = €800,000 or effectively 8%.

Question 20

	Floating rate	Fixed rate
Company X	Euribor*	12%
Company Y	Euribor + 0.3%	13.5%*
	0.3%	1.5% Arbitrage opportunity = 1.2%

If this is divided equally they will both reduce their cost of borrowing by 0.6%.
   Since X wants variable* it will pay Euribor – 0.6% and as Y wants a fixed rate* it will pay 12.9%.
   Suggested swap as follows
   Company X should borrow at 12% fixed and company Y at Euribor + 0.3% floating.

	Company X	Company Y
Pays to the bank	(12%)	(Euribor + 0.3%)
Pays in the swap	(Euribor)	(12.6%)
Receives in the swap	12.6%	Euribor
Net interest cost	(Euribor – 0.6%)	(12.9%)

Here company X pays Euribor and company Y pays 12.6% under the terms of the swap.

CHAPTER 18

Question 1

(a) Roy's criterion
$R_1 = 7\%$

Fund	A	B	C
Mean return	13	17	21
Standard Deviation (σ)	5	9	12
Difference From 7% (σ)	–1.2	–1.11	–1.17
Probability of Return <7%	11.51%	13.35%	12.1%

A has an 11.51% chance of delivering a return of 7% or less, B has a 13.35% chance of such a return, while C has a 12.1% chance. Therefore **A** is preferred portfolio.

(b) Kataoka's criterion
$\alpha = 13\%$.

From the standard normal distribution tables it can be seen that the bottom 13% of the distribution (13% in the left-hand tail of the distribution) occurs at 1.13 standard deviation below the mean. This holds for all normal distributions. Thus the value of R_1 can be calculated for each fund as 1.13 standard deviations below the mean i.e.

$$R_1 = R_p - 1.13\sigma$$

Portfolio	A	B	C
R_p	13	17	21
σ_p	5	9	12
R_1 =	7.35	6.83	7.44

The results indicate that 13% of the time fund A will fall below 7.35% return, fund B will fall below 6.83% while fund C will fall below 7.44%. Since fund C produces the highest floor it is the preferred portfolio.

(c) Telser's criterion
$R_1 = 7\%$ (minimum desired return)
$\alpha = 13\%$ (acceptable risk level)

Fund	A	B	C
Mean return	13	17	21
Standard Deviation (σ)	5	9	12
Difference From 7% (σ)	–1.2	–1.11	–1.17
Probability of Return <7%	11.51%	13.35%	12.1%
Obeys constraint?	Yes	No	Yes

Fund B fails the constraint since it has a greater than 13% (13.35%) chance of falling below a 7% return in any period. Both funds A and C meet the constraint. Of these two, fund C has the highest average return and is therefore the preferred portfolio.

Question 2

(a) Roy's criterion
$R_1 = 5\%$

Fund	A	B	C
Mean return	12	15	20
Standard Deviation (σ)	4	7	10
Difference From 5% (σ)	−1.75	−1.43	−1.5
Probability of Return <7%	4.01%	7.64%	6.68%

A has an 4.01% chance of delivering a return of 5% or less, B has a 7.64% chance of such a return, while C has a 6.68% chance. Therefore A is preferred portfolio.

(b) Kataoka's criterion
$\alpha = 8\%$.

From the standard normal distribution tables it can be seen that the bottom 8% of the distribution (8% in the left-hand tail of the distribution) occurs at 1.41 standard deviation below the mean. This holds for all normal distributions. Thus the value of Rl can be calculated for each fund as 1.41 standard deviations below the mean, i.e.

$$R_1 = R_p - 1.41\sigma$$

Portfolio	A	B	C
R_p	12	15	20
σ_p	4	7	10
R_1 =	6.36	5.13	5.90

The results indicate that 8% of the time fund A will fall below 6.36% return, fund B will fall below 5.13% while fund C will fall below 5.90%. Since fund A produces the highest floor it is the preferred portfolio.

(c) Telser's criterion
$R_1 = 5\%$ (minimum desired return)
$\sigma = 8\%$ (acceptable risk level)

Fund	A	B	C
Mean return	12	15	20
Standard Deviation (σ)	4	7	10
Difference From 5% (σ)	−1.75	−1.43	−1.5
Probability of Return <5%	4.01%	7.64%	6.68%
Obeys constraint?	Yes	Yes	Yes

Each of the funds A, B and C meet the constraint. Since fund C has the highest average return it is the preferred portfolio.

Question 4

The Sharpe measure
$R_f = 4\%$
$R_A = 11\%$
$\sigma_A = 5\%$
$\sigma_B = 14\%$
$R_B = 7\%$

The Sharpe measure for the two funds is:

Fund A $\quad \dfrac{11 - 4}{5} = 1.4$

Fund B $\quad \dfrac{14 - 4}{7} = 1.43$

Fund A earned 1.4 % return for each 1% of risk carried while Fund B earned 1.43% return for each 1% of risk carried. Fund B, is delivering a greater return for the level of risk attached and is therefore the preferred fund.

Question 5

The Treynor measure:

$R_f = 6\%$
$R_m = 9\%$
$R_a = 13\%$
$\beta_a = 1.4$
$R_b = 14\%$
$\beta_b = 1.2$

The Treynor measure for the two funds and the market average is:

Market Average $\quad \dfrac{9 - 6}{1} = 3$

Fund A $\quad \dfrac{13 - 6}{1.4} = 5$

Fund B $\quad \dfrac{14 - 6}{1.2} = 6.67$

Both funds are paying excess returns higher than the market average. Fund A earned an excess return of 5% when the risk level is neutralised to the market average while Fund B earned an excess return of 6.67% when the risk level is neutralised to the market average. Fund B is therefore paying an excess return higher than Fund A. Fund B is therefore the preferred fund.

Question 6

Differential return (total risk) measure

$R_f = 6\%$
$R_m = 11\%$
$\sigma_m = 5\%$
$R_A = 16\%$
$\sigma_A = 8\%$
$R_B = 9\%$
$\sigma_B = 6\%$

$$E(R_i) = R_f + (E(R_m) - R_f) \times \frac{\sigma_i}{\sigma_m}$$

The expected return on Fund A is:

$$6 + (11 - 6) \times \frac{8}{5} = 14\%$$

The actual return on Fund A was 16%.
The differential return is therefore 16% – 14% = 2%.
Fund A has therefore achieved a return 2% above that which could have been achieved by simply borrowing at the risk-free rate and investing in the market portfolio.
The expected return on Fund B is:

$$6 + (11 - 6) \times \frac{6}{5} = 12\%$$

The actual return on Fund B was 9%.
The differential return is therefore 9% – 12% = – 3%.
Fund B has therefore achieved a return 3% below that which could have been achieved by simply borrowing at the risk-free rate and investing in the market portfolio.
Fund A is therefore the preferred portfolio.

Question 7

Jensen measure

$R_f = 7\%$
$R_m = 10\%$
$R_A = 11\%$
$\beta_a = 1.4$
$R_B = 13\%$
$\beta = 1.6$

$$E(R_i) = R_f + \beta_i(E(R_m) - R_f)$$

The expected return on Fund A is:

$$7 + 1.4(10 - 7) = 11.2\%$$

The actual return on Fund A was 11%.

The differential return is therefore 11% − 11.2% = −0.2%.

Fund A has therefore achieved a return 0.2% below that which could have been achieved by simply borrowing at the risk-free rate and investing in the market portfolio.

The expected return on Fund B is:

$$7 + 1.6(10 - 7) = 11.8\%$$

The actual return on Fund B was 13%.

The differential return is therefore 13% − 11.8% = 1.2%.

Fund B has therefore achieved a return 1.2% above that which could have been achieved by simply borrowing at the risk-free rate and investing in the market portfolio.

Fund B is therefore the preferred.

CHAPTER 19

Question 5

Some possible reasons:
  (i) Usually the acquiring company is much bigger with a larger number of shares. Therefore, the gains made from mergers are spread more sparsely among shares.
 (ii) The managers of the acquiring company may not be acting in the best interest of the shareholders.
(iii) The merger may have been anticipated, and the gains incorporated into the share price before the merger.
(iv) In an era of 'merger mania', the demand for takeovers may be pushing the price (cost) of acquisition up to the point where the NPV = zero.

Question 7

The main reason is that 'reverse synergy' is possible. This is possible because the smaller entity can manage and focus more clearly on its core business, and, of course, performance evaluation is now easier, financial reports and stock prices are now separated from the mire of consolidated accounts.

Question 10

(i) $K_e = R_{fr} + RP_m(\beta)$
  $= 0.07 + 0.08(0.8) = 13.4\%$

Therefore the current price of Patterson is:
  $= D_1/K_e - g = €1.50/0.134 - 0.06 = €20.27.$

(ii) $K_e = R_{fr} + RP_m(\beta)$
  $= 7\% + 8\%(1.1) = 15.8\%$

Therefore, the value of Patterson to Murphy (per share) is:

  $= D_1/K_e - g = €1.50/0.158 - 0.07 = €17.04$

Range in values per share: €20.27 to €17.04.

Question 14

The value of firm B to Firm A is:
  $V_b{}^* = \Delta V + V_b$
  $= €1m + (2,500,000 \times €40)$
  $= €101m.$
Firm B wants €50 per share. Firm A would have to pay €50 x 2,500,000 = €125,000,000.
  The NPV is:
  $NPV = V_b{}^* - Cost$
  $= €101m - €1.25m$
  $= (€24m).$
This is a negative NPV, so Firm A should not purchase the share at €50.

CHAPTER 20

Question 1

The price of both bonds at a 10% yield and 9% yield can be calculated using 5.2 (chapter 5) and the procedure in section 20.1. This gives the following results:

Price at 10% yield *Finance* bond	=	106.55
Price at 9% yield of *Finance* bond	=	109.19
Price volatility of *Finance* bond	=	2.48%
Price at 10% yield *Treasury* bond	=	106.55
Price at 9% yield of *Treasury* bond	=	107.94*
Price volatility of *Treasury* bond	=	1.30%

*The assumption of early redemption results in the redemption value being paid in two months' time along with the normal coupon, but with no further payments thereafter. The price is therefore calculated as

$$\text{Price} = \frac{109.50}{(1.09)^{0.16}} = 107.94$$

Question 2

(a) The cash flow from the bond is as follows:

End-Year	1	2	3	4	5
Cashflow	40	40	40	40	1040

The cashflow is discounted at varying rates until two rates are found which give a present value either side of €800. As before these rates should be one percentage point apart. The true cost of finance can be approximated between these two trial rates by linear interpolation.

Since the payments of €40 form an annuity, the present value can be found using 5.2 (chapter 5).

A discount rate of 9% produces a present values of €805.52. A discount rate of 10% produces a present value of €772.55. The answer is therefore between 9 and 10%. The answer can be approximated by linear interpolation:

$$\frac{x}{1} = \frac{5.52}{32.97} = 0.17$$

The answer is approximated at 9.2%

(b) The annual cashflow and debt position can be shown as follows:

End-Year	Finance Cost @9.2%	Interest Paid	Debt
0			800.00
1	73.60	40	833.60
2	76.69	40	870.29
3	80.07	40	910.36
4	83.75	40	954.11
5	87.78	1040	1.89

The small positive balance at the end of year five is simply a rounding error as the true cost of finance is slightly below 9.2%.

Question 3

(a) 1 July 1997
The price on this date is calculated using 5.2 (chapter 5) with the following parameters

$P_t = 9.12$ (€12 less tax @ 24%)
$r = 0.07$
$n = 5$

This gives a price of €108.69
   Note that the investor buying the bond on this day does not get the coupon payment on that date, but must wait until one year later to receive her first income from the bond.

1 May 1997
An investor buying the bond on this day is getting the same as the person buying it on 1 July 1997 plus an extra €9.12 in two month's time. The price paid should reflect this extra payment, but also the fact that it is purchased earlier. The price is therefore

$$\text{Price } 31/05/097 = \frac{\text{Price } 01/07/97 + €9.12}{(1.07)^{1/6}} = €116.49$$

25 June 1997
This is similar to the above except that the discount period is 6 days rather than two months. The price is therefore:

$$\text{Price } 25/06/097 = \frac{\text{Price } 01/07/97 + €9.12}{(1.07)^{6/365}} = €117.68$$

(b) 1 July 1997

$$\text{Gross income yield} = \frac{12.00}{108.69} \times 100 = 11.04\%$$

1 May 1997

$$\text{Gross income yield} = \frac{12.00}{116.49} \times 100 = 10.30\%$$

25 June 1997

$$\text{Gross income yield} = \frac{12.00}{117.68} \times 100 = 10.20\%$$

Question 7

Since Bond B is issued and redeemed at par, the true average annual cost of finance is equal to the coupon rate, i.e. 10%. It is sufficient therefore to determine whether the true average annual cost of finance of Bond A is above or below 10%. The cash flow from the bond is as follows:

Bond A

End-Year	1	2	3	4	5
Cashflow	20	50	80	120	1350

A discount rate of 10% produces a present value of €1,039.81 A discount rate higher than 10% would be required to bring the present value down to €1,000. Therefore the true average annual cost of finance of Bond A is above 10%.

Question 15

(a) First find the price on 1/08/00
The price on this date is calculated using 5.2 (chapter 5) with the following parameters:

$P_t = 6.00$
$i = 0.09$
$n = 8$

This gives a price of €83.40.
   Note that the investor buying the bond on this day does not get the coupon payment on that date, but must wait until one year later to receive her first income from the bond.

Next calculate the price on 31 July 2000
An investor buying the bond on this day is getting the same as the person buying it on 1 August 2000 plus an extra €6.00 in one day's time. Since they are both parting with their money at virtually the same time the buyer on the 31 July should pay an extra €6.00 for the bond. The price on this date is therefore €89.40

(i) 26 May 2000

An investor buying the bond on this date gets the same cash flow as the investor buying it on 31 July 2000. However she has to part with her money about 66 days earlier and so the price paid on this date should be lower to reflect this. Thus the price of the bond on this date should be €89.40 discounted for 66 days at a rate of 9% p.a. This produces a price of €88.02

$$\text{Price } 26/05/00 = \frac{\text{Price } 31/07/00}{(1.09)^{66/365}} = €88.02$$

(ii) 31 January 2000

An investor buying the bond on this date gets the same cash flow as the investor buying it on 31 July 2000. However she has to part with her money about 6 months earlier and so the price paid on this date should be lower to reflect this. Thus the price of the bond on this date should be €89.40 discounted for 6 months at a rate of 9% p.a. This produces a price of €85.63

$$\text{Price } 31/01/00 = \frac{\text{Price } 31/07/00}{(1.09)^{1/2}} = €85.63$$

(iii) 26 August 2000

First find the price on 31 July 2001 as shown above but changing n to 7. This gives a value of €90.90. An investor buying the bond on the 26 August 2001 gets the same cash flow as the investor buying it on 31 July 2001. However she has to part with her money 339 days earlier and so the price paid on this date should be lower to reflect this. Thus the price of the bond on this date should be €90.90 discounted for 339 days at a rate of 9% p.a. This produces a price of €83.91

$$\text{Price } 26/08/00 = \frac{\text{Price } 31/07/01}{(1.09)^{339/365}} = €83.91$$

(iv) 26 May 2001

Similar to part (i), the price on 31 July 2001 should be calculated and then discounted for 66 days. An investor buying the bond on this date gets the same cash flow as the investor buying it on 31 July 2001. However she has to part with her money 66 days earlier and so the price paid on this date should be lower to reflect this. Thus the price of the bond on this date should be €90.90 discounted for 66 days at a rate of 9% p.a. This produces a price of €89.49

$$\text{Price } 26/05/01 = \frac{\text{Price } 31/07/01}{(1.09)^{66/365}} = €89.49$$

(v) 1 August 2000

The price on this date is calculated using 5.2 with the following parameters:

$P_t = 6.00$

$i = 0.09$

$n = 3$

This gives a price of €92.41.

Note that the investor buying the bond on this day does not get the coupon payment on that date, but must wait until one year later to receive her first income from the bond.

(b)

	Date	Price
(a) (i)	26/05/00	88.02
(a) (ii)	31/01/00	85.63

(a) (ii) < (a)(i) because the cashflow is similar irrespective of the date, but the purchaser has to part with his/her money earlier in (a)(ii)

	Date	Price
(a)(i)	26/05/00	88.02
(a)(iii)	26/08/00	83.91

(a)(iii) < (a)(i) because purchase on 26/05/00 generates an extra coupon payment of €6 (on 01/08/00). This outweighs the effect of earlier purchase.

CHAPTER 21

Question 1

(a) This is a similar to example 21.5 in the text.
The parameters required to find the original payment and the outstanding balance after 48 payments are

PV = 25,000
n = 144 months
r = 0.008 per month

The original payment is got from 21.1 and works out at €293.02. The outstanding balance after the payment at time 48 is made is got from 21.3 above and works out at €19,582.70.

Since Ann makes no payments in time 49, 50 and 51, this balance will be charged interest at the rate on 0.8% per month for the next 3 months (i.e. until time 51). The balance at time 51 will therefore be €20,056.46.

The required number of payments can be calculated from 21.1 using the following parameters.

PV = 20,056.46
P_t = 293.02
r = 0.008
n = unknown number of payments to be calculated

This produces an answer of 99.5. This can be interpreted as 99 full payments and one final smaller payment.

The last three lines of the amortisation schedule are therefore months 98, 99 and 100 of a new schedule when the payments resume. To show the last three lines, the outstanding balance after 97 payments must be calculated. Using 21.3 with the following parameters:

PV = 20,056.46
P_t = 293.02
k = 97 months
r = 0.008 per month

This works out as €733.54.

Amortisation Schedule

Time	Payment	Interest	Capital	Balance
97				733.54
98	293.02	5.87	287.15	446.39
99	293.02	3.57	289.45	156.94
100	158.20	1.26	156.94	0.00

(b) The balance at time 51 is, from (a) above, equal to 20,056.46. The balance at time 54 can be got be drawing up three lines of the amortisation schedule as follows:

Time	Payment	Interest	Capital	Balance
51				20,056.46
52	293.02	160.45	132.57	19,923.89
53	293.02	159.39	133.63	19,790.26
54	293.02	158.32	134.70	19,655.56

The rate of interest now changes to 0.009 per month. Since the payment stays the same as before, the term of the loan must be increased further. The required number of payments can be calculated from 21.1 using the following parameters:

PV = 19,655.56
P_t = 293.02
r = 0.009
n = unknown number of payments to be calculated

This produces an answer of 103.3. This can be interpreted as 103 more full payments from this point and one final smaller payment.

The last line of the amortisation schedule is therefore month 104 of a new schedule starting at time 55. To show the last line, the outstanding balance after 103 payments must be calculated. Using 21.3 with the following parameters:

PV = 19,655.56
P_t = 293.02
k = 103 months
r = 0.009 per month

This works out as €89.86

Amortisation Schedule

Time	Payment	Interest	Capital	Balance
103				89.86
104	90.67	0.81	89.86	0.00

(c) Calculate the balance on the loan at the time the re-financing option becomes available using 21.3 with k = 48.

Balance at time 48 = 19,582.70

The borrower needs to borrow this amount plus the penalty in order to redeem the loan.

Penalty
OB at time 48 = 19,582.70
OB at time 54 = 18,748.01 (if payments continued as originally agreed)
Capital paid (time 49–54) = 834.69
Total paid (time 49–54) = 1,758.12
Interest paid (time 49–54) = 923.43

Penalty = 923.43 + 200 = 1.123.43

Need to borrow 19582.70 + 1123.43 = 20706.13

The choice is now between continuing an existing loan valued at 19582.70 at a rate of interest of 9.6% p.a. compounded monthly or a loan of 20706.13 at a rate of interest of 8.4% p.a. compounded monthly each to be paid off over 8 years with monthly payments.
The new periodic payment can be calculated from 21.1 with

PV = 20,706.13
n = 96
r = 0.007

This produces a payment of €296.94.

Since 296.94 > 293.02 the borrower should not re-finance the loan.

Question 2

(a) Gross payment

Annuity
The monthly payment is calculated from 21.1 above as £811.41.

Endowment
The monthly payment to the bank is calculated as €80,000 × 0.008= 640
Add the endowment policy premium   = 220
Total   = 860

(b) and (c) Net Payments

Interest Paid
Annuity

		Year 1			Year 12
Outstanding Balance	Time 0	80,000.00	Time 132	32,607.20
	Time 12	77,355.77	Time 144	25,517.20
Capital Paid	Year 1	2,644.23	Year 12	7,090.00
Total Paid	Year 1	9,736.92	Year 12	9,736.92
Interest Paid	Year 1	7,092.69	Year 12	2,646.92

Endowment
Interest paid = 640 x 12 = 7,680

Tax Relief

Annual	Annuity Y1	Annuity Y12	Endowment
Interest Paid	7,092.69*	2,646.92	7,680.00*
Tax Allowance	5,000.00	2,646.92	5,000.00
Tax Relief	1,100.00	582.32	1,100.00
Monthly Tax Relief	91.67	48.53	91.67

* Note that interest paid is above maximum allowable of €5,000

Gross Payment	811.41	811.41	860.00
Tax Relief	91.67	48.53	91.67
Net Payment	719.74	762.88	768.33

(d) Change in the rate of interest
    The rate of interest changes at the end of the 11 year.
    Calculate the loan balance at this point.

Annuity

Outstanding Balance @ time 132 using 21.3 = 32607.20

Endowment

Balance = original loan size = 80,000

New monthly payment

Annuity

The outstanding balance is treated conceptually like a new loan at this point. The periodic payment can be found using 21.1.

PV = 32607.20*

r = 0.0065

n = 48

P_t = unknown payment size to be calculated.

* Balance at the time the new interest rate becomes operational.

The monthly payment works out at €792.98.

Endowment

The monthly payment to the bank is calculated as €80,000 × 0.007 = 560

Add the endowment policy premium = 220

Total = 780

Net Payments

Interest Paid:

Annuity

Year 12

Outstanding balance	Time 132	32,607.20 (start of 'new' loan)
	Time 144	25,380.06
Capital paid	year 12	7,227.14
Total paid	year 12	9,515.76
Interest paid	year 12	2,288.62

Endowment

Interest paid = 560 × 12 = 6,720

Tax relief

Annual	Annuity Y12	Endowment
Interest paid	2,288.62	6,720.00 (>5,000)
Tax allowance	2,288.62	5,000.00
Tax relief	503.50	1,100.00
Monthly tax relief	41.96	91.67

Gross payment	792.98	780.00
Tax relief	41.96	91.67
Net payment	751.02	688.33

Question 3

The repayment stream involves two separate annuities
- an annual payment of €1,500
- a monthly payment to be determined.

First find the value of aloan which the annual payment stream can support. To do this the annual effective rate of interest must be determined. With a monthly rate of 1.1%, the annual effective rate is 14.03%.

The loan size sustainable by these payments is found from 21.1 with the following parameters:

P_t = 1,500
n = 7 years
r = 0.1403 per year

This gives a loan size of 6,426.57. The remainder of the total loan of €35,000 must be repaid with monthly payments. The size of this 'second' notional loan is €35,000 – €6,426.57 = €28,573.43. The monthly payment required to pay this off can be found from 21.1 with the following parameters:

PV = 28,573.43
n = 84 months
r = 0.011 per month

This produces a monthly payment of 522.92.

Amortisation Schedule

Time	Payment	Interest	Capital	Balance
0				35,000.00
1	522.92	385.00	137.92	34,862.08
2	522.92	383.48	139.44	34,722.64
3	522.92	381.95	140.97	34,581.67
81				2,986.26*
82	522.92	32.85	490.07	2,496.19
83	522.92	27.46	495.46	2,000.73
84	522.74 + 1,500	22.01	2,000.73	0.00

*The outstanding balance at time 81 involves two calculations.

The outstanding balance on the 'monthly' loan can be found from 21.3 with the following parameters:

PV = 28,573.43
Pt = 522.92
k = 81 months
r = 0.011 per month
This produces an outstanding balance of 1,534.69.

The balance on the 'annual' loan can be found by simply discounting the remaining payment of 1,500 back for three months, i.e.

$$\frac{1,500}{(1.011)^3} = 1,451.57$$

The total outstanding balance is the sum of the two components i.e. 1,534.69 + 1,451.57 = 2,986.26

(b) Outstanding balance at end year three is calculated, in two parts as shown above.

PV = 28,573.43
P_t = 522.92
k = 36 months
r = 0.011 per month

This produces an outstanding balance of €19,419.90
   The balance on the 'annual' loan can be found by using 21.4 with:

P_t = 1,500
n = 7
k = 3 years
r = 0.1403 per month

This produces a value of €4,367.88.
The total outstanding balance is therefore €23,787.78.
   First find the value of loan which the remaining annual payments can support. To do this the annual effective rate of interest must be determined. With a monthly rate of 1.2%, the annual effective rate is 15.39%.
   The loan size sustainable by these payment is found from 21.1 with the following parameters:

P_t = 1,500
n = 4 years
r = 0.1539 per year

This gives a loan size of 4,248.90. The remainder of the total outstanding balance on the loan of €23,787.78 must be repaid with monthly payments. The size of this 'second' notional loan is €23,787.78 – €4,248.90 = €19,538.88. The monthly payment required to pay this off can be found from 21.1 with the following parameters:

PV = 19,538.88
n = 48 months
r = 0.012 per month

This produces a monthly payment of €537.86.

Amortisation Schedule

Time	Payment	Interest	Capital	Balance
81				3,022.73*
82	537.86	36.27	501.59	2,521.14
83	537.86	30.25	507.61	2,013.53
84	537.69 + 1,500	24.16	2,013.53	0.00

*The outstanding balance at time 81 involves two calculations.

The outstanding balance on the 'monthly' loan can be found from 21.3 with the following parameters:

PV = 19,538.88
P_t = 537.86
k = 45 months
r = 0.012 per month

This produces an outstanding balance of 1,575.46.

The balance on the 'annual' loan can be found by simply discounting the remaining payment of 1,500 back for three months, i.e.

$$\frac{1500}{(1.012)^3} = 1,447.27$$

The total outstanding balance is the sum of the two components i.e. 1,575.46 + 1,447.277 = 3,022.73

Appendix 2
Mathematical Tables

Future value of €1 at the end of t periods (FVIF) = $(1+r)^t$

Years (t)	Interest Rate (r)								
	1%	2%	3%	4%	5%	6%	7%	8%	9%
1	1.0100	1.0200	1.0300	1.0400	1.0500	1.0600	1.0700	1.0800	1.0900
2	1.0201	1.0404	1.0609	1.0816	1.1025	1.1236	1.1449	1.1664	1.1881
3	1.0303	1.0612	1.0927	1.1249	1.1576	1.1910	1.2250	1.2597	1.2950
4	1.0406	1.0824	1.1255	1.1699	1.2155	1.2625	1.3108	1.3605	1.4116
5	1.0510	1.1041	1.1593	1.2167	1.2763	1.3382	1.4026	1.4693	1.5386
6	1.0615	1.1262	1.1941	1.2653	1.3401	1.4185	1.5007	1.5869	1.6771
7	1.0721	1.1487	1.2299	1.3159	1.4071	1.5036	1.6058	1.7138	1.8280
8	1.0829	1.1717	1.2668	1.3686	1.4775	1.5938	1.7182	1.8509	1.9926
9	1.0937	1.1951	1.3048	1.4233	1.5513	1.6895	1.8385	1.9990	2.1719
10	1.1046	1.2190	1.3439	1.4802	1.6289	1.7908	1.9672	2.1589	2.3674
11	1.1157	1.2434	1.3842	1.5395	1.7103	1.8983	2.1049	2.3316	2.5804
12	1.1268	1.2682	1.4258	1.6010	1.7959	2.0122	2.2522	2.5182	2.8127
13	1.1381	1.2936	1.4685	1.6651	1.8856	2.1329	2.4098	2.7196	3.0658
14	1.1498	1.3195	1.5126	1.7317	1.9799	2.2609	2.5785	2.9372	3.3417
15	1.1610	1.3459	1.5580	1.8009	2.0789	2.3966	2.7590	3.1722	3.6425
16	1.1726	1.3728	1.6047	1.8730	2.1829	2.5404	2.9522	3.4259	3.9703
17	1.1843	1.4002	1.6528	1.9479	2.2920	2.6928	3.1588	3.7000	4.3276
18	1.1961	1.4282	1.7024	2.0258	2.4066	2.8543	3.3799	3.9960	4.7171
19	1.2081	1.4568	1.7535	2.1068	2.5270	3.0256	3.6165	4.3157	5.1417
20	1.2202	1.4859	1.8061	2.1911	2.6533	3.2071	3.8697	4.6610	5.6044

Interest Rate (r)									
Period (t)	10%	12%	14%	15%	16%	18%	20%	24%	28%
1	1.1000	1.1200	1.1400	1.1500	1.1600	1.1800	1.2000	1.2400	1.2800
2	1.2100	1.2544	1.2996	1.3225	1.3456	1.3924	1.4400	1.5376	1.6384
3	1.3310	1.4049	1.4815	1.5209	1.5609	1.6430	1.7280	1.9066	2.0972
4	1.4641	1.5735	1.6890	1.7490	1.8106	1.9388	2.0736	2.3642	2.6844
5	1.6105	1.7623	1.9254	2.0114	2.1003	2.2878	2.4883	2.9316	3.4360
6	1.7716	1.9738	2.1950	2.3131	2.4364	2.6996	2.9860	3.6352	4.3980
7	1.9487	2.2107	2.5023	2.6600	2.8262	3.1855	3.5832	4.5077	5.6295
8	2.1436	2.4760	2.8526	3.0590	3.2784	3.7589	4.2998	5.5895	7.2058
9	2.3579	2.7731	3.2519	3.5179	3.8030	4.4355	5.1598	6.9310	9.2234
10	2.5937	3.1058	3.7072	4.0456	4.4114	5.2338	6.1917	8.5944	11.806
11	2.8531	3.4785	4.2262	4.6524	5.1173	6.1759	7.4301	10.657	15.112
12	3.1384	3.8960	4.8179	5.3503	5.9360	7.2876	8.9161	13.215	19.343
13	3.4523	4.3635	5.4924	6.1528	6.8858	8.5994	10.699	16.386	24.759
14	3.7975	4.8871	6.2613	7.0757	7.9875	10.147	12.839	20.319	31.691
15	4.1772	5.4736	7.1379	8.1371	9.2655	11.974	15.407	25.196	40.565
16	4.5950	6.1304	8.1372	9.3576	10.748	14.129	18.488	31.243	51.923
17	5.0545	6.8660	9.2765	10.761	12.468	16.672	22.186	38.741	66.461
18	5.5599	7.6900	10.575	12.375	14.463	19.673	26.623	48.039	85.071
19	6.1159	8.6128	12.056	14.232	16.777	23.214	31.948	59.568	108.89
20	6.7275	9.6463	13.743	16.367	19.461	27.393	38.338	73.864	139.38

Mathematical Table

Present value of €1 to be received after t periods = $1/(1+r)^t$
Present Value of €1 (PVIF)

Period (t)	1%	2%	3%	4%	5%	6%	7%	8%	9%
1	0.9901	0.9804	0.9709	0.9615	0.9524	0.9434	0.9346	0.9259	0.9174
2	0.9803	0.9612	0.9426	0.9246	0.9070	0.8900	0.8734	0.8573	0.8417
3	0.9706	0.9423	0.9151	0.8890	0.8638	0.8396	0.8163	0.7938	0.7722
4	0.9610	0.9238	0.8885	0.8548	0.8227	0.7921	0.7629	0.7350	0.7084
5	0.9515	0.9057	0.8626	0.8219	0.7835	0.7473	0.7130	0.6806	0.6499
6	0.9420	0.8880	0.8375	0.7903	0.7462	0.7050	0.6663	0.6302	0.5963
7	0.9327	0.8706	0.8131	0.7599	0.7107	0.6651	0.6227	0.5835	0.5470
8	0.9235	0.8535	0.7894	0.7307	0.6768	0.6274	0.5820	0.5403	0.5019
9	0.9143	0.8368	0.7664	0.7026	0.6446	0.5919	0.5439	0.5002	0.4604
10	0.9053	0.8203	0.7441	0.6756	0.6139	0.5584	0.5083	0.4632	0.4224
11	0.8963	0.8043	0.7224	0.6496	0.5847	0.5268	0.4751	0.4289	0.3875
12	0.8874	0.7885	0.7014	0.6246	0.5568	0.4970	0.4440	0.3971	0.3555
13	0.8787	0.7730	0.6810	0.6006	0.5303	0.4688	0.4150	0.3677	0.3262
14	0.8700	0.7579	0.6611	0.5775	0.5051	0.4423	0.3878	0.3405	0.2992
15	0.8613	0.7430	0.6419	0.5553	0.4810	0.4173	0.3624	0.3152	0.2745
16	0.8528	0.7284	0.6232	0.5339	0.4581	0.3936	0.3387	0.2919	0.2519
17	0.8444	0.7142	0.6050	0.5134	0.4363	0.3714	0.3166	0.2703	0.2311
18	0.8360	0.7002	0.5874	0.4936	0.4155	0.3503	0.2959	0.2502	0.2120
19	0.8277	0.6864	0.5703	0.4746	0.3957	0.3305	0.2765	0.2317	0.1945
20	0.8195	0.6730	0.5537	0.4564	0.3769	0.31 18	0.2584	0.2145	0.1784

	Interest Rate (r)								
Period (t)	10%	12%	14%	15%	16%	18%	20%	24%	28%
1	0.9091	0.8929	0.8772	0.8696	0.8621	0.8475	0.8333	0.8065	0.7813
2	0.8264	0.7972	0.7695	0.7561	0.7432	0.7182	0.6944	0.6504	0.6104
3	0.7513	0.7118	0.6750	0.6575	0.6407	0.6086	0.5787	0.5245	0.4768
4	0.6830	0.6355	0.5921	0.5718	0.5523	0.5158	0.4823	0.4230	0.3725
5	0.6209	0.5674	0.5194	0.4972	0.4761	0.4371	0.4019	0.3411	0.2910
6	0.5645	0.5066	0.4556	0.4323	0.4104	0.3704	0.3349	0.2751	0.2274
7	0.5132	0.4523	0.3996	0.3759	0.3538	0.3139	0.2791	0.2218	0.1776
8	0.4665	0.4039	0.3506	0.3269	0.3050	0.2660	0.2326	0.1789	0.1388
9	0.4241	0.3606	0.3075	0.2843	0.2630	0.2255	0.1938	0.1443	0.1084
10	0.3855	0.3220	0.2697	0.2472	0.2267	0.1911	0.1615	0.1164	0.0847
11	0.3505	0.2875	0.2366	0.2149	0.1954	0.1619	0.1346	0.0938	0.0662
12	0.3186	0.2567	0.2076	0.1869	0.1685	0.1372	0.1122	0.0757	0.0517
13	0.2897	0.2292	0.1821	0.1625	0.1452	0.1163	0.0935	0.0610	0.0404
14	0.2633	0.2046	0.1597	0.1413	0.1252	0.0985	0.0779	0.0492	0.0316
15	0.2394	0.1827	0.1401	0.1229	0.1079	0.0835	0.0649	0.0397	0.0247
16	0.2176	0.1631	0.1229	0.1069	0.0930	0.0708	0.0541	0.0320	0.0193
17	0.1978	0.1456	0.1078	0.0929	0.0802	0.0600	0.0451	0.0258	0.0150
18	0.1799	0.1300	0.0946	0.0808	0.0691	0.0508	0.0376	0.0208	0.0118
19	0.1635	0.1161	0.0829	0.0703	0.0596	0.0431	0.0313	0.0168	0.0092
20	0.1486	0.1037	0.0728	0.0611	0.0514	0.0365	0.0261	0.0135	0.0072

Mathematical Table

Present value of an annuity of €1 per period for t periods =[1-1/(1+r)^t]/r
Present Value of €1 Ordinary Annuity (PVIFA)

Periods (t)	Interest Rate (r)								
	1%	2%	3%	4%	5%	6%	7%	8%	9%
1	0.9901	0.9804	0.9709	0.9615	0.9524	0.9434	0.9346	0.9259	0.9174
2	1.9704	1.9416	1.9135	1.8861	1.8594	1.8334	1.8080	1.7833	1.7591
3	2.9410	2.8839	2.8286	2.7751	2.7232	2.6730	2.6243	2.5771	2.5313
4	3.9020	3.8077	3.7171	3.6299	3.5460	3.4651	3.3872	3.3121	3.2397
5	4.8534	4.7135	4.5797	4.4518	4.3295	4.2124	4.1002	3.9927	3.8897
6	5.7955	5.6014	5.4172	5.2421	5.0757	4.9173	4.7665	4.6229	4.4859
7	6.7282	6.4720	6.2303	6.0021	5.7864	5.5824	5.3893	5.2064	5.0330
8	7.6517	7.3255	7.0197	6.7327	6.4632	6.2098	5.9713	5.7466	5.5348
9	8.5660	8.1622	7.7861	7.4353	7.1078	6.8017	6.5152	6.2469	5.9952
10	9.4713	8.9826	8.5302	8.1109	7.7217	7.3601	7.0236	6.7101	6.4177
11	10.3676	9.7868	9.2526	8.7605	8.3064	7.8869	7.4987	7.1390	6.8052
12	11.2551	10.5753	9.9540	9.3851	8.8633	8.3838	7.9427	7.5361	7.1607
13	12.1337	11.3484	10.6350	9.9856	9.3936	8.8527	8.3577	7.9038	7.4869
14	13.0037	12.1062	11.2961	10.5631	9.8986	9.2950	8.7455	8.2442	7.7862
15	13.8651	12.8493	11.9379	11.1184	10.3797	9.7122	9.1079	8.5595	8.0607
16	14.7179	13.5777	12.5611	11.6523	10.8378	10.1059	9.4466	8.8514	8.3126
17	15.5623	14.2919	13.1661	12.1657	11.2741	10.4773	9.7632	9.1216	8.5436
18	16.3983	14.9920	13.7535	12.6593	11.6896	10.8276	10.0591	9.3719	8.7556
19	17.2260	15.6785	14.3238	13.1339	12.0853	11.1581	10.3356	9.6036	8.9501
20	18.0456	16.3514	14.8775	13.5903	12.4622	11.4699	10.5940	9.8181	9.1285

Periods (t)	Interest Rate (r)								
	10%	12%	14%	15%	16%	18%	20%	24%	28%
1	0.9091	0.8929	0.8772	0.8696	0.8621	0.8475	0.8333	0.8065	0.7813
2	1.7355	1.6901	1.6467	1.6257	1.6052	1.5656	1.5278	1.4568	1.3916
3	2.4869	2.4018	2.3216	2.2832	2.2459	2.1743	2.1065	1.9813	1.8684
4	3.1699	3.0373	2.9137	2.8550	2.7982	2.6901	2.5887	2.4043	2.2410
5	3.7908	3.6048	3.4331	3.3522	3.2743	3.1272	2.9906	2.7454	2.5320
6	4.3553	4.1114	3.8887	3.7845	3.6847	3.4976	3.3255	3.0205	2.7594
7	4.8684	4.5638	4.2883	4.1604	4.0386	3.8115	3.6046	3.2423	2.9370
8	5.3349	4.9676	4.6389	4.4873	4.3436	4.0776	3.8372	3.4212	3.0758
9	5.7590	5.3282	4.9464	4.7716	4.6065	4.3030	4.0310	3.5655	3.1842
10	6.1446	5.6502	5.2161	5.0188	4.8332	4.4941	4.1925	3.6819	3.2689
11	6.4951	5.9377	5.4527	5.2337	5.0286	4.6560	4.3271	3.7757	3.3351
12	6.8137	6.1944	5.6603	5.4206	5.1971	4.7932	4.4392	3.8514	3.3868
13	7.1034	6.4235	5.8424	5.5831	5.3423	4.9095	4.5327	3.9124	3.4272
14	7.3667	6.6282	6.0021	5.7245	5.4675	5.0081	4.6106	3.9616	3.4587
15	7.6061	6.8109	6.1422	5.8474	5.5755	5.0916	4.6755	4.0013	3.4834
16	7.8237	6.9740	6.2651	5.9542	5.6685	5.1624	4.7296	4.0333	3.5026
17	8.0216	7.1196	6.3729	6.0472	5.7487	5.2223	4.7746	4.0591	3.5177
18	8.2014	7.2497	6.4674	6.1280	5.8178	5.2732	4.8122	4.0799	3.5294
19	8.3649	7.3658	6.5504	6.1982	5.8775	5.3162	4.8435	4.0967	3.5386
20	8.5136	7.4694	6.6231	6.2593	5.9288	5.3527	4.8696	4.1103	3 5458

Mathematical Table

Future value of an annuity of €1 per period for t periods = $[(1+r)^t-1]/r$
Future Value of a €1 Ordinary Annuity (FVIF)

Periods (t)	Interest Rate (r)								
	1%	2%	3%	4%	5%	6%	7%	8%	9%
1	1.0000	1.0000	1.0000	1.0000	1.0000	1.0000	1.0000	1.0000	1.0000
2	2.0100	2.0200	2.0300	2.0400	2.0500	2.0600	2.0700	2.0800	2.0900
3	3.0301	3.0604	3.0909	3.1216	3.1525	3.1836	3.2149	3.2464	3.2781
4	4.0604	4.1216	4.1836	4.2465	4.3101	4.3746	4.4399	4.5061	4.5731
5	5.1010	5.2040	5.3091	5.4163	5.5256	5.6371	5.7507	5.8666	5.9847
6	6.1520	63081	6.4684	6.6330	6.8019	6.9753	7.1533	7.3359	7.5233
7	7.2135	7.4343	7.6625	7.8983	8.1420	8.3938	8.6540	8.9228	9.2004
8	8.2857	8.5830	8.8932	9.2142	9.5491	9.8975	10.260	10.637	11.028
9	9.3685	9.7546	10.159	10.583	11.027	11.491	11.978	12.488	13.021
10	10.462	10.950	11.464	12.006	12.578	13.181	13.816	14.487	15.193
11	11.567	12.169	12.808	13.486	14.207	14.972	15.784	16.645	17.560
12	12.683	13.412	14.192	15.026	15.917	16.870	17.888	18.977	20.141
13	13.809	14.680	15.618	16.627	17.713	18.882	20.141	21.495	22.953
14	14.947	15.974	17.086	18.292	19.599	21.015	22.550	24.215	26.019
15	16.097	17.293	18.599	20.024	21.579	23.276	25.129	27.152	29.361
16	17.258	18.639	20.157	21.825	23.657	25.673	27.888	30.324	33.003
17	18.430	20.012	21.762	23.698	25.840	28.213	30.840	33.750	36.974
18	19.615	21.412	23.414	25.645	28.132	30.906	33.999	37.450	41.301
19	20.811	22.841	25.117	27.671	30.539	33.760	37.379	41.446	46.018
20	22.019	24.297	26.870	29.778	33.066	36.786	40.995	45.762	51.160

Periods (t)	Interest Rate (r)								
	10%	12%	14%	15%	16%	18%	20%	24%	28%
1	1.0000	1.0000	1.0000	1.0000	1.0000	1.0000	1.0000	1.0000	1.0000
2	2.1000	2.1200	2.1400	2.1500	2.1600	2.1800	2.2000	2.2400	2.2800
3	3.3100	3.3744	3.4396	3.4725	3.5056	3.5724	3.6400	3.7716	3.9184
4	4.6410	4.7793	4.9211	4.9934	5.0665	5.2154	5.3680	5.6842	6.0156
5	6.1051	6.3528	6.6101	6.7424	6.8771	7.1542	7.4416	8.0484	8.6999
6	7.7156	8.1152	8.5355	8.7537	8.9775	9.4420	9.9299	10.980	12.136
7	9.4872	10.089	10.730	11.067	11.414	12.142	12.916	14.615	16.534
8	11.436	12.300	13.233	13.727	14.240	15.327	16.499	19.123	22.163
9	13.579	14.776	16.085	16.786	17.519	19.086	20.799	24.712	29.369
10	15.937	17.549	19.337	20.304	21.321	23.521	25.959	31.643	38.593
11	18.531	20.655	23.045	24.349	25.733	28.755	32.150	40.238	50.398
12	21.384	24.133	27.271	29.002	30.850	34.931	39.581	50.895	65.510
13	24.523	28.029	32.089	34.352	36.786	42.219	48.497	64.110	84.853
14	27.975	32.393	37.581	40.505	43.672	50.818	59.196	80.496	109.61
15	31.772	37.280	43.842	47.580	51.660	60.965	72.035	100.82	141.30
16	35.950	42.753	50.980	55.717	60.925	72.939	87.442	126.01	181.87
17	40.545	48.884	59.118	65.075	71.673	87.068	105.93	157.25	233.79
18	45.599	55.750	68.394	75.836	84.141	103.74	128.12	195.99	300.25
19	51.159	63.440	78.969	88.212	98.603	123.41	154.74	244.03	385.32
20	57.275	72.052	91.025	102.44	115.38	146.63	186.69	303.60	494.21

Z	0.00	0.01	0.02	0.03	0.04	0.05	0.06	0.07	0.08	0.09
Normal Distribution										
0.0	0.5000	0.5040	0.5080	0.5120	0.5160	0.5199	0.5239	0.5279	0.5319	0.5359
0.1	0.5398	0.5438	0.5478	0.5517	0.5557	0.5596	0.5636	0.5675	0.5714	0.5753
0.2	0.5793	0.5832	0.5871	0.5910	0.5948	0.5987	0.6026	0.6064	0.6103	0.6141
0.3	0.6179	0.6217	0.6255	0.6293	0.6331	0.6368	0.6406	0.6443	0.6480	0.6517
0.4	0.6554	0.6591	0.6628	0.6664	0.6700	0.6736	0.6772	0.6808	0.6844	0.6879
0.5	0.6915	0.6950	0.6985	0.7019	0.7054	0.7088	0.7123	0.7157	0.7190	0.7224
0.6	0.7257	0.7291	0.7324	0.7357	0.7389	0.7422	0.7454	0.7486	0.7517	0.7549
0.7	0.7580	0.7611	0.7642	0.7673	0.7704	0.7734	0.7764	0.7794	0.7823	0.7852
0.8	0.7881	0.7910	0.7939	0.7967	0.7995	0.8023	0.8051	0.8078	0.8106	0.8133
0.9	0.8159	0.8186	0.8212	0.8238	0.8264	0.8289	0.8315	0.8340	0.8365	0.8389
1.0	0.8413	0.8438	0.8461	0.8485	0.8508	0.8531	0.8554	0.8577	0.8599	0.8621
1.1	0.8643	0.8665	0.8686	0.8708	0.8729	0.8749	0.8770	0.8790	0.8810	0.8830
1.2	0.8849	0.8869	0.8888	0.8907	0.8925	0.8944	0.8962	0.8980	0.8997	0.9015
1.3	0.9032	0.9049	0.9066	0.9082	0.9099	0.9115	0.9131	0.9147	0.9162	0.9177
1.4	0.9192	0.9207	0.9222	0.9236	0.9251	0.9265	0.9279	0.9292	0.9306	0.9319
1.5	0.9332	0.9345	0.9357	0.9370	0.9382	0.9394	0.9406	0.9418	0.9429	0.9441
1.6	0.9452	0.9463	0.9474	0.9484	0.9495	0.9505	0.9515	0.9525	0.9535	0.9545
1.7	0.9554	0.9564	0.9573	0.9582	0.9591	0.9599	0.9608	0.9616	0.9625	0.9633
1.8	0.9641	0.9649	0.9656	0.9664	0.9671	0.9678	0.9686	0.9693	0.9699	0.9706
1.9	0.9713	0.9719	0.9726	0.9732	0.9738	0.9744	0.9750	0.9756	0.9761	0.9767
2.0	0.9772	0.9778	0.9783	0.9788	0.9793	0.9798	0.9803	0.9808	0.9812	0.9817
2.1	0.9821	0.9826	0.9830	0.9834	0.9838	0.9842	0.9846	0.9850	0.9854	0.9857
2.2	0.9861	0.9864	0.9868	0.9871	0.9875	0.9878	0.9881	0.9884	0.9887	0.9890
2.3	0.9893	0.9896	0.9898	0.9901	0.9904	0.9906	0.9909	0.9911	0.9913	0.9916
2.4	0.9918	0.9920	0.9922	0.9925	0.9927	0.9929	0.9931	0.9932	0.9934	0.9936
2.5	0.9938	0.9940	0.9941	0.9943	0.9945	0.9946	0.9948	0.9949	0.9951	0.9952
2.6	0.9953	0.9955	0.9956	0.9957	0.9959	0.9960	0.9961	0.9962	0.9963	0.9964
2.7	0.9965	0.9966	0.9967	0.9968	0.9969	0.9970	0.9971	0.9972	0.9973	0.9974
2.8	0.9974	0.9975	0.9976	0.9977	0.9977	0.9978	0.9979	0.9979	0.9980	0.9981
2.9	0.9981	0.9982	0.9982	0.9983	0.9984	0.9984	0.9985	0.9985	0.9986	0.9986
3.0	0.9987	0.9987	0.9987	0.9988	0.9988	0.9989	0.9989	0.9989	0.9990	0.9990

Mean = 0

Standard Deviation = 1

Number in body of table gives probability of occurrence between minus infinity and the relevant z value

Example: The probability of finding an observation between minus infinity and 1.73 is 0.9582 or 95.82%

To find the probability of an observation below a negative number, subtract the probability shown in the table for the equivalent positive number, from 1

Example: The probability of an observation below –1.4 is found by $1 - 0.9192 = 0.0808 = 8.08\%$

Appendix 3
Irish Government Euro Denominated Bonds Outstanding (31/12/00)

Bond	Title	euro (m)	Maturity Date
9%	Government Bond 2001	113.0	15/07/01
8%	Capital Loan 2001	22.2	15/10/01
6.5%	Treasury Bond 2001	2,055.3	18/10/01
9 1/4%	Capital Stock 2003	204.4	11/07/03
8 1/4%	Exchequer Bond 2003	19.8	30/10/03
2 3/4	**Treasury Bond 2002 ****	3,031.2	18/10/02
14 3/4%	Development Stock 2002–04	25.7	01/02/02
6 1/4%	Treasury Bond 2004	257.4	18/10/04
3.5%	**Treasury Bond 2005 ****	5,376.1	18/10/05
12 1/2%	Capital Stock 2005	15.6	15/12/05
8%	Treasury Bond 2006	119.7	18/08/06
9%	Capital Stock 2006	136.7	01/09/06
8 1/4%	Capital Stock 2008	2.5	30/07/08
6%	Treasury Bond 2008	74.1	18/08/08
8 1/2%	Capital Stock 2010	15.3	01/10/10
4%	**Treasury Bond 2010 ****	6,594.4	18/04/10
8 3/4%	Capital Stock 2012	43.5	30/09/12
8 1/4%	Treasury Bond 2015	12.0	18/08/15
4.6%	**Treasury Bond 2016 ****	3,665.6	18/04/16
		Total 21,784.5	

Note: Bonds marked ** are currently designated as Benchmark Bonds.
Source: National Treasury Management Agency.

Glossary of Terms

Abnormal return: A return which is greater than the market return after adjusting for systematic risk

Accounts payable period: The time between receiving stock and paying for it.

Accounts receivable financing: Short-term loans involving the factoring of accounts receivable.

Accounts receivable period: The time between the sale of stock and the collection of the amount due.

Accrued interest: Interest earned but not yet paid.

Acid test ratio: *See* Quick Ratio.

Additional Funds Needed (AFN): The external funds required when the forecasted growth in assets exceeds the forecasted growth in liabilities and equity.

Agency costs: Costs incurred by principals (shareholders and/or creditors) to monitor (prevent or minimise) agency problems and therefore to contribute to the maximisation of shareholder value.

Agency problem: The conflict of interest between managers (agents) and principals (shareholders and/or creditors).

Ageing schedule: A schedule used to show the proportion of debtors balance outstanding for a particular period.

American Depository Receipt (ADR): Securities issued in the United States which represent shares of a foreign company and which therefore allow those shares to be traded in the United States.

American option: An option that can be exercised at any time before the final exercise date.

Annual compounding: Computing future values where interest is earned on interest that is paid each year.

Annual percentage rate: The true annual interest rate charged by the lender, taking into account the timing of interest payments and capital.

Annuity due: An annuity where the cash flow payments occur at the beginning of the period.

Annuity: A stream of equal annual cash flows for a limited number of periods.

Ask price: The price a dealer is willing to accept for a security, i.e. the price a dealer is willing to sell a security.

Authorised share capital: The maximum amount of share capital that a company is allowed to issue.

Average collection period: The average number of days it takes to collect debts from customers.

Balance sheet: A statement showing an economic unit's assets, liabilities and equity at a given point in time.

Balloon payment: Most of the repayment of a loan is made near or at the maturity date.

Base rate: The reference rate of interest that forms the basis for interest rate on bank loans, deposits and overdrafts.

Basis point: 0.01 per cent

Bearer: The owner of a share or security.

Beta: A measure of nondiversifiable risk.

Bid price: The price a dealer is willing to pay for a security.

Bid-ask spread: The difference between the bid price and the asked price.

Bill of exchange: A commitment in writing to pay a certain sum of money at a certain specified point in time. A bill of exchange can be sold (discounted) before its maturity date at less than face value.

Bird in the hand theory: A theory on dividend policy which states that investors prefer (place a higher value on) 1 of dividends than 1 reinvested in the company.

Bonds: Securities that pay the owner of the security a certain amount at some time in the future and which may pay interest at regular intervals over the life of the security.

Bonus issue: The issue of additional shares to existing shareholders in accordance to their current holding of shares.

Book value: Balance sheet value.

Book building: Underwriters ask financial institutions to provide nonbinding indications as to the number of shares they are interested in purchasing and the price they are willing to pay in a new or secondary issue of shares.

Book-to-market value: The ratio of balance sheet value (book value) to market value of shares.

Bootstrapping game: This is the 'price-earnings' game where a company can increase its earnings per share by acquiring another company with a lower earning per share.

Broker: A person who assists in bringing buyers and sellers together.

Buffer stock: The level of stock that is held to prevent 'stock-outs'.

Business risk: The equity risk that arises because of fluctuations in operating income.

Buy-back: Repurchase of shares.

Call option: The option to buy an asset at some specified date or exercise price on or before a specified exercise date.

Cap: An agreement setting the upper limit on the interest rate on a floating rate note.

Capital Asset Pricing Model (CAPM): The relationship between the required rate of return and the beta coefficient or the nondiversifiable risk of the firm.

Capital budgeting: The evaluation of long-term investment proposals discounting all cash flows to the present.

Capital Market Line (CML): The risk-return combinations available when the market portfolio and risk-free borrowing or lending is combined.

Capital market: Financial market that trades long-term securities.

Capital rationing: The procedure that sets a limit on the amount of cash available for any new investment project.

Capital structure: The mix of equity capital and long-term debt capital.

Carrying cost: The variable cost per unit of carrying an item of stock for a specific period of time.

Cash conversion cycle: The time between cash disbursement and cash collection.

Clientele dividend theory: The dividend theory that states that firms should set their dividends in a way that matches their clients' (shareholders') consumption or tax position.

Commercial paper: Short-term unsecured debt issued by large corporations or financial institutions.

Conglomerate merger: Where two firms, which operate in unrelated areas, combine.

Conversion price: The share price at which convertible bonds may be converted.

Convertible bonds: Bonds that give the right to the holder to exchange the bonds at some future date for ordinary shares at some predetermined price.

Corporate valuation: The sum of the present value of free cash flow during the horizon period and the present value of the free cash flows after the horizon period.

Cost of capital: The rate of return required by providers of capital to compensate for the risk they take on.

Coupon interest payments: Interest payments made at regular intervals as promised at the time when the bond was issued.

Credit period: The time it takes, on average, between the purchase of inputs and the payment for them.

Credit rating: A procedure in which those seeking credit are compared to some standard indicators of creditworthiness and are then scored accordingly.

Creditor: A person to whom a debt is owed.

Cum-rights: Shares that are purchased prior to the ex-rights date, giving the purchaser the right to subscribe for new shares under the rights issue.

Current assets: Liquid assets that can be converted into cash, usually within a year.

Current liabilities: Liabilities due to be paid, usually within one year.

Current yield: The interest paid on a bond divided by the current price of the bond.

Dawn raid: In acquisitions, the acquirer acts with such alacrity in buying the shares of the target company that the raider builds up a substantial holding in the target company before the target company's management has time to react.

Dealer: A person who makes a living buying and selling assets.

Debenture: A bond with specified redemption dates and usually secured against specific assets (mortgage debenture) or against a floating charge on the company's assets.

Debtor collection period: The number of days it takes on average to collect debts from customers.

Default risk premium: That part of a bond yield or nominal interest rate that represents compensation for the possibility of default on the promised interest and principal payments.

Degree of Operating Leverage (DOL): The proportionate change in operating income divided by the proportionate change in sales.

Derivative security: Financial asset that represents a claim on another financial asset.

Dilution: Existing shareholders suffer a loss in value in relation to book value, market value, ownership of shares, or earnings per share.

Discount loan: A loan in which the interest is paid in advance by deducting it from the amount borrowed.

Discount rate: The rate used when calculating the present value of future cash flows.

Discount yield: The yield an investor receives by purchasing a security at less than face value and redeeming it at maturity at face value.

Discounted cash flow valuation: The process of valuing an investment by calculating the sum of the present value of all future cash flows.

Discounted payback: The time needed to recover initial cash outflows after discounting cash inflows at the appropriate required rate of return.

Diversification effect: The process of portfolio selection where the fluctuations of the assets offset each other, reducing the overall volatility or risk of the portfolio.

Divestiture: To divest or remove assets from a company.

Dividend cover: The number of times the profit available for distribution to shareholders exceeds the actual dividend paid.

Dividend payout ratio: The ratio of dividends paid to net income.

Dividend Valuation Models (DVM): The value of a share is the sum of the present value of the expected future cash flows (dividends) from holding that share.

Dividend yield: A shares annual dividend divided by its current market price.

Dividend: The proportion of profit paid to ordinary shareholders, at the discretion of the board of directors.

DuPont formula: This relates the firm's net profit and total asset turnover to its return on total assets (ROA).

EASDAQ: European Associated of Securities Dealers Automated Quotation. A stock exchange aimed at fast growing companies.

Economic Order Quantity (EOQ): A model to determine an item's optimal order quantity. The order quantity that minimises carrying costs and order costs.

Economic Value Added (EVA): This is net operating profit after taxes (NOPAT) – after tax euro cost of capital (including the cost of equity capital).

Efficient Market Hypothesis (EMH): Asserts that organised capital markets are efficient. Security prices reflect all public information available, and prices react immediately to new information. Securities are fairly priced and therefore investors need not waste time looking for stocks that are 'mispriced'.

Employee Share Ownership Plans (ESOPs): Devices to promote employee share ownership in their company.

Equity multiplier: The ratio of total assets to equity.

Equity sweetener: Gives bond holders the right to participate in the favourable performance of the company by exercising an option to purchase shares.

Euro: The name of the single European currency.

European option: Options that can only be exercised on the expiration date.

Exchange rate risk: The risk associated with having international business where relative currency values can vary.

Exchange rate: The units of one currency needed to purchase one unit of another currency.

Ex-dividend: A share that is trading without having entitlement to forthcoming dividend.

Expected return: The return expected to be generated on a risky asset.

Ex-rights: A share that is trading without the entitlement to the forthcoming rights issue.

Face Value: also par value. The amount that is promised to be paid to the holder of the bond at maturity.

Factoring: The management practice of selling accounts receivable (debtors) to another firm or factor.

Financial leverage: A change in operating income causes a more than proportionate change in net income because of the fixed nature of financial costs.

Financial risk: The risk of the firm being unable to cover the fixed financial obligations of interest payments, lease payments.

Firm specific risk: Risk associated specifically with individual firms, such as poor management and industrial relations problems.

Fisher effect: The relationship between nominal returns, real returns and inflation.

Five 'Cs' of credit: Character, capacity, capital, collateral and conditions.

Fixed assets: Assets that are normally held for long periods of time.

Floating Rate Note (FRN): A note whose interest rate varies with short-term interest rates.

Flotation costs: Fees that are paid to bankers when new securities are issued.

Flotation: The issue of company shares for the first time on the stock exchange.

Forward Rate Agreement (FRA): An agreement struck between two parties about the future level of interest rates. If the market interest rate deviates from the agreed level compensation is paid by one party to the other.

Forward rate: The exchange rate used for future delivery of an asset.

Free cash flow: Cash flow that is free to distribute to shareholders and creditors because it is not needed for investment in fixed assets or working capital.

Friendly mergers: When two companies agree to a proposed merger.

Future value: The value an asset will have in the future.

Gearing: (Leverage) The proportion of debt in the overall capital structure.

Gilts: Fixed interest government bonds traded on the stock exchange.

Going concern value: The value of a business if it continues to operate.

Golden parachutes: A stipulation that managers will receive very large payments if the firm is acquired. Used as a defensive tactic in mergers.

Goodwill: The difference in the amount paid for a firm (the purchase price) and its book value.

Gordon's growth model: The dividend valuation model using the assumption of constant growth.

Greenmail: Shareholders will offer to sell their shareholding to the company at a substantial premium in return for not selling to a hostile bidder for the company.

Growth stock: Shares in a company that can invest money that will earn more than the opportunity cost of capital.

Hedging: The process of buying one security and selling another in order to reduce risk. The process of reducing the firm's exposure to price fluctuations.

Holding company: A company whose only purpose is to hold shares in other companies.

Homemade dividend: Individual investors make their own dividends by selling shares.

Horizontal merger: Merger between two companies that operate in the same line of activity.

Hostile merger: Where the target company's management is opposed to the merger.

Hurdle rate: The required minimum acceptable rate of return management needs from a project before the project is accepted.

Income stock: Shares of companies that provide high dividend payouts but have very few (if any) profitable investment opportunities.

Incremental cash flow: Cash flows that only occur if a particular project is undertaken.

Incremental cost: The change in costs as a result of a small change in output.

Incremental revenue: The change in revenue as a result of a small change in output.

Indenture: The contract between the company issuing the bond and the purchaser of the bond.

Index trackers: A managed investment fund such as unit-linked funds, designed to match the returns on a stock market index.

Initial Public Offering (IPO): A private company issues new shares to the public to become a publicly quoted company.

Insider trading: Trading in shares on the basis of privileged information, i.e. information not in the public domain.

Institutional investor: Financial institutions that invest other companies' shares.

Interest cover: The number of times the income of a company exceeds the interest paid to service the company's debts.

Interest Rate Parity (IRP): The interest rate differential between two countries is equal to the percentage difference between the forward and the spot exchange rate.

Interest rate risk: The risk of an adverse change in interest rates on the company's performance.

Interest rate spread: The difference between the interest rate charged by a bank on loans and the rate it pays on deposits.

Interim dividend: Dividends paid on the basis of half yearly results.

Internal growth rate: The maximum growth rate a company can achieve without resorting to outside finance.

Internal Rate of Return (IRR): The discount rate where investment projects have zero net present value.

Inventory financing: Using inventory as collateral for a loan.

Inventory period: The time between acquiring stock and selling stock.

Inverted yield curve: A yield curve that is downward sloping, indicating that long-term borrowing costs are cheaper than short-term borrowing costs.

Issued share capital: Total amount of the authorised share of capital that is issued.

Junk bond: Debt with below 'investment grade bond' ratings.

Just-in-time (JIT) inventory: A system of inventory control in which stock items needed are delivered 'just-in-time' to be used as they are needed.

Lead-time: The time between placing an order and the order being delivered.

Leveraged buyouts (LBOs): The acquisition of a company, unit or subsidiary in which a large percentage of the money used to buy the shares is borrowed. Usually involving incumbent management.

Lien: The claim by lenders on specified assets.

Liquidation: The ending of the firm as a going concern.

Liquidity preference theory: Theory suggesting that longer-term interest rates are higher than short-term interest rates, causing the yield curve to be upward sloping.

Liquidity risk premium: The additional interest demanded by lenders to compensate for holding an asset that is not easy to sell at a fair price.

Liquidity: The ability of a firm to meet its short–term obligations at the fall due.

Marginal cost of capital (MCC): The weighted average cost of capital (WACC) of the next euro amount of capital that is raised.

Market maker: A dealer who creates a market in securities by either buying or selling them.

Market risk: Also called systematic risk or nondiversifiable risk. The risk that cannot be diversified away.

Market Value Added (MVA): The difference between the market value of a firm and its book value.

Matching principle: The maturity of debt matches the maturity of the projects financed by that debt. Short-term assets are financed by short-term debt and long-term assets are financed by long-term debt.

Maximum sustainable growth rate: The growth rate a firm can maintain without adding equity capital.

Merger: Where two firms combine under one ownership.

Mezzanine finance: Unsecured debt that carries high risk and the possibility of high returns.

Moderate working capital financing: The approach to financing in which temporary current assets are financed with short-term finance, and permanent current assets and fixed assets are financed with long-term finance.

Money market: Wholesale financial markets in which short-term securities are traded.

Mutual fund: A managed investment fund, the shares of which are sold to investors.

Mutually exclusive projects: Projects that compete against each other and where only one of the mutually exclusive projects may be accepted.

Net Present Value (NPV): The projects initial investment minus the present value of its cash inflows discounted at the firm's appropriate cost of capital.

Net working capital: Current assets less current liabilities.

Net worth: The book value of a company's ordinary shares, share premium and retained earnings. Total assets minus total liabilities.

Nominal rate of interest: The real rate of interest plus various premiums. The actual interest rate charged by the supplier of funds.

Noncash items: Expenses charged against company earnings that do not involve a movement of cash, e.g. depreciation.

Nondiversifiable risk: That part of total risk that cannot be diversified away. Nondiversifiable risks include inflation and interest rate risk.

Off balance sheet financing: Any financing that is not shown as a liability on the company's balance sheet.

Offer for sale: A method used in selling shares in a new issue.

Offer price: The price market at which makers sell shares.

Official List: The list of securities admitted for trading on the Irish Stock Exchange.

Operating cash flow: Cash flow generated from the normal operating activities of the business.

Operating cycle: The time between buying stock and the collection of cash from debtors.

Operating leverage: The extend to which a company or a project relies on fixed costs.

Opportunity cost: The most productive or most valuable alternative sacrificed if a particular investment is undertaken.

Option: A contract that gives the owner the right to buy or sell a specified asset at a fixed price on or before a given date.

Order-driven trading system: Buy and sell orders are entered on a central computer system, and the computer automatically matches buyers and sellers according to the price and volume they entered.

Ordinary shares: This is the equity capital of a firm. Ordinary shareholders are the owners of the company and are therefore entitled to all distributable profits after debt holders have been paid.

Over-the-counter market (OTC): An intangible market used for the purchase and sale of securities not traded on organised markets. Most notable of the OTC market is the NASDAQ.

Overtrading: When the company has insufficient working capital to finance the level of trading activity.

Par value: Also 'face value'. The stated value of an ordinary share shown on the share certificate.

Partnership: An unincorporated business owned by two or more people.

Payback period: The amount of time a capital project will take to generate sufficient cash flows to cover the initial cash outflow.

Payout ratio: Dividends as a proportion of earnings per share.

Pension fund: Financial institutions that obtain money from workers, invest the funds and provide a pension upon retirement.

Performance spread: The percentage difference between the actual rate of return and the required rate of return on an investment.

Perpetuity: An investment that provides a level stream of cash flows into perpetuity.

Placing: A method of issuing shares in the primary market where shares are offered to the broker's private clients or a selected group of financial institutions.

Poison pill: An issue of securities that are convertible into ordinary, if the merger goes ahead. Designed to make the firm unattractive to the hostile acquiring firm.

Portfolio: A selected group pf assets.

Pre-emption right: The right of existing shareholders to subscribe for any additional issue of shares.

Preference shares: Securities issued by a company providing a given dividend to be paid before any dividends are paid to holders of common shares.

Present value: The current euro value of a future amount.

Price/earning (P/E) ratio: The number of times the current market price of a share covers the earnings per share. It indicates the amount investors are willing to pay for each euro of a firm's earnings. Share price divided by earnings per share.

Primary market: The financial market in which securities are initially issued.

Principal-agent problem: Problem shareholders (principals) have in ensuring that managers (agents) act in the interest of the shareholders.

Profitability index: A ratio of the present value of the cash inflows from a project to the present value of the cash outflows.

Pro-forma financial statements: Projected financial statements.

Promissory note: A legal document signed by the borrower agreeing to the terms of the loan.

Proprietorship: An unincorporated business owned by one person.

Prospectus: A document issued to provide information about a company during an IPO.

Proxy battle: An attempt by a group of shareholders (non-management) to gain control of the management of the firm by soliciting a sufficient number of proxy votes.

Public offering: The sale of bonds or shares to the general public.

Put option: An option to sell a given number of shares on or before a specified future date at a specified price.

Quick ratio: The ratio of current assets less stock to current liabilities. Also 'acid test' ratio.

Random walk theory: Share price movements are independent of one another. The share price in any particular day cannot be predicted by looking at the previous day's price.

Real rate of interest: The nominal interest rate adjusted for inflation.

Redemption: The repayment of the principal amount at maturity.

Relevant cash flows: The incremental after-tax cash outflow and the consequent cash inflows that result from a particular capital investment.

Required return: The rate of return required by investors to compensate for the level of risk.

Residual theory of dividends: The theory that the dividends paid by a firm should be what are left over after all acceptable investment projects have been undertaken.

Retained earnings: The cumulative amount of all earnings that have been retained (after dividends have been paid) since the company's inception.

Return on equity (ROE): The rate of return earned by the owners on their investment.

Return on total assets (ROA): The rate of return management generates on its assets.

Reverse stock split: Used as a method of increasing the share price by exchanging a certain number of outstanding shares for one new ordinary share.

Rights issue: An invitation to existing shareholders to purchase additional shares in the company in proportion to their existing holdings.

Risk free rate of return: The rate of return investor looks for to take on a project where there is no risk other than the risk of inflation.

Risk-return trade-off: The higher the risk the higher the rate of return required to compensate for that risk and the lower the risk the lower the rate of return required to compensate for the lower risk.

Safety stocks: Extra stocks that can be drawn down when usage rates and lead times are greater than was expected.

Seasoned equity offering: A new issue of securities to the public by a company that has previously issued securities.

Secondary market: The market where securities previously issued are traded.

Security Market Line (SML): An upward sloping straight line representing the relationship between expected return and beta.

Semi-annual compounding: Compounding of interest over two periods in the year.

Sensitivity analysis: Assessing the effect on NPV when one variable is changed.

Share dividend: The payment of a dividend in the form of shares instead of cash.

Share split: This is a free issue of shares to existing shareholders, commonly used to lower the share price.

Simple interest: Interest earned on the principal amount only.

Sinking fund: Regular payments into a fund in order to repay a debt.

Spontaneous financing: A form of financing that arises from the normal operations of the firm, e.g., creditors and accruals.

Spot market: The market for immediate transactions, e.g. spot interest rates, spot exchange rates. This is the opposite to arranging transactions to take place some time in the future, e.g. options and future markets.

Straight bond value: The price at which a convertible bond would sell without its conversion feature.

Straight bond: A bond that is not convertible and has no conversion features.

Striking price: The exercise price of an option.

Strong form efficiency: All relevant information both public and private is reflected in the market price of the share.

Subordinated debt: Also junior debt. Debt over which senior debt takes priority.

Subsidiaries: Companies controlled by holding companies.

Sunk costs: Costs that have already been incurred and cannot be reversed. Sunk costs should be ignored in investment appraisal.

Swop: A procedure where two companies lend to each other on the basis of different terms, e.g. one on a fixed rate and the other on a floating rate. With an interest rate swop one company arranges with another company to swop interest rate payments.

Swoption: An option to have a swop at some later date.

Syndicate: A group of underwriters who are formed to share the risk and sell the issue together.

Synergy: Where the combined entity will have a value greater than the sum of the individual parts.

Systematic risk: See market risk.

Tangible asset: Physical assets such as plant and machinery, vehicles, fixtures and fittings.

Target cash balance: The optimum or desired cash holdings a company should have, determined by the trade off between carrying costs and shortage costs.

Tender offer: A public offer to buy securities.

Term loans: Loans of usually one to five years.

Term structure of interest rates: The relationship between the interest rate and the time to maturity.

Time interest earned ratio: Measures the ability of a company to meet its fixed interest obligations. Profit before interest and tax divided by payments.

Total Shareholder Return (TSR): The total return a shareholder receives from holding a share. This is dividend income plus capital gains from the increase in the share price, divided by the initial share price.

Underpricing: When securities are issued below their current market price.

Underwriter: The procedure where an underwriting firm (investment bank), buys a security issue from the company issuing the security at a price below which the underwriting firm plans to sell it to the market. The issuer gets a guaranteed amount of cash and the underwriter takes on the risk of price changes between the time of purchase and the time of sale.

Uniform price auction: An auction system where all successful bidders will pay the same price for the shares.

Unit trusts: An investment organisation, which attracts funds from individuals in return for units of investment in shares and bonds.

Unsecured loan: Loans that have no assets pledged as collateral in the event of default.

Value based management: The approach to management, which states that the primary purpose is shareholder value maximisation.

Variable cost: Costs that change as a result of changes in output.

Variable rate bond: The interest rate payable varies with variations in short-term interest rates.

Venture capital: Capital to finance new firms.

Vertical merger: Merger between a customer and a supplier.

Warehouse receipt: A document providing evidence that a company owns stocks of goods held in a warehouse.

Warrant: The holder of a security is given the option to purchase a certain number of shares in the issuing company, at a certain price, at some specified date.

Weighted average cost of capital (WACC): The weighted average of the components of the optimum capital structure, i.e. the cost of equity and the after tax cost of debt.

Winner's curse: This is the problem faced by investors who are not well informed. The average investor will find difficulty in getting an allocation of shares in a successful IPO (one whose share price goes up) because there won't be enough shares to go around. If the average investor 'wins' and gets his/her entire allocation, it could be because the more informed investors avoided the issue.

Working capital: A company's short-term assets and short-term liabilities.

Yield curve: A graph showing the time to maturity of a bond and the interest rate. The term structure of interest rates.

Yield: Income from a security expressed as a percentage of its market price.

Zero coupon bond: Bonds that do not pay regular interest. They are issued at a discount to their par value and redeemed at par, providing a capital gain.

References and Further Reading

CHAPTER 1

The *Economist* magazine, *The Irish Times*, the *Sunday Business Post*, *The Financial Times*—all have very useful sections on finance and should be regular reading material for students of finance.

Brigham, Gaphenski, Erhardt, *Financial Management, Theory and Practice*.
Eakins, S., *Finance, Investments Institutions & Management*.
Gallagher, T.J., Andrew, J.D., *Financial Management, Principles and Practice*.
Kelly, K., *New Rules for the New Economy*.
Quinlan, J. and Stevens, K., *101 Trends Every Investor should know about the Global Economy*.

For a discussion on agency theory, see:
Jemsen, M.C., Meckling, W.H., 'Theory of the Firm, Managerial Behaviour, Agency Costs and Ownership Structure', *Journal of Financial Economics*.
Seitz, N., 'Shareholder Goals, Firm Goals and Firm Financing Decisions', *Financial Management*.

CHAPTER 2

Bingham, Gapenski and Ehrhardt, *Financial Management—Theory and Practice*.
Copeland, T., Koller, T. and Murrin, J. *Valuation: Measuring and Managing the Value of Companies*, Wiley & Sons 1992.
Stewart, G. Bennett, *The Quest for Value*, HarperCollins 1991.

CHAPTER 3

There are many sources of financial information available, some of which are as follows:

The Internet—Some companies make their annual reports available on the Internet.
Extel—a company that specialises in providing financial information on an entire range of companies.
Stockbroking firms provide information on a regular basis on the companies they analyse.

Newspapers—news articles, market data along with daily prices of securities. *The Irish Times* and the *Sunday Business Post* along with *The Financial Times* are important sources of up-to-date financial information.

The Irish Stock Market Annual

Chen, Kung, H. and Shimerda, T.A., 'An empirical analysis of useful financial ratios', *Financial Management*, Spring 1981.

Dun & Bradstreet, *Key Business Ratios*.

McKenzie, W., *Guide to Using and Interpreting Company Accounts*, 2nd ed., *Financial Times*/Pitman Publishing.

Ross, Westerfield, Jordan, *Fundamentals of Corporate Finance*, 5th ed., Irwin McGraw Hill.

Brigham, Gaphenski, Ehrhardt, *Financial Management, Theory and Practice*.

Gallagher, A., *Principles of Financial Management*, Prentice-Hall.

CHAPTER 4

Most introductory financial textbooks include a section on the time value of money. Two useful recent texts are:

Bradley, T. and Patton, P., *Essential Mathematics for Economics and Business*, John Wiley & Sons 1998.

Swift, L., *Mathematics and Statistics for Business, Management and Finance*, MacMillan Press Ltd 1997.

A more advanced treatment is available in:

Ross, S.A., Westerfield, R.W. and Jaffe, J.F., *Corporate Finance*, 2nd ed, Irwin 1988

CHAPTER 5

Bradley, T. and Patton, P., *Essential Mathematics for Economics and Business*, John Wiley & Sons 1998.

Swift, L., *Mathematics and Statistics for Business, Management and Finance*, MacMillan Press Ltd 1997

Elton, E.J. & Gruber, M.J., *Modern Portfolio Theory and Investment Analysis*, 4th ed, John Wiley & Sons 1991.

Ross, S.A., Westerfield, R.W. and Jaffe, J.F., *Corporate Finance*, 2nd ed, Irwin 1988.

CHAPTER 6

For an excellent treatment of company valuations and the use of FCF and DCF, see:
Brigham, Gapenski and Ehrhardt, *Financial Management, Theory and Practice*.

For further reading on company valuations and the concept of the 'horizon period', see:
Brealey and Myers, *Principles of Corporate Finance*, 6th ed., Irwin McGraw Hill.

For advanced studies on company valuation methods, see:
Copeland, Koller and Murring, *Valuation*.

For a clear exposition of cash flow valuation methods, see:

Rappaport, A., *Creating Shareholder Value*, New York Free Press 1986.

Gordon, M.J. and Shapiro, E., 'Capital Equipment Analysis: The Required Rate of Profit', *Management Science*, 3 October 1956.

CHAPTER 7

Arnold, G., *Corporate Financial Management*, FT / Pitman Publishing 1999.

Atrill, P., *Financial Management for Non-Specialists*, Prentice-Hall 1997.

BPP Manual, *Financial Strategy*, 2000.

Brealey and Myers, *Principles of Corporate Finance*.

Corr, A.V., *The Capital Expenditure Decision*, NAASMAC Canada 1983.

Diacogiannis, P.G., *Financial Management (A modelling approach using spreadsheets)*, McGraw Hill 1994.

Diacogiannis and Lai, R., 'Survey on the investment and financing of the companies in the USM', Warick Paper in *Management*, no. 33, April 1989.

Drury, C., *Management and Cost Accounting*, Chapman and Hall 1996.

Drury, C., Braund, S., Osborn, P. and Tayes, M., 'A survey of managing accounting practises in U.K. manufacturing companies', Certified Research Report 32, ACCA 1993.

Gitman, L.J. and Forrester, J.R. Jr., 'A survey of capital budgeting techniques used by major US firms', *Financial Management*, Autumn, 66–71, 1977.

Green, P.J. and McIlkenny, P., *Capital Budgeting Practices in Irish Listed Companies*, IAFA 1991.

Horngren, C., Bhimani, A., Foster, G. and Datar, S., *Management and Cost Accounting*, Prentice-Hall 1999.

Levy, H. and Sarnat, M., *Capital Investment and Financing Decisions*, Prentice-Hall 1994.

Lucey, B., McHugh, G. and McCabe, P., 'An Analysis of the Investment Appraisal Practices of Irish Companies', *Irish Business and Administrative Review*, vol. 15, 1995.

McLaney, E., *Business Finance*, FT / Prentice-Hall 2000.

McIntyre, A. and Coulthurst, N., 'Capital Budgeting in a Medium Sized Business', CIMA Research Report 1986.

Pike, R.H., 'An Empirical Study of the Adoption of Sophisticated Capital Budgeting Practices and Decision Making Effectiveness', *Accounting and Business Research*, 341–52, 1988.

Samuels, J.M., Wilkes, F.M. and Brayshaw, R.E. 'Management of Company Finance', *ITBP* 1995.

Pike, R. and Neale, B., *Corporate Finance and Investments: Decisions and Strategies*, Prentice-Hall 1999.

Samuels, Wilkes and Brayshaw, *Management of Company Finance*.

Sangster, A., 'Capital Investment Appraisal Techniques: A Survey of Current Usage', *Journal of Business Finance and Accounting* 20(3) 1993.

Solnick, B., *International Investments*, Addison Wesley 2000.

Watson, D. and Head, T., *Corporate Finance (Principles and Practice)* FT / Pitman Publishing 1999.

Weston, J.F. and Copeland, T. E., *Managerial Finance*, Cassell, London 1988.

CHAPTER 8

Arnold, G., *Corporate Financial Management*.

Baskin, J.B. (1989) 'An empirical investigation into the pecking order hypothesis', *Financial Management*, vol. 18, pp. 26–35.

Brealey and Myers (1999) *Principles of Corporate Finance*.

Diacogiannis (1994) *Financial Management*.

Donaldson, G. (1961) *Corporate Debt Capacity*, Harvard University Press.

Durand, D. (1952) *The Cost of Debt and Equity Funds for Business: Trends and Problems of Measurement*.

Conference on Research in Business Finance 1952.

Hill, A. (1998) *Corporate Finance Framework*, Pitman Publishing.

Homaifar, G., Zeitz, J. and Benkato, O. (1994) 'An empirical model of capital structure: some new evidence'. *Journal of Business Finance and Accounting* (January).

McLaney, E. (2000) *Business Finance Theory and Practice*, Pitman Publishing.

Masulis, R. (1980) 'The effect of capital structure changes on security prices', *Journal of Financial Economics* (June).

Miller, M. (1977) 'Leverage', *Journal of Finance*.

Miller, M. (1991) 'Debt and Taxes', *American Economic Review*, vol. 32, pp. 261–75.

Modigliani, F. and Miller, M. (1958) 'Cost of Capital, Corporation Finance and the Theory of Investment', *American Economic Review*, vol. 48, pp. 261–96.

Modigliani and Miller (1963) 'Corporate Income Taxes and the Cost of Capital: A Correction', *American Economic Review*, vol. 53, pp. 433–43.

Myers, S.(1984) 'The capital structure puzzle', *Journal of Finance*, vol. 39, pp. 575–92.

Samuels, Wilkes and Brayshaw *Management of Company Finance*.

Watson, D. and Head, T. (1999) *Corporate Finance (Principles and Practice)*.

CHAPTER 9

Arnold G., *Corporate Financial Management*.

Brealey and Myers, *Principles of Corporate Finance*.

Buckley, A., *Multinational Finance*, Prentice-Hall 2000.

Chen, N., 'Some Empirical Tests of the Theory of Arbitrage Pricing', *Journal of Finance*, 38: 1393–1414, Dec. 1983.

Diacogiannis, *Financial Management*.

Fama, E. and Macbeth, J., 'Risk Return and Equilibrium: Empirical Tests', *Journal of Political Economy*, 81: 607–36, May 1973.

Lintner J., 'The Valuation of Risk Assets and the Selection of Risky Investments in Stock Portfolios and Capital Budgets', *Review of Economics and Statistics*, 47: 13–37, Feb. 1967.

McLaney, E., *Business Finance*.

Markowitz, H., 'Portfolio Selection', *Journal of Finance* 7: 77–91, March 1952.

Pike and Neale, *Corporate Finance and Investments: Decisions and Stategies*.

Roll, R. and Ross, S., 'An Empirical Investigation of the Arbitrage Pricing Theory', *Journal of Finance*, 35: 1073–1103, Dec. 1980.

Ross, S., 'The Arbitrage Theory of Capital Asset Pricing', *Journal of Economic Theory*, 13: 341–60, Dec. 1976.

Samuels, Wilkes and Brayshaw, *Management of Company Finance*.
Sharpe W., 'Capital Asset Prices: A Theory of Market Equilibrium under Conditions of Risk', *Journal of Finance*, 19: 425–42, Sept. 1964.
Watson and Head, *Corporate Finance (Principles and Practice)*.

CHAPTER 10

For an advanced discussion and a clear exposition of company valuations see:
Brealey and Myers, *Principles of Corporate Finance*.
Brigham Gapenski and Ehrhardt, *Financial Management Theory and Practice*.
Copeland, Koller and Murrin, *Valuation, Measuring and Managing the Value of Companies*.

For additional reading on financial forecasting and planning, the following texts are excellent:
Eakins, Stanley G., *Finance, Investments, Institutions & Management*, Addison-Wesley.
Ross, Westerfield and Jordan, *Fundamentals of Corporate Finance*.

An excellent discussion on EVA and MVA is given in:
Ehrbar A., *Stern Stewart's EVA—the Real Key to Creating Wealth*.

CHAPTER 11

Arnold, *Corporate Financial Management*.
Brealey & Myers, *Principles of Corporate Finance*.
Brennan, Pierce, *Irish Company Accounts—Regulation and Reporting*, Oak Tree Press.
Bringham, Gapenski and Ehrhardt, *Financial Management—Theory and Practice*.
Dixon, *Financial Management*, Longman.
Eakins, *Finance, Investments, Institutions & Management*.
Westerfield Ross, and Jordan, *Fundamental of Corporate Finance*.

CHAPTER 12

The classic article, that is often quoted but seldom read, on dividend policy is:
Miller, Merton and Modigliani, 'Dividend Policy, Growth and the Valuation of Shares', *Journal of Business*, October 1961.

For a discussion on optimum investment policy, see:
Gordan, Myrton, J., 'Optimal Investment and Financing Policy', *Journal of Finance*, May 1963.

For a discussion on the clientele effect and taxes, see:
Richardson Pettit, R., 'Taxes, Transactions Costs and the Clientele Effect of Dividends', *Journal of Financial Economics*, December 1977.

See also:
Elton & Gruber, 'Marginal Stockholder Tax Rates and the Clientele Effect', *Review of Economics and Statistics*, February 1970.

For the classic article on the way firms set their dividend policy, see:
Litner, John, 'Distribution of Incomes of Corporations Among Dividends, Retained Earnings and Taxes', *American Economic Review*, May 1956.
On the relevancy of dividend policy, see:
Hayes, Linda S., 'Fresh Evidence that Dividends Don't Matter', *Fortune*, 4 May 1981.

For a review of the 'bird in the hand' theory, see:
Gordon, 'Dividends, Earnings and Stock Prices', *Review of Economics and Statistics*, May 1956.

For a study on the information content of dividends, see:
Bhattacharya, S., 'Imperfect Information, Dividend Policy and the Bird in the Hand Fallacy', *Bell Journal of Economics and Management Science*, Spring 1972.

The Bank of England produced a special on dividend policy:
Bank of England Quarterly Review, August 1993.

Of special interest to students who would like to take a further look at dividend policy, see an excellent series of articles in:
Financial Management, Autumn 1998.
Bingham, Gapenski and Ehrhardt, *Financial Management—Theory and Practice*.
Brealey & Myers, *Principles of Corporate Finance*.
Gallagher & Andrew, *Financial Management—Principles and Practice*.
Ross, Westerfield and Jordan, *Fundamentals of Corporate Finance*.

CHAPTER 13

Arnold, G, 'Corporate Financial Management'.
Baumol, William, 'The Transactions Demand for Cash: An Inventory Theoretic Approach', *Quarterly Journal of Economics*, Nov. 1952.
Bingham, Gaphenski and Ehrhardt, *Financial Management, Theory and Practice*.
Davis, E.W. and Collier, P.A., *Treasury Management in the UK*, Association of Corporate Treasurers.
Gallagher and Andrew, *Financial Management—Principles and Practice*.
Gentry, J., Vaidyanathan, R. and Hei Wai Lee, 'A Weighted Cash Conversion Cycle', *Financial Management*, Spring 1990.
Gentry, J.A., 'State of the Art of Short-Run Financial Management', *Financial Management*, Summer 1988.
Journal of Cash Management, The (US).
Ross, Westerfield and Jordan, *Fundamentals of Corporate Finance*.

CHAPTER 14

For further additional textbook reading:

Arnold, *Corporate Financial Management.*

Department of Enterprise, Trade and Employment, *How to Finance your Business,* Government Publications Office, Molesworth St, Dublin 2.

Eakins, *Finance, investments, institutions & Management.*

Ross, Westerfield and Jordan, *Fundamentals of Corporate Finance.*

CHAPTER 15

Arnold, *Corporate Financial Management.*

Brigham, Gaphenski and Ehrhardt, *Financial Management.*

Carty, P., 'The Economics of Expansion', *Accountancy*, March 1994 (on sources of finance).

Central Bank of Ireland Bulletin, for information on various deposit and other selected interest rates.

Davies, H., 'Finance for Small Firms', the *Bank of England Quarterly Bulletin*, February 1994.

Department of Enterprise, Trade and Employment, *How to Finance your Business.*

European Central Bank, *Monthly Bulletin*—useful for main interest rate trends in the euro zone and other monetary aggregates.

Gallagher and Andrew, *Financial Management—Principles and Practice.*

O'Kane, B., *Starting a Business in Ireland*, 2nd ed., Oak Tree Press.

Ross, Westerfield & Jordan, *Fundamentals of Corporate Fiance.*

Wynn, G.L., Sources of UK Short-term and Medium-term Debt', *Handbook of Corporate Finance*, London.

CHAPTER 16

Information on the operation of the Irish bond market is available from the National Treasury Management Agency (NTMA) and from the banks and stock-broking companies.

Information on the Irish pension fund industry is available from the Irish Association of Pension Funds (IAPF) and from the National Pensions Board.

Information on the Irish unit-linked fund industry is contained in the MoneyMate and Moneymate Plus databases, published by The Software Vineyard, Dublin.

CHAPTER 17

Arnold, *Corporate Financial Management.*

BPP *Financial Strategy 2000.*

Barnes, E. and Donnelly, R., An investigation into the Hedging Effectiveness of the Irish Interest Rate Futures Market', *Irish Business and Administrative Review* 1995.

Brett, M., *How to Read the Financial Pages*, 4th ed., London: Century 1995.

Buckley, *Multinational Finance.*

Demirag, I. and Goddard, S., *Financial Management for International Business*, McGraw-Hill 1994.

Eales, B., *Financial Risk Management*, McGraw-Hill 1995.

Levi, M., *International Finance*, 3rd ed., New York: McGraw-Hill 1996.

Madura, J., *International Financial Management*, West Publishing Company 1995.

O'Sullivan, R., 'Irish Credit Institutions' Participation in Single Currency Derivatives Markets', *Central Bank of Ireland Quarterly Bulletin*, Winter 1995.

Price Waterhouse, *Corporate Treasury Control and Performance Standards*, Dublin 1995

Taylor, F., *Mastering Foreign Exchange and Currency Options*, London: Pitman Publishing 1997.

Walsh, D., 'Risk management using derivative securities', *Managerial Finance*, vol. 21, no. 1, pp. 43–65, 1995.

Watson and Head, *Corporate Finance (Principles and Practice)*.

CHAPTER 18

Many textbooks on investment cover the area of risk-adjusted return analysis in some detail. The area of safety-first investment is not normally covered as well. For an excellent treatment of both topics see:

Elton, E.J. and Gruber, M.J., *Modern Portfolio Theory and Investment Analysis*, 4th ed, John Wiley & Sons 1991.

CHAPTER 19

For a discussion on acquisitions that offer no economic gain, see:

Myers, S.C., 'A Framework for Evaluating Mergers', in S.C. Myers ed., *Modern Developments in Financial Management*, F.A. Praeger, Inc. Publishers 1976.

For a discussion on the effect of increased borrowing on merger gains, see:

Lewellen, W.G., 'A Pure Financial Rationale for the Conglomerate Merger', *Journal of Finance*, 26 May 1971.

For a discussion on post-merger share price performance, see:

Franks, J.R., Harris, R.S. and Titman, S., The Postmerger Share-Price Performance of Acquiring Firms', *Journal of Financial Economics*, 29 March 1991.

For a discussion on proxy contests, see:

Dodd, P. and Warner J., 'On Corporate Governance: A Study of Proxy Contests', *Journal of Financial Economics*, 2 April 1985.

For a discussion of the 1980s merger wave, see:

Shleifer, A. and Vishney, E.W., 'The Takeover Wave of the 1980s', *Journal of Applied Corporate Finance*, Autumn 1991.

See also:

'The Best and Worst Deals of the 1980s: What We Learned from All Those Mergers, Acquisitions and Takeovers', *Business Week*, 15 January 1990.

For a discussion on whether the shareholders of the acquiring firm or the acquired firm benefit most mergers, see:

Black, B. and Grundfest J., 'Shareholder Gains from Takeovers and Restructurings between 1981 and 1986: $162 billion Is a Lot of Money', *Journal of Applied Corporate Finance*, Spring 1988.

Elgers, P. and Clarke, J., 'Merger Types and Shareholder Returns: Additional Evidence', *Financial Management*, Summer 1980.

Manson, S., Stark, A. and Thomas, H.M., 'A Cash Flow analysis of the Operational Gains from Mergers', Chartered Association of Certified Accountants—Research Report 35, London 1994.

Meeks, G., *Disappointing Marriage: A Study of the Gains from Mergers*, Cambridge University Press.

Rappaport, *Creating Shareholder Value*, (chapter 9).

For discussions on LBOs, the spring 1989 edition of the *Journal of Applied Corporate Finance* provides a number of articles.

For a discussion on the cultural and personnel side of mergers, see:

Cartwright, S. and Cooper, C., *Mergers and Acquisitions: The Human Factor*, Oxford: Butterworth Heinemann.

Also, on societal costs and benefits of mergers, see:

Cowling, K., Stoneman, P. and Cubbin, J., *Mergers and Economic Performance*, Cambridge: Cambridge University Press.

For a discussion on the UK experience of mergers and acquisitions, see:

Coopers & Lybrand and OC & C, 'A Review of Acquisition Experience of Major UK Companies', London: Coopers & Lybrand (1993).

For a case study on mergers, see:

Baker, G.P., 'Beatrice: A Study in the Creation and Destruction of Value', *Journal of Finance*, July 1992.

For more detailed textbook treatment of mergers and acquisitions, see:

Brealey & Myers, *Principles of Corporate Finance*.

Ross, Westerfield & Jordan, *Fundamentals of Corporate Finance*.

Brigham, Gapenski & Ehrhardt, *Financial Management, Theory and Practice*.

CHAPTER 20

Accounting Standards Board, *Financial Reporting Standard 4 'Capital Instruments'*, 1993

Bradley, T. and Patton, P., *Essential Mathematics for Economics and Business*, John Wiley & Sons 1998.

Elton, E.J. and Gruber, M.J., *Modern Portfolio Theory and Investment Analysis*, 4th ed, John Wiley & Sons 1991.

Ross, S.A., Westerfield, R.W. and Jaffe, J.F., *Corporate Finance*, 2nd ed, Irwin 1988.

CHAPTER 21

Information on the products and services offered by Irish mortgage providers is available from the main banks and building societies.

Bradley, T. and Patton, P., *Essential Mathematics for Economics and Business*, John Wiley & Sons 1998.

Swift, L., *Mathematics and Statistics for Business, Management and Finance*, MacMillan Press Ltd 1997

Zima, P. & Brown, R.L., *Contemporary Mathematics of Finance*, Schaums Outline Series, 1984.

Index